POCKET
WORLD ATLAS

POCKET
WORLD ATLAS

Bay Books
Sydney and London,

Bay Books,
Sydney and London,
in association with John Bartholomew & Son Ltd,
Edinburgh.

Published by Bay Books

National Library of Australia Card Number and
ISBN 1-86378-016-5
B 91

CONTENTS

viii-ix   World Physical
x-xi   World Political
xii-xiii   World Time Zones
xiv-xv   World Environment
xvi   Key to Symbols

1   Arctic Ocean
2-3   North America – Political
4-5   Canada, West
6-7   Canada, East
8-9   USA, West
10-11   USA, East
12   USA, Alaska
13   Canada Pacific
14-15   Lower Canada, USA North-East
16   Washington – New York – Boston
17   USA, South-East
18-19   USA, South-Central
20   USA, Pacific NW
21   USA, Pacific S
22   San Francisco & Los Angeles
23   Central Mexico
24-25   Mexico & Central America
26-27   Caribbean
28   South America - Political
29   South America, South
30   South America, Central
31   South America, NE

32-33	South America, North
34	Central Argentina
35	South-East Brazil
36-37	Europe – Political
38-39	Scandinavia
40-41	British Isles
42-43	England & Wales
44	Scotland, North
45	Ireland
46	Paris - Brussels – Ruhr
47	Alps
48-49	France
50-51	Spain
52-53	Italy
54-55	The Balkans
56-57	Germany & Austria
58-59	East-Central Europe
60-61	Central European Russia
62	USSR – Political
63	USSR, East
64-65	USSR, West
66-67	South Asia – Political
68-69	East Asia
70-71	South-East Asia
72-73	Central China
74	Japan & Korea
75	Central Japan
76-77	Indo-China & Singapore

78	Indonesia, Central
79	Philippines
80–81	Middle East
82–83	India & West China
84–85	India, NW & Pakistan
86	India, NE & Bangladesh
87	India, South & Sri Lanka
88–89	Africa – Political
90–91	Iran and the Gulf
92–93	Turkey, Syria & Iraq
94	Israel & Lebanon
95	Africa, North-East
96–97	Africa, West
98–99	Africa, Central
100–101	Africa, South
102–103	Atlantic Ocean
104–105	Australasia
106–107	Australia
108–109	Australia South-East
110–111	New Zealand
112	Antarctica

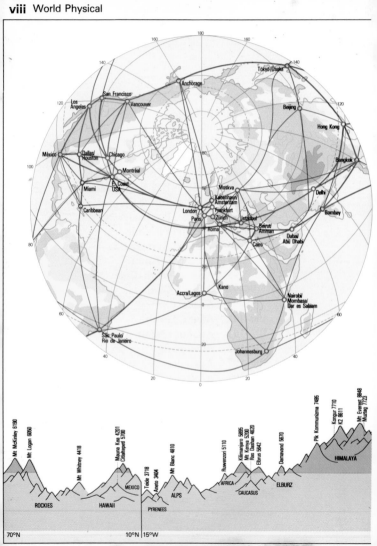

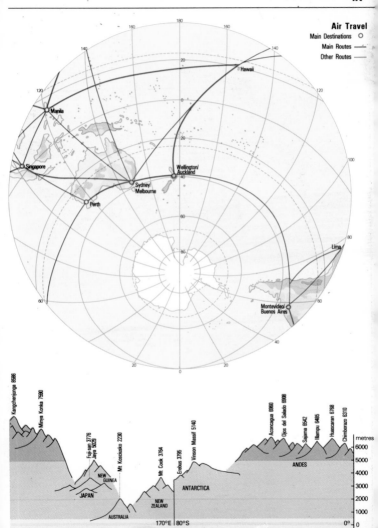

Air Travel
Main Destinations ○
Main Routes ——
Other Routes ——

Greenland (Den.)

Alaska (USA)

ICELAND
Reykjavík

C A N A D A

Vancouver
Seattle
Portland
Winnipeg
Ottawa
Montreal
Toronto

IRELAND
U.K.
London

Paris
FRAN

San Francisco
UNITED STATES
OF AMERICA
Chicago
New York
Philadelphia
Washington

Atlanta

PORTUGAL
Lisboa
Madrid
SPAIN

Los Angeles
Dallas
New
Orleans
Houston

Açores
(Port.)

ATLANTIC

Canary Is.
(Sp.)
Rabat
Casablanca
MOROCCO
ALGE

Hawaii (USA)

Miami

THE
BAHAMAS

Western
Sahara

MAURITANIA
Nouakchott
MALI

Guadalajara
México
CUBA
JAMAICA
HAITI
DOM. REP.

CAPE VERDE IS
THE GAMBIA
GUINEA-BISSAU
SENEGAL
Bamako
BURKINA

PACIFIC

GUATEMALA
EL SALVADOR
BELIZE
HONDURAS
NICARAGUA

COSTA RICA
PANAMA

Caracas
VENEZUELA

TRINIDAD & TOBAGO
GUYANA
SURINAM
FR. GUIANA

GUINEA
SIERRA LEONE
LIBERIA
IVORY COAST

Equator

Galapagos Is.
(Ec.)

Bogotá
COLOMBIA
Quito
ECUADOR

OCEAN

Lima
PERU

B R A Z I L

Recife
Salvador

OCEAN

OCEAN

La Paz
BOLIVIA

PARAGUAY
Asunción

Brasília

Rio de Janeiro
São Paulo

Santiago
CHILE

Buenos
Aires
URUGUAY
Montevideo

ARGENTINA

• Denotes capital cities

Falkland Is.
(UK)
S. Georgia
(UK)

Major Cities		Sŏul *South Korea*	6879	**Europe**	'000
by Continent	**Pop.**	Manila *Philippines*	5901	London *UK*	12 075
Oceania	'000	Jakarta *Indonesia*	5849	Paris *France*	8613
Sydney *Australia*	2874	Delhi *India*	5277	Moskva *USSR*	8099
Melbourne *Australia*	2578	Bangkok *Thailand*	5154	Leningrad *USSR*	4638
Brisbane *Australia*	943	Tehrān *Iran*	4496	Madrid *Spain*	3188
Adelaide *Australia*	883	Tianjin *China*	4280	Berlin *E Ger.-W Ger.*	3056
Perth *Australia*	809	Madras *India*	4277	Roma *Italy*	2830
Auckland *New Zealand*	766	Karachi *Pakistan*	4000	Birmingham *UK*	2748
Asia	'000	Shenyang *China*	3600	Manchester *UK*	2687
Tōkyō *Japan*	11 696	Dhākā *Bangladesh*	3459	Kiyev *USSR*	2144
Shanghai *China*	10 820	Saigon *Vietnam*	3420	Athínai *Greece*	2101
Calcutta *India*	9166	Baghdād *Iraq*	3206	Budapest *Hungary*	2064
Beijing *China*	8626	T'ai-pei *Taiwan*	3050	Bucureşti *Romania*	1934
Bombay *India*	8203	Bangalore *India*	2914	Tashkent *USSR*	1779
		İstanbul *Turkey*	2773	Barcelona *Spain*	1755

North and Central America	'000	South America	'000	Africa	'000
New York *USA*	16 120	Buenos Aires *Argentina*	9910	Cairo *Egypt*	6588
México *Mexico*	14 750	São Paulo *Brazil*	8584	Alexandria *Egypt*	2320
Los Angeles *USA*	11 496	Rio de Janeiro *Brazil*	5184	Kinshasa *Zaire*	2008
Chicago *USA*	7868	Santiago *Chile*	4039	Casablanca *Morocco*	1753
Philadelphia *USA*	5549	Lima *Peru*	3969	Johannesburg *South Africa*	1536
San Francisco *USA*	5182	Bogotá *Colombia*	3831	Alger *Algeria*	1503
Detroit *USA*	4618	Caracas *Venezuela*	2576	Lagos *Nigeria*	1477
Boston *USA*	3448	Belo Horizonte *Brazil*	1815	El Giza *Egypt*	1247
Houston *USA*	3102	Salvador *Brazil*	1526	Addis Ababa *Ethiopia*	1133
Washington *USA*	3060	Medellín *Colombia*	1442	Cape Town *South Africa*	1108
Toronto *Canada*	2999	Fortaleza *Brazil*	1339	Dar es Salaam *Tanzania*	870
Dallas *USA*	2975	Montevideo *Uruguay*	1314	Durban *South Africa*	851
Cleveland *USA*	2834	Recife *Brazil*	1241	Abidjan *Ivory Coast*	850
Montréal *Canada*	2828	Brasília *Brazil*	1203	Ibadan *Nigeria*	847
Miami *USA*	2640	Pôrto Alegre *Brazil*	1159	Nairobi *Kenya*	835

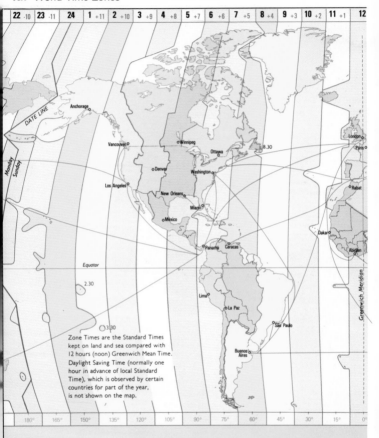

| 22 -10 | 23 -11 | 24 | 1 +11 | 2 +10 | 3 +9 | 4 +8 | 5 +7 | 6 +6 | 7 +5 | 8 +4 | 9 +3 | 10 +2 | 11 +1 | 12 |

DATE LINE

Monday
Sunday

Anchorage

Vancouver · Winnipeg
Ottawa
Denver · Washington
Los Angeles
New Orleans
Miami
Mexico

8.30

London
Paris

Rabat

Dakar

Abidjan

Panama · Caracas

Equator

2.30

Lima

La Paz

São Paulo

3.30

Greenwich Meridian

Buenos
Aires

Zone Times are the Standard Times
kept on land and sea compared with
12 hours (noon) Greenwich Mean Time.
Daylight Saving Time (normally one
hour in advance of local Standard
Time), which is observed by certain
countries for part of the year,
is not shown on the map.

| 180° | 165° | 150° | 135° | 120° | 105° | 90° | 75° | 60° | 45° | 30° | 15° | 0° |

Journey Times

Sail (via Cape)
164 days

Steam (via Cape)
43 days

Steam (via Suez)
30 days

Supertanker
(via Cape)
28 days

Singapore ←

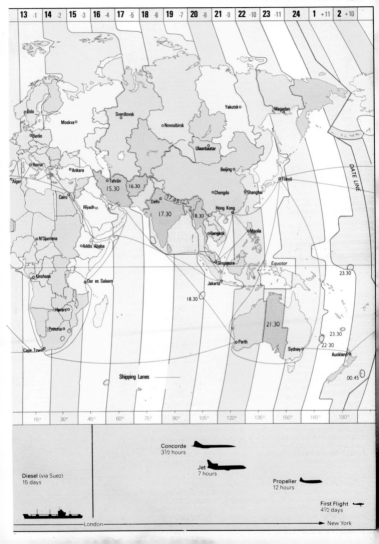

| 13 | -1 | 14 | -2 | 15 | -3 | 16 | -4 | 17 | -5 | 18 | -6 | 19 | -7 | 20 | -8 | 21 | -9 | 22 | -10 | 23 | -11 | 24 | 1 | +11 | 2 | +10 |

Oslo
Berlin
Moskva
Sverdlovsk
Novosibirsk
Yakutsk
Magadan
Roma
Ankara
Tehrān 15.30 16.30
Alger
Cairo
Ulaanbaatar
Beijing
Tōkyō
Rīyadh
Delhi 17.30 18.30
Chengdu
Shanghai
Hong Kong
N'Djamena
Addis Ababa
Bangkok
Manila
Singapore Equator
Kinshasa
Dar es Salaam
Jakarta 18.30
23.30
Harare
Pretoria
21.30
Cape Town
Perth
23.30
Sydney 22.30
Auckland
00.45

DATE LINE

Shipping Lanes

15° 30° 45° 60° 75° 90° 105° 120° 135° 150° 165° 180°

Concorde
3½ hours

Jet
7 hours

Propeller
12 hours

Diesel (via Suez)
15 days

First Flight
4½ days

London → New York

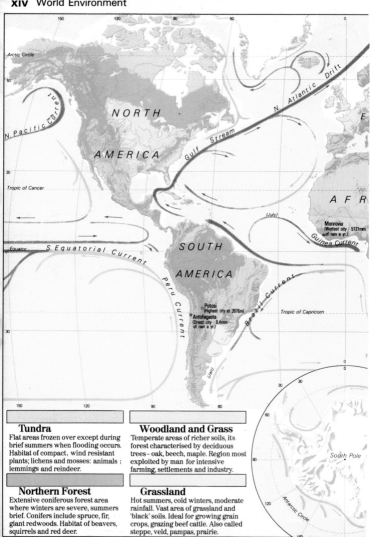

Tundra
Flat areas frozen over except during brief summers when flooding occurs. Habitat of compact, wind resistant plants; lichens and mosses: animals ; lemmings and reindeer.

Northern Forest
Extensive coniferous forest area where winters are severe, summers brief. Conifers include spruce, fir, giant redwoods. Habitat of beavers, squirrels and red deer.

Woodland and Grass
Temperate areas of richer soils, its forest characterised by deciduous trees - oak, beech, maple. Region most exploited by man for intensive farming, settlements and industry.

Grassland
Hot summers, cold winters, moderate rainfall. Vast area of grassland and 'black' soils. Ideal for growing grain crops, grazing beef cattle. Also called steppe, veld, pampas, prairie.

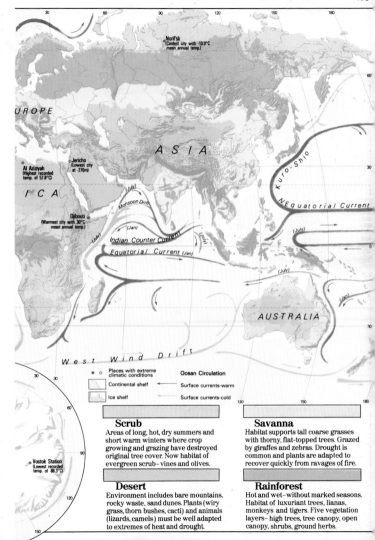

EUROPE

ASIA

AFRICA

AUSTRALIA

Al Azizyah
(Highest recorded temp. of 57.8°C)

Jericho
(Lowest city at -270m)

Norilsk
(Coolest city with -10.9°C mean annual temp.)

Djibouti
(Warmest city with 30°C mean annual temp.)

Monsoon Drift (July)

(July)

(Jan)

Indian Counter Current

Equatorial Current (Jan)

(July)

(July)

(July)

(Jan)

Kuro-Shio

N Equatorial Current

West Wind Drift

Vostok Station
(Lowest recorded temp. of -88.3°C)

● ○ Places with extreme climatic conditions

Ocean Circulation

Continental shelf — Surface currents-warm

Ice shelf — Surface currents-cold

Scrub
Areas of long, hot, dry summers and short warm winters where crop growing and grazing have destroyed original tree cover. Now habitat of evergreen scrub–vines and olives.

Desert
Environment includes bare mountains, rocky waste, sand dunes. Plants (wiry grass, thorn bushes, cacti) and animals (lizards, camels) must be well adapted to extremes of heat and drought.

Savanna
Habitat supports tall coarse grasses with thorny, flat-topped trees. Grazed by giraffes and zebras. Drought is common and plants are adapted to recover quickly from ravages of fire.

Rainforest
Hot and wet–without marked seasons. Habitat of luxuriant trees, lianas, monkeys and tigers. Five vegetation layers– high trees, tree canopy, open canopy, shrubs, ground herbs.

OCEAN DEPTHS

MAX. DEPTH IN METRES		MAX. DEPTH IN METRES	
7455	**Indian Ocean**	9219	**Atlantic Ocean**
6400	West Indian Basin	5449	Arctic Basin
6400	Madagascar Basin	5449	Eurasian Basin
5875	Arabian Basin	4994	Canadian Basin
5824	Somali Basin	4846	Greenland Basin
5778	Natal Basin	3960	Norwegian Basin
5660	South West Indian Basin		
4153	Oman Basin	9219	West Atlantic Basin
7455	East Indian Basin	9219	Puerto Rico Trench
6857	Diamantina Trench	8264	South Sandwich Trench
6840	Berlin Trench	7756	South Antilles Basin
6656	Cuvier Basin	6995	North American Basin
6350	West Australian Basin	6671	Guayana Basin
6335	Keeling Basin	6537	Brazilian Basin
6090	Central Indian Basin	6212	Argentinian Basin
		5883	Newfoundland Basin
11034	**Pacific Ocean**	4459	Labrador Basin
10540	West Pacific Basin		
10540	Philippine Trench	7856	East Atlantic Basin
10047	Kermadec Trench	7292	Cape Verde Basin
9165	New Hebrides Trench	6501	Canary Basin
9140	South Solomon Trench	6325	West European Basin
8412	Japan Trench	6040	Sierra Leone Basin
8066	Peru-Chile Trench	6013	Angola Basin
7388	Santa Cruz Basin	5834	Iberian Basin
6950	East Caroline Basin	5695	Guinea Basin
		5457	Cape Basin
6972	**Atlantic/Indian South Polar Basin**		

Adjoining Oceans:

7680	Aleutian Trench
5649	Venezuelan Basin
4950	Yucatan Basin
4535	Colombian Basin
4376	Mexican Basin

Source: Statistisches Jahrbuch 1984. Kohlhammer, Wiesbaden, 1984.

WORLD'S LONGEST RIVERS

River   *Length (km)*   Termination/Confluence

EUROPE

Volga   *3685*   Caspian Sea
Danube   *2858*   Black Sea
Dnepr   *2285*   Black Sea
Kama   *2032*   Volga
Don   *1970*   Sea of Azov
Pechora   *1809*   Barents Sea
Oka   *1480*   Volga
Belaya   *1420*   Kama
Dnestr   *1411*   Black Sea
Rhine   *1320*   North Sea
Vyatka   *1314*   Kama
Elbe   *1165*   North Sea
Desna   *1130*   Dnepr
Duena   *1020*   Baltic Sea
Loire   *1020*   Atlantic Ocean
Tajo   *1007*   Atlantic Ocean

AFRICA

Nile   *6671*   Mediterranean
Zaire   *4374*   Atlantic Ocean
Niger   *4184*   Atlantic Ocean
Zambesi   *2736*   Indian Ocean
Orange   *2092*   Atlantic Ocean
Okavango   *1800*   Okavango Delta
Limpopo   *1600*   Indian Ocean
Voita   *1600*   Atlantic Ocean
Senegal   *1430*   Atlantic Ocean
Chari   *1400*   Chad

AMERICA

North America

Mackenzie   *4241*   North Sea
Mississippi   *3778*   Gulf of Mexico
Missouri   *3725*   Mississippi
Rio Grande   *3034*   Gulf of Mexico
Yukon   *2849*   Bering Sea
Nelson   *2575*   Hudson Bay
Arkansas   *2333*   Mississippi
Colorado   *2333*   Gulf of California
Ohio   *2102*   Mississippi

Columbia   *1953*   Bering Sea
St Lawrence   *1170*   Atlantic Ocean

South America

Amazon   *6437*   Atlantic Ocean
Paraná   *4264*   Atlantic Ocean
Sao Francisco   *3199*   Atlantic Ocean
Tocantins   *2699*   Atlantic Ocean
Orinoco   *2575*   Atlantic Ocean
Paraguay   *2549*   Paraná
Uraguay   *1609*   La Plata
Magdalena   *1538*   Caribbean

ASIA

Yangtze   *5472*   East China Sea
Huanghe   *4667*   Yellow Sea
Amur   *4345*   Sea of Okhotsk
Ob   *4345*   North Sea
Lena   *4313*   North Sea
Mekong   *4184*   South China Sea
Yenisei   *4092*   North Sea
Euphrates   *3597*   Persian Gulf
Indus   *2897*   Arabian Sea
Brahmaputra   *2896*   Gulf of Bengal
Tarim   *2750*   Lop-nor
Amudarya   *2539*   Aral Sea
Ural   *2535*   Caspian Sea
Kolyma   *2513*   North Sea
Ganges   *2511*   Gulf of Bengal
Zaluen   *2414*   Indian Ocean
Irawadi   *2092*   Indian Ocean
Tigris   *1899*   Persian Gulf
Angara   *1852*   Yenisei
Kura   *1515*   Caspian Sea
Godavari   *1445*   Gulf of Bengal
Kizilirmak   *1151*   Black Sea
Zelenga   *1024*   Lake Baikal

AUSTRALIA AND OCEANIA

Darling   *2740*   Murray
Murray   *2570*   Great Australian Bight

Source: Statistisches Jahrbuch 1984. Kohlhammer. Wiesbaden, 1984.

INTERSTATE ROAD DISTANCES

Sydney–Melbourne
Hume Highway 877km
Princes Highway 1058km
Olympic Way 961km

Sydney–A'delaide
Mid-Western Highway 1418km
Sturt Highway 1427km
Barrier Highway 1668km

Melbourne–Adelaide
Western and Dukes Highways 726km
Princes Highway West 910km

Sydney–Brisbane
Pacific Highway 998km
New England Highway 1027km

Brisbane–Cairns
Bruce Highway 1727km

Adelaide–Perth
Eyre Highway 2718km

Adelaide–Darwin
Stuart Highway 3101km

Sydney–Darwin
Via Dubbo, Bourke, Charleville & Mt Isa 4169km

Brisbane–Darwin
Via Roma & Mt Isa 3679km

Perth–Darwin
North West Coastal Highway 4205km

AUSTRALIAN AIR DISTANCES

All distances are expressed in kilometres by means of the Great Circle Distance formula. A Great Circle Distance is the shortest distance between any two points of the globe, over the earth's surface.

		Darwin - Singapore	3350
Adelaide - Alice Springs	1316	Darwin - Sydney	3154
Adelaide - Auckland	3258		
Adelaide - Brisbane	1617	Hobart - Melbourne	617
Adelaide - Broken Hill	426	Hobart - Sydney	1040
Adelaide - Canberra	972	Hobart - Townsville	2622
Adelaide - Darwin	2619		
Adelaide - Hobart	1172	Melbourne - Nadi	3871
Adelaide - Melbourne	643	Melbourne - New York	16711
Adelaide - Perth	2120	Melbourne - Noumea	2689
Adelaide - Sydney	1166	Melbourne - Paris	16771
		Melbourne - Perth	2707
Brisbane - Cairns	1392	Melbourne - Rome	15971
Brisbane - Canberra	951	Melbourne - San Francisco	12657
Brisbane - Darwin	2852	Melbourne - Singapore	6040
Brisbane - Great Keppel Island	518	Melbourne - Sydney	707
Brisbane - Lord Howe Island	739	Melbourne - Tel Aviv	13750
Brisbane - Melbourne	1376	Melbourne - Tokyo	8148
Brisbane - Mount Isa	1572	Melbourne - Vancouver	13204
Brisbane - Perth	3611	Melbourne - Wellington	2595
Brisbane - Rockhampton	520		
Brisbane - Sydney	747	Perth - Port Hedland	1312
Brisbane - Townsville	1114	Perth - Rome	13342
		Perth - Singapore	3909
Canberra - Darwin	3141	Perth - Sydney	3284
Canberra - Hobart	850		
Canberra - Melbourne	470	Sydney - Tel Aviv	14177
Canberra - Perth	3091	Sydney - Tokyo	7807
Canberra - Sydney	237	Sydney - Toronto	15567
		Sydney - Townsville	1689
Darwin - Denpasar	1766	Sydney - Vancouver	12584
Darwin - Hong Kong	4263	Sydney - Wellington	2233
Darwin - Jakarta	2720	Sydney - Zurich	16595
Darwin - Kuala Lumpur	3674		
Darwin - London	13888		
Darwin - Mount Isa	1297		
Darwin - Perth	2651		

Source: Transport Australia. Air Transport Statistics.

CLIMATE ZONES IN AUSTRALIA

CLASSIFICATION	SEASONAL CHARACTERISTICS	
	Summer	Winter
Summer Rainfall — Tropical	Heavy periodic rains (heavier in coastal & highland areas) Hot generally Humid in coastal areas	Generally rainless Mild to warm Dry
Summer Rainfall — Subtropical	Heavy periodic rains (heavier in coastal & highland areas) Mainly hot Humid in highlands & coastal areas	Some significant rain Mild
Winter Rainfall (moderate to heavy) — Temperate	Irregular rain, mostly light Warm to hot	Reliable rain (moderate to heavy) Cool to mild
Winter Rainfall (mainly moderate) — Temperate	Mostly light irregular rain Warm to hot	Reliable rain (mainly moderate) Cool to cold
Arid (mainly summer rain) — Subtropical	Variable rain Hot to extreme Very dry	Mainly irregular light rain Mild to warm Dry
Arid (winter or non-seasonal rain) — Warm Temperate to Subtropical	Very irregular rain Hot to extreme Very dry	Variable rain, mainly light Cool to mild Dry

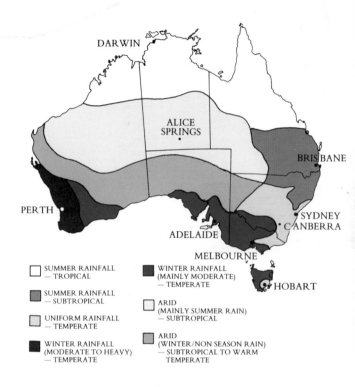

EXTREME MINIMUM TEMPERATURES
(All years to July 1982)

STATION	°C	DATE	STATION	°C	DATE
New South Wales —			South Australia —		
Charlotte Pass	– 22.2	14.7.1945	Yongala	– 8.2	20.7.1976
		22.8.1947	Yunta	– 7.7	19.7.1976
Kiandra	– 20.6	2.8.1929	Western Australia —		
Kosciusko Hotel	– 14.4	3.7.1929	Booylgoo	– 6.7	12.7.1969
		6.7.1939	Wandering	– 5.7	1.6.1964
Cooma	– 11.2	13.7.1898	Tasmania —		
Victoria —			Shannon	– 13.0	30.6.1983
Mount Hotham	– 12.8	13.8.1947	Butlers Gorge	– 13.0	30.6.1983
Omeo	– 11.7	15.6.1965	Tarraleah	– 13.0	30.6.1983
Bairnsdale	– 7.2	16.8.1896	Northern Territory —		
Queensland —			Alice Springs	– 7.5	12.7.1976
Stanthorpe	– 11.0	4.7.1895	Tempe Downs	– 6.9	24.7.1971
Mitchell	– 9.4	15.8.1979	Australian Capital		
Nanango	– 9.3	16.7.1918	Territory —		
			Canberra	– 10.0	19.7.1924
					11.7.1971

Source: Year Book Australia 1984. A.B.S. Cat. no. 1301.0

EXTREME MAXIMUM TEMPERATURES
(All years to July 1982)

STATION	°C	DATE	STATION	°C	DATE
New South Wales —			Western Australia —		
Bourke	52.8	17.1.1877	Eucla	50.7	22.1.1906
Walgett	50.1	2.1.1903	Mundrabilla	49.8	3.1.1979
Wilcannia	50.0	11.1.1939	Forrest	49.8	13.1.1979
Victoria —			Madura	49.4	7.1.1971
Mildura	50.8	6.1.1906	Tasmania —		
Swan Hill	49.4	18.1.1906	Bushy Park	40.8	26.12.1945
Queensland —			Hobart	40.8	4.1.1976
Cloncurry	53.1	16.1.1889	Northern Territory —		
Winton	50.7	14.12.1888	Finke	48.3	2.1.1960
Birdsville	50.0	24.12.1972	Jervois	47.5	3.1.1978
South Australia —			Australian Capital		
Oodnadatta	50.7	2.1.1960	Territory —		
Kyancutta	49.3	9.1.1939	Canberra (Acton)	42.8	11.1.1939

HIGHEST DAILY RAINFALLS
(All years to July 1981)

STATE	STATION	DATE	AMOUNT
			mm
New South Wales	Dorrigo	21.2.1954	809
	Cordeaux River	14.2.1898	574
Victoria	Balook	18.2.1951	275
	Hazel Park	1.12.1934	267
Queensland	Bellenden Ker (Top Station)	4.1.1979	1 140
	Crohamhurst	3.2.1893	907
	Finch Hatton	18.2.1958	878
	Mount Dangar	20.1.1970	869
South Australia	Stansbury	18.2.1946	222
	Stirling	17.4.1889	208
Western Australia	Whim Creek	3.4.1898	747
	Kilto	4.12.1970	635
	Fortescue	3.5.1890	593
Tasmania	Cullenswood	22.3.1954	352
	Mathinna	5.4.1929	337
Northern Territory	Roper Valley	15.4.1963	545
	Groote Eylandt	28.3.1953	513

Source: Year Book Australia 1984. A.B.S. Cat. no. 1301.0.

HIGHEST RAINFALL INTENSITIES IN SPECIFIED PERIODS
(millimetres)

STATION AND PERIOD OF RECORD	YEARS OF COMPLETE RECORDS	PERIOD IN HOURS				
		1	3	6	12	24
		mm	*mm*	*mm*	*mm*	*mm*
Adelaide *1897-1980*	80	69	133	141	141	141
Alice Springs *1951-1980*	28	75	77	87	108	150
Brisbane *1911-1980*	67	88	144	182	265	327
Broome *1948-1979*	32	112	157	185	313	351
Canberra *1932-1979*	44	51	68	71	89	139
Carnarvon *1956-1979*	24	32	63	83	95	108
Charleville *1953-1980*	28	42	66	75	111	142
Cloncurry *1953-1975*	20	59	118	164	173	204
Darwin (Airport) *1953-1980*	25	88	138	214	260	277
Esperance *1963-1979*	15	23	45	62	68	79
Hobart *1911-1980*	67	28	56	87	117	168
Meekatharra *1953-1979*	25	33	67	81	99	112
Melbourne *1878-1980*	90	79	83	86	97	130
Mildura *1953-1977*	23	49	60	65	65	91
Perth *1946-1980*	33	32	38	47	64	93
Sydney *1913-1979*	63	97	135	166	190	282
Townsville *1953-1980*	26	88	158	235	296	319

Source: Pluviograph records in Bureau of Meteorology archives.

BOUNDARIES

	International
	International under Dispute
	Cease Fire Line
	Autonomous or State
	Administrative
	Maritime (National)

LETTERING STYLES

CANADA   Independent Nation

FLORIDA   State, Province or Autonomous Region

Gibraltar (U.K.)   Sovereignty of Dependent Territory

Lothian   Administrative Area

LANGUEDOC   Historic Region

Loire *Vosges*   Physical Feature or Physical Region

TOWNS AND CITIES

Square symbols denote capital cities   *Population*

◨ ◉	**New York**	over 5 000 000
■ ●	**Montréal**	over 1 000 000
◻ ○	Ottawa	over 500 000
▪ •	**Québec**	over 100 000
◻ ○	St John's	over 50 000
▫ ○	Yorkton	over 10 000
▫ ○	Jasper	under 10 000
		Built-up-area

LAKE FEATURES

	Permanent
	Seasonal

OTHER FEATURES

	River
	Seasonal River
⹀	Pass, Gorge
	Dam, Barrage
	Waterfall, Rapid
	Aqueduct
	Reef
▲ 4231	Summit, Peak
.217	Spot Height, Depth
⌣	Well
△	Oil Field
▲	Gas Field
Gas / Oil	Oil / Natural Gas Pipeline
Gemsbok Nat. Pk	National Park
⛬ UR	Historic Site
	Main Railway
	Other Railway
- - - - - -	Under Construction
—+—+—	Rail Tunnel
- - - - - -	Rail Ferry
	Canal
⊕	International Airport
✦	Other Airport

For pages 102-103, 104-105 only:

	0	Sea Level
	200m	
	2000m	
	4000m	
	6000m	
		Depth

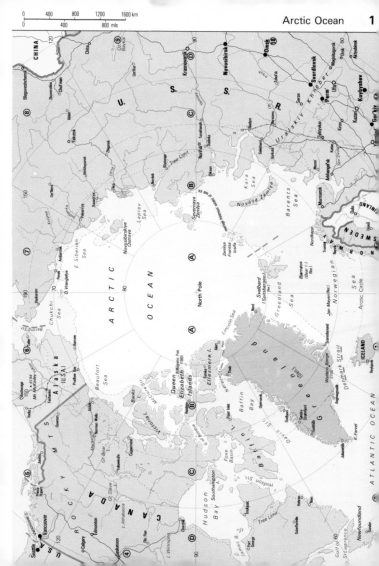

Arctic Ocean

0   400   800   1200   1600 km
0   400   800 mls

CHINA

U.   S.   S.   R.

Blagoveshchensk   Chita   Onon
Chul'man   Aldan   Lake Baykal   Krasnoyarsk   Novosibirsk   Omsk   Sverdlovsk   Kuybyshev   Kyzyl   Perm'   Ufa   Kazan'   Orsk   Gor'kiy

Yakutsk   Zhigansk   Olekminsk   Tiksi   Norad   Tunguska   Uralskiy   Serov   Khrebet   Magnitogorsk
Tree Limit   Norilsk   Dudinka   Turukhansk   Salekhard   Sob   Sev. Dvina   Pechora   Arkhangel'sk

Olenek   Kanaky   Khatanga   Kara Sea   Novaya Zemlya   Barents Sea   Murmansk   Nordkapp
Indigirka   Novosibirskiye Ostrova   Severnaya Zemlya   Zemlya Frantsa Iosifa   FINLAND   SWEDEN   NORWAY   Tromsø

Kolyma   Lena   Laptev Sea   ARCTIC   OCEAN   North Pole   Svalbard (Spitsbergen)   Bjørnøya (Bear I.)   Jan Mayen (Nor.)   Norwegian Sea   Arctic Circle

E. Siberian Sea   Novyye Sibirskiye Ostrova   Greenland Sea   Denmark Strait   ICELAND   Reykjavik

Chukchi Sea   Bering Strait   Barrow   Beaufort Sea   MacKenzie   Banks I.   Lincoln Sea   GREENLAND (Dan.)   Scoresbysund   Angmagssalik   C. Farvel

Alaska (U.S.A.)   Mt. McKinley   Prudhoe Bay   Queen Elizabeth Islands   Magnetic Pole (1980)   Ellesmere I.   Baffin Bay   Upernavik   Godhavn   Davis Strait
ROCKY   MTS   Fairbanks   Whitehorse   Victoria I.   Gt. Bear L.   Coppermine   Boothia   Gt. Slave L.   Foxe Basin   Baffin I.   Frobisher Bay   Julianehåb
Vancouver   Seattle   Edmonton   Calgary   Saskatoon   CANADA   L. Winnipeg   Churchill   Hudson Bay   Southampton I.   Hudson Str.   Fort Chimo   Tree Limit   Newfoundland
USA   Regina   Fort George   James B.   Moosonee   Gulf of St Lawrence   ATLANTIC OCEAN

ATLANTIC OCEAN

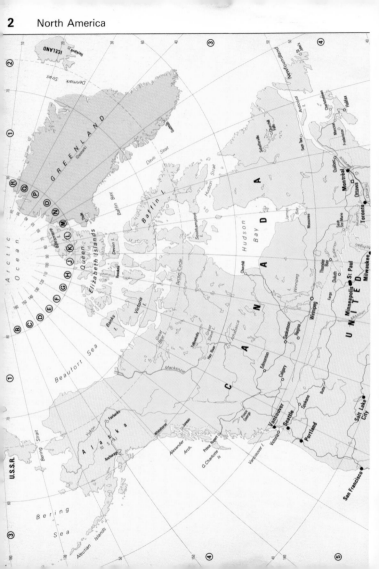

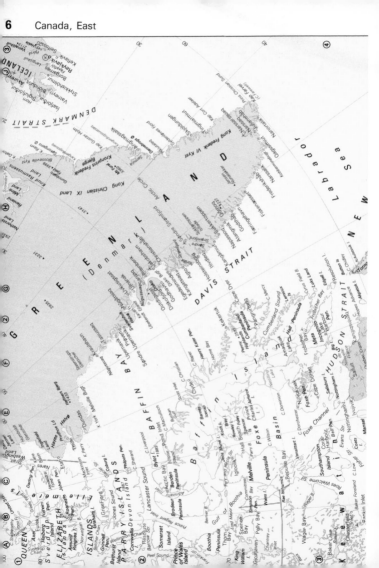

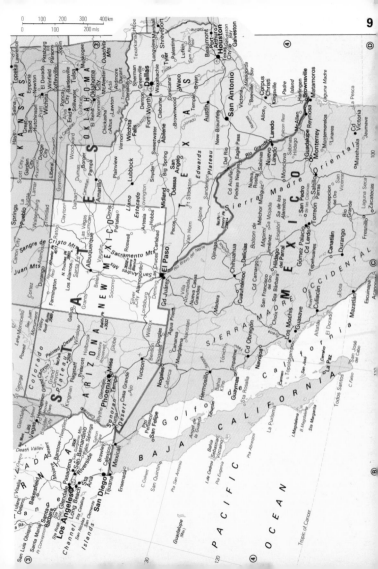

MANITOBA

ONTARIO

QUÉBEC

NEW BRUNSWICK

MAINE

NEW HAMPSHIRE

VERMONT

NEW YORK

MICHIGAN

WISCONSIN

MINNESOTA

IOWA

ILLINOIS

INDIANA

OHIO

PENNSYLVANIA

WEST VIRGINIA

VIRGINIA

MARYLAND

James Bay

St Lawrence

Lake Superior

Lake Huron

Lake Michigan

Lake Erie

Lake Ontario

Lake Winnipeg

Winnipeg

Minneapolis
St Paul

Kansas City

Chicago

Milwaukee

Madison

Des Moines

Duluth

Detroit

Toronto

Montréal

Ottawa

Boston

Providence

Hartford

New York
Newark
New Jersey

Philadelphia

Baltimore

Washington

Buffalo

Cleveland

Columbus

Cincinnati

Indianapolis

Pittsburgh

Thunder Bay

Sudbury

Sault Ste Marie

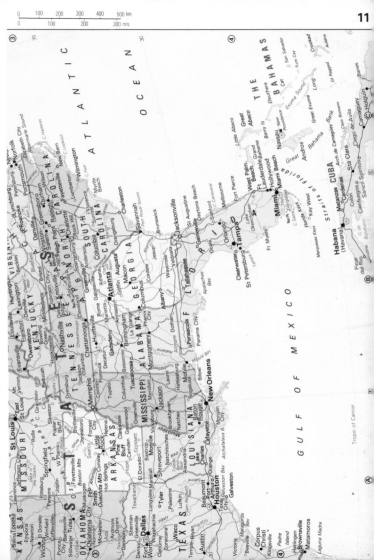

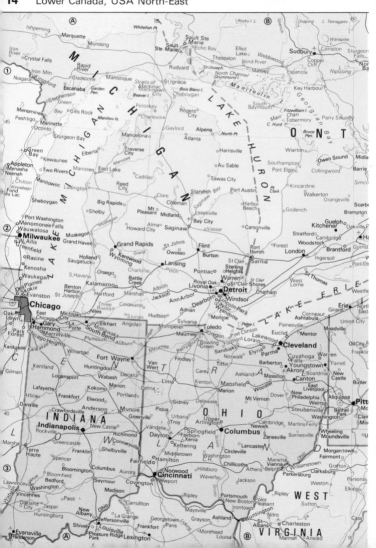

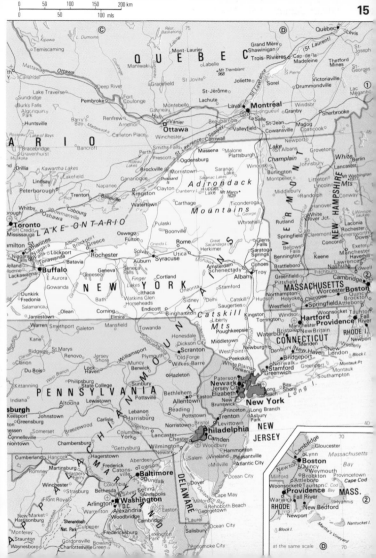

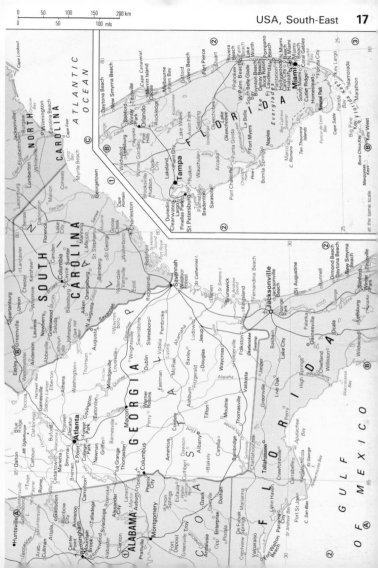

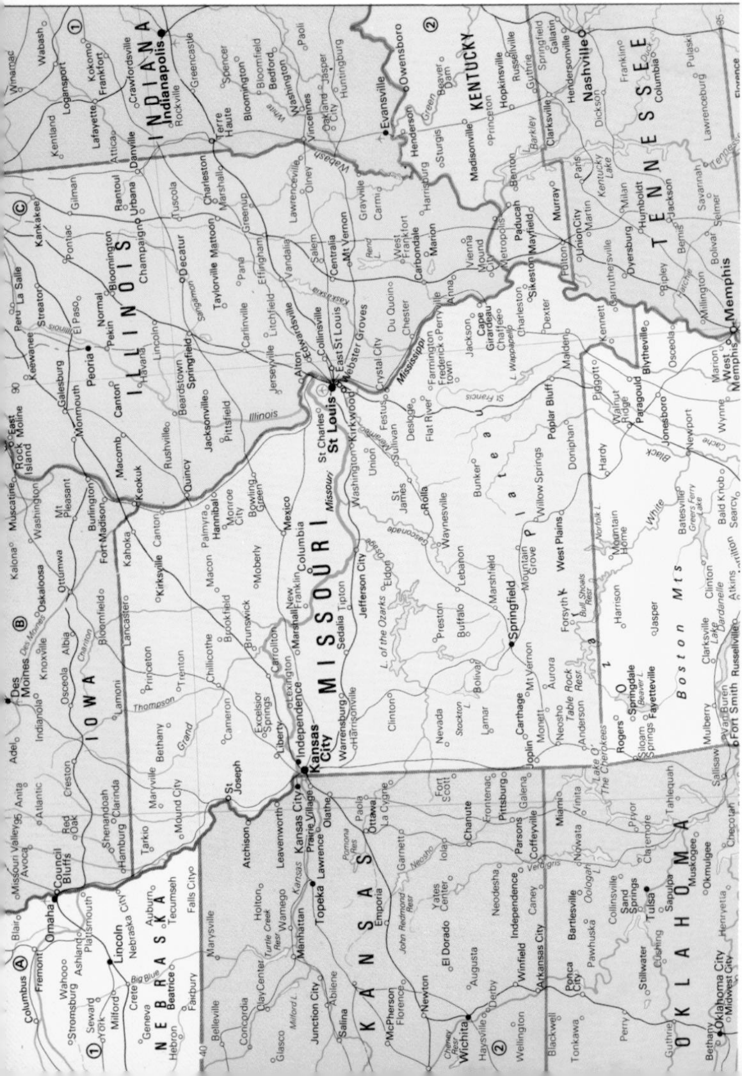

Map of the South-Central USA showing parts of:

- INDIANA
- KENTUCKY
- TENNESSEE
- ILLINOIS
- MISSOURI
- IOWA
- NEBRASKA
- KANSAS
- OKLAHOMA

Major cities and places include: Indianapolis, Nashville, Memphis, St Louis, East St Louis, Kansas City, Springfield, Omaha, Lincoln, Wichita, Tulsa, Oklahoma City, Des Moines, Council Bluffs, Peoria, Evansville, Paducah, Jefferson City, Columbia, St Joseph, Independence, Topeka, Lawrence, Fort Smith, Fayetteville.

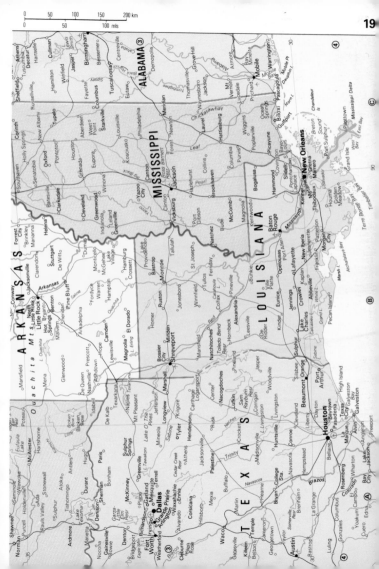

Map — Southern United States

Scale: 0 50 100 150 200 km · 0 50 100 mls

ALABAMA ③

Athens, Decatur, Hartselle, Cullman, Sheffield, Russellville, Hamilton, Winfield, Jasper, Lewis Smith L., Birmingham, Bessemer, Centreville, Grove Hill, Fayette, Tuscaloosa, Columbus, Eutaw, Demopolis, Thomasville, Waynesboro, Mt. Vernon, Jackson, Atmore, Bay Minette, Warrington, Mobile, Chickasaw, Prichard, Mobile Bay, Dauphin I.

MISSISSIPPI

Corinth, New Albany, Holly Springs, Tupelo, Aberdeen, West Point, Starkville, Louisville, Philadelphia, Newton, Meridian, Southaven, Senatobia, Oxford, Pontotoc, Houston, Eupora, Kosciusko, Forest, Hattiesburg, Wiggins, Ocean Springs, Biloxi, Gulfport, Batesville, Clarksdale, Grenada, Winona, Jackson, Clinton, Hazlehurst, Collins, Laurel, Columbia, Purvis, Poplarville, Picayune, Pearl R., Cleveland, Greenwood, Indianola, Greenville, Leland, Yazoo City, Vicksburg, Brookhaven, McComb, Magnolia, Kentwood, Bogalusa, Covington, Slidell, Bay St. Louis, Pascagoula

LOUISIANA

Forest City, Marianna, Helena, Clarendon, De Witt, Stuttgart, Dumas, McGehee, Monticello, Lake Village, Tallulah, St. Joseph, Ferriday, Natchez, Fort Gibson, Baton Rouge, Hammond, Laplace, Kenner, New Orleans, Marrero, Gretna, Port Sulphur, Grand Isle, Bastrop, Monroe, Crossett, Homer, Ruston, Jonesboro, Winnfield, Columbia, Catahoula L., Pineville, Alexandria, Bunkie, Opelousas, Port Allen, New Iberia, Franklin, Patterson, Morgan City, Houma, Thibodaux, Raceland

ARKANSAS

Poteau, Mena, De Queen, Nashville, Glenwood, Hope, Prescott, Magnolia, El Dorado, Camden, Hampton, Warren, Fordyce, Pine Bluff, Little Rock, Benton, Bryant, Hot Springs, Malvern, Arkadelphia, Ouachita R., Saline R., Conway, Mt. Ouachita, L. Ouachita

TEXAS

Shawnee, Seminole, Wewoka, Holdenville, McAlester, Ada, Stonewall, Atoka, Tishomingo, Durant, Denison, Sherman, Bonham, Paris, Sulphur Springs, Mt. Pleasant, Naples, Jefferson, Marshall, Longview, Kilgore, Henderson, Carthage, Center, Nacogdoches, Lufkin, Rusk, Jacksonville, Palestine, Athens, Crockett, Livingston, Cleveland, Woodville, Jasper, Newton, De Ridder, Kinder, Lake Charles, Jennings, Crowley, Kaplan, Abbeville, Sulphur, Orange, Beaumont, Port Arthur, Galveston, Texas City, La Marque, Pasadena, Baytown, Houston, Bellaire, Liberty, Dayton, Alvin, Angleton, Lake Jackson, Freeport, Richmond, Rosenberg, Wharton, Bay City, Edna, Columbus, La Grange, Bastrop, Luling, Gonzales, Cuero

Ardmore, Marietta, Nocona, Bowie, Gainesville, Denton, Fort Worth, Arlington, Dallas, Garland, Mesquite, Richardson, Irving, Grand Prairie, Cleburne, Glen Rose, Waxahachie, Ennis, Corsicana, Hillsboro, Mexia, Buffalo, Madisonville, Navasota, Bryan, College Station, Brenham, Hempstead, Conroe, Huntsville, Trinity, Marlin, Temple, Killeen, Gatesville, Georgetown, Taylor, Austin, Waco, McKinney, Terrell, Mineola, Tyler, Canton, Kaufman

De Kalb, Texarkana, Idabell, Broken Bow L., Pauls Valley, Ada, Ardmore

L. Texoma, Lake Tawakoni, Lake O' The Pines, Toledo Bend Res., Sam Rayburn Res., Sabine L., Galveston Bay, Matagorda Bay

50 100 150 200 km
50 100 mls

A 125 Parksville
Gibsons Horseshoe Bay Vancouver
Port Alberni
Nanaimo Vancouver
Richmond
New Westminster
Barkley Sd
Bamfield
Ladysmith
Cowichan
Blaine
Abbotsford
Hope Princeton
Agassiz Skagit Mtn *2356
Keremeos
C A N A D A
Okanagan Falls
Oliver
Oroville
Castlegar
Grand Forks Trail
Salmo
Creston
Metaline Falls
Ione
Priest
Bonners Ferry

Port Renfrew
Duncan
Sidney
Victoria
Esquimalt
Sooke
San Juan
Anacortes
Bellingham
Mt Baker *3285
Concrete
Mt Logan *2733
Tonasket
Republic
Omak
Okanogan
Franklin D. Roosevelt Lake
Colville
Newport
Sandpoint
Priest River
Spirit Lake

C. Flattery
Str of Juan de Fuca
Port Angeles
Olympic Nat. Park
Mt Olympus *2428
Mt Vernon
North Cascades Nat. Pk.
Glacier Peak *3221
Brewster
Columbia
Grand Coulee
Banks
Wilbur
Chelan
Coeur d'Alene Lake
Spokane
Medical Lake Cheney
Plummer
Coeur d'Alene
Kellogg

Forks
Edmonds
Seattle
Bremerton
Bellevue
Renton
Wenatchee
Ephrata
Odessa
Moses Lake
Ritzville
St Maries

① Hoquiam
Shelton
Olympia
Tacoma
Port Orchard
Kent
Auburn
Puyallup
Snoqualmie Pass
W A S H I N G T O N
Ellensburg
Selah
Yakima
Colfax
Pullman
Moscow
Kendrick
Potlatch

Aberdeen
Grays Hbr
Raymond
Willapa B
South Bend
Shelton
Centralia
Chehalis
Winlock
Mt Rainier *4392
Mount Rainier Nat. Park
Naches
Toppenish
Sunnyside
Richland
Pasco
Kennewick
Dayton
Clarkston
Lewiston

C. Disappointment
Astoria
Seaside
Longview Kelso
Rainier
Woodland
St Helens
Mt St Helens *2950
Mt Adams *3751
Goldendale
Columbia
Walla Walla
Umatilla
Snake
C O L U M B I A

Tillamook
Portland
Hillsboro
Lake Oswego
Newberg
Oregon City
Camas
Vancouver
White Salmon
Hood River
The Dalles
Arlington
Echo
Pendleton
Wallowa
Enterprise
La Grande
Riggins

45
Lincoln City
McMinnville
Woodburn
Salem
Mt Wilson *1707
Mt Hood *3427
Condon
Blue Mountains
Ukiah
Wallowa Sacajawea *2997 Pk
Hells Canyon
He Devil Mtn *2853
Midvale

Newport
Corvallis
Albany
Lebanon
Stayton
Idanha
Mt Jefferson *3199
Spray
Long Creek
Baker
Weiser
Payette
Ontario

Yachats
Florence
Eugene
Springfield
Lowell
Sweet Home
Redmond
Three Sisters *3156
Bend
Prineville
Madras
Dayville
Canyon City John Day
Unity
Caldwell
Nampa
Vale
Emmett

Reedsport
Cottage Grove
Oakridge
La Pine
O R E G O N
Brothers
Burns
Drewsey
Crane
Murphy
Jordan Valley

Coos Bay
N.Bend
Umpqua
Oakland
Crescent
High Desert
Silver Lake
Harney Basin
Harney L.
Malheur L.
Owyhee Mts

125
Myrtle Point
Roseburg
Myrtle Creek
Canyonville
Mt Thielsen *2799
Crater L.
Mt Scott *2721
Chiloquin
Upper Klamath L.
Jordan Valley
Oxbow

C. Blanco
Port Orford
Prospect
Nat. Pk.
Wolf Creek
Grants Pass
Mt McLoughlin *2894
Upper Klamath L.
Bly
Valley Falls

②
Gold Beach
Central Point
Medford
Ashland
Klamath Falls
Lakeview
Steens Mtn
Warner Mts

Brookings
O'Brien
Hornbrook
Dorris
Willow Ranch
Clear L. Resr
Goose L.
Denio
Mc Dermitt

Pt St George
Crescent City
Klamath
Yreka
K l a m a t h
Canby
Alturas
Middle Alkali L.
Upper L.
Black Rock Desert

Klamath
M t s
Weed
Mt Shasta *4317
Mount Shasta
Adin
N E V A D A
Santa Rosa Ra
Winnemucca
Golconda

B
Arcata
Eureka
Fortura
McCloud
Dunsmuir
C A L I F O R N I A
Project City
Redding Nat. Pk.
Lassen Pk *3187
Eagle L.
Susanville
Rye Patch Resr
Imlay
Battle Mountain
Mt Tobin *2979
C
120

0 50 100 150 200 km
0 50 100 mls

Humboldt Bay
Arcata
Eureka Weaverville
Fortuna

Dunsmuir Adin
Shasta Burney
Project City
Redding Lassen Pk.
Nat. Pk. 3187
Chester Eagle L
Almanor
Susanville Honey L.

Garberville
40
Cummings

Fort Bragg

Paradise
Chico
Oroville
Grass Quincy
Valley
Donner Pass
Feather R. Mid. Fork

Ukiah
Lakeport
Pt Arena

Clear L.

Williams
Marysville
Yuba City
Roseville
Colfax
Auburn
Placerville
Sutter Creek
San Andreas

Reno Sparks
Virginia City
Silver City
Carson City
Stewart
S. Lake Tahoe
Yerington
Schurz
Gabbs

Healdsburg
Santa
Rosa
Bodega Head
Napa
Vacaville
Fairfield
Vallejo
Antioch
Concord
Woodland
Davis
Carmichael
Sacramento
Galt
Lodi
Stockton
Oakdale
Sonora
Bridgeport
Coaldale

San Rafael
Berkeley Oakland
San Francisco
Daly City
San Mateo
Redwood City
Sunnyvale
Santa Clara
San Jose
Los Gatos
Alameda
Hayward
Livermore
Modesto
Turlock
Gustine
Merced
Madera
Pinedale
Fresno
Bishop
Big Pine

Santa Cruz
Watsonville
Monterey Bay
Pt Pinos
Monterey
Gonzales
Salinas
Los Banos
Kings
Canyon
Nat. Park
Independence
Lone Pine

King City
Coalinga
Hanford
Lemoore
Tulare
Visalia
Exeter
Porterville
Sequoia
Nat. Park
Mt Whitney
4418
Keeler

Paso Robles
Wasco
Oildale
Bakersfield
Delano
Arvin
Inyokern
Johannesburg

Morro Bay
San Luis
Obispo
Grover City
Santa
Maria
Lompoc
Tehachapi Mts
Tehachapi Pass
Mojave
Barstow

Pt Conception
Santa Barbara Chan.
Santa Barbara
Santa Paula
Fillmore
Ventura
Oxnard
Lancaster
Victorville

San Miguel
Santa Cruz
Santa Rosa
Channel Islands
Burbank
Beverly Hills
Santa Monica
Torrance
Los Angeles
Glendale
Pasadena
San Bernardino
Redlands
Pomona
Riverside
Anaheim
Santa Ana
Long Beach
Huntington Beach
Laguna Beach
San
Clemente
Santa Catalina
San Clemente
Oceanside
Carlsbad
Vista
Escondido
San Diego
Chula Vista
Tijuana
Tecate
Descanso

PACIFIC OCEAN

COAST RANGE
Sacramento Valley
SIERRA
Diablo Range
Santa Lucia Range
San Joaquin Valley
CALIFORNIA
NEVADA
NEVADA

Pyramid L.
Stillwater Ra.
Humboldt R.
Winnemucca Golconda
Emigrant Pass
Rye Patch Resr
Imlay
Battle Mountain
Mr Tobin 2979
Lovelock
Fernley
Fallon
Eastgate
Austin
Summit Mtn 3188
Shoshone Mts
Wildcat Pk 3203
Mt Jefferson 3642
Monitor Ra.
Warm Springs
Tonopah
Goldfield
Boundary Peak 4005
Piper Pk 2680
White Mtn 4342
Mono L.
Yosemite Nat. Park
El Portal
Mariposa
Pine Flat Resr
Panamint Range
Death Valley
Telescope Peak 3368

Winters

Donner Pass
Lake Tahoe

Kern R.

San Jacinto Pk 3301
Mt San Antonio 3068
Palomar Mt
Palm Springs

El
Cajon
National
City
La

Gulf of
Santa Catalina

Kaweah R.

USA, Hawaii

Kauai Channel
Hanalei
Kauai 1573
Mana Lihue
Niihau
Kaena Pt
Kahuku Pt
Oahu
Wahiawa
Pearl City
Pearl Harbor
Honolulu
Kailua
Kauai Chan.
Molokai
Kaunakakai
Lanai
Lanai City
Kahoolawe
Kalohi Chan.
Pailolo Chan.
Kahului
Wailuku
Maui
Hana
3055
Kealakekua Chan.
Alenuihaha Channel
Kailua
Waimea
Mauna Kea 4201
Hilo
Hakalau
Hawaii
Mauna Loa 4169
Kilauea
Crater
Hawaii Volcanoes Nat. Park 1243
Milolii
Ka Lae (South Cape)
Naalehu
Pahoa

PACIFIC OCEAN

160
20 N
155
20N

0 50 100 200 km
0 50 100 mls

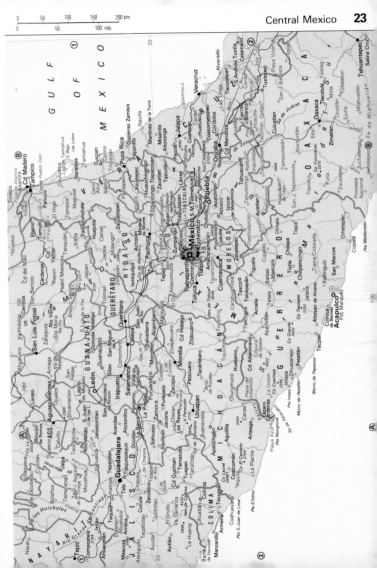

Scale

0 200 400 600 km
0 100 200 300 mls

United States region

Ft Smith · Memphis · Huntsville · Chattanooga · Gainesville · Athens · SOUTH · Florence · Columbia · C. Canaveral · (E)
ster · Little Rock · Tupelo · Columbus · Gadsden · Atlanta · CAROLINA · Orangeburg
Hot Springs · ARKANSAS · Greenwood · Tuscaloosa · Birmingham · Augusta · Charleston
Pine Bluff · Greenville · Macon · Savannah
wo · Monroe · Jackson · Meridian · Montgomery · GEORGIA
Shreveport · MISSISSIPPI · Phenix · Columbus · Albany · Waycross · Brunswick
mont · LOUISIANA · Vicksburg · ALABAMA · City · Dothan · Valdosta
Lufkin · Natchez · Laurel · Jacksonville
Alexandria · Hattiesburg · Tallahassee · St Augustine
Lake · Baton · Mobile · Pensacola · Panama City · Gainesville · Daytona Beach
Charles · Lafayette · Rouge · Biloxi · Apalachee B · Ocala
Pt Arthur · New Orleans · Orlando · C. Canaveral
Orange · Melbourne
Galveston · Clearwater · Tampa · Ft Pierce · Little Abaco · THE
St Petersburg · W Palm · Great Abaco · BAHAMAS
Tampa Bay · Lake · Beach · Berry Is · Eleuthera
Ft Myers · Okeechobee · Lake Worth · Gd · New · Nassau · Exuma Sound · Cat Is
Ft Lauderdale · Bahama · Providence
Hollywood · Berry Is · Andros · Great · Rum
Miami · Miami Beach · Exuma · Cay
The Everglades · Long I
C. Sable · Andros

Gulf of Mexico / Caribbean

GULF   OF   MEXICO

Key West · Marquesas Keys · Straits of Florida · Great Bahama Bank

Habana (Havana) · Matanzas · Arch. de · Camagüey
Cárdenas · Camagüey · Cayo Romano
Pinar del Río · Colon · Sta Clara · Morón · Ciego de Ávila
Yucatan Channel · Guane · G. de Batabanó · Cienfuegos · Sancti Spíritus · CUBA · Holguín · Ban
Progreso · C. San Antonio · Victoria de · las Tunas · Bayamo · Guant
Mérida · C. Catoche · I. de la · Jardines · Manzanillo · Santiago
Juventud · de la Reina · Sta.Cruz · de Cuba
Tizimín · G. de Guacanayabo
Ticul · Valladolid · I. de · Little Cayman · Cayman Brac · Port
Campeche · Peto · Cozumel · (U.K.) · Anton
YUCATAN · B.de la Ascensión · Grand Cayman · Montego Bay · Kingsto
ruz · Cd del · Escárcega · (U.K.) · Spanish Town · JAMAICA
Andrés · Carmen · Chetumal · Bco Chinchorro · Pedro Cays
xtla · Frontera · L. de Términos · Ambergris Cay · (Jam.)
Coatzacoalcos · Villahermosa · Belize · Turneffe I.
Minatitlán · Perdosico · BELIZE · Stann Creek · Is. de la Bahía · C A R I B B E A N
Istmo · Tuxtla · Flores · Belmopan · Trujillo · L. de Caratasca
de · Gutiérrez · Pta Gorda · Pto · S E A
Tehuantepec · San Cristóbal · G. de · Cortés · Tela · La Ceiba
alina · Comitán · HONDURAS · Paulaya · Cayos Miskitos
Cruz · Tonalá · S. Pedro Sula · Serrana Bank
o de · Huixtla · GUATEMALA · Cobán · Juticalpa · (U.S.A. & Col.) · I. de Providencia
antepec · Tapachula · Comayagua · (Col.)
Quezaltenango · Guatemala · Tegucigalpa · Bonanza · I. de San Andrés
Escuintla · Sta Ana · Pto Cabezas · (Col.)
San José · San Salvador · San · Prinzapolca
Sonsonate · S Miguel · La Unión · Matagalpa
EL SALVADOR · Chinandega · León · NICARAGUA · Bluefields
G. de Fonseca · Managua · L. de Managua
Masaya · Granada · Is del Maíz
San Juan · L. de · (Nic. & USA)
del Sur · Nicaragua · San Juan del Norte
G. de Papagayo · COSTA
Pen. de · Puntarenas · Alajuela · G. de los · Colón · Pta S. Blas
Nicoya · San José · Limón · Mosquitos
G.de Nicoya · Cartago · RICA · L. de · P · Panamá
Pto Cortés · Chiriquí · La Chorrera
Pen. de Osa · David · Arch. de
G. Dulce · Pto · Santiago · Chitré · las Perlas
Armuelles · Golfo
Pen. de · de
G. de · Azuero · Panamá
Chiriqui · Pta
Solano

90 · (D) · (E)

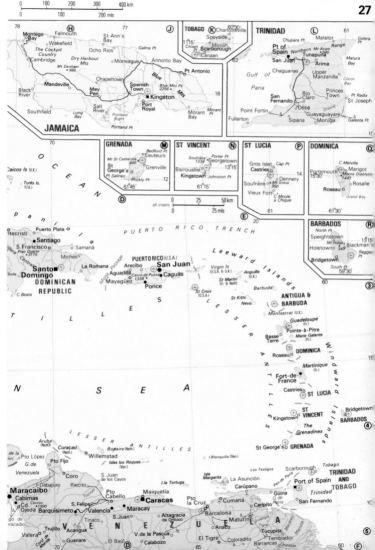

200 400 600 km
100 200 300 mls

La Serena
Coquimbo
Rivadavia
C. de Toro
Grl Manuel Belgrano 6380 6250
La Rioja
Sumampa
Reconquista
Goya
Mercedes
Uruguaiana
Cruz Alta
Sta Maria
BRAZIL
Cachoeira do Sul

Vera
Santa Fe
Corrientes
Paso de los Libres
Alegrete
Artigas
Rivera
do Livramento
Bagé

Punitaqui
Illapel
Los Vilos
Ovalle
Jáchal
Cruz del Eje
S. Agustin
L. Mar Chiquita
Rafaela
Santa Fe
Concordia
Salto
Tacuarembó
Melo

San Juan
Mercedario 6770
Aconcagua 6960
Córdoba
Va Dolores
S.Francisco
Alta Gracia
Paraná
Concepción
La Paz
Paysandú
Durazno

Viña del Mar
Valparaíso
Quillota
S. Felipe
Mendoza
Tupungato 6800
San Luis
Villa María
Bell Ville
Entre Ríos
Rosario
San Nicolás
URUGUAY
Trinidad
Florida
Treinta y Tres

Santiago
S. Antonio
S. Bernardo
Rancagua
Pichilemu
Vol Maipo 5290
S. Rafael
Mercedes
Río Cuarto
Cda de Gómez
Pergamino
Junín
Buenos Aires
Colonia
Avellaneda
La Plata
Montevideo
Maldonado
Rocha
Punta del Este

Curicó
Talca
Constitución
S. Fernando
Grl Alvear
Va Huidobro
Lincoln
Chivilcoy
Mercedes
Canelones
Punta de la Plata

Cauquenes
Linares
S. Carlos
Chillán
Mendoza
Bardas Blancas
Telén
Grl Pico
Trenque Lauquen
Pehuajó
Las Flores
Chascomús
Dolores

Talcahuano
Concepción
Coronel
Tomé
Vol Domuyo 4800
ARGENTINA
La Pampa
Sta Rosa
Guaminí
Carhué
Olavarría
Azul
Tandil
Ayacucho
Va Gesell

Lebu
Los Ángeles
Angol
Carahue
Temuco
Villarrica
Longuimay
Zapala
Neuquén
Grl Roca
Choele Choel
Río Negro
Tres Arroyos
Cnl Pringles
Balcarce
Bahía Blanca
Necochea
Claromecó
Punta Alta
Mar del Plata
Miramar

Toltén
Loncoche
Valdivia
Los Lagos
La Unión
Osorno
Vol Lanín 3740
Emb. El Chocón
S. Antonio Oeste
Carmen de Patagones
Viedma

Pto Varas
Puerto Montt
Ancud
I. de Chiloé
Castro
Achao
Paso Limay
Nahuel Huapi
S. Carlos de Bariloche
El Bolsón
Maquinchao
Valcheta
Golfo San Matías

Esquel
Chubut
Melimoyu 2400
Las Plumas
Chubut
Trelew
Gaimán
Rawson
Pto Madryn
Pto Pirámides

Archipiélago de las Chones
Pto Aisén
Coihaique
L. Musters
L. Colhué
Golfo San Jorge
Camarones
C. Dos Bahías

Pen. de Taitao
G. de Penas
San Valentín 4058
Sarmiento
L. Buenos Aires
Caleta Olivia
Comodoro Rivadavia
Colonia Las Heras

ATLANTIC OCEAN

Campana
Esmeralda
Madre de Dios
Hanover
O'Higgins
L. Gral Carrera
L. Cochrane
Deseado
Las Heras
C Tres Puntas
Deseado
Pta Médanos

Lautaro 3380
Santa Cruz
S. Martín
S. Julián
Sta Cruz

Pto Natales
Muralión
L. Argentino
L. Viedma
Calafate
Bahía Grande
Río Turbio
Río Gallegos

FALKLAND ISLANDS
(ISLAS MALVINAS)
(U.K.)
Jason Is
West Falkland
Weddell
East Falkland
C. Dolphin
Stanley
Falkland Sd

Arch. de la Reina Adelaida
Pen. Muñoz Gamero
Pen. Brecknock
Punta Arenas
Est. de Magallanes
Pen. de Brunswick
Desolación
Río Grande
Tierra del Fuego
Isla Grande de Tierra del Fuego
Santa Inés

Beauchene Is

at the same scale
Shag Rocks
South Georgia
(U.K.)
C. Alexandra
C. Disappointment
Grytviken

Londonderry
Hoste
Navarino
Ushuaia
C. San Diego
I. de los Estados
Is Wollaston
C. de Hornos (C. Horn)
Diego Ramírez

0 200 400 600 km
0 100 200 300 mils

A 50 B 45 C 40 D 35 E

Equator

Belém
I. de Marajó
B. de Marajó
C. Maguarinho
Salinópolis
Bragança
Capanema
Cametá
Abaetetuba
Pará
Pinheiro
Alcântara
Monção
São Luís
Rosário
Parnaíba
Camocim
Acaraú
Itapipoca
Caucaia
Fortaleza (Ceará)
Rocas
I. Fernando de Noronha

Tucuruí
Jatobá
Bacabal
Chapadinha
Coroatá
Caxias
Campo Maior
Piripiri
Sobral
Sta Quitéria
Canindé
Aracati
Maranhão
Codó
Teresina
Castelo
Crateús
Nova Russas
Quixadá
Morada N.
C E A R Á
Areia Branca
Macau Pta do Calcanhar
Mossoró
Natal

Imperatriz
Marabá
Grajaú
Pto Franco
Florano
Oeiras
Picos
Mombaça
Taua
Acopiara
Iguatu
Patu
RIO GRANDE DO NORTE
Caicó

Araguaína
Carolina
Balsas
P I A U I
J. do Norte
Crato
Sousa
Cabedelo
João Pessoa
Campina Grande

C. do Araguaia
S. Raimundo Nonato
Paulistana
Salgueiro
Ouricuri
P A R A Í B A
Caruaru
Limoeiro
Olinda
Recife (Pernambuco)
Japa batão

B R A Z I L
Petrolina
Juazeiro
P E R N A M B U C O
Garanhuns
Palmeira dos Ind.
Barreiros

Cach. de P. Afonso
Propriá
Arapiraca
A L A G O A S
Maceió
Penedo

B A H I A
Barra
Jacobina
Sen. do Bonfim
Lagarto
S E R G I P E
Aracajú
Estância

Ibotirama
R. de Jacuípe
Serrinha
Alagoinhas

Barreiras
Bom Jesus da Lapa
Iaçu
Cachoeira
Feira de S.
Castro Alves
Salvador (Bahia)

Aruanã
Uruaçu
Caetité
Chapada Diamantina
Vitória da Conquista
Valença
Ipiaú
Jequié
Itabuna
Ilhéus

G O I Á S
Ceres
Formosa
Januária
Porteirinha
Salinas
Itapetinga
Canavieiras

Goiás
Pirenópolis
Anápolis
Iporá
Goiânia
Brasília
São Francisco
Montes Claros
Araçuaí
Sa do Chifre
Belmonte
Pôrto Seguro

A T L A N T I C
O C E A N

Caldas Novas
Rio Verde
Jataí
Itumbiara
Goiandira
Paracatu
João Pinheiro
Pirapora
Corinto
Curvelo
Diamantina
Gov. Valadares
Teófilo Otôni
Nanuque
Itamaraju

Uberlândia
M I N A S
Araguari
Catalão
Patos de Minas
Sete Lagoas
Itabira
São Mateus
Linhares

Iturama
Uberaba
Araxá
G E R A I S
Divinópolis
Belo Horizonte
Carangola
Caratinga
Conselheiro Lafaiete
Manhuaçu
E S P Í R I T O
Colatina
Cnl Fabriciano
Cariacica
S A N T O
Vitória
Vila Velha

Pres. Vargas
Fernandópolis
S. José do Rio Preto
Barretos
Franca
Passos
São João del Rei
Lavras
Juiz de Fora
Barbacena
Ponte Nova
Caravelas
Itaperuna
Cachoeiro de Itapemirim

Araçatuba
Catanduva
S Ã O
P A U L O
Ribeirão Prêto
Poços de Caldas
Volta Redonda
Barra Mansa
Nova Friburgo
Petrópolis
S. João da Barra
Campos

Tupã
Marília
Limeira
Piracicaba
Campinas
Jundiaí
Magé
Rio de Janeiro
Niterói

Pres. Prudente
Assis
Bauru
São Carlos
Araraquara
Sorocaba
Itapetininga
Itapeva
São Paulo
Santos
São Vicente
Itanhaém

Ourinhos
Londrina
Jacarezinho
Apucarana
Itatiba
Juquiá
Iguape

Castro
Ponta Grossa
Guarapuava
União da Vitória
Mafra
Curitiba
Paranaguá
São Francisco do Sul

Tropic of Capricorn

45 C 40 D 35 E

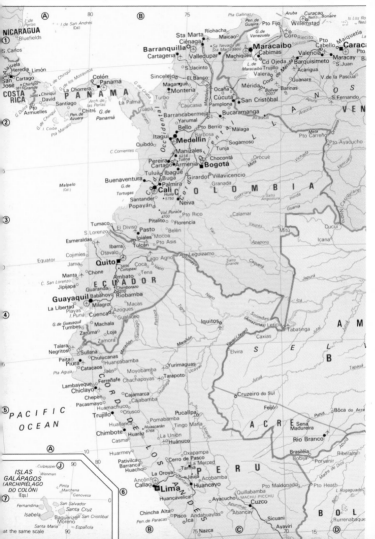

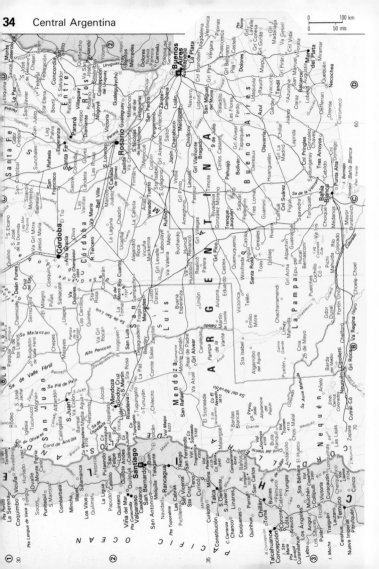

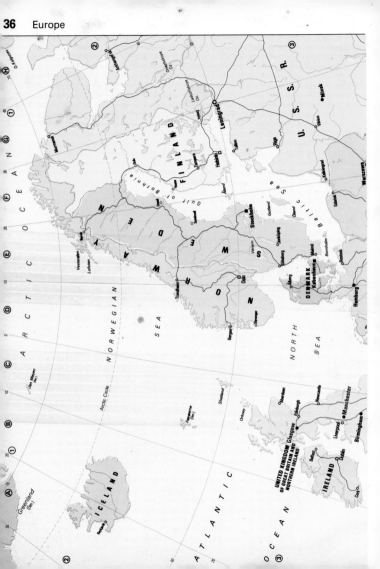

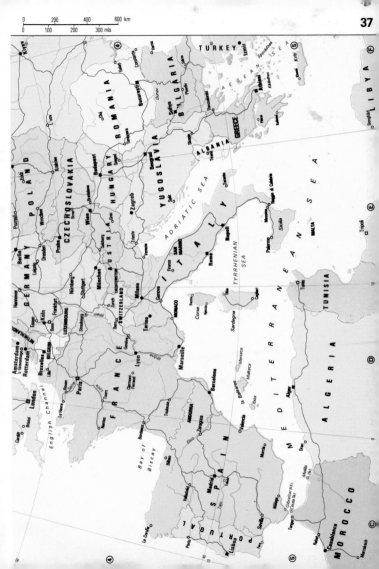

BARENTS SEA

ARCTIC OCEAN

NORWEGIAN SEA

ICELAND

Reykjavík
Akureyri
Vatnajökull
Hvannadalshnúkur 2119

Faroyar (Dan)
Tórshavn

FINLAND

Murmansk
Kol'skiy Poluostrov
Karel'skaya ASSR

Kuopio
Jyväskylä

Narvik
Kiruna
Boden
Luleå
Skellefteå
Umeå
Örnsköldsvik
Härnösand
Sundsvall
Östersund
Trondheim
Steinkjer
Ålesund
Molde
Kristiansund

Arctic Circle

N O R W E G I A N   S E A

NORWAY

Bergen
Stord
Lervik
Sunnhordland
Skaldö
Haugesund
Karmöy
Nordhordland (E)
Dalsfjorden

Shetland
Herma Ness
Unst
Fetlar
Yell
Whalsay
Isbister
St Magnus B
Lerwick
Foula
Sumburgh Hd

Fair Isle

Orkney
Westray
Rousay
Sanday
Sule Skerry
Kirkwall
Stromness
Stronsay
Hoy
Scapa Flow
Stack Skerry
Duncansby Hd

N O R T H

S E A

Thurso
Wick
Helmsdale
Ben Hope
927
C. Wrath
Ben More
Assynt
998
Dingwall
Inverness
Dornoch
Dornoch Firth
Moray Firth

N Rona
Sula Sgeir
Butt of Lewis
Flannan Is
Stornoway
Lewis
Harris
N Uist
S Uist
Barra
St Kilda

O u t e r   H e b r i d e s

The Minch

Ullapool
Kyle of Lochalsh
Mallaig
Fort Augustus
Fort William
Ben Nevis
1344
Skye
Portree
Rum
Eigg
Coll
Tiree
Mull
Colonsay
Jura
Islay
Oban
L. Awe
F. of Lorn
L Lomond
Campbeltown
Rathlin I.

SCOTLAND
Ben Macdui
1309
Braemar
Grampians
Spey
Don
Dee
Fraserburgh
Peterhead
Buchan Ness
Aberdeen
Stonehaven
Montrose
Arbroath
St Andrews
Banff
Elgin
Tay
L Tay
Perth
F. of Tay
Kirkcaldy
F. of Forth
Forth
Edinburgh
Stirling
White Coomb
822
Moffat
Galashiels
Hawick
St Abbs Hd
Berwick-upon-Tweed
Holy I
Glasgow
Motherwell
Paisley
Greenock
Irvine
Kilmarnock
Ayr
F. of Clyde
Arran
Merrick
843
Nith
Dumfries
Girvan
Stranraer
Larne
Luce B
Kirkcudbright
Solway Firth
Carlisle
Penrith
P e n n i n e s

Morpeth
Newcastle upon Tyne
Gateshead
S. Shields
Sunderland
Blyth
Durham
Hartlepool

N. IRELAND
Ballymena
Belfast
Coleraine
Londonderry
Omagh
Lough Neagh
Bangor
Foyle
Main
Tory I.
Errigal
752
Erne
Donegal
Rossan Pt
Assan L
Donegal B
Bann

0 50 100 150 200 km
0 50 100 mls

③ ④

NETHERLANDS

's-Gravenhage (Den Haag)
Rotterdam
Antwerpen
Gent Bruxelles (Brussel)
BELGIUM
Mechelen
Brugge
Oostende
Vlissingen
Dunkerque Gent
Calais Kortrijk Tournai Mons
St-Omer Lille Douai Valenciennes
Boulogne Béthune Arras Cambrai
Le Touquet Abbeville
St-Quentin
Laon
Amiens
Beauvais Compiègne Soissons
Noyon
Senlis
Neufchâtel Rouen Pontoise Meaux
Dieppe **Paris**
Le Tréport Versailles **FRANCE**
Rambouillet Melun Provins
Chartres Étampes Fontainebleau
Évreux Dreux
Le Havre Lisieux
Bolbec Elbeuf Louviers
Honfleur
Deauville
Bayeux Caen
Cherbourg
C. de la Hague
St-Lô
Valognes
Coutances
Granville
Mont-St-Michel
St-Malo Dinan
St-Brieuc
Dinard
Guingamp
Morlaix Lannion
Brest
L'Ouessant
Roscoff
Jersey Guernsey Channel Is. (U.K.)
Golfe de St-Malo
St Helier St Peter Port
Alderney
C. de la Hève
Pte de Barfleur
Mayenne Alençon
Domfront Argentan
Fougères
Avranches

ENGLAND
London
Great Yarmouth
Lowestoft
King's Lynn Norwich
Newmarket Ipswich
Cambridge Felixstowe Harwich
Peterborough Colchester
Bedford Chelmsford Southend
Luton
Northampton
Leicester
Nottingham Grimsby
Lincoln
Derby
Coventry
Birmingham
Worcester
Gloucester
Oxford
Reading Windsor
Maidstone Canterbury
Crawley Folkestone
Guildford Dover
Winchester Hastings
Brighton Eastbourne
Southampton Portsmouth
Isle of Wight
Bournemouth
Weymouth
Torbay
Plymouth
Exeter
Barnstaple
Bude
Newquay
Truro
Falmouth
Penzance Land's End
Isles of Scilly
Lizard Pt
Prawle Pt

Swansea Cardiff Bristol Bath Salisbury
Newport Weston-super-Mare
Taunton
WALES
Aberystwyth Brecon
Builth Wells
Carmarthen
Pembroke
Fishguard
St David's Hd
Cardigan Bay
Bangor Holyhead Birkenhead
Aberdovey
Pwllheli

Liverpool Manchester
Stoke Crewe Chester
Warrington Bolton
Shrewsbury Wolverhampton
Stafford
Preston Blackpool
Bradford Leeds
Harrogate Huddersfield
Sheffield Doncaster
York Hull
Halifax
Lancaster Morecambe
Kendal
Scafell Pike 3210
Barrow-in-Furness
Isle of Man Douglas
Middlesbrough Scarborough
Darlington
Yorkshire Moors
Flamborough Hd
Spurn Hd
The Wash
Yare
Trent
Ouse
Severn
Wye
Exe
Dartmoor
Exmoor
Lundy I.
Bristol Chan.

IRISH SEA

REP. OF IRELAND
Dublin
Baile Átha Cliath
Dún Laoghaire
Newry
Dundalk
Drogheda
Portadown
Armagh
Monaghan
Cavan
Longford
Mullingar
Athlone
Roscommon
Sligo
Ballina
Castlebar
Galway
Ennis
Limerick
Tipperary
Nenagh
Thurles
Kilkenny
Carlow
Portlaoise
Wicklow
Arklow
Bray
Wexford
Rosslare
Waterford
Dungarvan
Clonmel
Cork
Youghal
Tralee
Killarney
Dingle
Bantry
Killybegs
C. Clear
Old Hd of Kinsale
St George's Chan.
Wicklow Mts
L. Neagh
L. Erne
L. Derg
L. Corrib
L. Mask
Galway B.
Clew B.
Achill Hd
Aran Is.
Slyne Hd
Dingle B.

English Channel

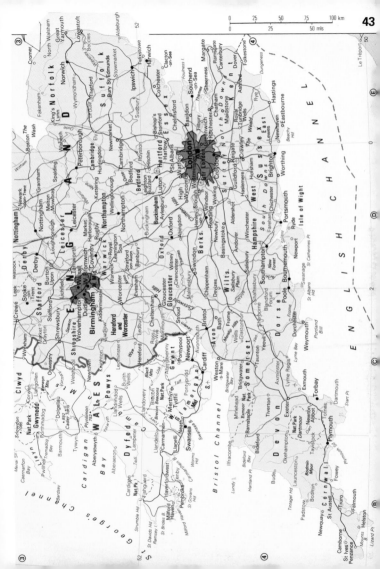

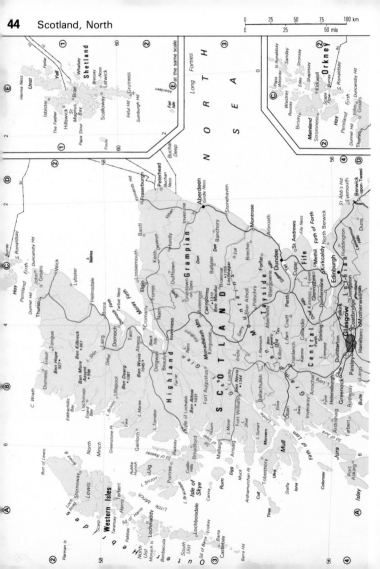

Scale
0 — 25 — 50 — 75 — 100 km
0 — 25 — 50 mls

North Sea

Shetland
Unst
Fetlar
Yell
Whalsay
Bressay
St Magnus Bay
Hillswick
Brae
Gruness
Lerwick
Scalloway
Sumburgh Hd
Fair Isle
Foula
Papa Stour
The Faither
Herma Ness
Muckle Flugga
Isbister
Esha Ness
John o' Groats

Orkney
N. Ronaldsay
Sanday
Stronsay
Westray
Papa Westray
Rousay
Eday
Shapinsay
Kirkwall
Mainland
Stromness
Scapa Flow
Hoy
S. Ronaldsay
Duncansby Hd
Burray
Pentland Firth
Thurso
Dunnet Hd

Buchan Deep
Long Forties

Peterhead
Buchan Ness
Fraserburgh
Kinnairds Hd
Aberdeen
Girdle Ness
Stonehaven
Montrose
Arbroath
Brechin
Forfar
Dundee
St Andrews
North Berwick
Firth of Forth
Methil
Kirkcaldy
Edinburgh
Berwick-upon-Tweed
St Abb's Hd
Eyemouth
Duns
Lammermuir Hills
Haddington
Lothian
Fife
Dunfermline
Kinross
Perth
Crieff
Stirling
Falkirk
Coatbridge
Motherwell
Hamilton
Glasgow
Paisley
Greenock
Helensburgh
Dumbarton
Largs

Banff
Keith
Deveron
Huntly
Turriff
Ellon
Inverurie
Ythan
Oldmeldrum
Grampian
Dufftown
Don
Ballater
Banchory
Dee
Braemar
Lochnagar
Blairgowrie
Pitlochry
Blair Atholl
Tayside
Aberfeldy
Loch Tay
Killin
Callander
L. Earn
L. Katrine
Central
L. Lomond
Arrochar
Inveraray
Rothesay
Bute
Ardrishaig
Port Askaig
Islay
Jura
Sd of Jura
Colonsay

Lossiemouth
Elgin
Forres
Nairn
Grantown-on-Spey
Cairngorms
Ben Macdui 1309
Aviemore
Monadhliath Mts
Kingussie
Spey
Cromarty
Inverness
Black Isle
Dingwall
Ben Wyvis 1046
Strathspey
Ben Attow 1031
Loch Ness
Fort Augustus
Glen Garry
Glen Moriston
Loch Lochy
Ben Nevis 1344
Fort William
Glencoe
Ballachulish
Loch Linnhe
Morvern
Mull
Tobermory
Staffa
Iona
Oban
L. Awe
Loch Etive
L. Fyne
Loch Leven

Highland
SCOTLAND
Grampian Mts

Wick
Lybster
Helmsdale
Brora
Golspie
Dornoch
Dornoch Firth
Tain
Alness
Invergordon
Beauly
Dornie
Kyle of Lochalsh
Glenelg
L. Duich
L. Hourn
Mallaig
Arisaig
Morar
L. Morar
L. Shiel
L. Nevis
Knoydart

Thurso
Halkirk
Dunbeath
Latheron
Lairg
Loch Shin
Bonar Bridge
Ben More Assynt 998
Ben Klibreck 961
Ben Hope 927
Tongue
Durness
C. Wrath
Kinlochbervie
Scourie
Lochinver
Ben More 962
Loch Assynt
Ullapool
Loch Broom
Little Loch Broom
Gruinard Bay
Gairloch
Loch Maree
Ben Eighe
Loch Torridon
Applecross
Shieldaig

Duncansby Hd
S. Ronaldsay
Hoy
Pentland Firth
Dunnet Hd

Pentland Firth

Western Isles
Butt of Lewis
Stornoway
Lewis
Harris
Tarbert
N. Harris
Sd of Harris
Loch Boisdale
North Uist
Lochmaddy
Benbecula
Monach Is
South Uist
Eriskay
Barra
Castlebay
Barra Hd
Sd of Barra
Berneray
Pabbay
Little Minch
The Minch
North Minch
Greenstone Pt
Rubha Reidh
Rubha Hunish
Portree
Isle of Skye
Raasay
Sd of Raasay
Scalpay
Broadford
Cuillin Hills
Soay
Canna
Rum
Eigg
Muck
Ardnamurchan Pt
Coll
Tiree
Ulva
Flannan Is

Braden
Buckie

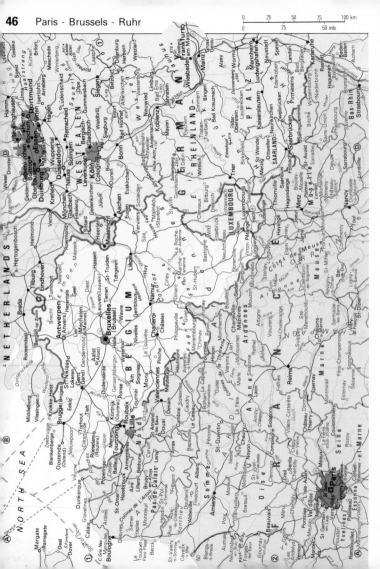

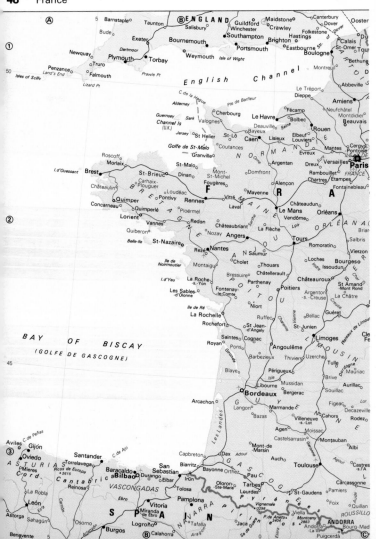

Barnstaple Taunton **E N G L A N D** Guildford Maidstone Canterbury Dover Ooster
Bude Salisbury Winchester Crawley Folkestone Dover
Newquay Exeter Bournemouth Southampton Brighton Hastings Calais Tour
Plymouth Torbay Weymouth Portsmouth Eastbourne Boulogne St-Omer
Penzance Land's End *Dartmoor* *Isle of Wight* Montreuil Bethune
Isles of Scilly Truro Falmouth *Prawle Pt* Abbeville
Lizard Pt Le Tréport

E n g l i s h   C h a n n e l Dieppe Amiens
Neufchâtel
C. de la Hague Pte de Barfleur Fécamp Montdidier
Alderney Cherbourg Le Havre Bolbec Rouen Beauvais
Guernsey Sark Valognes Deauville *Seine* Elbeuf Louviers
Channel Is St Helier St-Lô Bayeux Lisieux Evreux Mantes Cergy Pontoise
(U.K.) Jersey Caen Argentan Dreux Versailles **Paris**
Roscoff Golfe de St-Malo Coutances N O R M A N D I E Rambouillet Chartres Étampes FRANCE
Morlaix St-Malo Granville Mont-St-Michel Domfront Alençon Fontainebleau
I. d'Ouessant Brest St-Brieuc Dinan Fougères Mayenne M R A
Châteaulin Carhaix-Plouguer Loudéac Vitré Châteaudun
Quimper Pontivy Rennes Laval Le Mans Orléans ORLÉANA
Concarneau Quimperlé Ploërmel Vendôme *Loir*
Lorient Vannes Redon Châteaubriant La Flèche Tours Romorantin Vierzon
Quiberon Nozay Angers Saumur Loches Bourges Issoudun Salbris
Belle-Ile St-Nazaire Rezé Nantes Cholet Thouars Châteauroux St Amand-Mont Rond
Ile de Noirmoutier Montaigu Châtellerault Poitiers Argenton-s.-Creuse La Châtre
I. d'Yeu La Roche-s-Yon Bressuire Parthenay P O I T O U
Les Sables-d'Olonne Fontenay-le-Comte Niort Bellac Guéret
Ile de Ré La Rochelle Ruffec St Jean-d'Angely St-Junien Limoges
Rochefort Cognac Angoulême L I M O U S I N Uzerche
B A Y   O F   B I S C A Y Saintes Pons Thiviers Tulle
(GOLFE DE GASCOGNE) Royan Barbezieux Périgueux Brive
45 Blaye Isle Mussidan Souillac Aurillac
Libourne Bergerac Figeac Decazeville
Bordeaux Rodez
Arcachon Langon Marmande Villeneuve-s.-Lot Cahors
Bazas Agen Moissac Montauban Albi
Capbreton Dax Mont-de-Marsin Castelsarrasin Castres
Avilés C. de Peñas Gijón *Adour* Auch Toulouse Carcassonne
Oviedo C. de Ajo Biarritz Orthez Pau Tarbes St-Gaudens Pamiers
A S T U R I A S Santander Bayonne Oloron-Ste-Marie Lourdes Foix Quillan
Torrelavega Baracaldo San Sebastian Irún *Pyrénées* Andorra
Mieres *Picos de Europa* Durango Eibar Tolosa Jaca Vignemale Montcenti Bourg-Mad
La Robla Reinosa VASCONGADAS Pamplona N A R R A P.de Aneto **ANDORRA**
León Vitoria *Ebro* A R La Vi
Astorga Sahagún Miranda de Ebro Burgos Logroño Calahorra Se de Urgel Puigcerdá
Benavente Osorno Tafalla Aragón Fig

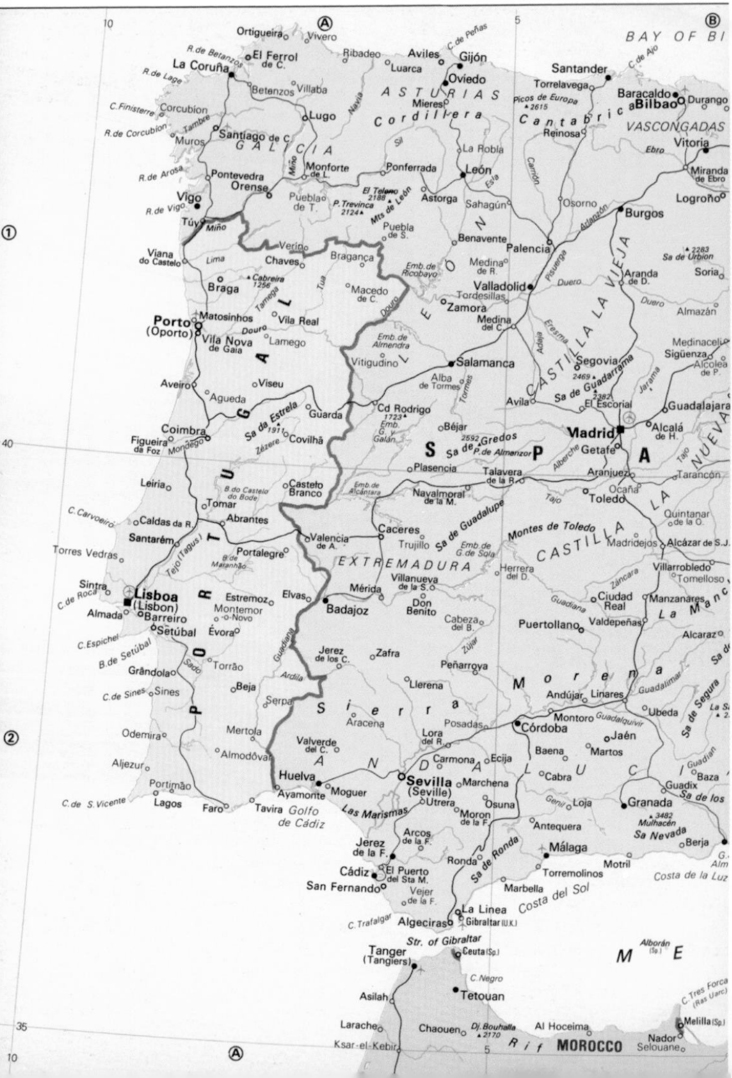
10
A
5
B
1
2
40
35
BAY OF BI
Ortigueira
Vivero
R.de Betanzos
El Ferrol de C.
Ribadeo
Aviles
C. de Peñas
Gijón
La Coruña
R.de Lage
Luarca
Oviedo
Santander
C. de Ajo
Torrelavega
Baracaldo
Durango
Bilbao
Betenzos
Villaba
ASTURIAS
Mieres
Picos de Europa
2615
C.Finisterre
Corcubion
Tambre
Lugo
Navia
Cordillera Cantabrica
Reinosa
VASCONGADAS
R.de Corcubion
Muros
Santiago de C.
GALICIA
Sil
La Robla
Ebro
Vitoria
Miño
Monforte de L.
Ponferrada
León
Carrión
Miranda de Ebro
R.de Arosa
Pontevedra
Orense
El Teleno 2188
Astorga
Esla
Vigo
Puebla de T.
P. Trevinca 2124
Mts de León
Sahagún
Osorno
Logroño
R.de Vigo
Túy
Miño
Puebla de S.
Arlanzón
Burgos
Benavente
Verín
Palencia
Bragança
LEÓN
Pisuerga
2283
Sa de Urbion
Viana do Castelo
Lima
Chaves
Medina de R.
Emb. de Ricobayo
Soria
Cabreira 1256
Tua
Aranda de D.
Braga
Macedo de C.
Valladolid
Duero
Tamega
Tordesillas
CASTILLA LA VIEJA
Douro
Zamora
Duero
Almazán
Matosinhos
Porto (Oporto)
Vila Real
Medina del C.
Eresma
Douro
Adaja
Vila Nova de Gaia
Lamego
Emb. de Almendra
Medinaceli
Sigüenza
Alcolea de P.
Vitigudino
Salamanca
Segovia
2469
Aveiro
Viseu
Alba de Tormes
Tormes
Sa de Guadarrama
Jarama
Agueda
Avila
2382
El Escorial
Guadalajara
Sa da Estrela
Guarda
Cd Rodrigo
1723
Emb. G. y Galán
Coimbra
1911
Béjar
Madrid
Alcalá de H.
Figueira da Foz
Mondego
Zêzere
Covilhã
2592 Gredos
Sa de
P. de Almanzor
Getafe
SPAIN
Alberche
NUEVA
Tajo
Plasencia
Talavera de la R.
Aranjuez
Tarancón
Leiria
B. do Castelo do Bode
Castelo Branco
Emb. de Alcántara
Navalmoral de la M.
Tajo
Ocaña
Toledo
LA
Tomar
C. Carvoeiro
Quintanar de la O.
Caldas da R.
Abrantes
Montes de Toledo
Sa de Guadalupe
CASTILLA
Santarém
Caceres
Madridejos
Alcázar de S.J.
Tejo (Tagus)
Valencia de A.
Trujillo
Emb. de G. de Sola
Torres Vedras
Portalegre
B. de Maranhão
EXTREMADURA
Herrera del D.
Villarrobledo
Zancara
Tomelloso
Sintra
C. de Roca
Lisboa (Lisbon)
Mérida
Villanueva de la S.
Estremoz
Elvas
Guadiana
Ciudad Real
Manzanares
La Mancha
Almada
Barreiro
Montemor o-Novo
Badajoz
Don Benito
Cabeza del B.
Puertollano
Valdepeñas
C. Espichel
Setúbal
Évora
Zújar
Alcaraz
B. de Setúbal
PORTUGAL
Guadiana
Jerez de los C.
Zafra
Sado
Torrão
Peñarroya
Sierra Morena
Sa de
Grândola
Ardila
Guadalimar
Beja
Llerena
C. de Sines
Sines
Serpa
Andújar
Linares
Sa de Segura
Sierra
Ubeda
La S
Aracena
Posadas
Montoro
Guadalquivir
Odemira
Mertola
Córdoba
Lora del R.
Jaén
Valverde del C.
Almodôvar
Baena
Martos
Aljezur
Carmona
Ecija
Guadian
ANDALUCIA
Baza
Cabra
Portimão
Huelva
Sevilla (Seville)
Marchena
Guadix
C. de S. Vicente
Lagos
Faro
Ayamonte
Moguer
Sa de los
Genil
Loja
Granada
Tavira
Golfo de Cádiz
Utrera
Osuna
Las Marismas
Moron de la F.
3482 Mulhacén
Antequera
Sa Nevada
Arcos de la F.
Jerez de la F.
Sa de Ronda
Málaga
Berja
Ronda
Motril
Cádiz
El Puerto del Sta M.
Torremolinos
Costa de la Luz
San Fernando
Vejer de la F.
Marbella
Costa del Sol
La Linea
C. Trafalgar
Algeciras
Gibraltar (U.K.)
Str. of Gibraltar
Alborán (Sp.)
Tanger (Tangiers)
Ceuta (Sp.)
ME
C. Negro
Tetouan
Asilah
C. Tres Forcas (Ras Uarc)
Larache
Chaouen
Dj. Bouhalla 2170
Al Hoceima
Melilla (Sp.)
Nador
Ksar-el-Kebir
Rif
MOROCCO
Selouane

0 50 100 150 200 km
0   50   100 mls

51

SCAY
Capbreton
San
Sebastian
Eibar
Biarritz
Bayonne
Irún
Tolosa
Mont-de-
Marsan
Dax
Adour
Auch
Toulouse
Albi
Castres-
s.l'A
Nîmes
Montpellier
Arles
Salon-d.-P.
Aix-en-Provence
Aubagne
Marseille
Toulon
Hyères
Martigues
Golfe du Lion
Sète
Narbonne
Béziers
Carcassonne
Quillan
Aude
Foix
Pamiers
St-Gaudens
FRANCE
Pau
Oloron-
Ste-Marie
Tarbes
Lourdes
Pyrénées
Vignemale
▲3298
P.de Aneto
▲3404
Montcenis
2883
Andorra
La Vieja
ANDORRA
Bourg-Madame
Puigcerdá
Viella
Pamplona
NAVARRA
Jaca
Aragón
Sa de Guara
Huesca
Barbastro
Segre
Sa del Codi
Figueras
C. de Creus
Perpignan
ROUSSILLON
Tafalla
Calahorra
Alfaro
Tudela
Tarazona
Alagón
Zaragoza
Emb. de
Mequinenza
Lérida
CATALUÑA
Sabadell
Tarrasa
Granollers
Mataró
Badalona
Barcelona
Gerona
San Feliú de G.
Costa Brava
Vich
Tar
Calatayud
Daroca
Monreal
del C.
Gállego
Sa de Albarracín
Guadalope
Caspe
Reus
Valls
Villanueva-y-G.
Tarragona
Ebro
Tortosa
Golfo
de
San Jorge
C. de Tortosa
Amposta
Vinaroz
Benicarló
Torreblanca
IN
Teruel
▲2019
Peñarroya
Sa de Gudar
Sarrión
Castellón de la P.
Is Columbretes
C. Formentor
Menorca
C. de Caballeria
Ciudadela
Mahón
C. Binibeca
Alcudia
Capdepera
40
Serrania de Cuenca
Cuenca
Emb. de
Alarcón
Segorbe
Villarreal
Sagunto
Turia
Golfo de
Valencia
Mallorca
▲1445
Mayor
Palma
de Mallorca
Manacor
Santañy
C. de Salinas
Cabrera
Motilla
del P.
Cabriel
La Roda
Utiel
VALENCIA
Valencia
Alcira
Júcar
Gandía
Denia
C. de la Nao
Ibiza
S. Antonio
Abad
Ibiza
Formentera
ISLAS BALEARES
(BALEARIC ISLANDS)
(Sp.)
Albacete
Almansa
Jardín
Alcaraz
MURCIA
Hellín
Elda
Villena
Alcoy
Benidorm
Alicante
Elche
Segura
Cieza
Orihuela
Caravaca
Murcia
Costa Blanca
Totana
Lorca
C. de Palos
Cartagena
Sagra
▲182
Húercal
Overa
G. de
Mazarrón
Aguilas
Filabres
Vera
Almería
C. de Gata
M E D I T E R R A N E A N   S E A
Ghazaouet
Beni-Saf
Ain
Temouchent
Mers el Kebir
Oran
C. Ferrat
Arzew
Sig
O. Tlélat
Mohammadia
Sidi-bel-Abbès
Mascara
Relizane
Mina
Frenda
C. Gharbi
Tiaret
Plat. du Sersou
Z. Chergui
Bou Saâda
Monts des
Ouled Naïl
35
Bosquet
Mostaganém
Ech Cheliff
Khemis
Cheliff
Miliana
Médéa
Ténès
Cherchell
Boufarik
Blida
Alger
(Algiers)
El Harrach
Dellys
Tizi
Ouzou
Bejaia
(Bougie)
Djurdjura
Beni
Mansour
Sétif
Kherrata
Soummam
O. Isser
Bouïra
Rabalou
Ksar El
Boukhari
Ain
Oussera
Ain el
Hadjel
M'Sila
Bj bou
Arréridj
Mts du Hodna
Chott
el Hodna
Barika
Bou Saâda
Ouassel
Z. Gharbi
A L G E R I A
Massif de l'Ouarsenis
Dahra
Chélif
Shossa
1
2
3

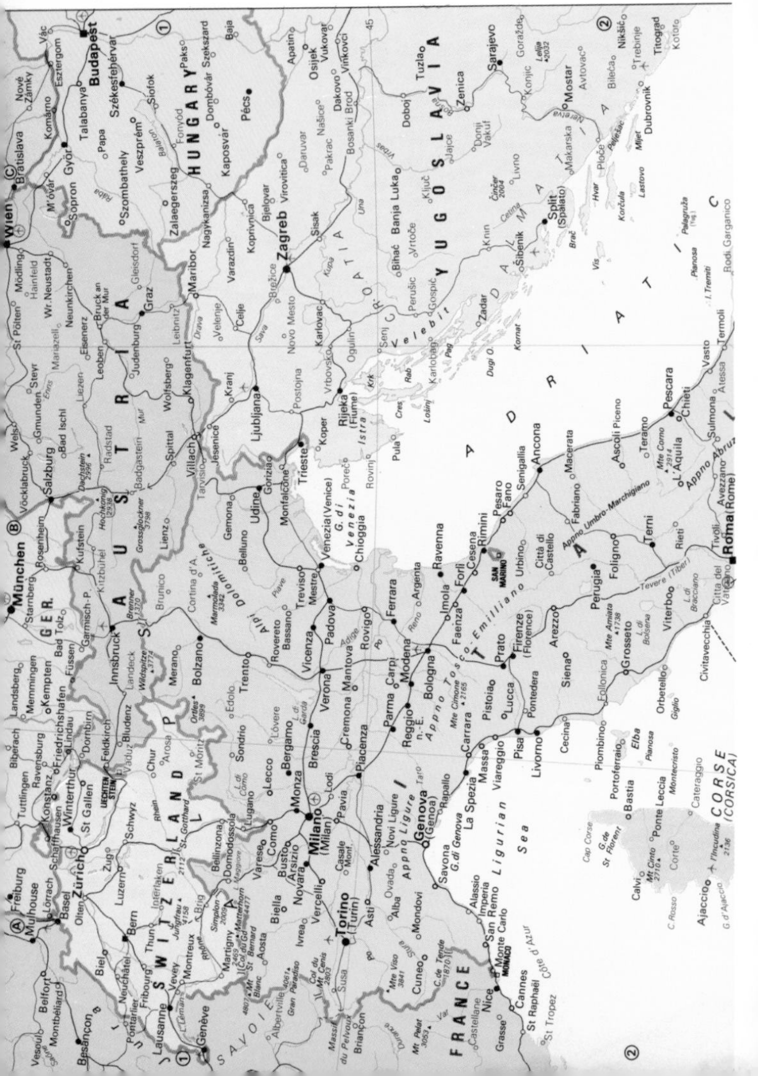

SWITZERLAND
AUSTRIA
HUNGARY
YUGOSLAVIA
FRANCE
GER.
ITALIA
ADRIATIC
CORSE (CORSICA)
Ligurian Sea
G. di Venezia
Milano (Milan)
Torino (Turin)
Genova (Genoa)
Venezia (Venice)
Firenze (Florence)
Roma (Rome)
Bologna
Verona
Padova
Trieste
Zagreb
Ljubljana
Wien
Budapest
München
Zürich
Bern
Genève
Innsbruck
Salzburg
Graz
Sarajevo
Split (Spalato)
Rijeka (Fiume)
Ancona
Pescara
Perugia
Pisa
Livorno
Nice
Monte Carlo
MONACO
SAN MARINO
LIECHTEN STEIN
Appno Tosco-Emilliano
Appno Ligure
Dolomitiche

0 50 100 150 200 km
0 50 100 mls

Southern Italy, Sicily, Sardinia, Tunisia

Seas
ADRIATIC SEA
IONIAN SEA
TYRRHENIAN SEA
MEDITERRANEAN SEA

Mainland Italy
Brindisi
Lecce
C. Sta Maria di Leuca
Gallipoli
Maglie
Otranto
Monopoli
Manduria
Bari
Molfetta
Taranto
Golfo di Taranto
Barletta
Andria
Matera
Le Murge
Altamura
Potenza
Appno Lucano
Metaponto
Corigliano Calabro
Rossano
Pta Alice
Crotone
C. Rizzuto
Vieste
Mts Gargano 1056
Manfredonia
Foggia
S. Severo
Campobasso
Castrovillari
Mte Pollino 2248
La Sila
Catanzaro
G. di Squillace
Nicastro
Paola
Cosenza
Pta Stilo
Isernia
Avellino
Appno Napoletano
Benevento
Sapri
G. di Policastro
Paolini
Vibo Valentia
Montalto 1959
Monte Donato
Capo Spartivento
Reggio di Calabria
Locri
Palmi
Str. de Messina
Caserta
Vesuvio 1277
Napoli (Naples)
Torre del
Pozzuoli
Ischia
Capri
Sorrento
Salerno
Eboli
Agropoli
Formia
Gaeta
Terracina
Anzio
I. Ponziane
Latina
Ostia
Lido di Ostia
Sora
Frosinone
Cassino
Mte Meleto 2050
rese
Stromboli

Sicily
SICILIA (SICILY)
Messina
Giarre
Acireale
Catania
Siracusa (Syracuse)
Noto
C. di Correnti
Mtti Nebrodi
Lentini
Barcellona
Etna 3323
Paterno
Enna
Caltanissetta
Caltagirone
Gela
Vittoria
Modica
Ragusa
Cefalù
Palermo
Bagheria
Termini
Licata
Agrigento
Sciacca
Castelvetrano
Alcamo
Patricò
Partinico
Trapani
C. San Vito
Marsala
Mazara del Vallo
Is. Egadi
Ustica
Isole Lipari
Lipari
Salina
Filicudi
Alicudi
Vulcano
Panarea

Malta
Malta Channel
Sicilian Channel
Pantelleria
MALTA
Gozo
Valletta
Mdina

Sardinia
SARDEGNA (SARDINIA)
Porto Vecchio
Bonifacio
Strait of Bonifacio
Sta Teresa di G.
Sartène
Asinara
Porto Torres
Sassari
Alghero
Olbia
Nuoro
I. Monte Ortu
L'Ortobene
Mte Gennargentu 1835
Muravera
Oristano
G. di Oristano
S. Pietro
S. Antioco
Iglesias
Carbonia
Cagliari
C. Carbonara
C. Teulada
C. Spartivento
Arbatax
Simbiola
Macomer
Sanluri

Tunisia
TUNISIA
Tunis
Bizerte
G. de Tunis
Kelibia
Nabeul
Hammamet
Golfe de Hammamet
Sousse
Monastir
Mokrine
M'saken
Kairouan
Mateur
Menzel
Haïq el Oued
Enfida
Dj Zaghouan 1295
Zaghouan
Kairouan
Ghardimaou
Medjerda
Béja
Jendouba
Le Kef
Kalaat Khasba
Makthar
Tébessa
Oued Mellègue
Annaba (Bône)
Guelma
Souk Ahras
Mts de la Medjerda
Tabarka
C. Serrat
C. Blanc
C. Bon
El Kala
Kalaat es Senam

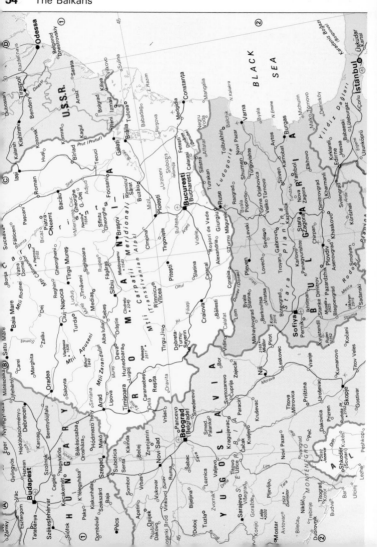

50 100 150 200 km
50 100 mls

TURKEY

GREECE

AEGEAN SEA

IONIAN SEA

Sea of Marmara

SPORADHES (DHODHEKANISOS)

KIkládhes (Cyclades)

Sea of Crete

Mírtoan Sea

IÓNIOI NÍSOI (Ionian Islands)

Strait of Otranto

Athínai (Athens)

Thessaloníki (Salonica)

İzmir

Bursa

Ródhos

Kríti

Pátrai

Vólos

Lárisa

Khalkís

Piraévs

Lésvos

Khíos

Sámos

Límnos

Kérkira (Corfu)

NORTH SEA

BALTIC SEA

S W E D E N

D E N M A R K

Jylland

Kattegat

Göteborg · Borås · Mölndal
Jönköping · Nässjö · Växjö · Karlskrona
Kalmar · Öland
Västervik · Hultsfred · Oskarshamn · Mönsterås
Karlshamn · Ronneby
Helsingborg · Helsingör · Lund · Malmö
Halmstad · Varberg · Laholm · Ängelholm
Halmstad · Ystad · Trelleborg

Bornholm · Rönne

Skagen · Frederikshavn · Ålborg
Thisted · Hjörring · Viborg · Randers · Grenå
Herning · Silkeborg · Århus
Esbjerg · Kolding · Vejle · Fredericia
Varde · Horsens
Odense · Svendborg · Nyborg
København (Copenhagen) · Roskilde · Köge
Næstved · Vordingborg · Nakskov
Lolland · Falster · Gedser
Sönderborg · Flensburg · Åbenrå · Haderslev

Rügen · Stralsund · Greifswald · Anklam
Sassnitz · Rostock · Warnemünde
Wismar · Schwerin

POLAND
Szczecin · Poznań · Gorzów Wlkp.
Koszalin · Słupsk · Stargard
Kostrzyn · Gubin

Berlin · Potsdam · Brandenburg · Oranienburg
Neuruppin · Eberswalde · Frankfurt
Cottbus · Finsterwalde

GERMANY

SCHLESWIG-HOLSTEIN
Kiel · Neumünster · Lübeck · Travemünde
Heide · Husum · Itzehoe · Elmshorn
Hamburg · Lauenburg · Stade · Buxtehude
Cuxhaven · Bremerhaven · Bremen

NIEDERSACHSEN
Oldenburg · Wilhelmshaven · Emden · Leer
Meppen · Lingen · Nordhorn · Osnabrück
Celle · Hannover · Braunschweig · Wolfsburg
Hildesheim · Hameln · Minden · Paderborn
Kassel · Göttingen · Northeim

Magdeburg · Halberstadt · Dessau
Wittenberg · Bitterfeld · Halle · Bernburg

NORDRHEIN-WESTFALEN
Münster · Bielefeld · Gütersloh · Hamm
Bochum · Dortmund · Essen · Duisburg
Düsseldorf · Wuppertal · Hagen · Wesel
Krefeld · Venlo · Mönchen

NETHERLANDS
Amsterdam · 's-Gravenhage (Den Haag)
Rotterdam · Utrecht · Leiden · Haarlem
Leeuwarden · Groningen · Assen · Zwolle
Apeldoorn · Arnhem · Nijmegen · Eindhoven
Tilburg · Breda · Dordrecht · Den Helder
Alkmaar · Hilversum · Amersfoort
Enschede · Hengelo · Deventer

BELGIUM
Antwerpen (Anvers) · Gent · Brugge
Bruxelles (Brussel) · Mechelen
Oostende · Brugge · Tourcoing · Dunkerque

East-Central Europe map

Opochka, Pustoshka, Polotsk, Novopolotsk, Glubokoye, Lepel, Borisov, Zhodino, **Minsk**, Osipovichi, Cherven, Zhlobin

B E L O R U S S I A N   S. S. R.

Molodechno, Vileyka, Smorgon, Rakov, Dzerzhinsk, Slutsk, Soligorsk

Postavy, Svir, Nieman, Lida, Novogrudok, Stolbtsy, Baranovichi, Luninets, Stolin, Dubrovitsa, Sarny

U. S. S. R.

Pinsk, Bereza, Ivatsevichi, Kobrin, Pruzhany, Malorita, Ratno, Matsiyovka

Daugavpils, Zarasai, Utena, Ukmerge, Vilnius, Vileyka, Oshmyany, Ivye, Mosty, Volkovysk, Grodno, Brest

Riga, Jurmala, Jelgava, Dobele, Bauska, Birzai, Pasvalys, Panevezys, Kedainiai, Jonava, Kaisiadorys, Pabrade, Varena, Druskininkai, Alytus, Bialystok, Bielsk Podlaski, Biala Podlaska

L A T V I S K A Y A   S. S. R.
L I T O V S K A Y A   S. S. R.

Tukums, Ogre, Lielupe, Daugava, Livani, Jekabpils, Radviliskis, Siauliai, Kelme, Raseiniai, Jurbarkas, Taurage, Neman

Kaunas (Kovno), Suwalki, Augustow, Elk, Grajewo, Lomza, Zambrow, Ostroleka, Ostrow Mazowiecka, Siedlice, Lukow Podlaski, Wlodawa

Ventspils, Kuldiga, Saldus, Telsiai, Mazeikiai, Priekule, Plunge

R. S. F. S. R.

Svetlogorsk, Sovetsk, **Kaliningrad (Königsberg)**, Gusev, Chernyakhovsk, Bartoszyce, Ketrzyn, Elk, Kolno, Szczytno

Roja, Cesis, Pieriga, Riezekne, Ludza

Ventspils, Liepaja, Klaipeda, Silute, Tilsit

Gotland, Visby, Klintehamn, Hemse, Burgsvik

B A L T I C

Wladyslawowo, Gulf of Gdansk (Gulf of Danzig), Braniewo, Elblag, Malbork, Olsztyn, Ostroda, Nidzica, Ciechanow, Pultusk, Nowy Dwor, **Warszawa**, Minsk M., Siedlce, Otwock, Pruszkow, Sochaczew, Zyrardow, Skierniewice, Radom, Tomasz. Maz., Deblin, Pulawy

Leba, Lebork, Slupsk, Koscierzyna, Starogard Gdanski, Chojnice, Swiecie, Chelmno, **Torun**, Inowroclaw, Wloclawek, Gostynin, Kutno, Plock, Sierpc, Mlawa, Brodnica, Grudziadz, Kwidzyn, Tczew, Sopot, **Gdynia**, **Gdansk (Danzig)**

Ustka, Slawno, Koszalin, Swidwin, Szczecinek, Jastrowie, Pila, Bory Tucholskie, Chelmza, Zrogo, Bydgoszcz, Gniezno, Wrzesnia, Konin, **Poznan**, Sroda, Jarocin, Pleszew, Kalisz, Zdunska Wola, **Lodz**, Pabianice, Zgierz, Lowicz, Kolo

P O L A N D

Bornholm, Ronne

Kolobrzeg, Karlino, Bialogard, Stargard, Choszczno, Krzyz, Myslibarz, **Szczecin**, Gryfino, Pyrzyce, Pniewy, **Gorzow Wlkp.**, Skwierzyna, Miedzyrzecz, Swiebodzin, **Zielona Gora**, Nowa Sol, Leszno, Gostyn, Rawicz, Glogow, Szprotawa, Zary, Zagan

Nassjo, Eksjo, Hultsfred, Vetlanda, Vaggeryd, Vastervik, Oskarshamn, Monsteras, Oland, Kalmar, Almhult, Nybro, Ronneby, **Karlskrona**, Hassleholm, Kristianstad, Simrishamn, Ystad

S W E D E N

Jonkoping, Varnamo, Ljungby, Markaryd

Sassnitz, Rugen, Anklam, Swinoujscie, Prenzlau, Eberswalde, **Frankfurt an der Oder**, Fürstenwalde, Oder, Spree, Cottbus, Guben, Krosno, Slubice

Oder

0 50 100 150 200 km
0 50 100 mls

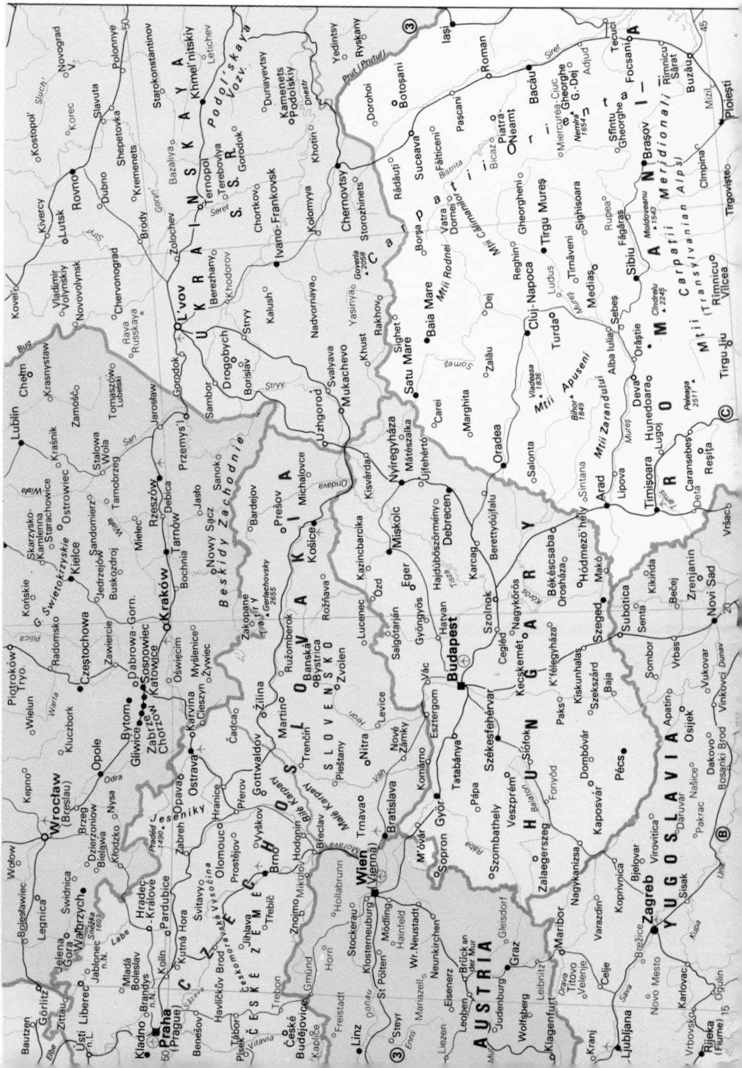

U K R A I N S K A — S.S.R.

U K R A I N E

P O L A N D

C Z E C H O S L O V A K I A

Č E S K É Z E M Ě

S L O V E N S K O

H U N G A R Y

A U S T R I A

Y U G O S L A V I A

R O M A N I A

Carpații Meridionali (Transylvanian Alps)

Mţii Apuseni

Mţii Zărandului

Beskidy Zachodnie

Novograd · Polonnye · Starokonstantinov · Leichov · Yedintsy · Ryskany · Iaşi · Roman

Kostopol' · Slavuta · Shepetovka · Kamenets-Podol'skiy · Khotin · Dorohoi · Botoşani · Bacău

Lutsk · Rovno · Dubno · Ternopil' · Chernovtsy · Rădăuţi · Suceava · Fălticeni · Piatra · Bistriţa · Gheorghe

Kovel' · Vladimir-Volynskiy · Novovolynsk · L'vov · Ivano-Frankovsk · Kolomyya · Baia Mare · Satu Mare · Dej · Reghin · Sibiu · Braşov · Câmpina

Chełm · Zamość · Rava Russkaya · Przemyśl · Drohobych · Uzhgorod · Mukachevo · Oradea · Arad · Timişoara · Reşiţa · Ploieşti

Lublin · Kraśnik · Stalowa Wola · Rzeszów · Jarosław · Sanok · Michalovce · Košice · Debrecen · Békéscsaba · Subotica · Novi Sad

Radom · Kielce · Tarnów · Nowy Sącz · Prešov · Miskolc · Eger · Szolnok · Kecskemét · Szeged · Zrenjanin

Częstochowa · Kraków · Oświęcim · Žilina · Ružomberok · Zvolen · Budapest · Székesfehérvár · Pécs · Osijek

Opole · Gliwice · Katowice · Ostrava · Olomouc · Brno · Bratislava · Győr · Szombathely · Zagreb · Sisak

Wrocław (Breslau) · Opole · Ostrava · Praha (Prague) · Wien (Vienna) · Graz · Maribor · Ljubljana · Rijeka (Fiume)

Görlitz · Liberec · Pardubice · České Budějovice · Linz · Klagenfurt · Celje · Novo Mesto

Mţii Rodnei · Mţii Călimani · Moldoveanu 2543 · Negoiu 2546 · Bihor 1849 · Gerlachovský 2655

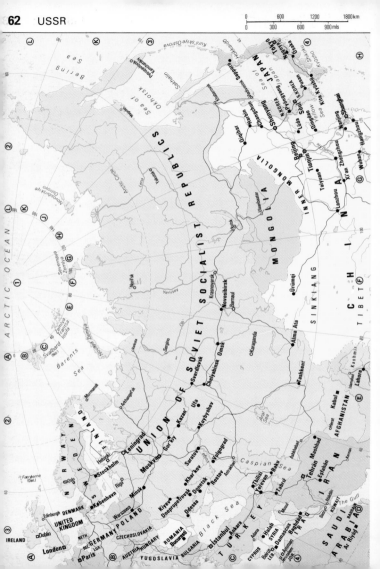

0   300   600   900 mils
0   600   1200   1800 km

ARCTIC OCEAN

Bering Sea

Sea of Okhotsk

UNION OF SOVIET SOCIALIST REPUBLICS

JAPAN

MONGOLIA

INNER MONGOLIA

CHINA

SINKIANG

TIBET

Barents Sea

Svalbard

NORWAY

SWEDEN

FINLAND

Leningrad

Moskva

Gor'kiy

Kazan'

Ufa

Kuybyshev

Sverdlovsk

Chelyabinsk

Omsk

Novosibirsk

Barnaul

Krasnoyarsk

Karaganda

Alma Ata

Tashkent

Aral Sea

Caspian Sea

Volgograd

Saratov

Rostov

Donetsk

Khar'kov

Kiyev

Dnepropetrovsk

Odessa

Black Sea

Minsk

Riga

Helsinki

Stockholm

København

Oslo

Edinburgh

Dublin

London

Paris

IRELAND

UNITED KINGDOM

DENMARK

GERMANY

POLAND

NETH

BEL

LUX

CZECHOSLOVAKIA

AUSTRIA

HUNGARY

YUGOSLAVIA

ROMANIA

BULGARIA

Bucureşti

Warszawa

Murmansk

Arkhangel'sk

Noril'sk

Yenisey

Lena

Ob

Arctic Circle

Severnaya Zemlya

Novaya Zemlya

Zemlya Frantsa Iosifa

TURKEY

Ankara

Istanbul

Adana

CYPRUS

SYRIA

Damascus

LEB

ISR

JOR

IRAQ

Baghdad

Al Başrah

Al Kuwayt

KUWAIT

The Gulf

SAUDI ARABIA

Ar Riyāḍ

IRAN

Tehrān

Eşfahān

Mashhad

Tabrīz

Baku

Tbilisi

Yerevan

AFGHANISTAN

Kabul

Herāt

Kashmir

Lahore

Srinagar

MONGOLIA

Ulaanbaatar

Ürümqi

Beijing

Tianjin

Lanzhou

Xi'an

Zhengzhou

Wuhan

Hangzhou

Nanjing

Shanghai

Taiwan

Shenyang

Dalian

Qingdao

Jinan

Harbin

Qiqihar

Changchun

Sea of Japan

Vladivostok

Khabarovsk

NORTH KOREA

SOUTH KOREA

Seoul

Tōkyō

Yokohama

Nagoya

Ōsaka

Kyōto

Kita-Kyūshū

Fukuoka

Sapporo

Hokkaidō

Sakhalin

Kuril'skiye Ostrova

Petropavlovsk-Kamchatskiy

Kamchatka

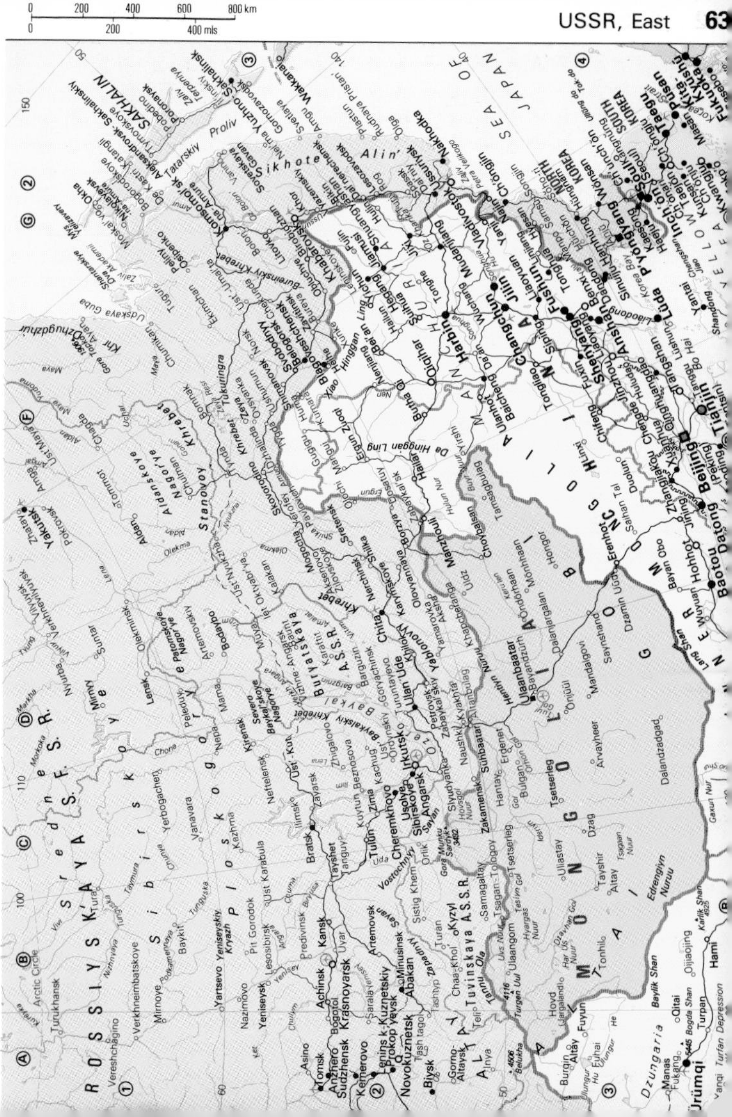

0 200 400 600 800 km
0 200 400 mls

SAKHALIN

Sikhote Alin'

SEA OF JAPAN

JAPAN

MONGOLIA

CHINA

Ulan-Ude · Chita · Irkutsk · Bratsk · Kansk · Achinsk · Krasnoyarsk · Tomsk · Kemerovo · Novokuznetsk · Biysk · Abakan

ROSSIYSKAYA S.F.S.R.

Sredne Sibirskoye Ploskogor'ye

Tuvinskaya A.S.S.R.

Buryatskaya A.S.S.R.

Vladivostok · Khabarovsk

Beijing (Peking) · Tianjin · Baotou · Dagong · Hohhot

Ulaanbaatar

Yakutsk

Arctic Circle

Stanovoy Khrebet

Yablonovyy Khrebet

Yenisey · Lena · Angara

SOUTH KOREA · NORTH KOREA

YELLOW SEA

Drungaria

Ulan Gom · Hovd · Tsetserleg · Dzüünharaa

Altay · Dalandzadgad

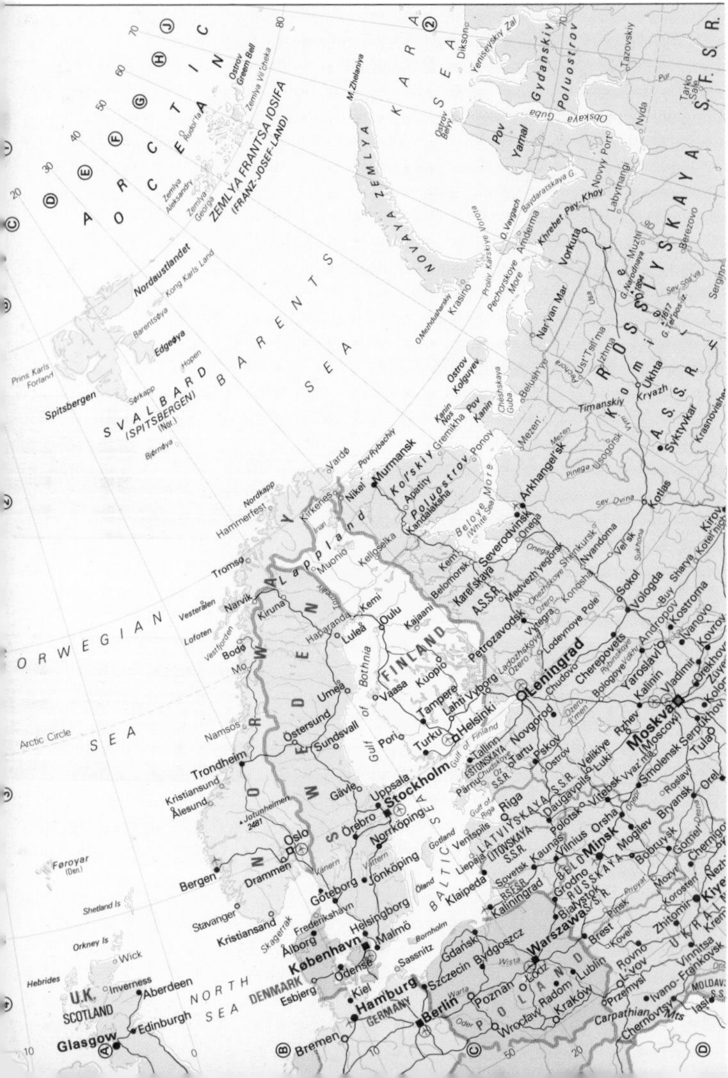

A R C T I C

O C E A N

ZEMLYA FRANTSA IOSIFA
(FRANZ-JOSEF-LAND)

Nordaustlandet

Kong Karls Land

Barentsöya

Edgeøya

Hopen

Prins Karls Forland

Spitsbergen

Sörkapp

SVALBARD
(SPITSBERGEN)
(Nor.)

Bjørnøya

NOVAYA ZEMLYA

KARA SEA

Gydanskiy Poluostrov

Dikson

Ostrov Belyy

Poluostrov Yamal

Obskaya Guba

R. S. F. S. R.

B A R E N T S

S E A

Ostrov Kolguyev

Murmansk

Kol'skiy Poluostrov

Kandalaksha

Arkhangel'sk

Severodvinsk

Timanskiy Kryazh

K O M I A. S. S. R.

Syktyvkar

Ukhta

Vorkuta

N O R W E G I A N

S E A

Arctic Circle

Tromsø

Narvik

Lofoten

Vesterålen

Bodø

Mo

Hammerfest

Nordkapp

Kirkenes

Vardø

Lappland

Kiruna

Gällivare

Muonio

Kemijärvi

Kemi

Oulu

Luleå

Gulf of Bothnia

Umeå

F I N L A N D

Vaasa

Kuopio

Tampere

Turku

Helsinki

Kem'

Belomorsk

Beloye More
(White Sea)

KAREL'SKAYA
A. S. S. R.

Petrozavodsk

Onezhskoye Ozero

Vologda

Cherepovets

Yaroslavl'

Leningrad

Moskva
(Moscow)

Novgorod

Pskov

N O R D E N

Trondheim

Östersund

Sundsvall

Namsos

Kristiansund

Ålesund

Jotunheimen
2481

S W E D E N

Gävle

Oslo

Drammen

Örebro

Uppsala

Stockholm

Norrköping

Vänern

Vättern

Gotland

Bergen

Stavanger

Kristiansand

Göteborg

Jönköping

Riga

LATVIYSKAYA
S. S. R.

Ventspils

Liepāja

Klaipėda

LITOVSKAYA
S. S. R.

Kaunas

Vilnius

Kaliningrad

BELORUSSKAYA
S. S. R.

Minsk

B A L T I C   S E A

Bornholm

Faeroyar
(Den.)

Shetland Is

Orkney Is

Wick

Hebrides

Inverness

Aberdeen

U.K.
SCOTLAND

Edinburgh

Glasgow

N O R T H

S E A

DENMARK

København

Helsingborg

Malmö

Frederikshavn

Skagerrak

Ålborg

Esbjerg

Kiel

Hamburg

GERMANY

Bremen

Berlin

Szczecin

Gdańsk

Gdynia

Sassnitz

Odra

Poznań

P O L A N D

Wrocław

Kraków

Łódź

Warszawa

Lublin

Radom

Brest

Białystok

Grodno

MOLDAV

Kiyev

Carpathian

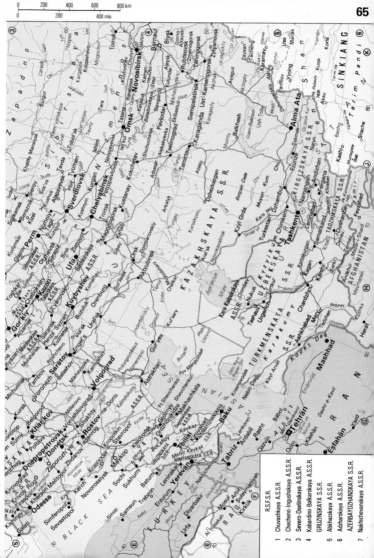

R.S.F.S.R.
1. Chuvashskaya A.S.S.R.
2. Checheno-Ingushstkaya A.S.S.R.
3. Severo-Osetinskaya A.S.S.R.
4. Kabardino-Balkarskaya A.S.S.R.
GRUZINSKAYA S.S.R.
5. Abkhazskaya A.S.S.R.
6. Adzharskaya A.S.S.R.
AZERBAYDZHANSKAYA S.S.R.
7. Nakhichevanskaya A.S.S.R.

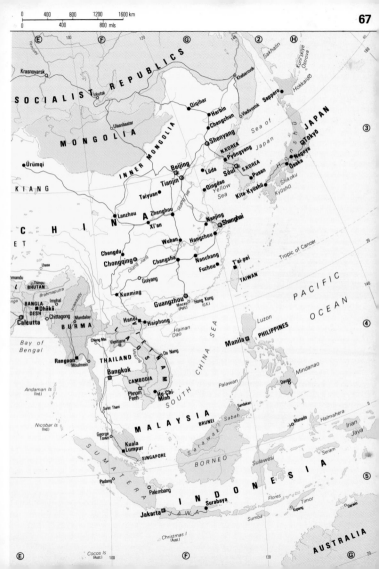

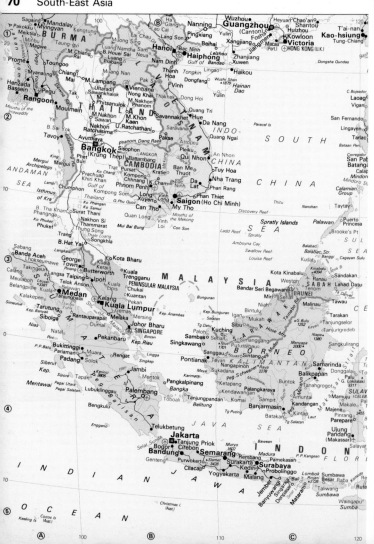

0 200 400 600 800 km
0 200 400 mls

Chia-i
TAIWAN (FORMOSA) Ⓓ
Tai-tung (China Nat. Rep.)
Ping-tung

PACIFIC Ⓔ 140 Ⓕ C

Farallon de Pajaros
20
Maug Is.

Luzon Strait
Babuyan Is
C Engaño
Aparri
Tuguegarao
Ilagan
Baguio
Dagupan
Baler
Cabanatuan
Quezon City
Manila
Polilio Is.
Daet
Boac
Naga
Legazpi
Romblon
Masbate
Oras
Panay
Roxas
Catbalogan
Iloilo
Bacolod
Cebu
Negros
Siaton
Bohol Sea
Butuan
Manukan
Ozamiz
L. Lanao
Zamboanga
Cotabato
Isabela
Basilan
Jolo
General
Santos
Sulu Arch.

Batan Is

LUZON

PHILIPPINES

Catanduanes

Bulan
Catarman
Samar
Guiuan
Leyte
Dinagat
10497
Surigao
Siargao
Cagayan de Oro
MINDANAO
Davao
Digos
Tinaca Pt

Parece Vela

Asuncion
Agrihan
Pagan
Alamagan
Guguan
Sarigan
Anatahan
Farallon
de Medinilla
Saipan
Tinian
Rota

Northern
Marianas

OCEAN

Ⓝ 140 Ⓕ C

Guam
(U.S.A.)
Nero Deep
9637

Mariana Deep
9818
Challenger Deep
11033

Ulithi
Fais
Gafer I.

Yap
Ngulu
Faraulep
Sorol
Woleai
Ifalik
Lamotrek

Trust Terr. of the PACIFIC ISLANDS (USA)
Palau
Islands
Koror

Rep. of Belau

CAROLINE

ISLANDS

Fed. States of
Micronesia
Sonsorol
Pulo Anna
Merir

Kepulauan
Talaud
Karakelong
Tahuna
Sangine
Kepulauan
Sangihe

Tobi

Helen Reef

Mapia

Equator
Ninigo Group
Wuvulu

LEBES

SEA

Buol
Kuandang
Gorontalo
Manado
Belang
Togian
Kep. Togian
Luwuk
Poso
VESI
ESI
opio
Towuti
Kendari
Kolaka
Natampone
Kabaena
Baubau
ESIA
S E A

Morotai
Tobelo
Ternate
Halmahera
Teluk
Weda
Bacan
Miangoi
Obi
Kep.
Sula
Mangole
Taliabu
Peleng
Banggai
Buru
Seram
Ambon
Namlea

Waigeo
Selat Dampier
Kwoka
2000
Sorong
Cendrawasih
Manokwari
Peg. Arfak
2935
Numfoor
Yapen
Teluk
Berau
Faktak
Bula
Miaool
Supiori
Biak

Tg d'Urville
Sarmi
Jayapura

Teluk
Cendrawasih

IRIAN
Dom
1340
Pegunungan Maoke
Pk Jaya
Angemuk
3741
Pk Mandala
4702

PAPUA
NEW GUINEA
Aitape
Wewak
Schouten Is
Karkar

Mt
Hagen
Central
4359
Gorok

MOLUCCAS
CERAM SEA
Piru
3019
Namlea

Kep. Banda
Adi
Kokonau
Kep. Kai
Wokam
Kep.
Aru
Trangan
Kobroör
Dobo

JAYA

Kokonau

NEW

PAPUA
GUINEA
Kikori
Kerema

Mendi
Kubor
Murray

Kuber
Bulolo
Wai

BANDA
SEA
Butung
Wowoni
Muna
Tukangbesi

Nila
Teun
Damar
Yamdena
Kepulauan
Tanimbar
Saumlaki
Selaru

P.Kolepom
Tk Flamingo
Tanahmerah

Merauke
Komoran
Tg Vals

Gulf of
Papua
Daru
Saibai
Port More

Flores
Ende
Lomblen
Alor
Wetar
Romang
Selat Wetar
Kep. Leti
Babar
Sermata

Oekusi
Atambua
TIMOR
Kupang
Roti
Savu Sea
Sawu

ARAFURA SEA

Mulgrave I.
Sept.
Banks I.
C. York
Thursday I.
Pr.of Wales I.
Somerset
Torres Strait
C. Grenville

Albatross B.
Weipa
Iron
Range
CORA

Great
Barrier Rf

TIMOR SEA Ⓓ

C.V. Diemen
Melville I.
Bathurst I.
Clarence Str.
Croker I.
Cobourg Pen.
Dundas Str.
Darwin
Arnhem Land
Wessel Is
C. Arnhem
Pen.
Nhulunbuy

AUSTRALIA

140 Ⓕ

SEA

Changchun
Jilin
Shenyang
Liaoning
Anshan
Fushun
Dandong
KOREA BAY
Lüda (Dairen)
Yingkou
Jinzhou
Qinhuangdao
Tangshan
Tianjin (Tientsin)
Beijing (Peking)
BO HAI
Bohai Wan
Hebei
Baoding
Shijiazhuang
Handan
Zhangjiakou
Chengde
Yantai
Qingdao (Tsingtao)
Zibo
Weifang
Jinan (Tsinan)
Shandong
YELLOW SEA (HUANG HAI)
Lianyungang
Xuzhou
Jiangsu
Nanjing
Huainan
Anhui
Bengbu
Kaifeng
Zhengzhou
Henan
Luoyang
Nanyang
Xi'an (Sian)
Shaanxi
Baoji
Taiyuan
Shanxi
Datong
Baotou
Hohhot
Nei Mongol
MONGOLIA
Erenhot
Yinchuan
Ningxia
Lanzhou
Xining
Qinghai
Gansu
Qin Ling
Mu Us Shamo
Tengger Shamo
Badain Jaran Shamo

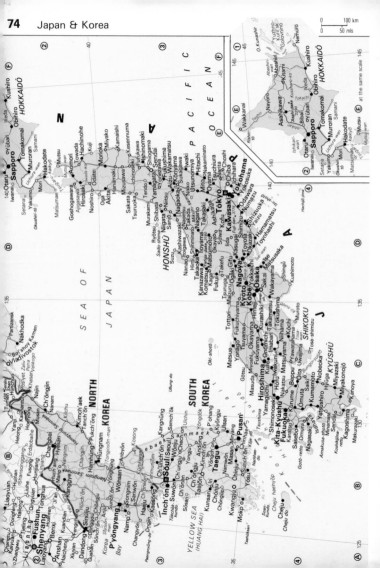

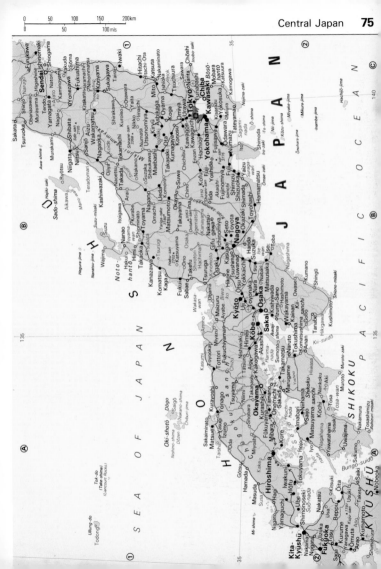

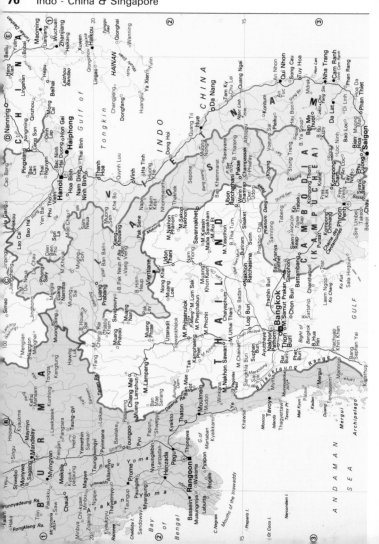

0 100 200 300 400 km
0 100 200 mls

PACIFIC

OCEAN

Dongsha
Quindao

Luzon
Strait

Batan
Islands
Basco

Balintang Channel

Babuyan Islands

Babuyan Channel Cape Engaño

Cape Bojeador

Laoag
2934
Aparri

Bangued
Vigan Tuguegarao

Ilagan

San
Fernando Solano Santiago
La Trinidad Mt Pulog 2929
Baguio Bayombong
Lingayen Dagupan
San Carlos San
Camiling Jose Baler
Tarlac Cabanatuan

Cordillera Central

LUZON

Sierra Madre

PHILIPPINE

Angeles Gapan
San Antonio San Fernando
Olongapo Malolos Polillo
Manila Quezon City Islands
Cavite Santa Cruz Calagua
Corregidor San Pablo Lamon Jose Panganiban
Lipa Lucban Daet
Batangas Lucena Sipocot Catanduanes
Lubang Boac Naga
Islands Iriga Virac
Calapan Marinduque Mayon 2421
Sablayan Mt Halcon Legazpi
2586 Sorsogon Gubat
MINDORO Mt Baco Bulan
2488 Sibuyan Masbate Catarman
San Jose Romblon Calbayog Oras
Tablas Sea SAMAR
Busuanga Calamian Catbalogan
Calamian Kalibo
Group Semirara Pandan Roxas Visayan San
Culion Islands Sea Isidro
Linapacan Strait Cuyo PANAY Bogo Carigara Tacloban
El Islands Cadiz Escalante Ormoc Burauen Guiuan
Nido Iloilo Silay Danao Baybay Leyte •10497
Taytay Dalanganem Bacolod Cebu Gulf Dinagat •10265
Cleopatra Islands La Carlota Lapu-Lapu
Needle Dumaran Binalbagan Maasin
Roxas Cuyo Bais Surigao Siarao
PALAWAN Islands Tanjay Tagbilaran
Puerto Cagayan Sipalay Dumaguete Siquijor Butuan
Princesa Islands Siaton Camiguin Gingoog
Aborlan Dipolog Lazi Cagayan
Mt Dapitan Oroquieta de Oro
Mantalingajan Tubbataha Manukan Iligan
2054 Reefs Liloy Ozamiz Marawi Malaybalay
Brooke's Mt Dapak 2550 Bislig
Point Pagadian MINDANAO
Balabac SULU SEA Zamboanga Malabang Tagum
Pen Cotabato Davao
Banggi Cagayan Sulu Zamboanga Moro Piang Mt Apo 2954 Mati
Kota Isabela Gulf Digos
Kinabulu Basilan Lais Cape San Agustin
Mt Palin Telok Pangutaran General
1216 Group Jolo Jolo Santos
Bandau Sandakan Parang Samales
Ranau Group Tinaca Point
Mt Kinabalu Labuk Tapul
SABAH Group Tawi-Tawi CELEBES Sarangani
Bingkor Malaysia Tawitawi Islands
Teniom Kuamut SEA Kepulauan
Kuamut Brassey Ra. Kawio
Tomani 1606 Bum Bum
Kalabakan Mt Magdalena Sempurna Kepulauan
1346 Nenusa
Tawau Karakelong

SOUTH

CHINA

SEA

PALAWAN

Palawan Passage

Balabac Strait

SULU
ARCHIPELAGO

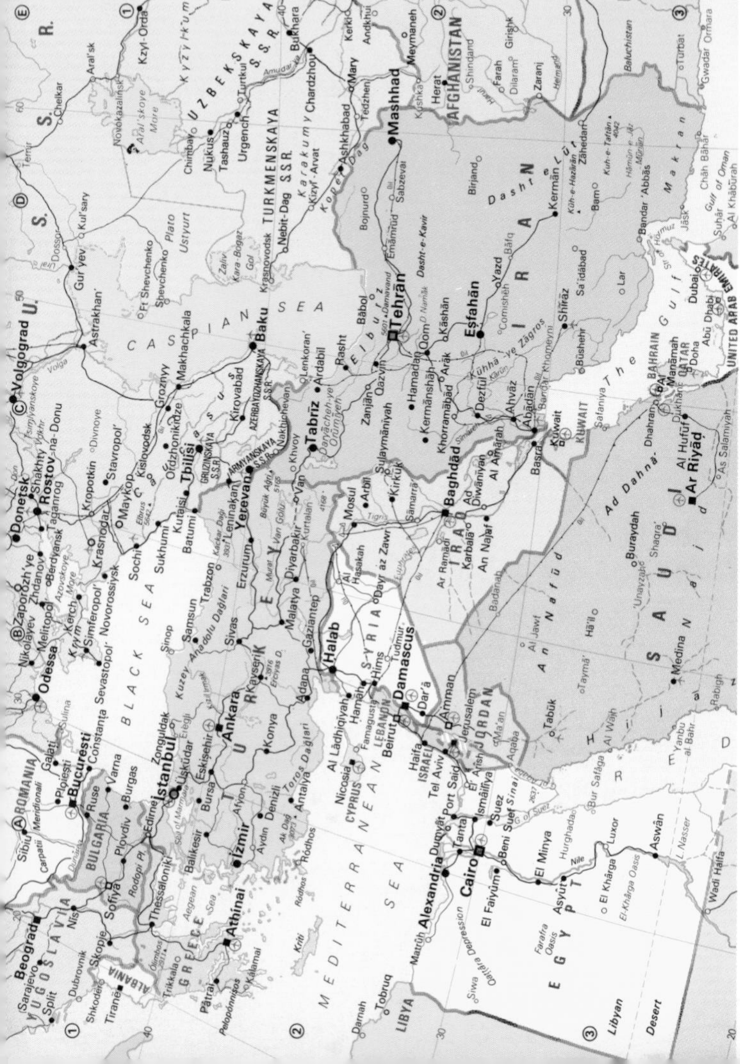

U.S.S.R.

Aral'sk
Kzyl-Orda
Kara-Kazakstan
Novokazalinsk
Chelkar

UZBEKSKAYA S.S.R.
Nukus
Urgench
Turtkul'
Bukhara
Chardzhou
Kerki
Andkhoy
Meymaneh

TURKMENSKAYA S.S.R.
Chardzhou
Mary
Tedzhen
Ashkhabad
Nebit-Dag
Kizyl-Arvat

AFGHANISTAN
Herat
Shindand
Farah
Dilaram
Zaranj

Mashhad
Sabzevar
Bojnurd
En?abad
Neyshabur
Birjand
Dasht-e Lut
Kerman
Kuh-e Taftan
Zahedan
Makran
Chah Bahar
Gwatar
Gulf of Oman

CASPIAN SEA
Astrakhan'
Gur'yev
Makhachkala
Baku
Krasnovodsk

Tehran
Qom
Esfahan
Yazd
Shiraz
Kerman
Bam
Lar
Bandar 'Abbas
Jask
Bandar Khomeyni

I R A N

Tabriz
Rasht
Qazvin
Hamadan
Arak

Volgograd U.
Rostov-na-Donu
Donetsk
Zaporozh'ye
Stavropol'
Krasnodar
Grozny
Ordzhonikidze
Tbilisi
Yerevan

BLACK SEA

Odessa
Nikolayev
Sevastopol'
Simferopol'

ROMANIA
Bucuresti
Galati
Constanta

BULGARIA
Sofiya
Plovdiv
Burgas
Varna

YUGOSLAVIA
Beograd
Skopje

ALBANIA
Tirane

Athinai
Thessaloniki

T U R K E Y
Ankara
Istanbul
Izmir
Konya
Sivas
Samsun
Trabzon
Erzurum

Halab
Damascus
Beirut
LEBANON
S Y R I A
Hims
Hama

I R A Q
Mosul
Kirkuk
Baghdad
Karbala'
An Najaf
Basra

ISRAEL
Tel Aviv
Jerusalem
Haifa

JORDAN
Amman

KUWAIT

BAHRAIN
QATAR
Doha
Abu Dhabi
UNITED ARAB EMIRATES
Dubai

Ar Riyad

S A U D I   A R A B I A
Medina
Mecca
Jiddah
Ad Dahna
An Nafud

MEDITERRANEAN SEA

CYPRUS
Nicosia

Alexandria
Cairo
E G Y P T
Suez
Port Said
Asyut
Luxor
Aswan
Lake Nasser

LIBYA
Tobruk

Libyan Desert

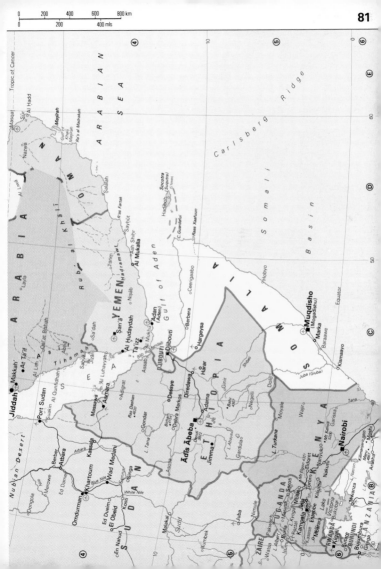

0   200   400   600   800 km
0   200   400 mls

Tropic of Cancer

④   ⑤   ⑥

Ⓔ

Masqat
Sūr
Majirah
Al Ḥadd

A R A B I A N   S E A

Nazwá

O M A N

Gulf of Masirah
Khalij Maşirah
Ra's al Madrakah

Al Layá

Carlsberg   Ridge

Ⓓ

Ash Sharīgh
Ra's Fartak

Socotra
(Suqutra)

Ṣalālah

Ⓓ

R u b '   a l   K h ā l ī

Taríf
Ḥabaroot

Layla

Hadibo

R a s   C a a r d a f u i

Thamarit

 Raas Xaafuun

Ash Shiḥr

Al 'Uqlah

Ḥaḍramawt
Tarīm

Sayhut
Ash Shiḥr
Al Mukalla

A R A B I A

At Ṭāif
Bi'r Fardān

Y E M E N

Şan'ā'
Nişāb

Gulf of Aden

Ḥobyo

S o m a l i   B a s i n

Qal'at Bishah

Al Luḥayyah
Sa'dah

Caluula
C. Guardafui

Bi'b al Mandab
Ceerigaabo

Makkah
Jiddah

Sabyā
Jīzān

Al Ḥudaydah

'Adan
(Aden)
Al Mukha
Djibouti
Assab

Berbera

Muqdisho
(Mogadishu)
Marka

Equator

Tihamah

Ta'izz

DJIBOUTI
Hargeysa

S O M A L I A

Baraawe

Port Sudan
Sawākin

'Asmara
Massawa

Ras Dashan
▲4620

Ḥārar
Dirēdawa
Dēssiē

Girīr

Shebele

Kismaayo

Nubian Desert

Berber
Atbara
Karima

Al Qunfudhah

Ⓒ

'Adigrat
Gonder

Ⓒ

Dolo
Juba (Giuba)

Dongola
Merowe

Atbara

Ṣinga

L. Tana
Debra Markos

Adama
Bahr
▲4307

E T H I O P I A

Nagēlī

Moyale

Wajir

Tana

Garissa

Ⓑ

Omdurman
Khartoum
Wad Medani

Blue Nile

Ādis Ābeba

Gardulaa

L. Turkana

Mt Kenya
4321▲
Embu

Nairobi

Ed Damer
Kassala

White Nile

Jimma
Ā'osa

Eldoret
Nakuru

Kitale

Kakamega
Kisumu
L. Victoria

Kigumu

El Obeid
Wad Medani

U G A N D A

K E N Y A

④   ⑤   ⑥

Ed Dueim
En Nahud
Kosti

Malakal

Sudd

Juba
Rumbek

Gulu

Lira
Soroti

Jinja
Kampala
Entebbe
Masaka

Nairobi
Machakos

Mt Kilimanjaro 5895▲
Arusha

N u b i a n   D e s e r t

S U D A N

Nimule

ZAIRE
Watsa

Butare
Bukavu

R W A N D A
Kigali
Mwanza
B U R U N D I
Bujumbura

Kisii
Musoma
Bukoba

T A N Z A N I A

Gitega

④   ⑤   ⑥

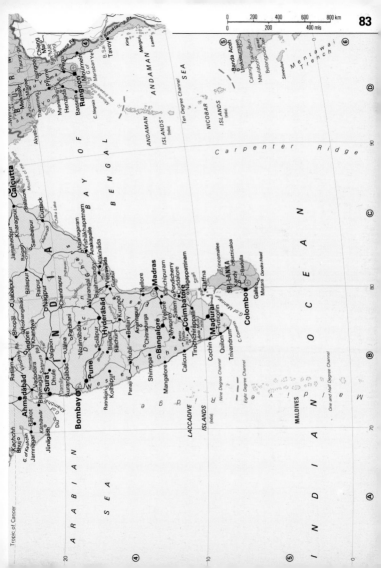

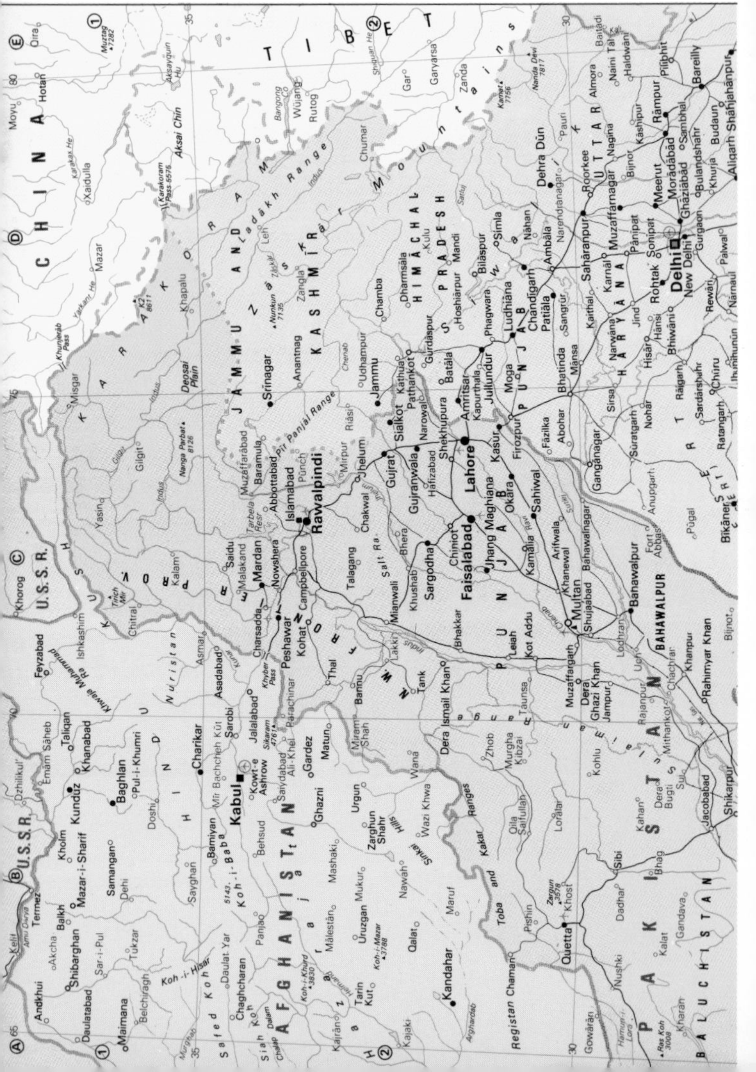

T I B E T

C H I N A

U.S.S.R.

K A R A K O R A M

Aksai Chin

Karakoram Pass 5575

Ladákh Range

Z a n s k a r   M o u n t a i n s

H I N D U   K U S H

K A S H M I R

JAMMU

Srinagar

Deosai Plain

Nanga Parbat 8126

Gilgit

Pir Panjal Range

Muzaffarabad

Baramula

Anantnag

Leh

Chamba

H I M A C H A L   P R A D E S H

Dharmsala

Mandi

Simla

Kulu

Bilaspur

Hoshiarpur

Dehra Dún

Roorkee

Saharanpur

Muzaffarnagar

Bijnor

Moradabad

Rampur

Bareilly

Budaun

Aligarh

Meerut

Delhi

New Delhi

U T T A R   P R A D E S H

H A R Y A N A

P U N J A B

Chandigarh

Patiala

Ludhiana

Jullundur

Amritsar

Lahore

Gujranwala

Sialkot

Jammu

Jhelum

Rawalpindi

Islamabad

Abbottabad

Peshawar

Mardan

Nowshera

K h y b e r   P a s s

Kohat

Bannu

Dera Ismail Khan

Faisalabad

Sargodha

Jhang Maghiana

Multan

Bahawalpur

Bahawalnagar

Rahimyar Khan

P U N J A B

B A H A W A L P U R

S A L T   R A N G E

A F G H A N I S T A N

Kabul

Charikar

Jalalabad

Gardez

Ghazni

Kandahar

Quetta

B A L U C H I S T A N

Baghlan

Kunduz

Mazar-i-Sharif

Balkh

Kabir Koh

K O H - I - B A B A

S U L A I M A N   R A N G E

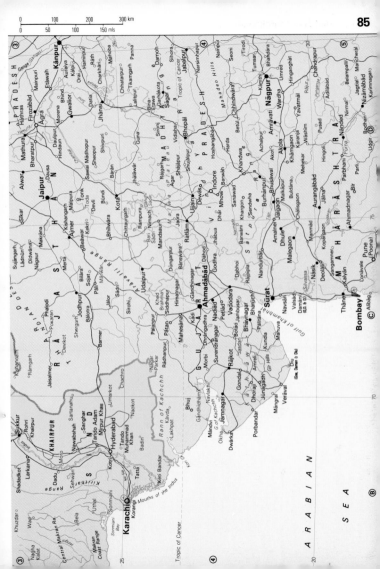

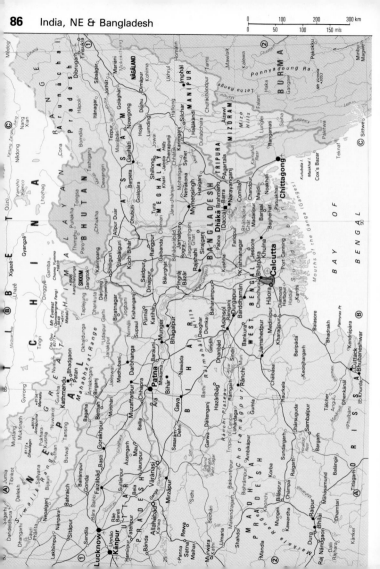

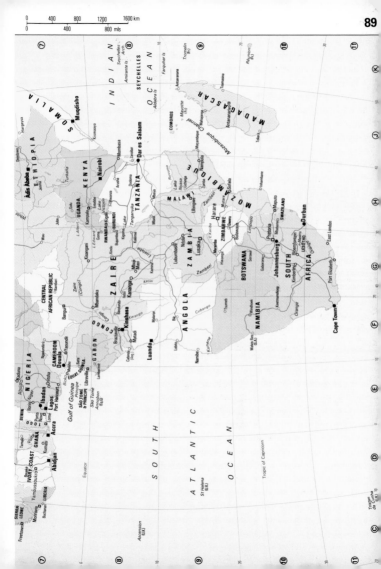

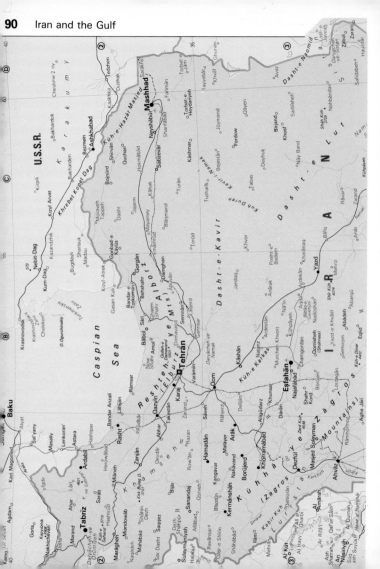

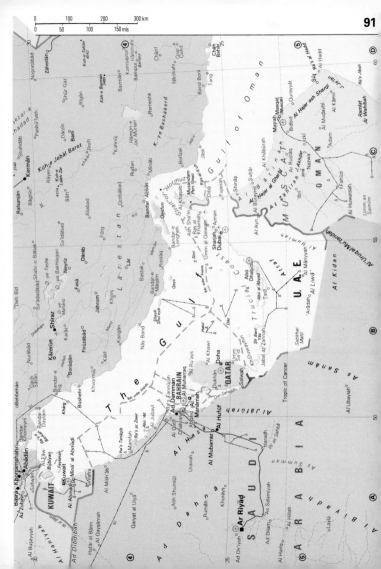

SAUDI ARABIA · **OMAN** · **U.A.E.** · **QATAR** · **BAHRAIN** · **KUWAIT**

0   100   200   300 km
0   50   100   150 mls

Gulf of Oman

The Gulf

MUSCAT/'UMAN

OMAN

Al Ḥajar ash Sharqī

Maṣqaṭ (Muscat)

Al Ḥajar al Gharbī

J. al Akhḍar

Nizwá

Ras Al Ḥadd

Sūr

Al Ḥadd

Ramlat Al Waḥībah

Rafsanjān
Kermān
Kūh-ye Jebāl Barez
Bam
Bāyenū-e Jāz Mūriān
Bandar 'Abbās
Strait of Hormuz
Qeshm
Ras Musandam Pen. ('Umān)
Al Khaşab
Dibā

Lārestān

Shīrāz
Kāzerūn
Lār
Bandar-e Lengeh
Sīrrī
Umm al Qaywayn
Dubai
Sharjah
Abū Zabī (Abu Dhabi)

U.A.E.

Al Liwā'

Al Kidan

As Sanam

Tropic of Cancer

Al 'Ubaylah

QATAR

Dūḥah (Doha)
Ar Rayyān
Salwah

Dukhān

Al Khawr

BAHRAIN

Al Muḥarraq
Al Manāmah
Ad Dammām
Al Khubar
Al Qaṭīf
Aḍ Ḍahrān

Al Hufūf

Al Jubayl

Al Jafūrah

Ad Dahnā'

SAUDI ARABIA

Aṣ Ṣammān

Ar Riyāḍ

Ad Dir'īyah

Ad Dilam

Al Hilāh

Al Kharj

Laylā

KUWAIT

Al Kuwayt
Al Aḥmadī
Mīnā' al Aḥmadī
Al Wafrah

Al Baṣrah
Al Fāw
Khorramshahr
Ābādān

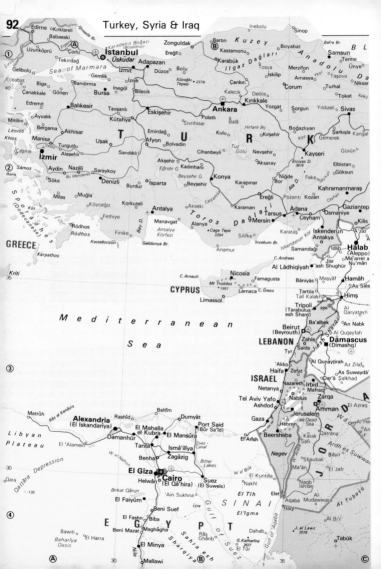

①

②

③

④

Ⓐ **Ⓑ** **Ⓒ**

Edirne Kırklareli
Karadeniz Boğazı Babaeski Inebolu Sinop
Uzunköprü Ereğli Çorlu Zonguldak Bartın Boyabat Bafra Br. Samsun
Gelibolu **Istanbul** Kastamonu Terme Ünye
Üsküdar Adapazarı Karabük Ilgaz Dağları Merzifon Tosya İskilip Amasya Taşova Niksar
Eceabat Biga İzmit Bolu Düzce Köroğlu 2378 Çankırı Delice Çorum Turhal Tokat
Çanakkale Gönen Bursa İnegöl Bilecik Tepesi Kalecik Sorgun Yıldızeli Sivas
Edremit Balıkesir Tavşanlı Eskişehir **Ankara** Kırıkkale Yozgat Boğazlıyan Şarkışla Kangal
Ayvalık Bergama Akhisar Kütahya Sivrihisar Polatlı Balâ Kırşehir Gemerek
Mitilini Emirdağ Kulu Kızı Kayseri Gürün
Lésvos Manisa Uşak Afyon Bolvadin Cihanbeyli Nevşehir Erciyas D. Elbistan
Khios **İzmir** Turgutlu Alaşehir Sandıklı Tuz Aksaray 3916 Feke Göksun
Çeşme Aydın Nazilli Sarayköy Eğridir G. Kadınhanı Gölü Niğde Bor Ala D. Kahramanmaraş
Sámos Söke Bü Menderes Denizli İsparta Konya Karapınar Pozantı Kozan Gaziantep
Ikaria Muğla Beyşehir G. Karaman Ereğli Tarsus Adana Osmaniye
Kós Köyceğiz Burdur Korkuteli Akseki Toros Dağları Ceyhan Kilis
Ródhos Fethiye Antalya Manavgat Alanya Karataş İskenderun Â'zâz
GREECE Ródhos Finike Antalya Körfezi Çağa Tepe Silifke Samandağı İdlib **Halab**
Kárpathos Kastellórizon Gelidonya Br. 2294 İncekum Br. İskenderun Kör. (Aleppo)
Kríti Anamur C. Andreas Jisr Ma'arret a Nu'mân
Samandağı ash Shughûr
35 C. Arnauti Al Lâdhiqîyah Hamâh
Nicosia Famagusta Bâniyâs Masyâf As-Sala
CYPRUS Mt Tróodos Larnaca C. Greco Tartûs Hims
1951 Limassol Tall Kalakh Al Qaryatayn
M e d i t e r r a n e a n Tripoli 3086
(Tarabulus An Nabk
esh Shām) Ba'labek Al Qutayfah
S e a Beirut Zahle **Damascus**
(Beyrouth) Saida (Dimashq)
LEBANON Tyr Al Qunaytirah As Zilaf
'Akko Zefat As Suwaydâ'
Haifa Nazareth Irbid Dar'a Salkhad
ISRAEL Netanya Mafraq
Tel Aviv Yafo Nablus Zarqa **Amman**
Matrûh Râs el Kenâyis Ashdod Jerusalem Al Azraq
Alexandria Rashîd Dumyât Gaza 352 Dead Ardh es Suwwân
(El Iskandariya) Baltîm Hebron Sea
El Mahalla Port Said El 'Arîsh Beersheba Kârak Sâfi
Damanhûr el Kubra (Bûr Sa'îd) Negev Shaubak Bâyir
El 'Alamein El Mansûra Suez Ma'ân El Jafr
Libyan Tanta Ismâ'îlîya Canal El Kuntilla
Benha Bitter El Tîh Naqb
Plateau Zagâzig Lakes Nakhl Ishtâr
El Tûr Qara Qattâra Depression 1274 'Ain Sukhna SINAI Aqaba Al Mudawwara At Tubayq
- 133 Helwân Suez El 'Igma
El Gîza (El Suweis) Elat Haql
Cairo Birkat Qârûn Dahab Al Bi'r
El Faiyûm (El Qâ'hira) Râs Ghârib J. al Lawz
Bawiti El Fashn Beni Suef Gulf of G. Katharîna 2578 Tabûk
Bahariya Biba 2637
Oasis El Harra Beni Mazar Maghâgha Gulf of Aqaba
El Minya Sharqiya Nile
Mallawi

30 **30** **35**

Scale

0 50 100 200 300 km
0 50 100 150 mls

B L A C K   S E A

Cam Br. Ordu Tirebolu Giresun

Ûlari

Batumi

Trabzon Rize Çayeli Artvin Ardahan

Akhalsikhe Akhalkalaki Rustavi

Kuba

Leninakan Kirovakan Kirovabad Geokchay Shemakha Sumgait

Mingechaurskoye Vdkhr

U. S. S. R.

Kazakh

Gümüşhane Bayburt Mescit D. ▲3236 Sarıkamış

Kars Kağızman

Kamo Sevan ●Yerevan Agdam Kazi Magomed

Yevlakh

Sal'yany

Aras
Horāsan

Büyük Ağrı Ararat 5165

Göris Kapydzhik 3906▲ Nakhichevan'

Igdir Alyat

Refahiye 2160 Zara Erzincan Aşkale Erzurum Eleşkirt Ağrı Doğubayazıt

Patnos Erciş Diyadin

Maku

Khvoy

Dzhulfa Marand Ahar Lari 4821 Kuh-ye Sabalan

Masally Lenkoran Astara

Divriği Tunceli Bingöl Muş Süphan D. Erciş

Van Gölü Van 2775 Gevaş Salmas Orūmīyeh

Daryācheh-ye Orūmīyeh Tabrīz Sarāb Herowābād Ardabīl Hashtpar

E Y Elazığ Keban Brj. Palu Ergani Silvan Batman Siirt Pervari

Bitlis Hakkâri Mor D. 3810

Kūh-e Sahand 3710 Marāgheh Hashtrūd Miāneh

Malatya Gölbaşı Adıyaman Hilvan Siverek Diyarbakır Dicle Midyat Cizre

Mardin Nusaybin Zakho Amādīyah Rawāndiz

Miandowāb Shāhīn Dezh Kirk Bulag D. 3707 Zanjān Qeydar Bijār Razan Row'ān

Beşni Nizip Urfa Akçakale Ceylanpınar Ra's al 'Ayn J.'Abd al 'Azīz 920 Al Qāmishlī Al Hasakah Jalāh Tall 'Afar

Naqadeh Mahābād Sar Dasht Saqqez

Sanandaj Qorveh 35

Jarābulus Manbij El Bāb Buhayrat al Asad Ar Raqqah As Sabkhah Sinjār Al Badī Al Hadr

Mosul Arbīl Dūkān Sulaymānīyah Halabja Allābād

Bīsotūn Kermānshāh Hamadān Kangavar Nahāvand

'mīyah

S Y R I A

Dayr az Zawr Mayādīn

Tudmur Al Bū Kamāl 'Anah Al Qā'im Al Hadīthah

Tikrīt Sāmarrā Al Miqdādīyah Khānaqīn Qasr-e Shīrīn Shāhābād

Borūjerd Khorramābād

Sab'Bi'ār Tubul ash Sham

Mileh Tharthar Hawr al Habbānīyah Hīt Ar Ramādī Al Fallūjah

Ba'qūbah Al Khālis Ilām

Kabīr Kūh Mehrān Simareh Lūristān

Mubayyir W. Hawrān

●Baghdād As Suwayrah

Dehlorān Dezfūl

Ar Rutbah W. al Ghdaf Bahr al Mīlh Karbalā Al Musayyib An Nu'mānīyah Al Kūt Ali al Gharbī

Ahvāz

I R A Q

Badiyat ash Shām

W. al Ubayyid An Najaf Al Hillah Ad Dīwānīyah Al Hayy Al 'Amārah

Al Qurnah Khorramshahr

Turayf Al Jālamīd W. Mirah Nukhayb Abū Sukhayr As Samāwah Ash Shatrah Qal'at Sālih

Ithah Nabk Al Harrah 'Al 'Isawīyah Badanah Ad Duwayd As Salmān Ash Shabakh An Nāsirīyah Sūq ash Suyūkh Hawr al Hammār

Basra Az Zubayr Abādān Al Fāw Būbīyan

Sirhān Al Widyān Shabrā Al Busayyah Safwan

Mughayra Al Jawf Al Hawjā Sakākah Rafhah Al Jumaymah Niṣāb Al Ahmadī Minā' al Ahmadī Al Wafra

Al Qalībah

S A U D I   A R A B I A

Al Ḥijārah Al Hānīyah Ad Dibdibah

KUWAIT Falakah Kuwait

Jubbah An Nafūd At Tawsiyah Hafar al Bāţin Al Qayṣamah Al Mish'āb Qaryat al

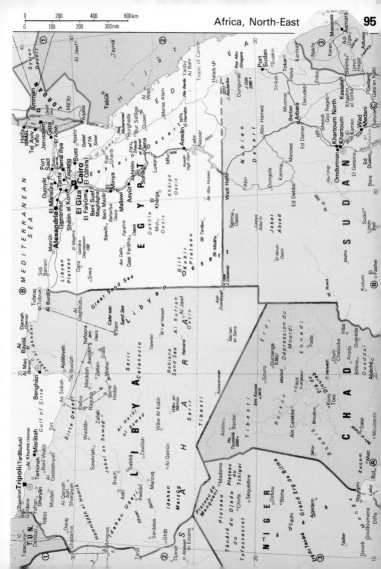

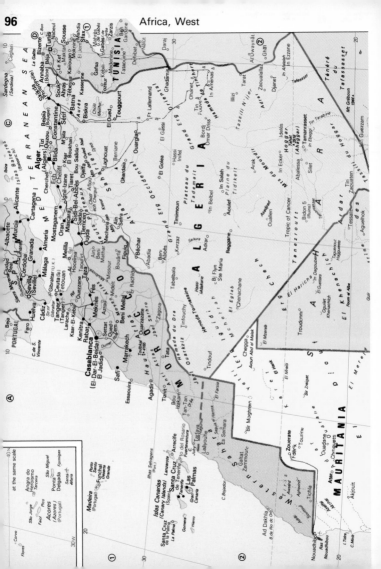

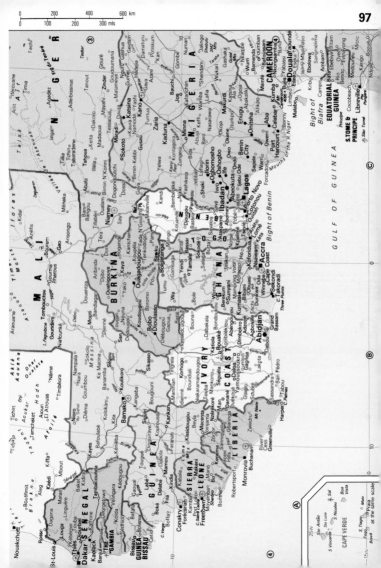

Ⓐ Tanout

Ⓑ Kanem

Ⓒ Kutum

Zinder Gouré Ngigimi Mao Salal Arada Biltine Guéréda Geneina El Fasher S U

Tessaoua Matameye Goudoumaria Diffa Lake Bol Massakori Oum Hadjer Abéché Ouaddai Zalingei Umm Keddada En Na

Nguru Gashua Chad Ndjamena Bokoro Mongo Am Dam Goz-Beida 3071 Jebel Marra Ed Da'ein El Muglad

Daura Yashi Geidam Maiduguri Kousséri (Ft Lamy) Massénya Mangalmé Nyala Taweisha Buram

Kano Gaya Hadejia Damaturu Bama Baguirmi Melfi Deli Am Timan Birao Raga Deim Zubeir Bahr

Katsina Potiskum Mokolo Bongor Bousso Sarh Harazé Ouanda Djallé Djéma

N I G E R I A Maroua Moundou Doba Dik Maro Ndélé **C E N T R A L A F R I C A N R E P U B L I C** Massif des Bongo Haute Kotto Yalinga

Jos Bauchi Gombe Numan Yola Garoua Léré Pala Lai Batangafo Bria Zémio

Kafanchan Wamba Shendam Wukari Gashaka Pala Bocaranga Bossangoa Bakala Bambari Bakouma Gwane

Makurdi Lafia Jalingo Poli Tcholliré Ngaoundéré Bozoum Bouar Dekoa Sibut Kouango Rafai Doruma

C A M E R O O N Tibati Meiganga Garoua Boulaï Carnot Boali Damara Bangassou Monga Bondo Niangar

Mamfé Wum Nkambé Bafia Bertoua Berbérati Boda Bangui Zongo Mobaye Yakoma Uele Bambili

Kumba Bamenda Foumban Nanga Eboko Abong Nola Mbaiki Libenge Gemena Monveda Aketi Buta Isiro Lienart

Buea Bafoussam Yaoundé Yokadouma Betou Bozene Lisala Bumba Banalia

Douala Edéa Eséka Mbalmayo Impfondo Makanza Bongandanga Yahuma Yambinga Kisangani (Stanleyville) Angumu

EQUAT. GUINEA Ebolowa Sangmélima Ouesso Basankusu Isangi Boyoma Falls Lubutu

Bata Ebebiyin Bitam Souanké Mbandaka (Coquilhatville) Befale Djolu Yatolema Ubundu Punia Walik

Libreville Medouneu Oyem Mekambo Pikounda Mompono Bokungu Ikela Opala Lubutu

Kango Mitzic Makokou Mbenza Fort Rousset Boende Bikoro Kiri Monkoto Lomela Kindu Shabunda

GABON Njolé Booué Kellé Liranga **Z A I R E** Loto Kalima Pangi Kibombo Kingombe

Lambaréné Lastoursville Mouila Moanda Djambala Ngabe Mushie Nioki Dekese Punia

Omboué Fougamou Koulamoutou Sibiti Mayama Bandundu Oshwe Bena Dibele Lodja Onema Kasongo Sentery

Mayumba Tchibanga Mossendjo Madingou Mouyondzi Brazzaville Kinshasa (Leopoldville) Masi Manimba Idiofa Mweka Lusambo Dimbelenge Kabinda Kabalo

Luobomo Madingo Kayes Buco Zongo Ndjili Kikwit Charlesville Luebo Makumbi Kananga (Luluabourg) Mbuji-Mayi Manono

Pte Noire Cabinda Tshela Luozi Madimba Popokabaka Gungu Tshikapa Dibaya Mwene Ditu Kabongo Mitwaba

Matadi Mbanza Ngungu Kasongo Lunda Kahemba Luiza Kamina

Boma Maquela do Zombo Sanza Luachimo Kapanga Lubudi

Ambriz Tomboco Damba Quimbele Marimba Camaxilo Canzar Kaniama

Luanda Caxito Nova Caipemba Bungo Cuango Lubalo Verissimo Sarmento Sandoa Kolwezi (Jadotville)

Dondo Malanje Saurimo Kasaji Mutshatsha Guba

Quibala Mussende Nova Gaia Cacolo Nova Chaves Caianda Dilolo Tenke Kitw

Sumbe (Novo Redondo) Andulo Luena Cazombo Lucusse Luau Likasi Mwinilunga Kipushi Chililabombwe Chingola

A N G O L A Luanguinga Macondo Mujimbeji Solwezi Zambezi Lumbala

200　400　600 km
100　200　300 mls

SUDAN

Keren　Massawa
Kassala　Barentu　Adi　Asmara
Khashm　Girba　Ugai
el Girba　Umm　Marsa Fatma
El Geteina　Hagar　Aduwa　Adigrat　Edd
Wad　El Gezira　Gedaref　Ras Dashan　Makale
Medani　Qala'en Nahl　4620　Sokota　Assab　Obock
El Obeid　El Dueim　Singa　Gallabat　Dabat　3657
Ed　Sennar　Gondar　Tandaho　DJIBOUTI　Djibouti　Zeila
Kosti　Hawata　L. Tana　Bahar　Waldia　L. Abbe
Er Rahad　Jebelein　Dunkur　Dar　Dangila　Dessye　Bikhili
Umm Ruwaba　Rashad　Rosieres　Burye　Debra Tabor　Debra Mts
Renk　Belfodio　Debra Birhan
Dilling　Asosa　Nejo　ETHIOPIA　Awash　Dire Dawa
Kaka　Paloich　Lekemti　Adis　Adama　Ahmar Mts　Harar
Abyei　Malakal　Dembidollo　Abeba　Aselle　Golocha
Bentiu　Nasir　Gore　Koma　Jimma　Goba　Ginir
Wau　Ayod　Akobo　Tori　Soddo　Shashamanna
Meshra　Er Req　Duk　Abera　Yirga　Mendebo　Hara
Tonj　Rumbek　Faiwil　Maji　Alem　Mts　Fanna
Yirol　Bor　Pibor Post　Bako　Arba Minch　Negelli
Amadi　Juba　Gardula　El Goran
Maridi　Mongalla　Swamp　Guba　Belet Uen
Torit　Lokitaung　Mega　Moyale　Dolo
Yambio　Laylo　Yei　Nimule　Lodwar　Lake Turkana　Mandera
Dungu　Faradje　Moyo　Kitgum　Mt Kulal　Buna　Xuddur
Watsa　Aru　Gulu　Moroto　2293　Baardheere
Mungbere　Pakwach　Lira　Mt Nyiru　Marsabit　Wajir
Bunia　Soroti　Kangetem　Afmadu
Masindi　Mt Elgon　Kitale　Isiolo　Mado Gashi　Jilib
UGANDA　Hoima　4321　Eldoret　Garissa　Giamame
Kampala　KENYA
Ruwenzori　Kakamega　Nanyuki　Equator
Goma　Jinja　Kisumu　Nakuru　Nyeri　Kismaayo
Kigali　Entebbe　Masaka　Kericho　Naivasha　Thika
RWANDA　Lake Victoria　Bukoba　Nairobi　Machakos
Butare　Kibungu　Nansio　Mwanza　Kajiado
BURUNDI　Biharamulo　Makindu　Patta I.
Bujumbura　Gitega　Musoma　Serengeti Nat. Park　Malindi
Kigoma　Nyakabindi　Ngorongoro Crater　Moshi
Uvinza　Nzega　Arusha　Tsavo　Voi　Mombasa
Kaliua　Shinyanga　Sekenke　Mbulu　Kwale
TANZANIA　Tabora　Singida　Kondoa　Masai Steppe　Tanga　Pemba I.
Manyoni　Dodoma　Korogwe
Kitunda　Mpwapwa　Handeni
Mpanda　Rungwa　Kilosa　Morogoro　Zanzibar
Sumbawanga　Chunya　Mikumi　Bagamoyo　Dar es Salaam
Mbeya　Iringa　Ifakara　Mafia I.
Tukuyu　Njombe　Mahenge　Mohoro
Tunduma　Liwale　Kilwa Kivinje
Mbala　Manda　Nachingwea　Lindi　Mtwara
Kasama　Songea　Masasi　Newala　COMOROS
Moroni　Grande Comore

Gulf of Aden
Ta'izz
Al Mukha (Mocha)　Adan (Aden)
Str. of Bab el Mandeb
Ras Khanzira　Karin
Berbera　Ceerigaabo
Guban
Hargeysa　Burco
Caynabo　Laas Caanood
Dagabur　Awarem　Damot
Ogaden　Warder　Galadi
Imi　Danan
SOMALIA
Baydhabo　Wanle Weyne　Jowhar
Buur Hakaba　Afgooye　Uarsciek
Marka　Muqdisho (Mugadishu)
Baraawe

SEYCHELLES
Aldabra Is.
Assumption

SOMALIA (inset at the same scale)
Candala　Alula
Baargaal　Guardafui
Boosaaso
Laas Qoray　Hordiyo
Ceerigaabo　Laz Daua　Ras Xaafuun
Carcar Mts　Bender Beyla
Qardho
Nugaal　Laas Caanood Damot　Eyl
El Hamure
Gaalkacyo　Dabaro
Garoowe
Hobyo

① Luanda

ZAIRE

ANGOLA

ZAMBIA

Lusaka

ZIMBABWE

NAMIBIA

BOTSWANA

Kalahari Desert

Windhoek

Great Namaland

Gemsbok Nat. Pk.

TRANSVAAL

Pretoria
Johannesburg

ORANGE FREE STATE

Bloemfontein

LESOTHO

SOUTH AFRICA

CAPE PROVINCE

Great Karroo

MAURITIUS
St Denis   Port Louis   Round I.
Réunion (Fr.)

Cape Town
Cape of Good Hope

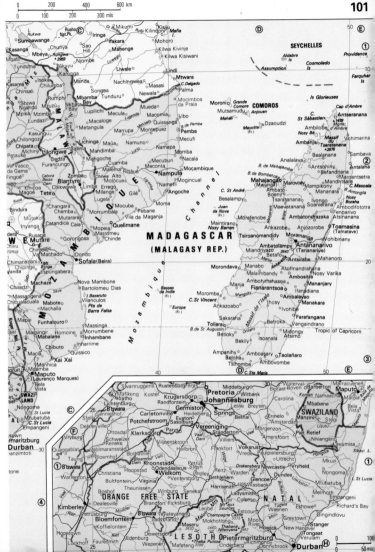

Map labels

Scale: 0 200 400 600 km / 0 100 200 300 mils

SEYCHELLES

Providence, Aldabra Is, Assumption, Cosmoledo Is, Farquhar Is

COMOROS — Moroni, Grande Comore, Mutsamudu, Anjouan, Mahéli, Mayotte (Fr.), Dzaoudzi, Is Glorieuses, Cap d'Ambre, Antseranana

C. Delgado, Mocimboa da Praia, Palma, Newala, Masasi, Nachingwea, Songea, Tunduru

Rukwa, Mikumi, Kilindoni, Mafia, Kisiu, Ruaha Nat.Pk., Iringa, Ifakara, Mahenge, Kilwa Kivinje, Kilwa Kisiwani, Lindi, Mtwara

Sumbawanga, Chunya, Sao Hill, Njombe, Liwale, Lupilichi, Mbamba Bay, Nkhata Bay, Metangula, Lichinga, Maúa, Mandimba

C. St Sébastien, Ambilobe, Nosy Bé, Ambanja, Massif OU Tsaratanana 2876, Vohimarina, Nosy Boraha, Antongila, Maroantsetra, Mandritsara, Befandriana, Antsohihy, Sambava, Antalaha, C. Masoala

Analalava, B. de Mahajamba, Mahajanga (Majunga), Marovoay, Mampikony, Ambato-Boeny, Tsaratanana, Maevatanana, Besalampy, Maintirano, Nosy Barren, Morafenobe, Tsiroanomandidy, Miandrivazo, Betafo

MADAGASCAR (MALAGASY REP.)

Antananarivo (Tananarive), Mahanoro, Toamasina (Tamatave), Moramanga, Vohibinany, Anjozorobe, Ambatondrazaka, Ambatolampy, Antsirabe

Morondava, Manabo, Malaimbandy, Ambohimahasoa, Fianarantsoa, Ifanadiana, Mananjary, Manakara, Farafangana, Vangaindrano

Morombe, Mangoky, Ankazoabo, Sakaraha, Toliara, C. St Vincent, B. de St Augustin, Onilahy, Betioky, Bekily, Isoanala, Midongy Atsimo, Tropic of Capricorn, Ampanihy, Ambovombe, Amboasary, Beloha, Tsihombe, Taolañaro, C. Ste Marie

Bassas da India (Fr.), Juan de Nova (Fr.), Europa (Fr.)

Mozambique region

Mozambique Channel, Mozambique, Moma, Angoche, Gilé, Mocuba, Pebane, Vila da Magania, Mopeia, Marromeu, Chinde, Quelimane, Sofala (Beira)

Nampula, Mecuburi, Nametil, Meconta, Nacala, Memba, Namapa, Namuno, Mahoche, Cuamba, Malema, Ribáuè, Alto Molócuè, Errego, Milange, Lugela

Pemba, Ilbo, P. de Pemba, Quissanga, Marrupa, Macaloge, Metangula, Mecufi

Teto, Tete, Changara, Chemba, Caia, Catandica, Mutarara, Chikwawa, Limbe, Blantyre, Zomba, Dedza

Mutoko, Inyanga, Rusape, Mutare, Chimoio, Vila Machado, Dondo, Gorongosa

Chimanimani, Mt Binga 2436, Chipinge, Espungabera, Nova Mambone, Bartolomeu Dias, Machaze, Save, I. Bazaruto, Vilanculos, Pta de Barra Falsa

Chiredzi, Massangena, Chicualacuala, Mabote, Machaila, Funhalouro, Massinga, Morrumbene, Inhambane, Inharrime, Quissico

Mapai, Pafuri, Massingir, Homoine, Chibuto, Manhica, Xai Xai, Maputo (Lourenço Marques), Bela Vista

SWAZILAND

Inset map (South Africa)

Swartruggens, Rustenburg, Brits, Middelburg, Waterval Boven, Belfast, Barberton, Marracuene, Maputo, Bela Vista

Mafikeng, Koster, Pretoria, Witbank, Carolina, Komati, Namaacha, Mbabane, **SWAZILAND**, Manzini, Siteki

Lichtenburg, Randfontein, Johannesburg, Germiston, Springs, Leslie, Breyten, Ermelo, Amsterdam, Piet Retief, Nhlangano, Lavumisa

Ottosdal, Klerksdorp, Parys, Sasolburg, Vereeniging, Standerton, Morgenzon, Amersfoort, Pongola, Mkuzi, Sibayi L.

Delareyville, Schweizer Reneke, Wolmaransstad, Vijoenskroon, Heilbron, Frankfort, Villiers, Volksrust, Paulpietersburg, Utrecht, Nongoma, L. St Lucia

Quaggasblat, Taung, Bothaville, Kroonstad, Odendaalsrus, Welkom, Petrus Steyn, Reitz, Warden, Vrede, Newcastle, Vryheid, Dundee, Glencoe, Mkuzi, Melmoth, Empangeni

Warrenton, Christiana, Hoopstad, Bultfontein, Virginia, Ventersburg, Senekal, Bethlehem, Harrismith, Ladysmith, Colenso, Weenen, Eshowe, Gingindlovu, Richard's Bay

Kimberley, Boshof, Theunissen, Winburg, Drakensberg Mts, Mooi River, Greytown, Stanger, Tugaat, Verulam, **Durban**

Dealesville, Brandfort, Ficksburg, Thaba Nchu, Mokhotlong, **LESOTHO**, Thabana-Ntlenyana 3482, Estcourt, Howick, New Hanover, Pinetown

Petrusburg, Bloemfontein, Dewetsdorp, Wepener, **ORANGE FREE STATE**, **NATAL**

Koffiefontein, Edenburg, **Pietermaritzburg**, Richmond, Donnybrook, Ixopo

Hopetown, Luckhoff, Fauresmith, Trompsburg, Mafeteng, Puthadi-tjhaba

Durban, **B'tswana**

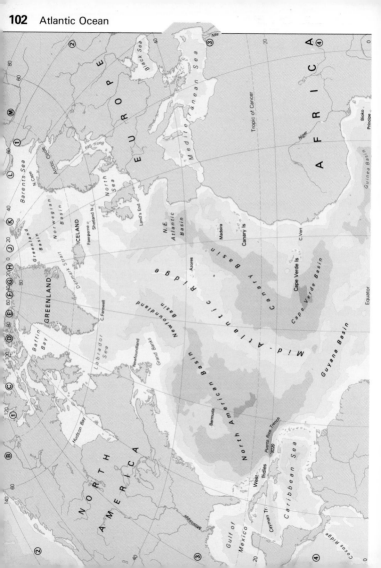

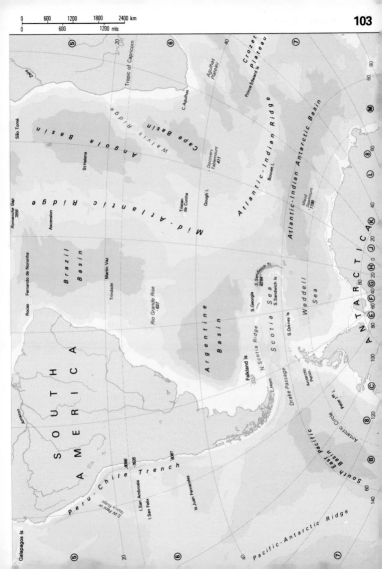

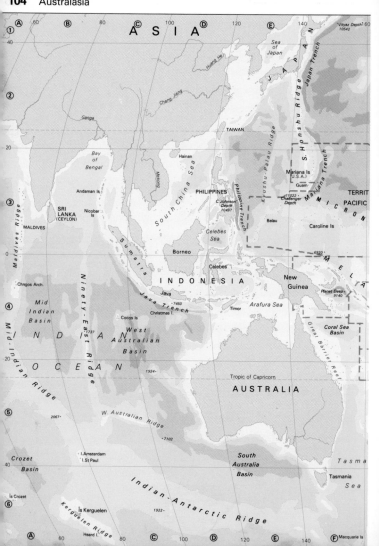

Ⓐ 60 Ⓑ 80 Ⓒ 100 Ⓓ 120 Ⓔ 140 Vityaz Depth 160 10542

① 40

A S I A

Sea of Japan

② Chang Jiang

Huang He

J A P A N

S. Honshu Ridge

Japan Trench

Ganga

TAIWAN

20

Bay of Bengal

Hainan

Mariana Is (U.S.A.)
Guam

Kyushu-Palau Ridge

Mariana Trench

TERRIT PACIFIC

Andaman Is

Mekong

Philippine Trench

M I C R O N

③ SRI LANKA (CEYLON)
Nicobar Is

South China Sea

PHILIPPINES

C. Johnson Depth 10497

11022 Challenger Depth

Belau

Caroline Is

MALDIVES

Maldives Ridge

Celebes Sea

0

Chagos Arch.

Sumatra

Borneo

Celebes

6920

M E L A

New Guinea

Planet Deep 9140

④ Mid Indian Basin

Ninety East Ridge

I N D O N E S I A

Java

Java Trench

7450

Christmas I.

Cocos Is

West Australian Basin

Timor

Arafura Sea

Coral Sea Basin

Great Barrier Reef

Mid-Indian Ridge

I N D I A N

20

1924

Tropic of Capricorn

A U S T R A L I A

⑤ 2067

W. Australian Ridge

7102

O C E A N

Crozet Basin

I. Amsterdam I. St Paul

South Australia Basin

Tasma

Tasmania Sea

40

Is Crozet

Indian-Antarctic Ridge

Tasmania

⑥ Kerguelen Ridge

Is Kerguelen

1922

Heard I.

Ⓐ 60 Ⓑ 80 Ⓒ 100 Ⓓ 120 Ⓔ 140 Ⓕ Macquarie Is

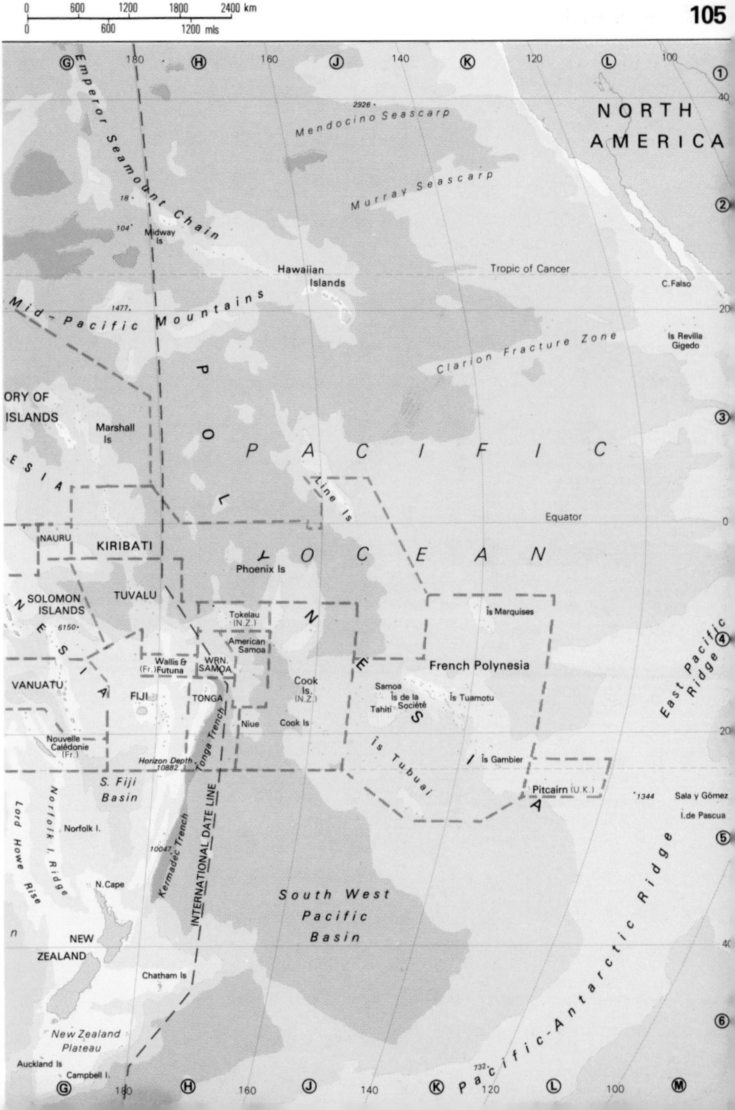

Scale bar: 0 — 600 — 1200 — 1800 — 2400 km / 0 — 600 — 1200 mils

NORTH AMERICA

Emperor Seamount Chain

Mendocino Seascarp   2926

Murray Seascarp

Mid-Pacific Mountains

104   Midway Is

1477

Tropic of Cancer

C.Falso

Hawaiian Islands

Is Revilla Gigedo

Clarion Fracture Zone

PACIFIC OCEAN

P O L Y N E S I A

ORY OF ISLANDS

...ESIA

Marshall Is

NAURU   KIRIBATI

SOLOMON ISLANDS

6150

TUVALU

Line Is

Equator

Phoenix Is

Tokelau (N.Z.)

WRN SAMOA

Wallis & Futuna (Fr.)

American Samoa

Cook Is (N.Z.)

Samoa

Is Marquises

French Polynesia

VANUATU

FIJI   TONGA

Cook Is

Niue

Samoa

Is de la Société

Tahiti

Is Tuamotu

Nouvelle-Calédonie (Fr.)

Horizon Depth 10882

(Tonga Trench)

Is Tubuai

Is Gambier

Pitcairn (U.K.)

1344   Sala y Gómez

i.de Pascua

East Pacific Ridge

S. Fiji Basin

Lord Howe Rise

Norfolk I. Ridge

Norfolk I.

10047

(Kermadec Trench)

INTERNATIONAL DATE LINE

N.Cape

South West Pacific Basin

NEW ZEALAND

New Zealand Plateau

Chatham Is

Auckland Is

Campbell I.

732   *Pacific-Antarctic Ridge*

180   160   140   120   100

G   H   J   K   L   M

① ② ③ ④ ⑤ ⑥

Scale: 0 200 400 600 800 km / 0 200 400 mls

140

Darwe
Gulf of Papua
Poppondetta
Trobriands
New Georgia
Santa Isabel
SOLOMON ISLANDS
(E)
(F)

Port Moresby
Kokoda
D'Entrecasteaux Islands
Woodlark
PAPUA
Saibai
(1)

Torres Strait
Pr. of Wales
Somerset
York
NEW GUINEA
Port Stanley Rge.
Kupiano
Alotau
Samarai
Misima
Louisiade Arch.
Florida Is
Malaita
Honiara
Guadalcanal
Maramasike
Stewart Is

Weipa
Cape York Peninsula
C. Grenville
Iron Range
Tagula
Rossel
San Cristobal

of
aria
Coen
Princess Charlotte B.
Emerald

Wellesley Is
Mitchell River
Laura
Cooktown
C o r a l
Rennell
976?

Normanton
Gilbert
Mt Bartle Frere 1612
Cairns
Innisfail
Coral Sea
Island Territories
Willis Group
(2)

Croydon
Forsayth
Ravenshoe
Palm Is
Coringa Is
Récifs d'Entrecasteaux

Cloncurry
Hughenden
Ingham
Townsville
Charters Towers
Ayr
Bowen
S
Marion Reef
Îles Chesterfield (Fr.)

Richmond
Collinsville
Proserpine
e
Îles Bélep

elwyn
Winton
Clermont
Mackay
Sarina
Northumberland Is
Swain Reefs
a
Bellona Reefs
20
Muéo
Bourail
Lifu

QUEENSLAND
Longreach
Barcaldine
Mount Morgan
Emerald
Mariborough
Caro
Nouvelle Calédonie
Nouméa
Île des Pins

Barco
Blackall
Rockhampton
Gladstone
Tropic of Capricorn

Windorah
Dividing
Theodore
Taroom
Bundaberg
Fraser I. Gt Sandy I.
Maryborough
Gympie
P A C I F I C
(3)

Quilpie
Charleville
Roma
Dalby
Miles
Toowoomba
Brisbane
Ipswich
O C E A N

Milparinka
Cunnamulla
St George
Goondiwindi
Warwick
Stanthorpe
Lismore
Casino
Grafton

Bourke
Walgett
Moree
Glen Innes
Inverell
Armidale
Roger Mtn 1615

Cobar
Nyngan
Narrabri
Tamworth
Port Macquarie
Norfolk I. (Aust)
30

Wilcannia
Broken Hill
Menindee
Ivanhoe
NEW SOUTH WALES
Dubbo
Mt Barrington 1585
Taree
Lord Howe I. (Aust)

L. Frome
Cobar
G
Orange
Cessnock
Maitland
Newcastle

Cooma
Bathurst
Lithgow
Sydney
Wollongong
170

Griffith
Cootamundra
Junee
Goulburn
Canberra A.C.T.

Mildura
Hay
Wagga Wagga
Jerilderie
Murray
Yass
Mt Kosciusko 2230
(4)

elaide
Murray Bridge
Balranald
Deniliquin
Shepparton
Albury
Bombala
Australian Alps

Horsham
VICTORIA
Bendigo
Orbost
T A S M A N

Hamilton
Ararat
Ballarat
Melbourne
Sale
Bairnsdale

Port Fairy
Warrnambool
Portland
Colac
Geelong
Morwell
Wonthaggi
Wilson's Prom.

King I.
Bass Strait
Furneaux Group
Flinders
C. Barren
S E A

C. Grim
Smithton
Burnie
Devonport
Launceston
St Mary's

Queenstown
Mt Ossa 1617
NEW ZEALAND
C. Farewell
Nelson

Geeveston
Hobart
TASMANIA
Westport
South Island
Greymouth

South West C.
South East C.
(D)
(E)
150
160
(F)
(G)

140

NORTHERN TERRITORY
(A)

QUEENS

Simpson
Desert

Pedirka

Alberga

Oodnadatta
Mt Dutton

Peake
Warrina
Conway
Edwards Ck
Lake
Eyre
(North)

Anna Ck
William Ck

Beresford
Coward
Springs
Bopeechee
Callanna

Millers Creek

Mount Eba
Parakylia
Bon Bon
Andamooka

Kingoonya
Coondambo

L Everard
Nukey
Bluff
Gawler Ranges
Poochera

Buckleboo
Kyancutta

Port
Kenny
Locke
Elliston

Mt Hope
Yeelanna
Cummins

Port Lincoln
C. Carnot

C. Catastrophe

C. Borda

C. du Couedic

Birdsville

Dutrie
Betoota
Moonda L
Haddon
Corner
Cooper Ck

Pandie Pandie
L Ulcowaranie
Haddon Downs
Yamma Yamma

Peera Peera
Poolanna L
Cordillo Downs
Clifton Hills
Durham Downs

Eromanga

Thargomindah

Adavale

Thylunga

Quilpie Cheepie

Toompine
Humeburn
Dundoo

Warburton
Kallakoopa

Warrandirinna

Cooper
Basn

Innamincka
Wilson

Mcomba
Orientos

Sturt

Desert
Narylico

Etadunha

L Gregory

Ft Grey

L. Blanche
Lake Stewart
Tibooburra
Milparinka

Tilcha

Marree
Callabonna
Yandama

L. Callabonna

Yancannia
Tongo

White Cliffs

Cunnamulla
Eulo

Thargomindah

Dynevor
Downs

Calwarro

Hungerford

Eringonia

Yantabulla
Wanaaring
Fords Bridge
Goombalie

Louth

Tilpa

Cobar

Lyndhurst
Leigh Creek

Mt Hack
Beltana

Mt Eba

Woomera

Binman

Parachilna

Lake
Frome

Wilcannia

L. Poopelloe

Tandou L

L. Mern
419

Hawker

SOUTH

AUSTRALIA

Port Augusta

Whyalla
Port Pirie

Iron Knob

Kimba
Carappe Hill
Cleve
Cowell

Kadina
Wallaroo
Moonta

Snowtown

Gawler

Mt Remarkable
Wilmington
Orroroo

Quorn
Carrieton

Baratta

Peterborough
Oakbank

Canopus

Olary

Burtundy

Silverton
Cockburn
Mingary

Broken Hill

Menindee L

Meninee

Mount
Manara

Ivanhoe

Conoble

Mossgiel

Gilgunnia

Trida

Willandra

Hillston

EYRE

PENINSULA

Tumby
Bay
Hardwicke B

Minlaton

Maitland

Yorke

YORKE

Ps

Wilmington

Jamestown
Crystal
Brook

Burra

Eudunda

Kapunda
Nuriootpa

Kadina

Balaklava

Wakerie

Renmark

Berri

Loxton

Barmera

Murray

Meringur

Red Cliffs

Mildura

Wentworth

V. Victoria

Hatfield

Pooncarie

Booligal

Goolgowi

Maude

Riverina

Balranald

Lachlan

Darlington Point

Griffith

Hay

Wa

Griff

Kulwin

Robinvale

Moulamein

Kyabram

C. Spencer
Investigator Strait

Kingscote

Kangaroo I.

Elizabeth
Strathalbyn

Adelaide

Murray Bridge

Mt Lofty

Tailem Bend
Coolwia

Meningie

Willoughby

Pinnaroo

Cowangie

Patchewollock

Ouyen

Nyah West

Swan Hill
Sea Lake

Keith

Tintinara

Bordertown

Naracoorte

Padthaway

Wolseley

Yanac

Nhill

Jeparit

Warracknabeal

Rainbow

Yaapeet

Birchip

Charlton

Echuca

Rochester

Numurkah

Shepparton

Benalla

Kerang

Sea Lake

Speed

Deniliquin

Finley

Jerilderie

Berrigan

Corow

Wa

Great Australian Bight

Penola

Balmoral

Casterton

Millicent

Mount Gambier
Port MacDonnell

Hamilton
Branxholme
Heywood

Portland

C. Nelson

Penola

Stawell

Ararat

Horsham

Murtoa

Dimboola

Nhill

Donald

Inglewood

St Arnaud

Bendigo

Castlemaine

Maryborough

Creswick

VICTORIA

Seymour

Kilmore

Kyneton

Healesville

Ballarat

Bacchus Marsh

Melbourne

Geelong

Queenscliff

Phillip
I

Dandenong

Hastings
Cowes

Colac

Coramamabul

Apollo Bay

Lorne

Wonthaggi

Mortlake

Camperdown

Warrnambool

Port Campbell

Pt Fairy

C. Otway

0 100 200 300 km
0 50 100 150 mls

Augathella C
Morven
L A N D
914 Mt Hutton
Injune
Taroom Mundubbera
Biggenden **Maryborough**
Gayndah
Mitchell
Mungallala
Muckadilla
Roma
Wallumbilla
Miles
Chinchilla
Dalby
Murgon
Wondai
Goomeri
Kilcoy
Gympie
Tewantin
Coroy
Maroochydore
Caloundra
Jackson
Condamine
Tara
Dirranbandi
Surat
Glenmorgan
Meandarra
Toogoolawah
Crows Nest
Moreton I.
Redcliffe
Toowoomba
Pittsworth
Oakey
Ipswich **Brisbane** ①
Cambooya
Stradbroke I.
Beenleigh
Beaudesert
Gold Coast
Tweed Heads
Warwick
Killarney
Murwillumbah
Kyogle
Mullumbimby
C. Byron
P A C I F I C
Stanthorpe
Texas
Tenterfield
Casino
Ballina
Lismore
Woodburn
New Angledool
Ashley
Garah
Moree
Warialda
Deepwater
Yamba
Maclean
Grafton
Lightning Ridge
Collarenebri
Gwydir
Bingara
Inverell
Glen Innes
30
Walgett
Burren Jct.
Narrabri
Wee Waa
Barraba
Guyra
Dorrigo
Glenreagh
Coff's Harbour
O C E A N
Coonamble
Baradine
Manilla
Uralla
Armidale
Bellingen
Nambucca Heads
Macksville
Smoky C.
Coonabarabran
Gunnedah
Walcha
Kempsey
Tamworth
Quirindi
Wingham
Wauchope
Port Macquarie
Gilgandra
Coolah
Merriwa
Scone
Gloucester
Taree
C. Hawke
Dubbo
Wellington
Mudgee
Muswellbrook
Singleton
Forster
Tuncurry
Dungog
Sugarloaf Pt.
Wollongong
Nowra
Jervis Bay
Canberra
ACT
Goulburn

TASMANIA
Bass Strait
Wilson's Promontory
King I.
Furneaux
Flinders I.
Group
Lady Barron
Cape Barren I.
Banks Strait
Whitemark
Smithton
Wynyard
Burnie
Ulverstone
Devonport
Latrobe
St Helens
Launceston
St Marys
Deloraine
Longford
Campbell Town
Queenstown
Mt Ossa
Derwent Br.
Oatlands
Freycinet Peninsula
Strahan
New Norfolk
Hobart
Huonville
Geeveston
Port Davey
S.W. Cape
Bruny I.
S.E. Cape
Tasman Pen.
S. Pillar

at the same scale

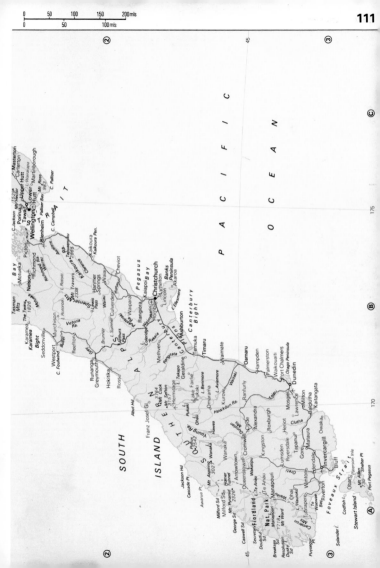

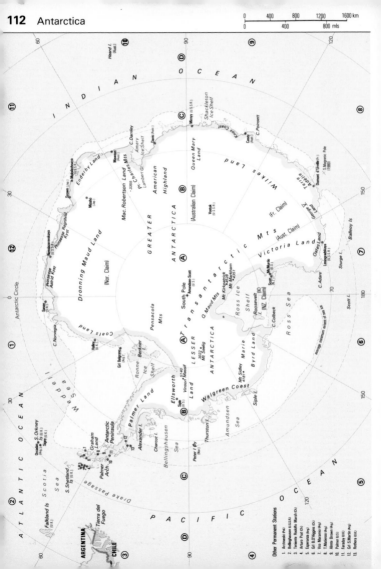

Other Permanent Stations
1. Arctowski (Pol.)
2. Bellingshausen (U.S.S.R.)
3. Teniente Rodolfo Marsh (Ch.)
4. Frei/Prat (Ch.)
5. Esperanza (Arg.)
6. Grl B.O'Higgins (Ch.)
7. Vice Marambio (Arg.)
8. T.Matienzo (Arg.)
9. Almte Brown (Arg.)
10. Palmer (U.S.)
11. Faraday (U.K.)
12. Grl G.I.San Martín (Arg.)
13. Rothera (U.K.)

Index

In the index, the first number refers to the page, and the following letter
and number to the section of the map in which the index entry
can be found. For example, 48C2 **Paris** means that Paris can
be found on page 48 where column C and row 2 meet.

Abbreviations used in the index

Afghan	Afghanistan	Germ	Germany	Phil	Philippines	Arch	Archipelago
Alb	Albania	Hung	Hungary	Pol	Poland	B	Bay
Alg	Algeria	Ind	Indonesia	Port	Portugal	C	Cape
Ant	Antarctica	Irish Rep	Ireland	Rom	Romania	Chan	Channel
Arg	Argentina	Leb	Lebanon	S Arabia	Saudi Arabia	Gl	Glacier
Aust	Australia	Lib	Liberia	Scot	Scotland	I(s)	Island(s)
Bang	Bangladesh	Liech	Liechtenstein	Sen	Senegal	Lg	Lagoon
Belg	Belgium	Lux	Luxembourg	S Africa	South Africa	L	Lake
Bol	Bolivia	Madag	Madagascar	Switz	Switzerland	Mt(s)	Mountain(s)
Bulg	Bulgaria	Malay	Malaysia	Tanz	Tanzania	O	Ocean
Burk	Burkina	Maur	Mauritania	Thai	Thailand	P	Pass
Camb	Cambodia	Mor	Morocco	Turk	Turkey	Pen	Peninsula
Can	Canada	Mozam	Mozambique		Union of	Plat	Plateau
CAR	Central African Republic	Neth	Netherlands		Soviet Socialist	Pt	Point
Czech	Czechoslovakia	NZ	New Zealand	USSR	Republics	Res	Reservoir
Den	Denmark	Nic	Nicaragua		United States	R	River
Dom Rep	Dominican Republic	N Ire	Northern Ireland	USA	of America	S	Sea
El Sal	El Salvador	Nig	Nigeria	Urug	Uruguay	Sd	Sound
Eng	England	Nor	Norway	Ven	Venezuela	Str	Strait
Eq Guinea	Equatorial Guinea	Pak	Pakistan	Viet	Vietnam	V	Valley
Eth	Ethiopia	PNG	Papua New Guinea	Yugos	Yugoslavia		
Fin	Finland	Par	Paraguay	Zim	Zimbabwe		

A

57B2 **Aachen** Germany
46C1 **Aalst** Belg
38K6 **Äänekoski** Fin
47C1 **Aarau** Switz
47B1 **Aare** R Switz
72A3 **Aba** China
97C4 **Aba** Nig
99D2 **Aba** Zaire
91A3 **Ābādān** Iran
90B3 **Ābādeh** Iran
96B1 **Abadla** Alg
35B1 **Abaeté** Brazil
31B1 **Abaeté** R Brazil
31B2 **Abaetetuba** Brazil
72D1 **Abagnar Qi** China
97C4 **Abakaliki** Nig
63B2 **Abakan** USSR
97C3 **Abala** Niger
96C2 **Abalessa** Alg
32C6 **Abancay** Peru
90B3 **Abarqū** Iran
74E2 **Abashiri** Japan
74E2 **Abashiri-wan** B
 Japan
71F4 **Abau** PNG
99D2 **Abaya** L Eth
99D1 **Abbai** R Eth
99E1 **Abbe** L Eth
48C1 **Abbeville** France
19B4 **Abbeville** Louisiana,
 USA
17B1 **Abbeville** S Carolina,
 USA
45B2 **Abbeyfeale** Irish Rep
47C2 **Abbiategrasso** Italy
20B1 **Abbotsford** Can
84C2 **Abbottabad** Pak
61H3 **Abdulino** USSR
98C1 **Abéché** Chad
39F7 **Åbenrå** Den
97C4 **Abeokuta** Nig
99D2 **Abera** Eth
43B3 **Aberaeron** Wales

15C3 **Aberdeen** Maryland,
 USA
100B4 **Aberdeen** S Africa
44C3 **Aberdeen** Scot
8D2 **Aberdeen** S Dakota,
 USA
8A2 **Aberdeen**
 Washington, USA
4J3 **Aberdeen L** Can
44C3 **Aberfeldy** Scot
43C4 **Abergavenny** Wales
43B3 **Aberystwyth** Wales
81C4 **Abhā** S Arabia
90A2 **Abhar** Iran
97B4 **Abidjan** Ivory Coast
18A2 **Abilene** Kansas, USA
9D3 **Abilene** Texas, USA
43D4 **Abingdon** Eng
7B4 **Abitibi** R Can
7C5 **Abitibi,L** Can
61F5 **Abkhazskaya**
 Republic, USSR
84C2 **Abohar** India
97C4 **Abomey** Benin
98B2 **Abong Mbang** Cam
79A4 **Aborlan** Phil
98B1 **Abou Deia** Chad
91A4 **Abqaiq** S Arabia
50A2 **Abrantes** Port
95C2 **Abri** Sudan
106A3 **Abrolhos** Is Aust
8B2 **Absaroka Range** Mts
 USA
91B5 **Abū al Abyad** I UAE
91A4 **Abū 'Alī** I S Arabia
91B5 **Abu Dhabi** UAE
95C3 **Abu Hamed** Sudan
97C4 **Abuja** Nig
33D5 **Abunã** Brazil
32E6 **Abuná** R Bol
93D3 **Abū Sukhayr** Iraq
111B2 **Abut Head** C NZ
95C3 **Abu 'Urug** Well
 Sudan
99D1 **Abuye Meda** Mt Eth

99C1 **Abu Zabad** Sudan
99D2 **Abwong** Sudan
56B1 **Åby** Den
94B3 **Aby 'Aweigila** Well
 Egypt
99C2 **Abyei** Sudan
24B2 **Acambaro** Mexico
24B2 **Acaponeta** Mexico
24B3 **Acapulco** Mexico
31D2 **Acaraú** Brazil
32D2 **Acarigua** Ven
24C3 **Acatlán** Mexico
23B2 **Acatzingo** Mexico
97B4 **Accra** Ghana
85D4 **Achalpur** India
29B4 **Achao** Chile
47D1 **Achensee** L Austria
46E2 **Achern** Germany
41A3 **Achill I** Irish Rep
63C2 **Achinsk** USSR
53C3 **Acireale** Italy
26C2 **Acklins** I Caribbean S
32C6 **Acobamba** Peru
29B2 **Aconcagua** Mt Chile
31D3 **Acopiara** Brazil
88B4 **Açores** Is Atlantic O
47C2 **Acqui** Italy
108A2 **Acraman,L** Aust
 Acre = **'Akko**
32C5 **Acre** State, Brazil
22C3 **Acton** USA
23B1 **Actopan** Mexico
19A3 **Ada** USA
50B1 **Adaja** R Spain
91C5 **Adam** Oman
99D2 **Adama** Eth
35A2 **Adamantina** Brazil
98B2 **Adamaoua** Region,
 Nig/Cam
47D1 **Adamello** Mt Italy
16C1 **Adams** USA
87B3 **Adam's Bridge** India/
 Sri Lanka
13D2 **Adams L** Can
8A2 **Adams,Mt** USA

87C3 **Adam's Peak** Mt
 Sri Lanka
81C4 **'Adan** Yemen
92C2 **Adana** Turk
60D5 **Adapazari** Turk
11ZB7 **Adare,C** Ant
108B1 **Adavale** Aust
47C2 **Adda** R Italy
91A4 **Ad Dahna'** Region,
 S Arabia
96A2 **Ad Dakhla** Mor
91B4 **Ad Damman**
 S Arabia
91A4 **Ad Dibdibah** Region,
 S Arabia
91A5 **Ad Dilam** S Arabia
91A5 **Ad Dir'iyah** S Arabia
93D3 **Ad Diwaniyah** Iraq
81C4 **Ad Dīl** Yemen
91A5 **Ad Duwayd** S Arabia
108C4 **Adelaide** Aust
4J3 **Adelaide Pen** Can
22D3 **Adelanto** USA
 Aden = **'Adan**
81C4 **Aden,G of** Yemen/
 Somalia
97C3 **Aderbissinat** Niger
94C2 **Adhra** Syria
71E4 **Adi** I Indon
52B1 **Adige** R Italy
99D1 **Adigrat** Eth
85D5 **Adilabad** India
20B2 **Adin** USA
15D2 **Adirondack Mts**
 USA
99D2 **Ādīs Ābeba** Eth
95C3 **Adi Ugai** Eth
93C2 **Adiyaman** Turk
54C1 **Adjud** Rom
4E4 **Admiralty I** USA
6B2 **Admiralty Inlet** B
 Can
87B1 **Adoni** India
48B3 **Adour** R France
96A2 **Adrar** Region, Maur

96C2 Adrar *Mts* Alg
96A2 Adrar Soutouf *Region, Mor*
98C1 Adré Chad
95A2 Adri Libya
47E2 Adria Italy
14B2 Adrian Michigan, USA
52B2 Adriatic *S* Italy/Yugos
99D1 Aduwa Eth
97B4 Adzopé Ivory Coast
55B3 Aegean *S* Greece
80E2 Afghanistan Republic, Asia
99E2 Afgooye Somalia
97C4 Afikpo Nig
38G6 Afjord Nor
96C1 Aflou Alg
99E2 Afmedu Somalia
97A3 Afollé *Region, Maur*
94B2 Afula Israel
92B2 Afyon Turk
95A3 Agadem Niger
97C3 Agadez Niger
96B1 Agadir Mor
85D4 Agar India
86C2 Agartala India
20B1 Agassiz Can
97B4 Agboville Ivory Coast
93E1 Agdam USSR
75B1 Agematsu Japan
48C3 Agen France
90A3 Agha Jari Iran
96A2 Aghwinit *Well Mor*
47D2 Agno *R* Italy
47E1 Agordo Italy
48C3 Agout *R* France
85D3 Agra India
53C2 Agri *R* Italy
93D2 Agri Turk
53B3 Agrigento Italy
55B3 Agrinion Greece
34A3 Agrio *R* Chile
53B2 Agropoli Italy
61H2 Agryz USSR
6E3 Agto Greenland
27D3 Aguadilla Puerto Rico
24B1 Agua Prieta Mexico
24B2 Aguascalientes Mexico
23A1 Aguascalientes State, Mexico
35C1 Aguas Formosas Brazil
50A1 Agueda Port
96C3 Aguelhok Mali
50B2 Aguilas Spain
23A2 Aguililla Mexico
100B4 Agulhas,C S Africa
79C4 Agusan *R* Phil
Ahaggar = Hoggar
93E2 Ahar Iran
110B1 Ahipara *B* NZ
85C4 Ahmadābād India
87A1 Ahmadnagar India
99E2 Ahmar *Mts* Eth
46D1 Ahr *R* Germany
46D1 Ahrgebirge *Region, Germany*
23A1 Ahuacatlán Mexico
23A1 Ahualulco Mexico
39G7 Åhus Sweden
90B2 Ahuvān Iran
90A3 Ahvāz Iran
26A4 Aiajuela Costa Rica
47B1 Aigle Switz
47B2 Aiguille d'Arves *Mt* France
47B2 Aiguille de la Grand Sassière *Mt* France
75B1 Aikawa Japan
17B1 Aiken USA
73A5 Ailao Shan *Upland* China
35C1 Aimorés Brazil
96B1 Ain Beni Mathar Mor
95B2 Ain Dalla *Well* Egypt
51C2 Ain el Hadjel Alg
95A3 Ain Galakka Chad
96B1 Ain Sefra Alg

92B4 'Ain Sukhna Egypt
75A2 Aioi Japan
96B2 Aioun Abd el Malek *Well Maur*
97B3 Aïoun El Atrouss Maur
30C2 Aiquile Bol
97C3 Aïr *Desert Region* Niger
13E2 Airdrie Can
46B1 Aire France
42D3 Aire *R* Eng
46C2 Aire *R* France
6C3 Airforce *I* Can
47C1 Airolo Switz
4E3 Aishihik Can
12G2 Aishihik *L* Can
46B2 Aisne Department, France
49C2 Aisne *R* France
71F4 Aitape PNG
58D1 Aiviekste *R* USSR
72B2 Aixa Zuogi China
49D3 Aix-en-Provence France
47A2 Aix-les-Bains France
86B2 Aiyar Res India
55B3 Aiyion Greece
55B3 Aiyna *I* Greece
86C2 Āīzawl India
100A3 Aizeb *R* Namibia
74E3 Aizu-Wakamatsu Japan
52A2 Ajaccio Corse
23B2 Ajalpan Mexico
95B1 Ajdabiyah Libya
74E2 Ajigasawa Japan
91C4 Ajman UAE
85C3 Ajmer India
9B3 Ajo USA
23A2 Ajuchitan Mexico
55C3 Ak *R* Turk
75B1 Akaishi-sanchi *Mts* Japan
87B1 Akalkot India
111B2 Akaroa NZ
75A2 Akashi Japan
61J3 Akbulak USSR
93C2 Akçakale Turk
96A2 Akchar *Watercourse* Maur
55C3 Akdağ *Mt* Turk
98C2 Aketi Zaïre
93D1 Akhalkalaki USSR
93D1 Akhalsikhe USSR
55B3 Akharnaí Greece
12D2 Akhiok USA
92A2 Akhisar Turk
58D1 Akhiste USSR
95C2 Akhmim Egypt
61G4 Akhtubinsk USSR
60D4 Akhtyrka USSR
75A2 Aki Japan
7A4 Akimiski *I* Can
74E3 Akita Japan
96A3 Akjoujt Maur
94B2 'Akko Israel
4E3 Aklavik Can
97B3 Aklé Aouana *Desert Region* Maur
99D2 Akobo Sudan
99D2 Akobo *R* Sudan
84B1 Akoha Afghan
85D4 Akola India
85D4 Akot India
6D3 Akpatok *I* Can
55B3 Ákra Kafirévs *C* Greece
55B3 Ákra Maléa *C* Greece
38A2 Akranes Iceland
55C3 Ákra Sídheros *C* Greece
55B3 Ákra Spátha *C* Greece
55B3 Ákra Taínaron *C* Greece
10B2 Akron USA
94A1 Akrotiri *B* Cyprus

84D1 Aksai Chin *Mts* China
92B2 Aksaray Turk
61H3 Aksay USSR
84D1 Aksayquin Hu *L* China
92B2 Akşehir Turk
92B2 Akseki Turk
63D2 Aksenovo Zilovskoye USSR
68D1 Aksha USSR
82C1 Aksu China
61J4 Aktumsyk USSR
65G4 Aktyubinsk USSR
38B1 Akureyri Iceland
65K5 Akzhal USSR
11B3 Alabama State, USA
11B3 Alabama *R* USA
92C2 Ala Daǧlari *Mts* Tur
61F5 Alagir USSR
47B2 Alagna Italy
31D3 Alagoas State, Brazil
31D4 Alagoinhas Brazil
51B1 Alagón Spain
93E4 Al Ahmadi Kuwait
25D3 Alajuela Costa Rica
12B2 Alakanuk USA
38L5 Alakurtti USSR
93E3 Al Amārah Iraq
21A2 Alameda USA
23B1 Alamo Mexico
9C3 Alamogordo USA
9C3 Alamosa USA
39H6 Åland *I* Fin
92B2 Alanya Turk
17B1 Alapaha *R* USA
65H4 Alapayevsk USSR
92A2 Alaşehir Turk
68B3 Ala Shan *Mts* China
4C3 Alaska State, USA
4D4 Alaska,G of USA
12C3 Alaska Pen USA
4C3 Alaska Range *Mts* USA
52A2 Alassio Italy
12D1 Alatna *R* USA
61G3 Alatyr USSR
108B2 Alawoona Aust
91C5 Al'Ayn UAE
82B2 Alayskiy Khrebet *Mts* USSR
49D3 Alba Italy
92C2 Al Bāb Syria
51B2 Albacete Spain
50A1 Alba de Tormes Spain
93D2 Al Badi Iraq
54B1 Alba Iulia Rom
54A2 Albania Republic, Europe
106A4 Albany Aust
17B1 Albany Georgia, USA
15D2 Albany New York, USA
8A2 Albany Oregon, USA
7B4 Albany *R* Can
34B2 Albardón Arg
91C5 Al Batinah *Region, Oman*
107E3 Albatross *B* Aust
95B1 Al Baydā Libya
11C3 Albemarle Sd USA
50B1 Alberche *R* Spain
108A1 Alberga Aust
46B1 Albert France
5G4 Alberta Province, Can
99D2 Albert,L Uganda/Zaïre
10A2 Albert Lea USA
99D2 Albert Nile *R* Uganda
49D2 Albertville France
49C3 Albi France
18B1 Albia USA
33G2 Albina Suriname
14B2 Albion Michigan, USA
15C2 Albion New York, USA
92C4 Al Bi'r S Arabia
91A5 Al Biyadh *Region, S Arabia*
50B2 Alborán *I* Spain

39G7 Ålborg Den
95A1 Al Brayqah Libya
93D3 Al Bū Kamāl Syria
47C1 Albula *R* Switz
9C3 Albuquerque USA
91C5 Al Buraymi Oman
95B1 Al Burdi Libya
107D4 Albury Aust
93E3 Al Buṣayyah Iraq
50B1 Alcalá de Henares Spain
53B3 Alcamo Italy
51B1 Alcañiz Spain
31C2 Alcântara Brazil
50B2 Alcaraz Spain
50B2 Alcázar de San Juan Spain
51B2 Alcira Spain
35D1 Alcobaça Brazil
50B1 Alcolea de Pinar Spain
51B2 Alcoy Spain
51C2 Alcudia Spain
89J8 Aldabra *Is* Indian O
63E2 Aldan USSR
63E2 Aldanskaya Nagor'ye *Upland* USSR
43E3 Aldeburgh Eng
43B4 Alderney *I* UK
43D4 Aldershot Eng
97A3 Aleg Maur
35B2 Alegrete Brazil
34C2 Alejandro Roca Arg
30H6 Alejandro Selkirk *I* Chile
63G2 Aleksandrovsk Sakhalinskiy USSR
65J4 Alekseyevka USSR
60E3 Aleksin USSR
58B1 Alem Sweden
35C2 Além Paraíba Brazil
49C2 Alençon France
21C4 Alenuihaha Chan Hawaiian Is
Aleppo = Ḥalab
6D1 Alert Can
49C3 Alès France
52A2 Alessandria Italy
64B3 Ålesund Nor
12C3 Aleutian Range *Mts* USA
4E4 Alexander Arch USA
100A3 Alexander Bay S Africa
17A1 Alexander City USA
112C3 Alexander *I* Ant
111A3 Alexandra NZ
29G8 Alexandra,C South Georgia
6C2 Alexandra Fjord Can
95B1 Alexandria Egypt
11A3 Alexandria Louisiana, USA
10A2 Alexandria Minnesota, USA
10A2 Alexandria Virginia, USA
55C2 Alexandroúpolis Greece
13C2 Alexis Creek Can
94B2 Aley Leb
65K4 Aleysk USSR
93D3 Al Fallūjah Iraq
51B1 Alfaro Spain
54C2 Alfatar Bulg
93E3 Al Fāw Iraq
35B2 Alfenas Brazil
55B3 Alfiós *R* Greece
47D2 Alfonsine Italy
35C2 Alfonzo Cláudio Brazil
35C2 Alfredo Chaves Brazil
61J4 Alga USSR
34B3 Algarrobo del Águila Arg
50A2 Algeciras Spain
96C1 Alger Alg
96B2 Algeria Republic, Africa
53A2 Alghero Sardegna

Algiers = Alger
15C1 Algonquin Park Can
91C5 Al Hadd Oman
93D3 Al Hadithah Iraq
92C3 Al Hadithah S Arabia
93D2 Al Hadr Iraq
91C5 Al Hajar al Gharbī Mts Oman
91C5 Al Hajar ash Sharqī Mts Oman
93C3 Al Hamad Desert Region Jordan/ S Arabia
93E4 Al Haniyah Desert Region Iraq
91A5 Al Hariq S Arabia
93C3 Al Harrah Desert Region S Arabia
95A2 Al Harūj al Aswad Upland Libya
91A4 Al Hasa Region, S Arabia
93D2 Al Hasakah Syria
93C4 Al Hawjā' S Arabia
93E3 Al Hayy Iraq
94C2 Al Hijanah Syria
93D3 Al Hillah Iraq
91A5 Al Hillah S Arabia
96B1 Al Hoceima Mor
91A4 Al Hufūf S Arabia
91B5 Al Humrah Region, UAE
91C5 Al Huwatsah Oman
90A2 Al'īābad Iran
91C4 Aliabad Iran
55B2 Aliākmon R Greece
93E3 Ali al Gharbī Iraq
87A1 Alībag India
51B2 Alicante Spain
9D4 Alice USA
106C3 Alice Springs Aust
53B3 Alicudi I Italy
84D3 Aligarh India
90A3 Alīgūdarz Iran
84B2 Ali-Khel Afghan
55C3 Aliminiá I Greece
86B1 Alipur Duär India
14B2 Aliquippa USA
22B2 Alisal USA
93C3 Al' Isawiyah S Arabia
100B4 Aliwal North S Africa
95B2 Al Jaghbūb Libya
93D3 Al Jālamīd S Arabia
95B2 Al Jawf Libya
93C4 Al Jawf S Arabia
93D2 Al Jazīrah Desert Region Syria/Iraq
50A2 Aljezur Port
91A4 Al Jubayl S Arabia
91C5 Al Kāmil Oman
93D2 Al Khābūr R Syria
91C5 Al Khabūrah Oman
91C4 Al Khasab Oman
91B4 Al Khawr Qatar
95A1 Al Khums Libya
91B5 Al Kidan Region, S Arabia
94C2 Al Kiswah Syria
56A2 Alkmaar Neth
95B2 Al Kufrah Oasis Libya
93E3 Al Kūt Iraq
92C2 Al Lādhiqīyah Syria
86A1 Allahābād India
94C2 Al Lajāh Mt Syria
12D1 Allakaket USA
76B2 Allanmyo Burma
95C2 'Allaqi Watercourse Egypt
17B1 Allatoona L USA
15C2 Allegheny R USA
10C3 Allegheny Mts USA
17B1 Allendale USA
111A3 Allen,Mt NZ
15C2 Allentown USA
87B3 Alleppey India
49C2 Aller R France
47D1 Allgäu Mts Germany

8C2 Alliance USA
81C3 Al Lith S Arabia
91B5 Al Liwā Region, UAE
109D1 Allora Aust
14B2 Alma Michigan, USA
82B1 Alma Ata USSR
50A2 Almada Port
Al Madīnah = Medina
71F2 Almagan I Pacific O
91B4 Al Manāmah Bahrain
93D3 Al Ma'nīyah Iraq
21A1 Almanor,L USA
51B2 Almansa Spain
13B1 Alma Peak Mt Can
91B5 Al Māriyyah UAE
95B1 Al Marj Libya
50B1 Almazán Spain
35C1 Almenara Brazil
50B2 Almeria Spain
61H3 Al'met'yevsk USSR
56C1 Älmhult Sweden
93E3 Al Miqdādīyah Iraq
112C3 Almirante Brown Base Ant
34A1 Almirante Latorre Chile
55B3 Almirós Greece
91A4 Al Mish'āb S Arabia
74D3 Almodóvar Port
84D3 Almora India
91A4 Al Mubarraz S Arabia
92C4 Al Mudawwara Jordan
91C5 Al Mudaybi Oman
91B4 Al Muharraq Bahrain
81C4 Al Mukalla Yemen
81C4 Al Mukhā Yemen
93D3 Al Musayyib Iraq
44B3 Alness Scot
93E3 Al Nu'mānīyah Iraq
42D2 Alnwick Eng
71D4 Alor I Indon
77C4 Alor Setar Malay
Alost = Aalst
107E2 Alotau PNG
106B3 Aloysius,Mt Aust
34C3 Alpachiri Arg
14B1 Alpena USA
47B2 Alpes du Valais Mts Switz
52B1 Alpi Dolomitiche Mts Italy
47B2 Alpi Graie Mts Italy
9C3 Alpine Texas, USA
47C1 Alpi Orobie Mts Italy
47B2 Alpi Pennine Mts Italy
47C1 Alpi Retiche Mts Switz
47D1 Alpi Venoste Mts Italy
52A1 Alps Mts Europe
95A1 Al Qaddāhiyah Libya
94C1 Al Qadmüs Syria
93D3 Al Qā'im Iraq
93C4 Al Qalibah S Arabia
93D2 Al Qamishli Syria
95A1 Al Qaryah Ash Sharqīyah Syria
92C3 Al Qaryatayn Syria
91A4 Al Qātif S Arabia
95A2 Al Qatrūn Libya
91A4 Al Qaysāmah S Arabia
94C2 Al Quatayfah Syria
92C3 Al Qunaytirah Syria
81C4 Al Qunfidhah S Arabia
93E3 Al Qurnah Iraq
94C1 Al Quşayr Syria
92C3 Al Qutayfah Syria
56B1 Als I Den
49D2 Alsace Region, France
57B2 Alsfeld Germany
42C2 Alston Eng
38J5 Alta Nor
29D2 Alta Gracia Arg
27D5 Altagracia de Orituco Ven
68A2 Altai Mts Mongolia
17B1 Altamaha R USA

33G4 Altamira Brazil
23B1 Altamira Mexico
53C2 Altamura Italy
68C1 Altanbulag Mongolia
71F4 Altape PNG
24B2 Altata Mexico
63A3 Altay China
63B3 Altay Mongolia
63A2 Altay Mts USSR
47C1 Altdorf Switz
46D1 Altenkirchen Germany
34B3 Altiplanicie del Payún Plat Arg
47B1 Altkirch France
101C2 Alto Molócue Mozam
10A3 Alton USA
15C2 Altoona USA
34B2 Alto Pencoso Mts Arg
35A1 Alto Sucuriú Brazil
23B2 Altotonga Mexico
23A2 Altoyac de Alvarez Mexico
82C2 Altun Shan Mts China
20B2 Alturas USA
9D3 Altus USA
91B5 Al'Ubaylah S Arabia
99F1 Alula Somalia
93C4 Al Urayq Desert Region S Arabia
91B5 Al'Uruq al Mu'taridah Region, S Arabia
9D2 Alva USA
23B2 Alvarado Mexico
19A3 Alvarado USA
39G6 Älvdalen Sweden
19A4 Alvin USA
38J5 Alvsbyn Sweden
80B3 Al Wajh S Arabia
85D3 Alwar India
93D3 Al Widyān Desert Region Iraq/ S Arabia
72A2 Alxa Yougi China
93D2 Alyat USSR
39J8 Alytus USSR
46E2 Alzey Germany
23B2 Amacuzac R Mexico
99D2 Amadi Sudan
93D2 Amādīyah Iraq
6C3 Amadjuak L Can
74B4 Amakusa-shotō I Japan
39G7 Åmål Sweden
63D2 Amalat R USSR
55B3 Amaliás Greece
85D4 Amalner India
69E4 Amami I Japan
69E4 Amami gunto Arch Japan
100C4 Amanzimtoti S Africa
33G3 Amapá Brazil
33G3 Amapá State, Brazil
9C3 Amarillo USA
23A1 Amatitan Mexico
Amazonas = Solimões
32D4 Amazonas State, Brazil
28C3 Amazonas R Brazil
84D2 Ambāla India
80A2 Ambalangoda Sri Lanka
101D3 Ambalavao Madag
98B2 Ambam Cam
101D2 Ambanja Madag
1C7 Ambarchik USSR
32B4 Ambato Ecuador
101D2 Ambato-Boeny Madag
101D2 Ambatolampy Madag
101D2 Ambatondrazaka Madag
57C3 Amberg Germany
25D3 Ambergris Cay I Belize
86A2 Ambikāpur India
101D2 Ambilobe Madag
101D3 Amboasary Madag
101D2 Ambodifototra Madag

101D3 Ambohimahasoa Madag
71D4 Ambon Indon
101D3 Ambositra Madag
98B3 Ambriz Angola
98C1 Am Dam Chad
64H3 Amderma USSR
24B2 Ameca Mexico
23B2 Amecameca Mexico
34C2 Ameghino Arg
56B2 Ameland I Neth
16C2 Amenia USA
112B10 American Highland Ant
105H4 American Samoa Is Pacific O
17B1 Americus USA
101G1 Amersfoort S Africa
112C10 Amery Ice Shelf Ant
55B3 Amfilokhia Greece
55B3 Amfissa Greece
63F1 Amga USSR
63F1 Amgal R USSR
69F2 Amgu USSR
69F1 Amgun' R USSR
99D1 Amhara Region Eth
7D5 Amherst Can
16C1 Amherst Massachusetts, USA
82B2 Amhūr India
48C2 Amiens France
75B1 Amino Japan
94B1 Amioune Leb
89K8 Amirante Is Indian O
86B1 Amkhapalli Nepal
92C3 Amman Jordan
38K6 Ämmänsaario Fin
56B2 Ammersfoort Neth
80E1 Amoda'ya R USSR
90B2 Amol Iran
55C3 Amorgós I Greece
7C5 Amos Can
Amoy = Xiamen
101D3 Ampanihy Madag
35B2 Amparo Brazil
51C1 Amposta Spain
85D4 Amrāvati India
85C4 Amreli India
84C2 Amritsar India
56A2 Amsterdam Neth
101H1 Amsterdam S Africa
15D2 Amsterdam USA
98C1 Am Timan Chad
88L3 Amu Darya R USSR
6A2 Amund Ringes I Can
4F2 Amundsen G Can
112B4 Amundsen S Ant
112A Amundsen-Scott Base Ant
78D3 Amuntai Indon
63E2 Amur R USSR
33E2 Anaco Ven
8B2 Anaconda USA
20B1 Anacortes USA
55C3 Anáfi I Greece
93D3 'Anah Iraq
21B3 Anaheim USA
87B2 Anaimalai Hills India
83C4 Anakapalle India
12E1 Anaktuvuk P USA
101D2 Analalava Madag
92B2 Anamur Turk
75A2 Anan Japan
87B2 Anantapur India
31B5 Anápolis Brazil
90C3 Anār Iran
90B3 Anārak Iran
71F2 Anatahan I Pacific O
30D9 Añatuya Arg
74B3 Anbyŏn N Korea
22C4 Anacapa Is USA
4D3 Anchorage USA
30C2 Ancohuma Mt Bol
32B6 Ancón Peru
52B2 Ancona Italy
16C1 Ancram USA

29B4 Ancud Chile
69E2 Anda Chile
34A3 Andacollo Arg
108A1 Andado Aust
32C6 Andahuaylas Peru
38F6 Andalsnes Nor
50A2 Andalucia Region, Spain
17A1 Andaman Is
83D4 Andaman Is Burma
83D4 Andaman S Burma
108A2 Andamooka Aust
38H5 Andenes Nor
47C1 Andermatt Switz
57B2 Andernach Germany
14A2 Anderson Indiana, USA
18B2 Anderson Missouri, USA
17B1 Anderson S Carolina, USA
4F3 Anderson R Can
87B1 Andhra Pradesh State, India
55B3 Andikithira I Greece
65J5 Andizhan USSR
65H6 Andkhui Afghan
74B3 Andong S Korea
51C1 Andorra Principality, SW Europe
51C1 Andorra-La-Vella Andorra
43D4 Andover Eng
35A2 Andradina Brazil
12B2 Andreafsky USA
92B2 Andreas,C Cyprus
53C2 Andria Italy
11C4 Andros I The Bahamas
55B3 Ándros I Greece
87A2 Androth I India
50B2 Andújar Spain
100A2 Andulo Angola
97C4 Anécho Togo
97C3 Anéfis Mali
34B3 Añelo Arg
63C2 Angarsk USSR
38H6 Ánge Sweden
24A2 Angel de la Guarda I Mexico
79B2 Angeles Phil
39G7 Ängelholm Sweden
109C1 Angellala Creek R Aust
22B1 Angels Camp USA
71E4 Angemuk Mt Indon
48B2 Angers France
76C3 Angkor Hist Site Camb
41C3 Anglesey I Wales
19A4 Angleton USA
6G3 Angmagssalik Greenland
101D2 Angoche Mozam
29B3 Angol Chile
14B2 Angola Indiana, USA
100A2 Angola Republic, Africa
103H6 Angola Basin Atlantic O
12H3 Angoon USA
48C2 Angoulême France
96A1 Angra do Heroismo Açores
35C2 Angra dos Reis Brazil
34C3 Anguil Arg
27E3 Anguilla I Caribbean S
26B2 Anguilla Cays Is Caribbean S
86B2 Angul India
99C3 Angumu Zaire
56C1 Anholt I Den
73C4 Anhua China
72D3 Anhui Province, China
12C2 Aniak USA
35B1 Anicuns Brazil

46B2 Anizy-le-Château France
4C3 Anjak USA
48B2 Anjou Republic, France
101D2 Anjouan I Comoros
101D2 Anjozorobe Madag
74B3 Anju N Korea
72B3 Ankang China
92B2 Ankara Turk
101D2 Ankaratra Mt Madag
101D3 Ankazoabo Madag
101D2 Ankazobe Madag
56C2 Anklam Germany
76D3 An Loc Viet
73B4 Anlong China
73C3 Anlu China
18C2 Anna USA
96C1 'Annaba Alg
92C3 An Nabk S Arabia
92C3 An Nabk Syria
108A1 Anna Creek Aust
80C3 An Nafūd Desert S Arabia
93D3 An Najaf Iraq
42C2 Annan Scot
15C3 Annapolis USA
86A1 Annapurna Mt Nepal
14B2 Ann Arbor USA
94C1 An Nāsirah Syria
93E3 An Nāsirīyah Iraq
47B2 Annecy France
47B1 Annemasse France
76D3 An Nhon Viet
73A5 Anning China
17A1 Anniston USA
89E8 Annobon I Eq Guinea
49C2 Annonay France
27J1 Annotto Bay Jamaica
73D3 Anqing China
72B2 Ansai China
57C2 Ansbach Germany
26C3 Anse d'Hainault Haiti
72E1 Anshan China
73B4 Anshun China
97C3 Ansongo Mali
14B3 Ansted USA
92C2 Antakya Turk
101D2 Antalaha Madag
92B2 Antalya Turk
92B2 Antalya Körfezi B Turk
101D2 Antananarivo Madag
112C1 Antarctic Circle Ant
112C3 Antarctic Pen Ant
96B2 Anti-Atlas Mts Mor
7D5 Anticosti I Can
27E3 Antigua I Caribbean S
Anti Lebanon = Jebel esh Sharqi
21A2 Antioch USA
19A3 Antlers USA
30B3 Antofagasta Chile
45C1 Antrim County, N Ire
45C1 Antrim N Ire
45C1 Antrim Hills N Ire
101D2 Antseranana Madag
101D2 Antsirabe Madag
101D2 Antsohihy Madag
76D3 An Tuc Viet
46C1 Antwerpen Belg
45C2 An Uaimh Irish Rep
84C3 Anupgarh India
87C3 Anuradhapura Sri Lanka
Anvers = Antwerpen
4B3 Anvik USA
63B3 Anxi China
72C2 Anyang China
72A3 A'nyêmqên Shan Upland China
47C2 Anza R Italy
13E1 Anzac Can
65K4 Anzhero-Sudzhensk USSR
53B2 Anzio Italy
74E2 Aomori Japan

52A1 Aosta Italy
97B3 Aoukar Desert Region Maur
96C2 Aoulef Alg
95A2 Aozou Chad
30E3 Apa R Brazil/Par
11B4 Apalachee B USA
17B2 Apalachicola USA
17A2 Apalachicola B USA
23B2 Apan Mexico
64E3 Apatity USSR
32C3 Apaporis R Colombia
35A2 Aparecida do Taboado Brazil
79B2 Aparri Phil
54A1 Apatin Yugos
64E3 Apatity USSR
24B3 Apatzingan Mexico
56B2 Apeldoorn Neth
35B2 Apiai Brazil
33F2 Apoera Surinam
108B3 Apollo Bay Aust
79C4 Apo,Mt Phil
17A2 Apopka,L USA
30F2 Aporé R Brazil
10A2 Apostle Is USA
10A2 Apostle L USA
23A1 Apozol Mexico
11B3 Appalachian Mts USA
52A3 Appennino Abruzzese Mts Italy
52A2 Appennino Ligure Mts Italy
53C2 Appennino Lucano Mts Italy
53B2 Appennino Napoletano Mts Italy
52B2 Appennino Tosco-Emilliano Mts Italy
52B2 Appennino Umbro-Marchigiano Mts Italy
47C1 Appenzell Switz
42C2 Appleby Eng
14A2 Appleton Wisconsin, USA
30F3 Apucarana Brazil
23B1 Apulco Mexico
32D2 Apure R Ven
92C4 Aqaba Jordan
92B4 'Aqaba,G of Egypt/S Arabia
90B3 'Aqdā Iran
30E3 Aquidauana Brazil
23A2 Aquila Mexico
86A1 Ara India
17A1 Arab USA
81D4 Arabian S Asia/Arabian Pen
31D4 Aracajú Brazil
31D2 Aracati Brazil
31B2 Araçatuba Brazil
50A2 Aracena Spain
31C5 Araçuai Brazil
94B3 Arad Israel
60B4 Arad Rom
96C1 Arada Chad
91B5 'Arādah UAE
106C1 Arafura S Indon/Aust
30F2 Aragarças Brazil
51B1 Aragón Region, Spain
50B1 Aragón R Spain
33G6 Araguaia R Brazil
31B3 Araguaina Brazil
31B5 Araguari Brazil
35B1 Araguari R Brazil
75B1 Arai Japan
96C2 Arak Alg
90A3 Arāk Iran
76A2 Arakan Yoma Mts Burma
87B2 Arakkonam India
93E2 Araks R USSR
Aral S = Aral'skoye More
80E1 Aral'sk USSR

65G5 Aral'skoye More S USSR
40B2 Aran I / Irish Rep
41B3 Aran Is Irish Rep
50B1 Aranda de Duero Spain
23A1 Arandas Mexico
50B1 Aranjuez Spain
75A2 Arao Japan
97B3 Araouane Mali
29E2 Arapey R Urug
31D4 Arapiraca Brazil
35A2 Arapongas Brazil
30G4 Ararangua Brazil
31B6 Araraquara Brazil
35B2 Araras Brazil
107D4 Ararat Aust
93D2 Ararat USSR
93D1 Aras R Turk
75C1 Arato Japan
32D2 Arauca R Ven
34A3 Arauco Chile
32C2 Arauca Colombia
85C4 Arāvalli Range Mts India
31B5 Araxá Brazil
99D2 Arba Minch Eth
53A3 Arbatax Sardegna
93D2 Arbīl Iraq
47A1 Arbois France
39H6 Arbrå Sweden
44C3 Arbroath Scot
47A1 Arc France
47B2 Arc R France
48B3 Arcachon France
17B2 Arcadia USA
20B2 Arcata USA
23A2 Arcelia Mexico
26B2 Archipiélago de Camaguey Arch Cuba
29B6 Archipiélago de la Reina Adelaida Arch Chile
29B4 Archipiélago de las Chones Arch Chile
32B2 Archipiélago de las Perlas Arch Panama
35B2 Arcos Brazil
50A2 Arcos de la Frontera Spain
1C1 Arctic Circle
4E3 Arctic Red Can
4E3 Arctic Red R Can
4D3 Arctic Village USA
112C2 Arctowski Base Ant
54C2 Arda R Bulg
65F6 Ardabil Iran
93D1 Ardahan Turk
39F6 Ardal Nor
96C2 Ardar des Iforas Upland Alg/Mali
45C2 Ardee Irish Rep
90B3 Ardekān Iran
46C2 Ardennes Department, France
57A2 Ardennes Region, Belg
90B3 Ardestan Iran
92C3 Ardh es Suwwan Desert Region Jordan
50A2 Ardila R Port
109C2 Ardlethan Aust
9D3 Ardmore USA
44A3 Ardnamurchan Pt Scot
46A1 Ardres France
44B3 Ardrishaig Scot
42B2 Ardrossan Scot
27D3 Arecibo Puerto Rico
31D2 Areia Branca Brazil
21A2 Arena,Pt USA
30B2 Arequipa Peru
52B2 Arezzo Italy
52B2 Argenta Italy
49C2 Argentan France

46B2 Argenteuil France
28C1 Argentina Republic,
S America
103F7 Argentine Basin
Atlantic O
48C2 Argenton-sur-Creuse
France
54C2 Argeş R Rom
84B2 Arghardab R Afghan
55B3 Argolikós Kólpos G
Greece
46C2 Argonne Region,
France
55B3 Argos Greece
55B3 Argostólion Greece
22B3 Arguello,Pt USA
106B2 Argyle,L Aust
56C1 Arhus Den
100A3 Ariamsvlei Namibia
34C2 Arias Arg
97B3 Aribinda Burkina
30B2 Arica Chile
84C2 Arifwala Pak
Arihā = Jericho
27L1 Arima Trinidad
35B1 Arinos Brazil
33F6 Arinos R Brazil
23A2 Ario de Rosales
Mexico
27L1 Aripo,Mt Trinidad
33E5 Aripuana Brazil
33E5 Aripuana R Brazil
48A3 Arisaig Scot
87B2 Ariskere India
13B2 Aristazabal I Can
34B3 Arizona Arg
9B3 Arizona State, USA
39G7 Ärjäng Sweden
61F3 Arkadak USSR
19B3 Arkadelphia USA
65H4 Arkalyk USSR
11A3 Arkansas State, USA
11A3 Arkansas R USA
18A2 Arkansas City USA
64F3 Arkhangel'sk USSR
41B3 Arklow Irish Rep
50B1 Arlanzón R Spain
47D1 Arlberg P Austria
49C3 Arles France
19A3 Arlington Texas, USA
15C3 Arlington Virginia,
USA
20B1 Arlington
Washington, USA
97C3 Arlit Niger
57B3 Arlon Belg
Armageddon=
Megiddo
45C1 Armagh County, N Ire
45C1 Armagh N Ire
61F5 Armavir USSR
23A2 Armenia Mexico
32B3 Armenia Colombia
107E4 Armidale Aust
13D2 Armstrong Can
65F5 Armyanskaya SSR
Republic, USSR
7C3 Arnaud R Can
92B2 Arnauti C Cyprus
56B2 Arnhem Neth
106C2 Arnhem,C Aust
106C2 Arnhem Land Aust
22B1 Arnold USA
15C1 Arnprior Can
46E1 Arnsberg Germany
100A3 Aroab Namibia
47C2 Arona Italy
12B2 Aropuk L USA
52A1 Arosa Switz
97A3 Arquipélago dos
Bijagós Arch
Guinea-Bissau
93D3 Ar Ramādi Iraq
42B2 Arran I Scot
93C2 Ar Raqqah Syria
49C1 Arras France
96A2 Arrecife Canary Is
34C2 Arrecifes Arg

23A1 Arriaga Mexico
93E3 Ar Rifā't Iraq
93E3 Ar Rihāb Desert
Region Iraq
91A5 Ar Riyāḍ S Arabia
44B3 Arrochar Scot
111A2 Arrowtown NZ
23B1 Arroyo Seco Mexico
91B4 Ar Ru'ays Qatar
91C5 Ar Rustaq Oman
93D3 Ar Rutbah Iraq
47D2 Arsiero Italy
49D2 Arsizio Italy
61G2 Arsk USSR
55B3 Árta Greece
23A2 Arteaga Mexico
63B2 Artemovsk USSR
63D2 Artemovskiy USSR
9C3 Artesia USA
11B2 Arthurs P NZ
6B2 Artic Bay Can
29E2 Artigas Urug
4H3 Artillery L Can
48C1 Artois Region, France
112C2 Arturo Prat Base Ant
71D1 Artvin Turk
99D2 Aru Zaïre
33G6 Aruanã Brazil
27C4 Aruba I Caribbean S
86B1 Arun R Nepal
86C1 Arunachal Pradesh
Union Territory,
India
87B3 Aruppukkottai India
99D3 Arusha Tanz
98C2 Aruwimi R Zaïre
68C2 Arvayheer Mongolia
47B2 Arve R France
7C5 Arvida Can
38H5 Arvidsjaur Sweden
39G7 Arvika Sweden
21B2 Arvin USA
94B1 Arwad I Syria
61F2 Arzamas USSR
84C2 Asadabad Afghan
52A2 Asti R Japan
75C3 Astipálaia I Greece
87A2 Asahi R Japan
74E2 Asahi dake Mt Japan
74E2 Asahikawa Japan
86B2 Asansol India
95A2 Asawanwah Well
Libya
61K2 Asbest USSR
15D2 Asbury Park USA
103H5 Ascension I Atlantic O
57B3 Aschaffenburg
Germany
56C2 Aschersleben
Germany
52B2 Ascoli Piceno Italy
47C1 Ascona Switz
96C2 Asedjrad Upland Alg
38H6 Åsele Sweden
99D2 Åselle Eth
54B2 Asenovgrad Bulg
46C2 Asfeld France
61J2 Asha USSR
17B1 Ashburn USA
111B2 Ashburton NZ
106A3 Ashburton R Aust
92B3 Ashdod Israel
19B3 Ashdown USA
11B3 Asheville USA
109D1 Ashford Aust
43E4 Ashford Eng
74D3 Ashikaga Japan
75A2 Ashizuri-misaki Pt
Japan
65G6 Ashkhabad USSR
10B3 Ashland Kentucky,
USA
18A1 Ashland Nebraska,
USA
14B2 Ashland Ohio, USA
8A2 Ashland Oregon, USA
109C1 Ashley Aust
16B2 Ashokan Res USA
94B3 Ashqelon Israel
93D3 Ash Shabakh Iraq

91C4 Ash Sha'm UAE
93D2 Ash Sharqāt Iraq
93E3 Ash Shatrah Iraq
81C4 Ash Shihr Yemen
91A4 Ash Shumlul S Arabia
14B2 Ashtabula USA
7D4 Ashuanipi L Can
92C3 'Aşī R Syria
47D2 Asiago Italy
53A2 Asinara I Medit S
45K6 Asino USSR
93D2 Aşkale Turk
39G7 Askersund Sweden
84C1 Asmar Afghan
95C3 Asmara Eth
75A2 Aso Japan
99D1 Asosa Eth
111A2 Aspiring,Mt NZ
92C2 Assad Syria
91A5 As Salamiyah
S Arabia
92C2 As Salamīyah Syria
93D3 As Salman Iraq
86C1 Assam State, India
93E3 As Samāwah Iraq
91B5 As Şanām Region,
S Arabia
92C3 As Sanamayn Syria
56B2 Assen Neth
56B1 Assens Den
95A1 As Sidrah Libya
5H5 Assiniboia Can
5G4 Assiniboine,Mt Can
30F3 Assis Brazil
92C3 As Sukhnah Syria
91A5 As Summan Region,
S Arabia
99E3 Assumption I
Seychelles
92C3 As Suwaydā' Syria
93D3 As Suwayrah Iraq
93E2 Astara USSR
52A2 Asti Italy
75C3 Astipálaia I Greece
50A1 Astorga Spain
8A2 Astoria USA
61G4 Astrakhan' USSR
50A1 Asturias Region,
Spain
30E4 Asunción Par
90D2 Aswa R Uganda
80B3 Aswân Egypt
95C2 Aswân High Dam
Egypt
95C2 Asyût Egypt
92C3 As Zilaf Syria
97C4 Atakpamé Togo
71D4 Atambua Indon
6E3 Atangmik Greenland
96A2 Atar Maur
65J5 Atasu USSR
95C3 Atbara Sudan
65H4 Atbasar USSR
11A4 Atchafalaya B USA
10A3 Atchison USA
16B3 Atco USA
23A1 Atenguillo Mexico
52B2 Atessa Italy
46B1 Ath Belg
13E2 Athabasca Can
5H4 Athabasca R Can
5H4 Athabasca L Can
45B2 Athenry Irish Rep
Athens = Athinai
11B3 Athens Georgia, USA
14B3 Athens Ohio, USA
19A3 Athens Texas, USA
16B3 Athens Texas, USA
41B3 Athlone Irish Rep
16C1 Athol USA
55B3 Áthos Mt Greece
45C2 Athy Irish Rep
98B1 Ati Chad
7A5 Atikoken Can
61F3 Atkarsk USSR
18B2 Atkins USA
23B2 Atlacomulco Mexico

11B3 Atlanta Georgia, USA
14B2 Atlanta Michigan,
USA
18A1 Atlantic USA
10C3 Atlantic City USA
16B2 Atlantic Highlands
USA
103H8 Atlantic Indian Basin
Atlantic O
103H7 Atlantic Indian Ridge
Atlantic O
96C1 Atlas Saharien Mts
Alg
4E4 Atlin Can
4E4 Atlin L Can
94B2 'Atlit Israel
23B2 Atlixco Mexico
23B2 Atmore USA
101D3 Atofinandrahana
Madag
12D3 Atognak I USA
19A3 Atoka USA
23A1 Atotonilco Mexico
32B2 Atoyac R Mexico
32B2 Atrato R Colombia
91B5 Attaf Region, UAE
81C3 At Ta'if S Arabia
94C2 At Tall Syria
17A1 Attalla USA
12D3 Attawapiskat Can
7B4 Attawapiskat R Can
93D3 At Taysīyah Desert
Region S Arabia
14A2 Attica Indiana, USA
16C2 Attigny France
16D2 Attleboro
Massachusetts, USA
76D3 Attopeu Laos
92C4 At Tubayq Upland
S Arabia
34B3 Atuel R Arg
39H7 Atvidaberg Sweden
22B2 Atwater USA
49D3 Aubagne France
46C2 Aube Department,
France
49C3 Aubenas France
17A1 Auburn Alabama,
USA
21A2 Auburn California,
USA
14A2 Auburn Indiana, USA
18A1 Auburn Nebraska,
USA
15C2 Auburn New York,
USA
20B1 Auburn Washington,
USA
48C3 Auch France
110B1 Auckland NZ
105G6 Auckland Is NZ
48C3 Aude R France
7B4 Auden Can
47B1 Audincourt France
107B B1 Audine Aust
57C3 Augsburg Germany
106A4 Augusta Aust
11B3 Augusta Georgia,
USA
18A2 Augusta Kansas, USA
10D2 Augusta Maine, USA
12D3 Augustine I USA
58C2 Augustow Pol
106A3 Augustus,Mt Aust
46A2 Aumale France
85D3 Auraiya India
85D5 Aurangabad India
96C1 Aures Mts Alg
48C2 Aurillac France
8C3 Aurora Colorado, USA
10B2 Aurora Illinois, USA
14B3 Aurora Indiana, USA
18B2 Aurora Mississippi,
USA
100A3 Aus Namibia
14B2 Au Sable USA
10A2 Austin Minnesota,
USA

21B2 Austin Nevada, USA
9D3 Austin Texas, USA
107D4 Australian Alps Mts Aust
37E4 Austria Federal Republic, Europe
46A1 Authie R France
32A2 Autlán Mexico
49C2 Autun France
49C2 Auvergne Region, France
49C2 Auxerre France
46B1 Auxi-le-Châteaux France
22C4 Avallon France
22C4 Avalon USA
7E5 Avalon Pen Can
35B2 Avaré Brazil
90D3 Avaz Iran
94B3 Avedat Hist Site Israel
33F4 Aveiro Brazil
50A1 Aveiro Port
29E2 Avellaneda Arg
53B2 Avellino Italy
46B1 Avesnes-sur-Helpe France
39H6 Avesta Sweden
52B2 Avezzano Italy
44C3 Aviemore Scot
111B2 Aviemore,L NZ
47B2 Avigliana Italy
49C3 Avignon France
50B1 Avila Spain
50A1 Avilés Spain
47D1 Avisio R Italy
108B3 Avoca R Aust
43C4 Avon County, Eng
43D4 Avon R Dorset, Eng
43D3 Avon R Warwick, Eng
43C4 Avonmouth Wales
17B2 Avon Park USA
46B2 Avre R France
54A2 Avtovac Yugos
94C2 A'waj R Syria
74D4 Awaji-shima L Japan
99E2 Awarem Eth
111A2 Awarua Pt NZ
99E2 Awash Eth
99E2 Awash R Eth
75B1 Awa-shima / Japan
111B2 Awatere R NZ
95A2 Awbārī Libya
98C2 Aweil Sudan
95B2 Awjilah Libya
96A2 Awserd Well Mor
6A2 Axel Heiburg I Can
43C4 Axminster Eng
75B1 Ayabe Japan
29E3 Ayacucho Arg
32C6 Ayacucho Peru
65K5 Ayaguz USSR
82C2 Ayakkum Hu L China
50A2 Ayamonte Spain
63F2 Ayan USSR
32C6 Ayauiri Peru
92A2 Aydin Turk
55C3 Áyios Evstrátios I Greece
43D4 Aylesbury Eng
13D2 Aylmer,Mt Can
94C2 'Ayn al Fijah Syria
93D2 'Ayn Zälah Iraq
95B2 Ayn Zuwayyah Well Libya
99D2 Ayod Sudan
42B2 Ayr Aust
42B2 Ayr Scot
42B2 Ayr R Scot
42B2 Ayre,Pt of Eng
52C2 Aytos Bulg
76C3 Aytthaya Thai
23A1 Ayutla Mexico
55C3 Ayvacik Turk
55C3 Ayvalik Turk
86A1 Azamgarh India
97B3 Azaouad Desert Region Mali
97D3 Azare Nig
92C2 A'Zaz Syria

Azbine = Aïr
96A2 Azzeffal R Maur
65F5 Azerbaydzhanskaya SSR Republic, USSR
32B4 Azogues Ecuador
Azores = Açores
98C1 Azoum R Chad
60E4 Azovskoye More S USSR
96B1 Azrou Mor
34D3 Azucena Arg
32A2 Azuero,Pen de Panama
29E3 Azul Arg
94C2 Az-Zabdäni Syria
91C5 Az Zähirah Mts Oman
93E3 Az Zubayr Iraq

B

94B2 Ba'abda Leb
92C3 Ba'albek Leb
94B3 Ba'al Hazor Mt Israel
99E2 Baardheere Somalia
54C2 Babadag Rom
92A1 Babaeski Turk
32B4 Babahoyo Ecuador
81C4 Bāb al Mandab Str Djibouti/Yemen
71D4 Babar I Indon
99D3 Babati Tanz
60E2 Babayevo USSR
14B2 Baberton USA
13B1 Babine R Can
5F4 Babine L Can
90B2 Bābol Iran
79B2 Babuyan Chan Phil
79B2 Babuyan Is Phil
31C2 Bacabal Brazil
71D4 Bacan I Indon
60C4 Bacău Rom
76D1 Bac Can Viet
108B3 Bacchus Marsh Aust
82B2 Bachu China
4J3 Back R Can
12J2 Backbone Ranges Mts Can
76D1 Bac Ninh Viet
79B3 Bacolod Phil
79B3 Baco,Mt Phil
87B2 Badagara India
72A1 Badain Jaran Shamo Desert China
50A2 Badajoz Spain
51C1 Badalona Spain
93D3 Badanah S Arabia
46D2 Bad Bergzabern Germany
46D1 Bad Ems Germany
47C1 Baden Switz
57B3 Baden-Baden Germany
57B3 Baden-Württemberg State, Germany
57C3 Badgastein Austria
22C2 Badger USA
57B2 Bad-Godesberg Germany
57B2 Bad Hersfeld Germany
46D1 Bad Honnef Germany
85B4 Badin Pak
52B1 Bad Ischl Austria
93C3 Badiyat ash Sham Desert Region Jordan/Iraq
57B3 Bad-Kreuznach Germany
46D1 Bad Nevenahr-Ahrweiler Germany
47C1 Bad Ragaz Switz
57C3 Bad Tolz Germany
87C3 Badulla Sri Lanka
50B2 Baena Spain
97A3 Bafatá Guinea-Bissau
4H2 Baffin Region Can
6C2 Baffin B Greenland/Can
6C2 Baffin I Can
98B2 Bafia Cam
97A3 Bafing R Mali

97A3 Bafoulabé Mali
98B2 Bafoussam Cam
90C3 Bāfq Iran
60E5 Bafra Burun Pt Turk
91C4 Bäft Iran
98C2 Bafwasende Zaïre
86A1 Bagaha India
87B1 Bägalkot India
99D3 Bagamoyo Tanz
29F2 Bagé Brazil
93D3 Baghdād Iraq
87B2 Bai Bureau de Bang
91C2 Bāghin Iran
84B1 Baghlan Afghan
49C3 Bagnols-sur-Cèze France
97B3 Bagoé R Mali
79B2 Baguio Phil
86B1 Bahäduräbäd India
11C4 Bahamas,The Is Caribbean S
86B2 Baharampur India
99D1 Bahar Dar Eth
92A4 Bahariya Oasis Egypt
84C3 Bahawalpur Pak
84C3 Bahawalpur Province, Pak
85C3 Bahawathagar Pak
31C4 Bahia State, Brazil
29D3 Bahía Blanca Arg
29D3 Bahía Blanca B Arg
34A3 Bahía Concepción Chile
35C2 Bahía da Ilha Grande B Brazil
24B2 Bahía de Banderas B Mexico
24C2 Bahía de Campeche B Mexico
25D3 Bahía de la Ascension B Mexico
24B3 Bahía de Petacalco B Mexico
96A2 Bahía de Rio de Oro B Mor
35C2 Bahía de Sepetiba B Brazil
29C6 Bahía Grande B Arg
9B4 Bahia Kino Mexico
24A2 Bahía Magdalena B Mexico
24A2 Bahía Sebastia Vizcaino B Mexico
86A1 Bahraich India
91C4 Bahrain Sheikdom, Arabian Pen
93D3 Bahr al Milh L Iraq
98C2 Bahr Aouk R Chad/CAR
98C2 Bahrat Lut = Dead S
98C2 Bahr el Arab Watercourse Sudan
99D2 Bahr el Ghazâl R Sudan
98B1 Bahr el Ghazal Watercourse Chad
101H1 Baia de Maputo B Mozam
31B2 Baia de Marajó B Brazil
101D2 Baia de Pemba B Mozam
31C2 Baia de São Marcos B Brazil
50A2 Baia de Setúbal B Port
31D4 Baia de Todos os Santos B Brazil
100A2 Baia dos Tigres Angola
60B4 Baia Mare Rom
98B2 Baibokoum Chad
69E2 Baicheng China
101E2 Baie Antongila B Madag

7D5 Baie-Comeau Can
101D2 Baie de Bombetoka B Madag
101D2 Baie de Mahajamba B Madag

101D3 Baie de St Augustin B Madag
94B2 Baie de St Georges B Leb
10D2 Baie des Chaleurs B Can
7C4 Baie-du-Poste Can
72B3 Baihe China
72C3 Bai He R China
93D3 Ba'ïji Iraq
86A2 Baikunthpur India
Baile Atha Cliath = Dublin
52C2 Bäilesti Rom
46B1 Bailleul France
72A3 Baima China
17B1 Bainbridge USA
12B2 Baird Inlet USA
4B3 Baird Mts USA
72D1 Bairin Youqi China
72D1 Bairin Zuoqi China
107D4 Bairnsdale Aust
79B4 Bais Phil
54A1 Baja Hung
9B3 Baja California State, Mexico
24A1 Baja California Pen Mexico
61J2 Bakal USSR
98C2 Bakala CAR
97A3 Bakel Sen
8C2 Baker Montana, USA
8B2 Baker Oregon, USA
4J3 Baker Foreland Pt Can
4J3 Baker L Can
4J3 Baker Lake Can
8A2 Baker,Mt USA
16E5 Bakersfield USA
90C2 Bakharden USSR
90C2 Bakhardok USSR
60D3 Bakhmach USSR
38C1 Bakkaflói B Iceland
99D2 Bako Eth
99E2 Bako Eth
72B4 Bakouma CAR
65F5 Baku USSR
92B2 Balâ Turk
79A4 Balabac I Phil
70C3 Balabac Str Malay
78C2 Balaikarangan Indon
108A2 Balaklava Aust
61G3 Balakovo USSR
86A2 Balángir India
61F3 Balashov USSR
86B2 Balasore India
80A3 Balät Egypt
52C1 Balaton L Hung
54C2 Balbriggan Irish Rep
29E3 Balcarce Arg
54C2 Balchik Bulg
111B3 Balclutha NZ
18B2 Bald Knob USA
17B1 Baldwin USA
9C3 Baldy Peak Mt USA
Balearic Is = Islas Baleares
78C2 Baleh R Malay
79B2 Baler Phil
61H2 Balezino USSR
106A1 Bali I Indon
92A2 Balikesir Turk
93C2 Balikh R Syria
78D3 Balikpapan Indon
79B2 Balintang Chan Phil
78C4 Bali S Indon
35A1 Baliza Brazil
84B1 Balkh Afghan
65J5 Balkhash USSR
44B3 Ballachulish Scot
45B2 Ballaghaderreen Irish Rep
42B2 Ballantrae Scot
4G2 Ballantyne Str Can
87B2 Ballapur India
107D4 Ballarat Aust
44C3 Ballater Scot
112C7 Balleny Is Ant
86A1 Ballia India

109D1 **Ballina** Aust
41B3 **Ballina** Irish Rep
45B2 **Ballinasloe** Irish Rep
45B2 **Ballinrobe** Irish Rep
45B1 **Ballycastle** N Ire
45C1 **Ballycastle** N Ire
45C1 **Ballymena** N Ire
45C1 **Ballymoney** N Ire
45B1 **Ballyshannon**
    Irish Rep
45B2 **Ballyvaghan** Irish Rep
108B3 **Balmoral** Aust
34C2 **Balnearia** Arg
84B3 **Balochistan** Region,
    Pak
100A2 **Balombo** Angola
109C1 **Balonn** R Aust
85C3 **Balotra** India
86A1 **Balrāmpur** India
107D4 **Balranald** Aust
31B3 **Balsas** Brazil
23B2 **Balsas** Mexico
24B3 **Balsas** R Mexico
60C4 **Balta** USSR
39H7 **Baltic S** N Europe
92B3 **Baltim** Egypt
45B3 **Baltimore** Irish Rep
10C3 **Baltimore** USA
86B1 **Bālurghāt** India
61H4 **Balykshi** USSR
91C4 **Bam** Iran
98B1 **Bama** Nig
97B3 **Bamako** Mali
98C2 **Bambari** CAR
17B1 **Bamberg** USA
57C3 **Bamberg** Germany
98C2 **Bambili** Zaïre
35B2 **Bambuí** Brazil
98B2 **Bamenda** Cam
13C3 **Bamfield** Can
98B2 **Bamingui** R CAR
98B2 **Bamingui Bangoran**
    National Park CAR
84B2 **Bamiyan** Afghan
91D4 **Bampur** Iran
91D4 **Bampur** R Iran
98C2 **Banalia** Zaïre
97B3 **Banamba** Mali
76C3 **Ban Aranyaprathet**
    Thai
76C2 **Ban Ban** Laos
77C4 **Ban Betong** Thai
45C1 **Banbridge** N Ire
43D3 **Banbury** Eng
44C3 **Banchory** Scot
25D3 **Banco Chinchorro** *Is*
    Mexico
15C1 **Bancroft** Can
86A1 **Bānda** India
70A3 **Banda Aceh** Indon
97B4 **Bandama** R Ivory
    Coast
91C4 **Bandar Abbās** Iran
90A2 **Bandar Anzalī** Iran
91B4 **Bandar-e Daylam** Iran
91B4 **Bandar-e Lengheh**
    Iran
91B4 **Bandar-e Māqām** Iran
91B4 **Bandar-e Rīg** Iran
90B2 **Bandar-e Torkoman**
    Iran
91A3 **Bandar Khomeyni** Iran
78C2 **Bandar Seri Begawan**
    Brunei
71D4 **Banda S** Indon
91C4 **Band Boni** Iran
35C2 **Bandeira** *Mt* Brazil
97B3 **Bandiagara** Mali
60C5 **Bandirma** Turk
45B3 **Bandon** Irish Rep
98B3 **Bandundu** Zaïre
78B4 **Bandung** Indon
26B2 **Banes** Cuba
13D2 **Banff** Can
44C3 **Banff** Scot
5G4 **Banff** Can
13D2 **Banff Nat Pk** Can
87B2 **Bangalore** India

98C2 **Bangassou** CAR
70C3 **Banggi** I Malay
76D2 **Bang Hieng** R Laos
78B3 **Bangka** I Indon
78A3 **Bangko** Indon
76C3 **Bangkok** Thai
82C3 **Bangladesh** Republic,
    Asia
84D2 **Bangong Co** L China
10D2 **Bangor** Maine, USA
45D1 **Bangor** N Ire
16B2 **Bangor** Pennsylvania,
    USA
42B3 **Bangor** Wales
78D3 **Bangsalsembera**
    Indon
76B3 **Bang Saphan Yai** Thai
79B2 **Bangued** Phil
98B2 **Bangui** CAR
100C2 **Bangweulu** L Zambia
77C4 **Ban Hat Yai** Thai
76C2 **Ban Hin Heup** Laos
76C3 **Ban Houei Sai** Laos
76B3 **Ban Hua Hin** Thai
97B3 **Bani** R Mali
97C3 **Bani Bangou** Niger
95A1 **Bani Walid** Libya
92C2 **Baniyas** Syria
94B2 **Baniyas** Syria
52C2 **Banja Luka** Yugos
78C3 **Banjarmasin** Indon
97A3 **Banjul** The Gambia
77B4 **Ban Kantang** Thai
76D2 **Ban Khemmarat** Laos
77B4 **Ban Khok Kloi** Thai
71F5 **Banks I** Aust
5E4 **Banks I** British
    Columbia, Can
4F2 **Banks I** Northwest
    Territories, Can
20C1 **Banks L** USA
111B2 **Banks Pen** NZ
109C4 **Banks Str** Aust
86B2 **Bankura** India
76B2 **Ban Mae Sariang** Thai
76B2 **Ban Mae Sot** Thai
76D3 **Ban Me Thuot** Viet
45C1 **Bann** R N Ire
77B4 **Ban Na San** Thai
84C2 **Bannu** Pak
34A3 **Baños Maule** Chile
76C2 **Ban Pak Neun** Laos
77C4 **Ban Pak Phanang** Thai
76D3 **Ban Ru Kroy** Camb
76B3 **Ban Sai Yok** Thai
76C3 **Ban Sattahip** Thai
59B3 **Banská Bystrica** Czech
85C4 **Bānswāra** India
77B4 **Ban Tha Kham** Thai
76D2 **Ban Thateng** Laos
76C2 **Ban Tha Tum** Thai
41B3 **Bantry** Irish Rep
41A3 **Bantry** B Irish Rep
76D3 **Ban Ya Soup** Viet
78C4 **Banyuwangi** Indon
72C3 **Baofeng** China
76C1 **Bao Ha** Viet
72B3 **Baoji** China
76D3 **Bao Loc** Viet
68B4 **Baoshan** China
72C1 **Baotou** China
86A1 **Bāpatla** India
46B1 **Bapaume** France
93D3 **Ba'Qūbah** Iraq
32J7 **Baquerizo Morena**
    Ecuador
54A2 **Bar** Yugos
99D1 **Bara** Sudan
99E2 **Baraawe** Somalia
78D3 **Barabai** Indon
86A1 **Bāra Banki** India
65J4 **Barabinsk** USSR
65J4 **Barabinskaya Step**
    Steppe USSR
50B1 **Baracaldo** Spain
26C2 **Baracoa** Cuba
94C2 **Baradá** R Syria
109C2 **Baradine** Aust

87A1 **Bārāmati** India
84C2 **Baramula** Pak
85D3 **Bārān** India
79B3 **Barangas** Phil
4E4 **Baranof I** USA
60C3 **Baranovichi** USSR
108A2 **Baratta** Aust
86B1 **Barauni** India
31C6 **Barbacena** Brazil
27F4 **Barbados** I
    Caribbean S
51C1 **Barbastro** Spain
101H1 **Barberton** S Africa
48B2 **Barbezieux** France
32C2 **Barbösa** Colombia
27E3 **Barbuda** I
    Caribbean S
107D3 **Barcaldine** Aust
    Barce = Al Marj
53C3 **Barcellona** Italy
51C1 **Barcelona** Spain
33E1 **Barcelona** Ven
107D3 **Barcoo** R Aust
34B3 **Barda del Medio** Arg
95A2 **Bardaï** Chad
29C3 **Bardas Blancas** Arg
86B2 **Barddhaman** India
59C3 **Bardejov** Czech
47C2 **Bardi** Italy
47B2 **Bardonecchia** Italy
43B3 **Bardsey** I Wales
84D3 **Bareilly** India
64D2 **Barentsøya** I
    Barents S
64E2 **Barents S** USSR
95C3 **Barentu** Eri
86A2 **Bargarh** India
47B2 **Barge** Italy
63D2 **Barguzin** USSR
63D2 **Barguzin** R USSR
63D2 **Bari** Italy
53C2 **Bari** Italy
51D2 **Barika** Alg
32C2 **Barinas** Ven
86B2 **Baripāda** India
85C4 **Bari Sādri** India
86C2 **Barisal** Bang
78C3 **Barito** R Indon
95A2 **Barjuj** *Watercourse*
    Libya
73A3 **Barkam** China
18C2 **Barkley,L** USA
13B3 **Barkley Sd** Can
100B4 **Barkly East** S Africa
106C2 **Barkly Tableland** *Mts*
    Aust
46C2 **Bar-le-Duc** France
106A3 **Barlee,L** Aust
106A3 **Barlee Range** *Mts*
    Aust
53C2 **Barletta** Italy
85C3 **Barmer** India
108B2 **Barmera** Aust
43B3 **Barmouth** Wales
42D2 **Barnard Castle** Eng
65K4 **Barnaul** USSR
16B3 **Barnegat** USA
16B3 **Barnegat B** USA
6C2 **Barnes Icecap** Can
17B1 **Barnesville** Georgia,
    USA
14B3 **Barnesville** Ohio, USA
42D3 **Barnsley** Eng
43B4 **Barnstaple** Eng
97C4 **Baro** Nig
86C1 **Barpeta** India
32D1 **Barquisimeto** Ven
31C4 **Barra** Brazil
44A3 **Barra** I Scot
109D2 **Barraba** Aust
23A2 **Barra de Navidad**
    Mexico
35C2 **Barra de Piraí** Brazil
35A1 **Barra do Garças** Brazil
50A2 **Barragem do Castelo**
    do Bode *Res* Port
50A2 **Barragem do**
    Maranhão Port

44A3 **Barra Head** *Pt* Scot
31C6 **Barra Mansa** Brazil
32B6 **Barranca** Peru
32C2 **Barrancabermeja**
    Colombia
33E2 **Barrancas** Ven
30E4 **Barranqueras** Arg
32C1 **Barranquilla** Colombia
44A3 **Barra,Sound of** *Chan*
    Scot
16C1 **Barre** USA
34B2 **Barreal** Arg
31C4 **Barreiras** Brazil
50A2 **Barreiro** Port
31D3 **Barreiros** Brazil
107D5 **Barren,C** Aust
12D3 **Barren Is** USA
31B6 **Barretos** Brazil
13E2 **Barrhead** Can
14C2 **Barrie** Can
13C2 **Barrière** Can
108B2 **Barrier Range** *Mts*
    Aust
107E4 **Barrington,Mt** Aust
27N2 **Barrouaillie** St Vincent
4C2 **Barrow** USA
45C2 **Barrow** R Irish Rep
106C3 **Barrow Creek** Aust
106A3 **Barrow I** Aust
42C2 **Barrow-in-Furness**
    Eng
6A2 **Barrow Str** Can
15C1 **Barry's Bay** Can
87B1 **Barsi** India
9B3 **Barstow** USA
49C2 **Bar-sur-Aube** France
33F2 **Bartica** Guyana
92B1 **Bartin** Turk
107D2 **Bartle Frere,Mt** Aust
9D3 **Bartlesville** USA
101C3 **Bartolomeu Dias**
    Mozam
58C2 **Bartoszyce** Pol
78C4 **Barung** I Indon
85D4 **Barwāh** India
85C4 **Barwāni** India
109C1 **Barwon** R Aust
98B2 **Basankusu** Zaïre
34D2 **Basavilbas** Arg
79B1 **Basco** Phil
52A1 **Basel** Switz
53C2 **Basento** R Italy
13E2 **Bashaw** Can
79B1 **Bashi Chan** Phil
61H3 **Bashkirskaya ASSR**
    Republic, USSR
79A4 **Basilan** I Phil
43E4 **Basildon** Eng
43D4 **Basingstoke** Eng
9B2 **Basin Region** USA
93E3 **Basra** Iraq
46D2 **Bas-Rhin** Department,
    France
76D3 **Bassac** R Camb
13E2 **Bassano** Can
52B1 **Bassano** Italy
47D2 **Bassano del Grappa**
    Italy
97C4 **Bassari** Togo
101C3 **Bassas da India** I
    Mozam Chan
76A2 **Bassein** Burma
27E3 **Basse Terre**
    Guadeloupe
97C4 **Bassila** Benin
22C2 **Bass Lake** USA
107A4 **Bass Str** Aust
39G7 **Båstad** Sweden
91B4 **Bāstak** Iran
86A1 **Basti** India
52A2 **Bastia** Corse
57B3 **Bastogne** Belg
19B3 **Bastrop** Louisiana,
    USA
19A3 **Bastrop** Texas, USA
98A2 **Bata** Eq Guinea

Batakan

78C3 Batakan Indon
84D2 Batala India
68B3 Batang China
98B2 Batangafo CAR
79B1 Batan Is Phil
35B2 Batanis Brazil
15C2 Batavia USA
109D3 Batemans Bay Aust
17B1 Batesburg USA
18B2 Batesville Arkansas, USA
19C3 Batesville Mississippi, USA
43C4 Bath Eng
15C2 Bath New York, USA
98B1 Batha R Chad
107D4 Bathurst Aust
7D5 Bathurst Can
4F2 Bathurst,C Can
106C2 Bathurst I Aust
4H2 Bathurst I Can
4H3 Bathurst Inlet B Can
90B3 Batïäq-e-Gavkhûni Salt Flat Iran
109C3 Batlow Aust
93D2 Batman Turk
96C1 Batna Alg
11A3 Baton Rouge USA
94B1 Batroun Leb
78A3 Battambang Camb
87C3 Batticaloa Sri Lanka
13F2 Battle R Can
10B2 Battle Creek USA
7E4 Battle Harbour Can
20C2 Battle Mountain USA
78D2 Batukelau Indon
65F5 Batumi USSR
77C5 Batu Pahat Malay
78A3 Baturaja Indon
94B2 Bat Yam Israel
71D4 Baubau Indon
97C3 Bauchi Nig
47B2 Bauges Mts France
7E4 Bauld,C Can
47B1 Baumes-les-Dames France
63D2 Baunt USSR
31B6 Bauru Brazil
35A1 Baus Brazil
57C2 Bautzen Germany
78C4 Baween I Indon
95B2 Bawiti Egypt
97B3 Bawku Ghana
76B2 Bawlake Burma
108A2 Bawlen Aust
17B1 Baxley USA
25E2 Bayamo Cuba
78D4 Bayan Indon
72A1 Bayandalay Mongolia
68C2 Bayandzürh Mongolia
68B3 Bayan Har Shan Mts China
72A1 Bayan Mod China
72B1 Bayan Obo China
47A2 Bayard P France
12J3 Bayard,Mt Can
79B3 Baybay Phil
93D1 Bayburt Turk
10B2 Bay City Michigan, USA
19A4 Bay City Texas, USA
76B2 Bay Dağları Turk
64H3 Baydaratskaya Guba B USSR
99E2 Baydhabo Somalia
48B2 Bayeux France
47D3 Bayerische Alpen Mts Germany
57C3 Bayern State, Germany
92C3 Bâyir Jordan
68C1 Baykalsky Khrebet Mts USSR
63B1 Baykit USSR
63B3 Baylik Shan Mts China/Mongolia
61J3 Baymak USSR

79B2 Bayombang Phil
48B3 Bayonne France
57C3 Bayreuth Germany
19C3 Bay St Louis USA
15D2 Bay Shore USA
15C1 Bays,L of Can
68A2 Baytik Shan Mts China
Bayt Lahm=Bethlehem
19B4 Baytown USA
50B2 Baza Spain
59D3 Bazaliya USSR
48B3 Bazas France
73B3 Bazhong China
91D4 Bazmān Iran
92C3 Bcharré Leb
16B3 Beach Haven USA
43E4 Beachy Head Eng
16C2 Beacon USA
101D2 Bealanana Madag
18B1 Beardstown USA
Bear I = Bjørnøya
22B1 Bear Valley USA
8D2 Beatrice USA
44C2 Beatrice Oilfield N Sea
13C1 Beatton R Can
5F4 Beatton River Can
29E6 Beauchene Is Falkland Is
109D1 Beaudesert Aust
1B5 Beaufort S Can
100B4 Beaufort West S Africa
15D1 Beauharnois Can
44B3 Beauly Scot
21B3 Beaumont California, USA
11A3 Beaumont Texas, USA
49C2 Beaune France
48C2 Beauvais France
13F1 Beauval Can
12E1 Beaver Alaska, USA
13F2 Beaver R Saskatchewan, Can
4D3 Beaver Creek Can
12E1 Beaver Creek USA
18C2 Beaver Dam Kentucky, USA
13E2 Beaverhill L Can
14A1 Beaver I USA
18B2 Beaver L USA
13D1 Beaverlodge Can
85C3 Beawar India
34B2 Beazley Arg
31B5 Bebedouro Brazil
43E3 Beccles Eng
54B1 Bečej Yugos
96B1 Béchar Alg
12C3 Becharof L USA
11B3 Beckley USA
43D3 Bedford County, Eng
43D3 Bedford Eng
14A3 Bedford Indiana, USA
27M2 Bedford Pt Grenada
4D2 Beechey Pt USA
109C3 Beechworth Aust
109D1 Beenleigh Aust
92B3 Beersheba Israel
Beer Sheva = Beersheba
94B3 Beér Sheva R Israel
9D4 Beeville USA
98C2 Befale Zaïre
101D2 Befandriana Madag
109C3 Bega Aust
91B4 Behbehān Iran
12H3 Behm Canal Sd USA
90B2 Behshahr Iran
84B2 Behsud Afghan
69E2 Bei'an China
73B5 Beihai China
72D2 Beijing China
73B1 Beilu China
73B4 Beipan Jiang R China
72E1 Beipiao China
Beira = Sofala
92C3 Beirut Leb

68B2 Bei Shan Mts China
94B2 Beit ed Dîne Leb
94B3 Beit Jala Israel
50A2 Beja Port
96C1 Beja Tunisia
96C1 Bejaïa Alg
50A1 Béjar Spain
90C3 Bejestān Iran
59C3 Békéscsaba Hung
101D3 Bekily Madag
86A1 Bela India
85B3 Bela Pak
78C2 Belaga Malay
16A3 Bel Air USA
87B1 Belamoalli India
71D3 Belang Indon
70A3 Belangpidie Indon
71E3 Belau Republic, Pacific O
104E3 Belau I Pacific O
101C3 Bela Vista Mozam
70A3 Belawan Indon
61J2 Belaya R USSR
6A2 Belcher Chan Can
7C4 Belcher Is Can
84B1 Belchiragh Afghan
61H3 Belebey USSR
31B2 Belém Brazil
32B3 Belén Colombia
34C3 Belén Urug
9C3 Belen USA
99E2 Belet Uen Somalia
45D1 Belfast N Ire
101H1 Belfast S Africa
45D1 Belfast Lough Estuary N Ire
42D2 Belford Eng
49D2 Belfort France
87A1 Belgaum India
56A2 Belgium Kingdom, N W Europe
60E3 Belgorod USSR
60D4 Belgorod Dnestrovskiy USSR
Belgrade = Beograd
95A2 Bel Hedan Libya
78B3 Belinyu Indon
78B3 Belitung I Indon
25D3 Belize Belize
25D3 Belize Republic, Cent America
48C2 Bellac France
5F4 Bella Coola Can
47C2 Bellagio Italy
19A4 Bellaire USA
52B1 Bellano Italy
87B1 Bellary India
109C1 Bellata Aust
47B2 Belledonne Mts France
8C2 Belle Fourche USA
49D2 Bellegarde France
17B2 Belle Glade USA
7E4 Belle I Can
48B2 Belle-Ile I France
7E4 Belle Isle,Str of Can
7C5 Belleville Can
18A2 Belleville Kansas, USA
20B1 Bellevue Washington, USA
109D2 Bellingen Aust
8A2 Bellingham USA
112C2 Bellingshausen Base Ant
112C3 Bellingshausen S Ant
52A2 Bellinzona Switz
32B2 Bello Colombia
107E3 Bellona Reefs Nouvelle Calédonie
22B1 Bellota USA
15D2 Bellows Falls USA
63B3 Bell Pen Can
52B1 Belluno Italy
29D2 Bell Ville Arg
31D5 Belmonte Brazil
25D3 Belmopan Belize
45B1 Belmullet Irish Rep

69E1 Belogorsk USSR
101D3 Beloha Madag
31C5 Belo Horizonte Brazil
10B2 Beloit Wisconsin, USA
64E3 Belomorsk USSR
61J3 Beloretsk USSR
60C3 Belorusskaya SSR Republic, USSR
101D2 Belo-Tsiribihina Madag
64E3 Beloye More S USSR
60E1 Beloye Ozero L USSR
60E1 Belozersk USSR
14B3 Belpre USA
108A2 Beltana Aust
19A3 Belton USA
59D3 Bel'tsy USSR
16B2 Belvidere New Jersey, USA
98B3 Bembe Angola
97C3 Bembéréke Benin
10A2 Bemidji USA
36G3 Bena Nor
98C3 Bena Dibele Zaïre
108C3 Benalla Aust
84B3 Ben Attow Mt Scot
50A1 Benavente Spain
44A3 Benbecula I Scot
106A4 Bencubbin Aust
8A2 Bend USA
44B3 Ben Dearg Mt Scot
99F2 Bender Beyla Somalia
60C4 Bendery USSR
107D4 Bendigo Aust
57C3 Benešov Czech
53B2 Benevento Italy
83C4 Bengal,B of Asia
96D1 Ben Gardane Tunisia
72D3 Bengbu China
95B1 Benghāzi Libya
78A2 Bengkalis Indon
78A3 Bengkulu Indon
100A2 Benguela Angola
92B3 Benha Egypt
44B2 Ben Hope Mt Scot
99C2 Beni Zaïre
32D6 Béni R Bol
96B1 Beni Abbes Alg
51C1 Benicarló Spain
7A5 Benidji USA
51B2 Benidorm Spain
51C2 Beni Mansour Alg
95C2 Beni Mazar Egypt
96B1 Beni Mellal Mor
97C4 Benin Republic, Africa
97C4 Benin City Nig
95C2 Beni Suef Egypt
44B2 Ben Kilbreck Mt Scot
44B3 Ben Lawers Mt UK
109C4 Ben Lomond Mt Aust
44C3 Ben Macdui Mt Scot
44B2 Ben More Assynt Mt Scot
111B2 Benmore,L NZ
44B3 Ben Nevis Mt Scot
15D2 Bennington USA
94B2 Bennt Jbail Leb
98B2 Bénoué R Cam
9C3 Benson USA
71D4 Benteng Indon
99C2 Bentiu Sudan
18B3 Benton Arkansas, USA
18C2 Benton Kentucky, USA
14A2 Benton Harbor USA
97C4 Benue R Nig
45B1 Benwee Hd C Irish Rep
44B3 Ben Wyvis Mt Scot
72E1 Benxi China
54B2 Beograd Yugos
86A2 Beohari India
74C4 Beppu Japan
55A2 Berat Alb
99D1 Berber Sudan
99E1 Berbera Somalia
98B2 Berbérati CAR
46A1 Berck France

60C4	Berdichev USSR
60E4	Berdyansk USSR
97B4	Berekum Ghana
22B2	Berenda USSR
5J4	Berens R Can
5J4	Berens River Can
108A1	Beresford Aust
59C3	Berettyóújfalu Hung
58D2	Bereza USSR
59C3	Berezhany USSR
65G4	Berezniki USSR
60D4	Berezovka USSR
64H3	Berezovo USSR
92A2	Bergama Turk
52A1	Bergamo Italy
39F6	Bergen Nor
46C1	Bergen op Zoom Neth
48C3	Bergerac France
46D1	Bergisch-Gladbach Germany
12F2	Bering GI USA
1C6	Bering Str USA/USSR
91C4	Berizak Iran
50B2	Berja Spain
8A3	Berkeley USA
112B2	Berkner I Ant
54B2	Berkovitsa Bulg
16C1	Berkshire County, Eng
16C1	Berkshire Hills USA
13D2	Berland R Can
56C2	Berlin Germany
56C2	Berlin State, Germany
15D2	Berlin New Hampshire, USA
30D3	Bermejo Bol
30D4	Bermejo R Arg
3M5	Bermuda / Atlantic O
52A1	Bern Switz
16B2	Bernardsville USA
34C3	Bernasconi Arg
56C2	Bernburg Germany
47B1	Berner Oberland Mts Switz
6B2	Bernier R Can
57C3	Berounka R Czech
108B2	Berri Aust
96C1	Berriane Alg
48C2	Berry Region, France
22A1	Berryessa,L USA
11C4	Berry Is The Bahamas
98B2	Bertoua Cam
45B2	Bertraghboy B Irish Rep
15C2	Berwick USA
42C2	Berwick-upon-Tweed Eng
43C3	Berwyn Mts Wales
101D2	Besalampy Madag
49D2	Besançon France
59C3	Beskidy Zachodnie Mts Pol
93C2	Besni Iran
94B3	Besor R Israel
11B3	Bessemer USA
101D2	Betafo Madag
50A1	Betanzos Spain
94B3	Bet Guvrin Israel
101G1	Bethal S Africa
100A3	Bethanie Namibia
18B1	Bethany Missouri, USA
18A2	Bethany Oklahoma, USA
4B3	Bethel Alaska, USA
16C2	Bethel Connecticut, USA
14B2	Bethel Park USA
15C3	Bethesda USA
94B3	Bethlehem Israel
101G1	Bethlehem S Africa
15C2	Bethlehem USA
48C1	Bethune France
101D3	Betioky Madag
108B1	Betoota Aust
98B2	Betou Congo
82A1	Betpak Dala Steppe USSR
101D3	Betroka Madag

7D5	Betsiamites Can
86A1	Bettiah India
12D1	Bettles USA
47C2	Béttola Italy
85D4	Betul India
85D3	Betwa R India
46D1	Betzdorf Germany
12C3	Beverley,L USA
16D1	Beverly USA
21B3	Beverly Hills USA
97B4	Beyla Guinea
87B2	Beypore India
	Beyrouth = Beirut
92B2	Beyşehir Turk
92B2	Beyşehir Gölü L Turk
94B2	Beyt Shean Israel
47C1	Bezau Austria
60E2	Bezhetsk USSR
49C3	Béziers France
52C3	Beznosova USSR
86B1	Bhadgaon Nepal
87C1	Bhadrachalam India
86B2	Bhadrakh India
87B2	Bhadra Res India
87B2	Bhadravati India
84B3	Bhag Pak
86B1	Bhagalpur India
84C2	Bhakkar Pak
82D3	Bhamo Burma
85D4	Bhandara India
85D3	Bharatpur India
85C4	Bharuch India
86B2	Bhatiapara Ghat Bang
84C2	Bhatinda India
87A2	Bhatkal India
86B2	Bhatpara India
85C4	Bhavnagar India
84C2	Bhera Pak
86A1	Bheri R Nepal
86A2	Bhilai India
85C3	Bhilwara India
87C1	Bhimavaram India
85D3	Bhind India
84B3	Bhiwani India
87B1	Bhongir India
85D4	Bhopal India
86B2	Bhubaneshwar India
85B4	Bhuj India
85D4	Bhusawal India
82C3	Bhutan Kingdom, Asia
71E4	Biak I Indon
58C2	Biala Podlaska Pol
58B2	Bialograd Pol
58C2	Bialystok Pol
38A1	Biargtangar C Iceland
90C2	Biarjmand Iran
48B3	Biarritz France
47C1	Biasca Switz
92B4	Biba Egypt
74E2	Bibai Japan
100A2	Bibala Angola
57B3	Biberach Germany
97B4	Bibiani Ghana
54C1	Bicaz Rom
50A1	Bida Nig
87B1	Bidar India
91C5	Bidbid Oman
43B4	Bideford Eng
43B4	Bideford B Eng
96C2	Bidon 5 Alg
100A2	Bié Angola
52A1	Biel Switz
59B2	Bielawa Pol
56B2	Bielefeld Germany
47B1	Bieler See L Switz
52A1	Biella Italy
58C2	Bielsk Podlaski Pol
76D3	Bien Hoa Viet
53B2	Biferno R Italy
92A1	Biga Turk
55C3	Bigadiç Turk
19C3	Big Black R USA
18A1	Big Blue R USA
17B2	Big Cypress Swamp USA

4D3	Big Delta USA
49D2	Bigent Germany
13F2	Biggar Can
5H4	Biggar Kindersley Can
109D1	Biggenden Aust
12G3	Bigger,Mt Can
8C2	Bighorn R USA
76C3	Bight of Bangkok B Thai
97C4	Bight of Benin B W Africa
97C4	Bight of Biafra B Cam
6C3	Big I Can
47C1	Bignasco Switz
97A3	Bignona Sen
21B2	Big Pine USA
17B2	Big Pine Key USA
22C3	Big Pine Mt USA
14A2	Big Rapids USA
5H4	Big River Can
9C3	Big Spring USA
7A4	Big Trout L Can
7B4	Big Trout Lake Can
52C2	Bihać Yugos
86B1	Bihar India
86B2	Bihar State, India
99D3	Biharamulo Tanz
60B4	Bihor Mt Rom
87B1	Bijapur India
87C1	Bijapur India
90A2	Bijar Iran
86A1	Bijauri Nepal
54A2	Bijeljina Yugos
73B4	Bijie China
84D3	Bijnor India
84C3	Bijnot Pak
94B2	Bikaner India
94B2	Bikfaya Leb
69F2	Bikin USSR
98B3	Bikoro Zaire
85C3	Bilara India
84D2	Bilaspur India
86A2	Bilaspur India
76B3	Bilauktaung Range Mts Thai
50B1	Bilbao Spain
59B3	Bílé R Czech
54A2	Bileća Yugos
92B1	Bilecik Turk
98C2	Bili R Zaire
79B3	Biliran I Phil
8C2	Billings USA
98A3	Bilma Niger
11B3	Biloxi USA
98C1	Biltine Chad
85D4	Bina-Etawa India
79B3	Binalbagan Phil
101C2	Bindura Zim
100B2	Binga Zim
98A2	Binga Mt Zim
109D1	Bingara Aust
57B3	Bingen Germany
10C2	Binghamton USA
78D1	Bingkor Malay
93D2	Bingöl Turk
72D3	Binhai China
72A2	Bintan I Indon
78A3	Bintuhan Indon
78C2	Bintulu Malay
29B3	Bió Bió R Chile
102J4	Bioko I Atlantic O
87B1	Bir India
95B2	Bir Abu Husein Well Egypt
95B2	Bi'r al Harash Well Libya
98C1	Birao CAR
86B1	Biratnagar Nepal
12E1	Birch Creek USA
108B3	Birchip Aust
5G4	Birch Mts Can
7A4	Bird Can
106C3	Birdsville Aust
106C2	Birdum Aust
86A1	Birganj Nepal
94A3	Bir Gifgafa Well Egypt
94A3	Bir Hasana Well Egypt

35A2	Birigui Brazil
90C3	Birjand Iran
92B4	Birkat Qarun L Egypt
46D2	Birkenfeld Germany
42C3	Birkenhead Eng
60C4	Birlad Rom
94A3	Bir Lahfân Well Egypt
43C3	Birmingham Eng
11B3	Birmingham USA
95B2	Bir Misâha Well Egypt
96A2	Bir Moghrein Maur
94B3	Birin Kebbi Nig
97C3	Birni N'Konni Nig
69F2	Birobidzhan USSR
45C2	Birr Irish Rep
51C2	Bir Rabalou Alg
109C1	Birrie R Aust
44C2	Birsay Scot
61J2	Birsk USSR
95B2	Bir Tarfâwi Well Egypt
63B2	Biryusa USSR
39J7	Birzai USSR
96B2	Bir Zreigat Well Maur
48A2	Biscay,B of France/ Spain
17B2	Biscayne B USA
46D2	Bischwiller France
73B4	Bishan China
8B3	Bishop USA
42D2	Bishop Auckland Eng
43E4	Bishop's Stortford Eng
86A2	Bishrampur India
96C1	Biskra Alg
79C4	Bislig Phil
8C2	Bismarck USA
90A3	Bisotün Iran
97A3	Bissau Guinea-Bissau
10A1	Bissett Can
5G4	Bistcho L Can
54C1	Bistrita R Rom
98B2	Bitam Gabon
57B3	Bitburg Germany
46D2	Bitche France
93D2	Bitlis Turk
55B2	Bitola Yugos
56C2	Bitterfeld Germany
100A4	Bitterfontein S Africa
92B3	Bitter Lakes Egypt
8B2	Bitterroot Range Mts USA
74D3	Biwa-ko L Japan
99E1	Biyo Kaboba Eth
65K4	Biysk USSR
96C1	Bizerte Tunisia
51C2	Bj bou Arréridj Alg
52C1	Bjelovar Yugos
64C2	Bj Flye Ste Marie Alg
64C2	Bjørnøya / Barents S
12F1	Black R USA
18B2	Black R USA
107D3	Blackall Aust
42C3	Blackburn Eng
4D3	Blackburn,Mt USA
13E2	Black Diamond Can
5H5	Black Hills USA
44B3	Black Isle Pen Scot
27R3	Blackman's Barbados
43C4	Black Mts Wales
43C3	Blackpool Eng
27H1	Black River Jamaica
8B2	Black Rock Desert USA
65E5	Black S USSR/Europe
45A1	Blacksod B Irish Rep
109D2	Black Sugarloaf Mt Aust
97B3	Black Volta R Ghana
41B3	Blackwater R Irish Rep
18A2	Blackwell USA
54B2	Blagoevgrad Bulg
63E2	Blagoveshchensk USSR
20B1	Blaine USA
44C3	Blair Atholl Scot
44C3	Blairgowrie Scot

Blakely

17B1	Blakely USA
108A1	Blanche,L Aust
34A2	Blanco R Arg
34B1	Blanco R Arg
8A2	Blanco,C USA
7E4	Blanc Sablon Can
43C4	Blandford Forum Eng
46B1	Blangy-sur-Bresle France
46B1	Blankenberge Belg
101C2	Blantyre Malawi
48B2	Blaye France
109C2	Blayney Aust
111B2	Blenheim NZ
96C1	Blida Alg
14B1	Blind River Can
108A2	Blinman Aust
78C4	Blitar Indon
15D2	Block I USA
16D2	Block Island Sd USA
101G1	Bloemfontein S Africa
101G1	Bloemhof S Africa
101G1	Bloemhof Dam Res S Africa
33F3	Blommesteinmeer L Surinam
38A1	Blonduós Iceland
45B1	Bloody Foreland C Irish Rep
14A3	Bloomfield Indiana, USA
18B1	Bloomfield Iowa, USA
10B2	Bloomington Illinois, USA
14A3	Bloomington Indiana, USA
14A2	Bloomsburg USA
78C4	Blora Indon
6H3	Blosseville Kyst Mts Greenland
57B3	Bludenz Austria
11B3	Bluefield USA
32A1	Bluefields Nic
26B3	Blue Mountain Peak Mt Jamaica
16A2	Blue Mts USA
109D2	Blue Mts Aust
27J1	Blue Mts Jamaica
8A2	Blue Mts USA
	Blue Nile = Bahr el Azraq
99D1	Blue Nile R Sudan
4G3	Bluenose L Can
11B3	Blue Ridge Mts USA
13D2	Blue River Can
45B1	Blue Stack Mt Irish Rep
111A3	Bluff NZ
106A4	Bluff Knoll Mt Aust
30G4	Blumenau Brazil
49D2	Blundez Austria
20B2	Bly USA
12E3	Blying Sd USA
42D2	Blyth Eng
11B3	Blythe USA
11B3	Blytheville USA
97A4	Bo Sierra Leone
79B3	Boac Phil
72D2	Boading China
14B2	Boardman USA
63C3	Boatou China
33E3	Boa Vista Brazil
97A4	Boa Vista I Cape Verde
76E1	Bobai China
47C2	Bóbbio Italy
97B3	Bobo Dioulasso Burkina
60C3	Bobruysk USSR
17B2	Boca Chica Key I USA
32D5	Bôca do Acre Brazil
35C1	Bocaiúva Brazil
98B2	Bocaranga CAR
17B2	Boca Raton USA
59C3	Bochnia Pol
56B2	Bocholt Germany
46D1	Bochum Germany
100A2	Bocoio Angola

98B2	Boda CAR
63D2	Bodaybo USSR
21A2	Bodega Head Pt USA
95A3	Bodélé Region Chad
38J5	Boden Sweden
47C1	Bodensee L Switz/Germany
87B1	Bodhan India
87B2	Bodināyakkanūr India
43B4	Bodmin Eng
43B4	Bodmin Moor Upland Eng
38G5	Bodø Nor
63G2	Bodorodskoye USSR
55D5	Bodrum Turk
98C3	Boende Zaïre
97A3	Boffa Guinea
76B2	Bogale Burma
19C3	Bogalusa USA
109C2	Bogan R Aust
97B3	Bogandé Burkina
64G3	Bogarnes Iceland
92C2	Bogazlyan Turk
61K2	Bogdanovich USSR
68A2	Bogda Shan Mt China
100A3	Bogenfels Namibia
109D1	Boggabilla Aust
109C2	Boggabri Aust
45B2	Boggeragh Mts Irish Rep
79B3	Bogo Phil
109C3	Bogong,Mt Aust
78B4	Bogor Indon
61H2	Bogorodskoye USSR
32C3	Bogotá Colombia
63A2	Bogotol USSR
86B2	Bogra Bang
72D2	Bo Hai B China
46B2	Bohain-en-Vermandois France
72D2	Bohai Wan B China
57C3	Böhmer-Wald Upland Germany
79B4	Bohol I Phil
79B4	Bohol S Phil
35A1	Bois R Brazil
14B1	Bois Blanc I USA
8B2	Boise USA
96A2	Bojador,C Mor
79B2	Bojeador,C Phil
90C2	Bojnūrd Iran
97A3	Boké Guinea
109C1	Bokhara R Aust
39F7	Boknafjord Inlet Nor
98B3	Boko Congo
76C3	Bokor Camb
98C3	Bokungu Zaïre
98B1	Bol Chad
97A3	Bolama Guinea-Bissau
23A1	Bolaños Mexico
23A1	Bolanos R Mexico
48C2	Bolbec France
97B4	Bole Ghana
59B2	Boleslawiec Pol
97B3	Bolgatanga Ghana
60C4	Bolgrad USSR
34C3	Bolívar Arg
18B2	Bolívar Missouri, USA
18C2	Bolívar Tennessee, USA
30C2	Bolivia Republic, S America
38H6	Bollnäs Sweden
109C1	Bollon Aust
32C1	Bolívar Mt Ven
52B2	Bologna Italy
60D2	Bologoye USSR
69F2	Bolon USSR
61G3	Bol'shoy Irgiz R USSR
74C2	Bol'shoy Kamen USSR
65F5	Bol'shoy Kavkaz Mts USSR
61G4	Bol'shoy Uzen R USSR
9C4	Bolson de Mapimi Desert Mexico
43C3	Bolton Eng

92B1	Bolu Turk
38A1	Bolungarvik Iceland
92B2	Bolvadin Turk
52B1	Bolzano Italy
98B3	Boma Zaïre
107D4	Bombala Aust
87A1	Bombay India
99D2	Bombo Uganda
35B1	Bom Despacho Brazil
86C1	Bomdila India
97A4	Bomi Hills Lib
31C4	Bom Jesus da Lapa Brazil
63E2	Bomnak USSR
99C2	Bomokandi R Zaïre
98C2	Bomu R CAR/Zaïre
27D4	Bonaire I Caribbean S
12F2	Bona,Mt USA
25D3	Bonanza Nic
7E5	Bonavista Can
108A2	Bon Bon Aust
98C2	Bondo Zaïre
97B4	Bondoukou Ivory Coast
	Bône = 'Annaba
33E3	Bonfim Guyana
98C2	Bongandanga Zaïre
98B1	Bongor Chad
19A3	Bonham USA
53A2	Bonifacio Corse
52A2	Bonifacio,Str of Chan Medit S
	Bonin Is = Ogasawara Gunto
17B2	Bonita Springs USA
57B2	Bonn Germany
20C1	Bonners Ferry USA
12H1	Bennet Plume R Can
13E2	Bonnyville Can
97A4	Bonthe Sierra Leone
99E1	Booaaso Somalia
108B2	Booligal Aust
109D1	Boonah Aust
15C3	Boonville USA
109C2	Boorowa Aust
6A2	Boothia,G of Can
6A2	Boothia Pen Can
98B3	Booué Gabon
108A1	Bopeechee Aust
99D2	Bor Sudan
92B2	Bor Turk
54B2	Bor Yugos
8B2	Borah Peak Mt USA
39G7	Borås Sweden
91B4	Borāzjān Iran
108A3	Borda,C Aust
48B3	Bordeaux France
4G2	Borden I Can
6B2	Borden Pen Can
16B2	Bordentown USA
42C2	Borders Region, Scot
108B3	Bordertown Aust
96C2	Bordj Omar Dris Alg
96C1	Borens River Can
38A2	Borgarnes Iceland
3C3	Borger USA
39H7	Borgholm Sweden
47C2	Borgosia Italy
47D1	Borgo Valsugana Italy
59C3	Borislav USSR
61E3	Borisoglebsk USSR
60C3	Borisov USSR
60E3	Borisovka USSR
95A3	Borkou Region Chad
39H6	Borlänge Sweden
47C2	Bórmida Italy
47D1	Bórmio Italy
78D1	Borneo I Malay/Indon
39H7	Bornholm I Den
55C3	Bornova Turk
98C2	Boro R Sudan
79B3	Boromo Burkina
60D2	Borovichi USSR
106C2	Borroloola Aust
51C4	Borsa Rom
90A3	Borūjed Iran
90B3	Borūjen Iran
58B2	Bory Tucholskie Region, Pol

63D2	Borzya USSR
54A1	Bosanski Brod Yugos
73B5	Bose China
101G1	Boshof S Africa
54A2	Bosna R Yugos
75C1	Bōsō-hantō B Japan
	Bosporus = Karadeniz Boğazi
51C2	Bosquet Alg
98B2	Bossangoa CAR
98B2	Bossémbélé CAR
19B3	Bossier City USA
65K5	Bosten Hu L China
43D3	Boston Eng
10C2	Boston USA
11A3	Boston Mts USA
85C4	Botad India
54B2	Botevgrad Bulg
101G1	Bothaville S Africa
64C3	Bothnia,G of Sweden/Fin
100B3	Botletli R Botswana
60C4	Botoşani Rom
100B3	Botswana Republic, Africa
53C3	Botte Donato Mt Italy
46D1	Bottrop Germany
35B2	Botucatu Brazil
7E5	Botwood Can
97B4	Bouaké Ivory Coast
98B2	Bouar CAR
96B1	Bouârfa Mor
98B2	Bouca CAR
51C2	Boufarik Alg
	Bougie = Bejaïa
97B3	Bougouni Mali
46C2	Bouillon France
96B2	Bou Izakarn Mor
46D2	Boulay-Moselle France
8C2	Boulder Colorado, USA
9B3	Boulder City USA
22A2	Boulder Creek USA
48C1	Boulogne France
98B2	Boumba R CAR
97B4	Bouna Ivory Coast
8B3	Boundary Peak Mt USA
97B4	Boundiali Ivory Coast
107F3	Bourail Nouvelle Calédonie
97B3	Bourem Mali
49D2	Bourg France
49D2	Bourg de Péage France
48C2	Bourges France
48C3	Bourg-Madame France
49C2	Bourgogne Region, France
47B2	Bourg-St-Maurice France
108C2	Bourke Aust
43D4	Bournemouth Eng
96C1	Bou Saâda Alg
98B1	Bousso Chad
97A3	Boutilimit Maur
103J7	Bouvet I Atlantic O
34D2	Bovril Arg
13E2	Bow R Can
107D2	Bowen Aust
19A3	Bowie Texas, USA
13E2	Bow Island Can
11B3	Bowling Green Kentucky, USA
18B2	Bowling Green Missouri, USA
14B2	Bowling Green Ohio, USA
15C3	Bowling Green Virginia, USA
15C2	Bowmanville Can
109D2	Bowral Aust
13C2	Bowron R Can
72D3	Bo Xian China
72D2	Boxing China
92B1	Boyabat Turk

98B2 **Boyali** CAR
5J4 **Boyd** Can
16B2 **Boyertown** USA
13E2 **Boyle** Can
41B3 **Boyle** Irish Rep
45C2 **Boyne** R Irish Rep
72D3 **Boyntoon Beach** USA
98C2 **Boyoma Falls** Zaïre
55C3 **Bozca Ada** I Turk
55C3 **Boz Dağlari** Mts Turk
8B2 **Bozeman** USA
Bozen = Bolzano
98B2 **Bozene** Zaïre
98B2 **Bozoum** CAR
47B2 **Bra** Italy
52C2 **Brač** I Yugos
15C1 **Bracebridge** Can
95A2 **Brach** Libya
38H6 **Bräcke** Sweden
17B2 **Bradenton** USA
42D3 **Bradford** Eng
44E1 **Brae** Scot
44C3 **Braemar** Scot
50A1 **Braga** Port
34C3 **Bragado** Arg
50A1 **Bragana** Port
31B2 **Bragança** Brazil
35B2 **Bragança Paulista**
    Brazil
86C2 **Brahman-Baria** Bang
86B2 **Brāhmani** R India
86C1 **Brahmaputra** R India
7E5 **Braie Verte** Can
60C4 **Brăila** Rom
10A2 **Brainerd** USA
97A3 **Brakna** Region, Maur
5F4 **Bralorne** Can
14C2 **Brampton** Can
33E3 **Branco** R Brazil
100A3 **Brandberg** Mt
    Namibia
56C2 **Brandenburg**
    Germany
56C2 **Brandenburg** State,
    Germany
101G1 **Brandfort** S Africa
8D2 **Brandon** Can
100B4 **Brandvlei** S Africa
57C2 **Brandys nad Lebem**
    Czech
58B2 **Braniewo** Pol
10B2 **Brantford** Can
108B3 **Branxholme** Aust
7D5 **Bras d'Or L** Can
35C1 **Brasil de Minas** Brazil
32D6 **Brasiléia** Brazil
31B5 **Brasilia** Brazil
54C1 **Brasov** Rom
78D1 **Brassay Range** Mts
    Malay
59B3 **Bratislava** Czech
63C2 **Bratsk** USSR
15D2 **Brattleboro** USA
56C2 **Braunschweig**
    Germany
97A4 **Brava** I Cape Verde
9B3 **Brawley** USA
45C2 **Bray** Irish Rep
6C3 **Bray** I Can
13D2 **Brazeau** R Can
13D2 **Brazeau,Mt** Can
28D4 **Brazil** Republic,
    S America
103G5 **Brazil Basin** Atlantic O
9D3 **Brazos** R USA
98B3 **Brazzaville** Congo
57C3 **Brdy** Upland Czech
111A3 **Breaksea Sd** NZ
110B1 **Bream B** NZ
78B4 **Brebes** Indon
44C3 **Brechin** Scot
46C1 **Brecht** Belg
59B3 **Břeclav** Czech
43C4 **Brecon** Wales
43C4 **Brecon Beacons** Mts
    Wales
43B3 **Brecon Beacons Nat**
    Pk Wales

56A2 **Breda** Neth
100B4 **Bredasdorp** S Africa
38H6 **Bredbyn** Sweden
61J3 **Bredy** USSR
15C2 **Breezewood** USA
47C1 **Bregenz** Austria
47C1 **Bregenzer Ache** R
    Austria
38A1 **Breiðafjörður** B
    Iceland
47C2 **Brembo** R Italy
17A1 **Bremen** USA
56B2 **Bremen** Germany
56B2 **Bremerhaven**
    Germany
20B1 **Bremerton** USA
19A3 **Brenham** USA
57C3 **Brenner** P Austria/
    Italy
47D2 **Breno** Italy
47D2 **Brenta** R Italy
22B2 **Brentwood** USA
52B1 **Brescia** Italy
    Breslau = Wrocław
47D1 **Bressanone** Italy
44E1 **Bressay** I Scot
48B2 **Bressuire** France
48B2 **Brest** France
58C2 **Brest** USSR
48B2 **Bretagne** Region,
    France
46B2 **Breteuil** France
16B2 **Breton Woods** USA
110B1 **Brett,C** NZ
109C1 **Brewarrina** Aust
16C2 **Brewster** New York,
    USA
20C1 **Brewster** Washington,
    USA
101G1 **Breyten** S Africa
52C1 **Brežice** Yugos
98C2 **Bria** CAR
49D3 **Briancon** France
49C2 **Briare** France
21B2 **Bridgeport** California,
    USA
15D2 **Bridgeport**
    Connecticut, USA
19A3 **Bridgeport** Texas,
    USA
22C1 **Bridgeport Res** USA
16B3 **Bridgeton** USA
27F4 **Bridgetown** Barbados
7D5 **Bridgewater** Can
16D2 **Bridgewater** USA
43C4 **Bridgwater** Eng
43C4 **Bridgwater B** Eng
42D2 **Bridlington** Eng
109C4 **Bridport** Aust
47B1 **Brienzer See** L Switz
46C2 **Briey** France
52A1 **Brig** Switz
8B2 **Brigham City** USA
109C3 **Bright** Aust
43D4 **Brighton** Eng
46E1 **Brilon** Germany
55A2 **Brindisi** Italy
19B3 **Brinkley** USA
107E3 **Brisbane** Aust
15D2 **Bristol** Connecticut,
    USA
43C4 **Bristol** Eng
15D2 **Bristol** Pennsylvania,
    USA
16D2 **Bristol** Rhode Island,
    USA
11B3 **Bristol** Tennessee,
    USA
12B3 **Bristol B** USA
43B4 **Bristol Chan** Eng/
    Wales
4D3 **British Mts** USA
5F4 **British Columbia**
    Province, Can
6B1 **British Empire Range**
    Mts Can
101G1 **Brits** S Africa
100B4 **Britstown** S Africa

48C2 **Brive** France
59B3 **Brno** Czech
17B1 **Broad** R USA
7C4 **Broadback** R Can
44A2 **Broad Bay** Inlet Scot
44B3 **Broad Law** Mt Scot
5H4 **Brochet** Can
4G2 **Brock** I Can
15C2 **Brockport** USA
16D1 **Brockton** USA
15C2 **Brockville** Can
6B2 **Brodeur Pen** Can
42B2 **Brodick** Scot
58B2 **Brodnica** Pol
60C3 **Brody** USSR
19B3 **Broken Bow**
    Oklahoma, USA
19B3 **Broken Bow L** USA
107D4 **Broken Hill** Aust
47C2 **Broni** Italy
38G5 **Brønnøysund** Nor
16C2 **Bronx** Borough, New
    York, USA
79A4 **Brooke's Point** Phil
18B2 **Brookfield** Missouri,
    USA
11A3 **Brookhaven** USA
20B2 **Brookings** Oregon,
    USA
8D2 **Brookings** South
    Dakota, USA
16D1 **Brookline** USA
16C2 **Brooklyn** Borough,
    New York, USA
5G4 **Brooks** Can
12C3 **Brooks,L** USA
12A1 **Brooks Mt** USA
4C3 **Brooks Range** Mts
    USA
17B2 **Brooksville** USA
109D1 **Brooloo** Aust
106B2 **Broome** Aust
44C2 **Brora** Scot
20B2 **Brothers** USA
95A3 **Broulkou** Chad
13E3 **Browning** USA
9D4 **Brownsville** USA
9D3 **Brownwood** USA
46B1 **Bruay-en-Artois**
    France
106A3 **Bruce,Mt** Aust
14B1 **Bruce Pen** Can
59B3 **Brück an der P**
    Austria
    Bruges = Brugge
46B1 **Brugge** Belg
46D1 **Brühl** Germany
78C2 **Brunei** Sultanate,
    S E Asia
52B1 **Brunico** Italy
111B2 **Brunner,L** NZ
11B3 **Brunswick** Georgia,
    USA
18B2 **Brunswick**
    Mississippi, USA
29B6 **Brunswick,Pen de**
    Chile
109C4 **Bruny I** Aust
61F1 **Brusenets** USSR
26A3 **Brus Laguna**
    Honduras
    Brüssel = Bruxelles
56A2 **Bruxelles** Belg
18B2 **Bryan** USA
108A2 **Bryan,Mt** Aust
60D3 **Bryansk** USSR
59B2 **Bryant** USA
59B2 **Brzeg** Pol
93E4 **Būbiyan** I Kuwait/Iraq
99D3 **Bubu** R Tanz
32C2 **Bucaramanga**
    Colombia
44D3 **Buchan** Oilfield N Sea
97A4 **Buchanan** Lib
44D3 **Buchan Deep** N Sea
6C2 **Buchan G** Can
40C2 **Buchan Ness** Pen
    Scot

7E5 **Buchans** Can
34C2 **Buchardo** Arg
    Bucharest = Bucureşti
47C1 **Buchs** Switz
43D3 **Buckingham** Eng
12B1 **Buckland** USA
12B1 **Buckland** R USA
108A2 **Buckleboo** Aust
98B3 **Buco Zau** Congo
54C2 **Bucureşti** Rom
59B3 **Budapest** Hung
84D3 **Budaun** India
43B4 **Bude** Eng
19B3 **Bude** USA
61F5 **Budennovsk** USSR
34A2 **Buéa** Cam
22B3 **Buellton** USA
98A2 **Buéa** Cam
22B3 **Buellton** USA
34B2 **Buena Esperanza** Arg
32B3 **Buenaventura**
    Colombia
23A2 **Buenavista** Mexico
29E2 **Buenos Aires** Arg
29D3 **Buenos Aires** State,
    Arg
18B2 **Buffalo** Mississippi,
    USA
10C2 **Buffalo** New York,
    USA
8C2 **Buffalo** South Dakota,
    USA
19A3 **Buffalo** Texas, USA
8C2 **Buffalo** Wyoming,
    USA
101H1 **Buffalo** R S Africa
13E2 **Buffalo L** Alberta, Can
5G3 **Buffalo L** Northwest
    Territories, Can
5H4 **Buffalo Narrows** Can
17B1 **Buford** USA
54C2 **Buftea** Rom
59C2 **Bug** R Pol/USSR
32B3 **Buga** Colombia
90B2 **Bugdayli** USSR
61H3 **Bugulma** USSR
61H3 **Buguruslan** USSR
93C2 **Buhayrat al Asad** Res
    Syria
41C3 **Builth Wells** Wales
34A2 **Buin** Chile
99C3 **Bujumbura** Burundi
98C3 **Bukama** Zaïre
99C3 **Bukavu** Zaïre
80E2 **Bukhara** USSR
78C2 **Bukit Batubrok** Mt
    Indon
70B4 **Bukittinggi** Indon
99D3 **Bukoba** Tanz
78D3 **Buku Gandadiwata** Mt
    Indon
71E4 **Bula** Indon
79B3 **Bulan** Phil
84D3 **Bulandshahr** India
100B3 **Bulawayo** Zim
55C3 **Buldan** Turk
85D4 **Buldāna** India
68C2 **Bulgan** Mongolia
54B2 **Bulgaria**
    Republic, Europe
47B1 **Bulle** Switz
111B2 **Buller** R NZ
109C3 **Buller,Mt** Aust
106A4 **Bullfinch** Aust
108B1 **Bulloo** R Aust
108B1 **Bulloo Downs** Aust
108B1 **Bulloo L** Aust
18B2 **Bull Shoals Res** USA
34A3 **Bulnes** Chile
71F4 **Bulolo** PNG
101G1 **Bultfontein** S Africa
98C2 **Bumba** Zaïre
76B2 **Bumphal Dam** Thai
99D2 **Buna** Kenya
106A4 **Bunbury** Aust
45C1 **Buncrana** Irish Rep
107E3 **Bundaberg** Aust
109D2 **Bundarra** Aust
85D3 **Būndi** India

25E2 Camagüey,Arch de Is Cuba
30B2 Camaná Peru
30C3 Camargo Bol
22C3 Camarillo USA
29C4 Camarones Arg
20B1 Camas USA
98B3 Camaxilo Angola
98B3 Cambatela Angola
76C3 Cambodia Republic, S E Asia
43B4 Camborne Eng
49C1 Cambrai France
14B2 Cambrian Mts Wales
14B2 Cambridge Can
43D3 Cambridge County, Eng
43E3 Cambridge Eng
27H1 Cambridge Jamaica
15C3 Cambridge Maryland, USA
15D2 Cambridge Massachussets, USA
110C1 Cambridge NZ
14B2 Cambridge Ohio, USA
4H3 Cambridge Bay Can
60E5 Cam Burun Pt Turk
11A3 Camden Arkansas, USA
109D2 Camden Aust
15D3 Camden New Jersey, USA
17B1 Camden South Carolina, USA
18B2 Cameron Missouri, USA
19A3 Cameron Texas, USA
4H2 Cameron I Can
111A3 Cameron Mts NZ
98A2 Cameroon Federal Republic, Africa
98A2 Cameroun Mt Can
31B2 Cametá Brazil
79B4 Camiguin I Phil
79B2 Camiling Phil
17B1 Camilla USA
22B1 Camino USA
30D3 Camiri Bol
31C2 Camocim Brazil
106C2 Camooweal Aust
34D2 Campana I
29A5 Campana I Chile
13B2 Campania I Can
111B2 Campbell,C NZ
13B2 Campbell I Can
105G6 Campbell I NZ
4E3 Campbell,Mt Can
84C2 Campbellpore Pak
5F5 Campbell River Can
7D5 Campbellton Can
109D2 Campbelltown Aust
42B2 Campbeltown Scot
25C3 Campeche Mexico
108B3 Camperdown Aust
31D3 Campina Grande Brazil
31B6 Campinas Brazil
35B1 Campina Verde Brazil
98A2 Campo Cam
52B2 Campobasso Italy
35B2 Campo Belo Brazil
35B1 Campo Florido Brazil
30D4 Campo Gallo Arg
30F3 Campo Grande Brazil
31C2 Campo Maior Brazil
30F3 Campo Mourão Brazil
35C2 Campos Brazil
35B1 Campos Altos Brazil
47D1 Campo Tures Italy
76D3 Cam Ranh Viet
5G4 Camrose Can
100A2 Camucuio Angola
27K1 Canaan Tobago
16C1 Canaan USA
100A2 Canacupa Angola
2F3 Canada Dominion, N America
29D2 Cañada de Gomez Arg

9C3 Canadian R USA
60C5 Canakkale Turk
34B3 Canalejas Arg
13D2 Canal Flats Can
24A1 Cananea Mexico
102G3 Canary Basin Atlantic O
Canary Is = Islas Canarias
23A2 Canas Mexico
24B2 Canatlán Mexico
11B4 Canaveral,C USA
31D5 Canavieiras Brazil
107D4 Canberra Aust
20B2 Canby California, USA
99F1 Candala Somalia
55C3 Çandarli Körfezi B Turk
16C2 Candlewood,L USA
29E2 Canelones Urug
18A2 Caney USA
100A2 Cangamba Angola
100B2 Cangombe Angola
72D2 Cangzhou China
7D4 Caniapiscau R Can
7D4 Caniapiscau,L Can
53B3 Canicattí Italy
31D2 Caninde Brazil
92B1 Çankırı Turk
13D2 Canmore Can
44A3 Canna I Scot
87B2 Cannanore India
49D3 Cannes France
109C3 Cann River Aust
34H1 Cañoas Brazil
13D1 Canoe L Can
9C3 Canon City USA
108B2 Canopus Aust
5H4 Canora Can
109C2 Canowindra Aust
45C2 Cansore Pt Irish Rep
43E4 Canterbury Eng
111B2 Canterbury Bight B NZ
111B2 Canterbury Plains NZ
77D4 Can Tho Viet
Canton = Guangzhou
13 Canton Mississippi, USA
18B1 Canton Missouri, USA
10B2 Canton Ohio, USA
12E2 Cantwell USA
20C2 Canyon City USA
12J2 Canyon Range Mts Can
20B2 Canyonville USA
98C3 Canzar Angola
76D1 Cao Bang Viet
31B2 Capanema Brazil
35B2 Capão Bonito Brazil
48B3 Capbreton France
24B2 Cap Corrientes C Mexico
52A2 Cap Corse C Corse
101D2 Cap d'Ambre C Madag
48B2 Cap de la Hague C France
15D1 Cap-de-la-Madeleine Can
6C3 Cap de Nouvelle-France C Can
51C2 Capdepera Spain
23A2 Cap de Tancitiario C Mexico
109C4 Cape Barren I Aust
103J6 Cape Basin Atlantic O
7E5 Cape Breton I Can
97B4 Cape Coast Ghana
15D2 Cape Cod B USA
6C3 Cape Dorset Can
17C1 Cape Fear R USA
18C2 Cape Girardeau USA
6B3 Cape Henrietta Maria C Can
Cape Horn = Cabo de Hornos
104E3 Cape Johnston Depth Pacific O
35C1 Capelinha Brazil
4B3 Cape Lisburne USA

100A2 Capelongo Angola
15D3 Cape May USA
5F5 Cape Mendocino USA
98B3 Capenda Camulemba Angola
4F2 Cape Perry Can
100B4 Cape Province S Africa
7A4 Cape Tatnam Can
100A4 Cape Town S Africa
102G4 Cape Verde Is Atlantic O
102G4 Cape Verde Basin Atlantic O
12F3 Cape Yakataga USA
107D2 Cape York Pen Aust
46A1 Cap Gris Nez C France
26C3 Cap-Haitien Haiti
31B2 Capim R Brazil
27P2 Cap Moule à Chique C St Lucia
53C3 Capo Isola de Correnti C Italy
53C3 Capo Rizzuto C Italy
55A3 Capo Santa Maria di Leuca C Italy
53B3 Capo San Vito Italy
53C3 Capo Spartivento C Italy
27P2 Cap Pt St Lucia
53B2 Capri I Italy
100B2 Caprivi Strip Region, Namibia
52A2 Cap Rosso C Corse
102H4 Cap Vert C Sen
32C4 Caquetá R Colombia
54B2 Caracal Rom
33E3 Caracaraí Brazil
32D1 Caracas Ven
35B2 Caraguatatuba Brazil
29B3 Carahue Chile
35C1 Caraí Brazil
35C2 Carandaí Brazil
31C6 Carangola Brazil
54B1 Caransebeş Rom
107P2 Carappee Hill Mt Aust
26A3 Caratasca Honduras
35C1 Caratinga Brazil
51B2 Caravaca Spain
35D1 Caravelas Brazil
18C2 Carbondale Illinois, USA
53A3 Carbonia Sardegna
7E5 Carborear Can
5G4 Carcaion Can
99E1 Carcar Mts Somalia
48C3 Carcassonne France
4E3 Carcross Can
23B2 Cardel Mexico
25D2 Cárdenas Cuba
23B1 Cárdenas Mexico
43C4 Cardiff Wales
43B3 Cardigan Wales
43B3 Cardigan B Wales
13E2 Cardston Can
54B1 Careí Rom
33F4 Carenero Brazil
34A2 Carén Chile
14B2 Carey USA
48B2 Carhaix-Plouguer France
29D3 Carhué Arg
31C6 Cariacica Brazil
5J4 Caribou Can
5G4 Caribou Mts Alberta, Can
5F4 Caribou Mts British Columbia, Can
79B3 Carigara Phil
32D1 Caripito Ven
33E1 Caripito Ven
15C1 Carleton Place Can
101G1 Carletonville S Africa
18C2 Carlinville USA
42C2 Carlisle Eng
15C2 Carlisle USA
34C3 Carlos Arg

35C1 Carlos Chagas Brazil
45C2 Carlow County, Irish Rep
45C2 Carlow Irish Rep
21B3 Carlsbad California, USA
9C3 Carlsbad New Mexico, USA
54H5 Carlyle Can
12G2 Carmacks Can
47B2 Carmagnola Italy
43B4 Carmarthen Wales
43B4 Carmarthen B Wales
22B2 Carmel California, USA
16C2 Carmel New York, USA
94B2 Carmel,Mt Israel
34D2 Carmelo Urug
34C2 Carmel Valley USA
9B4 Carmen I Mexico
29D4 Carmen de Patagones Arg
35B1 Carmi USA
21A2 Carmichael USA
35B1 Carmo do Paranaiba Brazil
50A2 Carmona Spain
106A3 Carnarvon Aust
100A4 Carnarvon S Africa
35D1 Carncacá Brazil
45C1 Carndonagh Irish Rep
106B5 Carnegie,L Aust
98B2 Carnot CAR
108A2 Carnot,C Aust
17B2 Carol City USA
31B3 Carolina Brazil
101H1 Carolina S Africa
17C1 Carolina Beach USA
104F3 Caroline Is Pacific O
60B4 Carpathians Mts E Europe
59D3 Carpaţii Orientali Mts Rom
106C2 Carpentaria,G of Aust
83C5 Carpenter Ridge Indian O
49D3 Carpentras France
52B2 Carpi Italy
22C3 Carpinteria USA
17B2 Carrabelle USA
52B2 Carrara Italy
41B3 Carrauntoohill Mt Irish Rep
45C2 Carrickmacross Irish Rep
45B2 Carrick on Shannon Irish Rep
45C2 Carrick-on-Suir Irish Rep
108A2 Carrieton Aust
8D2 Carrington USA
50B1 Carrión R Spain
10A2 Carroll USA
17A1 Carrollton Georgia, USA
14A3 Carrollton Kentucky, USA
18B2 Carrollton Missouri, USA
18C2 Carruthersville USA
60E5 Carsamba Turk
92B2 Carsamba R Turk
8B3 Carson City USA
14B2 Carsonville USA
26B4 Cartagena Colombia
51B2 Cartagena Spain
32B3 Cartago Colombia
25D4 Cartago Costa Rica
111C2 Carterton NZ
18B2 Carthage Missouri, USA
15C2 Carthage New York, USA
19B3 Carthage Texas, USA
106B2 Cartier I Timor S
7E4 Cartwright Can
31D3 Caruaru Brazil

33E1 Carúpano Ven
46B1 Carven France
34A2 Casablanca Chile
96B1 Casablanca Mor
35B2 Casa Branca Brazil
9B3 Casa Grande USA
52A1 Casale Monferrato Italy
47D2 Casalmaggiore Italy
34C3 Casares Arg
13C3 Cascade Mts Can/USA
111A2 Cascade Pt NZ
8A2 Cascade Range Mts
USA
30F3 Cascavel Brazil
53B2 Caserta Italy
112C9 Casey Base Ant
45C2 Cashel Irish Rep
34C2 Casilda Arg
107E3 Casino Aust
32B5 Casma Peru
51B1 Caspe Spain
8C2 Casper USA
65G6 Caspian S USSR
14C3 Cass USA
100B2 Cassamba Angola
46B1 Cassel France
12J3 Cassiar Can
4E3 Cassiar Mts Can
35A1 Cassilândia Brazil
53B2 Cassino Italy
22C3 Castaic USA
34B2 Castaño R Arg
47D2 Castelfranco Italy
49D3 Castellane France
34D3 Castelli Arg
51B2 Castellón de la Plana
Spain
31C3 Castelo Brazil
50A2 Castelo Branco Port
48C3 Castelsarrasin France
53B3 Castelvetrano Italy
108B3 Casterton Aust
50B1 Castilla La Nueva
Region, Spain
50B1 Castilla La Vieja
Region, Spain
41B3 Castlebar Irish Rep
44A3 Castlebay Scot
42C2 Castle Douglas Scot
20C1 Castlegar Can
45B2 Castleisland Irish Rep
108B3 Castlemain Aust
45B2 Castlerea Irish Rep
109C2 Castlereagh Aust
48C3 Castres-sur-l'Agout
France
27E4 Castries St Lucia
29A4 Castro Arg
30F3 Castro Brazil
31D4 Castro Alves Brazil
53C3 Castrovillari Italy
22B2 Castroville USA
111A2 Caswell Sd NZ
25E2 Cat / The Bahamas
79B3 Catabalogan Phil
32A5 Catacaos Peru
35C2 Cataguases Brazil
19B3 Catahoula L USA
35B1 Cataláo Brazil
51C1 Cataluña Region, Spain
30C4 Catamarca Arg
30C4 Catamarca State, Arg
101C2 Catandica Mozam
79B3 Catanduanes I Phil
31B6 Catanduva Brazil
53C3 Catania Italy
53C3 Catanzaro Italy
108A2 Catastrophe,C Aust
26C5 Catatumbo R Ven
16A2 Catawissa USA
23B2 Catemaco Mexico
49D3 Cateur Corse
52A2 Catéggio Corse
98B3 Catete Angola
97A3 Catio Guinea-Bissau
7A4 Cat Lake Can
13D3 Catlegar Can

107E3 Cato I Aust
25D2 Catoche,C Mexico
16A3 Catoctin Mt USA
15C3 Catonsville USA
34C3 Catrilo Arg
15D2 Catskill USA
15D2 Catskill Mts USA
32C2 Cauca R Colombia
31D2 Caucaia Brazil
32B2 Caucasia Colombia
Caucasus = Bol'shoy
Kavkaz
46B1 Caudry France
98B3 Caungula Angola
29B3 Cauquenes Chile
87B2 Cauvery R India
49D3 Cavaillon France
47D1 Cavalese Italy
97B4 Cavally R Lib
45C2 Cavan County,
Irish Rep
45C2 Cavan Irish Rep
79B3 Cavite Phil
31C2 Caxias Brazil
32C4 Caxias Brazil
30F4 Caxias do Sul Brazil
98B3 Caxito Angola
17B1 Cayce USA
93D1 Çayeli Turk
33G3 Cayenne French
Guiana
46A1 Cayeux-sur-Mer
France
25E3 Cayman Brac /
Caribbean S
26A3 Cayman Is
Caribbean S
26A3 Cayman Trench
Caribbean S
99E2 Caynabo Somalia
25E3 Cayo Romano / Cuba
25D3 Cayos Miskitos Is Nic
26A2 Cay Sal / Caribbean S
100B2 Cazombo Angola
Ceará = Fortaleza
31C3 Ceara State, Brazil
79B3 Cebu Phil
79B3 Cebu / Phil
16B3 Cecilton USA
52B2 Cecina Italy
8B3 Cedar City USA
19A3 Cedar Creek Res USA
5J4 Cedar L Can
10A2 Cedar Rapids USA
17A1 Cedartown USA
24A2 Cedros I Mexico
106C4 Ceduna Aust
99E2 Ceelbuur Somalia
99E1 Ceerigaabo Somalia
53B3 Cefalù Italy
59B3 Cegléd Hung
100A2 Cela Angola
24B2 Celaya Mexico
Celebes = Sulawesi
70C3 Celebes S S E Asia
14B2 Celina USA
52C1 Celje Yugos
56C2 Celle Germany
71E4 Cendrawasih Pen
Indon
47C2 Ceno R Italy
19B3 Center USA
16C2 Center Moriches USA
17A1 Center Point USA
47D2 Cento Italy
44B3 Central Region, Scot
98B2 Central African
Republic Africa
16D2 Central Falls USA
18C2 Centralia Illinois, USA
8A2 Centralia Washington,
USA
20B2 Central Point USA
71F4 Central Range Mts
PNG
16A3 Centreville Maryland,
USA
78C4 Cepu Indon

Ceram = Seram
71D4 Ceram Sea Indon
34C3 Cereales Arg
31B5 Ceres Brazil
100A4 Ceres S Africa
22B2 Ceres USA
48C2 Cergy-Pontoise France
52C2 Cerignola Italy
60C5 Cernavodă Rom
9C4 Cerralvo I Mexico
23A1 Cerritos Mexico
34B2 Cerro Aconcagua Mt
Arg
23B1 Cerro Azul Mexico
34A3 Cerro Campanario Mt
Chile
34C2 Cerro Champaqui Mt
Arg
23A2 Cerro Cuachaia Mt
Mexico
23B1 Cerro de Astillero
Mexico
34B2 Cerro de Olivares Mt
Arg
32B6 Cerro de Pasco Mt
Peru
27D3 Cerro de Punta Mt
Puerto Rico
23A2 Cerro El Cantado Mt
Mexico
34B3 Cerro El Nevado Mt
Arg
23A2 Cerro Grande Mts
Mexico
34A2 Cerro Juncal Mt Arg/
Chile
23A1 Cerro la Ardilla Mts
Mexico
34B1 Cerro las Tortolas Mt
Arg
23A2 Cerro Laurel Mt Mexico
34A3 Cerro Mercedario Mt
Arg
34A3 Cerro Murallón Mt Chile
27C4 Cerron Mt Ven
34B3 Cerro Payún Mt Arg
23B2 Cerro Penón del Rosario
Mt Mexico
34B2 Cerro Sosneado Mt
Arg
23A2 Cerro Teotepec Mt
Mexico
34B2 Cerro Tupungato Mt
Arg
23B2 Cerro Yucuyacau Mt
Mexico
47C2 Cervo R Italy
52B2 Cesena Italy
60B2 Cēsis USSR
57C3 České Budějovice
Czech
57C3 České Země Region,
Czech
59B3 Českomoravská
Vysočina U Czech
55C3 Çeşme Turk
107E4 Cessnock Aust
52C2 Cetina R Yugos
98B1 Ceuta N W Africa
92C2 Ceyhan Turk
92C2 Ceyhan R Turk
93C2 Ceylanpınar Turk
Ceylon = Sri Lanka
63B2 Chaa-Khol USSR
48C2 Chaâteaudun France
47B1 Chablais Region,
France
34C2 Chacabuco Arg
32B5 Chachapoyas Peru
34B3 Chacharramendi Arg
84C3 Chachran Pak
30D4 Chaco State, Arg
98B1 Chad Republic, Africa
98B1 Chad L C Africa
34B3 Chadileuvu R Arg
8C2 Chadron USA
18C2 Chaffee USA
85A3 Chagai Pak
63F2 Chagda USSR

84B2 Chaghcharan Afghan
104B4 Chagos Arch Indian O
27L1 Chaguanas Trinidad
91D4 Chāh Bahār Iran
76C2 Chai Badan Thai
86B2 Chāibāsa India
76C3 Chaine des
Cardamomes Mts
Camb
98C4 Chaine des Mitumba
Mts Zaïre
76C2 Chaiyaphum Thai
34D2 Chajari Arg
84C2 Chakwal Pak
30B2 Chala Peru
100C2 Chalabesa Zambia
84A2 Chalap Dalam Mts
Afghan
73C4 Chaling China
85C4 Chālisgaon India
12F1 Chalkyitsik USA
46C2 Challerange France
46C2 Châlons sur Marne
France
49C2 Chalon sur Saône
France
57C3 Cham Germany
84B2 Chaman Pak
84D2 Chamba India
85D3 Chambal R India
15C3 Chambersburg USA
49D2 Chambéry France
46B2 Chambly France
85A3 Chambor Kalat Pak
90B3 Chamgordan Iran
34B2 Chamical Arg
47F2 Chamonix France
86A2 Champa India
49C2 Champagne Region,
France
101G1 Champagne Castle Mt
Lesotho
47A1 Champagnole France
10B2 Champaign USA
76D3 Champassak Laos
10C2 Champlain,L USA
87B2 Chämräjnagar India
3084 Chañaral Chile
34A3 Chanco Chile
4D3 Chandalar USA
4D3 Chandalar R USA
84D2 Chandigarh India
86C2 Chandpur Bang
85D5 Chandrapur India
91D4 Chanf Iran
101C2 Changara Mozam
74B2 Changbai China
69E2 Changchun China
73C4 Changde China
68E4 Chang-hua Taiwan
76D2 Changjiang China
73D3 Chang Jiang R China
74B2 Changjin N Korea
73C4 Changsha China
72E3 Changshu China
74A2 Changtu China
72B2 Changwu China
74B3 Changyŏn N Korea
72C2 Changzhi China
73D3 Changzhou China
72E1 Chaoyang China
48B2 Channel Is UK
9B3 Channel Is USA
7E5 Channel Port-aux-
Basques Can
76C3 Chanthaburi Thai
46B2 Chantilly France
18A2 Chanute USA
73D5 Chaoàn China
73D5 Chao'an China
73D3 Chao Hu L China
76C3 Chao Phraya R Thai
72E1 Chaoyang China
31C4 Chapada Diamantina
Mts Brazil
31C2 Chapadinha Brazil
23A1 Chapala Mexico
23A1 Chapala,Lac de L
Mexico

61H3	Chapayevo USSR
30F4	Chapecó Brazil
27H1	Chapelton Jamaica
7B5	Chapleau Can
61E3	Chaplygin USSR
112C3	Charcot I Ant
80E2	Chardzhou USSR
48C2	Charente R France
98B1	Chari R Chad
98B1	Chari Baguirmi Region, Chad
84B1	Charikar Afghan
18B1	Chariton R USA
33F2	Charity Guyana
85D3	Charkhāri India
46C1	Charleroi Belg
18C2	Charleston Illinois, USA
18C2	Charleston Missouri, USA
11C3	Charleston S Carolina, USA
10B3	Charleston W Virginia, USA
98C3	Charlesville Zaïre
107D3	Charleville Aust
49C2	Charleville-Mézières France
14A1	Charlevoix USA
14B2	Charlotte Michigan, USA
11B3	Charlotte N Carolina, USA
17B2	Charlotte Harbor B USA
10C3	Charlottesville USA
7D5	Charlottetown Can
27K1	Charlotteville Tobago
108B3	Charlton Aust
10C1	Charlton I Can
84C2	Charsadda Pak
107D3	Charters Towers Aust
48C2	Chartres France
29E3	Chascomús Arg
13D2	Chase Can
48B2	Châteaubriant France
48C2	Châteaudun France
48B2	Châteaulin France
48C2	Châteauroux France
46D2	Château-Salins France
49C2	Château-Thierry France
46C1	Châtelet Belg
48C2	Châtellerault France
43E4	Chatham Eng
7D5	Chatham New Brunswick, Can
16C1	Chatham New York, USA
14B2	Chatham Ontario, Can
13A2	Chatham Sd Can
12H3	Chatham Str USA
49C2	Châtillon France
47B2	Châtillon Italy
16B3	Chatsworth USA
17B1	Chattahoochee USA
17A1	Chattahoochee R USA
11B3	Chattanooga USA
76A1	Chauk Burma
49D2	Chaumont France
46B2	Chauny France
73A3	Chau Phu Viet
50A1	Chaves Port
50B2	Chazaouet Alg
34C2	Chazón Arg
32C2	Chcontá Colombia
57C2	Cheb Czech
65F4	Cheboksary USSR
10B2	Cheboygan USA
74B3	Chech'on S Korea
85C3	Chechro Pak
18A2	Checotah USA
76A2	Cheduba I Burma
108B1	Cheepie Aust
96B2	Chegga Maur
100C2	Chegutu Zim
20B1	Chehalis USA
74B4	Cheju S Korea
74B4	Cheju do I S Korea
74B4	Cheju-haehyŏp Str S Korea
63F2	Chekunda USSR
26U1	Chelan,L USA
90B2	Cheleken USSR
34B3	Chelforo Arg
80D1	Chelkar USSR
59C2	Chelm Pol
58B2	Chelmno Pol
43C4	Chelmsford Eng
65H4	Chelyabinsk USSR
101C2	Chemba Mozam
57C2	Chemnitz Germany
84D2	Chenab R India/Pak
96B2	Chenachane Alg
20C1	Cheney USA
18A2	Cheney Res USA
72D1	Chengde China
73A3	Chengdu China
72E2	Chengshan Jiao Pt China
73C4	Chenxi China
73C4	Chen Xian China
73D3	Chen Xian China
32B5	Chepén Peru
34B2	Chepes Arg
48C2	Cher R France
23A2	Cheran Mexico
17C1	Cheraw USA
48B2	Cherbourg France
96C1	Cherchell Alg
63C2	Cheremkhovo USSR
60E2	Cherepovets USSR
60D4	Cherkassy USSR
61F5	Cherkessk USSR
60D3	Chernigov USSR
60D2	Chernobyl USSR
60C4	Chernovtsy USSR
61J2	Chernukha USSR
60B3	Chernyakhovsk USSR
61G4	Chernyye Zemli Region, USSR
18A2	Cherokees,L o'the USA
34A3	Cherquenco Chile
86C1	Cherrapunji India
60C3	Cherven' USSR
59C2	Chervonograd USSR
10C3	Chesapeake B USA
43C3	Cheshire County, Eng
16C1	Cheshire USA
64F3	Chëshskaya Guba B USSR
21A1	Chester California, USA
43C3	Chester Eng
18C2	Chester Illinois, USA
16C1	Chester Massachusets, USA
15C3	Chester Pennsylvania, USA
17B1	Chester S Carolina, USA
16A3	Chester USA
42D3	Chesterfield Eng
6A3	Chesterfield Inlet Can
16A3	Chestertown USA
25D3	Chetumal Mexico
13C1	Chetwynd Can
12J2	Chevak USA
111B2	Cheviot NZ
40C2	Cheviots Hills Eng/Scot
13D3	Chewelah USA
8C2	Cheyenne USA
86A1	Chhapra India
85D4	Chhatarpur India
85D4	Chhindwāra India
86B1	Chhuka Bhutan
73E5	Chia'i Taiwan
100A2	Chiange Angola
76C2	Chiang Kham Thai
76B2	Chiang Mai Thai
47B2	Chiavenna Italy
74E3	Chiba Japan
100A2	Chibia Angola
7C4	Chibougamau Can
75A1	Chiburi-jima I Japan
101C3	Chibuto Mozam
101B2	Chicago USA
14A2	Chicago Heights USA
12G3	Chichagof I USA
43D4	Chichester Eng
75B1	Chichibu Japan
69G4	Chichi-jima I Japan
11B3	Chickamauga L USA
19C3	Chickasawhay R USA
9D3	Chickasha USA
12F2	Chicken USA
32A5	Chiclayo Peru
8A3	Chico USA
29C4	Chico R Arg
101C2	Chicoa Mozam
15D2	Chicopee USA
7C5	Chicoutimi Can
101C3	Chicualacuala Mozam
87B2	Chidambaram India
6D3	Chidley,C Can
17B2	Chiefland USA
99C3	Chiengi Zambia
47B2	Chieri Italy
46C2	Chiers R France
47C1	Chiesa Italy
47D2	Chiese R Italy
52B2	Chieti Italy
72D1	Chifeng China
12C3	Chigidak,Mt USA
4C3	Chignik Mts USA
23B2	Chignahuapán Mexico
12C3	Chignik USA
24B2	Chihuahua Mexico
87B2	Chik Ballāpur India
87B2	Chikmagalūr India
12C2	Chikuminuk L USA
101C2	Chikwawa Malawi
76A1	Chi-kyaw Burma
87C1	Chilakalūrupet India
23B2	Chilapa Mexico
87B3	Chilaw Sri Lanka
28B6	Chile Republic
34B2	Chilecito Mendoza, Arg
100B2	Chililabombwe Zambia
86B2	Chilka L India
13C2	Chilko R Can
13C2	Chilkotin R Can
34A3	Chillán Chile
34D3	Chillar Arg
18B2	Chillicothe Missouri, USA
14B3	Chillicothe Ohio, USA
13C3	Chilliwack Can
86B1	Chilmari India
101C2	Chilongozi Zambia
22D2	Chiloquin USA
24C3	Chilpancingo Mexico
43D4	Chiltern Hills Upland Eng
14A2	Chilton USA
101C2	Chilumba Malawi
69E4	Chi-lung Taiwan
101C2	Chilwa L Malawi
100C2	Chimanimani Zim
46C1	Chimay Belg
65G5	Chimbay USSR
32B4	Chimborazo Mt Ecuador
32B5	Chimbote Peru
65H5	Chimkent USSR
101C2	Chimoio Mozam
67E3	China Republic, Asia
	China National Republic = Taiwan
25D3	Chinandega Nic
32B6	Chincha Alta Peru
109D1	Chinchilla Aust
101C2	Chinde Mozam
86C2	Chindwin R Burma
100B2	Chingola Zambia
100A2	Chinguar Angola
96A2	Chinguetti Maur
74B3	Chinhae S Korea
100C2	Chinhoyi Zim
12D3	Chiniak,C USA
84C2	Chiniot Pak
74B3	Chinju S Korea
98C2	Chinko R CAR
75B1	Chino Japan
101C2	Chinsali Zambia
52B1	Chioggia Italy
101C2	Chipata Zambia
101C3	Chipinge Zim
87B1	Chiplūn India
43C4	Chippenham Eng
10A2	Chippewa Falls USA
32A4	Chira R Peru
87C1	Chirāla India
101C3	Chiredzi Zim
95A2	Chirfa Niger
32A2	Chiriquí Mt Panama
54C2	Chiripan Bulg
32A2	Chirripo Grande Mt Costa Rica
100B2	Chirundu Zim
100B2	Chisamba Zambia
73B4	Chishui He R China
47B2	Chisone R Italy
68D1	Chita USSR
100A2	Chitado Angola
100A2	Chitembo Angola
12F2	Chitina USA
12F2	Chitina R USA
87B2	Chitradurga India
84C1	Chitral Pak
32A2	Chitré Panama
86C2	Chittagong Bang
85C4	Chittaurgarh India
87B2	Chittoor India
100B2	Chitungwiza Zim
47D1	Chiusa Italy
47B2	Chivasso Italy
29D2	Chivilcoy Arg
100C2	Chivu Zim
75A1	Chizu Japan
29C3	Choele Choel Arg
34C3	Choique Arg
24B2	Choix Mexico
58B2	Chojnice Pol
99D1	Choke Mts Eth
48B2	Cholet France
23B2	Cholula Mexico
100B2	Choma Zambia
86B1	Chomo Yummo Mt China/India
57C2	Chomutov Czech
63C1	Chona R USSR
74B3	Ch'ŏnan S Korea
76C3	Chon Buri Thai
32A4	Chone Ecuador
74B2	Ch'ŏngjin N Korea
74B3	Chongju S Korea
74B3	Ch'ŏngju S Korea
100A2	Chongoroi Angola
73B4	Chongqing China
74B3	Chŏngŭp S Korea
74B3	Chŏnju S Korea
86B1	Chooyu Mt China/Nepal
59D3	Chortkov USSR
74B3	Ch'ŏrwŏn N Korea
59B2	Chorzow Pol
74E3	Choshi Japan
34A3	Chos-Malal Arg
58B2	Choszczno Pol
86A2	Chotanāgpur Region, India
96C1	Chott Melrhir Alg
22B2	Chowchilla USA
63D3	Choybalsan Mongolia
6A3	Chantrey Inlet B Can
61H2	Chaykovskiy USSR
111B2	Christchurch NZ
101G1	Christiana S Africa
6D2	Christian,C Can
12H3	Christian Sd USA
6E3	Christianshab Greenland
104D4	Christmas I Indian O

61G2 **Christopol** USSR
65J5 **Chu** USSR
65J5 **Chu** *R* USSR
29C4 **Chubut** State, Arg
29C4 **Chubut** *R* Arg
76D2 **Chudovo** USSR
64D4 **Chudskoye Ozer** *L*
    USSR
4D3 **Chugach Mts** USA
12E2 **Chugiak** USA
75A1 **Chūgoku-sanchi** *Mts*
    Japan
29F2 **Chui** Brazil
29B3 **Chuillán** Chile
77C5 **Chukai** Malay
76D2 **Chu Lai** Viet
21B3 **Chula Vista** USA
12E2 **Chulitna** USA
63E2 **Chulman** USSR
32A5 **Chulucanas** Peru
30C2 **Chulumani** Bol
65K4 **Chulym** USSR
63A2 **Chulym** *R* USSR
63B2 **Chuma** USSR
84D2 **Chumar** India
63F2 **Chumikan** USSR
77B3 **Chumphon** Thai
74B3 **Ch'unch'ŏn** S Korea
86B2 **Chunchura** India
74B3 **Ch'ungju** S Korea
    Chungking=Chongqing
99D3 **Chunya** Tanz
63C1 **Chunya** *R* USSR
27L1 **Chupara** Pt Trinidad
30C3 **Chuquicamata** Chile
52A1 **Chur** Switz
86C2 **Churāchāndpur** India
7A4 **Churchill** USA
7D4 **Churchill** *R* Labrador,
    Can
7A4 **Churchill** *R* Manitoba,
    Can
7A4 **Churchill,C** Can
7D4 **Churchill Falls** Can
5H4 **Churchill** *L* Can
84C3 **Chūru** India
23A2 **Churumuco** Mexico
61J2 **Chusovoy** USSR
61G2 **Chuvashskaya ASSR**
    Republic, USSR
68B4 **Chuxiong** China
76D3 **Chu Yang Sin** *Mt* Viet
76B3 **Cianjur** Indon
47D2 **Ciano d'Enza** Italy
35A2 **Cianorte** Brazil
58C2 **Ciechanow** Pol
25E2 **Ciego de Avila** Cuba
32C1 **Ciénaga** Colombia
25D2 **Cienfuegos** Cuba
59B3 **Cieszyn** Pol
51B2 **Cieza** Spain
92B2 **Cihanbeyli** Turk
23A2 **Cihuatlán** Mexico
78B4 **Cijulang** Indon
78B4 **Cilacap** Indon
54C1 **Cimpina** Rom
51C1 **Cinca** *R* Spain
52C2 **Čincer** *Mt* Yugos
10B3 **Cincinnati** USA
54B1 **Cindrelu** *Mt* Rom
55C3 **Cine** *R* Turk
46C1 **Ciney** Belg
34B3 **Cipolletti** Arg
4C3 **Circle** Alaska, USA
14B3 **Circleville** USA
78B4 **Cirebon** Indon
43D4 **Cirencester** Eng
47D2 **Citadella** Italy
100A4 **Citrusdal** S Africa
52B2 **Citta del Vaticano** Italy
52B2 **Città di Castello** Italy
24B2 **Ciudad Acuña** Mexico
23A2 **Ciudad Altamirano**
    Mexico
33E2 **Ciudad Bolivar** Ven
24B2 **Ciudad Camargo**
    Mexico

25C3 **Ciudad del Carmen**
    Mexico
23B1 **Ciudad del Maiz**
    Mexico
51C1 **Ciudadela** Spain
33E2 **Ciudad Guayana** Ven
24B3 **Ciudad Guzman**
    Mexico
23A2 **Ciudad Hidalgo**
    Mexico
24B1 **Ciudad Juárez** Mexico
9C4 **Ciudad Lerdo** Mexico
24C2 **Ciudad Madero**
    Mexico
23B2 **Ciudad Mendoza**
    Mexico
24B2 **Ciudad Obregon**
    Mexico
27C4 **Ciudad Ojeda** Ven
33E2 **Ciudad Piar** Ven
50B2 **Ciudad Real** Spain
50A1 **Ciudad Rodrigo** Spain
24C2 **Ciudad Valles** Mexico
24C2 **Ciudad Victoria**
    Mexico
52B2 **Civitavecchia** Italy
93D2 **Cizre** Turk
43E4 **Clacton-on-Sea** Eng
5G4 **Claire,L** Can
14C2 **Clairton** USA
47A1 **Clairvaux** France
17A1 **Clamecy** France
100A4 **Clanwilliam** S Africa
45C2 **Clara** Irish Rep
34D3 **Claraz** Arg
45B3 **Clare** County,
    Irish Rep
14B2 **Clare** USA
45A2 **Clare** *I* Irish Rep
15D2 **Claremont** USA
18A2 **Claremore** USA
45B2 **Claremorris** Irish Rep
109D1 **Clarence** *R* Aust
111B2 **Clarence** *R* NZ
106C2 **Clarence Str** Aust
12H3 **Clarence Str** USA
19B3 **Clarendon** USA
7E5 **Clarenville** Can
5G4 **Claresholm** Can
18A1 **Clarinda** USA
15C2 **Clarion** Pennsylvania,
    USA
24A3 **Clarión** *I* Mexico
15C2 **Clarion** *R* USA
105J3 **Clarion Fracture Zone**
    Pacific O
11B3 **Clark Hill Res** USA
14B2 **Clark,Pt** Can
14B3 **Clarksburg** USA
11A3 **Clarksdale** USA
12C3 **Clarks Point** USA
20C1 **Clarkston** USA
18B2 **Clarksville** Arkansas,
    USA
35A1 **Claro** *R* Brazil
29D3 **Claromecó** Arg
18A2 **Clay Center** USA
44D2 **Claymore** Oilfield
    N Sea
13B3 **Clayoquot Sd** Can
9C3 **Clayton** New Mexico,
    USA
15C2 **Clayton** New York,
    USA
45B2 **Clear,C** Irish Rep
12E3 **Cleare,C** USA
13D1 **Clear Hills** *Mts* Can
21A2 **Clear L** USA
20B2 **Clear Lake Res** USA
13D2 **Clearwater** Can
11B3 **Clearwater** USA
13E1 **Clearwater** *R* Can
13C2 **Clearwater** *L* Can
9D3 **Cleburne** USA
22B1 **Clements** USA
79A3 **Cleopatra Needle** *Mt*
    Phil
107D3 **Clermont** Aust

46B2 **Clermont** France
46C2 **Clermont-en-Argonne**
    France
49C2 **Clermont-Ferrand**
    France
46D1 **Clervaux** Germany
47D1 **Cles** Italy
108A2 **Cleve** Aust
42D2 **Cleveland** County, Eng
19B3 **Cleveland** Mississippi,
    USA
10B2 **Cleveland** Ohio, USA
11B3 **Cleveland** Tennessee,
    USA
19A3 **Cleveland** Texas, USA
41B3 **Clew** *B* Irish Rep
45A2 **Clifden** Irish Rep
109D1 **Clifton** Aust
16B2 **Clifton** New Jersey,
    USA
14A1 **Clifton Hills** Aust
13F3 **Climax** Can
18B2 **Clinton** Arkansas,
    USA
5F4 **Clinton** Can
16C2 **Clinton** Connecticut,
    USA
16D1 **Clinton**
    Massachusetts, USA
19B3 **Clinton** Mississippi,
    USA
18B2 **Clinton** Missouri, USA
16B2 **Clinton** New Jersey,
    USA
4H3 **Clinton-Colden L**
    Can
21A3 **Clipperton I** Pacific O
30C2 **Cliza** Bol
45B3 **Clonakilty** Irish Rep
107D3 **Cloncurry** Aust
45C1 **Clones** Irish Rep
45C2 **Clonmel** Irish Rep
10A2 **Cloquet** USA
12C2 **Cloudy Mt** USA
22C2 **Clovis** California, USA
9C3 **Clovis** New Mexico,
    USA
60B4 **Cluj** Rom
54B1 **Cluj-Napoca** Rom
47B1 **Cluses** France
47C2 **Clusone** Italy
111A3 **Clutha** *R* NZ
43C3 **Clwyd** County, Wales
6D2 **Clyde** Can
111A3 **Clyde** NZ
42B2 **Clyde** *R* Scot
23A2 **Coahuayana** Mexico
23A2 **Coalcomán** Mexico
13E2 **Coaldale** Can
21B2 **Coaldale** USA
21A2 **Coalinga** USA
33E5 **Coari** *R* Brazil
17A1 **Coastal Plain** USA
4E4 **Coast Mts** Can
8A2 **Coast Ranges** *Mts*
    USA
42B2 **Coatbridge** Scot
23B2 **Coatepec** Mexico
16B3 **Coatesville** USA
15D1 **Coaticook** Can
6B3 **Coats I** Can
112B1 **Coats Land** Region,
    Ant
25C3 **Coatzacoalcos** Mexico
7C5 **Cobalt** Can
25C3 **Cobán** Guatemala
107D4 **Cobar** Aust
109C3 **Cobargo** Aust
45B3 **Cobh** Irish Rep
32D6 **Cobija** Bol
16B1 **Cobleskill** USA
51B2 **Cobo de Palos** *C*
    Spain
7C5 **Cobourg** Can
106C2 **Cobourg Pen** Aust
57C2 **Coburg** Germany
32B4 **Coca** Ecuador
32C4 **Coca** USA
30C2 **Cochabamba** Bol

46D1 **Cochem** Germany
87B3 **Cochin** India
13E2 **Cochrane** Alberta, Can
7B5 **Cochrane** Ontario, Can
108B2 **Cockburn** Aust
16A3 **Cockeysville** USA
27H1 **Cockpit Country,The**
    Jamaica
25D3 **Coco** *R* Honduras/Nic
98A2 **Cocobeach** Gabon
27L1 **Cocos B** Trinidad
104C4 **Cocos Is** Indian O
10C2 **Cod,C** USA
111A3 **Codfish I** NZ
7D4 **Cod I** Can
47C2 **Codigoro** Italy
31C2 **Codó** Brazil
47C2 **Codogno** Italy
32A3 **Cojimíes** Ecuador
50A1 **Coimbra** Port
32C3 **Coimbatore** India
50A1 **Coimbra** Port
35B6 **Coihaique** Chile
87B2 **Coimbatore** India
29B5 **Coihaique** Chile
87B2 **Coimbatore** India
50A1 **Coimbra** Port
108A2 **Coffin B** Aust
109D2 **Coff's Harbour** Aust
23B2 **Cofre de Perote** *Mt*
    Mexico
48B2 **Cognac** France
52C2 **Cohoes** USA
108B3 **Cohuna** Aust
29B5 **Coihaique** Chile
87B2 **Coimbatore** India
50A1 **Coimbra** Port
101G1 **Colenso** S Africa
45C1 **Coleraine** N Ire
111B2 **Coleridge,L** NZ
100B4 **Colesberg** S Africa
22C1 **Coleville** USA
21A2 **Colfax** California, USA
19B3 **Colfax** Louisiana, USA
20C1 **Colfax** Washington,
    USA
24B3 **Colima** Mexico
23A2 **Colima** State, Mexico
34A2 **Colina** Chile
44A3 **Coll** *I* Scot
109C1 **Collarenebri** Aust
108A2 **Colle de Tende** *P*
    France/Italy
12E2 **College** USA
17B1 **College Park** Georgia,
    USA
16A3 **College Park**
    Washington, USA
19A3 **College Station** USA
106A4 **Collie** Aust
106B2 **Collier B** Aust
46A1 **Collines de L'Artois**
    Mts France
46A2 **Collines de Thiérache**
    France
14B2 **Collingwood** Can
110B2 **Collingwood** NZ
19C3 **Collins** Mississippi,
    USA
4H2 **Collinson Pen** Can
107D3 **Collinsville** Aust
18C2 **Collinsville** Illinois,
    USA

18A2 Collinsville Oklahoma, USA
34A3 Collipulli Chile
49D2 Colmar France
Cologne = Köln
35B2 Colômbia Brazil
32B3 Colombia Republic, S America
15C3 Colombo Sri Lanka
87B3 Colombo Sri Lanka
25D2 Colon Cuba
32B2 Colón Panama
29E2 Colonia Urug
34D2 Colonia del Sacramento Urug
34B3 Colonia 25 de Mayo Arg
29C5 Colonia Las Heras Arg
44A3 Colonsay I Scot
23A1 Colotlán Mexico
27E5 Coloradito Ven
8C3 Colorado State, USA
9B3 Colorado R Arizona, USA
29D3 Colorado R Buenos Aires, Arg
9D3 Colorado R Texas, USA
9B3 Colorado Plat USA
8C3 Colorado Springs USA
22D3 Colton USA
16A3 Columbia Maryland, USA
19C3 Columbia Mississippi, USA
10A3 Columbia Missouri, USA
15C2 Columbia Pennsylvania, USA
11B3 Columbia S Carolina, USA
11B3 Columbia Tennessee, USA
13D2 Columbia R Can
8A2 Columbia R USA
5G4 Columbia,Mt Can
20C1 Columbia Plat USA
11B3 Columbus Georgia, USA
14A3 Columbus Indiana, USA
11B3 Columbus Mississippi, USA
8D2 Columbus Nebraska, USA
10B2 Columbus Ohio, USA
19A4 Columbus Texas, USA
20C1 Colville USA
4C3 Colville R USA
110C1 Colville,C NZ
4F3 Colville USA
42C3 Colwyn Bay Wales
47E2 Comacchio Italy
22B1 Comanche Res USA
25D3 Comayagua Honduras
34A2 Combarbalá Chile
45C2 Comeragh Mts Irish Rep
86C2 Comilla Bang
25C3 Comitán Mexico
46C2 Commercy France
6B3 Committees B Can
52A1 Como Italy
29C5 Comodoro Rivadavia Arg
23A1 Comonfort Mexico
87B3 Comorin,C India
101D2 Comoros Is Indian O
49C2 Compiègne France
23A1 Compostela Mexico
34B2 Comte Salas Arg
86C1 Cona China
97A4 Conakry Guinea
34B2 Concarán Arg
48B2 Concarneau France
35D1 Conceiçao da Barra Brazil
31B3 Conceição do Araguaia Brazil
35C1 Conceição do Mato Dentro Brazil
29B3 Concepción Chile

30E3 Concepción Par
29E2 Concepción R Arg
24B2 Concepcion del Oro Mexico
34D2 Concepcion del Uruguay Arg
9A3 Conception,Pt USA
35B2 Conchas Brazil
9C4 Conchos R Mexico
21A2 Concord California, USA
10C2 Concord New Hampshire, USA
29E2 Concordia Arg
8D3 Concordia USA
20B1 Concrete USA
109D1 Condamine Aust
107D4 Condobolin Aust
20B1 Condon USA
46C1 Condroz Mts Belg
17A1 Conecuh R USA
47E2 Conegliano Italy
89F8 Congo Republic, Africa
89F8 Congo R Congo
Congo,R = Zaire
14B1 Coniston Can
45B2 Connaught Region, Irish Rep
14B2 Conneaut USA
10C2 Connecticut State, USA
15D2 Connecticut R USA
15C2 Connellsville USA
45B2 Connemara,Mts of Irish Rep
14A3 Connersville USA
108B2 Conoble Aust
19A3 Conroe USA
35C2 Conselheiro Lafaiete Brazil
77D4 Con Son Is Viet
Constance,L=Bodensee
60C5 Constanta Rom
18A1 Constantine Alg
12C3 Constantine,C USA
29B3 Constitución Chile
13F3 Consul Can
31C4 Contas R Brazil
23B2 Contreras Mexico
4H3 Contuoyto L Can
11A3 Conway Arkansas, USA
15D2 Conway New Hampshire, USA
17C1 Conway South Carolina, USA
108A1 Conway,R Wales
42C3 Conwy Wales
106C3 Cooper Pedy Aust
110B2 Cook Str NZ
13B2 Cook,C Can
4C3 Cook Inlet B USA
105H4 Cook Is Pacific O
111B2 Cook,Mt NZ
107D2 Cooktown Aust
108C1 Coolabah Aust
108C1 Cooladdi Aust
109C2 Coolah Aust
109C2 Coolamon Aust
108A4 Coolgardie Aust
109C3 Cooma Aust
109C2 Coonabarabran Aust
109C2 Coonamble Aust
108B2 Coonbah Aust
108A2 Coondambo Aust
87A2 Coondapoor India
87B2 Coongoola Aust
87B2 Coonoor India
108B1 Cooper Basin Aust
106C3 Cooper Creek Aust
108B1 Cooper Creek R Aust
108A3 Coorong,The Aust
109D1 Cooroy Aust
20B2 Coos B USA
20B2 Coos Bay USA
107D4 Cootamundra Aust
45C1 Cootehill Irish Rep

23B2 Copala Mexico
23B2 Copala Mexico
Copenhagen= København
30B4 Copiapó Chile
47D2 Copparo Italy
12F2 Copper R USA
4D3 Copper Centre USA
14B1 Copper Cliff Can
4G3 Coppermine Can
4G3 Coppermine R Can
Coquihatville = Mbandaka
30B4 Coquimbo Chile
54B2 Corabia Rom
17B2 Coral Gables USA
6B3 Coral Harbour Can
107D2 Coral S Aust/PNG
104F4 Coral Sea Basin Pacific O
107E2 Coral Sea Island Territories Aust
108B3 Corangamite,L Aust
33F3 Corantijn R Surinam/Guyana
46B2 Corbeil-Essonnes France
50A1 Corcubion Spain
11B3 Cordele USA
50A1 Cordillera Cantabrica Mts Spain
26C3 Cordillera Central Mts Dom Rep
79B2 Cordillera Central Mts Phil
34B2 Cordillera de Ansita Mts Arg
32B5 Cordillera de los Andes Mts Peru
30C4 Cordillera del Toro Mts Arg
32C2 Cordillera de Mérida Ven
34A3 Cordillera de Viento Mts Arg
25D3 Cordillera Isabelia Mts Nic
32B3 Cordillera Occidental Mts Colombia
32B3 Cordillera Oriental Mts Colombia
108B1 Cordillo Downs Aust
29D2 Córdoba Arg
24C3 Córdoba Mexico
50B2 Córdoba Spain
29D2 Córdoba State, Arg
4D3 Cordova USA
Corfu = Kérkira
109D2 Coricudgy,Mt USA
53C2 Corigliano Calabro Italy
11B3 Corinth Mississippi, USA
31C5 Corinto Brazil
45B2 Cork County, Irish Rep
41B3 Cork Irish Rep
92A1 Corlu Turk
31C5 Cornel Fabriciano Brazil
35A2 Cornélio Procópio Brazil
7E5 Corner Brook Can
109C3 Corner Inlet B Aust
15C2 Corning USA
7C5 Cornwall Can
43B4 Cornwall County, Eng
43B4 Cornwall,C Eng
4H2 Cornwall I Can
6A2 Cornwallis I Can
110C1 Coromandel Pen NZ
110C1 Coromandel Range Mts NZ
22D4 Corona California, USA

13E2 Coronation Can
4G3 Coronation G Can
34C2 Coronda Arg
29B3 Coronel Chile
34D3 Coronel Brandsen Arg
34D3 Coronel Dorrego Arg
35C1 Coronel Fabriciano Brazil
30E4 Coronel Oviedo Par
29D3 Coronel Pringles Arg
34D3 Coronel Suárez Arg
34D3 Coronel Vidal Arg
30B2 Coropuna Mt Peru
109C3 Corowa Aust
49D3 Corps France
9D4 Corpus Christi USA
9D4 Corpus Christi,L USA
79B3 Corregidor I Phil
35A1 Corrente R Mato Grosso, Brazil
30E4 Corrientes Arg
30E4 Corrientes State, Arg
19B3 Corrigan USA
106A4 Corrigin Aust
107E2 Corringe Is Aust
109C3 Corryong Aust
52A2 Corse I Medit S
42B2 Corsewall Pt Scot
Corsica = Corse
52A2 Corsicana USA
9C3 Cortez USA
52B1 Cortina d'Ampezzo Italy
15C2 Cortland USA
23A2 Coruca de Catalan Mexico
93D1 Çoruh R Turk
60E5 Çorum Turk
30E2 Corumbá Brazil
35B1 Corumba R Brazil
35B1 Corumbaiba Brazil
20B2 Corvallis USA
46A1 Corvo I Açores
43C3 Corwen Wales
23B2 Coscomatopec Mexico
53C3 Cosenza Italy
101D1 Cosmoledo Is Seychelles
34C2 Cosquín Arg
51B2 Costa Blanca Region, Spain
51C1 Costa Brava Region, Spain
50B2 Costa de la Luz Region, Spain
50B2 Costa del Sol Region, Spain
22D4 Costa Mesa USA
25D3 Costa Rica Republic, Cent America
79B4 Cotabato Phil
30C3 Cotagaita Bol
49D3 Côte d'Azur Region, France
46C2 Côtes de Meuse Mts France
97C4 Cotonou Benin
32B4 Cotopaxi Mt Ecuador
43C4 Cotswold Hills Upland Eng
20B2 Cottage Grove USA
56C2 Cottbus Germany
108A3 Couedic,C du Aust
20C1 Couer d'Alene L USA
46B2 Coulommiers France
15C1 Coulonge R Can
22B2 Coulterville USA
4B3 Council USA
8D2 Council Bluffs USA
52A2 Courmayeur Italy
13B3 Courtenay Can
Courtrai = Kortrijk
48B2 Coutances France
43D3 Coventry Eng
50A1 Covilhã Spain
17B1 Covington Georgia, USA

19B3 Covington Louisiana, USA
109C2 Cowal,L Aust
108B3 Cowangie Aust
15D1 Cowansville Can
108A1 Coward Springs Aust
24B2 Cowell Aust
108C3 Cowes Aust
20B1 Cowichan L Can
20B1 Cowitz R USA
109C2 Cowra Aust
30F2 Coxim Brazil
16C1 Coxsackie USA
86C2 Cox's Bazar Bang
22B2 Coyote USA
23A2 Coyuca de Benitez Mexico
100B4 Cradock S Africa
8C2 Craig USA
57C3 Crailsheim Germany
54B2 Craiova Rom
15D2 Cranberry L USA
5G5 Cranbrook Can
20C2 Crane Oregon, USA
16D2 Cranston USA
20B2 Crater L USA
20B2 Crater Lake Nat Pk USA
31C3 Crateus Brazil
31D3 Crato Brazil
14A2 Crawfordsville USA
17B1 Crawfordville USA
43D4 Crawley Eng
5H4 Cree L Can
46B2 Creil France
47C2 Crema Italy
52B1 Cremona Italy
46B2 Crépy-en-Valois France
52B2 Cres I Yugos
20B2 Crescent City USA
34C2 Crespo Arg
13D3 Creston Can
18B1 Creston USA
17A1 Crestview USA
108B3 Creswick Aust
47A1 Crêt de la Neige Mt France
Crete = Kríti
18A1 Crete USA
55B3 Crete,S of Greece
48C2 Creuse R France
43C3 Crewe Eng
44B3 Crianlarich Scot
30G4 Criciúma Brazil
44C3 Crieff Scot
12G3 Crillon,Mt USA
35B1 Cristalina Brazil
52C1 Croatia Region, Yugos
78D1 Crocker Range Mts Malay
19A3 Crocket USA
106C2 Croker I Aust
44C3 Cromarty Scot
43E3 Cromer Eng
111A3 Cromwell NZ
11C4 Crooked I The Bahamas
13C2 Crooked R Can
8D2 Crookston USA
109C2 Crookwell Aust
109D1 Croppa Creek Aust
11A3 Crossett USA
12G3 Cross Sd USA
53C3 Crotone Italy
19B3 Crowley USA
27K1 Crown Pt Tobago
109D1 Crows Nest Aust
107D2 Croydon Aust
43D4 Croydon Eng
104B5 Crozet Basin Indian O
4F2 Crozier Chan Can
30F4 Cruz Alta Brazil
25E3 Cruz,C Cuba
29D2 Cruz del Eje Arg
35C2 Cruzeiro Brazil
32C5 Cruzeiro do Sul Brazil
13C1 Crysdale,Mt Can

108A2 Crystal Brook Aust
18B2 Crystal City Missouri, USA
14A1 Crystal Falls USA
101C2 Cuamba Mozam
100B2 Cuando R Angola
100A2 Cuangar Aust
Cuango,R = Kwango,R
34C2 Cuarto R Arg
24B2 Cuauhtémoc Mexico
23B2 Cuautla Mexico
25D2 Cuba Republic, Caribbean S
100A2 Cubango R Angola
100A2 Cuchi Angola
100A2 Cuchi R Angola
34C3 Cuchillo Có Arg
32D3 Cucuí Brazil
32C2 Cúcuta Colombia
87B2 Cuddalore India
87B2 Cuddapah India
108A3 Cue Aust
32B4 Cuenca Ecuador
51B1 Cuenca Spain
24C3 Cuernavaca Mexico
19A4 Cuero USA
30C2 Cuiabá Brazil
30E2 Cuiabá R Brazil
23B2 Cuicatlan Mexico
35C1 Cuieté R Brazil
44A3 Cuillin Hills Mts Scot
98B3 Cuilo R Angola
100A2 Cuito R Angola
100A2 Cuito Cunavale Angola
23A2 Cuitzeo Mexico
77D3 Cu Lao Hon I Viet
109C3 Culcairn Aust
109C1 Culgoa R Aust
24B2 Culiacán Mexico
79A3 Culion I Phil
17A1 Cullman USA
47A2 Culoz France
15C3 Culpeper I USA
32J7 Culpepper I Ecuador
17B2 Culter Ridge USA
111B2 Culverden NZ
33E1 Cumaná Ven
10C3 Cumberland Maryland, USA
11B3 Cumberland R USA
6D3 Cumberland Pen Can
6D3 Cumbernauld Sd Can
42C2 Cumbria Eng
21A2 Cummings USA
108A2 Cummins Aust
42B2 Cumnock Scot
34A3 Cunco Chile
100A2 Cunene R Angola/ Namibia
52A2 Cuneo Italy
107D3 Cunnamulla Aust
44C3 Cupar Scot
54B2 Cuprija Yugos
27D4 Curaçao I Caribbean S
34A3 Curacautín Chile
34B3 Curaco R Arg
34A3 Curanilahue Chile
34A3 Curepto Chile
29B2 Curicó Chile
30G4 Curitiba Brazil
108A2 Curnamona Aust
100A2 Curoca R Angola
31C5 Curvelo Brazil
18A2 Cushing USA
33B4 Cutbank R Can
17B1 Cuthbert USA
34B3 Cutral-Có Arg
86B2 Cuttack India
100A2 Cuvelai Angola
56B2 Cuxhaven Germany
14B2 Cuyahoga Falls USA
79B3 Cuyo Is Phil
32C6 Cuzco Peru
99C3 Cyangugu Zaïre
Cyclades = Kikládhes
13F3 Cypress Hills Mts Can
92B3 Cyprus Republic, Medit S

6D3 Cyrus Field B Can
59B3 Czechoslovakia Republic, Europe
59B2 Częstochowa Pol

D

76C1 Da R Viet
69E2 Da'an China
94C3 Dab'a Jordan
27C4 Dabajuro Ven
99E2 Dabaro Somalia
73B3 Daba Shan Mts China
99D1 Dabat Eth
85C4 Dabhoi India
73C3 Dabie Shan U China
97A3 Dabola Guinea
97B4 Dabou Ivory Coast
59B2 Dabrowa Gorn Pol
57C3 Dachau Germany
52B1 Dachstein Mt Austria
73A3 Dada He R China
17B2 Dade City USA
84B3 Dadhar Pak
85B3 Dadu Pak
68C3 Dadu He R China
79B3 Daet Phil
73B4 Dafang China
73B2 Daga R Burma
99E2 Dagabur Eth
99D1 Dagana Sen
66F5 Dagestanskaya ASSR Republic, USSR
79B3 Dagupan Phil
92B4 Dahab Egypt
63E3 Da Hinggan Ling Mts China
17B1 Dahlonega USA
85C4 Dāhod India
95A2 Dahra Libya
51C2 Dahra Region, Alg
86A1 Dailekh Nepal
34C3 Daireaux Arg
Dairen = Lüda
69F4 Daitō Is Pacific O
93D3 Dajarra Aust
97A3 Dakar Sen
95B2 Dakhla Oasis Egypt
97C3 Dakoro Niger
54B2 Dakovica Yugos
54A1 Dakovo Yugos
100B2 Dala Angola
97A3 Dalaba Guinea
72D1 Dalai Nur L China
68C2 Dalandzadgad Mongolia
79B3 Dalanganem Is Phil
68C2 Dalanjargalan Mongolia
76D3 Da Lat Viet
107E3 Dalby Aust
39F7 Dalen Nor
42C2 Dales,The Upland Eng
17A1 Daleville USA
9C3 Dalhart USA
4E2 Dalhousie,C Can
9D3 Dallas USA
20B1 Dalles,The USA
5E4 Dall I USA
86A2 Dalli Rajhara India
97C3 Dallol R Niger
97C3 Dallol Bosso R Niger
52C2 Dalmatia Region Yugos
69F2 Dal'nerechensk USSR
97B4 Daloa Ivory Coast
73B4 Dalou Shan Mts China
86A2 Dāltenganj India
17B1 Dalton Georgia, USA
16C1 Dalton Massachusetts, USA
106C2 Daly R Aust
21A2 Daly City USA
106C2 Daly Waters Aust
79B4 Damaguete Phil
85C4 Damān India
92B3 Damanhûr Egypt

71D4 Damar I Indon
98B2 Damara CAR
92C3 Damascus Syria
16A3 Damascus USA
97D3 Damaturu Nig
90B2 Damavand Iran
98B3 Damba Angola
87C3 Dambulla Sri Lanka
90B2 Damghan Iran
99E2 Damoh India
99E2 Damot Eth
94B2 Damour Leb
106A3 Dampier Aust
84A3 Dana Jordan
22C2 Dana,Mt USA
97B4 Danané IG
76D2 Da Nang Viet
79B3 Danao Brazil
70A3 Danau Tobu L Indon
71D4 Danau Tuwuti L Indon
73A3 Danbu China
15D2 Danbury USA
86A1 Dandeldhura Nepal
87A1 Dandeli India
108C3 Dandenong Aust
74A2 Dandong China
100A4 Danger Pt S Africa
99D1 Dangila Eth
7E4 Danguard Jenson Land Region Can
62E4 Daniels Harbour Can
6G3 Dannebrogs Øy I Greenland
110C2 Dannevirke NZ
87C1 Dantewāra India
Danube = Donau
10B2 Danville Illinois, USA
11B3 Danville Kentucky, USA
16A2 Danville Pennsylvania, USA
11C3 Danville Virginia, USA
Danzig = Gdańsk
73C4 Dao Xian China
73B4 Daozhen China
79B4 Dapiak,Mt Phil
79B3 Dapitan Phil
68B3 Da Qaidam China
94C2 Dar'a Syria
91B4 Dārāb Iran
95A1 Daraj Libya
90B3 Dārān Iran
92C3 Dar'a Salkhad Syria
86B1 Darbhanga India
22C1 Dardanelle USA
1882 Dardanelle,L USA
99D3 Dar es Salaam Tanz
110B1 Dargaville NZ
17B1 Darien USA
Darjeeling = Dārjiling
86B1 Dārjiling India
107D4 Darling R Aust
109C1 Darling Downs Aust
6C1 Darling Pen Can
108B2 Darlington Aust
42D2 Darlington Eng
17C1 Darlington USA
57B3 Darmstadt Germany
95B1 Darnah Libya
108B2 Darnick Aust
4F3 Darnley B Can
112C10 Darnley,C Ant
51B1 Daroca Spain
98C2 Dar Rounga Region, CAR
43C4 Dartmoor Moorland Eng
43C4 Dartmoor Nat Pk Eng
7D5 Dartmouth Can
43C4 Dartmouth Eng
107D1 Daru PNG
52C1 Daruvar Yugos
106C2 Darwin Aust
91B4 Daryācheh-ye Bakhtegan L Iran
91B4 Daryācheh-ye Mahārlū L Iran

90B3 Daryächeh-ye Namak *Salt Flat* Iran
90D3 Daryächeh-ye-Sistan *Salt L* Iran/Afghan
91B4 Daryächeh-ye Tashk *L* Iran
80C2 Daryächeh-ye Orümiyeh *L* Iran
91C4 Därzin Iran
91B4 Das *I* UAE
73C3 Dashennonglia *Mt* China
90C2 Dasht Iran
90B3 Dasht-e-Kavir *Salt Desert* Iran
90C3 Dasht-e Lut *Salt Desert* Iran
90D3 Dasht-e Naomid *Desert Region* Iran
85D3 Datia India
72A2 Datong China
72C1 Datong China
72A2 Datong He *R* China
79B4 Datu Piang Phil
39K7 Daugava *R* USSR
60C2 Daugavpils USSR
6D1 Dauguard Jensen Land Greenland
84A1 Daulatabad Afghan
85D3 Daulpur India
46D1 Daun Germany
87A1 Daund India
5H4 Dauphin Can
16A2 Dauphin USA
49D2 Dauphiné *Region*, France
97C3 Daura Nig
85D3 Dausa India
87B2 Dāvangere India
79C4 Davao Phil
79C4 Davao G Phil
22A2 Davenport California, USA
10A2 Davenport Iowa, USA
32A2 David Panama
4D3 Davidson Mts USA
21A2 Davis USA
112C10 Davis *Base* Ant
7D4 Davis Inlet Can
6E3 Davis Str Greenland/Can
61J3 Davlekanovo USSR
47C1 Davos Switz
99E2 Dawa *R* Eth
73A4 Dawan China
84B2 Dawat Yar Afghan
91B4 Dawhat Salwah *B* Qatar/S Arabia
76B2 Dawna Range *Mts* Burma
4E3 Dawson Can
17B1 Dawson Georgia, USA
107D3 Dawson *R* Aust
5F4 Dawson Creek Can
13D2 Dawson,Mt Can
12G2 Dawson Range *Mts* Can
73A3 Dawu China
73C3 Dawu China
48B3 Dax France
73B3 Daxian China
73B5 Daxin China
73A3 Daxue Shan *Mts* China
73C4 Dayong China
94C2 Dayr 'Ali Syria
94C1 Dayr 'Atiyah Syria
93D2 Dayr az Zawr Syria
10B3 Dayton Ohio, USA
19B4 Dayton Texas, USA
20C1 Dayton Washington, USA
11B4 Daytona Beach USA
73C4 Dayu China
78D3 Dayu Indon
72D2 Da Yunhe *R* China
20C2 Dayville USA
73B3 Dazhu China

100B4 De Aar S Africa
26C2 Deadman's Cay The Bahamas
92C3 Dead S Israel/Jordan
46A1 Deal Eng
101G1 Dealesville S Africa
13B2 Dean *R* Can
34C2 Deán Funes Arg
14B2 Dearborn USA
4F3 Dease Arm *B* Can
4E4 Dease Lake Can
8B3 Death V USA
48C2 Deauville France
97B4 Debakala Ivory Coast
12B2 Debauch Mt USA
27L1 Débé Trinidad
59C2 Debica Pol
58C2 Deblin Pol
97B3 Débo,L Mali
99D2 Debra Birhan Eth
99D1 Debra Markos Eth
99D1 Debra Tabor Eth
59C3 Debrecen Hung
81C2 Decatur Alabama, USA
17B1 Decatur Georgia, USA
10B3 Decatur Illinois, USA
14B2 Decatur Indiana, USA
48C3 Decazeville France
73A4 Dechang China
97B3 Dédougou Burkina
101C2 Dedza Malawi
42B2 Dee *R* Dumfries and Galloway, Scot
42C3 Dee *R* Eng/Wales
44C3 Dee *R* Grampian, Scot
15C1 Deep River Can
16C2 Deep River USA
109D1 Deepwater Aust
7E5 Deer Lake Can
8B2 Deer Lodge USA
34D3 Defferrari Arg
17A1 De Funiak Springs USA
68B3 Dêgê China
106A3 De Grey *R* Aust
91B3 Deh Bid Iran
84B1 Dehi Afghan
96D1 Dehibat Tunisia
87B3 Dehiwala-Mt Lavinia Sri Lanka
90A3 Dehlorän Iran
84D2 Dehra Dün India
86A2 Dehri India
98C2 Deim Zubeir Sudan
94B2 Deir Abu Sa'id Jordan
94C1 Deir el Ahmar Leb
60B4 Dej Rom
18C2 De Kalb Texas, USA
63G2 De Kastri USSR
98C3 Dekese Zaire
98B2 Dekoa CAR
106B1 Dekusi Indon
9B3 Delano USA
10C3 Delaware State, USA
14B2 Delaware USA
15C2 Delaware *R* USA
10C3 Delaware B USA
109C3 Delegate Aust
47B1 Delemont Switz
101D2 Delgado C Mozam
84D3 Delhi India
15D2 Delhi New York, USA
92B1 Delice Turk
24B2 Delicias Mexico
90B3 Delijän Iran
47B1 Delle France
22D4 Del Mar USA
39F8 Delmenhorst Germany
4B3 De Long Mts USA
109C4 Deloraine Aust
5H5 Deloraine Can
17B2 Delray Beach USA
9C4 Del Rio USA
8B3 Delta USA
12E2 Delta *R* USA
12E2 Delta Junction USA

99D2 Dembidollo Eth
46C1 Demer *R* Belg
9C3 Deming USA
54C2 Demirköy Turk
49C1 Denain France
82A2 Denau USSR
42C3 Denbigh Wales
12B2 Denbigh,C Can
78B3 Dendang Indon
46C1 Dendermond Belg
99D2 Dendi *Mt* Eth
46B1 Dêndre *R* Belg
72B1 Dengkou China
72C3 Deng Xian China
Den Haag = 's-Gravenhage
27H1 Denham,Mt Jamaica
56A2 Den Helder Neth
51C2 Denia Spain
107D4 Deniliquin Aust
20C2 Denio USA
9D3 Denison Texas, USA
12D3 Denison,Mt USA
92A2 Denizli Turk
39F7 Denmark Kingdom, Europe
1C1 Denmark Str Greenland/Iceland
27P2 Dennery St Lucia
78D4 Denpasar Indon
16B3 Denton Maryland, USA
9D3 Denton Texas, USA
107E1 D'Entrecasteaux Is PNG
47B1 Dents du Midi *Mt* Switz
8C3 Denver USA
98B2 Déo *R* Cam
86B2 Deoghar India
85C5 Deolali India
84D1 Deosai Plain India
95B3 Dépression du Mourdi Chad
19B3 De Queen USA
84C3 Dera Pak
84B3 Dera Bugti Pak
84C2 Dera Ismail Khan Pak
106B2 Derby Aust
16C2 Derby Connecticut, USA
43D3 Derby County, Eng
43D3 Derby Eng
9D3 Derby Kansas, USA
60E3 Dergachi USSR
19B3 De Ridder USA
Derna = Darnah
95C3 Derudeb Sudan
109C4 Derwent Bridge Aust
34B2 Desaguadero Arg
34B2 Desaguadero *R* Bol
30C2 Desaguadero *R* Bol
21B3 Descanso Mexico
20B2 Deschutes *R* USA
29C5 Deseado Arg
29C5 Deseado *R* Arg
47D2 Desenzano Italy
96A1 Deserta Grande *I* Medeira
30C4 Desierto de Atacama *Desert* Chile
18B2 Desloge USA
10A2 Des Moines Iowa, USA
60D3 Desna *R* USSR
29B6 Desolación *I* Chile
14A2 Des Plaines USA
56C2 Dessau Germany
99D1 Dessye Eth
12G2 Destruction Bay Can
46A1 Desvres France
54B1 Deta Rom
100B2 Dett Zim
10B2 Detroit USA
76D3 Det Udom Thai
54B1 Deva Rom
56B2 Deventer Neth
44C3 Deveron *R* Scot
85C3 Devikot India

22C2 Devil Postpile Nat Mon USA
22C1 Devils Gate *P* USA
Devil's Island = Isla du Diable
8D2 Devils Lake USA
12H3 Devils Paw *Mt* Can
43D4 Devizes Eng
85D3 Devli India
55B2 Devoll *R* Alb
43B4 Devon County, Eng
6A2 Devon I Can
107D5 Devonport Aust
86C1 Dewangiri Bhutan
85D4 Dewàs India
101G1 Dewetsdorp S Africa
11B3 Dewey Res USA
19B3 De Witt USA
18C2 Dexter Missouri, USA
73A3 Deyang China
90C3 Deyhuk Iran
90A3 Dezful Iran
72D2 Dezhou China
90A2 Dezh Shāhpūr Iran
91B4 Dhahran S Arabia
86C2 Dhākā Bang
87B2 Dhamavaram India
86A2 Dhamtari India
86B2 Dhanbad India
86A1 Dhangarhi Nepal
86B1 Dhankuta Nepal
85D4 Dhār India
87B2 Dharmapuri India
84D2 Dharmsāla India
97B3 Dhar Oualata *Desert Region* Maur
86A1 Dhaulagiri *Mt* Nepal
86B2 Dhenkānai India
94B3 Dhibah Jordan
55C3 Dhíkti Ori *Mt* Greece
55C3 Dhodhekánisos *Is* Greece
55B3 Dhomokós Greece
87B1 Dhone India
85C4 Dhoraji India
85C4 Dhrāngadhra India
86B1 Dhuburi India
85C4 Dhule India
22B2 Diablo,Mt USA
21A2 Diablo Range *Mts* USA
34C2 Diamante Arg
34B2 Diamante *R* Arg
31C5 Diamantina Brazil
107D3 Diamantina *R* Aust
86B2 Diamond Harbours India
22B1 Diamond Springs USA
91C4 Dibā UAE
98C3 Dibaya Zaire
86C1 Dibrugarh India
8C2 Dickinson USA
1B10 Dickson USSR
14A2 Dickson City USA
93D2 Dicle *R* Turk
13E2 Didsbury Can
85C3 Didwäna India
97B3 Diébougou Burkina
46D2 Diekirch Lux
97B3 Diéma Mali
76C1 Dien Bien Phu Viet
56B2 Diepholz Germany
48C2 Dieppe France
46C1 Diest Belg
46D2 Dieuze France
7D5 Digby Can
49D3 Digne France
49C2 Digoin France
79C4 Digos Phil
71E4 Digul *R* Indon
86C1 Dihang *R* India
Dijlah = Tigris
49C2 Dijon France
98B2 Dik Chad
99E1 Dikhil Djibouti
46B1 Diksmuide Belg
82A2 Dilaram Afghan
76D3 Di Linh Viet

46E1 Dillenburg Germany
99C1 Dilling Sudan
12C3 Dillingham USA
8B2 Dillon USA
16A2 Dillsburg USA
100B2 Dilolo Zaire
　Dimashq = Damascus
98C3 Dimbelenge Zaire
97B4 Dimbokro Ivory Coast
54C2 Dimitrovgrad Bulg
61G3 Dimitrovgrad USSR
94B3 Dimona Israel
86C1 Dimpãpur India
79C3 Dinagat I Phil
81B1 Dinajpur India
48B2 Dinan France
46C1 Dinant Belg
94B2 Dinar Turk
99D1 Dinder R Sudan
87B2 Dindigul India
72B2 Dingbian China
86B1 Dinggyê China
41A3 Dingle Irish Rep
41A3 Dingle B Irish Rep
97A3 Dinguiraye Guinea
44B3 Dingwall Scot
72A2 Dingxi China
72D2 Ding Xian China
76D1 Dinh Lap Viet
22C2 Dinuba USA
97A3 Diouloulou Sen
86C1 Diphu India
99E2 Dirê Dawa Eth
106A3 Dirk Hartog I Aust
95A3 Dirkou Niger
109C1 Dirranbandi Aust
99E2 Dirri Somalia
29G8 Disappointment,C
　South Georgia
20B1 Disappointment,C USA
106B3 Disappointment,L Aust
108B3 Discovery B Aust
103J7 Discovery Tablemount
　Atlantic O
47C1 Disentis Muster Switz
6E3 Disko Greenland
6E3 Disko Bugt B Greenland
6E3 Diskorjord Greenland
58D1 Disna USSR
35B1 Distrito federal Federal
　District, Brazil
85C4 Diu India
79C4 Diuat Mts Phil
31C6 Divinópolis Brazil
61F4 Divnoye USSR
93C2 Divriği Turk
22B1 Dixon California, USA
5E4 Dixon Entrance Sd Can/
　USA
13D1 Dixonville Can
93E3 Diyālā R Iraq
65F6 Diyarbakir Turk
90A3 Diz R Iran
98B2 Dja R Cam
95A2 Djadi R Alg
95A2 Djado,Plat du Niger
98B3 Djambala Congo
96C2 Djanet Alg
50A2 Djebel Bouhalla Mt Mor
51C2 Djelfa Alg
98C2 Djéma CAR
97B3 Djenné Mali
97B3 Djibo Burkina
99E1 Djibouti Djibouti
99E1 Djibouti Republic, E
　Africa
98C2 Djolu Zaire
97C4 Djougou Benin
97D2 Djugu Zaire
38C2 Djúpivogur Iceland
51C2 Djurdjura Mts Alg
60E2 Dmitrov USSR
60E3 Dnepr R USSR
60D4 Dneprodzerzhinsk USSR
60E4 Dnepropetrovsk USSR
60C3 Dneprovskaja
　Nizmennost' Region,
　USSR

60B4 Dnestr R USSR
60D2 Dno USSR
98B2 Doba Chad
58C1 Dobele USSR
34C3 Doblas Arg
71E4 Dobo Indon
54A2 Doboj Yugos
54B2 Dobreta-Turnu-Severin
　Rom
60D3 Dobrush USSR
31C5 Doce R Brazil
30D3 Doctor R P Peña Arg
87B2 Dod India
87B2 Doda Betta Mt India
　Dodecanese =
　Sporádhes
9C3 Dodge City USA
99D3 Dodoma Tanz
97C3 Dogondoutchi Niger
93D2 Doğubayazit Turk
91B4 Doha Qatar
7C5 Dolbeau Can
49D2 Dôle France
43C3 Dolgellau Wales
99E2 Dolo Eth
47D1 Dolomitche Mts Italy
29E3 Dolores Arg
34D2 Dolores Urug
23A1 Dolores Hidalgo
　Mexico
4G3 Dolphin and Union Str
　Can
29E6 Dolphin,C Falkland Is
71E4 Dom Mt Indon
65G4 Dombarovskiy USSR
38F6 Dombås Nor
46D2 Dombasle-sur-Meurthe
　France
54A1 Dombóvár Hung
48B2 Domfront France
27E3 Dominica I
27C3 Dominican Republic
　Caribbean S
6C3 Dominion,C Can
7E4 Domino,C Can
68D1 Domna USSR
52A1 Domodossola Italy
78D4 Dompu Indon
29B3 Domuyo Mt Arg
109D1 Domville,Mt Aust
65H4 Dom-yanskoya USSR
44C3 Don R Scot
61F4 Don R USSR
45C1 Donaghadee N Ire
57C3 Donau R Germany
57C3 Donauwörth Germany
50A2 Don Benito Spain
42D3 Doncaster Eng
98B3 Dondo Angola
101C2 Dondo Mozam
87C3 Dondra Head C
　Sri Lanka
45B1 Donegal County,
　Irish Rep
45B1 Donegal Irish Rep
40B3 Donegal B Irish Rep
45B1 Donegal Mts Irish Rep
60E4 Donetsk USSR
73C4 Dong'an China
106A3 Dongara Aust
73A4 Dongchuan China
76D2 Dongfang China
74B2 Dongfeng China
70C4 Donggala Indon
68B3 Donggi Cona L China
74A3 Donggou China
70C4 Dongguang China
73C5 Dongguan Dao I China
72A1 Dong He R China
76D2 Dong Hoi Viet
73C5 Dong Jiang R China
75D3 Dongola Sudan
73D5 Dongshan China
68D4 Dongsha Qundao I
　China
72C2 Dongsheng China
72E3 Dongtai China

73C4 Dongting Hu L China
73B5 Dongxing China
73D3 Dongzhi China
18B2 Doniphan USA
52C2 Donji Vakuf Yugos
38G5 Dönna I Nor
21A2 Donner P USA
46D2 Donnersberg Mt
　Germany
101G1 Donnybrook S Africa
22B2 Don Pedro Res USA
12D1 Doonerak,Mt USA
79B4 Do Qu R China
47B2 Dora Baltea R Italy
49D2 Dorbirn Austria
43C4 Dorchester Eng
6C3 Dorchester,C Can
48C2 Dordogne R France
56A2 Dordrecht Neth
13F2 Doré L Can
13F2 Doré Lake Can
97B3 Dori Burkina
46B2 Dormans France
57B3 Dornbirn Austria
44B3 Dornoch Scot
44B3 Dornoch Firth Estuary
　Scot
38H6 Dorotea Sweden
109D2 Dorrigo Aust
20B2 Dorris USA
43C4 Dorset County, Eng
46D1 Dorsten Germany
56B2 Dortmund Germany
98C2 Doruma Zaire
83D2 Dosatuy USSR
84B1 Doshi Afghan
22B2 Dos Palos USA
97C3 Dosso Niger
65G5 Dossor USSR
11B3 Dothan USA
104J1 Dual France
98A2 Douala Cam
109D1 Double Island Pt Aust
49D2 Doubs R France
111A3 Doubtful Sd NZ
97B3 Douentza Mali
22B2 Douglas Arizona, USA
42B2 Douglas Eng
82D2 Douglas Georgia, USA
17B1 Douglas Georgia, USA
8C2 Douglas Wyoming,
　USA
12A1 Douglas,C USA
13B2 Douglas Chan Can
53A2 Douglas,Mt USA
46B1 Doullens France
45C1 Doun County, N Ire
30F3 Dourados Brazil
50A1 Douro R Port
15C3 Dover Delaware, USA
43E4 Dover Eng
15D2 Dover New
　Hampshire, USA
16B2 Dover New Jersey,
　USA
14B2 Dover Ohio, USA
43D3 Dover R Eng
41D3 Dover,Str of UK/
　France
18B3 Downington USA
42B2 Downpatrick N Ire
13C2 Downton,Mt USA
16B2 Doylestown USA
75A1 Dözen I Japan
96A2 Dr'aa R Mor
35A2 Dracena Brazil
16D1 Dracut USA
49D3 Draguignan France
101C3 Drakensberg Mts
　S Africa
101G1 Drakensberg Mt
　S Africa
103E7 Drake Pass Pacific/
　Atlantic O
55B2 Dráma Greece
39G7 Drammen Nor
38A1 Drangajökull Iceland
52C1 Drava R Yugos

13D2 Drayton Valley Can
49C2 Dreux France
57C2 Dresden Germany
48C2 Dreux France
20C2 Drewsey USA
54B2 Drin R Alb
58D1 Drissa R USSR
45C2 Drogheda Irish Rep
59C3 Drogobych USSR
112B12 Dronning Maud Land
　Region, Ant
30D3 Dr P.P. Penã Par
5G4 Drumheller Can
14B1 Drummond I USA
15D1 Drummondville Can
58C2 Druskininksi USSR
12G3 Dry B USA
7A5 Dryden USA
27H1 Dry Harbour Mts
　Jamaica
76B3 Duang I Burma
91C4 Dubai UAE
5H3 Dubawnt R Can
5H3 Dubawnt L Can
107D4 Dubbo Aust
45C2 Dublin County,
　Irish Rep
17B1 Dublin USA
60E2 Dubna USSR
60C3 Dubno USSR
15C2 Du Bois USA
13B2 Dubose,Mt Can
58D2 Dubrovica USSR
54A2 Dubrovnik Yugos
10A2 Dubuque USA
46D2 Dudelange Lux
1C10 Dudinka USSR
43C3 Dudley Eng
97B4 Duékoué Ivory Coast
50B1 Duero R Spain
44C3 Dufftown Scot
52B2 Dugi Otok I Yugos
56B2 Duisburg Germany
93E3 Dükan Iraq
99D2 Duk Faiwil Sudan
91B4 Dukhän Qatar
73A4 Dukou China
68B3 Dulan China
34C2 Dulce R Arg
78C2 Dulit Range Mts
　Malay
86C2 Dullabchara India
10A2 Duluth USA
94C2 Duma Syria
78A2 Dumai Indon
79A3 Dumaran I Phil
9C3 Dumas USA
94C2 Dumayr Syria
42B2 Dumbarton Scot
42C2 Dumfries Scot
42B2 Dumfries and
　Galloway Region,
　Scot
86B2 Dumka India
15C1 Dumoine,L Can
112C8 Dumont d'Urville Base
　Ant
95C1 Dumyat Egypt
54C2 Dunărea R Rom
45C2 Dunany Head Pt
　Irish Rep
54B2 Dunav R Bulg
59D3 Dunayevtsy USSR
42C2 Dunbar Scot
5G4 Duncan Can
16A2 Duncannon USA
44C2 Duncansby Head Pt
　Scot
45C1 Dundalk Irish Rep
16A3 Dundalk USA
45C2 Dundalk B Irish Rep
6D2 Dundas Greenland
4G2 Dundas Pen Can
71E5 Dundas Str Aust
101H1 Dundee S Africa
44C3 Dundee Scot
108B1 Dundoo Aust

42B2 Dundrum B N Ire
111B3 Dunedin NZ
17B2 Dunedin USA
109C2 Dunedoo Aust
44C3 Dunfermline Scot
85C4 Dungarpur India
45C2 Dungarvan Irish Rep
43E4 Dungeness Eng
109D2 Dungog Aust
99C2 Dungu Zaïre
95C2 Dungunab Sudan
68B2 Dunhuang China
46B1 Dunkerque France
10C2 Dunkirk USA
99D1 Dunkur Eth
97B4 Dunkwa Ghana
41B3 Dun Laoghaire Irish Rep
45B3 Dunmanway Irish Rep
26B1 Dunmore Town The Bahamas
44C2 Dunnet Head Pt Scot
42C2 Duns Scot
20B2 Dunsmuir USA
111A2 Dunstan Mts NZ
46C2 Dun-sur-Meuse France
72D1 Duolun China
98B3 Duque de Braganca Angola
18C2 Du Quoin USA
94B3 Dura Israel
49D3 Durance R France
24B2 Durango Mexico
50B1 Durango Spain
9C3 Durango USA
29E2 Durano Urug
9D3 Durant USA
94C1 Duraykish Syria
101H1 Durban S Africa
46D1 Düren Germany
86A2 Durg India
86B2 Durgapur India
42D2 Durham County, Eng
42D2 Durham Eng
11C3 Durham N Carolina, USA
16D1 Durham New Hampshire, USA
108B1 Durham Downs Aust
54A2 Durmitor Mt Yugos
44B2 Durness Scot
55A2 Durrës Alb
108B1 Durrie Aust
45A3 Dursey I Irish Rep
55C3 Dursunbey Turk
110B2 D'Urville I NZ
90D2 Dushak USSR
73B4 Dushan China
82A2 Dushanbe USSR
111A3 Dusky Sd NZ
56B2 Düsseldorf Germany
73B4 Duyun China
92B1 Düzce Turk
60C2 Dvina R USSR
85B4 Dwärka India
6D3 Dyer,C Can
11B3 Dyersburg USA
43B3 Dyfed County, Wales
61F5 Dykh Tau Dağlari Mt USSR
108B1 Dynevor Downs Aust
68B2 Dzag Mongolia
63C3 Dzamin Uüd Mongolia
101D2 Dzaoudzi Mayotte
68C2 Dzavhan Mongolia
68B2 Dzavhan Gol R Mongolia
80E1 Dzhezkazgan USSR
61F2 Dzerzhinsk USSR
63E2 Dzhalinda USSR
63D3 Dzhambul USSR
60D4 Dzhankoy USSR
65H4 Dzhezkazgan USSR
84B1 Dzhilikul' USSR
65J5 Dzhungarskiy Alatau Mts USSR
59B2 Dzierzoniow Pol
62C1 Dzungaria Basin, China

E

7B4 Eabamet L Can
12F2 Eagle Alaska, USA
20B2 Eagle L California, USA
19A3 Eagle Mountain L USA
9C4 Eagle Pass USA
4E3 Eagle Plain Can
12E2 Eagle River USA
22B2 Earlimart USA
17B1 Easley USA
15C2 East Aurora USA
43E4 Eastbourne Eng
14A2 East Chicago USA
69E3 East China Sea China/Japan
83B4 Eastern Ghats Mts India
29E6 East Falkland I Falkland Is
12E1 East Fork R USA
21B2 Eastgate USA
16C1 Easthampton USA
16C2 East Hampton USA
14A2 East Lake USA
14B2 East Liverpool USA
100B4 East London S Africa
7C4 Eastmain Can
7C4 Eastmain R Can
17B1 Eastman USA
15C3 Easton Maryland, USA
15C2 Easton Pennsylvania, USA
16B2 East Orange USA
105L4 East Pacific Ridge Pacific O
17B1 East Point USA
42D3 East Retford Eng
11A3 East St Louis USA
1B7 East Siberian S USSR
43E4 East Sussex County, Eng
17B1 Eatonton USA
10A2 Eau Claire USA
71F3 Eauripik I Pacific O
23B1 Ebano Mexico
98B2 Ebebiyin Eq Guinea
56C2 Eberswalde Germany
73A4 Ebian China
65K5 Ebinur L China
52C3 Eboli Italy
98B2 Ebolowa Cam
51B1 Ebro R Spain
92A1 Eceabat Turk
96C1 Ech Cheliff Alg
72D2 Eching China
20C1 Echo USA
4G3 Echo Bay Can
46D2 Echternach Lux
108B3 Echuca Aust
50A2 Ecija Spain
6B2 Eclipse Sd Can
32B4 Ecuador Republic, S America
44C2 Eday I Scot
98C1 Ed Da'ein Sudan
95C3 Ed Damer Sudan
95C3 Ed Debba Sudan
44B2 Eddrachillis B Scot
99D1 Ed Dueim Sudan
109C4 Eddystone Pt Aust
98A2 Edea Cam
109C3 Eden Aust
42C2 Eden R Eng
101G1 Edenburg S Africa
111A3 Edendale NZ
46E1 Edenkoben Germany
46E1 Eder R Germany
6D3 Edgell I Can
64D2 Edgeeya I Barents O
16A3 Edgewood USA
94B3 Edh Dhahiriya Israel
55B2 Edhessa Greece
44C3 Edinburgh Scot
60C5 Edirne Turk

17B1 Edisto R USA
13D2 Edith Cavell,Mt Can
20B1 Edmonds USA
5G4 Edmonton Can
7D5 Edmundston Can
19A4 Edna USA
12H3 Edna Bay USA
52B1 Edolo Italy
94B3 Edom Region, Jordan
92A2 Edremit Turk
55C3 Edremit Körfezi B Turk
68B2 Edrengiyn Nuruu Mts Mongolia
5G4 Edson Can
34C3 Eduardo Castex Arg
12J2 Eduni,Mt Aust
108B3 Edward R Aust
99C3 Edward,L Uganda/Zaïre
108A1 Edwards Creek Aust
9C3 Edwards Plat Aust
18C2 Edwardsville USA
12H3 Edziza,Mt USA
12B2 Eek USA
46C1 Eeklo Belg
10B3 Effingham USA
6E3 Egedesminde Greenland
12C3 Egegik USA
59C3 Eger Hung
39H7 Egersund Nor
16B3 Egg Harbor City USA
4G2 Eglinton I Can
110B1 Egmont,C NZ
110B1 Egmont,Mt NZ
92B2 Eğridir Gölü L Turk
95B2 Egypt Republic, Africa
106B2 Eighty Mile Beach Aust
108C3 Eildon,L Aust
56B2 Eindhoven Neth
47C1 Einsiedeln Switz
94B3 Ein Yahav Israel
57C2 Eisenach Germany
57C3 Eisenerz Austria
46D1 Eitorf Germany
72A1 Ejin qi China
23B2 Ejutla Mexico
110C2 Eketahuna NZ
65J4 Ekibastuz USSR
63F2 Ekimchan USSR
92B3 Ek Mahalla el Kubra Egypt
39H7 Eksjo Sweden
5G4 Ekwan R Can
92A3 El'Alamein Egypt
92A3 El'Arish Egypt
92B4 Elat Israel
95B3 El'Atrun Oasis Sudan
93C2 Elazığ Turk
92C3 El Azraq Jordan
52B2 Elba I Italy
95C2 El Balyana Egypt
32C2 El Banco Colombia
55B2 Elbasan Alb
27D5 El Baúl Ven
57C2 Elbe R Germany
94C1 El Bega'a R Leb
14A2 Elberta USA
8C3 Elbert,Mt USA
17B1 Elberton USA
92C2 Elbistan Turk
58B2 Elblag Pol
29B4 El Bolson Arg
61F5 Elbrus Mt USSR
Elburz Mts = Reshteh-ye Alborz
21B3 El Cajon USA
19A4 El Campo USA
51B2 Elche Spain
51B2 Elda Spain

32B1 El Diviso Colombia
96B2 El Djouf Desert Region Maur
18B2 Eldon USA
11A3 El Dorado Arkansas, USA
35B2 Eldorado Brazil
9D3 El Dorado Kansas, USA
24B2 El Dorado Mexico
27D5 El Dorado Ven
99D2 Eldoret Kenya
22C1 Eleanor,L USA
96B2 El Eglab Region, Alg
50B1 El Escorial Spain
93D2 Eleşkirt Turk
11C4 Eleuthera I The Bahamas
92B4 El Faiyûm Egypt
96B2 El Farsia Well Mor
98C1 El Fasher Sudan
92B4 El Fashn Egypt
50A1 El Ferrol del Caudillo Spain
99C1 El Fula Sudan
96C1 El Gassi Alg
99D1 El Geteina Sudan
99D1 El Gezira Region, Sudan
94B3 El Ghor V Israel/Jordan
10B2 Elgin Illinois, USA
44C3 Elgin Scot
92B3 El Giza Egypt
96C1 El Golea Alg
99D2 Elgon,Mt Uganda/Kenya
99E2 El Goran Eth
23A2 El Grullo Mexico
96B2 El Guettara Well Mali
99E2 El Hamurre Somalia
96B2 El Haricha Desert Region Mali
92A4 El Harra Egypt
51C2 El Harrach Alg
99D1 El Hawata Sudan
23B1 El Higo Arg
34A3 El Huecu Arg
92B4 El'Igma Desert Region Egypt
12B2 Elim USA
4H2 Elira,C Can
Elisabethville = Lubumbashi
39K6 Elisenvaara Fin
El Iskandariya = Alexandria
61F4 Elista USSR
106C4 Elizabeth Aust
15D2 Elizabeth USA
11C3 Elizabeth City USA
17C1 Elizabethton N Carolina, USA
16A2 Elizabethtown Pennsylvania, USA
96B1 El Jadida Mor
92C3 El Jafr Jordan
99D1 El Jebelein Sudan
96D1 El Jem Tunisia
58C2 Elk Pol
16B3 Elk R Maryland, USA
14B3 Elk R W Virginia, USA
99D1 El Kamlin Sudan
22B1 Elk Grove USA
El Khalil = Hebron
80B3 El Khârga Egypt
80B3 El-Khârga Oasis Egypt
14A2 Elkhart USA
96B2 El Khenachich Desert Region Mali
54C2 Elkhovo Bulg
14C3 Elkins USA
8B2 Elko USA
16B3 Elkton USA
92B3 El Kuntilla Egypt
99C1 El Lagowa Sudan
4H2 Ellef Ringnes I Can
8A2 Ellensburg USA

16B2 Ellenville USA
6B2 Ellesmere I Can
111B2 Ellesmere,L NZ
16A3 Ellicott City USA
100B4 Elliot S Africa
7B5 Elliot Lake Can
94B3 El Lisan Pen Jordan
112B3 Ellsworth Land Region Ant
95B1 El Maghra L Egypt
92B3 El Mansûra Egypt
16B3 Elmer USA
96B3 El Merelé Desert Region Maur
34B2 El Milagro Arg
94B1 El Mina Leb
92B4 El Minya Egypt
22B1 Elmira California, USA
10C2 Elmira New York, USA
98C1 El Muglad Sudan
96B2 El Mzereb Well Mali
79A3 El Nido Phil
99D1 El Obeid Sudan
23A2 El Oro Mexico
96C1 El Oued Alg
9C3 El Paso USA
21A2 El Porta USA
22C2 El Portal USA
50A2 El Puerto del Sta Maria Spain
El Qâhira = Cairo
El Quds = Jerusalem
94B3 El Quseima Egypt
9D3 El Reno USA
4E3 Elsa Can
25D3 El Salvador Republic, Cent America
22D4 Elsinore L USA
57C2 Elsterwerde Germany
El Suweis = Suez
50A1 El Teleno Mt Spain
110B1 Eltham NZ
33E2 El Tigre Ven
92B4 El Tîh Desert Region Egypt
34C2 El Tío Arg
20C1 Eltopia USA
92B4 El Tûr Egypt
87C1 Elûru India
50A2 Elvas Port
32C5 Elvira Brazil
34A2 El Volcán Chile
14A2 Elwood USA
43E3 Ely Eng
10A2 Ely Minnesota, USA
8B3 Ely Nevada, USA
14B2 Elyria USA
90B2 Emâmrûd Iran
58B1 Eman R Sweden
61J4 Emba USSR
61J4 Emba R USSR
29C3 Embalse Cerros Colorados L Arg
51B2 Embalse de Alarcón Res Spain
50A2 Embalse de Alcántara Res Spain
50A2 Embalse de Almendra Res Spain
50A2 Embalse de Garcia de Sola Res Spain
33E2 Embalse de Guri L Ven
51B1 Embalse de Mequinenza Res Spain
50A2 Embalse de Ricobayo Res Spain
29E2 Embalse de Rio Negro Res Urug
29C3 Embalse El Chocón L Arg
29C4 Embalse Florentine Ameghino L Arg
50A1 Embalse Gabriel y Galan Res Spain

30D3 Embarcación Arg
5G4 Embarras Portage Can
47B2 Embrun France
99D3 Embu Kenya
56B2 Emden Germany
73A4 Emei China
56B2 Emden Germany
9C4 Emerald Aust
107D3 Emerald Aust
7D4 Emeri Can
5J5 Emerson Can
21B1 Emigrant P USA
95A3 Emi Koussi Mt Chad
34B3 Emilo Mitre Arg
92B2 Emirdağ Turk
16B2 Emmaus USA
56B2 Emmen Neth
20C2 Emmett USA
16A3 Emmitsburg USA
12B2 Emmonak USA
16A3 Emory Peak Mt USA
24A2 Empalme Mexico
101H1 Empangeni S Africa
30E4 Empedrado Par
105G1 Emperor Seamount Chain Pacific O
18A2 Emporia Kansas, USA
56B2 Ems R Germany
44B2 Enard B Scot
23A1 Encarnacion Mexico
30E4 Encarnación Par
97B4 Enchi Ghana
22D4 Encinitas USA
35C1 Encruzilhada Brazil
106B1 Ende Indon
13D2 Enderby Can
112C11 Enderby Land Region, Ant
15C2 Endicott USA
12D1 Endicott Mts USA
47D1 Engadin Mts Switz
79D2 Engaño,C Phil
94B3 En Gedi Israel
47C1 Engelberg Switz
61G3 Engel's USSR
78A4 Enggano I Indon
41C3 England Country, UK
7E4 Englee Can
41C3 English Channel Eng/ France
97B3 Enji Well Maur
39H7 Enköping Sweden
53B3 Enna Italy
99C1 En Nahud Sudan
95B3 Ennedi Region Chad
109C1 Enngonia Aust
41B3 Ennis Irish Rep
19A3 Ennis Texas, USA
45C2 Enniscorthy Irish Rep
45C1 Enniskillen N Ire
45B2 Ennistimon Irish Rep
94B2 Enn Nâqoura Leb
57C3 Enns R Austria
39F8 Enschede Neth
24A1 Ensenada Mexico
73B3 Enshi China
99D2 Entebbe Uganda
17A1 Enterprise Alabama, USA
20C1 Enterprise Oregon, USA
97C4 Enugu Nig
75B1 Enzan Japan
49C2 Epernay France
16A2 Ephrata Pennsylvania, USA
20C1 Ephrata Washington, USA
49D2 Epinal France
46A2 Epte R France
100A3 Epukiro Namibia
34C3 Epu pel Arg
90B3 Eqlid Iran
89D7 Equator
98A2 Equatorial Guinea Republic, Africa
47C2 Erba Italy
46D2 Erbeskopf Mt Germany
34A3 Ercilla Chile

93D2 Erciş Turk
92C2 Erciyas Daglari Mt Turk
74B2 Erdaobaihe China
72C1 Erdene Mongolia
68C2 Erdenet Mongolia
95B3 Erdi Region Chad
30F4 Erechim Brazil
92B1 Ereğli Turk
92B2 Ereğli Turk
68D2 Erenhot China
50B1 Eresma R Spain
61F3 Erfrud Germany
57C2 Erfurt Germany
93C2 Ergani Turk
96B2 Erg Chech Desert Region Alg
95A3 Erg du Djourab Desert Chad
97D3 Erg Du Ténéré Desert Region Niger
92A1 Ergene R Turk
96B2 Erg Iguidi Region Alg
58D1 Ergli USSR
98B1 Erguig R Chad
62D2 Ergun' USSR
68D1 Ergun R China
63E2 Ergun Zuoqi China
95C3 Eriba Sudan
10C2 Erie USA
10B2 Erie,L Can/USA
42B2 Erin Port Eng
44A3 Eriskay I Scot
46D1 Erkelenz Germany
57C3 Erlangen Germany
19B3 Erling,L USA
101G1 Ermelo S Africa
87B3 Ernakulam India
87B2 Erode India
108A1 Eromanga Aust
96B1 Er Rachidia Mor
99D1 Er Rahad Sudan
101C2 Errego Mozam
40B2 Errigal Mt Irish Rep
41A3 Erris Head Pt Irish Rep
99D1 Er Roseires Sudan
94B2 Er Rummân Jordan
57C2 Erzgebirge Upland Germany
93C2 Erzincan Turk
65F6 Erzurum Turk
48C3 Esara R Spain
56B1 Esbjerg Den
9C4 Escalón Mexico
10B2 Escanaba USA
25C3 Escárcega Mexico
46C2 Esch Lux
21B3 Escondido USA
24B2 Escuinapa Mexico
25C3 Escuintla Guatemala
98B2 Eséka Cam
51C1 Esera R Spain
90B3 Esfahân Iran
101H1 Eshowe S Africa
110C1 Eskdale NZ
38C1 Eskifjörður Iceland
39H7 Eskilstuna Sweden
4E3 Eskimo L Can
7A3 Eskimo Point Can
92B2 Eskisehir Turk
50A1 Esla R Spain
29A5 Esmeralda I Chile
32B3 Esmeraldas Ecuador
26B2 Esmeralda Cuba
49C3 Espalion France
14B1 Espanola USA
32J7 Española I Ecuador
106B4 Esperance Aust
34C2 Esperanza Arg
112C2 Esperanza Base Ant
35C1 Espírito Santo State, Brazil
101C3 Espungabera Mozam
29B4 Esquel Arg
20B1 Esquimalt Can
34D2 Esquina Arg
94C2 Es Samra Jordan
96B1 Essaouira Mor

96A2 Es Semara Mor
56B2 Essen Germany
33F3 Essequibo R Guyana
43E4 Essex County, Eng
14B2 Essexville USA
57B3 Esslingen Germany
48B2 Essonne France
31D4 Estância Brazil
101G1 Estcourt S Africa
47D2 Este Italy
46B2 Esternay France
30D3 Esteros Par
5H5 Estevan Can
17B1 Estill USA
Estonskaya SSR
Republic, USSR
29B6 Estrecho de Magallanes Str Chile
50A2 Estremoz Port
59B3 Esztergom Hung
108A1 Etadunna Aust
46C2 Etam France
48C2 Etampes France
108A1 Etamunbanie,L Aust
46A1 Etaples France
85D3 Etäwah India
99D2 Ethiopia Republic, Africa
23B2 Etla Mexico
53B3 Etna Mt Italy
12A3 Etolin I USA
12H2 Etolin Str USA
6C2 Eton Can
100A2 Etosha Nat Pk Namibia
100A2 Etosha Pan Salt L Namibia
17B1 Etowah R USA
46D2 Ettelbruck Lux
109C2 Euabalong Aust
14B2 Euclid USA
109C3 Eucumbene,L Aust
46B2 Eudunda Aust
19A2 Eufala L USA
17A1 Eufaula USA
8A2 Eugene USA
108C1 Eulo Aust
19B3 Eunice Louisiana, USA
46D1 Eupen Germany
93D3 Euphrates R Iraq
19C3 Eupora USA
48C2 Eure R France
20B2 Eureka California, USA
8B3 Eureka Can
8B3 Eureka Nevada, USA
8B3 Eureka Sd Can
108C3 Euroa Aust
109C1 Eurombah R Aust
101D3 Europa I Mozam Chan
57B2 Euskirchen Germany
13B2 Eutsuk L Can
13D2 Evansburg Can
6B1 Evans,C Can
7C4 Evans,L Can
6B3 Evans Str Can
14A2 Evanston Illinois, USA
8B2 Evanston Wyoming, USA
11B3 Evansville Indiana, USA
101G1 Evaton S Africa
106C4 Everard,L Aust
82C3 Everest,Mt China/ Nepal
8A2 Everett Washington, USA
16C1 Everett,Mt USA
11B4 Everglades,The Swamp USA
43D3 Evesham Eng
98B2 Evinayong Eq Guinea
39F7 Evje Nor
47B1 Evolène Switz
50A2 Évora Port
48C2 Evreux France
55B3 Évvoia I Greece
98B3 Ewo Congo

22C1 Excelsior Mt USA
18B2 Excelsior Springs USA
21B2 Exeter California, USA
43C4 Exeter Eng
15D2 Exeter New Hampshire, USA
43C4 Exmoor Nat Pk Eng
43C4 Exmouth Eng
50A2 Extremadura Region, Spain
25E2 Exuma Sd The Bahamas
99D3 Eyasi L Tanz
42C2 Eyemouth Scot
99E2 Eyl Somalia
106B4 Eyre R Aust
106C3 Eyre Creek R Aust
106C3 Eyre,L Aust
106C4 Eyre Pen Aust
79B3 Eyte i Phil
23A1 Ezatlan Mexico
55C3 Ezine Turk

F

4G3 Faber L Can
39G7 Fåborg Den
52B2 Fabriano Italy
95A3 Fachi Niger
95B3 Fada Chad
97C3 Fada N'Gourma Burkina
52B2 Faenza Italy
6E3 Faeringehavn Greenland
98B2 Fafa R CAR
99E2 Fafan R Eth
54B1 Făgăras Rom
46C1 Fagnes Region, Belg
97B3 Faguibine,L L Mali
91C5 Fahud Oman
96A1 Faiol i Açores
4D3 Fairbanks USA
7A5 Fairbault USA
14B3 Fairborn USA
8D2 Fairbury USA
16A3 Fairfax USA
21A2 Fairfield California, USA
16C2 Fairfield Connecticut, USA
14B3 Fairfield Ohio, USA
45C1 Fair Head Pt N Ire
40C2 Fair Isle i Scot
111B2 Fairlie NZ
14B3 Fairmont W Virginia, USA
13D1 Fairview Can
4E4 Fairweather,Mt USA
71F3 Fais i Pacific O
84C2 Faisalabad Pak
8C2 Faith USA
44E1 Faither,The Pen Scot
86A1 Faizãbãd India
43E3 Fakenham Eng
39G7 Fåköping Sweden
86C2 Falam Burma
24C2 Falcon Res Mexico/USA
97A3 Falémé R Mali/Sen
39G7 Falkenberg Sweden
42C2 Falkirk Scot
29D6 Falkland Is Dependency, S Atlantic
29E6 Falkland Sd Falkland Is
22D4 Fallbrook USA
8B3 Fallon USA
15D2 Fall River USA
18A1 Falls City USA
43B4 Falmouth Eng
27H1 Falmouth Jamaica
16D2 Falmouth Massachusetts, USA
100A4 False B S Africa
24A2 Falso,C Mexico
56C2 Falster i Den

54C1 Fălticeni Rom
39H6 Falun Sweden
92B2 Famagusta Cyprus
46C1 Famenne Region, Belg
76B2 Fang Thai
99D2 Fangak Sudan
73E5 Fang liao Taiwan
52B2 Fano Italy
112C3 Faraday Base Ant
99C2 Faradje Zaïre
101D3 Farafangana Madag
95B2 Farafra Oasis Egypt
80E2 Farah Afghan
71F2 Faralon de Medinilla i Pacific O
97A3 Faranah Guinea
71F3 Faraulep i Pacific O
43D4 Fareham Eng
Farewell,C = Kap Farvel
107G5 Farewell,C NZ
110B2 Farewell Spit Pt NZ
8D2 Fargo USA
94B2 Fari'a R Israel
10A2 Faribault USA
86B2 Faridpur Bang
90C2 Farīmān Iran
18B2 Farmington Missouri, USA
9C3 Farmington New Mexico, USA
22B2 Farmington Res USA
42D2 Farne Deep N Sea
47D2 Farnham,Mt USA
12H2 Faro Can
50A2 Faro Port
39H7 Fåro i Sweden
89K9 Farquhar is Indian O
44B3 Farrar R Scot
14B2 Farrell USA
53A3 Fársala Greece
91B4 Fasã Iran
45B3 Fastnet Rock Irish Rep
60C3 Fastov USSR
86A1 Fatehpur India
13D1 Father Can
30F2 Fatima du Sul Brazil
101G1 Fauresmith S Africa
47B2 Faverges France
7B4 Fawn R Can
38H6 Fax R Sweden
38A2 Faxaflóri R Iceland
95A3 Faya Chad
11A3 Fayetteville Arkansas, USA
11C3 Fayetteville N Carolina, USA
93E4 Faylakah i Kuwait
84C2 Fãzilka India
96A2 Fdérik Maur
11C3 Fear,C USA
21A2 Feather Middle Fork R USA
48C2 Fécamp France
34D2 Federación Arg
34D2 Federal Arg
71F3 Federated States of Micronesia is Pacific O
56C2 Fehmarn i Germany
32C5 Feijó Brazil
73C5 Feilai Xai Bei Jiang R China
110C2 Feilding NZ
100C2 Feira Zambia
31DA Feira de Santan Brazil
92C2 Feke Turk
57B3 Feldkirch Austria
34D2 Feliciano R Arg
41D3 Felixstowe Eng
47D1 Feltre Italy
38G6 Femund L Nor
74A2 Fengcheng China
73B4 Fengdu China
72D1 Fenging China
73B3 Fengjie China
72B3 Feng Xian China
72C1 Fengzhen China
72C2 Fen He R China

101D2 Fenoarivo Atsinanana Madag
60E5 Feodosiya USSR
90C3 Ferdow Iran
46B2 Fère-Champenoise France
82B2 Fergana USSR
45C1 Fermanagh County, N Ire
45B2 Fermoy Irish Rep
47D1 Fern Mt Italy
32J7 Fernandina i Ecuador
14B1 Fernandina Beach USA
103G5 Fernando de Noronha i Atlantic O
35A2 Fernandópolis Brazil
20B1 Ferndale USA
21B2 Fernley USA
52B2 Ferrara Italy
32B5 Ferreñafe Peru
19B3 Ferriday USA
96B1 Fès Mor
18B2 Festus USA
54C2 Fetesti Rom
92A2 Fethiye Turk
61H5 Fetisovo USSR
44E1 Fetlar i' Scot
84C1 Feyzabad Afghan
101D3 Fianarantsoa Madag
99D2 Fiche Eth
101G1 Ficksburg S Africa
47D2 Fidenza Italy
55A2 Fier Alb
47D1 Fiera Di Primeiro Italy
44C3 Fife Region, Scot
44C3 Fife Ness Pen Scot
48C3 Figeac France
50A1 Figueira da Foz Port
51C1 Figueras Spain
96B1 Figuig Mor
105G4 Fiji is Pacific O
30D3 Filadelfia Par
54B2 Filiaşi Rom
55B3 Filiatrá Greece
53B3 Filicudi i Italy
21B3 Fillmore California, USA
44B3 Findhorn R Scot
10C2 Findlay USA
13D2 Findlay,Mt USA
15C2 Finger Lakes USA
92B2 Finike Turk
106C3 Finke R Aust
108A1 Finke Flood Flats Aust
64D3 Finland Republic, N Europe
39J7 Finland,G of N Europe
5F4 Finlay R Can
5F4 Finlay Forks Can
108C3 Finley Aust
38H5 Finnsnes Nor
71F4 Finschhafen PNG
47C1 Finsteraarhorn Mt Switz
56C2 Finterwalde Germany
45C1 Fintona N Ire
111A3 Fiordland Nat Pk NZ
94B2 Fiq Syria
93C2 Firat R Turk
22B2 Firebaugh USA
52B2 Firenze Italy
34C2 Firmat Arg
85D3 Firozābād India
84C2 Firozpur India
39H7 Firspång Sweden
44A3 Firth of Clyde Estuary Scot
44C3 Firth of Forth Estuary Scot
44A3 Firth of Lorn Estuary Scot
40C2 Firth of Tay Estuary Scot
91B4 Firuzabad Iran
100A3 Fish R Namibia
22C2 Fish Camp USA

16C2 Fishers I USA
6B3 Fisher Str Can
43B4 Fishguard Wales
6E3 Fiskenaesset Greenland
46B2 Fismes France
15D2 Fitchburg USA
17B1 Fitful Head Pt Scot
17B1 Fitzgerald USA
7A Fitzroy R Aust
106B2 Fitzroy Crossing Aust
14B1 Fitzwilliam I Can
Fiume = Rijeka
99C3 Fizi Zaïre
9B3 Flagstaff USA
42D2 Flamborough Head C Eng
8C2 Flaming Gorge Res Eng
44A2 Flannan Isles Is Scot
12J2 Flat R Can
13E3 Flathead R USA
8B2 Flathead L USA
18B2 Flat River USA
8A2 Flattery,C USA
42C3 Fleetwood Eng
39F7 Flekkefjord Nor
69G4 Fleming Deep Pacific O
16B2 Flemington USA
56B2 Flensburg Germany
47B1 Fleurier Switz
106C4 Flinders i Aust
107D4 Flinders i Aust
107D2 Flinders R Aust
106C4 Flinders Range Mts Aust
5H4 Flin Flon Can
10B2 Flint USA
42C3 Flint Wales
11B3 Flint R USA
46B1 Flixecourt France
17A1 Florala USA
Florence = Firenze
11B3 Florence Alabama, USA
18A2 Florence Kansas, USA
20B2 Florence Oregon, USA
11C3 Florence S Carolina, USA
32B3 Florencia Colombia
46C2 Florenville Belg
25D3 Flores Guatemala
96A1 Flores i Açores
106B1 Flores i Indon
34D3 Flores R Arg
70C4 Flores S Indon
31C3 Floriano Brazil
30G4 Florianópolis Brazil
25D2 Florida State, USA
29E2 Florida Urug
17B2 Florida B USA
17B2 Florida City USA
107E1 Florida Is Solomon Is
11B4 Florida Keys Is USA
11B4 Florida,Strs of USA
55B2 Florina Greece
38F6 Florø Nor
47D1 Fluchthorn Mt Austria
54C1 Focsani Rom
53C2 Foggia Italy
97A4 Fogo i Cape Verde
48C3 Foix France
6C3 Foley i Can
52B2 Foligno Italy
43E4 Folkestone Eng
17B1 Folkston USA
52B2 Follonica Italy
22B1 Folsom USA
22B1 Folsom L L USA
5H4 Fond-du-Lac Can
10B2 Fond Du Lac USA
48C2 Fontainebleau France
18B2 Fontenac USA
48B2 Fontenay-le-Comte France
52C1 Fonyód Hung
Foochow = Fuzhou

12D2 Foraker,Mt USA	5G3 Fort Smith Can	40C2 Frazerburgh Scot	75C1 Funabashi Japan
46D2 Forbach France	4G3 Fort Smith Region,	16B3 Frederica USA	96A1 Funchal Medeira
109C2 Forbes Aust	Can	56B1 Fredericia Den	35C1 Fundão Brazil
97C4 Forcados Nig	11A3 Fort Smith USA	15C3 Frederick Maryland,	7D5 Fundy,B of Can
38F6 Forde Nor	9C3 Fort Stockton USA	USA	101C3 Funhalouro Mozam
108C1 Fords Bridge Aust	20B2 Fortuna California,	15C3 Fredericksburg	72D3 Funing China
19B3 Fordyce USA	USA	Virginia, USA	73B5 Funing China
97A4 Forécariah Guinea	5G4 Fort Vermillion Can	12H3 Frederick Sd USA	97C3 Funtua Nig
6G3 Forel,Mt Greenland	17A1 Fort Walton Beach	18B2 Fredericktown USA	73D4 Fuqing China
14B2 Forest USA	USA	7D5 Fredericton Can	101C2 Furancungo Mozam
17B1 Forest Park USA	14B2 Fort Wayne USA	6E3 Frederikshab	91C4 Fürg Iran
22A1 Forestville USA	44B3 Fort William Scot	Greenland	47C1 Furka P Switz
44C3 Forfar Scot	9C3 Fort Worth USA	39G7 Frederikshavn Den	107D5 Furneaux Group Is
46A2 Forges-les-Eaux	12F2 Fortymile R USA	15C2 Fredonia USA	Aust
France	12E1 Fort Yukon USA	39G7 Fredrikstad Nor	56C2 Fürstenwalde
20B1 Forks USA	73C5 Foshan China	16B2 Freehold USA	Germany
52B2 Forlì Italy	47B2 Fossano Italy	26B1 Freeport The Bahamas	57C3 Fürth Germany
51C2 Formentera I Spain	12G3 Foster,Mt USA	19A4 Freeport Texas, USA	74D3 Furukawa Japan
53B2 Formia Italy	98B3 Fougamou Gabon	97A4 Freetown Sierra Leone	6B3 Fury and Hecla St Can
96A1 Formigas / Açores	48B2 Fougères France	57C3 Freistadt Austria	74A2 Fushun Liaoning,
Formosa = Taiwan	44D1 Foula I Scot	106A4 Fremantle Aust	China
30E4 Formosa Arg	43E4 Foulness I Eng	22B2 Fremont California,	73A4 Fushun Sichuan, China
31D5 Formosa Brazil	111B2 Foulwind,C NZ	USA	74B2 Fusong China
30D5 Formosa State, Arg	98B2 Foumban Cam	18A1 Fremont Nebraska,	57C3 Füssen Germany
73D5 Formosa Str Taiwan/	49C1 Fourmies France	USA	72E2 Fu Xian China
China	55C3 Foúrnoi I Greece	14B2 Fremont Ohio, USA	72E1 Fuxin China
47D2 Fornovo di Taro Italy	97A3 Fouta Djallon Mts	33G3 French Guiana	72D1 Fuyang China
38D3 Faroyar Is	Guinea	Dependency,	72E1 Fuyuan Liaoning,
N Atlantic O	111B3 Foveaux Str NZ	S America	China
44C3 Forres Scot	43B4 Fowey Eng	109C4 Frenchmans Cap Mt	73A4 Fuyuan Yunnan, China
106B4 Forrest Aust	13D2 Fox Creek Can	Aust	68A2 Fuyun China
11A3 Forrest City USA	6B3 Foxe Basin G Can	105J4 French Polynesia Is	73D4 Fuzhou China
107D2 Forsayth Aust	6B3 Foxe Chan Can	Pacific O	56C1 Fyn / Den
39J6 Forssa Fin	6C3 Foxe Pen Can	24B2 Fresnillo Mexico	
109D2 Forster Aust	110C2 Foxton NZ	8B3 Fresno USA	**G**
18B2 Forsyth Missouri, USA	13F2 Fox Valley Can	22C2 Fresno R USA	
84C3 Fort Abbas Pak	45B2 Foynes Irish Rep	47A1 Fretigney France	99E2 Gaalkacyo Somalia
7B4 Fort Albany Can	100A4 Foz do Cuene Angola	46B1 Frévent France	21B2 Gabbs USA
31D2 Fortaleza Brazil	30F4 Foz do Iguaçu Brazil	109C4 Freycinet Pen Aust	100A2 Gabela Angola
44B3 Fort Augustus Scot	16A2 Frackville USA	97A3 Fria Guinea	96D1 Gabe's Tunisia
100B4 Fort Beaufort S Africa	34B2 Fraga Arg	22C2 Friant USA	22B2 Gabilan Range Mts
21A2 Fort Bragg USA	16D1 Framingham USA	22C2 Friant Dam USA	USA
8C2 Fort Collins USA	31B6 Franca Brazil	52A1 Fribourg Switz	98B3 Gabon Republic, Africa
15C1 Fort Coulogne Can	49C2 France	57B3 Friedrichshafen	100B3 Gaborone Botswana
27E4 Fort de France	Republic, Europe	Germany	54C2 Gabrovo Bulg
Martinique	10A2 Frances Can	6D3 Frobisher B Can	91B3 Gach Sārān Iran
17A1 Fort Deposit USA	12J2 Frances R Can	6D3 Frobisher Bay Can	17A1 Gadsden Alabama,
10A2 Fort Dodge USA	98B3 Franca Ville Gabon	5H4 Frobisher L Can	USA
106A3 Fortescue R Aust	49D2 Franche Comté	61F4 Frolovo USSR	10A1 Gads L Can
7A5 Fort Frances Can	Region, France	43C4 Frome Eng	53B2 Gaeta Italy
4F3 Fort Franklin Can	100B3 Francistown Botswana	108A1 Frome R Aust	71F3 Gaferut I Pacific O
7C4 Fort George Can	13B2 Francois L Can	43C4 Frome R Eng	96C1 Gafsa Tunisia
4F3 Fort Good Hope Can	14A2 Frankfort Indiana, USA	106C4 Frome,L Aust	60D2 Gagarin USSR
108B1 Fort Grey Aust	11B3 Frankfort Kentucky,	15C3 Front Royal USA	97B4 Gagnoa Ivory Coast
44B3 Forth R Scot	USA	15C3 Frontera Mexico	7D4 Gagnon Can
7B4 Fort Hope Can	101G1 Frankfort S Africa	53B2 Frosinone Italy	61F5 Gagra USSR
34B2 Fortin Uno Arg	57B2 Frankfurt Germany	82B1 Frunze USSR	86B1 Gaibanda India
4F3 Fort Laird Can	46E1 Frankfurt am Main	73C5 Fuchuan China	29C4 Gaimán Arg
96C1 Fort Lallemand Alg	Germany	24B2 Fuerte R Mexico	17B2 Gainesville Florida,
97A3 Fort Lamy = Ndjamena	56C2 Frankfurt-an-der-Oder	30E3 Fuerte Olimpo Par	USA
11B4 Fort Lauderdale USA	Germany	96A2 Fuerteventura I	17B1 Gainesville Georgia,
4F3 Fort Liard Can	57C3 Fränkischer Alb	Canary Is	USA
5G4 Fort Mackay Can	Upland Germany	72C2 Fugu China	19A3 Gainesville Texas,
5G5 Fort Macleod Can	14A3 Franklin Indiana, USA	68A2 Fuhai China	USA
5G4 Fort McMurray Can	19B4 Franklin Louisiana,	91C5 Fujairah UAE	42D3 Gainsborough Eng
4E3 Fort McPherson Can	USA	75B1 Fuji Japan	108A2 Gairdner,L Aust
108J2 Fort Madison USA	16D1 Franklin	73D4 Fujian Province, China	16A3 Gaithersburg USA
8C2 Fort Morgan USA	Massachusetts, USA	69F2 Fujin China	87B1 Gajendragarh India
11B4 Fort Myers USA	16B2 Franklin New Jersey,	75B1 Fujinomiya Japan	73D4 Ga Jiang R China
5F4 Fort Nelson Can	USA	74D3 Fuji-san Mt Japan	99E2 Galadi Eth
4F3 Fort Norman Can	14C2 Franklin Pennsylvania,	75B1 Fujisawa Japan	99D3 Galana R Kenya
17A1 Fort Payne USA	USA	75B1 Fuji-Yoshida Japan	103D6 Galapagos Is Pacific O
8C2 Fort Peck Res USA	4F2 Franklin B Can	73C4 Fukang China	42C2 Galashiels Scot
11B4 Fort Pierce USA	20C1 Franklin D Roosevelt L	74C3 Fukuchiyima Japan	54C1 Galati Rom
4G3 Fort Providence Can	USA	74C4 Fukue Japan	4C3 Galena Alaska, USA
5G3 Fort Resolution Can	4F3 Franklin Mts Can	74C3 Fukui Japan	18B2 Galena Kansas, USA
98B3 Fort Rousset Congo	4J2 Franklin Str Can	74C4 Fukuoka Japan	27L1 Galeota Pt Trinidad
7C4 Fort Rupert Can	64D5 Frankovsk USSR	74C4 Fukushima Japan	27L1 Galera Pt Trinidad
5F4 Fort St James Can	111B2 Franz Josef Glacier NZ	74C4 Fukuyama Japan	10A2 Galesburg USA
13C1 Fort St John Can	Franz-Joseph-Land =	16B3 Fulda USA	15C2 Galeton USA
13E2 Fort Saskatchewan	Zemlya Frantsa Iosifa	57B2 Fulda Germany	61F2 Galich USSR
Can	5F5 Fraser R Can	57B2 Fulda R Germany	50A1 Galicia Region, Spain
4F3 Fort Scott USA	44C3 Fraserburgh Scot	73B4 Fuling China	Galilee,S of = Tiberias,L
4E3 Fort Selkirk Can	107E3 Fraser I Aust	27L1 Fullarton Trinidad	27J1 Galina Pt Jamaica
7B4 Fort Severn Can	13B2 Fraser L Can	22D4 Fullerton USA	99D1 Gallabat Sudan
61H5 Fort Shevchenko	47B1 Frasne France	18C2 Fulton Kentucky, USA	47C2 Gallarate Italy
USSR	34D2 Fray Bentos Urug	15C2 Fulton New York, USA	
4F3 Fort Simpson Can		46C1 Fumay France	

87C3 Galle Sri Lanka
51B1 Gállego R Spain
    Gallipoli = Gelibolu
55A2 Gallipoli Italy
38J5 Gällivare Sweden
42B2 Galloway District
42B2 Galloway,Mull of C
    Scot
8C3 Gallup USA
22B1 Galt USA
96A2 Galtat Zemmour Mor
25C2 Galveston USA
11A4 Galveston B USA
34C2 Gálvez Arg
49D3 Galvi Corse
45B2 Galway County,
    Irish Rep
41B3 Galway Irish Rep
41B3 Galway B Irish Rep
86B1 Gamba Gabon
97B3 Gambaga Ghana
4A3 Gambell USA
97A3 Gambia R The Gambia/
    Sen
97A3 Gambia,The, Republic,
    Africa
98B3 Gamboma Congo
100A2 Gambos Angola
87C3 Gampola Sri Lanka
99E2 Ganale Dorya R Eth
15C2 Gananoque Can
    Gand = Gent
100A2 Ganda Angola
98C3 Gandajika Zaire
84B3 Gandava Pak
7E5 Gander Can
85C4 Gāndhidhām India
85C4 Gāndhinagar India
85D4 Gāndhi Sāgar L India
51B2 Gandia Spain
86B2 Ganga R India
85C3 Ganganar India
86C2 Gangaw Burma
72A2 Gangca China
82C2 Gangdise Shan Mts
    China
    Ganges = Ganga
86B1 Gangtok India
72B3 Gangu China
8C2 Gannett Peak Mt USA
72B2 Ganquan China
108A3 Gantheaume C Aust
39K8 Gantseviohi USSR
73D4 Ganzhou China
97C3 Gao Mali
72A2 Gaolan China
72C2 Gaoping China
97B3 Gaoua Burkina
97A3 Gaoual Guinea
72D3 Gaoyou Hu L China
73C5 Gaozhou China
49D3 Gap France
79B2 Gapan Phil
84D2 Gar China
109C1 Garah Aust
31D3 Garanhuns Brazil
21A1 Garberville USA
35B2 Garça Brazil
35A2 Garcias Brazil
47D2 Garda Italy
9C3 Garden City USA
14A1 Garden Pen USA
34D3 Gardey Arg
84B2 Gardez Afghan
16C2 Gardiners I USA
16D1 Gardner USA
47D2 Gardone Italy
99D2 Gardula Eth
47D2 Gargano Italy
85D4 Garhākota India
61K2 Gari USSR
5A3 Garies S Africa
99D3 Garissa Kenya
19A3 Garland USA
57C3 Garmisch-Partenkirchen
    Germany
90B2 Garmsar Iran
18A2 Garnett USA

8B2 Garnett Peak Mt USA
48C3 Garonne R France
44B3 Garry R Scot
78B4 Garut Indon
86A2 Garwa India
14A2 Gary USA
82C2 Garyarsa China
4H3 Gary L Can
93 Garza-Little Elm Res
    USA
90B2 Gasan Kuli USSR
48B3 Gascogne Region,
    France
18B2 Gasconade R USA
106A3 Gascoyne R Aust
98B2 Gashaka Nig
97D3 Gashua Nig
10D2 Gaspé Can
10D2 Gaspé,C Can
10D2 Gaspé Pen Can
94A1 Gata,C Cyprus
60C2 Gatchina USSR
42D2 Gateshead Eng
19A2 Gatesville USA
15C1 Gatineau Can
15C1 Gatineau R Can
109D1 Gatton Aust
86C1 Gauhāti India
58C1 Gauja R USSR
86A1 Gauri Phanta India
22B3 Gaviota USA
39H6 Gävle Sweden
108A2 Gawler Ranges Mts
    Aust
72A1 Gaxun Nur L China
86A2 Gaya India
97C3 Gaya Niger
14B1 Gaylord USA
109D1 Gayndah Aust
61H1 Gayny USSR
60C4 Gaysin USSR
92B3 Gaza Israel
97B4 Gbaringa Lib
58B2 Gdańsk Pol
58B2 Gdańsk,G of Pol
39K7 Gdov USSR
58B2 Gdynia Pol
94A3 Gebel Halāl Mt Egypt
95C2 Gebel Hamata Mt
    Egypt
92B4 Gebel Katherina Mt
    Egypt
94A3 Gebel Libni Mt Egypt
94A3 Gebel Maghāra Mt
    Egypt
99D1 Gedaref Sudan
55C3 Gediz R Turk
56C2 Gedser Den
46C1 Geel Belg
108B3 Geelong Aust
109C4 Geeveston Aust
97D3 Geidam Nig
46D1 Geilenkirchen
    Germany
99D3 Geita Tanz
73A5 Gejiu China
53B3 Gela Italy
46D1 Geldern Germany
55C2 Gelibolu Turk
92B2 Gelidonya Burun Turk
46D1 Gelsenkirchen
    Germany
39F8 Gelting Germany
77C5 Gemas Malay
46C1 Gembloux Belg
98B2 Gemena Zaïre
92C2 Gemerek Turk
92A1 Gemlik Turk
52B1 Gemona Italy
100B3 Gemsbok Nat Pk
    Botswana
98C1 Geneina Sudan
34C3 General Acha Arg
34B2 General Alvear
    Buenos Aires, Arg
34B2 General Alvear
    Mendoza, Arg

34C2 General Arenales Arg
34D3 General Belgrano Arg
112B2 General Belgrano Base
    Ant
112C2 General Bernardo
    O'Higgins Base Ant
34D3 General Conesa
    Buenos Aires, Arg
30D3 General Eugenio A
    Garay Par
34D3 General Guido Arg
34C3 General La Madrid Arg
34C2 General Levalle Arg
30C4 General Manuel
    Belgrano Mt Arg
34D3 General Paz
    Buenos Aires, Arg
34C3 General Pico Arg
34C2 General Pinto Arg
29C3 General Roca Arg
79C4 General Santos Phil
34C3 General Viamonte Arg
34C3 General Villegas Arg
15C2 Genesee R USA
15C2 Geneseo USA
    Geneva = Genève
18A1 Geneva Nebraska, USA
87B1 Geneva New York,
    USA
    Geneva, L of = Lac
    Léman
52A1 Genève Switz
50B2 Genil R Spain
    Genoa = Genova
109C3 Genoa Aust
52A2 Genoa Italy
32J7 Genovesa I Ecuador
46B1 Gent Belg
78B4 Genteng Indon
56C2 Genthin Germany
93E1 Geokchay USSR
100B4 George S Africa
7D4 George R Can
109C2 George,L USA
17B2 George,L Florida, USA
15D2 George,L New York,
    USA
111A2 George Sd NZ
109C4 George Town Aust
15C3 Georgetown Delaware,
    USA
33F2 Georgetown Guyana
14B3 Georgetown Kentucky,
    USA
77C4 George Town Malay
27N2 Georgetown St
    Vincent
17C1 Georgetown S
    Carolina, USA
19A3 Georgetown Texas,
    USA
97A3 Georgetown The
    Gambia
112C8 George V Land Region,
    Ant
17B1 Georgia State, USA
14B1 Georgia B Can
13C3 Georgia,Str of Can
60E3 Georgina R Aust
61F5 Georgiyevsk USSR
57C2 Gera Germany
46B1 Geraardsbergen Belg
111B2 Geraldine NZ
106A3 Geraldton Aust
10B2 Geraldton Can
94B3 Gerar R.Israel
4C3 Gerdine,Mt USA
12E2 Gerdova Peak Mt USA
77C4 Gerik Malay
60B4 Gerlachovsky Mt Pol
13C1 Germanson Lodge Can
56C2 Germany
    Republic, Europe
101G1 Germiston S Africa
46D1 Gerolstein Germany
51C1 Gerona Spain

46E1 Geseke Germany
99E2 Gestro R Eth
50B1 Getafe Spain
16A3 Gettysburg
    Pennsylvania, USA
93D2 Gevas Turk
55B2 Gevgelija Yugos
47B1 Gex France
94C2 Ghabāghib Syria
96C1 Ghadamis Libya
90B2 Ghaem Shahr Iran
86A1 Ghāghara R India
97B4 Ghana Republic,
    Africa
100B3 Ghanzi Botswana
96C1 Ghardaia Alg
95A1 Gharyan Libya
95A2 Ghāt Libya
84D3 Ghāziābād India
84C3 Ghazi Khan Pak
84B2 Ghazni Afghan
54C1 Gheorghe G-Dej Rom
54C1 Gheorgheni Rom
88E4 Ghudamis Alg
90D3 Ghurian Afghan
95B2 Gialo Libya
99E3 Giamame Somalia
53C3 Giarre Italy
100A3 Gibeon Namibia
50A2 Gibraltar Colony,
    SW Europe
50A2 Gibraltar,Str of Spain/
    Africa
106B3 Gibson Desert Aust
20B1 Gibsons Can
87B1 Giddalūr India
57B2 Giessen Germany
17B2 Gifford USA
74D3 Gifu Japan
42B2 Gigha I Scot
52A2 Giglio I Italy
50A1 Gijón Spain
107D2 Gilbert R Aust
13C2 Gilbert,Mt Can
101C2 Gilé Mozam
94B2 Gilead Region, Jordan
91B4 Gilf Kebir Plat Egypt
109C2 Gilgandra Aust
84C1 Gilgit Pak
84C1 Gilgit R Pak
108C2 Gilgunnia Aust
7A4 Gillam Can
108A2 Gilles L Aust
13B2 Gill I Can
14A1 Gills Rock USA
14A2 Gilman USA
22B2 Gilroy USA
8D1 Gimli Can
101H1 Gingindlovu S Africa
79C4 Gingoog Phil
99E3 Ginir Eth
55B3 Gióna Mt Greece
109C3 Gippsland Mts Aust
14B2 Girard USA
32C3 Girardot Colombia
44C3 Girdle Ness Pen Scot
93C1 Giresun Turk
59B3 Gir Hills India
98B2 Giri R Zaïre
86B2 Girīdih India
48B2 Gironde R France
42B2 Girvan Scot
111C2 Gisborne NZ
46A2 Gisors France
99C3 Gitega Burundi
    Giuba,B = Juba,R
54C2 Giurgiu Rom
46C1 Givet Belg
58C2 Gizycko Pol
55B2 Gjirokastër Alb
39G6 Gjovik Nor
7D5 Glace Bay Can
12G3 Glacier Bay Nat Mon
    USA
13E3 Glacier Nat Pk USA/
    Can
20B1 Glacier Peak Mt USA

6B2 Glacier Str Can
107E3 Gladstone
   Queensland, Aust
108A2 Gladstone S Aust,
   Aust
109C4 Gladstone Tasmania,
   Aust
14A1 Gladstone USA
38A1 Glama Mt Iceland
39G6 Glåma R Nor
46D2 Glan R Germany
47C1 Glarner Mts Switz
47C1 Glarus Switz
18A2 Glasco USA
8C2 Glasgow Montana,
   USA
42B2 Glasgow Scot
16B3 Glassboro USA
43C4 Glastonbury Eng
61H2 Glazov USSR
59B3 Gleisdorf Austria
110C1 Glen Afton NZ
16A3 Glen Burnie USA
101H1 Glencoe S Africa
9B3 Glendale Arizona,
   USA
22C3 Glendale California,
   USA
12E2 Glenhallen USA
109D1 Glen Innes Aust
109C4 Glenmorgan Aust
109D2 Glenreagh Aust
16A3 Glen Rock USA
19A3 Glen Rose USA
44C3 Glenrothes UK
15D2 Glens Falls USA
45B1 Glenties Irish Rep
19B3 Glenwood Arkansas,
   USA
8C3 Glenwood Springs
   USA
39F6 Glittertind Mt Nor
59B2 Gliwice Pol
9B3 Globe USA
58B2 Głogów Pol
38G5 Glomfjord Nor
109D2 Gloucester Aust
43C4 Gloucester Eng
16C1 Gloucester USA
58D1 Glubokoye USSR
60D3 Glukhov USSR
59B3 Gmünd Austria
57C3 Gmunden Austria
58B2 Gniezno Pol
100A3 Goabeg Namibia
87A1 Goa, Daman and Diu
   Union Territory,
   India
86C1 Goälpara India
99D2 Goba Eth
100A3 Gobabis Namibia
34C2 Gobernador Crespo
   Arg
34B3 Gobernador Duval Arg
72B1 Gobi Desert China/
   Mongolia
75B2 Gobo Japan
87B1 Godag India
87C1 Godāvari R India
14B2 Goderich Can
6E3 Godhavn Greenland
85C4 Godhra India
34B2 Godoy Cruz Arg
7A4 Gods L Can
6E3 Godthåb Greenland
   Godwin Austen = K2
35B1 Goiandira Brazil
35B1 Goianésia Brazil
35B1 Goiânia Brazil
35A1 Goiás Brazil
31B4 Goiás State, Brazil
35A2 Goio-Erê Brazil
99D2 Gojab R Eth
55C2 Gökçeada I Turk
55C3 Gökova Körfezi R
   Turk
92C2 Göksun Turk
63C3 Gol R USSR

86C1 Golāghāt India
93C2 Gölbaşi Turk
20C2 Golconda USA
20B2 Gold Beach USA
109D1 Gold Coast Aust
13D2 Golden Can
110B2 Golden B NZ
20B1 Goldendale USA
22A2 Golden Gate Chan
   USA
19B4 Golden Meadow USA
21B2 Goldfield USA
13B3 Gold River Can
58C2 Goleniow Pol
22C3 Goleta USA
52A2 Golfe d'Ajaccio G
   Corse
96D1 Golfe de Gabes G
   Tunisia
   Golfe de Gascogne =
   Biscay,Bay of
52A2 Golfe de St Florent G
   Corse
48B2 Golfe de St-Malo B
   France
49C3 Golfe du Lion G
   France
29B4 Golfo Corcovado G
   Chile
50B2 Golfo de Almeria G
   Spain
29B4 Golfo de Ancud G
   Chile
25D2 Golfo de Batabano G
   Cuba
50A2 Golfo de Cadiz G
   Spain
53A3 Golfo de Cagliari G
   Sardegna
24A1 Golfo de California G
   Mexico
25D3 Golfo de Chiriqui G
   Panama
25D3 Golfo de Fonseca G
   Honduras
26B2 Golfo de Guacanayabo
   G Cuba
32A4 Golfo de Guayaquil G
   Ecuador
26B5 Golfo del Darien G
   Colombia/Panama
32A2 Golfo de los Mosquitos
   G Panama
25D3 Golfo del Papagaya G
   Nic
51B2 Golfo de Mazarrón G
   Spain
25D4 Golfo de Nicoya G
   Costa Rica
53A3 Golfo de Oristano G
   Sardegna
25E4 Golfo de Panamá G
   Panama
25D3 Golfo de Papagayo G
   Costa Rica
27E4 Golfo de Paria G Ven
29B5 Golfo de Penas G
   Chile
49D3 Golfo de St Florent
   Corse
51C1 Golfo de San Jorge G
   Spain
24C3 Golfo de Tehuantepec
   G Mexico
32B3 Golfo de Torugas G
   Colombia
32B2 Golfo de Uraba G
   Colombia
51C2 Golfo de Valencia G
   Spain
27C4 Golfo de Venezuela G
   Ven
52A3 Golfo di Genova G
   Italy
53C3 Golfo di Policastro G
   Italy
53C3 Golfo di Squillace G
   Italy

53C2 Golfo di Taranto G
   Italy
52B2 Golfo di Venezia G
   Italy
25D4 Golfo Dulce G
   Costa Rica
29C5 Golfo San Jorge G Arg
29D4 Golfo San Matias G
   Arg
68B3 Golmud China
99E2 Golocha Eth
52C3 Golovin B USA
74F2 Golovnino USSR
99C3 Goma Zaire
97D3 Gombe Nig
60D3 Gomel USSR
96A2 Gomera I Canary Is
24B2 Gómez Palacio Mexico
63E2 Gonam R USSR
90C2 Gonbad-e Kāvūs Iran
86A1 Gonda India
85C4 Gondal India
99D1 Gondar Eth
92A1 Gönen Turk
55C3 Gonen R Turk
73A4 Gongga Shan Mt
   China
72A2 Gonghe China
97D3 Gongola R Nig
22B2 Gonzales California,
   USA
19A4 Gonzales Texas, USA
34C3 Gonzalez Chaves Arg
13C2 Good Hope Mt Can
8C2 Goodland USA
12B3 Goodnews Bay USA
109C1 Goodooga R Aust
42D3 Goole Eng
108C2 Goolgowi Aust
108A4 Goolma Aust
108C2 Goombalie Aust
109D1 Goomeri Aust
109D1 Goondiwindi Aust
7E4 Goose Bay Can
17C1 Goose Creek USA
20B2 Goose L USA
87B1 Gooty India
63C2 Gora Munku Sardyk Mt
   USSR
54A2 Goražde Yugos
4D3 Gordon USA
13E1 Gordon L Can
15C3 Gordonsville USA
98B2 Goré Chad
99D2 Gore Eth
111A3 Gore NZ
63F2 Gore Topko Mt USSR
45C1 Gorey Irish Rep
90B2 Gorgān Iran
93E2 Goris USSR
52B1 Gorizia Italy
65F4 Gor'kiy USSR
61F2 Gor'kovskoye
   Vodokhranilishche
   Res USSR
57C2 Görlitz Germany
60E4 Gorlovka USSR
22C3 Gorman USA
54C2 Gorna Orjahovica Bulg
68A1 Gorno-Altaysk USSR
69G2 Gornozavodsk USSR
61F2 Gorodets USSR
59C3 Gorodok Ukrainskaya
   S.S.R.
59D3 Gorodok Ukrainskaya
   S.S.R.
71F4 Goroka PNG
86A1 Gorakhpur India
101C2 Gorongosa Mozam
71D3 Gorontalo Indon
61K2 Goro Yurma Mt USSR
45B2 Gort Irish Rep
63C2 Goryachinsk USSR
59D3 Goryn' R USSR
59C2 Góry Świetokrzyskie
   Upland Pol

64G3 Gory Tel'pos-iz' Mt
   USSR
39H8 Gorzow Wielkopolski
   Pol
74E2 Goshogawara Japan
52C2 Gospić Yugos
54B2 Gostivar Yugos
58B2 Gostynin Pol
39G7 Göteborg Sweden
98B2 Gotel Mts Nig
39H7 Gotland I Sweden
74B4 Goto-retto I Japan
39H7 Gotska Sandön I
   Sweden
74C3 Götsu Japan
98B1 Goudoumaria Niger
103H7 Gough I Atlantic O
109C2 Goulburn Aust
97B3 Goumbou Mali
97B3 Goundam Mali
98B1 Gouré Niger
97B3 Gourma Rharous Mali
46A2 Gournay-en-Bray
   France
95A3 Gouro Chad
71E5 Gove Pen Aust
60B4 Goverla Mt USSR
35C1 Governador Valadares
   Brazil
86A2 Govind Ballabh Paht
   Sāgar L India
15C2 Gowanda USA
84B3 Gowärän Afghan
30E4 Goya Arg
98C1 Goz-Beida Chad
53B3 Gozo I Medit S
95C3 Goz Regeb Sudan
100B4 Graaff-Reinet S Africa
15C1 Gracefield Can
109C1 Grafton Aust
8D2 Grafton N Dakota, USA
14B3 Grafton W Virginia,
   USA
5E4 Graham I Can
13C1 Graham I Can
13E1 Graham L Can
100B4 Grahamstown S Africa
31B3 Grajaú Brazil
52C2 Grajewo Pol
55B2 Grámmos Mt Greece/
   Alb
44C3 Grampian Region, Scot
44B3 Grampian Mts Scot
32C3 Granada Colombia
25D3 Granada Nic
50B2 Granada Spain
15D1 Granby Can
96A2 Gran Canaria I
   Canary Is
30D4 Gran Chaco Region
   Arg
14A2 Grand R Michigan,
   USA
18B1 Grand R Missouri,
   USA
27Q2 Grand B Dominica
11C4 Grand Bahama I
   The Bahamas
7E5 Grand Bank Can
102F2 Grand Banks Atlantic O
97B4 Grand Bassam Ivory
   Coast
9B3 Grand Canyon USA
26A3 Grand Cayman I
   Caribbean S
13E2 Grand Centre Can
20C1 Grand Coulee USA
34B3 Grande R Arg
31C4 Grande R Bahia, Brazil
35B1 Grande R Minas
   Gerais/São Paulo,
   Brazil
13D2 Grande Cache Can
47A2 Grande Chartreuse
   Region, France
101D2 Grande Comore I
   Comoros
13D1 Grande Prairie Can

19A3 **Grande Prairie** USA
95A3 **Grand Erg de Bilma**
Desert Niger
96B2 **Grand erg Occidental**
Mts Alg
96C2 **Grand erg Oriental**
Mts Alg
7C4 **Grande Rivière de la**
Baleine *R* Can
20C1 **Grande Ronde** *R* USA
7D5 **Grand Falls** New
Brunswick, Can
7E5 **Grand Falls**
Newfoundland, Can
20C1 **Grand Forks** USA
8D2 **Grand Forks** USA
16B1 **Grand Gorge** USA
14A2 **Grand Haven** USA
19C3 **Grand Isle** USA
19B4 **Grand L** USA
15D1 **Grand Mère** Can
50A2 **Grândola** Port
5J4 **Grand Rapids** Can
14A2 **Grand Rapids**
Michigan, USA
10A2 **Grand Rapids**
Minnesota, USA
47B2 **Grand St Bernard** *P*
Italy/Switz
8B2 **Grand Teton** *Mt* USA
8B2 **Grand Teton Nat Pk**
USA
46A2 **Grandvilliers** France
25D1 **Grangeburg** USA
51C1 **Granollers** Spain
52A1 **Gran Paradiso** *Mt* Italy
47D1 **Gran Pilastro** *Mt*
Austria/Italy
43D3 **Grantham** Eng
21B2 **Grant,Mt** USA
44C3 **Grantown-on-Spey**
Scot
9C3 **Grants** USA
20B2 **Grants Pass** USA
48B2 **Granville** France
5H4 **Granville L** Can
35C1 **Grão Mogol** Brazil
49D3 **Grasse** France
21A2 **Grass Valley** USA
5H5 **Gravelbourg** Can
46B1 **Gravelines** France
100C3 **Gravelotte** S Africa
15C2 **Gravenhurst** Can
109D1 **Gravesend** Aust
12H3 **Gravina I** USA
12B2 **Grayling** USA
20B1 **Grays Harbor** *B* USA
14B3 **Grayson** USA
18C2 **Grayville** USA
59B3 **Graz** Austria
27H1 **Great J** Jamaica
11C4 **Great Abaco** *I*
The Bahamas
106B4 **Great Australian Bight**
G Aust
16B3 **Great B** New Jersey,
USA
112B10 **Greater Antarctic**
Region, Ant
26B2 **Greater Antilles** *Is*
Caribbean S
43D4 **Greater London**
County, Eng
43C3 **Greater Manchester**
County, Eng

25E2 **Great Exuma** *I*
The Bahamas
8B2 **Great Falls** USA
44B3 **Great Glen** *V* Scot
86B1 **Great Himalayan Range**
Mts Asia
11C4 **Great Inagua** *I*
The Bahamas
100B4 **Great Karroo** *Mts*
S Africa
109C4 **Great L** Aust
100A3 **Great Namaland**
Region, Namibia
42C3 **Great Ormes Head** *C*
Wales
11C4 **Great Ragged** *I*
The Bahamas
99D3 **Great Ruaha** *R* Tanz
15D2 **Great Sacandaga L**
USA
8B2 **Great Salt L** USA
95B2 **Great Sea Salt** Libya/
Egypt
106B3 **Great Sandy Desert**
Aust
8A2 **Great Sandy Desert**
USA
Great Sandy I=Fraser I
4G3 **Great Slave L** Can
107D5 **Great South B** USA
106B3 **Great Victoria Desert**
Aust
72B2 **Great Wall** China
43E3 **Great Yarmouth** Eng
94B1 **Greco,C** Cyprus
55B3 **Greece**
Republic, Europe
15C2 **Greece** USA
8C2 **Greeley** USA
6B1 **Greely Fjord** Can
14A1 **Green B** USA
14A2 **Green Bay** USA
14A3 **Greencastle** Indiana,
USA
16C1 **Greenfield**
Massachusetts, USA
14A2 **Greenfield** Wisconsin,
USA
13F2 **Green Lake** Can
6F2 **Greenland**
Dependency,
N Atlantic O
102H1 **Greenland Basin**
Greenland S
1B1 **Greenland S** Greenland
42B2 **Greenock** Scot
16C2 **Greenport** USA
16B3 **Greensboro** Maryland,
USA
11C3 **Greensboro** N Carolina,
USA
15C2 **Greensburg**
Pennsylvania, USA
18C2 **Greenup** USA
17A1 **Greenville** Alabama,
USA
97B4 **Greenville** Lib
19B3 **Greenville** Mississippi,
USA
16D1 **Greenville**
N Hampshire, USA
14B2 **Greenville** Ohio, USA
17B1 **Greenville** S Carolina,
USA
19A3 **Greenville** Texas, USA
43E4 **Greenwich** Eng
16C2 **Greenwich** USA
16B3 **Greenwood** Delaware,
USA
19B3 **Greenwood**
Mississippi, USA
17B1 **Greenwood** S Carolina,
USA
18B2 **Greers Ferry L** USA
108A1 **Gregory,L** Aust
107D2 **Gregory Range** *Mts*
Aust

56C2 **Greifswald** Germany
64F3 **Gremikha** USSR
56C1 **Grenå** Den
19C3 **Grenada** USA
27E4 **Grenada** *I* Caribbean S
27E4 **Grenadines,The** *Is*
Caribbean S
109C2 **Grenfell** Aust
49D2 **Grenoble** France
27M2 **Grenville** Grenada
107D2 **Grenville,C** Aust
20B1 **Gresham** USA
78A3 **Gresik** Jawa, Indon
78A3 **Gresik** Sumatera,
Indon
19B4 **Gretna** USA
111B2 **Grey** *R* NZ
12G2 **Grey Hunter Pk** *Mt*
Can
7E4 **Grey Is** Can
16C1 **Greylock,Mt** USA
111B2 **Greymouth** NZ
107D3 **Grey Range** *Mts* Aust
45C2 **Greystones** Irish Rep
101H1 **Greytown** S Africa
101F1 **Griekwastad** S Africa
17B1 **Griffith** USA
108C2 **Griffith** Aust
107D5 **Grim,C** Aust
15C2 **Grimsby** Can
42D3 **Grimsby** Eng
38B1 **Grímsey** *I* Iceland
13D1 **Grimshaw** Can
39F7 **Grimstad** Nor
47C1 **Grindelwald** Switz
6A2 **Grinnell Pen** Can
6B2 **Grise Fjord** Can
61H1 **Griva** USSR
39J7 **Grobina** USSR
58C2 **Grodno** USSR
86A1 **Gromati** *R* India
56B2 **Groningen** Neth
106C2 **Groote Eylandt** *I* Aust
100A2 **Grootfontein** Namibia
100B3 **Grootvloer** *Salt L*
S Africa
27P2 **Gros Islet** St Lucia
46E1 **Grosser Feldberg** *Mt*
Germany
52B2 **Grosseto** Italy
46E2 **Gross-Gerau** Germany
57C3 **Grossglockner** *Mt*
Austria
47E1 **Gross Venediger** *Mt*
Austria
12C3 **Grosvenor,L** USA
22B2 **Groveland** USA
21D2 **Grover City** USA
15D2 **Groveton** USA
61G5 **Groznyy** USSR
58B2 **Grudziadz** Pol
44C3 **Grünau** Namibia
44E2 **Grutness** Scot
65F5 **Gruzinskaya SSR**
Republic, USSR
61F3 **Gryazi** USSR
61F2 **Gryazovets** USSR
29G8 **Grytviken** South
Georgia
45A2 **Gt Blasket** *I* Irish Rep
35C2 **Guaçuí** Brazil
23A1 **Guadalajara** Mexico
50B1 **Guadalajara** Spain
107E1 **Guadalcanal** *I*
Solomon Is
50B2 **Guadalimar** *R* Spain
51B1 **Guadalope** *R* Spain
50B2 **Guadalqivir** *R* Spain
24B2 **Guadalupe** Mexico
3G6 **Guadalupe** *I* Mexico
27E3 **Guadeloupe** *I*
Caribbean S
50B2 **Guadian** *R* Spain
50A2 **Guadiana** *R* Port
50B2 **Guadix** Spain
32D6 **Guajará Mirim** Brazil
32C1 **Guajira,Pen de**
Colombia

32B4 **Gualaceo** Ecuador
34D2 **Gualeguay** Arg
34D2 **Gualeguaychú** Arg
71F2 **Guam** *I* Pacific O
34C3 **Guamini** Arg
77C5 **Gua Musang** Malay
23A1 **Guanajuato** Mexico
23A1 **Guanajuato** State,
Mexico
32D2 **Guanare** Ven
25D2 **Guane** Cuba
73C5 **Guangdong** Province,
China
73A3 **Guanghan** China
72C3 **Guanghua** China
73A4 **Guangmao Shan** *Mt*
China
73B5 **Guangnan** China
72B3 **Guangyuan** China
73D4 **Guangze** China
67F3 **Guangzhou** China
35C1 **Guanhães** Brazil
32D3 **Guania** *R* Colombia
27E5 **Guanipa** *R* Ven
26B2 **Guantánamo** Cuba
72D1 **Guanting Shuiku** *Res*
China
73B5 **Guanxi** Province,
China
73A3 **Guan Xian** China
32B2 **Guapa** Colombia
33E6 **Guaporé** *R* Brazil/Bol
30C2 **Guaqui** Bol
32D4 **Guaranda** Ecuador
30F4 **Guarapuava** Brazil
35B2 **Guaratinguetá** Brazil
50A1 **Guarda** Port
99F1 **Guardafui,C** Somalia
35B1 **Guarda Mor** Brazil
9C4 **Guasave** Mexico
47D2 **Guastalla** Italy
25C3 **Guatemala** Guatemala
25C3 **Guatemala** Republic,
Cent America
34C3 **Guatraché** Arg
32C3 **Guaviare** *R* Colombia
35B2 **Guaxupé** Brazil
27L1 **Guayaguayare**
Trinidad
32A4 **Guayaquil** Ecuador
24A2 **Guaymas** Mexico
34D2 **Guayquiraro** *R* Arg
99D2 **Guba** Eth
100B3 **Guban** *Region* Zaïre
99E2 **Guban** *Region*
Somalia
79B3 **Gubat** Phil
56C2 **Gubin** Pol
87B2 **Güdür** India
14B2 **Guelpho** Can
24A2 **Guenabacoa** Cuba
98C1 **Guéréda** Chad
48C2 **Guéret** France
48B2 **Guernsey** *I* UK
23A2 **Guerrero** State,
Mexico
99D2 **Gughe** *Mt* Eth
63E2 **Guigui** China
71F2 **Guguan** *I* Pacific O
109C2 **Guiargambone** Aust
73C4 **Guidong** China
97B4 **Guiglo** Ivory Coast
73C5 **Gui Jiang** *R* China
43D4 **Guildford** Eng
73C4 **Guilin** China
47B2 **Guillestre** France
72A2 **Guinan** China
97A3 **Guinea** Republic,
Africa
102H4 **Guinea Basin** Atlantic
O
97A3 **Guinea-Bissau**
Republic, Africa
97C4 **Guinea,G of** W Africa
26A2 **Güines** Cuba
97B3 **Guir** *Well* Mali
84C2 **Guiranwala** Pak
33E1 **Güiria** Ven

46B2 Guise France
79C3 Guian Phil
73B5 Gui Xian China
73B4 Guiyang China
73B4 Guizhou Province, China
85C4 Gujarāt State, India
84C2 Gujrāt Pak
87B1 Gulbarga India
58D1 Gulbene USSR
87B1 Guledagudda India
80D3 Gulf,The S W Asia
109C2 Gulgong Aust
73B4 Gulin China
12E2 Gulkana USA
12E2 Gulkana R USA
13E2 Gull L Can
13F2 Gull Lake Can
55C3 Güllük Körfezi B Turk
99D2 Gulu Uganda
109C1 Guluguba Aust
97C3 Gumel Nig
46D1 Gummersbach Germany
86A2 Gumpla India
93C1 Gümüşhane Turk
85D4 Guna India
99D1 Guna Mt Eth
109C3 Gundagai Aust
98B3 Gungu Zaïre
6H3 Gunnbjørn Fjeld Mt Greenland
109D2 Gunnedah Aust
87B1 Guntakal India
17A1 Guntersville USA
17A1 Guntersville L USA
87C1 Guntūr India
77C5 Gunung Batu Putch Mt Malay
78D3 Gunung Besar Mt Indon
78D2 Gunung Bulu Mt Indon
78A3 Gunung Gedang Mt Indon
78C2 Gunung Lawit Mt Malay
78C4 Gunung Lawu Mt Indon
78D2 Gunung Menyapa Mt Indon
78D2 Gunung Niapa Mt Indon
78A3 Gunung Patah Mt Indon
78C4 Gunung Raung Mt Indon
78A3 Gunung Resag Mt Indon
78D3 Gunung Sarempaka Mt Indon
78C4 Gunung Sumbing Mt Indon
77C5 Gunung Tahan Mt Malay
78A2 Gunung Talakmau Mt Indon
100A2 Gunza Angola
72D3 Guoyang China
84D2 Gurdaspur India
84D3 Gurgaon India
86A1 Gurkha Nepal
92C2 Gürün Turk
31B2 Gurupi R Brazil
100C2 Guruve Zim
72A1 Gurvan Sayhan Uul Upland Mongolia
61H4 Gur'yev USSR
65F5 Gurzinskaya Republic, USSR
97C3 Gusau Nig
58C2 Gusev USSR
74A3 Gushan China
61F2 Gus'khrustalnyy USSR
12G3 Gustavus USA
22B2 Gustine USA
11B3 Guston USA

56B2 Gütersloh Germany
18C2 Guthrie Kentucky, USA
18A2 Guthrie Oklahoma, USA
23B1 Gutiérrez Zamora Mexico
33F3 Guyana Republic, S America
102F4 Guyana Basin Atlantic O
72C1 Guyang China
48B3 Guyenne Region, France
9C3 Guymon USA
109D2 Guyra Aust
72B2 Guyuan China
109C2 Gwabegar Aust
85D3 Gwalior India
100B3 Gwanda Zim
98C2 Gwane Zaïre
82A3 Gwardar Pak
45B1 Gweebarra B Irish Rep
89G9 Gwelo Zim
43C4 Gwent County, Wales
100B2 Gweru Zim
109C1 Gwydir R Aust
43C3 Gwynedd Wales
65F5 Gyandzha USSR
86B1 Gyangzê China
68B3 Gyaring Hu L China
64J2 Gydanskiy Poluostrov Pen USSR
85B2 Gyirong China
6F3 Gyldenløves Fjord Greenland
109D1 Gympie Aust
59B3 Gyöngyös Hung
59B3 Györ Hung

H

38K6 Haapajärvi Fin
60B2 Haapsalu USSR
56A2 Haarlem Neth
46D1 Haarstrang Region, Germany
25D2 Habana Cuba
86C2 Habiganj Bang
74D4 Hachijo-jima I Japan
75B1 Hachiman Japan
74E2 Hachinohe Japan
75B1 Hachioji Japan
16B2 Hackettstown USA
108A2 Hack,Mt Aust
42C2 Haddington Scot
108B1 Haddon Corner Aust
108B1 Haddon Downs Aust
97D3 Hadejia Nig
97C3 Hadejia R Nig
94B2 Hadera Israel
56B1 Haderslev Den
81D4 Hadiboh Socotra
4H2 Hadley B Can
73B5 Hadong Vietnam
81C4 Hadramawt Region, Yemen
56C1 Hadsund Den
74B3 Haeju N Korea
91A4 Hafar al Bātin S Arabia
6D2 Haffners Bjerg Mt Greenland
84C2 Hafizabad Pak
86C1 Haflong India
38A2 Hafnafjóður Iceland
12B3 Hagemeister I USA
56B2 Hagen Germany
15C3 Hagerstown USA
75A2 Hagi Japan
73B5 Ha Giang Vietnam
46D2 Hagondange France
45B2 Hags Hd C Irish Rep
46D2 Haguenau France
96A2 Hagunia Well Mor
69G4 Haha-jima I Japan
68B3 Hah Xil Hu L China

74A2 Haicheng China
76D1 Hai Duong Viet
94B2 Haifa Israel
94B2 Haifa,B of Israel
72D2 Hai He R China
73C5 Haikang China
76E1 Haikou China
80C3 Ha'il S Arabia
86C2 Hailākāndi India
63D3 Hailar China
74B2 Hailong China
69E2 Hailun China
38J5 Hailuoto I Fin
76D2 Hainan I China
12G3 Haines USA
12G2 Haines Junction Can
59B3 Hainfeld Austria
73B5 Haiphong Vietnam
26C3 Haiti Republic, Caribbean S
95C3 Haiya Sudan
72A2 Haiyan China
72B2 Haiyuan China
72D3 Haizhou Wan B China
59C3 Hajdúböszörmény Hung
75B1 Hajiki-saki Pt Japan
86C2 Haka Burma
21C4 Hakalau Hawaiian Is
21C4 Hakalau Hawaiian Is
93D2 Hakkâri Turk
74E2 Hakodate Japan
75B1 Hakui Japan
74E2 Haku-san Mt Japan
92C2 Halab Syria
93E3 Halabja Iraq
95C2 Halaib Sudan
94C1 Halba Leb
56C2 Halberstadt Germany
79B3 Halcon,Mt Phil
39G7 Halden Nor
86B2 Haldia India
84D3 Haldwāni India
13C1 Halfway R Can
7D5 Halifax Can
42D3 Halifax Eng
6D1 Hall Basin Sd Can
6B3 Hall Beach Can
46C1 Halle Belg
56C2 Halle Germany
112B1 Halley Base Ant
39F6 Hallingdal R Nor
6D3 Hall Pen Can
106B2 Hall's Creek Aust
71D3 Halmahera I Indon
39G7 Halmstad Sweden
56B2 Haltern Germany
38J5 Halti Mt Nor
42C2 Haltwhistle Eng
91B4 Halul I Qatar
94B3 Haluza Hist Site Israel
75A2 Hamada Japan
96C2 Hamada de Tinrhert Desert Region Alg
96B2 Hamada du Dra Upland Alg
90A3 Hamadān Iran
96B2 Hamada Tounassine Region, Alg
92C2 Hamāh Syria
75B2 Hamamatsu Japan
39G6 Hamar Nor
87C3 Hambantota Sri Lanka
19B3 Hamburg Arkansas, USA
18A1 Hamburg Iowa, USA
15C3 Hamburg Pennsylvania, USA
56B2 Hamburg Germany
16C2 Hamden USA
39J6 Hämeenlinna Fin
106A3 Hamersley Range Mts Aust
74B2 Hamgyong Sanmaek Mts N Korea
74B2 Hamhŭng N Korea
68B2 Hami China
94B1 Hamidiyah Syria
108B3 Hamilton Aust

14C2 Hamilton Can
110C1 Hamilton NZ
14B3 Hamilton Ohio, USA
42B2 Hamilton Scot
7E4 Hamilton Inlet B Can
22B2 Hamilton,Mt USA
38K6 Hamina Fin
86A1 Hamirpur India
56B2 Hamm Germany
95A2 Hammādah al Hamra Upland Libya
38H6 Hammerdal Sweden
38J4 Hammerfest Nor
14A2 Hammond Illinois, USA
19B3 Hammond Louisiana, USA
16B3 Hammonton USA
111B3 Hampden NZ
43C4 Hampshire County, Eng
19B3 Hampton Arkansas, USA
91C4 Hāmūn-e Jaz Mūrian L Iran
84B3 Hamun-i-Lora Salt L Pak
21C4 Hana Hawaiian Is
21C4 Hanalei Hawaiian Is
74E3 Hanamaki Japan
72C2 Hancheng China
73C3 Hanchuan China
15C3 Hancock Maryland, USA
10B2 Hancock Michigan, USA
73C3 Handa Japan
72C2 Handan China
99D3 Handeni Tanz
72B2 Hanggin Qi China
39J7 Hangö Fin
73E3 Hangzhou China
73E3 Hangzhou Wan B China
111B2 Hanmer Springs NZ
13E2 Hanna Can
18B2 Hannibal USA
56B2 Hannover Germany
39G7 Hanöbukten B Sweden
76D1 Hanoi Viet
16A3 Hanover USA
29B6 Hanover I Chile
72B3 Han Shui China
72A3 Han Shui R China
85D3 Hānsi India
68C2 Hantay Mongolia
72B3 Hanzhong China
86B2 Hāora India
38J5 Haparanda Sweden
86C1 Hāpoli India
92C4 Haql S Arabia
91A5 Haradh S Arabia
75C1 Haramachi Japan
99E2 Harar Eth
101C2 Harare Zim
98C1 Haraze Chad
14B2 Harbor Beach USA
55B3 Harda India
39F6 Hardangerfjord Inlet Nor
46D2 Hardt Region, Germany
108A2 Hardwicke B Aust
18B2 Hardy USA
99E2 Hargeysa Somalia
94B3 Har Hakippa Mt Israel
68B3 Harhu L China
78A3 Hari R Indon
75A2 Harima-nada B Japan
56B2 Harlingen Neth
9D4 Harlingen USA
43E4 Harlow Eng
94B2 Har Meron Mt Israel
20C2 Harney Basin USA
20C2 Harney L USA
38H6 Härnösand Sweden

63B3 Har Nuur L Mongolia
97B4 Harper Lib
12F2 Harper,Mt USA
15C3 Harpers Ferry USA
94B3 Har Ramon Mt Israel
7C4 Harricanaw R Can
16B3 Harrington USA
7E4 Harrington Harbour Can
44A3 Harris District Scot
18C2 Harrisburg Illinois, USA
16A2 Harrisburg Pennsylvania,USA
101G1 Harrismith S Africa
18B2 Harrison USA
15C3 Harrisonburg USA
7E4 Harrison,C Can
13C3 Harrison L USA
18B2 Harrisonville USA
44A3 Harris,Sound of Chan Scot
14B2 Harrisville USA
42D3 Harrogate Eng
94B3 Har Saggi Mt Israel
38H5 Harstad Nor
12G2 Hart R Can
39F6 Härteigen Mt Nor
16C2 Hartford Connecticut,USA
14A2 Hartford Michigan, USA
38G6 Hartkjølen Mt Nor
108A2 Hart,L Aust
43B4 Hartland Pt Eng
42D2 Hartlepool Eng
19A3 Hartshorne USA
17B1 Hartwell Res USA
101F1 Hartz R S Africa
68B2 Har Us Nuur L Mongolia
43E4 Harwich Eng
84D3 Haryāna State, India
94B3 Hāsā Jordan
94B2 Hāsbaiya Leb
43D4 Haselmere Eng
75B2 Hashimoto Japan
90A2 Hashtpar Iran
90A2 Hashtrūd Iran
87B2 Hassan India
56B2 Hasselt Belg
96C2 Hassi Inifel Alg
96B2 Hassi Mdakane Well Alg
96C1 Hassi Messaoud Alg
108C3 Hastings Aust
43E4 Hastings Eng
8D2 Hastings Nebraska, USA
110C1 Hastings NZ
108B2 Hatfield Aust
12B1 Hathan Inlet USA
85D3 Hāthras India
76D2 Ha Tinh Viet
108B2 Hattah Aust
11C3 Hatteras,C USA
19C2 Hattiesburg USA
59B3 Hatvan Hung
76D3 Hau Bon Viet
99E2 Haud Region, Eth
39F7 Haugesund Nor
110C1 Hauhungaroa Range Mts NZ
13F1 Haultain R Can
110B1 Hauraki G NZ
111A3 Hauroko,I NZ
47C1 Hausstock Mt Switz
96B1 Haut Atlas Mts Mor
98C2 Haute Kotto Region, CAR
46C1 Hautes Fagnes Mts Belg
46B1 Hautmont Belg
96B1 Hauts Plateaux Mts Alg
90D3 Hauzdar Iran
18B1 Havana USA
Havana = Habana

87B3 Havankulam Sri Lanka
110C1 Havelock North NZ
43B4 Haverfordwest Wales
16D1 Haverhill USA
87B2 Hāveri India
16C2 Haverstraw USA
59B3 Havlíčkův Brod Czech
8C2 Havre USA
16A3 Havre de Grace USA
7D4 Havre-St-Pierre Can
54C2 Havsa Turk
21C4 Hawaii I Hawaiian Is
21C4 Hawaii Volcanoes Nat Pk Hawaiian Is
111A2 Hawea,L NZ
110B1 Hawera NZ
42C2 Hawick Scot
111A2 Hawkdun Range Mts NZ
110C Hawke B NZ
109D2 Hawke,C Aust
108A2 Hawker Aust
76B1 Hawng Luk Burma
93D3 Hawr al Habbaniyah L Iraq
93E3 Hawr al Hammár L Iraq
21B2 Hawthorne USA
108B2 Hay Aust
5G3 Hay R Can
46D2 Hayange France
4B3 Haycock USA
7A4 Hayes R Can
6D2 Hayes Halvø Region Greenland
12E2 Hayes,Mt USA
5G3 Hay River Can
18A2 Haysville USA
22A2 Hayward California, USA
86B2 Hazārībāg India
46B1 Hazebrouck France
19B3 Hazelhurst USA
4G2 Hazel Str Can
13B1 Hazelton Mts Can
6C1 Hazen L Can
94B3 Hazeva Israel
16B2 Hazleton USA
22A1 Healdsburg USA
108C3 Healesville Aust
12E2 Healy USA
104B6 Heard I Indian O
19A3 Hearne USA
10B2 Hearst Can
72D2 Hebei Province, China
109C1 Hebel Aust
72C2 Hebi China
72C2 Hebian China
7D4 Hebron Can
94B3 Hebron Israel
18A1 Hebron Nebraska, USA
5E4 Hecate Str Can
12H3 Heceta I USA
73B5 Hechi China
4G2 Hecla and Griper B Can
111C2 Hector,Mt NZ
38G6 Hede Sweden
39H6 Hedemora Sweden
20C1 He Devil Mt USA
56B2 Heerenveen Neth
46C1 Heerlen Neth
Hefa = Haifa
73D3 Hefei China
73B4 Hefeng China
69F2 Hegang China
75B1 Hegura-jima I Japan
94B3 Heidan R Jordan
56B2 Heide Germany
101G1 Heidelberg Transvaal, S Africa
57B3 Heidelberg Germany
63E2 Heihe China
101G1 Heilbron S Africa
57B3 Heilbronn Germany
56C2 Heiligenstadt Germany
38K6 Heinola Fin
73B4 Hejiang China

6J3 Hekla Mt Iceland
76C1 Hekou Viet
73A5 Hekou Yaozou Zizhixian China
72B2 Helan China
72B2 Helan Shan Mt China
19B3 Helena Arkansas, USA
8B2 Helena Montana, USA
22D3 Helendale USA
71E3 Helen Reef / Pacific O
44B3 Helensburgh Scot
91B4 Helleh R Iran
51B2 Hellin Spain
20C1 Hells Canyon R USA
46D1 Hellweg Region, Germany
22B2 Helm USA
80E2 Helmand R Afghan
100A3 Helmeringhausen Namibia
46C1 Helmond Neth
44C2 Helmsdale Scot
72C2 Helong China
39G7 Helsingborg Sweden
Helsingfors = Helsinki
56C1 Helsingør Den
38J6 Helsinki Fin
43B4 Helston Eng
89C3 Helwān Egypt
19A3 Hempstead USA
39H7 Hemse Sweden
72A3 Henan China
72C3 Henan Province, China
110B1 Hen and Chicken Is NZ
14A3 Henderson Kentucky, USA
9B3 Henderson Nevada, USA
19B3 Henderson Texas, USA
73E5 Heng-ch'un Taiwan
68B4 Hengduan Shan Mts China
56B2 Hengelo Neth
72B2 Hengshan China
72D2 Hengshui China
76D1 Heng Xian China
73C4 Hengyang China
77A4 Henhoaha Nicobar Is
43D4 Henley-on-Thames Eng
16B3 Henlopen,C USA
18A2 Henrietta Maria,C Can
6D3 Henry Kater Pen Can
68C2 Hentiyn Nuruu Mts Mongolia
76B2 Henzada Burma
73B5 Hepu China
80E2 Herat Afghan
5H4 Herbert Can
110C2 Herbertville NZ
46E1 Herborn Germany
26A4 Heredia Costa Rica
43C3 Hereford Eng
43C3 Hereford & Worcester County, Eng
46C1 Herentals Belg
47B1 Héricourt France
18A2 Herington USA
111A3 Heriot NZ
47C1 Herisau Switz
15D2 Herkimer USA
44E1 Herma Ness Pen Scot
109C2 Hermidale Aust
111B2 Hermitage NZ
Hermon,Mt = Jebel ash Shaykh
24A2 Hermosillo Mexico
16A2 Herndon Pennsylvania,USA
22C2 Herndon California, USA
46D1 Herne Germany
56B1 Herning Den
90A2 Herowābād Iran
50A2 Herrera del Duque Spain

16A2 Hershey USA
43D4 Hertford County, Eng
94B2 Herzliyya Israel
46C1 Hesbaye Region, Belg
46B1 Hesdin France
72B2 Heshui China
22D3 Hesperia USA
12H2 Hess R Can
57B2 Hessen State, Germany
22C2 Hetch Hetchy Res USA
42C2 Hexham Eng
73C5 He Xian China
73C5 Heyuan China
108B3 Heywood Aust
72B2 Heze China
17B2 Hialeah USA
110C1 Hicks Bay NZ
109C3 Hicks,Pt Aust
23B1 Hidalgo State, Mexico
24B2 Hidalgo del Parral Mexico
35B1 Hidrolândia Brazil
96A2 Hierro / Canary Is
75C1 Higashine Japan
74B4 Higashi-suidō Str Japan
20B2 High Desert USA
14B1 High Island USA
44B3 Highland Region, Scot
22D3 Highland USA
22C1 Highland Peak Mt USA
16B2 Highlands Falls USA
11B1 High Point USA
13D1 High Prairie Can
5G4 High River Can
17B2 High Springs USA
16B2 Hightstown USA
43D4 High Wycombe Eng
39J7 Hiiumaa / USSR
80C3 Hijaz Region, S Arabia
75B2 Hikigawa Japan
75B2 Hikone Japan
110B1 Hikurangi NZ
9C4 Hidalgo Mexico
9C4 Hidalgo del Parral Mexico
56B2 Hildesheim Germany
27N2 Hillaby,Mt Barbados
56C1 Hillerød Den
14B3 Hillsbo Ohio, USA
20B1 Hillsboro Oregon, USA
19A3 Hillsboro Texas, USA
108C2 Hillston Aust
44E1 Hillswick Scot
21C4 Hilo Hawaiian Is
93C2 Hilvan Turk
56B2 Hilversum Neth
84D2 Himachal Pradesh State, India
82D3 Himalaya Mts Asia
85C4 Himatnagar India
74C4 Himeji Japan
74D3 Himi Japan
92C3 Hims Syria
12E2 Hinchinbrook Entrance USA
12E2 Hinchinbrook I USA
85D3 Hindaun India
84B1 Hindu Kush Mts Afghan
87B2 Hindupur India
13D1 Hines Creek Can
85B3 Hinganghāt India
69E2 Hinggan Ling Upland China
85B3 Hingol R Pak
85D5 Hingoli India
38H5 Hinneya I Nor
11C1 Hinsdale USA
13D2 Hinton Can
34B2 Hipolito Itrogoyen Arg
86A2 Hirakud Res India
92B2 Hirfanli Baraji Res Turk

87B2 Hirihar India
74E2 Hirosaki Japan
74C4 Hiroshima Japan
46C2 Hirson France
54C2 Hirşova Rom
56B1 Hirtshals Den
84D3 Hisär India
2C3 Hispaniola /
  Caribbean S
94C1 Hisyah Syria
93D3 Hit Iraq
74E3 Hitachi Japan
75C1 Hitachi-Ota Japan
43D4 Hitchin Eng
38F6 Hitra / Nor
75A2 Hiuchi-nada B Japan
75A2 Hiwasa Japan
56B1 Hjørring Den
76B1 Hka R Burma
97C4 Ho Ghana
76D1 Hoa Binh Viet
76D3 Hoa De Viet
109C4 Hobart Aust
9C3 Hobbs USA
56B1 Hobro Den
13C2 Hobson L USA
99E2 Hobyo Somalia
  Ho Chi Minh = Saigon
57C3 Hochkönig Mt Austria
54B1 Hódmező'hely Hung
59B3 Hodonin Czech
74B2 Hoeryong N Korea
57C2 Hof Germany
38B2 Hofsjökull Mts
  Iceland
74C4 Hōfu Japan
9C2 Hoggar Upland Alg
46D1 Hohe Acht Mt
  Germany
72C1 Hohhot China
6J3 Höhn Iceland
68B3 Hoh Sai Hu China
82C2 Hoh Xil Shan Mts
  China
99D2 Hoima Uganda
86C1 Hojai India
75A2 Hojo Japan
110B1 Hokianga Harbour B
  NZ
111B2 Hokitika NZ
74E2 Hokkaido Japan
90C2 Hokmābād Iran
109C3 Holbrook Aust
9B3 Holbrook USA
19A2 Holdenville USA
87B2 Hole Narsipur India
27R3 Holetown Barbados
26B2 Holguin Cuba
111B2 Holitika NZ
12C2 Holitna R USA
59B3 Hollabrunn Austria
14A2 Holland USA
22B2 Hollister USA
19C3 Holly Springs USA
22C3 Hollywood California,
  USA
17B2 Hollywood Florida,
  USA
4G2 Holman Island Can
38J6 Holmsund Sweden
94B2 Holon Israel
56B1 Holstebro Den
6E3 Holsteinborg
  Greenland
14B2 Holt USA
18A2 Holton USA
12C2 Holy Cross USA
42B3 Holyhead Wales
42D2 Holy I Eng
43B3 Holy I Wales
16C1 Holyoke
  Massachusetts, USA
86C2 Homalin Burma
6D3 Home B Can
12D3 Homer Alaska, USA
19B3 Homer Louisiana,
  USA
111A2 Homer Tunnel NZ

17B1 Homerville USA
17B2 Homestead USA
17A1 Homewood USA
87B1 Homnābād India
101C3 Homoine Mozam
25D3 Hondo R Mexico
25D3 Honduras Republic,
  Cent America
25D3 Honduras,G of
  Honduras
39G6 Hønefoss Nor
15C2 Honesdale USA
21A1 Honey L USA
76C1 Hong R Viet
76D1 Hon Gai Viet
73A4 Hongguo China
73C4 Hong Hu L China
72B2 Honghui China
73C4 Hongjiang China
73C5 Hong Kong Colony,
  S E Asia
68D2 Hongor Mongolia
73B5 Hongshui He R China
72A3 Hongyuan China
72D3 Hongze Hu L China
107E1 Honiara Solomon Is
77C4 Hon Khoai / Camb
76B1 Hon Lan / Viet
38K4 Hønnigsvåg Nor
21C4 Honolulu Hawaiian Is
77C4 Hon Panjang / Viet
74D3 Honshu / Japan
20B1 Hood,Mt USA
20B1 Hood River USA
45C2 Hook Head C
  Irish Rep
12G3 Hoonah USA
12A2 Hooper Bay USA
101G1 Hoopstad S Africa
56A2 Hoorn Neth
9B3 Hoover Dam USA
12E2 Hope Alaska, USA
19B3 Hope Arkansas, USA
13C3 Hope Can
7D4 Hopedale Can
64D2 Hopen / Barents S
6D3 Hopes Advance,C Can
10B3 Hopetoun Aust
100B3 Hopetown S Africa
18C2 Hopkinsville USA
20B1 Hoquiam USA
93D1 Horasan Turk
99F1 Hordiyo Somalia
47C1 Horgen Switz
105H5 Horizon Depth
  Pacific O
91C4 Hormuz,Str of Oman/
  Iran
59B3 Horn Austria
6H3 Horn C Iceland
38H5 Hornavan L Sweden
19B3 Hornbeck USA
20B2 Hornbrook USA
111B2 Hornby NZ
7B5 Hornepayne Can
4F3 Horn Mts Can
42D3 Hornsea Eng
72B1 Horn Uul Mt
  Mongolia
30E3 Horqueta Par
15C2 Horseheads USA
56C1 Horsens Den
20B1 Horseshoe Bay Can
108B3 Horsham Aust
43C4 Horsham Eng
39G7 Horten Nor
4F3 Horton R Can
78C2 Hose Mts Malay
85D4 Hoshangābād India
84D2 Hoshiārpur India
87B1 Hospet India
7G4 Hoste / Chile
88B2 Hotan China
19B3 Hot Springs Arkansas,
  USA
8C2 Hot Springs S. Dakota,
  USA
4G3 Hottah Can

46A2 Houdan France
72C2 Houma China
19B4 Houma USA
16C2 Housatonic R USA
13B2 Houston Can
19C3 Houston Mississippi,
  USA
19A4 Houston Texas, USA
106A3 Houtman /s Aust
68B2 Hovd Mongolia
68C1 Hövsgol Nuur L
  Mongolia
14A2 Howard City USA
12C1 Howard P USA
109C3 Howe,C Aust
101H1 Howick S Africa
44C2 Hoy / Scot
39F6 Høyanger Nor
59B2 Hradec-Králové Czech
59B3 Hranice Czech
59B3 Hron R Czech
73E5 Hsin-chu Taiwan
73E5 Hsüeh Shan Mt
  Taiwan
72B2 Huachi China
32B6 Huacho Peru
72C1 Huade China
72D3 Huaibei China
72D3 Huaibin China
73C4 Huai He R China
73C4 Huaihua China
73C5 Huaiji China
72D3 Huainan China
69E4 Hua-lien Taiwan
32B5 Huallaga R Peru
32B5 Huallanca Peru
32B5 Huamachuco Peru
100A2 Huambo Angola
30C2 Huanay Bol
32B5 Huancabamba Peru
32B6 Huancavelica Peru
32B6 Huancayo Peru
73D3 Huangchuan China
  Huang Hai = Yellow S
72D2 Huang He R China
72B2 Huangling China
76D2 Huangliu China
73C3 Huangpi China
73D3 Huangshi China
34C3 Huanguelén Arg
73E4 Huangyan China
74B2 Huanren China
32B5 Huánuco Peru
30C2 Huanuni Bol
72B2 Huan Xian China
32B5 Huaráz Peru
32B6 Huarmey Peru
32B5 Huascarán Mt Peru
30B4 Huasco Chile
23B2 Huatusco Mexico
23B1 Huauchinango Mexico
23B2 Huautla Mexico
72C2 Hua Xian China
24B2 Huayapan R Mexico
73C3 Hubei Province, China
87B1 Hubli India
34C3 Hucal Arg
74B2 Huch'ang N Korea
42D3 Huddersfield Eng
39H6 Hudiksvall Sweden
17B2 Hudson Florida, USA
14B2 Hudson Michigan,
  USA
16C1 Hudson New York,
  USA
16C1 Hudson R USA
7B4 Hudson B Can
5H4 Hudson Bay Can
13C1 Hudson's Hope Can
6C3 Hudson Str Can
76D2 Hue Viet
23B1 Huejutla Mexico
50A2 Huelva Spain
23A2 Hueramo Mexico
51B2 Húercal Overa Spain
51B1 Huesca Spain
23B2 Huexotla Hist Site
  Mexico

107D3 Hughenden Aust
12D1 Hughes USA
86B2 Hugli R India
19A3 Hugo USA
73D4 Hui'an China
110C1 Huiarau Range Mts
  NZ
74B2 Huich'ŏn N Korea
74B2 Huifa He R China
32B3 Huila Mt Colombia
73D5 Huilai China
73A4 Huili China
74B2 Huinan China
34C2 Huinca Renancó Arg
25C3 Huixtla Mexico
73A4 Huize China
73C5 Huizhou China
23B2 Hujuápan de Léon
  Mexico
69F2 Hulin China
15C1 Hull Can
42D3 Hull Eng
58B1 Hultsfred Sweden
63D3 Hulun Nur L China
69E1 Huma China
33E5 Humaitá Brazil
100B4 Humansdorp S Africa
42D3 Humber R Eng
5H4 Humberside County,
  Eng
5H4 Humboldt Can
20C2 Humboldt R USA
20B2 Humboldt B USA
6D2 Humboldt Gletscher
  Gl Greenland
21B2 Humboldt L USA
108C1 Humeburn Aust
109C3 Hume,L Aust
100A2 Humpata Angola
22C2 Humphreys USA
38A1 Húnaflói B Iceland
73C4 Hunan Province,
  China
74C2 Hunchun China
13C2 Hundred Mile House
  Can
54B1 Hunedoara Rom
59B3 Hungary
  Republic, Europe
108B1 Hungerford Aust
74B3 Hūngnam N Korea
74B2 Hunjiang China
46D2 Hunsrück Mts,
  Germany
107D2 Hunter R Aust
13B2 Hunter I Can
109C4 Hunter Is Aust
12D2 Hunter,Mt USA
14A3 Huntingburg USA
43D3 Huntingdon Eng
14A2 Huntingdon Indiana,
  USA
14B3 Huntington W
  Virginia, USA
22C4 Huntington Beach
  USA
22C2 Huntington L USA
110C1 Huntly NZ
44C3 Huntly Scot
44C3 Hunt,Mt Can
108A1 Hunt Pen Aust
17A1 Huntsville Alabama,
  USA
15C1 Huntsville Can
19A3 Huntsville Texas, USA
76D2 Huong Khe Viet
71F4 Huon Peninsula Pen
  PNG
109C4 Huonville Aust
14B1 Hurd,C Can
80B3 Hurghada Egypt
8D2 Huron S Dakota, USA
14B1 Huron,L Can/USA
34A2 Hurtado Chile
111B2 Hurunui R NZ
38B1 Husavik Iceland
54C1 Huşi Rom
39G7 Huskvarna Sweden

12C1 Huslia USA
94B2 Husn Jordan
56B2 Husum Germany
109C1 Hutton,Mt Aust
72D2 Hutuo He R China
46C1 Huy Belg
72A2 Huzhu China
52C2 Hvar I Yugos
100B2 Hwange China
100B2 Hwange Nat Pk Zim
15D2 Hyannis USA
68B2 Hyargas Nuur L
Mongolia
5E4 Hydaburg Can
16C2 Hyde Park USA
87B1 Hyderābād India
85B3 Hyderabad Pak
49D3 Hyères France
12J2 Hyland R Can
8B2 Hyndman Peak Mt
USA
38K6 Hyrynsalmi Fin
13D1 Hythe Can
74C4 Hyūga Japan
39J6 Hyvikää Fin

I

31C4 Iaçu Brazil
54C2 Ialomiţa R Rom
54C1 Iaşi Rom
97C4 Ibadan Nig
32B3 Ibagué Colombia
54B2 Ibar R Yugos
32B3 Ibarra Ecuador
35B1 Ibiá Brazil
30E4 Ibicuí R Brazil
34D2 Ibicuy Arg
51C2 Ibiza Spain
51C2 Ibiza I Spain
101D2 Ibo Mozam
31C4 Ibotirama Brazil
91C5 'Ibrī Oman
32B6 Ica Peru
32D4 Ica R Brazil
32D3 Icana Brazil
38A1 Iceland Republic,
N Atlantic O
13C2 Ice Mt Can
87A1 Ichalkaranji India
74E3 Ichihara Japan
75B1 Ichinomiya Japan
74E3 Ichinoseki Japan
12F3 Icy B USA
4B2 Icy C USA
63B2 Ida R USSR
19B3 Idabell USA
8B2 Idaho USA
46D2 Idaho Falls USA
20B2 Idanha USA
46D2 Idar Oberstein
Germany
95A2 Idehan Marzūg Desert
Libya
95A2 Idehan Ubari Desert
Libya
96C2 Ideles Alg
68B2 Iderlyn Gol R
Mongolia
95C2 Idfu Egypt
55B3 Idhi Óros Mt Greece
55B3 Idhra I Greece
98B3 Idiofa Zaïre
12C2 Iditarod R USA
92C2 Idlib Syria
39K7 Idritsa USSR
100B4 Idutywa S Africa
55C3 Ierápetra Greece
46B1 Ieper Belg
91F3 Ifakara Tanz
71F3 Ifalik I Pacific O
101D3 Ifanadiana Madag
97C4 Ife Nig
97C3 Iférouane Niger
78C2 Igan Malay
35B2 Igarananva Brazil
93E2 Igdir Iran
39H6 Iggesund Sweden

34B2 Iglesia Arg
53A3 Iglesias Sardegna
6B3 Igloolik Can
10A2 Ignace Can
55B3 Igoumenítsa Greece
61H2 Igra USSR
23B2 Iguala Mexico
31B6 Iguape Brazil
35B2 Iguape Brazil
35B2 Iguatama Brazil
31D3 Iguatu Brazil
98A3 Iguéla Gabon
101D3 Ihosy Madag
74D3 Iida Japan
75B1 Iide-san Mt Japan
38K6 Iisalmi Fin
75A2 Iizuka Japan
97C4 Ijebu Ode Nig
56B2 Ijsselmeer S Neth
55C3 Ikaría I Greece
74E2 Ikeda Japan
98C3 Ikela Zaïre
54B2 Ikhtiman Bulg
12D3 Ikolik,C USA
101D2 Ikopa R Madag
79B2 Ilagan Phil
90A3 Ilām Iran
47C1 Ilanz Switz
13F1 Île à la Crosse Can
13F1 Île à la Crosse,L Can
89G8 Ilebo Zaïre
96D1 Île de Jerba I Tunisia
48B2 Île de Noirmoutier I
France
48B2 Île de Ré I France
107F3 Île des Pins I Nouvelle
Calédonie
48A2 Île d'Ouessant I
France
48B2 Île d'Yeu I France
61J3 Ilek R USSR
107F2 Îles Bélep Nouvelle
Calédonie
107E2 Îs Chesterfield
Nouvelle Calédonie
49D3 Îles d'Hyères Is
France
43B4 Ilfracombe Eng
92B1 Ilgaz Dağlari Mts Turk
101C3 Ilha Bazaruto I
Mozam
33G3 Ilha De Maracá I Brazil
33G4 Ilha de Marajó I Brazil
35B2 Ilha de São Sebastião
I Brazil
33G6 Ilha do Bananal
Region Brazil
35C2 Ilha Grande I Brazil
35B2 Ilha Santo Amaro I
Brazil
96A1 Ilhas Selvegens I
Atlantic O
31D4 Ilhéus Brazil
12C3 Iliamna L USA
12D2 Iliamna V USA
79B4 Iligan Phil
63G3 Il'inskiy USSR
55B3 Iliodhrómia I Greece
79B4 Illana B Phil
34A2 Illapel Chile
34A2 Illapel R Chile
97C3 Illéla Niger
47D1 Iller R Germany
4C4 Illimani Mt Bolivia
10A2 Illinois State, USA
18B2 Illinois R USA
96C2 Illizi Alg
30B2 Ilo Peru
79B3 Iloilo Phil
38J6 Ilomantsi Fin
97C4 Ilorin Nig
75A2 Imabari Japan
75B1 Imaichi Japan
60C1 Imatra Fin
30G4 Imbituba Brazil
99E2 Imi Eth
20C2 Imlay USA
47D1 Immenstadt Germany

52B2 Imola Italy
31B3 Imperatriz Brazil
52A2 Imperia Italy
98B2 Impfondo Congo
86C2 Imphal India
47D1 Imst Austria
12B1 Imuruk L USA
75B1 Ina Japan
96C2 In Afahleleh Well Alg
75B2 Inamba-jima I Japan
96C2 In Amenas Alg
38K5 Inari Fin
38K5 Inarijärvi L Fin
75C1 Inawashiro-ko L
Japan
96C2 In Belbel Alg
60E5 Ince Burun Pt Turk
92B2 Incekum Burun Pt
Turk
74B3 Inch'ŏn S Korea
96B2 In Dagouber Well
Mali
35B1 Indaia R Brazil
38H6 Indals R Sweden
21B2 Independence
California, USA
18A2 Independence Kansas,
USA
18B2 Independence
Missouri, USA
78A3 Inderagiri R Indon
61H4 Inderborskly USSR
83B3 India Federal
Republic, Asia
14A3 Indiana State, USA
15C2 Indiana USA
104C6 Indian-Antarctic Ridge
Indian O
14A3 Indianapolis USA
Indian Desert = Thar
Desert
7E4 Indian Harbour Can
104B4 Indian O
18B1 Indianola Iowa, USA
19B3 Indianola Mississippi,
USA
35B1 Indianópolis Brazil
76D2 Indo China Region,
S E Asia
70C4 Indonesia Republic,
S E Asia
85D4 Indore India
78B4 Indramayu Indon
48C2 Indre R France
85B3 Indus R Pak
96C2 In Ebeggi Well Alg
96C2 In Ecker Alg
92A1 Inegöl Turk
96D2 In Ezzane Alg
97C3 Ingal Niger
14B2 Ingersoll Can
107D2 Ingham Aust
6D2 Inglefield Land Region
Can
110B1 Inglewood NZ
109D1 Inglewood
Queensland, Aust
22C4 Inglewood USA
108B3 Inglewood Victoria,
Aust
38B2 Ingólfshöfôi I Iceland
57C3 Ingolstadt Germany
86B2 Ingrāj Bāzār India
96C3 In-Guezzam Well Alg
101C3 Inhambane Mozam
101C3 Inharrime Mozam
35B1 Inhumas Brazil
32D3 Inírida R Colombia
41B3 Inishbofin I Irish Rep
45A1 Inishéa I Irish Rep
45B2 Inishmaan I Irish Rep
45B2 Inishmore I Irish Rep
45B1 Inishmurray I
Irish Rep
41B3 Inishowen District,
Irish Rep
45A2 Inishshark I Irish Rep

45A2 Inishturk I Irish Rep
109C1 Injune Aust
12H3 Inklin Can
12H3 Inklin R Can
12C1 Inland L USA
47D1 Inn R Austria
108B1 Innamincka Aust
68C2 Inner Mongolia
Autonomous Region,
China
107D2 Innisfail Aust
12C2 Innoko R USA
57C3 Innsbruck Austria
98B3 Inongo Zaïre
58B2 Inowrocŵaw Pol
96C2 In Salah Alg
47B1 Interlaken Switz
24C3 Intexpec Mexico
47C2 Intra Italy
78D3 Intu Indon
75C1 Inubo-saki C Japan
7C4 Inukjuac Can
4E3 Inuvik Can
4F3 Inuvik Region Can
44B3 Inveraray Scot
111A3 Invercargill NZ
109D1 Inverell Aust
13D2 Invermere Can
44B3 Inverness Scot
44C3 Inverurie Scot
108A3 Investigator Str Aust
68A1 Inya USSR
101C2 Inyanga Zim
21B2 Inyokern USA
98B3 Inzia R Zaïre
55B3 Ioánnina Greece
18A2 Iola USA
44A3 Iona I Scot
100A2 Iôna Nat Pk Angola
20C1 Ione USA
Ionian Is = Ioníoi Nísoi
55A3 Ionian S Italy/Greece
55B3 Ioníoi Nísoi Is Greece
55C3 Íos I Greece
10A2 Iowa R USA
18B1 Iowa State, USA
18B1 Iowa City USA
35B1 Ipameri Brazil
35C1 Ipanema Brazil
61F4 Ipatovo USSR
32B3 Ipiales Colombia
77C5 Ipoh Malay
30F2 Iporá Brazil
57C2 Ipsala Turk
109D1 Ipswich Aust
43E3 Ipswich Eng
16D1 Ipswich USA
30B3 Iquique Chile
32C4 Iquitos Peru
55C3 Iráklion Greece
80D2 Iran Republic, S W
Asia
91D4 Īrānshahr Iran
23A1 Irapuato Mexico
93D3 Iraq Republic, S W
Asia
95A2 Irā Wan Watercourse
Libya
94B2 Irbid Jordan
61K2 Irbit USSR
36C3 Ireland Republic,
NW Europe
33F3 Ireng R Guyana
74B3 Iri S Korea
71E4 Irian Jaya Province,
Indon
82C3 Iriba Chad
79B3 Iriga Phil
99D3 Iringa Tanz
69E4 Iriomote I Japan
23G5 Iriri R Brazil
42B3 Irish S English Rep
12D1 Irikilik R USA
63C2 Irkutsk USSR
65J4 Irlysh USSR
108A2 Iron Knob Aust
14A1 Iron Mountain USA
107D2 Iron Range Aust
14A1 Iron River USA

Irontown

14B3 Irontown USA
10A2 Ironwood USA
10B2 Iroquois Falls Can
75B2 Iro-zaki C Japan
76A2 Irrawaddy,Mouths of the Burma
65H4 Irtysh R USSR
51B1 Irun Spain
42B2 Irvine Scot
19A3 Irving USA
79B4 Isabela Phil
32J7 Isabela I Ecuador
4H2 Isachsen Can
4H2 Isachsen,C Can
6H3 Isafjörðhur Iceland
74C4 Isahaya Japan
98C2 Isangi Zaïre
47D1 Isar R Italy
47D1 Isarco R Italy
44E1 Isbister Scot
47D1 Ischgl Austria
53B2 Ischia I Italy
75B2 Ise Japan
47D2 Iseo Italy
46D1 Iserlohn Germany
53B2 Isernia Italy
76B2 Ise-wan B Japan
69E4 Ishigaki I Japan
74E2 Ishikari R Japan
74E2 Ishikari-wan B Japan
65H4 Ishim USSR
65H4 Ishim R USSR
74E3 Ishinomaki Japan
75C1 Ishioka Japan
84C1 Ishkashim Afghan
14A1 Ishpeming USA
65J4 Isil'kul USSR
99D2 Isiolo Kenya
98C2 Isiro Zaïre
92C2 Iskenderun Turk
92C2 Iskenderun Körfezi B Turk
92B1 Iskilip Turk
65K4 Iskitim USSR
54B2 Iskur R Bulg
12H3 Iskut R Can/USA
23B2 Isla Mexico
34C3 Isla Bermejo I Arg
27E4 Isla Blanquilla Ven
32A2 Isla Coiba I Panama
9B4 Isla de Cedros I Mexico
29B4 Isla de Chiloé I Chile
25D2 Isla de Cozumel I Mexico
26C3 Isla de la Gonâve Cuba
26A2 Isla de la Juventud I Cuba
34D2 Isla de las Lechiguanas I Arg
3K8 Isla del Coco I Costa Rica
25D3 Isla del Maíz I Caribbean S
23B1 Isla de Lobos I Mexico
29D6 Isla de los Estados I Arg
28E2 Isla de Marajó I Brazil
105L5 Isla de Pascua I Pacific O
26A4 Isla de Providencia I Caribbean S
26A4 Isla de San Andres I Caribbean S
30G4 Isla de Santa Catarina I Brazil
33G2 Isla du Diable I French Guiana
31E2 Isla Fernando de Noronha I Brazil
29C6 Isla Grande de Tierra del Fuego I Arg/Chile
27D4 Isla la Tortuga I Ven
84C2 Islamabad Pak
24A2 Isla Magdalena I Mexico
27E4 Isla Margarita Ven
34A3 Isla Mocha Chile

17B2 Islamorada USA
10A1 Island L Can
108A2 Island Lg Aust
110B1 Islands,B of USA
32A4 Isla Puná I Ecuador
103D6 Isla San Ambrosia I Pacific O
103D6 Isla San Felix I Pacific O
24A2 Isla Santa Margarita I Mexico
34A3 Isla Santa Maria I Chile
51C2 Islas Baleares Is Spain
96A2 Islas Canarias Is Atlantic O
51C2 Islas Columbretes Is Spain
25D3 Islas de la Bahia Is Honduras
26A4 Islas del Maíz Is Caribbean S
33E1 Islas de Margarita I Ven
29C7 Islas Diego Ramírez Is Chile
32J7 Islas Galapagos Is Pacific O
30H6 Islas Juan Fernández Is Chile
32D1 Islas los Roques Is Ven
Islas Malvinas = Falkland Is
105L3 Islas Revilla Gigedo Is Pacific O
29C7 Islas Wollaston Is Chile
97A3 Isla Tidra I Maur
29B5 Isla Wellington I Chile
48C2 Isle R France
104B5 Isle Amsterdam I Indian O
43D4 Isle of Wight I Eng
10B2 Isle Royale I USA
104B5 Isle St Paul I Indian O
104A6 Isles Crozet I Indian O
105J4 Isles de la Société Is Pacific O
105K5 Isles Gambier Is Pacific O
101D2 Isles Glorieuses Is Madag
104B6 Isles Kerguelen Is Indian O
105K4 Isles Marquises Is Pacific O
105J4 Isles Tuamotu Is Pacific O
105J5 Isles Tubai Is Pacific O
22B1 Isleton USA
92B3 Ismâ'ilîya Egypt
101D3 Isoanala Madag
101C2 Isoka Zambia
53B3 Isola Egadi I Italy
53B2 Isola Ponziane I Italy
53C2 Isola Lipari Is Italy
53C2 Isoles Tremiti Is Italy
75B1 Isosaki Japan
92B2 Isparta Turk
94B2 Israel Republic, S W Asia
51C2 Isser R Alg
48C2 Issoire France
49C2 Issoudun France
92A1 İstanbul Turk
55B3 Istiáia Greece
25C3 Istmo de Tehuantepec Isthmus Mexico
17B2 Istokpoga,L USA
52B1 Istra Pen Yugos
35B1 Itaberai Brazil
35C1 Itabira Brazil
35C2 Itabirito Brazil
31D4 Itabuna Brazil
33F4 Itacoatiara Brazil
32B2 Itagui Colombia

33F4 Itaituba Brazil
30G4 Itajai Brazil
35B2 Itajuba Brazil
52B2 Italy Republic, Europe
35D1 Itamaraju Brazil
35C1 Itamarandiba Brazil
35C1 Itambacuri Brazil
35C1 Itambé m Brazil
86C1 Itánagar India
35B2 Itanhaém Brazil
35C1 Itanhém Brazil
35C1 Itanhém R Brazil
31D1 Itacobim Brazil
35B2 Itapecerica Brazil
35C2 Itaperuna Brazil
31C5 Itapetinga Brazil
35B3 Itapetininga Brazil
35B2 Itapeva Brazil
31D2 Itapipoca Brazil
35B1 Itapuranga Brazil
30E4 Itaquí Brazil
35C1 Itarantim Brazil
35B2 Itararé Brazil
35B2 Itararé R Brazil
35C2 Itaúna Brazil
35B1 Iténez R Brazil/Bol
15C2 Ithaca USA
98C2 Itimbiri R Zaïre
35C1 Itinga Brazil
6E3 Itivdleg Greenland
75B2 Ito Japan
74D3 Itoigawa Japan
33E6 Itonomas R Bol
35B2 Itu Brazil
35B1 Itumbiara Brazil
35A1 Iturama Brazil
30C3 Iturbe Arg
35B1 Iturutaba Brazil
56B2 Itzehoe Germany
65K4 Iurga USSR
58D2 Ivacevichi USSR
35A2 Ivaí R Brazil
38K5 Ivalo Fin
54A2 Ivangrad Yugos
108B2 Ivanhoe Aust
64D5 Ivano USSR
59C2 Ivano-Frankovsk USSR
61F2 Ivanovo USSR
65H3 Ivdel' USSR
98B2 Ivindo R Gabon
101D3 Ivohibe Madag
101D2 Ivongo Soanierana Madag
97B4 Ivory Coast Republic, Africa
52A1 Ivrea Italy
6C3 Ivujivik Can
74E3 Iwaki Japan
74C4 Iwakuni Japan
74E2 Iwanai Japan
97C4 Iwo Nig
69G4 Iwo Jima I Japan
23B1 Ixmiquilpa Mexico
23A2 Ixtapa Mexico
23A1 Ixtlán Mexico
75A2 Iyo Japan
75A2 Iyo-nada B Japan
65G4 Izhevsk USSR
64G3 Izhma USSR
91C5 Izki Oman
60C4 Izmail USSR
92A2 İzmir Turk
55C3 İzmir Körfezi B Turk
92A1 İznik Turk
55C2 İznik Golü L Turk
94C2 İzra' Syria
23B2 Izúcar de Matamoros Mexico
75B2 Izumi-sano Japan
75A1 Izumo Japan
74D4 Izu-shotō Is Japan

94C2 Jabal al 'Arab Syria
95A2 Jabal as Sawdā Mts Libya
91B5 Jabal az Zannah UAE
94C1 Jabal Halimah Mt Leb/Syria
83B3 Jabalpur India
59B2 Jablonec nad Nisou Czech
31D3 Jaboatão Brazil
35B2 Jaboticabal Brazil
51B1 Jaca Spain
23A1 Jacala Mexico
33F6 Jacareacanga Brazil
35B2 Jacareí Brazil
30F3 Jacarezinho Brazil
29C2 Jáchal Arg
35C1 Jacinto Brazil
13F2 Jackfish L Can
109C1 Jackson Aust
22B1 Jackson California, USA
14B2 Jackson Michigan, USA
19B3 Jackson Mississippi, USA
18C2 Jackson Missouri, USA
14B3 Jackson Ohio, USA
11B3 Jackson Tennessee, USA
111B2 Jackson,C NZ
111A2 Jackson Head Pt NZ
19B3 Jacksonville Arkansas, USA
17B1 Jacksonville Florida, USA
18B2 Jacksonville Illinois, USA
17C1 Jacksonville N Carolina, USA
19A3 Jacksonville Texas, USA
17B1 Jacksonville Beach USA
26C3 Jacmel Haiti
84B3 Jacobabad Pak
31C4 Jacobina Brazil
23A2 Jacona Mexico
Jadotville = Likasi
32B5 Jaén Peru
50B2 Jaén Spain
Jaffa = Tel Aviv Yafo
108A3 Jaffa,C Aust
87B3 Jaffna Sri Lanka
86B2 Jagannathganj Ghat Bang
87C1 Jagdalpur India
91C4 Jagin R Iran
87B1 Jagtial India
29F2 Jaguarão R Brazil
35B2 Jaguariaíva Brazil
91B4 Jahrom Iran
85D5 Jäina India
72A2 Jainca China
85D3 Jaipur India
85C3 Jaisalmer India
29H1 Jajarm Iran
52C2 Jajce Yugos
78B4 Jakarta Indon
6E3 Jakobshavn Greenland
38J6 Jakobstad Fin
23B2 Jalaca Mexico
84B2 Jalai-Kut Afghan
23B2 Jalapa Mexico
35A2 Jales Brazil
86B1 Jaleswar Nepal
85D4 Jalgaon India
97D4 Jalingo Nig
51B1 Jalón R Spain
95B2 Jalo Oasis Libya
85C3 Jalor India
34J1 Jalostotitlan Mexico
86B1 Jalpáiguri India
23B1 Jalpan Mexico
32A4 Jama Ecuador
26B3 Jamaica I Caribbean S
26B3 Jamaica Chan Caribbean S

J
95B1 Jabal al Akhdar Mts Libya

86B2 Jamalpur Bang	94B2 Jebel ash Shaykh *Mt*	74B2 Ji'an Jilin, China	18A2 John Redmond Res
78A3 Jambi Indon	Syria	73D4 Jiande China	USA
85C4 Jambussar India	95C2 Jebel Asoteriba *Mt*	73B4 Jiang'an China	11B3 Johnson City
7B4 James B Can	Sudan	73D4 Jiangbiancun China	Tennessee, USA
5J5 Jameston USA	94B3 Jebel Ed Dabab *Mt*	73A5 Jiangcheng China	17B1 Johnston USA
108A2 Jamestown Aust	Jordan	73D4 Jiang Jiang *R* China	27N2 Johnston Pt *St*
8D2 Jamestown	94B3 Jebel el Ata'ita *Mt*	73C5 Jiangmen China	Vincent
N Dakota, USA	Jordan	72D3 Jiangsu Province,	15C2 Johnstown
15C2 Jamestown New	92C3 Jebel esh Sharqi *Mts*	China	Pennsylvania, USA
York, USA	Leb/Syria	73C4 Jiangxi Province,	77C5 Johor Bharu Malay
16D2 Jamestown Rhode	94B3 Jebel Ithriyat *Mt*	China	49C2 Joigny France
Island, USA	Jordan	73A3 Jiangyou China	30G4 Joinville Brazil
23B2 Jamiltepec Mexico	91C5 Jebel Ja'lan *Mt* Oman	72D1 Jianping China	61H3 Jok *R* USSR
87B1 Jamkhandi India	94B2 Jebel Liban *Mts* Leb	73A5 Jianshui China	38H5 Jokkmokk Sweden
84C2 Jammu India	94C2 Jebel Ma'lūlā *Mt*	73A5 Jian Xi *R* China	93E2 Jolfa Iran
84D2 Jammu and Kashmir	Syria	73D4 Jianyang China	10B2 Joliet USA
State, India	98C1 Jebel Marra *Mt*	72E2 Jiaonan China	7C5 Joliette Can
85B4 Jamnagar India	Sudan	72E2 Jiao Xian China	79B4 Jolo Phil
84C3 Jampur Pak	94C3 Jebel Mudeisisat *Mt*	72E2 Jiaozhou Wan *B*	79B4 Jolo *I* Phil
38K6 Jämsä Fin	Jordan	China	82D2 Joma *Mt* China
86B2 Jamshedpur India	95C2 Jebel Oda *Mt* Sudan	72E2 Jiaozuo China	58C1 Jonava USSR
86B1 Janakpur Nepal	94B3 Jebel Qasr ed Deir *Mt*	73E3 Jiaxiang China	72A3 Jonê China
35C1 Janaúba Brazil	Jordan	68B3 Jiayuguan China	11A3 Jonesboro Arkansas,
90B3 Jandaq Iran	94B2 Jebel Um ed Daraj *Mt*	81B3 Jiddah S Arabia	USA
109D1 Jandowae Aust	Jordan	72D3 Jieshou China	19B3 Jonesboro Louisiana,
1B1 Jan Mayen *I*	95B2 Jebel Uveinat *Mt*	72C2 Jiexiu China	USA
Norwegian S	Sudan	72A3 Jigzhi China	6B2 Jones Sd Can
35C1 Januária Brazil	42C2 Jedburgh Scot	59B3 Jihlava Czech	58C1 Joniskis USSR
85D4 Jaora India	*Jedda = Jiddah*	99E2 Jilib Somalia	39G7 Jönköping Sweden
51 Japan Empire, E Asia	59C2 Jedrzejów Pol	69E2 Jilin China	11A3 Joplin USA
74C3 Japan,S of S E Asia	19B3 Jefferson Texas, USA	51B1 Jiloca *R* Spain	92C3 Jordan Kingdom,
104F2 Japan Trench	11A3 Jefferson City USA	9C4 Jiménez Coahuila,	S W Asia
Pacific O	8B3 Jefferson,Mt USA	Mexico	94B2 Jordan *R* Israel
32D4 Japurá *R* Brazil	14A3 Jeffersonville USA	99D2 Jimma Eth	20C2 Jordan Valley USA
93C2 Jarabulus Syria	60C2 Jekabpils USSR	72D2 Jinan China	86C1 Jorhāt India
35B1 Jaraguá Brazil	59B2 Jelena Gora Pol	84D3 Jind India	38J5 Jörn Sweden
50B1 Jarama *R* Spain	60B2 Jelgava USSR	72B2 Jingbian China	78C3 Jorong Indon
94B2 Jarash Jordan	78C4 Jember Indon	73D4 Jingdezhen China	39F7 Jørpeland Nor
30E3 Jardim Brazil	57C2 Jena Germany	76C1 Jinghong China	79B3 Jose Pañganiban Phil
51B2 Játiva *R* Spain	78C2 Jenaja *I* Indon	73C3 Jingmen China	106B2 Joseph Bonaparte G
26B2 Jardines de la Reina *Is*	47D1 Jenbach Austria	72B2 Jingning China	Aust
Cuba	94B2 Jenin Israel	73B4 Jing Xiang China	64B3 Jotunheimen *Mt* Nor
Jargalant = Hovd	19B3 Jennings USA	73D4 Jinhua China	94B2 Jouai'ya Leb
33G3 Jari *R* Brazil	59B2 Jensensky *Upland*	72D2 Jining Nei Monggol,	94B2 Jounie Leb
86C1 Jaria Jhānjail Bang	Czech	China	86C1 Jowal India
46C2 Jarny France	6F3 Jensen Nunatakker	72D3 Jining Shandong,	99E2 Jowhar Somalia
58B2 Jarocin Pol	*Mt* Greenland	China	12H2 Joy,Mt Can
59C2 Jaroslaw Pol	6B3 Jens Munk *I* Can	99D2 Jinja Uganda	5F5 Juan de Fuca,Str of
38G6 Järpen Sweden	108B3 Jeparit Aust	76C1 Jinping China	Can/USA
72B2 Jartai China	31D4 Jequié Brazil	73A4 Jinsha Jiang *R* China	101D2 Juan de Nova *I*
85C4 Jasdan India	35C1 Jequital *R* Brazil	73C4 Jinshi China	Mozam Chan
97C4 Jasikan Ghana	35C1 Jequitinhonha Brazil	72E1 Jinxi China	
94B3 Jāsk Iran	31C5 Jequitinhonha *R*	72E1 Jin Xian China	34D3 Juárez Arg
59C3 Jaslo Pol	Brazil	72E1 Jinzhou China	31D3 Juázeiro Brazil
29D6 Jason Is Falkland Is	50A2 Jerez de la Frontera	33E5 Jiparaná *R* Brazil	31D3 Juàzeiro do Norte
18B2 Jasper Arkansas, USA	Spain	32A4 Jipijapa Ecuador	Brazil
13D2 Jasper Can	50A2 Jerez de los Caballeros	23A2 Jiquilpan Mexico	99D2 Juba Sudan
17B1 Jasper Florida, USA	Spain	91C4 Jiroft Iran	99E2 Juba *R* Somalia
14A3 Jasper Indiana, USA	94B3 Jericho Israel	73B4 Jishou China	94B1 Jubail Leb
13D2 Jasper Nat Pk Can	108C3 Jerilderie Aust	94B3 Jisr esh Shughūr	93D3 Jubbah S Arabia
58B2 Jastrowie Pol	48B2 Jersey *I* UK	Syria	96A2 Juby,C Mor
35A1 Jataí Brazil	15C2 Jersey City USA	54B2 Jiu *R* Rom	51B2 Jucar *R* Spain
51B2 Játiva Spain	15C2 Jersey Shore USA	73D4 Jiujiang China	23B2 Juchatengo Mexico
31B2 Jatobá Brazil	18B2 Jerseyville USA	73A4 Jiulong China	23A1 Juchipila Mexico
35B2 Jau Brazil	92C3 Jerusalem Israel	73D4 Jiulong Jiang *R* China	23A1 Juchitan Mexico
32B6 Jauja Peru	109D3 Jervis B Aust	69F2 Jixi China	57C3 Judenburg Austria
86A1 Jaunpur India	13C2 Jervis Inlet *Sd* Can	94B3 Jiza Jordan	30B2 Juilaca Peru
Java = Jawa	52B1 Jesenice Yugos	81C4 Jizan S Arabia	31C6 Juiz de Fora Brazil
87B2 Javadi Hills India	86B2 Jessore Bang	97A3 Joal Sen	30C3 Jujuy State, Arg
Javari = Yavari	11B3 Jesup USA	35C1 João Monlevade	30C2 Juli Peru
70B4 Java S Indon	34C2 Jesus Maria Arg	Brazil	33F3 Julianatop *R*
106A2 Java Trench Indon	16D2 Jewett City USA	31E3 João Pessoa Brazil	Surinam
78B4 Jawa *I* Indon	54A2 Jezerce *Mt* Alb	35B1 João Pirheiro Brazil	6F3 Julianehåb Greenland
71F4 Jayapura Indon	58C2 Jeziora Mamry *L* Pol	33B2 Jocoli Arg	46D1 Jülich Germany
94C2 Jayrud Syria	58C2 Jezioro Śniardwy *L*	85C3 Jodhpur India	84D2 Jullundur India
96B2 Jbel Ouarkziz *Mts*	Pol	38K6 Joensuu Fin	86A1 Jumla Nepal
Mor	94B2 Jezzine Leb	46C2 Joeuf France	94B3 Jum Suwwāna *Mt*
96B1 Jbel Sarhro *Mt* Mor	85C4 Jhābua India	13D2 Joffre,Mt Can	Jordan
19B4 Jeanerette USA	85D4 Jhālāwār India	86B1 Jogbani India	85C4 Jünägadh India
97C4 Jebba Nig	84C2 Jhang Maghiana Pak	87A2 Jog Falls India	72D2 Junan China
93D2 Jebel 'Abd al 'Aziz *Mt*	85D3 Jhānsi India	101G1 Johannesburg	9D3 Junction City USA
Syria	86A2 Jhärsuguda India	S Africa	31B8 Jundiai Brazil
95B3 Jebel Abyad Sudan	84C2 Jhelum Pak	21B2 Johannesburg USA	4E4 Juneau USA
91C5 Jebel Akhdar *Mt*	84C2 Jhelum *R* Pak	6C2 Johan Pen Can	107D4 Junee Aust
Oman	11C3 J H Kerr L USA	12D1 John *R* USA	22C2 June Lake USA
92C4 Jebel al Lawz *Mt*	84D3 Jhunjhunün India	20C2 John Day USA	52A1 Jungfrau *Mt* Switz
S Arabia	69F2 Jiamusi China	20B1 John Day *R* USA	16A2 Juniata *R* USA
	73C4 Ji'an Jiangxi, China	44C2 John o'Groats Scot	

29D2 Junín Arg
73A4 Junlian China
31B6 Juquiá Brazil
99C2 Jur R Sudan
42B2 Jura I Scot
22A2 Jura Mts France
44B3 Jura,Sound of Chan Scot
94B3 Jurf ed Darāwīsh Jordan
60B2 Jürmala USSR
32D4 Juruá R Brazil
33F6 Juruena R Brazil
94C1 Jūsīyah Syria
34B2 Justo Daract Arg
32D4 Jutaí R Brazil
25D3 Juticalpa Honduras
Jutland = Jylland
90C3 Jūymand Iran
56B1 Jylland Pen Den
38K6 Jyväskylä Fin

K

82B2 K2 Mt China/India
90C2 Kaakhka USSR
101H1 Kaapmuiden S Africa
71D4 Kabaena I Indon
97A4 Kabala Sierra Leone
99D3 Kabale Rwanda
98C3 Kabalo Zaïre
99D2 Kabambare Zaïre
98C3 Kabinda Zaïre
90A3 Kabir Kuh Mts Iran
100B2 Kabompo Zambia
100B2 Kabompo R Zambia
98C3 Kabongo Zaïre
84B2 Kabul Afghan
85B4 Kachchh,G of India
61J2 Kachkanar USSR
63C2 Kachug USSR
76B3 Kadan Burma
78D3 Kadapongan I Indon
85C4 Kadi India
108A2 Kadina Aust
92B2 Kadınhanı Turk
87B2 Kadiri India
60E4 Kadiyevka USSR
100B2 Kadoma Zim
99C1 Kadugli Sudan
97C3 Kaduna Nig
97C3 Kaduna R Nig
97B2 Kadur India
97A3 Kaédi Maur
21C4 Kaena Pt Hawaiian Is
74B3 Kaesŏng N Korea
97C4 Kafanchan Nig
99C1 Kaffrine Sen
94C1 Kafrūn Bashūr Syria
100B2 Kafue Zambia
100B2 Kafue R Zambia
100B2 Kafue Nat Pk Zambia
74D3 Kaga Japan
65H6 Kagan USSR
92B2 Kağızman Turk
74C4 Kagoshima Japan
90C2 Kāhak Iran
99D3 Kahama Tanz
84B3 Kahan Pak
78C3 Kahayan R Indon
98B3 Kahemba Zaïre
46E1 Kahler Asten Mt Germany
91C4 Kahnūj Iran
18B1 Kahoka USA
21C4 Kahoolawe I Hawaiian Is
92C2 Kahramanmaraş Turk
21C4 Kahuku Pt Hawaiian Is
111B2 Kaiapoi NZ
33F2 Kaieteur Fall Guyana
72C3 Kaifeng China
110B1 Kaikohe NZ
111B2 Kaikoura NZ
111B2 Kaikoura Pen NZ
111B2 Kaikoura Range Mts NZ

73B4 Kaili China
21C4 Kailua Hawaiian Is
71E4 Kaimana Indon
75B2 Kainan Japan
97C3 Kainji Res Nig
110B1 Kaipara Harbour B NZ
73C5 Kaiping China
96D1 Kairouan Tunisia
22C2 Kaiser Peak Mt USA
57B3 Kaiserslautern Germany
74B2 Kaishantun China
58D2 Kaisiadorys USSR
110B1 Kaitaia NZ
111A3 Kaitangata NZ
84D3 Kaithal India
21C4 Kaiwi Chan Hawaiian Is
73B3 Kai Xian China
73A5 Kaiyuan Liaoning, China
74A2 Kaiyuan Yunnan, China
12C2 Kaiyuh Mts USA
38K6 Kajaani Fin
84B2 Kajaki Afghan
99D3 Kajiado Kenya
84B2 Kajrān Afghan
99D1 Kaka Sudan
99D2 Kakamega Kenya
75A2 Kake Japan
12I3 Kake USA
12D3 Kakhonak USA
65E5 Kakhovskoye Vodokhranilishche Res USSR
91B4 Kākī Iran
87C1 Kākināda India
75A2 Kakogawa Japan
4D2 Kaktovik USA
75C1 Kakuda Japan
55B3 Kalabáka Greece
78D1 Kalabakan Malay
100B2 Kalabo Zambia
61F3 Kalach USSR
61F4 Kalach-na-Donu USSR
86C2 Kaladan R Burma
21C4 Ka Lae I Hawaiian Is
100B3 Kalahari Desert Botswana
38J6 Kalajoki Fin
63D2 Kalakan USSR
70A3 Kalakepen Indon
84C1 Kalam Pak
55C3 Kálimnos I Greece
86B1 Kālimpang India
60E2 Kalinin USSR
60C3 Kaliningrad USSR
8B2 Kalispell USA
58B2 Kalisz Pol
99D3 Kaliua Tanz
38J5 Kalix R Sweden
100A3 Kalkfeld Namibia
100A3 Kalkrand Namibia
108A1 Kalkaroop R Aust
38K6 Kallávesi I Fin
55C3 Kallonís Kólpos B Greece
39H7 Kalmar Sweden
61G4 Kalmykskaya ASSR Republic, USSR

100B2 Kalomo Zambia
18B1 Kalona USA
13B2 Kalone Peak Mt Can
87A2 Kalpeni I India
85D3 Kālpi India
85A2 Kalat Khasba Tunisia
12B2 Kalskag USA
12C2 Kaltag USA
58C1 Kaluga USSR
39G7 Kalundborg Den
59C3 Kalush USSR
87B2 Kalyandurg India
60E2 Kalyazin USSR
61H1 Kama R USSR
74E3 Kamaishi Japan
84C2 Kamalia Pak
110C1 Kamanawa Mts NZ
100A2 Kamanjab Namibia
84D2 Kamat Mt India
87B3 Kamban India
61H2 Kambarka USSR
97A4 Kambia Sierra Leone
59D3 Kamenets Podolskiy USSR
61F3 Kamenka USSR
65K4 Kamen-na-Obi USSR
61K2 Kamensk-Ural'skiy USSR
5H3 Kamilukuak L Can
98C3 Kamina Zaïre
7A3 Kaminak L Can
75C1 Kaminoyama Japan
5F4 Kamloops Can
93E1 Kamo USSR
75C1 Kamogawa Japan
99D2 Kampala Uganda
77C5 Kampar Malay
78A2 Kampar R Indon
56B2 Kampen Neth
76B2 Kamphaeng Phet Thai
77C3 Kampot Camb
Kampuchea = Cambodia
91D4 Kamsaptar Iran
61J2 Kamskoye Vodokhranilishche Res USSR
85D4 Kāmthi India
61G3 Kamyshin USSR
61K2 Kamyshlov USSR
7C4 Kanaaupscow R Can
98C3 Kananga Zaïre
61G2 Kanash USSR
75B1 Kanayama Japan
74D3 Kanazawa Japan
4C3 Kanbisha USA
87B2 Kānchipuram India
84B2 Kandahar Afghan
64E3 Kandalaksha USSR
38L5 Kandalakshskaya Guba G USSR
97A3 Kandi Benin
109C2 Kandos Aust
87B3 Kandy Sri Lanka
15C2 Kane USA
6C1 Kane Basin B Can
98B1 Kanem Desert Region Chad
97B3 Kangaba Mali
22C1 Kangal Turk
6E3 Kangâmiut Greenland
91B4 Kangān Iran
77C4 Kangar Malay
106C4 Kangaroo I Aust
6E3 Kanga'tsiaq Greenland
90A3 Kangāvar Iran
72C1 Kangbao China
82C3 Kangchenjunga Mt Nepal
73A4 Kangding China
6G3 Kangerdlugssuaq B Greenland
6G3 Kangerdlugssvatsaiq B Greenland
99D2 Kangetet Kenya
74B2 Kanggye N Korea
7D4 Kangiqsualujjuaq Can

6C3 Kangiqsujuaq Can
7C3 Kangirsuk Can
74B3 Kangnŭng S Korea
98B2 Kango Gabon
68B2 Kangto Mt China
72B3 Kang Xian China
77D4 Kanh Hung Viet
98C3 Kaniama Zaïre
87B1 Kani Giri India
64F3 Kanin Nos Pt USSR
39J6 Kankaanpää Fin
14A2 Kankakee USA
14A2 Kankakee R USA
97B3 Kankan Guinea
86A2 Kānker India
87B3 Kanniyākumari India
97C3 Kano Nig
74C4 Kanoya Japan
86A1 Kānpur India
9D3 Kansas State, USA
18A2 Kansas R USA
10A3 Kansas City USA
73D5 Kanshi China
63B2 Kansk USSR
97C3 Kantchari Burkina
65K4 Kanthi India
12D2 Kantishna USA
12D2 Kantishna R USA
100B3 Kanye Botswana
68D4 Kao-hsiung Taiwan
100A2 Kaoka Veld Plain Namibia
97A3 Kaolack Sen
100B2 Kaoma Zambia
21C4 Kapaau Hawaiian Is
98C3 Kapanga Zaïre
6F3 Kap Cort Adelaer C Greenland
6H3 Kap Dalton C Greenland
39H7 Kapellskär Sweden
6F3 Kap Farvel C Greenland
6G3 Kap Gustav Holm C Greenland
62J1 Kapit Zambia
78C2 Kapit Malay
19B3 Kaplan USA
57C3 Kaplice Czech
77B4 Kapoe Thai
99C3 Kapona Zaïre
52C1 Kaposvár Hung
6C2 Kap Parry C Can
6H3 Kap Ravn C Greenland
78B3 Kapuas R Indon
108A2 Kapunda Aust
84D2 Kapurthala India
7B5 Kapuskasing Can
107D2 Kaputar Mt Aust
93E2 Kapydzhik Mt USSR
6D2 Kap Yozk C Greenland
92B1 Karabük Turk
55C2 Karacabey Turk
85B3 Karachi Pak
87A1 Kārād India
60E5 Kara Daglari Mt Turk
92B1 Karadeniz Boğazi Sd Turk
68D1 Karaftit USSR
65J5 Karaganda USSR
65J5 Karagayly USSR
1C4 Karaj Iran
92B2 Karak Jordan
65G5 Kara Kalpakskaya A.S.S.R. Republic, USSR
84D1 Karakax He R China
71D3 Karakelong I Indon
84D1 Karakoram Mts India
84D1 Karakoram P India/China
97A3 Karakoro R Maur/Sen
65G6 Karakumy Desert USSR
94B3 Karama Jordan

92B2 **Karaman** Turk
65K5 **Karamay** China
111B2 **Karamea** NZ
111B2 **Karamea Bight** B NZ
85D4 **Kāranja** India
92B2 **Karapınar** Turk
64H2 **Kara S** USSR
100A3 **Karasburg** Namibia
38K5 **Karasjok** Nor
65J4 **Karasuk** USSR
92C2 **Karataş** Turk
65H5 **Kara Tau** Mts USSR
76B3 **Karathuri** Burma
74J2 **Karatsu** Japan
91B4 **Karāz** Iran
93D3 **Karbalā'** Iraq
59C3 **Karcag** Hung
55B3 **Kardhítsa** Greece
64E3 **Karel'skaya ASSR** Republic, USSR
38J5 **Karesvando** Sweden
96B2 **Karet** Desert Region Maur
65K4 **Kargasok** USSR
97D3 **Kari** Nig
100B2 **Kariba** Zim
100B2 **Kariba L** Zim/Zambia
100B2 **Kariba Dam** Zim/Zambia
95C3 **Karima** Sudan
78B3 **Karimata** I Indon
86C2 **Karimganj** Bang
87B1 **Karimnagar** India
99E1 **Karin** Somalia
39J6 **Karis** Fin
99C3 **Karishimbe** Mt Zaïre
55B3 **Káristos** Greece
87A2 **Kārkal** India
71F4 **Karkar** I PNG
90A3 **Karkheh** R Iran
60D4 **Karkinitskiy Zaliv** B USSR
63B3 **Karlik Shan** Mt China
58B2 **Karlino** Pol
52C2 **Karlobag** Yugos
52C1 **Karlovac** Yugos
54C2 **Karlovo** Bulg
57C2 **Karlovy Vary** Czech
39G7 **Karlshamn** Sweden
39G7 **Karlskoga** Sweden
39H7 **Karlskrona** Sweden
57B3 **Karlsruhe** Germany
39G7 **Karlstad** Sweden
12D3 **Karluk** USA
86C2 **Karnafuli Res** Bang
84D3 **Karnal** India
87A1 **Karnataka** State, India
54C2 **Karnobat** Bulg
100B2 **Karoi** Zim
99D3 **Karonga** Malawi
95C3 **Karora** Sudan
78D3 **Karossa** Indon
55C3 **Kárpathos** I Greece
6E2 **Karrats Fjord** Greenland
93D1 **Kars** Turk
65H4 **Karsakpay** USSR
58D1 **Kārsava** USSR
80E2 **Karshi** USSR
38J6 **Karstula** Fin
94B1 **Kartaba** Leb
54C2 **Kartal** Turk
61K3 **Kartaly** USSR
90A3 **Kārūn** R Iran
86A1 **Karwa** India
87A2 **Kārwār** India
68D1 **Karymskoye** USSR
98B3 **Kasai** R Zaïre
100B2 **Kasaji** Zaïre
101C2 **Kasama** Zambia
99D3 **Kasanga** Tanz
87A2 **Kāsaragod** India
5H3 **Kasba L** Can
100B2 **Kasempa** Zambia
100B2 **Kasenga** Zaïre
99D2 **Kasese** Uganda
90B3 **Kāshān** Iran
12C2 **Kashegelok** USA

82B2 **Kashi** China
84D3 **Kāshipur** India
74D3 **Kashiwazaki** Japan
90C2 **Kashmar** Iran
66D3 **Kashmir** State, India
61F3 **Kasimov** USSR
18C2 **Kaskaskia** R USA
38J6 **Kaskinen** Fin
61K2 **Kasli** USSR
5G5 **Kaslo** Can
98C3 **Kasonga** Zaïre
98B3 **Kasongo-Lunda** Zaïre
55C3 **Kásos** I Greece
61G4 **Kaspiyskiy** USSR
95C3 **Kassala** Sudan
57B2 **Kassel** Germany
96C1 **Kasserine** Tunisia
100A2 **Kassinga** Angola
92B1 **Kastamonou** Turk
55B3 **Kastélli** Greece
92A2 **Kastellorizon** I Greece
55B2 **Kastoria** Greece
55C3 **Kástron** Greece
74D3 **Kasugai** Japan
75A1 **Kasumi** Japan
101C2 **Kasungu** Malawi
84C2 **Kasur** Pak
100B2 **Kataba** Zambia
98C3 **Katako-kombe** Zaïre
4D3 **Katalla** USA
63G2 **Katangli** USSR
106A4 **Katanning** Aust
55B2 **Katerini** Greece
5E4 **Kates Needle** Mt Can/USA
82D3 **Katha** Burma
106C2 **Katherine** Aust
85C4 **Kāthiāwār** Pen India
86B1 **Kathmandu** Nepal
84D2 **Kathua** India
86B1 **Katihār** India
100B2 **Katima Mulilo** Namibia
4C4 **Katmai,Mt** USA
12D3 **Katmai Nat Mon** USA
86A2 **Katni** India
109D2 **Katoomba** Aust
59B2 **Katowice** Pol
39H7 **Katrineholm** Sweden
97C3 **Katsina** Nig
97C4 **Katsina Ala** Nig
75C1 **Katsuta** Japan
75C1 **Katsuura** Japan
75B1 **Katsuyama** Japan
65H6 **Kattakurgan** USSR
39G7 **Kattegat** Str Den/Sweden
21C4 **Kauai** I Hawaiian Is
21C4 **Kauai Chan** Hawaiian Is
21C4 **Kaulakahi Chan** Hawaiian Is
21C4 **Kaunakakai** Hawaiian Is
60B3 **Kaunas** USSR
97C3 **Kaura Namoda** Nig
38J5 **Kautokeino** Nor
55B2 **Kavadarci** Yugos
55A2 **Kavajë** Alb
55B2 **Kavála** Greece
85B4 **Kāvda** India
75B1 **Kawagoe** Japan
75B1 **Kawaguchi** Japan
110B1 **Kawakawa** NZ
99C3 **Kawambwa** Zambia
86A2 **Kawardha** India
15C2 **Kawartha Lakes** Can
74D3 **Kawasaki** Japan
110C1 **Kawhia** NZ
110B1 **Kawhia** NZ
97B3 **Kaya** Burkina
12F3 **Kayak I** USA
78D2 **Kayan** R Indon
87B3 **Kāyankulam** India
97A3 **Kayes** Mali
92C2 **Kayseri** Turk
1B8 **Kazach'ye** USSR
93E1 **Kazakh** USSR

65G5 **Kazakhskaya SSR** Republic, USSR
61G2 **Kazan'** USSR
54C2 **Kazanlŭk** Bulg
69G4 **Kazan Retto** Is Japan
91B4 **Kāzerūn** Iran
61H1 **Kazhim** USSR
93E1 **Kazi Magomed** USSR
59C3 **Kazincbarcika** Hung
55B3 **Kéa** I Greece
21C4 **Kealaikahiki Chan** Hawaiian Is
8D2 **Kearney** USA
93C2 **Keban Baraji** Res Turk
97A3 **Kébémer** Sen
96C1 **Kebili** Tunisia
94C1 **Kebir** R Leb/Syria
38H5 **Kebnekaise** Mt Sweden
59B3 **Kecskemét** Hung
58C1 **Kedainiai** USSR
97A3 **Kédougou** Sen
17C4 **Keele** R Can
12H2 **Keele Pk** Mt Can
21B2 **Keeler** USA
15D2 **Keene** New Hampshire, USA
100A3 **Keetmanshoop** Namibia
18C1 **Keewanee** USA
6A3 **Keewatin** Region Can
55B3 **Kefallinía** I Greece
94B2 **Kefar Sava** Israel
38A2 **Keflavík** Iceland
5G4 **Keg River** Can
76B1 **Kehsi Mansam** Burma
108B3 **Keith** Aust
44C3 **Keith** Scot
4F3 **Keith Arm** B Can
8B3 **Kekertuk** Can
85D3 **Kekri** India
77C5 **Kelang** Malay
77C4 **Kelantan** R Malay
84B1 **Kelif** USSR
92C1 **Kelkit** R Turk
98B3 **Kellé** Congo
4F2 **Kellet,C** Can
20C1 **Kellogg** USA
64D3 **Kelloselkä** Fin
45C2 **Kells** Irish Rep
42B2 **Kells Range** Hills Scot
58C1 **Kelme** USSR
5G5 **Kelowna** Can
5F4 **Kelsey Bay** Can
42C2 **Kelso** Scot
20B1 **Kelso** USA
64E3 **Kem'** USSR
38L6 **Kem'** R USSR
97B3 **Ke Macina** Mali
13B2 **Kemano** Can
65K4 **Kemerovo** USSR
38J5 **Kemi** Fin
38K5 **Kemi** R Fin
38K5 **Kemijärvi** Fin
46C1 **Kempen** Region, Belg
26B2 **Kemps Bay** The Bahamas
109D2 **Kempsey** Aust
57C3 **Kempten** Germany
12D2 **Kenai** USA
12D3 **Kenai Mts** USA
12D2 **Kenai Pen** USA
99D2 **Kenamuke Swamp** Sudan
42C2 **Kendal** Eng
109D2 **Kendall** Aust
71D4 **Kendari** Indon
78C3 **Kendawangan** Indon
86B2 **Kendrāpāra** India
20C1 **Kendrick** USA
97A4 **Kenema** Sierra Leone
98B3 **Kenge** Zaïre
76B1 **Kengtung** Burma
100B3 **Kenhardt** S Africa
97A3 **Kéniéba** Mali
96B1 **Kenitra** Mor
45B3 **Kenmare** Irish Rep

45B3 **Kenmare** R Irish Rep
19B4 **Kenner** USA
18C2 **Kennett** USA
16B3 **Kennett Square** USA
20C1 **Kennewick** USA
5F4 **Kenny Dam** Can
7A5 **Kenora** Can
15D2 **Kenosha** USA
43E4 **Kent** County, Eng
20B1 **Kent** Washington, USA
14A2 **Kentland** USA
14B2 **Kenton** USA
4H3 **Kent Pen** Can
11B3 **Kentucky** State, USA
11B3 **Kentucky L** USA
19B3 **Kentwood** Louisiana, USA
14A2 **Kentwood** Michigan, USA
99D2 **Kenya** Republic, Africa
99D3 **Kenya,Mt** Kenya
18B1 **Keokuk** USA
86A2 **Keonchi** India
86B2 **Keonjhargarh** India
71E4 **Kepaluan Tanimbar** Arch Indon
59B2 **Kępno** Pol
78B2 **Kepulauan Anambas** Arch Indon
71E4 **Kepulauan Aru** Arch Indon
78B2 **Kepulauan Badas** Is Indon
71E4 **Kepulauan Banda** Arch Indon
71D4 **Kepulauan Banggai** I Indon
78B2 **Kepulauan Bunguran Seletan** Arch Indon
71E4 **Kepulauan Kai** Arch Indon
71D4 **Kepulauan Leti** I Indon
78A3 **Kepulauan Lingga** Is Indon
70A4 **Kepulauan Mentawi** Arch Indon
78A2 **Kepulauan Riau** Arch Indon
71D4 **Kepulauan Sabalana** Arch Indon
71D4 **Kepulauan Sangihe** Arch Indon
71D4 **Kepulauan Sula** I Indon
71D3 **Kepulauan Talaud** Arch Indon
78B2 **Kepulauan Tambelan** Is Indon
71E4 **Kepulauan Tanimbar** I Indon
71D4 **Kepulauan Togian** I Indon
71D4 **Kepulauan Tukambesi** Is Indon
87B2 **Kerala** State, India
108B3 **Kerang** Aust
39K6 **Kerava** Fin
60E4 **Kerch'** USSR
71F4 **Kerema** PNG
20C1 **Keremeos** Can
95C3 **Keren** Eth
104B6 **Kerguelen Ridge** Indian O
99D3 **Kericho** Kenya
78A3 **Kerinci** Mt Indon
99D2 **Kerio** R Kenya
80E2 **Kerki** USSR
55B3 **Kérkira** Greece
55A3 **Kérkira** I Greece
57C3 **Kerman** Iran
22B2 **Kerman** USA
90A3 **Kermānshāh** Iran
21B2 **Kern** R USA
13F2 **Kerrobert** Can
45B3 **Kerry** County, Irish Rep
17B1 **Kershaw** USA
78B3 **Kertamulia** Indon

63D3	Kerulen R Mongolia
96B2	Kerzaz Alg
55C2	Keşan Turk
74E3	Kesennuma Japan
38L5	Kestenga USSR
42C2	Keswick Eng
65K4	Ket R USSR
97C4	Kéta Ghana
78C3	Ketapang Indon
5E4	Ketchikan USA
97C3	Ketia Niger
85B4	Keti Bandar Pak
58C2	Ketrzyn Pol
43D3	Kettering Eng
14B3	Kettering USA
20C1	Kettle R Can
20C1	Kettle River Range Mts USA
7C3	Kettlestone B Can
90C3	Kevir-i Namak Salt Flat Iran
14A2	Kewaunee USA
14B1	Key Harbour Can
17B2	Key Largo USA
11B4	Key West USA
63C2	Kezhma USSR
54A1	K'feleghaza Hung
12B2	Kgun L USA
94C2	Khabab Syria
62H3	Khabarovsk USSR
85B3	Khairpur Pak
85B3	Khairpur Region, Pak
100B3	Khakhea Botswana
55C3	Khálki I Greece
55B2	Khalkidhiki Pen Greece
55B3	Khalkis Greece
61G2	Khalturin USSR
85C4	Khambhat,G of India
85D4	Khamgaon India
76C2	Kham Keut Laos
85C1	Khammam India
90A2	Khamseh Mts Iran
76C2	Khan R Laos
84B1	Khanabad Afghan
93E3	Khānaqīn Iraq
85D4	Khandwa India
84C2	Khanewal Pak
94C3	Khan ez Zabib Jordan
77D4	Khanh Hung Viet
55B3	Khaniá Greece
84C3	Khanpur Pak
65H3	Khanty-Mansiysk USSR
94B3	Khan Yunis Egypt
84D1	Khapalu India
68C2	Khapcheranga USSR
61G4	Kharabali USSR
86B2	Kharagpur India
91C4	Kharan Iran
84B3	Kharan Pak
90B3	Kharānaq Iran
91B4	Khārg I Iran
95C2	Khârga Oasis Egypt
85D4	Khargon India
60E4	Khar'kov USSR
54C2	Kharmanli Bulg
61F2	Kharovsk USSR
95C3	Khartoum Sudan
95C3	Khartoum North Sudan
74C2	Khasan USSR
95C3	Khashm el Girba Sudan
86C1	Khasi-Jaintia Hills India
54C2	Khaskovo Bulg
1B9	Khatanga USSR
76B3	Khawsa Burma
76C2	Khe Bo Viet
85C4	Khed Brahma India
51C2	Khemis Alg
96C2	Kherrata Alg
60D4	Kherson USSR
63D2	Khilok USSR
55C3	Khíos Greece
55C3	Khíos I Greece
60C4	Khmel'nitskiy USSR

59C3	Khodorov USSR
84B1	Kholm Afghan
76D3	Khong Laos
91B4	Khonj Iran
69F2	Khor USSR
91A3	Khoramshahr Iran
91B5	Khōr Duwayhin B UAE
84C1	Khorog USSR
90A3	Khorramābād Iran
90C3	Khosf Iran
84B2	Khost Pak
60C4	Khotin USSR
12C2	Khotol Mt USA
60C3	Khoyniky USSR
63F2	Khrebet Dzhugdzhur Mts USSR
90C2	Khrebet Kopet Dag Mts USSR
64H3	Khrebet Pay-khoy Mts USSR
82C1	Khrebet Tarbagatay Mts USSR
63E2	Khrebet Tukuringra Mts USSR
86B2	Khulna Bang
84D1	Khunjerab P China/India
90B3	Khunsar Iran
91A4	Khurays S Arabia
86B2	Khurda India
84D3	Khurja India
84C2	Khushab Pak
94B2	Khushnīyah Syria
90C3	Khust USSR
99C1	Khuwei Sudan
85B3	Khuzdar Pak
90D3	Khvāf Iran
61G3	Khvalynsk USSR
90C3	Khvor Iran
91B4	Khvormūj Iran
93D2	Khvoy Iran
84C1	Khwaja Muhammad Mts Afghan
84C2	Khyber P Afghan/Pak
99C3	Kiambi Zaire
19A3	Kiamichi R USA
12B1	Kiana USA
98B3	Kibangou Congo
98C3	Kibaya Tanz
98C3	Kibombo Zaire
99D3	Kibondo Tanz
99D3	Kibungu Rwanda
55B2	Kičevo Yugos
5G4	Kicking Horse P Can
97C3	Kidal Mali
43C3	Kidderminster Eng
97A3	Kidira Sen
110C1	Kidnappers,C NZ
56C2	Kiel Germany
59C2	Kielce Pol
56C2	Kieler Bucht B Germany
	Kiev = Kiyev
80E2	Kifab USSR
97A3	Kiffa Maur
89H8	Kigali Rwanda
12A2	Kigluaik Mts USA
99C3	Kigoma Tanz
75B2	Kii-sanchi Mts Japan
74C4	Kii-suido B Japan
54B1	Kikinda Yugos
55B3	Kikládhes Is Greece
71F4	Kikori PNG
98B3	Kikwit Zaire
21C4	Kilauea Crater Mt Hawaiian Is
4C3	Kilbuck Mts USA
74B2	Kilchu N Korea
109D1	Kilcoy Aust
45C2	Kildare County, Irish Rep
45C2	Kildare Irish Rep
19B3	Kilgore USA
99D3	Kilifi Kenya
99D3	Kilimanjaro Mt Tanz
99D3	Kilindoni Tanz
92C2	Kilis Turk

45B2	Kilkee Irish Rep
45C2	Kilkenny County, Irish Rep
45C2	Kilkenny Irish Rep
45B2	Kilkieran B Irish Rep
55B2	Kilkís Greece
45B1	Killala B Irish Rep
45C2	Killaloe Irish Rep
109D1	Killarney Aust
41B3	Killarney Aust
19A3	Killeen USA
12D1	Killik R USA
44B3	Killin Scot
55B3	Killíni Mt Greece
45B1	Killybegs Irish Rep
42B2	Kilmarnock Scot
61H2	Kil'mez USSR
99D3	Kilosa Tanz
41B3	Kilrush Irish Rep
99C3	Kilwa Zaire
99D3	Kilwa Kisiwani Tanz
99D3	Kilwa Kivinje Tanz
108A2	Kimba Aust
12F2	Kimball,Mt USA
13D3	Kimberley Can
101F1	Kimberley S Africa
106B2	Kimberley Plat Aust
74B2	Kimch'aek N Korea
74B3	Kimch'ŏn S Korea
55B3	Kími Greece
60E2	Kimry USSR
70C3	Kinabalu Mt Malay
78D1	Kinabatangan R Malay
14B2	Kincardine Can
13B1	Kincolith Can
13B3	Kinder USA
13F2	Kindersley Can
97A3	Kindia Guinea
98C3	Kindu Zaire
61H3	Kinel' USSR
61F2	Kineshma USSR
109D1	Kingaroy Aust
21A2	King City USA
5F4	Kingcome Inlet Can
7C4	King George Is Can
107D4	King I Aust
13B2	King I Can
106B2	King Leopold Range Mts Aust
8B3	Kingman USA
98C3	Kingombe Zaire
108A2	Kingoonya Aust
22C2	Kingsburg USA
21B2	Kings Canyon Nat Pk USA
108A3	Kingscote Aust
106B2	King Sd Aust
14A1	Kingsford USA
17B1	Kingsland USA
43E3	King's Lynn Eng
16C2	Kings Park USA
8B2	Kings Peak Mt USA
107C4	Kingston Aust
7C5	Kingston Can
25B3	Kingston Jamaica
15D2	Kingston New York, USA
111A3	Kingston NZ
27E4	Kingstown St Vincent
9D4	Kingsville USA
44B3	Kingussie Scot
4J3	King William I Can
100B4	King William's Town S Africa
98B3	Kinkala Congo
39G7	Kinna Sweden
44D3	Kinnairds Head Pt Scot
75B1	Kinomoto Japan
44C3	Kinross Scot
45B3	Kinsale Irish Rep
98B3	Kinshasa Zaire
78D3	Kintap Indon
42B2	Kintyre Pen Scot
13D1	Kinuso Can
99D2	Kinyeti Mt Sudan
55B3	Kiparissía Greece

55B3	Kiparissiakós Kólpos G Greece
15C1	Kipawa,L Can
99D3	Kipili Tanz
12B3	Kipnuk USA
45C2	Kippure Mt Irish Rep
100B2	Kipushi Zaire
55C3	Kirakira Solomon Is
65J5	Kirgizskaya SSR Republic, USSR
82B1	Kirgizskiy Khrebet Mts USSR
98B3	Kiri Zaire
105G4	Kiribati Is Pacific O
92B2	Kırıkkale Turk
60D2	Kirishi USSR
85B3	Kirithar Range Mts Pak
55C3	Kırkağaç Turk
36A2	Kirk Bulağ Dağh Mt Iran
42C2	Kirkby Eng
44C3	Kirkcaldy Scot
42B2	Kirkcudbright Scot
38K5	Kirkenes Nor
7B5	Kirkland Lake Can
112A	Kirkpatrick,Mt Ant
10A2	Kirksville USA
93D2	Kirkūk Iraq
44C2	Kirkwall Scot
18B2	Kirkwood USA
60D3	Kirov USSR
61G2	Kirov USSR
31J2	Kirovakan USSR
61J2	Kirovgrad USSR
60D4	Kirovograd USSR
61H2	Kirs USSR
92B2	Kirşehir Turk
56C2	Kiruna Sweden
75B1	Kiryū Japan
98C2	Kisangani Zaire
86B1	Kisarazu Japan
86D3	Kishanganj India
60C4	Kishinev USSR
75B2	Kishiwada Japan
99D3	Kisii Kenya
99D3	Kisiju Tanz
59B3	Kiskunhalas Hung
66F5	Kislovodsk USSR
99E3	Kismaayo Somalia
75B1	Kiso-sammyaku Mts Japan
97A4	Kissidougou Guinea
17B2	Kissimmee,L USA
99D3	Kisumu Kenya
59C3	Kisvárda Hung
97B3	Kita Mali
65H6	Kitab USSR
74C4	Kitakata Japan
74C4	Kita-Kyūshū Japan
90C4	Kitale Kenya
69C4	Kitami Japan
74E2	Kitami Japan
7B5	Kitchener Can
99D3	Kitgum Uganda
55B3	Kíthira I Greece
55B3	Kíthnos I Greece
94A1	Kíti,C Cyprus
4H3	Kitikmeot Region Can
5F4	Kitimat Can
38K5	Kitnen R Fin
75A2	Kitsuki Japan
15C2	Kittanning USA
38J5	Kittilä Fin
99D3	Kitunda Tanz
13B1	Kitwanga Can
100B2	Kitwe Zambia
57C3	Kitzbühel Austria
47E1	Kitzbühler Alpen Mts Austria
57C3	Kitzingen Germany
98C3	Kiumbi Zaire
12B1	Kivalina USA
59D2	Kivercy USSR
99C3	Kivu,L Zaire/Rwanda
4B3	Kiwalik USA
60D3	Kiyev USSR

61J2 Kizel USSR
92C2 Kizil R Turk
80D2 Kizyl-Arvat USSR
90B2 Kizyl-Atrek USSR
57C2 Kladno Czech
57C3 Klagenfurt Austria
60B2 Klaipėda USSR
8A2 Klamath USA
20B2 Klamath R USA
8A2 Klamath Falls USA
20B2 Klamath Mts USA
57C3 Klatovy Czech
12H3 Klawak USA
94B1 Kleiat Leb
101G1 Klerksdorp S Africa
60E2 Klin USSR
58B1 Klintehamn Sweden
60D3 Klintsy USSR
52C3 Ključ Yugos
59B2 Kłodzko Pol
12G2 Klondike R Can/USA
4D3 Klondike Plat Can/USA
59B3 Klosterneuburg Austria
12G2 Kluane R Can
12G2 Kluane L Can
12G2 Kluane Nat Pk Can
59B2 Kluczbork Pol
12G3 Klukwan USA
12E2 Klutina L USA
12E2 Knight 1 USA
43C3 Knighton Wales
52C2 Knin Yugos
106A4 Knob,C Aust
46B1 Knokke-Heist Belg
112C9 Knox Coast Ant
11B3 Knoxville Tennessee, USA
6H3 Knud Ramsussens Land Region Greenland
78B3 Koba Indon
6F3 Kobbermirebugt Greenland
74D4 Kobe Japan
56C1 København Den
57B2 Koblenz Germany
60B3 Kobrin USSR
71E4 Kobroör 1 Indon
12C1 Kobuk R USA
54B2 Kočani Yugos
76C3 Ko Chang 1 Thai
86B1 Koch Bihar India
47D1 Kochel Germany
6C3 Koch 1 Can
74C4 Kōchi Japan
12D3 Kodiak USA
12D3 Kodiak 1 USA
87B2 Kodikkarai India
90D2 Kodok Sudan
100A3 Koes Namibia
101G1 Koffiefontein S Africa
97B4 Koforidua Ghana
74D3 Kōfu Japan
75B1 Koga Japan
39G7 Køge Den
84C2 Kohat Pak
84B2 Koh-i-Baba Mts Afghan
84B1 Koh-i-Hisar Mts Afghan
84B2 Koh-i-Khurd Mt Afghan
86C1 Kohima India
84B1 Koh-i-Mazar Mt Afghan
84B3 Kohlu Pak
60C2 Kohtla Järve USSR
75B1 Koide Japan
12F2 Koidern Can
77A4 Koihoa Is Nicobar Is
74B4 Kŏje-do 1 S Korea
65H4 Kokchetav USSR
39J6 Kokemaki L Fin
38J6 Kokkola Fin
107D1 Kokoda PNG
14A2 Kokomo USA

71E4 Kokonau Indon
65K5 Kokpekty USSR
7D4 Koksoak R Can
100B4 Kokstad S Africa
76C3 Ko Kut 1 Thai
38L5 Kola USSR
71D4 Kolaka Indon
77B4 Ko Lanta 1 Thai
87B2 Kolār India
87B2 Kolār Gold Fields India
97A3 Kolda Sen
39F7 Kolding Den
87A1 Kolhapur India
12C3 Kolig USA
59B2 Kolin Czech
57B2 Köln Germany
58B2 Koło Pol
58B2 Kolobrzeg Pol
97B3 Kolokani Mali
60E2 Kolomna USSR
60C4 Kolomyya USSR
65K4 Kolpashevo USSR
68A2 Kolpekty USSR
55C3 Kólpos Merabéllou B Greece
55B2 Kólpos Singitikós G Greece
74E3 Kóriyama Japan
55B2 Kólpos Strimonikós G Greece
55B2 Kólpos Toronaíos G Greece
38L5 Kol'skiy Poluostrov Pen USSR
38G6 Kolvereid Nor
100B2 Kolwezi Zaïre
1C7 Kolyma R USSR
54B2 Kom Mt Bulg/Yugos
99D2 Koma Eth
97D3 Komaduga Gana R Nig
59B3 Komárno Czech
101H1 Komati R S Africa
74D3 Komatsu Japan
75A2 Komatsushima Japan
64G3 Komi A.S.S.R. Republic, USSR
70C4 Komodo 1 Indon
71E4 Komoran 1 Indon
75B1 Komoro Japan
55C2 Komotiní Greece
76D3 Kompong Cham Camb
76C3 Kompong Chhnang Mts Camb
77C3 Kompong Som Camb
76C3 Kompong Thom Camb
76D3 Kompong Trabek Camb
63F2 Komsomol'sk na Amure USSR
64A4 Konda R USSR
99D3 Kondoa Tanz
87B1 Kondukūr India
6G3 Kong Christian IX Land Region Greenland
6F3 Kong Frederik VI Kyst Mts Greenland
64C2 Kong Karls Land Is Barents S
78D2 Kongkemul Mt Indon
98C3 Kongolo Zaïre
39F7 Kongsberg Den
39G6 Kongsvinger Nor
Königsberg = Kaliningrad
58B2 Konin Pol
54A2 Konjic Yugos
61F1 Konosha USSR
75B1 Konosu Japan
60D3 Konotop USSR
63B2 Konsk USSR
59C2 Końskie Pol
49D2 Konstanz Germany
97C3 Kontagora Nig
76D3 Kontum Viet
92B2 Konya Turk
13D3 Kootenay R Can
85C5 Kopargaon India
6J3 Kópasker Iceland
38A2 Kópavogur Iceland

52B1 Koper Yugos
80D2 Kopet Dag Mts Iran/USSR
61K2 Kopeysk USSR
77C4 Ko Phangan 1 Thai
77B4 Ko Phuket 1 Thai
39H7 Köping Sweden
87B1 Koppal India
52C1 Koprivnica Yugos
86A2 Korangi Pak
86A2 Korba India
57B2 Korbach Germany
4B3 Korbuk R USA
55B2 Korçë Alb
52C2 Korčula 1 Yugos
72E2 Korea B China/Korea
74E4 Korea Str S Korea/Japan
59D2 Korec USSR
92B1 Körglu Tepesi Mt Turk
87A4 Korhogo Ivory Coast
85B4 Kori Creek India
55B3 Korinthiakós Kólpos G Greece
55B3 Kórinthos Greece
61K3 Korkino USSR
92B2 Korkuteli Turk
82C1 Korla China
52C1 Kornat 1 Yugos
60D5 Köroğlu Tepesi Mt Turk
99D3 Korogwe Tanz
108B3 Koroit Aust
71E3 Koror Palau Is, Pacific O
53C3 Kóros R Hung
60C3 Korosten USSR
95A3 Koro Toro Chad
12B3 Korovin 1 USA
69G2 Korsakov USSR
39G7 Korsør Den
46B1 Kortrijk Belg
55C3 Kós 1 Greece
77C4 Ko Samui 1 Thai
58B2 Koscierzyna Pol
59D2 Kosciusko Mt Aust
12H3 Kosciusko 1 USA
74E3 Koshikijima-retto 1 Japan
59C3 Košice Czech
74B3 Kosong N Korea
97B4 Kossou L Ivory Coast
101G1 Koster S Africa
99D1 Kosti Sudan
59D2 Kostopol' USSR
61F2 Kostroma USSR
56C2 Kostrzyn Pol
39H8 Koszalin Pol
85D3 Kota India
78A4 Kotaagung Indon
78D3 Kotabaharu Indon
78D3 Kotabaru Indon
77C4 Kota Bharu Indon
78A3 Kotabumi Indon
84C2 Kot Addu Pak
78D1 Kota Kinabulu Malay
87C1 Kotapad India
61G2 Kotel'nich USSR
61F4 Kotel'nikovo USSR
39K6 Kotka Fin
64F3 Kotlas USSR
12B2 Kotlik USA
54A2 Kotor Yugos
60C4 Kotovsk USSR
85B3 Kotri Pak
87C1 Kottagüdem India
87B3 Kottayam India
98C2 Kotto R CAR
87B3 Kottūru India
12B1 Kotzebue USA
4B3 Kotzebue Sd USA
97C3 Kouande Benin
98C2 Kouango CAR
97B3 Koudougou Burkina
98B3 Koulamoutou Gabon

97B3 Koulikoro Mali
97B3 Koupéla Burkina
33G2 Kourou French Guiana
97B3 Kouroussa Guinea
98B1 Kousséri Cam
39K6 Kouvola Fin
60B3 Kovel USSR
Kovno = Kaunas
61F2 Kovrov USSR
61F3 Kovylkino USSR
60E1 Kovzha R USSR
77C4 Ko Way 1 Thai
73C5 Kowloon Hong Kong
84B2 Kowt-e-Ashrow Afghan
92A2 Köyceğiz Turk
38L5 Koydor USSR
87A1 Koyna Res India
12B2 Koyuk USA
12B1 Koyuk R USA
12C2 Koyukuk USA
12C1 Koyukuk R USA
92C2 Kozan Turk
55B2 Kozáni Greece
61G2 Koz'modemyansk USSR
61F2 Koztroma USSR
75B2 Közu-shima 1 Japan
39F7 Kragerø Nor
54B2 Kragujevac Yugos
77B3 Kra,Isthmus of Burma/Malay
Krakatau = Rakata
94C1 Krak des Chevaliers Hist Site Syria
59B2 Kraków Pol
54B2 Kraljevo Yugos
60C4 Kramatorsk USSR
30H6 Kramfors Sweden
52B1 Kranj Yugos
61F4 Krapotkin USSR
61G1 Krasavino USSR
61J2 Krashnokamsk USSR
64G2 Krasino USSR
59C2 Krasnik Pol
61G3 Krasnoarmeysk USSR
60E5 Krasnodar USSR
61K2 Krasnotur'insk USSR
61J2 Krasnoufimsk USSR
61J3 Krasnousol'-skiy USSR
65G3 Krasnovishersk USSR
65G5 Krasnovodsk USSR
63B2 Krasnoyarsk USSR
59C2 Krasnystaw Pol
61G3 Krasnyy Kut USSR
60E4 Krasnyy Luch USSR
61G4 Krasnyy Yar USSR
76D3 Kratie Camb
6E2 Kraulshavn Greenland
56B2 Krefeld Germany
60D4 Kremenchug USSR
60D4 Kremenchugskoye Vodokhranilische Res USSR
59D2 Kremenets USSR
98A2 Krichi Cam
60D3 Krichev USSR
47E1 Krimml Austria
87B1 Krishna R India
86B2 Krishnagiri India
86B2 Krishnanagar India
39F7 Kristiansand Nor
39G7 Kristianstad Sweden
64B3 Kristiansund Nor
39G7 Kristinehamn Sweden
38J6 Kristiinankaupunki Fin
55B3 Kríti 1 Greece
60D4 Krivoy Rog USSR
52B1 Krk 1 Yugos
6G3 Kronprins Frederik Bjerge Mts Greenland
39K7 Kronshtadt USSR
101G1 Kroonstad S Africa
65F5 Kropotkin USSR
101G1 Krugersdorp S Africa

78A4 Krui Indon
55A2 Kruje Alb
58D2 Krupki USSR
12B1 Krusenstern,C USA
54B2 Kruševac Yugos
39K7 Krustpils USSR
12G3 Kruzof I USA
65E5 Krym Pen USSR
60D5 Krym R USSR
60E5 Krymsk USSR
58B2 Krzyz Pol
96C1 Ksar El Boukhari Alg
96B1 Ksar el Kebir Mor
70A3 Kuala Indon
77C5 Kuala Dungun Malay
77C4 Kuala Kerai Malay
77C5 Kuala Kubu Baharu
 Malay
77C5 Kuala Lipis Malay
77C5 Kuala Lumpur Malay
77C4 Kuala Trengganu
 Malay
78D1 Kuamut Malay
74A2 Kuandian China
77C5 Kuantan Malay
93E1 Kuba USSR
71F4 Kubar PNG
78C2 Kuching Malay
70C3 Kudat Malay
78C4 Kudus Indon
61H2 Kudymkar USSR
57C3 Kufstein Austria
90C3 Kuh Duren Upland
 Iran
91C4 Kuh-e Bazmān Mt
 Iran
90B3 Kūh-e Dinar Mt Iran
90C2 Kūh-e-Hazār Masjed
 Mts Iran
91C4 Kūh-e Jebāl Barez Mts
 Iran
90B3 Kūh-e Karkas Mts
 Iran
91C4 Kuh-e Laleh Zar Mt
 Iran
90A2 Kūh-e Sahand Mt Iran
91D4 Kuh e Taftān Mt Iran
90A2 Kūhhaye Sabalan Mts
 Iran
90A3 Kūhhā-ye Zāgros Mts
 Iran
38K6 Kuhmo Fin
90B3 Kūhpāyeh Iran
90C3 Kūhpāyeh Mt Iran
91C4 Kūh ye Bashākerd Mts
 Iran
90A2 Kūh ye Sabalan Mt
 Iran
100A3 Kuibis Namibia
4B4 Kuigillingok USA
12H3 Kuiu I USA
74E2 Kuji Japan
75A2 Kuju-san Mt Japan
12C3 Kukaklek L USA
54B2 Kukës Alb
77C5 Kukup Malay
91C4 Kül R Iran
55C3 Kula Turk
61J4 Kulakshi USSR
99D2 Kulal,Mt Kenya
55B2 Kulata Bulg
60B2 Kuldiga USSR
61H4 Kul'sary USSR
84D2 Kulu India
65J4 Kulunda USSR
108B2 Kulwin Aust
61G5 Kuma R USSR
75B1 Kumagaya Japan
78C3 Kumai Indon
74C4 Kumamoto Japan
75B2 Kumano Japan
54B2 Kumanovo Yugos
63E2 Kumara China
97B4 Kumasi Ghana
98A2 Kumba Cam
87B2 Kumbakonam India
61J3 Kumertau USSR

74B3 Kūmhwa S Korea
39H7 Kumla Sweden
87A2 Kumta India
82C1 Kümüx China
84C2 Kunar R Afghan
39K7 Kunda USSR
85C4 Kunda India
84B1 Kunduz Afghan
89F9 Kunene R Angola
39G7 Kungsbacka Sweden
61J2 Kungur USSR
76B1 Kunhing Burma
82B2 Kunlun Shan Mts
 China
73A4 Kunming China
74B3 Kunsan S Korea
38K6 Kuopio Fin
52C1 Kupa R Yugos
106B2 Kupang Indon
107D2 Kupiano PNG
12J3 Kupreanof I USA
60E4 Kupyansk USSR
82C1 Kuqa China
75B1 Kurabe Japan
74C4 Kurashiki Japan
75A1 Kurayoshi Japan
54C2 Kürdzhali Bulg
74C4 Kure Japan
60B2 Kuressare USSR
63A1 Kureyka R USSR
65H4 Kurgan USSR
88K6 Kuria Muria Is Oman
38J6 Kurikka Fin
 Kuril Is = Kuril'skiye
 Ostrova
69H2 Kuril'skiye Ostrova
 USSR
87B1 Kurnool India
75C1 Kuroiso Japan
111B2 Kurow NZ
109D2 Kurri Kurri Aust
60E3 Kursk USSR
51C1 Kurskiy Zaliv Lg
 USSR
68A2 Kuruktag R China
100B3 Kuruman S Africa
74C4 Kurume Japan
87C3 Kurunegala Sri Lanka
65K5 Kurunktag R China
61J2 Kusa USSR
55C3 Kuşadasi Körfezi B
 Turk
55C2 Kus Golü L Turk
74D4 Kushimoto Japan
74C2 Kushiro Japan
86B2 Kushtia Bang
61H3 Kushum R USSR
80E2 Kushra Afgan
65G4 Kushva USSR
12B2 Kuskokwim R USA
12B3 Kuskokwim B USA
12C2 Kuskokwim Mts USA
86A1 Kusma Nepal
74E2 Kussharo-ko L Japan
65H4 Kustanay USSR
92A2 Kütahya Turk
78D3 Kutai R Indon
59B3 Kutná Hora Czech
58B2 Kutno Pol
59B3 Kutu Zaire
86C2 Kutubdia I Bang
98C1 Kutum Sudan
7D4 Kuujjuaq Can
38K5 Kuusamo Fin
61J3 Kuvandyk USSR
93E4 Kuwait Kuwait
80C3 Kuwait Sheikdom,
 S W Asia
75B1 Kuwana Japan
65G4 Kuybyshev USSR
65J4 Kuybyshev USSR
61G3 Kuybyshevskoye
 Vodokhranilishche
 Res USSR
63C2 Kuytun USSR
60E5 Kuyucak Anadolu Daglari
 Mts Turk
61G3 Kuznetsk USSR

38J4 Kvaenangen Sd Nor
12C3 Kvichak USA
12C3 Kvichak R USA
12C3 Kvichak B USA
38G5 Kvigtind Mt Nor
38H5 Kvikkjokk Sweden
99D3 Kwale Kenya
74B3 Kwangju S Korea
98B3 Kwango R Zaire
100B2 Kwekwe Zim
12B2 Kwethluk USA
12B2 Kwethluk R USA
58B2 Kwidzyn Pol
71E4 Kwoka Mt Indon
108C3 Kyabram Aust
76B2 Kyaikami Burma
76B2 Kyaikto Burma
68C1 Kyakhta USSR
108A2 Kyancutta Aust
76B1 Kyaukme Burma
76B1 Kyauk-padaung
 Burma
76A2 Kyaukpyu Burma
40B2 Kyle of Lochalsh Scot
46D1 Kyll R Germany
108B3 Kyneton Aust
99D2 Kyoga L Uganda
74B3 Kyŏngju S Korea
74D3 Kyoto Japan
65H4 Kyshtym USSR
74C4 Kyūshū I Japan
104E3 Kyushu-Palau Ridge
 Pacific O
54B2 Kyustendil Bulg
68B1 Kyzyl USSR
65H5 Kyzylkum Desert
 USSR
65H5 Kzyl Orda USSR

L

99E2 Laas Caanood
 Somalia
46E1 Laasphe Germany
99E1 Laas Qoray Somalia
33E1 La Asunción Ven
96A2 Laâyoune Mor
23A1 La Barca Mexico
97A3 Labé Guinea
59B2 Labe R Czech
15D1 Labelle Can
17B2 La Belle USA
12G2 Laberge,L Can
78D1 Labi Brunei
13E2 la Biche,L Can
61F5 Labinsk USSR
94C1 Laboué Leb
34C2 Laboulaye Arg
7D4 Labrador Region Can
7D4 Labrador City Can
7E4 Labrador S Greenland/
 Can
33E5 Lábrea Brazil
78D1 Labuan I Malay
78B4 Labuhan Indon
76A2 Labutta Burma
65H3 Labytnangi USSR
46B2 La Capelle France
34C2 La Carlota Arg
79B3 La Carlota Phil
12J1 Lac Belot L Can
7C4 Lac Bienville L Can
83B4 Laccadive Is India
47B2 Lac d'Annecy L
 France
4G3 Lac de Gras L Can
47B1 Lac de Joux L Switz
47B1 Lac de Neuchâtel L
 Switz
23A2 Lac de Patzcuaro L
 Mexico
23A2 Lac de Sayula L
 Mexico
4F3 Lac des Bois L Can
47A2 Lac du Bourget L
 France

25D3 La Ceiba Honduras
108A3 Lacepede B Aust
48C2 La Châtre France
47B1 La-Chaux-de-Fonds
 Switz
94B3 Lachish Hist Site
 Israel
107D4 Lachlan R Aust
32B2 La Chorrera Panama
15D1 Lachute Can
7D4 Lac Joseph L Can
15C2 Lackawanna USA
5G4 Lac la Biche Can
4G3 Lac la Martre L Can
5H4 Lac la Ronge L Can
7C4 Lac L'eau Claire Can
52A1 Lac Léman L Switz/
 France
10C1 Lac Manouane L Can
15D1 Lac Megantic Can
7C4 Lac Mistassini L Can
13E2 Lacombe Can
15D2 Laconia USA
50A1 La Coruña Spain
10A2 La Crosse USA
9C3 Las Cruces USA
7A4 Lac Seul L Can
15D2 Lac Cygne USA
84D2 Ladākh Range India
85C3 Lādnūn India
73B5 Ladong China
60D1 Ladozhskoye Ozero L
 USSR
6B2 Lady Ann Str Can
101G1 Lady Barron Aust
101G1 Ladybrand S Africa
13C3 Ladysmith Can
101G1 Ladysmith S Africa
71F4 Lae PNG
76C3 Laem Ngop Thai
56C1 Laesø I Den
10B2 Lafayette Indiana,
 USA
11A3 Lafayette Louisiana,
 USA
46B2 La Fère France
46B2 La-Ferté-sous-Jouarre
 France
97C4 Lafia Nig
97C4 Lafiagi Nig
48B2 La Flèche France
96C1 La Galite I Tunisia
56C1 Lagan R Sweden
31D4 Lagarto Brazil
96C1 Laghouat Alg
35C2 Lagoa de Araruama
 Brazil
29F2 Lagoa dos Patos Lg
 Brazil
35C2 Lagoa Feia Brazil
32B4 Lago Agrio Ecuador
35C1 Lagoa Juparaná L
 Brazil
29F2 Lagoa mar Chiguita L
 Arg
29F2 Lagoa Mirim L Brazil/
 Urug
29B6 Lago Argentino L Arg
29B5 Lago Buenos Aires L
 Arg
29B5 Lago Cochrane L Arg/
 Chile
29C5 Lago Colhué Huapi L
 Arg
24B2 Lago de Chapala L
 Mexico
32A2 Lago de Chiriqui L
 Panama
23A2 Lago de Cuitzeo L
 Mexico
29B3 Lago de la Laja L
 Chile
53A2 Lago del Coghinas L
 Sardegna
32C2 Lago de Maracaibo L
 Ven
25D3 Lago de Nicaragua L
 Nic

32A1 Lago de Perlas L Nic
52B2 Lago di Bolsena L Italy
52B2 Lago di Bracciano L Italy
52A1 Lago di Como L Italy
47D2 Lago d'Idro L Italy
52B1 Lago di Garda L Italy
47C2 Lago di Lecco L Italy
47C2 Lago di Lugano L Italy
47D2 Lago d'Iseo L Italy
47C2 Lago d'Orta L Italy
29B5 Lago General Carrera L Chile
52A1 Lago Maggiore L Italy
29C5 Lago Musters L Arg
48B3 Lagon France
29B4 Lago Nahuel Haupi L Arg
29B5 Lago O'Higgins L Chile
53A2 Lago Omodeo L Sardegna
30C2 Lago Poopó L Bol
29B4 Lago Ranco L Chile
32D6 Lago Rogaguado L Bol
97C4 Lagos Nig
50A2 Lagos Port
29B5 Lago San Martin L Arg/Chile
24B2 Lagos de Moreno Mexico
30C2 Lago Titicaca Bol/Peru
29B5 Lago Viedma L Arg
8B2 La Grande USA
7C4 La Grande Rivière R Can
106B2 Lagrange Aust
11B3 La Grange Georgia, USA
14A3 La Grange Kentucky, USA
19A4 La Grange Texas, USA
33E2 La Gran Sabana Mts Ven
47B2 La Grave France
48B3 Lagroño Spain
34A3 Laguna Aluminé L Arg
21B3 Laguna Beach USA
34C3 Laguna Colorada Grande L Arg
79B3 Laguna de Bay Lg Phil
25D3 Laguna de Caratasca Lg Honduras
25D4 Laguna de Chiriquí L Panama
25D3 Laguna de Managua L Nic
25D3 Laguna de Nicaragua L Nic
26A4 Laguna de Perlas Lg Nic
23B1 Laguna de Pueblo Viejo L Mexico
24C2 Laguna de Tamiahua Lg Mexico
25C3 Laguna de Términos Lg Mexico
23A1 Laguna de Yuriria L Mexico
23B1 Laguna la Altamira Mexico
24C2 Laguna Madre Lg Mexico
34C2 Laguna Mar Chiquita L Arg
29B4 Laguna Nahuel Huapi L Arg
34C2 Laguna Paiva Arg
29B4 Laguna Ranco Chile
9C4 Laguna Seca Mexico
23B1 Laguna Tortugas L Mexico
70C3 Lahad Datu Malay
78A3 Lahat Indon

38J6 Lahia Fin
90B2 Lāhījān Iran
46D1 Lahn R Germany
46D1 Lahnstein Germany
84C2 Lahore Pak
39K6 Lahti Fin
23A2 La Huerta Mexico
98B2 Lai Chad
73B5 Laibin China
76C1 Lai Chau Viet
100B4 Laingsburg S Africa
44B2 Lairg Scot
78A3 Lais Indon
79C4 Lais Phil
72E2 Laiyang China
72D2 Laizhou Wan B China
34A3 Laja R Chile
30F4 Lajes Brazil
22D4 La Jolla USA
109C2 Lake Cargelligo Aust
11A3 Lake Charles USA
17B1 Lake City Florida, USA
17C1 Lake City S Carolina, USA
42C2 Lake District Region, Eng
22D4 Lake Elsinore USA
106C3 Lake Eyre Basin Aust
15C2 Lakefield Can
6D3 Lake Harbour Can
22C3 Lake Hughes USA
16B2 Lakehurst USA
19A4 Lake Jackson USA
13E2 Lake la Biche Can
17B2 Lakeland USA
7A5 Lake of the Woods Can
20B1 Lake Oswego USA
21A2 Lakeport USA
19B3 Lake Providence USA
111B2 Lake Pukaki NZ
109C3 Lakes Entrance Aust
22C2 Lakeshore USA
108B1 Lake Stewart Aust
15C1 Lake Traverse Can
8A2 Lakeview USA
20B1 Lakeview Mt USA
19B3 Lake Village USA
17B2 Lake Wales USA
22C4 Lakewood California, USA
16B2 Lakewood New Jersey, USA
14B2 Lakewood Ohio, USA
17B2 Lake Worth USA
86A1 Lakhimpur India
85B4 Lakhpat India
84C2 Lakki Pak
55B3 Lakonikós Kólpos G Greece
97B4 Lakota Ivory Coast
38K4 Laksefjord Inlet Nor
38K4 Lakselv Nor
34C2 La Laguna Arg
32A4 La Libertad Ecuador
34A2 La Ligua Chile
50A2 La Linea Spain
85D4 Lalitpur India
5H4 La Loche Can
13F1 la Loche,L Can
46C1 La Louvière Belg
26A4 La Luz Nic
7C5 La Malbaie Can
23B2 La Malinche Mt Mexico
50B2 La Mancha Region, Spain
9C3 Lamar Colorado, USA
18B2 Lamar Missouri, USA
19A4 La Marque USA
98B3 Lambaréné Gabon
32A5 Lambayeque Peru
112B10 Lambert GB Ant
16B2 Lambertville USA
4F2 Lamblon,C Can
47C2 Lambro R Italy
76C2 Lam Chi R Thai

50A1 Lamego Port
47B2 La Meije Mt France
32B6 La Merced Peru
21B3 La Mesa USA
55B3 Lamia Greece
42C2 Lammermuir Hills Scot
39G7 Lammhult Sweden
79B3 Lamon B Phil
18B1 Lamoni USA
71F3 Lamotrek I Pacific O
43B3 Lampeter Wales
99E3 Lamu Kenya
47D1 Lana Italy
21C4 Lanai I Hawaiian Is
21C4 Lanai City Hawaiian Is
42C2 Lanark Scot
76B3 Lanbi I Burma
76C1 Lancang R China
21B3 Lancaster California, USA
42C2 Lancaster Eng
18B1 Lancaster Mississippi, USA
15D2 Lancaster New Hampshire, USA
14B3 Lancaster Ohio, USA
10C3 Lancaster Pennsylvania, USA
17C1 Lancaster S Carolina, USA
6B2 Lancaster Sd Can
83B3 Landak R Indon
46E2 Landan Germany
57C3 Landeck Austria
8C2 Lander USA
34C2 Landeta Arg
57C3 Landsberg Germany
4F2 Lands End C Can
43B4 Land's End Pt Eng
57C3 Landshut Germany
39G7 Landskrona Sweden
17A1 Lanett USA
56B2 Langenhagen Germany
47B1 Langenthal Switz
42C2 Langholm Scot
38A2 Langjökull Mts Iceland
77B4 Langkawi I Malay
21B3 Langley Can
108C1 Langlo R Aust
47B1 Langnau Switz
49D2 Langres France
70A3 Langsa Indon
76D1 Lang Son Viet
48C3 Languedoc Region, France
29B3 Lanin Mt Arg
79B4 Lanoa,L Phil
16B2 Lansdale USA
7B4 Lansdowne House Can
16B2 Lansford USA
10B2 Lansing USA
47B1 Lanslebourg France
96A2 Lanzarote I Canary Is
72A2 Lanzhou China
47B2 Lanzo Torinese Italy
79B2 Laoag Phil
76C1 Lao Cai Viet
72D1 Laoha He R China
45C2 Laois County, Irish Rep
46B2 Laon France
32B6 La Oroya Peru
73C5 Laos Republic, S E Asia
49C2 Lapalisse France
25D3 La Palma Panama
96A2 La Palma I Canary Is
34B3 La Pampa State, Arg
30C2 La Paragua Ven
29E2 La Paz Arg
34B2 La Paz Arg

30C2 La Paz Bol
24A2 La Paz Mexico
69G2 La Perouse Str Japan/USSR
23A1 La Piedad Mexico
20B2 La Pine USA
19B3 Laplace USA
23A2 La Placita Mexico
29E2 La Plata Arg
13F1 La Plonge,L Can
14A2 La Porte USA
39K6 Lappeenranta Fin
38H5 Lappland Region Sweden/Fin
34C1 Laprida Arg
1B8 Laptev S USSR
38J6 Lapua Fin
79B3 Lapu-Lapu Phil
9B4 La Purisma Mexico
95B2 Laqiya Arba'in Well Sudan
30C3 La Quiaca Arg
52B2 L'Aquila Italy
91B4 Lār Iran
96B1 Larache Mor
8C2 Laramie USA
8C2 Laramie Range Mts USA
50B2 Larca Spain
9D4 Laredo USA
91B4 Larestan Region, Iran
Largeau = Faya
47B2 L'Argentière France
17B2 Largo USA
42A2 Largs Scot
90A2 Lāri Iran
30C4 La Rioja Arg
30C4 La Rioja State, Arg
55B3 Lárisa Greece
85B3 Larkana Pak
92B3 Larnaca Cyprus
94A1 Larnaca B Cyprus
45D1 Larne N Ire
50A1 La Robla Spain
46C1 La Roche-en-Ardenne Belg
48B2 La Rochelle France
47B1 La Roche-sur-Foron France
48B2 La Roche-sur-Yon France
51B2 La Roda Spain
27D3 La Romana Dom Rep
5H4 La Ronge Can
5H4 La Ronge,L Can
39F7 Larvik Nor
65J3 Lar'yak USSR
50B2 La Sagra Mt Spain
11C1 La Salle Can
18C1 La Salle USA
7C5 La Sarre Can
34C1 Las Avispas Arg
34A2 Las Cabras Chile
5G4 Lascombe Can
9C3 Las Cruces USA
26C3 La Selle Mt Haiti
72B2 Lasengmia China
30B4 La Serena Chile
29E3 Las Flores Arg
76B1 Lashio Burma
53C3 La Sila Mts Italy
90B2 Lāsjerd Iran
34A3 Las Lajas Arg
50B2 Las Marismas Marshland Spain
96A2 Las Palmas de Gran Canaria Canary Is
52A2 La Spezia Italy
29C4 Las Plumas Arg
34C2 Las Rosas Arg
20B2 Lassen Peak Mt USA
20B2 Lassen Volcanic Nat Pk USA
23B2 Las Tinaja Mexico
98B3 Lastoursville Gabon
52C2 Lastovo I Yugos
24B2 Las Tres Marias Is Mexico

34C2 Las Varillas Arg
9C3 Las Vegas USA
Latakia = Al Lādhiqīyah
53B2 Latina Italy
34B2 La Toma Arg
32D1 La Tortuga I Ven
79B2 La Trinidad Phil
109C4 Latrobe Aust
94B3 Latrun Israel
7C5 La Tuque Can
87B1 Lātūr India
60B2 Latviyskaya SSR Republic, USSR
107D5 Launceston Aust
43B4 Launceston Eng
29B4 La Unión Chile
25D3 La Unión El Salvador
23A2 La Unión Mexico
32B5 La Unión Peru
107D2 Laura Aust
15C3 Laurel Delaware, USA
16A3 Laurel Maryland, USA
11B3 Laurel Mississippi, USA
17B1 Laurens USA
17C1 Laurinburg USA
52A1 Lausanne Switz
78D3 Laut I Indon
29B5 Lautaro Mt Chile
46D2 Lauterecken Germany
15D1 Laval Can
48B2 Laval France
22B2 Laveaga Peak Mt USA
47C2 Laveno Italy
31B6 Lavras Brazil
4A3 Lavrentiya USSR
101H1 Lavumisa Swaziland
78D1 Lawas Malay
14A1 Lawksawk Burma
18A2 Lawrence Kansas, USA
15D2 Lawrence Massachusetts, USA
111A3 Lawrence NZ
14A3 Lawrenceville Illinois, USA
9D3 Lawton USA
91A5 Layla S Arabia
99D2 Laylo Sudan
23A2 Lázaro Cárdenas Mexico
99E1 Laz Daua Somalia
79B4 Lazi Phil
8C2 Lead USA
13F2 Leader Can
18A2 Leavenworth USA
58B2 Leba Pol
18B2 Lebanon Missouri, USA
20B2 Lebanon Oregon, USA
15C2 Lebanon Pennsylvania, USA
92C3 Lebanon Republic, S W Asia
101C3 Lebombo Mts Mozam/S Africa/Swaziland
58B2 Lebork Pol
47A2 Le Bourg-d'Oisans France
47B1 Le Brassus Switz
29B3 Lebu Chile
47B1 Le Buet Mt France
46B1 Le Cateau France
55A2 Lecce Italy
52A1 Lecco Italy
47D1 Lech R Austria
47D1 Lechtaler Alpen Mts Austria
49C2 Le Creusot France
43C3 Ledbury Eng
13E2 Leduc Can
16C1 Lee USA
45B3 Lee R Irish Rep
41C3 Leeds Eng
43C3 Leek Eng

56B2 Leer Germany
17B2 Leesburg Florida, USA
16A3 Leesburg Virginia, USA
19B3 Leesville USA
109C2 Leeton Aust
56B2 Leeuwarden Neth
106A4 Leeuwin,C Aust
22C2 Lee Vining USA
27E3 Leeward Is Caribbean S
94A1 Lefkara Cyprus
79B3 Legazpi Phil
47D2 Legnago Italy
59B2 Legnica Pol
33F2 Leguan Inlet Guyana
32C4 Leguizamo Colombia
84D2 Leh India
48C2 Le Havre France
62B2 Lehigh R USA
16B2 Lehighton USA
84C2 Leiah Pak
59B3 Leibnitz Austria
43D3 Leicester County, Eng
43D3 Leicester Eng
107C2 Leichhardt R Aust
56B2 Leiden Neth
46B1 Leie R Belg
106C4 Leigh Creek Aust
43D4 Leighton Buzzard Eng
56B2 Leine R Germany
45C2 Leinster Region, Irish Rep
57C2 Leipzig Germany
50A2 Leiria Port
39F7 Leirvik Nor
45B1 Leitrim County, Irish Rep
73C4 Leiyang China
73B5 Leizhou Bandao Pen China
73C5 Leizhou Wan B China
56A2 Lek R Neth
96C1 Le Kef Tunisia
99D2 Lekemti Eth
19B3 Leland USA
54A2 Lelija Mt Yugos
47B1 Le Locle Switz
48C2 Le Mans France
6D3 Lemieux Is Can
8C2 Lemmon USA
21B2 Lemoore USA
49C2 Lempdes France
86C2 Lemro R Burma
52C2 Le Murge Region, Italy
63C2 Lena R USSR
38L6 Lendery USSR
73C4 Lengshujiang China
82A1 Leninabad USSR
65F5 Leninakan USSR
60D2 Leningrad USSR
112B7 Leningradskaya Base Ant
61H3 Leninogorsk Tatar ASSR, USSR
68A1 Leninogorsk USSR
65K4 Leninsk-Kuznetskiy USSR
69F2 Leninskoye USSR
65F6 Lenkoran' USSR
46E1 Lenne R Germany
16C1 Lenox USA
46B1 Lens France
63D1 Lensk USSR
53B3 Lentini Italy
76B3 Lenya R Burma
52B1 Leoben Austria
43C3 Leominster Eng
16D1 Leominster USA
24B2 Leon Mexico
32B6 Leon Nic
50A1 Leon Region, Spain
50A1 León Spain
100A3 Leonardville Namibia
106B3 Leonora Aust
35C2 Leopoldina Brazil
Léopoldville = Kinshasa

60C3 Lepel USSR
73D4 Leping China
49C2 Le Puy France
98B2 Léré Chad
101G1 Leribe Lesotho
47C2 Lerici Italy
51C1 Lerida Spain
23A1 Lerma R Mexico
47D1 Lermoos Austria
55C3 Léros I Greece
44E1 Lerwick Scot
46A2 Les Andelys France
26C3 Les Cayes Haiti
47B2 Les Ecrins Mt France
73A4 Leshan China
54B2 Leskovac Yugos
48B3 Les Landes Region, France
101G1 Leslie S Africa
61H2 Lesnoy USSR
63B2 Lesosibirsk USSR
101G1 Lesotho Kingdom, S Africa
69F2 Lesozavodsk USSR
48B2 Les Sables-d'Olonne France
112A Lesser Antarctica Region, Ant
27D4 Lesser Antilles Is Caribbean S
13E1 Lesser Slave L Can
55C3 Lésvos I Greece
58B2 Leszno Pol
86C2 Letha Range Mts Burma
5G5 Lethbridge Can
33F3 Lethem Guyana
59D3 Letichev USSR
63D2 Let Oktyobr'ya USSR
78B2 Letong Indon
46A1 Le Touquet-Paris-Plage France
76B2 Letpadan Burma
48C1 Le Tréport France
47B1 Leuk Switz
57A2 Leuven Belg
55B3 Levádhia Greece
38G6 Levanger Nor
47B2 Levanna Mt Italy
71D5 Lévêque,C Aust
46D1 Leverkusen Germany
59B3 Levice Czech
47D2 Levico Italy
110C2 Levin NZ
7C5 Lévis Can
15D2 Levittown USA
55B3 Lévka Ori Mt Greece
55B3 Levkás Greece
55B3 Levkás I Greece
102B2 Lévqué,C Aust
54A1 Levski Bulg
43E4 Lewes Eng
40B2 Lewis I Scot
16A2 Lewisburg USA
111B2 Lewis P NZ
8B2 Lewis Range Mts USA
8B2 Lewiston Idaho, USA
10C2 Lewiston Maine, USA
8C2 Lewistown Montana, USA
15C2 Lewistown Pennsylvania, USA
19B3 Lewisville USA
11B3 Lexington Kentucky, USA
18B2 Lexington Missouri, USA
15C3 Lexington Park USA
79C3 Leyte G Phil
54A2 Lezhe Alb
73C3 Lhasa China
86B1 Lhazê China
70A3 Lhokseumawe Indon
86C1 Lhozhag China
68B4 Lhünze China
Liancourt Rocks = Tok-do

79C4 Lianga Phil
72B3 Liangdang China
73C5 Lianjiang China
73C5 Lianping China
73C5 Lian Xian China
72D3 Lianyungang China
72E1 Liaodong Bandao Pen China
72E1 Liaodong Wan B China
72E1 Liao He R China
72E1 Liaoning Province, China
72E1 Liaoyang China
72E1 Liaoyuan China
74B2 Liaoyuang China
4F3 Liard R Can
4F4 Liard River Can
46C2 Liart France
98B2 Liberal USA
9C3 Liberal USA
57C2 Liberec Czech
97A4 Liberia Republic, Africa
18B2 Liberty Missouri, USA
15D2 Liberty New York, USA
19B3 Liberty Texas, USA
48B3 Libourne France
23B2 Libres Mexico
98A2 Libreville Gabon
95A2 Libya Republic, N Africa
95B2 Libyan Desert Libya
95B1 Libyan Plat Egypt
53B3 Licata Italy
43D3 Lichfield Eng
101C2 Lichinga Mozam
101G1 Lichtenburg S Africa
14B3 Licking R USA
22B2 Lick Observatory USA
60C3 Lida USSR
39G7 Lidköping Sweden
53B2 Lido di Ostia Italy
52A1 Liechtenstein Principality, Europe
57B2 Liège Belg
58C1 Lielupe R USSR
57C3 Lienz Austria
60B2 Liepaja USSR
46C1 Lier Belg
47B1 Liestal Switz
15C1 Lièvre R Can
57C3 Liezen Austria
45C2 Liffey R Irish Rep
45C1 Lifford Irish Rep
107F3 Lifu I Nouvelle Calédonie
109C1 Lightning Ridge Aust
46C2 Ligny-en-Barrois France
101C2 Ligonha R Mozam
47C2 Liguria Region, Italy
52A2 Ligurian S Italy
21C4 Lihue Hawaiian Is
100B2 Likasi Zaïre
49C1 Lille France
46B1 Lillers France
38G6 Lillehammer Nor
39G7 Lillestrøm Nor
13C2 Lillooet Can
13C2 Lillooet R Can
101C2 Lilongwe Malawi
79B4 Liloy Phil
54A2 Lim R Yugos
32B6 Lima Peru
50A1 Lima Spain
10B2 Lima USA
92B3 Limassol Cyprus
45C1 Limavady N Ire
34B3 Limay R Arg
34B3 Limay Mahuida Arg
98A2 Limbe Cam
101C2 Limbe Malawi
57B2 Limburg W Gem
31B6 Limeira Brazil
45B2 Limerick County, Irish Rep

56B1 Limfjorden *L* Den
106C2 Limmen Bight *B* Aust
55C3 Limnos *I* Greece
31D3 Limoeiro Brazil
48C2 Limoges France
25D4 Limón Costa Rica
8C3 Limon USA
48C2 Limousin Region,
France
79A3 Linapacan Str Phil
29B3 Linares Chile
9D4 Linares Mexico
50B2 Linares Spain
68B4 Lincang China
29D2 Lincoln Arg
18A1 Lincoln California,
USA
42D3 Lincoln County, Eng
42D3 Lincoln Eng
18C1 Lincoln Illinois, USA
8D2 Lincoln Nebraska,
USA
15D2 Lincoln New
Hampshire, USA
111B2 Lincoln NZ
80A Lincoln *S* Greenland
20B2 Lincoln City USA
14B2 Lincoln Park USA
52A2 L'Incudina *Mt* Corse
57B3 Lindau Germany
33F2 Linden Guyana
39F7 Lindesnes *C* Nor
99D3 Lindi Tanz
98C2 Lindi *R* Zaire
101G1 Lindley *S* Africa
55C3 Lindos Greece
15C2 Lindsay Can
105J3 Line Is Pacific O
72C2 Linfen China
76D2 Lingao China
79B2 Lingayen Phil
56B2 Lingen Germany
73C4 Lingling China
73B5 Lingshan China
72C2 Lingshi China
97A3 Linguère Sen
73E4 Linhai Rhejiang,
China
31D5 Linhares Brazil
72B1 Linhe China
74B2 Linjiang China
39H7 Linköping Sweden
72D2 Linqing China
35B2 Lins Brazil
72A2 Lintao China
47C1 Linthal Switz
68D2 Linxi China
72A2 Linxia China
57C3 Linz Austria
79B3 Lipa Phil
53B3 Lipari *I* Italy
61E3 Lipetsk USSR
54B1 Lipova Rom
56B2 Lippe *R* Germany
46E1 Lippstadt Germany
99D3 Lira Uganda
98B3 Liranga Congo
98C2 Lisala Zaire
50A2 Lisboa Port
Lisbon = Lisboa
45C1 Lisburn N Ire
45B2 Liscannor B Irish Rep
73D4 Lishui China
73C4 Li Shui *R* China
60E4 Lisichansk USSR
48C2 Lisieux France
46B2 L'Isle-Adam France
47B1 L'Isle-sur-le-Doubs
France
107E3 Lismore Aust
45B2 Listowel Irish Rep
73B5 Litang China
94B2 Litani *R* Leb
33G3 Litani *R* Suriname
18C2 Litchfield USA
107E4 Lithgow Aust
16A2 Lititz USA
69F2 Litovko USSR

60B2 Litovskaya SSR
Republic, USSR
19A3 Little *R* USA
11C4 Little Abaco *I*
The Bahamas
110C1 Little Barrier *I* NZ
13E2 Little Bow *R* Can
25D3 Little Cayman *I*
Caribbean S
16B3 Little Egg Harbor *B*
USA
26C2 Little Inagua *I*
Caribbean S
77A4 Little Nicobar *I*
Nicobar Is
11A3 Little Rock USA
22D3 Littlerock USA
13D2 Little Smoky China
13D2 Little Smoky *R*
Can
16A3 Littlestown USA
15D2 Littleton New
Hampshire, USA
74B2 Liuhe China
73D5 Liuzhou China
55B3 Livanátais Greece
58D1 Livani USSR
12E1 Livengood USA
17B1 Live Oak USA
21A2 Livermore USA
7D5 Liverpool Can
42C3 Liverpool Eng
4E2 Liverpool B Can
42C3 Liverpool B Eng
6C2 Liverpool,C Can
109D2 Liverpool Range *Mts*
Aust
8B2 Livingston Montana,
USA
19B3 Livingston Texas,
USA
44C4 Livingstone UK
Livingstone =
Maramba
19A3 Livingston,L USA
52C2 Livno Yugos
60E3 Livny USSR
14B2 Livonia USA
52B2 Livorno Italy
99D3 Liwale Tanz
52B1 Ljubljana Yugos
38G6 Ljungan *R* Sweden
39G7 Ljungby Sweden
39H6 Ljusdal Sweden
38H6 Ljusnan *R* Sweden
43C4 Llandeilo Wales
43C4 Llandovery Wales
43D3 Llandrindod Wells
Wales
42C3 Llandudno Wales
43C4 Llanelli Wales
43C3 Llangollen Wales
9C3 Llano Estacado *Plat*
USA
24D2 Llanos Region,
Colombia/Ven
30D2 Llanos de Chiquitos
Region, Bol
50A2 Llerena Spain
43B3 Lleyn *Pen* Wales
63C2 Llimsk USSR
63C2 Llin USSR
89E7 Llorin Nig
5H4 Lloydminster Can
30C3 Llullaillaco *Mt* Arg/
Chile
30C3 Loa *R* Chile
49C2 Loan France
98B3 Loange *R* Zaire
100B3 Lobatse Botswana
98B2 Lobaye *R* CAR
34D3 Loberia Arg
100A2 Lobito Angola
34D3 Lobos Arg
47B2 Locano Italy
47C1 Locarno Switz
44B3 Loch Awe *L* Scot
44A3 Lochboisdale Scot

44A3 Loch Bracadale *Inlet*
Scot
44B3 Loch Broom *Estuary*
Scot
42B2 Loch Doon *L* Scot
44B3 Loch Earn *L* Scot
44B2 Loch Eriboll *Inlet* Scot
44B3 Loch Ericht *L* Scot
44B3 Loches France
44B3 Loch Etive *Inlet* Scot
44B3 Loch Ewe *Inlet* Scot
44B3 Loch Fyne *Inlet* Scot
44B3 Loch Hourn *Inlet* Scot
44B2 Lochinver Scot
44B3 Loch Katrine *L* Scot
44C3 Loch Leven *L* Scot
44B3 Loch Linnhe *Inlet*
Scot
44B3 Loch Lochy *L* Scot
44B3 Loch Lomond *L* Scot
44B3 Loch Long *Inlet* Scot
44B3 Loch Maree *L* Scot
44A3 Loch Morar *L* Scot
44C3 Lochnagar *Mt* Scot
44B3 Loch Ness *L* Scot
44B3 Loch Rannoch *L* Scot
44A2 Loch Roag *Inlet* Scot
44C3 Loch Sheil *L* Scot
44B2 Loch Shin *L* Scot
44A3 Loch Snizort *Inlet*
Scot
44B3 Loch Sunart *Inlet*
Scot
44B3 Loch Tay *L* Scot
44B3 Loch Torridon *Inlet*
Scot
108A2 Lock Aust
42C2 Lockerbie Scot
15C2 Lock Haven USA
15C2 Lockport USA
76D3 Loc Ninh Viet
53C3 Locri Italy
94B3 Lod Israel
108B3 Loddon *R* Aust
60D1 Lodeynoye Pole USSR
84C3 Lodhran Pak
52A1 Lodi Italy
21A2 Lodi USA
98C3 Lodja Zaire
47B1 Lods France
99D2 Lodwar Kenya
58B2 Łódź Pol
38G5 Lofoten *Is* Nor
8B2 Logan Utah, USA
4D3 Logan,Mt Can
14A2 Logansport Indiana,
USA
19B3 Logansport Louisiana,
USA
50B1 Logroño Spain
86A2 Lohárdaga India
39J6 Lohja Fin
76B2 Loikaw Burma
39J6 Loimaa Fin
48C2 Loir *R* France
49C2 Loire *R* France
32B4 Loja Ecuador
50B2 Loja Spain
38K5 Lokan Tekojärvi *Res*
Fin
46B1 Lokeren Belg
99D2 Lokitaung Kenya
58D1 Loknya USSR
98C3 Lokolo *R* Zaire
98C3 Lokoro *R* Zaire
6D3 Loks Land *I* Can
56C2 Lolland *I* Den
6D3 Lokolo Zaire
98C3 Lomami *R* Zaire
97A4 Loma Mts Sierra
Leone/Guinea
47C2 Lombardia Region,
Italy
71D4 Lomblen *I* Indon
78D4 Lombok *I* Indon
97C4 Lomé Togo
98C3 Lomela Zaire

98C3 Lomela *R* Zaire
60C2 Lomonosov USSR
47B1 Lomont Region,
France
21A3 Lompoc USA
58C2 Lomza Pol
87A1 Lonāvale India
29B3 Loncoche Chile
7B5 London Can
43D4 London Eng
45C1 Londonderry County,
N Ire
45C1 Londonderry N Ire
29B7 Londonderry *I* Chile
106B2 Londonderry,C Aust
30C4 Londres Arg
30F3 Londrina Brazil
21B2 Lone Pine USA
11C4 Long *I* The Bahamas
71F4 Long *I* PNG
78C2 Long Akah Malay
47E1 Longarone Italy
34A3 Longavi *Mt* Chile
27H2 Long B Jamaica
17C1 Long B USA
9B3 Long Beach California,
USA
15D2 Long Beach New York,
USA
51D2 Long Branch USA
73D5 Longchuan China
20C2 Long Creek USA
109C4 Longford Aust
45C2 Longford County,
Irish Rep
45C2 Longford Irish Rep
44D3 Long Forties *Region*
N Sea
72D1 Longhua China
7C4 Long I Can
10C2 Long I USA
16C2 Long Island Sd USA
7B4 Longlac Can
73B5 Longlin China
68D2 Longmont USA
78D2 Longnawan Indon
29B3 Longquimay Chile
107D3 Longreach Aust
72A2 Longnou Shan
Upland China
42C2 Longtown Eng
15D1 Longueuil Can
34A3 Longuimay Chile
46C2 Longuyon France
11A3 Longview Texas,
USA
8A2 Longview
Washington, USA
46C2 Longwy France
72A3 Longxi China
77D3 Long Xuyen Viet
73D4 Longyan China
73B5 Longzhou China
47D2 Lonigo Italy
49D2 Lons-le-Saunier
France
11C3 Lookout,C USA
99D3 Loolmalasin *Mt* Tanz
13D1 Loon R Can
45B2 Loop Hd *C* Irish Rep
76C3 Lop Buri Thai
95C2 Lopez *C* Gabon
68B2 Lop Nor *L* China
50A2 Lora del Rio Spain
10B2 Lorain USA
84B2 Loralai Pak
90B3 Lordegan Iran
107E4 Lord Howe *I* Aust
105G5 Lord Howe Rise
Pacific O
6A3 Lord Mayor B Can
9C3 Lordsburg USA
35B2 Lorena Brazil
47E2 Loreo Italy
23A1 Loreto Mexico
48B2 Lorient France
108B3 Lorne Aust
57B3 Lörrach Germany

49D2 **Lorraine** *Region*
France
9C3 Los Alamos USA
34A2 Los Andes Chile
29B3 Los Angeles Chile
34B2 Los Angeles USA
21A2 Los Banos USA
34B2 Los Cerrillos Arg
21A2 Los Gatos USA
52B2 Lošinj *I* Yugos
29B3 Los Lagos Chile
24B2 Los Mochis Mexico
22B3 Los Olivos USA
34A3 Los Sauces Chile
44C3 Lossiemouth Scot
27E4 Los Testigos *Is* Ven
29B2 Los Vilos Chile
48C3 Lot *R* France
34A3 Lota Chile
42C2 Lothian Region, Scot
99D2 Lotikipi Plain Sudan/
Kenya
98C3 Loto Zaïre
47B1 Lötschberg Tunnel
Switz
38K5 Lotta *R* Fin/USSR
48B2 Loudéac France
97A3 Louga Sen
41B3 Lough Allen *L*
Irish Rep
45C2 Lough Boderg *L*
Irish Rep
43D3 Loughborough Eng
45C2 Lough Bowna *L*
Irish Rep
45C1 Lough Carlingford *L*
N Ire
41B3 Lough Conn *L*
Irish Rep
41B3 Lough Corrib *L*
Irish Rep
41B3 Lough Derg *L* Irish Rep
45C2 Lough Derravaragh *L*
Irish Rep
4H2 Loughead I Can
41B3 Lough Ennell *L*
Irish Rep
41B3 Lough Erne *L* N Ire
40B2 Lough Foyle *Estuary*
N Ire/Irish Rep
45B3 Lough Neagh *L* N Ire
45C1 Lough Oughter *L*
Irish Rep
45B2 Loughrea Irish Rep
45C2 Lough Ree *L* Irish Rep
45B2 Lough Sheelin *L*
Irish Rep
45C2 Lough Strangford *L*
Irish Rep
45C1 Lough Swilly *Estuary*
Irish Rep
14B3 Louisa USA
70C3 Louisa Reef *I* S E Asia
107E2 Louise,L USA
107E2 Louisiade Arch
Solomon Is
11A3 Louisiana State, USA
17B1 Louisville Georgia,
USA
11B3 Louisville Kentucky,
USA
38L5 Loukhi USSR
48B3 Lourdes France
108C2 Louth Aust
45C2 Louth County,
Irish Rep
42D3 Louth Eng
Louvain = Leuven
48C2 Louviers France
60D2 Lovat *R* USSR
54B2 Lovech Bulg
21B1 Loveleck USA
9C3 Lovington USA
38L5 Lovozero USSR
8C2 Low,C Can
10C2 Lowell Massachusetts,
USA

20B2 Lowell Oregon, USA
16D1 Lowell USA
111B2 Lower Hutt NZ
7C4 Lower Seal,L Can
43E3 Lowestoft Eng
58B2 Łowicz Pol
108B2 Loxton Aust
5F4 Loyd George,Mt Can
54A2 Loznica Yugos
23A2 Loz Reyes Mexico
65H3 Lozva *R* USSR
98C3 Luacano Angola
98C3 Luachimo Angola
98C3 Lualaba *R* Zaïre
100B2 Luampa Zambia
100B2 Luân Angola
73D3 Lu'an China
98B3 Luanda Angola
100A2 Luando *R* Angola
100B2 Luanginga *R* Angola
76C1 Luang Namtha Laos
76C2 Luang Prabang Laos
98B3 Luangue *R* Angola
100C2 Luangwa *R* Zambia
72D1 Luan He *R* China
72D1 Luanping China
100B2 Luanshya Zambia
100B2 Luapula *R* Zaïre
50A1 Luarca Spain
98B3 Lubalo Angola
58D2 L'uban USSR
79B3 Lubang Is Phil
100A2 Lubango Angola
9C3 Lubbock USA
56C2 Lübeck Germany
98C3 Lubefu Zaïre
98C3 Lubefu *R* Zaïre
99C3 Lubero Zaïre
98C3 Lubilash *R* Zaïre
59C2 Lublin Pol
60D3 Lubny USSR
78C2 Lubok Antu Malay
98C3 Lubudi Zaïre
98C3 Lubudi *R* Zaïre
78A3 Lubuklinggau Indon
98C3 Lubumbashi Zaïre
98C3 Lubutu Zaïre
79B3 Lucban Phil
52B2 Lucca Italy
42B2 Luce *B* Scot
19C3 Lucedale USA
79B3 Lucena Phil
59B3 Lucenec Czech
Lucerne = Luzern
73C5 Luchuan China
56C2 Luckenwalde
Germany
101F1 Luckhoff S Africa
86A1 Lucknow India
100B2 Lucusse Angola
72E2 Lüda China
46D1 Lüdenscheid Germany
100A3 Lüderitz Namibia
84D2 Ludhiana India
14A2 Ludington USA
43C3 Ludlow Eng
54C2 Ludogorie *Upland*
Bulg
17B1 Ludowici USA
54B1 Luduş Rom
39H6 Ludvika Sweden
57B3 Ludwigsburg
Germany
57B3 Ludwigshafen
Germany
56C2 Ludwigslust Germany
98C3 Luebo Zaïre
98C3 Luema *R* Zaïre
98B3 Luembe *R* Angola
100A2 Luena Angola
100B2 Luene *R* Angola
72B3 Lüeyang China
73D5 Lufeng China
11A3 Lufkin USA
60C2 Luga USSR
60C2 Luga *R* USSR
52A1 Lugano Switz
60E4 Lugansk USSR

101C2 Lugela Mozam
101C2 Lugenda *R* Mozam
50A1 Lugo Spain
54B1 Lugoj Rom
72A3 Luhuo China
98B3 Lui *R* Angola
100B2 Luiana Angola
100B2 Luiana *R* Angola
**Luichow Peninsula =
Leizhou Bandao**
47C2 Luino Italy
98B2 Luionga *R* Zaïre
72B2 Luipan Shan *Upland*
China
100B2 Luishia Zaïre
68B4 Luixi China
98C3 Luiza Zaïre
73D3 Lujiang China
98B3 Lukenie *R* Zaïre
64E4 Luki USSR
98B3 Lukolela Zaïre
58C2 Luków Pol
98C3 Lukuga *R* Zaïre
100B2 Lukulu Zambia
38J5 Luleå Sweden
38J5 Luleå *R* Sweden
54C2 Lüleburgaz Turk
72C2 Lüliang Shan *Mts*
China
19A4 Luling USA
98C2 Lulonga *R* Zaïre
Luluabourg = Kananga
100B2 Lumbala Angola
11C3 Lumberton USA
78D1 Lumbis Indon
86C1 Lumding India
100B2 Lumeje Angola
111A3 Lumsden NZ
39G7 Lund Sweden
101C2 Lundazi Zambia
100C3 Lundi *R* Zim
43B4 Lundy *I* Eng
56C2 Lüneburg Germany
46C2 Lunéville France
100B2 Lunga *R* Zambia
86C2 Lunglei India
100A2 Lungue Bungo *R*
Angola
58D2 Luninec USSR
98B3 Luobomo Congo
101C3 Luocheng China
73B5 Luocheng China
73C5 Luoding China
72C3 Luohe China
72C3 Luo He *R* Henan,
China
72B2 Luo He *R* Shaanxi,
China
73C4 Luoxiao Shan *Hills*
China
72C3 Luoyang China
98B3 Luozi Zaïre
100B2 Lupane Zim
101C2 Lupilichi Mozam
Lu Qu = Tao He
30E4 Luque Par
45C1 Lurgan N Ire
101C2 Lurio *R* Mozam
90A3 Luristan Region, Iran
100B2 Lusaka Zambia
98C3 Lusambo Zaïre
100B2 Lushnje Alb
99D3 Lushoto Tanz
68B4 Lushui China
72E2 Lüshun China
43D4 Luton Eng
60C3 Lutsk USSR
99E2 Luuq Somalia
98C3 Luvua *R* Zaïre
99D3 Luwegu *R* Tanz
100C2 Luwingu Zambia
71D4 Luwuk Indon
46D2 Luxembourg *Grand
Duchy*, N W Europe
49D2 Luxembourg Lux
73A5 Luxi China
95C2 Luxor Egypt

61G1 Luza USSR
61G1 Luza *R* USSR
52A1 Luzern Switz
73B5 Luzhai China
73B4 Luzhi China
73B4 Luzhou China
79B2 Luzon *I* Phil
79B1 Luzon Str Phil
59C3 L'vov USSR
44C2 Lybster Scot
38H6 Lycksele Sweden
100B3 Lydenburg S Africa
8B3 Lyell,Mt USA
16A2 Lykens USA
43C4 Lyme B Eng
43C4 Lyme Regis Eng
11C3 Lynchburg USA
108A2 Lyndhurst Aust
15D2 Lynn USA
12G3 Lynn Canal *Sd* USA
17A1 Lynn Haven USA
5H4 Lynn Lake Can
5H3 Lynx L Can
49C2 Lyon France
12G3 Lyon Canal *Sd* USA
17B1 Lyons Georgia, USA
106A3 Lyons *R* Aust
47B2 Lys *R* Italy
61J2 Lys'va USSR
111B2 Lyttelton NZ
13C2 Lytton Can
22A1 Lytton USA
58D2 Lyubeshov USSR
60E2 Lyublino USSR

M

76C1 **Ma** *R* Viet
94B2 Ma'agan Jordan
94B2 Ma'alot Tarshiha
Israel
92C3 Ma'an Jordan
73D3 Ma'anshan China
92C2 Ma'arrat an Nu'mān
Syria
46C1 Maas *R* Neth
46C1 Maaseik Belg
79B3 Maasin Phil
57B2 Maastricht Belg
101C3 Mabalane Mozam
33F2 Mabaruma Guyana
42E3 Mablethorpe Eng
101C3 Mabote Mozam
58C2 Mabrita USSR
35C2 Macaé Brazil
58D2 M'adel USSR
9D3 McAlester USA
9D4 McAllen USA
101C2 Macaloge Mozam
33G3 Macapá Brazil
35C1 Macarani Brazil
32B4 Macas Ecuador
31D3 Macaú Brazil
73C5 Macau *Dependency*,
China
13C2 McBride Can
12F2 McCarthy Can
13A2 McCauley I Can
42C3 Macclesfield Eng
6B1 McClintock B Can
4H2 McClintock Chan Can
16A2 McClure USA
22B2 McClure,L USA
19B3 McComb USA
8C2 McCook USA
6C2 Macculloch,C Can
13C1 McCusker,Mt Can
4E4 McDame Can
20C2 McDermitt USA
13E2 Macdonald *R* Can
106C3 Macdonnell Ranges
Mts Aust
50A1 Macedo de Cavaleiros
Port
31D3 Maceió Brazil

97B4	Macenta Guinea
52B2	Macerata Italy
108A2	Macfarlane,L Aust
19B3	McGehee USA
45B3	MacGillycuddys Reeks *Mts* Irish Rep
4C3	McGrath USA
35B2	Machado Brazil
101C3	Machaila Mozam
99D3	Machakos Kenya
32B4	Machala Ecuador
101C3	Machaze Mozam
87B1	Macherla India
94B2	Machgharab Leb
87C1	Machilipatnam India
32C1	Machiques Ven
32C6	Machu-Picchu *Hist Site* Peru
101C3	Macia Mozam
109C1	MacIntyre *R* Aust
107D3	Mackay *R* Aust
106B3	Mackay,L Aust
14C2	McKeesport USA
13C1	Mackenzie Can
4F3	Mackenzie *R* Can
4E3	Mackenzie *B* Can
4G2	Mackenzie King I Can
4E3	Mackenzie Mts Can
14B1	Mackinac,Str of USA
14B1	Mackinaw City USA
12D2	McKinley,Mt USA
19A3	McKinney USA
6C2	Mackinson Inlet *B* Can
109D2	Macksville Aust
20B2	Mclaoughlin,Mt USA
109D1	Maclean Aust
100B4	Maclear S Africa
5G4	McLennan Can
13D2	McLeod Can
4G3	McLeod *B* Can
106A3	McLeod,L Can
13C1	McLeod Lake Can
4E3	Macmillan *R* Can
12H2	Macmillan *P* Can
20B1	McMinnville Oregon, USA
112B7	McMurdo *Base* Ant
13D2	McNaughton L Can
18B1	Macomb USA
53A2	Macomer Sardegna
101C2	Macomia Mozam
49C2	Mâcon France
11B3	Macon Georgia, USA
18B2	Macon Missouri, USA
100B2	Macondo Angola
18A2	McPherson USA
104F6	Macquarie *Is* Aust
97A4	Macquarie *R* Aust
109C4	Macquarie Harbour *B* Aust
109D2	Macquarie,L Aust
17B1	McRae USA
112B11	Mac. Robertson Land Region, Ant
45B3	Macroom Irish Rep
4G3	McTavish Arm *B* Can
108A1	Macumba *R* Aust
47C2	Macunaga Italy
4F3	McVicar Arm *B* Can
94B3	Mädabä Jordan
95A3	Madadi *Well* Chad
89J10	Madagascar *I* Indian O
95A2	Madama Niger
71F4	Madang PNG
97C3	Madaoua Niger
86C2	Madaripur Bang
90B2	Madau USR
15C1	Madawaska *R* Can
14A1	Madeira *I* Atlantic O
33E5	Madeira *R* Brazil
24B2	Madera Mexico
21A2	Madera USA
87A1	Madgaon India
86B1	Madhubani India
86A2	Madhya Pradesh State, India
87B2	Madikeri India
98B3	Madimba Zaïre
98B3	Madingo Kayes Congo
98B3	Madingou Congo
10B3	Madison Indiana, USA
10B2	Madison Wisconsin, USA
18C2	Madisonville Kentucky, USA
19A3	Madisonville Texas, USA
78C4	Madiun Indon
99D2	Mado Gashi Kenya
47D1	Madonna di Campiglio Italy
87C2	Madras India
20B2	Madras USA
29A6	Madre de Dios *I* Chile
32D6	Madre de Dios *R* Bol
87C3	Madras India
50B1	Madrid Spain
50B2	Madridejos Spain
78C4	Madura *I* Indon
87B3	Madurai India
75B1	Maebashi Japan
76B3	Mae Khlong *R* Thai
77B4	Mae Nam Lunang *R* Thai
76C2	Mae Nam Mun *R* Thai
76B2	Mae Nam Ping *R* Thai
101D2	Maevatanana Madag
101G1	Mafeteng Lesotho
109C3	Maffra Aust
99D3	Mafia *I* Tanz
101G1	Mafikeng S Africa
30G4	Mafra Brazil
92C3	Mafraq Jordan
32C2	Magangué Colombia
34D3	Magdalena Arg
24A1	Magdalena Mexico
26C4	Magdalena *R* Colombia
78D1	Magdalena,Mt Malay
7D5	Magdalen Is Can
56C2	Magdeburg Germany
31C6	Magé Brazil
78C4	Magelang Indon
47C1	Maggia *R* Switz
92B4	Maghâgha Egypt
45C1	Magherafelt N Ire
55A2	Maglie Italy
61J3	Magnitogorsk USSR
19B3	Magnolia USA
101C2	Magoé Mozam
15D1	Magog Can
23B1	Magosal Mexico
13E2	Magrath Can
7A3	Maguse River Can
76B1	Magwe Burma
90A2	Mahâbâd Iran
86B1	Mahabharat Range *Mts* Nepal
87A1	Mahad India
85D4	Mahadeo Hills India
101D2	Mahajanga Madag
100B3	Mahalapye Botswana
86A2	Mahânadi *R* India
101D2	Mahanoro Madag
16A2	Mahanoy City USA
87A1	Maharashtra State, India
86A2	Mähäsamund India
76C2	Maha Sarakham Thai
101D2	Mahavavy *R* Madag
87B1	Mahbübnagar India
71F1	Mahdia Tunisia
87B2	Mahe India
85D4	Mahekar India
101D2	Mahéli *I* Comoros
86A2	Mahendragarh India
99D3	Mahenge Tanz
85C4	Mahesana India
110C1	Mahia Pen NZ
85D3	Mahoba India
51C2	Mahón Spain
12J1	Mahony L Can
96D1	Mahrès Tunisia
85C4	Mahuva India
32C1	Maicao Colombia
47B1	Maiche France
43E4	Maidstone Eng
98B1	Maiduguri Nig
86A2	Maihar India
86C2	Maijdi Bang
76B3	Mail Kyun *I* Burma
84A1	Maimana Afghan
14B1	Main Chan Can
98B3	Mai-Ndombe *L* Zaïre
10D2	Maine State, USA
48B2	Maine *Region* France
44C2	Mainland *I* Scot
85D3	Mainpuri India
46A2	Maintenon France
101D2	Maintirano Madag
57B2	Mainz Germany
87A4	Maio *I* Cape Verde
34D3	Maipó *Mt* Arg/Chile
34D3	Maipú Arg
32D1	Maiquetía Ven
47B2	Maira *R* Italy
86C1	Mairäbari India
86C2	Maiskhal *I* Bang
107E4	Maitland New South Wales, Aust
108A2	Maitland S Australia, Aust
74D3	Maizuru Japan
70C4	Majene Indon
30B2	Majes *R* Peru
99D2	Maji Eth
72D2	Majia He *R* China
	Majunga = Mahajanga
99D1	Makale Eth
99C1	Makale Eth
86B1	Makalu *Mt* China/Nepal
98B2	Makanza Zaïre
52C2	Makarska Yugos
61F2	Makaryev USSR
	Makassar = Ujung Pandang
78D3	Makassar Str Indon
61H4	Makat USSR
97A4	Makeni Sierra Leone
60E4	Makeyevka USSR
100B3	Makgadikgadi *Salt Pan* Botswana
61G5	Makhachkala USSR
99D3	Makindu Kenya
88H5	Makkah S Arabia
7E4	Makkovik Can
59C3	Makó Hung
98B2	Makokou Gabon
110C1	Makorako,Mt NZ
98B2	Makoua Congo
85C3	Makräna India
85A3	Makran Coast Range *Mts* Pak
96C1	Makthar Tunisia
93D2	Mäkü Iran
98D3	Makumbi Zaïre
74C4	Makurazaki Japan
97C4	Makurdi Nig
79B4	Malabang Phil
87A2	Malabar Coast India
89E7	Malabo Bioko
77D4	Malacca,Str of S E Asia
32C2	Málaga Colombia
50B2	Málaga Spain
101D3	Malaimbandy Madag
107F1	Malaita *I* Solomon Is
99D2	Malakal Sudan
84C2	Malakand Pak
78C4	Malang Indon
98B3	Malange Angola
97C3	Malanville I Sweden
39H7	Mälaren *L* Sweden
34B3	Malargüe Arg
12F3	Malaspina Gl USA
93C2	Malatya Turk
101C2	Malawi Republic, Africa
	Malawi,L = Nyasa,L
79C4	Malaybalay Phil
90A3	Maläyer Iran
70B3	Malaysia Federation, S E Asia
93D2	Malazgirt Turk
58B2	Malbork Pol
56C2	Malchin Germany
18C2	Malden USA
83B5	Maldives *Is* Indian O
104B4	Maldives Ridge Indian O
29F2	Maldonado Urug
47D1	Male Italy
85C4	Malegaon India
59B3	Male Karpaty *Upland* Czech
101C2	Malema Mozam
84B2	Mälestän Afghan
61J3	Maleuz USSR
38H5	Malgomaj *L* Sweden
58B3	Malha *Well* Sudan
20C2	Malheur *L* USA
97B3	Mali Republic, Africa
78D1	Malinau Indon
99E3	Malindi Kenya
	Malines = Mechelen
40B2	Malin Head *Pt* Irish Rep
85D4	Maikala Range *Mts* India
85D4	Malkäpur India
55C2	Malkara Turk
54C2	Malko Türnovo Bulg
44B3	Mallaig Scot
95C2	Mallawi Egypt
47D1	Malles Venosta Italy
51C2	Mallorca *I* Spain
45B2	Mallow Irish Rep
38G6	Malm Nor
38J5	Malmberget Sweden
56B2	Malmédy Germany
43C4	Malmesbury Eng
100A4	Malmesbury S Africa
39G7	Malmö Sweden
61G2	Malmyzh USSR
79B3	Malolos Phil
15D2	Malone USA
101G1	Maloti *Mts* Lesotho
38F6	Måløy Nor
28A2	Malpelo *I* Colombia
34A2	Malpo *R* Chile
85D3	Mälpura India
8C2	Malta Montana, USA
53B3	Malta Channel Malta/Italy
53B3	Malta *I* Medit S
100A3	Maltahöhe Namibia
42D2	Malton Eng
39G6	Malung Sweden
87A1	Malvan India
19B3	Malvern USA
87C3	Malwa Plat India
65F5	Malyy Kavkaz *Mts* USSR
61G4	Malyy Uzen' *R* USSR
63D2	Mama USSR
71E4	Mamberamo *R* Indon
99C2	Mambasa Zaïre
98B2	Mamfé Cam
33D6	Mamoré *R* Bol
97A3	Mamou Guinea
101D2	Mampikony Madag
97B4	Mampong Ghana
94B3	Mamshit *Hist Site* Israel
100B3	Mamuno Botswana
97B4	Man Ivory Coast
21C4	Mana Hawaiian Is
101D3	Manabo Madag
33E4	Manacapuru Brazil
51C2	Manacor Spain
71D3	Manado Indon
25D3	Managua Nic
101D3	Manakara Madag
101D2	Mananara Madag
101D3	Mananjary Madag
111A3	Manapouri NZ
111A3	Manapouri,L NZ

86C1 Manas Bhutan
82C1 Manas China
65K5 Manas Hu L China
86A1 Manaslu Mt Nepal
16B2 Manasquan USA
33F4 Manaus Brazil
92B2 Manavgat Turk
93C2 Manbij Syria
42B2 Man,Calf of I Eng
87B1 Mancheral India
15D2 Manchester Connecticut, USA
42C3 Manchester Eng
10C2 Manchester New Hampshire, USA
16A2 Manchester Pennsylvania, USA
69E2 Manchuria Hist Region, China
91B4 Mand R Iran
101C2 Manda Tanz
35A2 Mandaguari Brazil
39F7 Mandal Nor
76B1 Mandalay Burma
68C2 Mandalgovi Mongolia
72A1 Mandal Ovoo Mongolia
8C2 Mandan USA
14A2 Mandelona USA
99E2 Mandera E Afr
26B3 Mandeville Jamaica
101C2 Mandimba Mozam
86A2 Mandla India
101D2 Mandritsara R Madag
85D4 Mandsaur India
53C2 Manduria Italy
85B4 Mandvi India
87B2 Mandya India
58D2 Manevichi USSR
42D3 Manfield Eng
53C2 Manfredonia Italy
98B1 Manga Desert Region Niger
110C1 Mangakino NZ
54C2 Mangalia Rom
98B1 Mangalmé Chad
87A2 Mangalore India
78B3 Manggar Indon
68B3 Mangnia China
101D2 Mangoky R Madag
71D4 Mangole I Indon
85B4 Mangral India
63E2 Mangui China
8D3 Manhattan USA
31C6 Manhuacu Brazil
101D2 Mania R Madag
101C2 Manica Mozam
7D5 Manicouagan R Can
7D4 Manicouagan Res Can
91A4 Manifah S Arabia
79B3 Manila Phil
109D2 Manilla Aust
97B3 Maninian Ivory Coast
86C2 Manipur State, India
86C2 Manipur R Burma
92A2 Manisa Turk
41C3 Man,Isle of Irish S
14A2 Manistee USA
14A2 Manistee R USA
14A1 Manistique USA
5H4 Manitoba Province, Can
5J4 Manitoba,L Can
13F2 Manito L Can
14A1 Manitou Is USA
7B5 Manitoulin I Can
14A2 Manitowoc USA
15C1 Maniwaki Can
32B2 Manizales Colombia
101D3 Manja Madag
106A4 Manjimup Aust
87B1 Mänjra R India
10A2 Mankato USA
97B4 Mankono Ivory Coast
12D2 Manley Hot Springs USA
110B1 Manly NZ

85C4 Manmäd India
78A3 Manna Indon
108A2 Mannahill Aust
87B3 Mannar Sri Lanka
87B3 Mannar,G of India
87B2 Mannärgudi India
78B3 Mannheim Germany
13D1 Manning Can
17B1 Manning USA
108A2 Mannum Aust
97A4 Mano Sierra Leone
71E4 Manokwari Indon
98C3 Monono Zaire
76B3 Manono Burma
75B1 Manor-wan B Japan
74B2 Manp'o N Korea
84D3 Mänsa India
100B2 Mansa Zambia
6B3 Mansel I Can
19B2 Mansfield Arkansas, USA
108C3 Mansfield Aust
19B3 Mansfield Louisiana, USA
16D1 Mansfield Massachusetts, USA
10B2 Mansfield Ohio, USA
15C2 Mansfield Pennsylvania, USA
71E2 Mansyu Deep Pacific O
32A4 Manta Ecuador
79A4 Mantalingajan,Mt Phil
32B6 Mantaro R Peru
22B2 Manteca USA
48C2 Mantes France
52B1 Mantova Italy
38J6 Mantta Fin
61F2 Manturovo USSR
79B4 Manuel Ribas Brazil
110B1 Manukau NZ
71F4 Manus I Pacific O
50B2 Manzanares Spain
25E2 Manzanillo Cuba
24B3 Manzanillo Mexico
63D3 Manzhouli USSR
94C3 Manzil Jordan
101C3 Manzini Swaziland
98B1 Mao Chad
72A2 Maomao Shan Mt China
73C5 Maoming China
101C3 Mapai Mozam
71E3 Mapia Is Pacific O
5H5 Maple Creek Can
101H1 Maputo Mozam
101H1 Maputo R Mozam
Ma Qu = Huange He
72A3 Maqu China
86B1 Maquan He R China
98B3 Maquela do Zombo Angola
29C4 Maquinchao Arg
31B3 Marabá Brazil
32C1 Maracaibo Ven
32D1 Maracay Ven
95A2 Marädah Libya
97C3 Maradi Niger
90A2 Marägheh Iran
99D2 Maralal Kenya
107F1 Maramasike I Solomon Is
100B2 Maramba Zambia
90A2 Marand Iran
31B2 Maranhão State, Brazil
109C1 Maranoa R Aust
32B4 Marañón R Peru
7B5 Marathon Can
17B2 Marathon Florida, USA
78D2 Maratua I Indon
23A2 Maravatio Mexico
79B4 Marawi Phil
34B2 Marayes Arg
50B2 Marbella Spain
106A3 Marble Bar Aust
100B3 Marblehall S Africa

16D1 Marblehead USA
57B2 Marburg Germany
57B2 Marche Belg
50A2 Marchena Spain
46C1 Marche-en-Famenne Belg
32J7 Marchena I Ecuador
17B2 Marco USA
34C2 Marcos Juárez Arg
12E2 Marcus Baker,Mt USA
15D2 Marcy,Mt USA
84C2 Mardan Pak
29E3 Mar del Plata Arg
93D2 Mardin Turk
99D1 Mardin R Eth
16B1 Margaretville USA
43E4 Margate Eng
54B1 Marghita Rom
109C4 Maria I Aust
104F3 Mariana Is Pacific O
13E1 Mariana Lake Can
104F3 Marianas Trench Pacific O
86C1 Mariäni India
19B3 Marianna Arkansas, USA
17A1 Marianna Florida, USA
7G4 Maria Van Diemen,C NZ
59B3 Mariazell Austria
52C1 Maribor Yugos
99C2 Maridi Sudan
112B5 Marie Byrd Land Region, Ant
27E3 Marie Galante I Caribbean S
39H6 Mariehamn Fin
46C1 Mariembourg Belg
33G2 Marienburg Surinam
100A3 Mariental Namibia
39G7 Mariestad Sweden
17B1 Marietta Georgia, USA
14B3 Marietta Ohio, USA
19A3 Marietta Oklahoma, USA
27Q2 Marigot Dominica
60B3 Marijampole USSR
31B6 Marilia Brazil
98B3 Marimba Angola
79B3 Marinduque I Phil
10B2 Marinette USA
30F3 Maringá Brazil
98C2 Maringa R Zaire
18B2 Marion Arkansas, USA
18C2 Marion Illinois, USA
10B2 Marion Indiana, USA
10B2 Marion Ohio, USA
17C1 Marion S Carolina, USA
11B3 Marion,L USA
107E2 Marion Reef Aust
21B2 Mariposa USA
22B2 Mariposa R USA
22B2 Mariposa Res USA
60C5 Marista R Bulg
60E4 Mariupol' USSR
61G2 Mariyskaya ASSR Republic, USSR
94B2 Marjayoun Leb
58D2 Marjina Gorki USSR
94B3 Marka Jordan
99E2 Marka Somalia
56C1 Markaryd Sweden
43C3 Market Drayton Eng
43D3 Market Harborough Eng
112A Markham,Mt Ant
22C1 Markleeville USA
16D1 Marlboro Massachusetts, USA
107D3 Marlborough Aust
46B2 Marle France
19A3 Marlin USA
48C3 Marmande France
55C2 Marmara Adi I Turk
92A1 Marmara,S of Turk

55C3 Marmaris Turk
14B3 Marmet USA
52B1 Marmolada Mt Italy
12D3 Marmot B USA
47A1 Marnay France
46B2 Marne Department, France
46B2 Marne R France
98B2 Maro Chad
101D2 Maroantsetra Madag
101C2 Marondera Zim
33G3 Maroni R French Guiana
109D1 Maroochydore Aust
98B1 Maroua Cam
101D2 Marovoay Madag
11B4 Marquesas Keys Is USA
10B2 Marquette USA
46A1 Marquise France
109C2 Marra R Aust
101H1 Marracuene Mozam
96B1 Marrakech Mor
106C3 Marree Aust
19B4 Marrero USA
101C2 Marromeu Mozam
101C2 Marrupa Mozam
95C2 Marsa Alam Egypt
99D2 Marsabit Kenya
53B3 Marsala Italy
49D3 Marseille France
12B2 Marshall Alaska, USA
14A3 Marshall Illinois, USA
14B2 Marshall Michigan, USA
18B2 Marshall Missouri, USA
11A3 Marshall Texas, USA
105G3 Marshall Is Pacific O
18B2 Marshfield Missouri, USA
26B1 Marsh Harbour The Bahamas
19B4 Marsh I USA
12H2 Marsh L Can
76B2 Martaban,G of Burma
78A3 Martapura Indon
78A3 Martapura Indon
15D2 Martha's Vineyard I USA
49D2 Martigny Switz
59B3 Martin Czech
111C2 Martinborough NZ
34B3 Martin de Loyola Arg
23B1 Martinez de la Torre Mexico
27E4 Martinique I Caribbean S
17A1 Martin,L USA
15C3 Martinsburg USA
14B2 Martins Ferry USA
103G6 Martin Vaz I Atlantic O
49D3 Martigues France
110C2 Marton NZ
50B2 Martos Spain
78D1 Marudi Malay
84B2 Maruf Afghan
75A2 Marugame Japan
85C3 Märwär India
65H6 Mary USSR
108B3 Maryborough Queensland, Aust
108B3 Maryborough Victoria, Aust
5F4 Mary Henry,Mt Can
10C3 Maryland State, USA
42C2 Maryport Eng
21A2 Marysville California, USA
18A2 Marysville Kansas, USA
20B1 Marysville Washington, USA
10A2 Maryville Iowa, USA
18B1 Maryville Missouri, USA
95A2 Marzuq Libya

Masada = Mezada
94B2 Mas'adah Syria
99D3 Masai Steppe *Upland Tanz*
99D3 Masaka Uganda
93E2 Masally USSR
74B3 Masan S Korea
101C2 Masasi Tanz
25D3 Masaya Nic
79B3 Masbate Phil
79B3 Masbate *I* Phil
96C1 Mascara Alg
23A1 Mascota Mexico
35D1 Mascote Brazil
101G1 Maseru Lesotho
66C3 Mashhad Iran
84B2 Mashaki Afghan
90C2 Mashhad Iran
98B3 Masi-Manimba Zaïre
99D2 Masindi Uganda
99C3 Masisi Zaïre
90A3 Masjed Soleyman Iran
101E2 Maskoula *C* Madag
10A2 Mason City USA
91C5 Masqat Oman
52B2 Massa Italy
10C2 Massachusetts State, USA
15D2 Massachusetts B USA
98B1 Massakori Chad
101C3 Massangena Mozam
95C3 Massawa Eth
15D2 Massena USA
98B1 Masséyna Chad
14B1 Massey USA
49C2 Massif Central *Mts* France
98B2 Massif de l'Adamaoua *Mts* Cam
26C3 Massif de la Hotte *Mts* Haiti
101D3 Massif de l'Isalo *Upland* Madag
98C2 Massif des Bongo *Upland* CAR
49D2 Massif du Pelvoux *Mts* France
101D2 Massif du Tsaratanana *Mt* Madag
14B2 Massillon USA
97B3 Massina Region, Mali
101C3 Massinga Mozam
101C3 Massingir Mozam
61H4 Masteksay USSR
111C2 Masterton NZ
74C4 Masuda Japan
92C2 Masvár Syria
98B3 Matadi Zaïre
25D3 Matagalpa Nic
7C4 Matagami Can
9D4 Matagorda B USA
110C1 Matakana I NZ
100A2 Matala Angola
87C3 Matale Sri Lanka
97A3 Matam Sen
97C3 Matameye Niger
24C2 Matamoros Mexico
95B2 Ma'tan as Sarra *Well* Libya
7D5 Matane Can
25D2 Matanzas Cuba
34A2 Mataquito *R* Chile
87C3 Matara Sri Lanka
106A1 Mataram Indon
30B2 Matarani Peru
51C1 Mataró Spain
111C2 Mataura NZ
24B2 Matehuala Mexico
27L1 Matelot Trinidad
53C2 Matera Italy
59C3 Mátészalka Hung
85D3 Mathura India
79A1 Mati Phil
78D3 Matisiri *I* Indon
43D3 Matlock Eng
33F6 Mato Grosso Brazil
33F6 Mato Grosso State, Brazil

30E2 Mato Grosso do Sul State, Brazil
101H1 Matola Mozam
91C5 Matrah Oman
92A3 Matrûh Egypt
74C3 Matsue Japan
74E2 Matsumae Japan
74D3 Matsumoto Japan
74D4 Matsusaka Japan
74C4 Matsuyama Japan
7B5 Mattagami *R* Can
15C1 Mattawa Can
52A1 Matterhorn *Mt* Italy/ Switz
26C2 Matthew Town The Bahamas
16C2 Mattituck USA
18C2 Mattoon USA
84B2 Matun Afghan
27L1 Matura B Trinidad
33E2 Maturín Ven
86A1 Mau India
101C2 Maúa Mozam
49C1 Maubeuge France
108B2 Maude Aust
103J8 Maud Seamount Atlantic O
21C4 Maui *I* Hawaiian Is
34A3 Maule *R* Chile
14B2 Maumee USA
14B2 Maumee *R* USA
100B2 Maun Botswana
21C4 Mauna Kea *Mt* Hawaiian Is
21C4 Mauna Loa *Mt* Hawaiian Is
4F3 Maunoir *L* Can
4F3 Maunoir,L Can
45C2 Mauriac France
96A2 Mauritania Republic, Africa
100B2 Mavinga Angola
86C2 Mawlaik Burma
112C10 Mawson *Base* Ant
78B3 Maya *I* Indon
63F2 Maya *R* USSR
93D2 Mayadïn Syria
11C4 Mayaguana *I* The Bahamas
27D3 Mayagüez Puerto Rico
97C3 Mayahi Niger
98B3 Mayama Congo
90C2 Mayamey Iran
42B2 Maybole Scot
10C3 May,C USA
108A2 Maydena Aust
46D1 Mayen Germany
48B2 Mayenne France
13D2 Mayerthorpe Can
18C2 Mayfield USA
61E5 Maykop USSR
65H6 Maymaneh Afghan
76B1 Maymyo Burma
4E3 Mayo Can
45B2 Mayo County, Irish Rep
16A3 Mayo USA
45B1 Mayo,Mts of Irish Rep
79B3 Mayon *Mt* Phil
51C2 Mayor *R* Spain
34C3 Mayor Buratovich Arg
110C1 Mayor I NZ
30D2 Mayor P Lagerenza Par
101D2 Mayotte *I* Indian O
27H2 May Pen Jamaica
16B3 May Point,C USA
47D1 Mayrhofen Austria
16B3 Mays Landing USA
14B3 Maysville USA
98B3 Mayumba Gabon
100B2 Mazabuka Zambia
84D1 Mazar China
94B3 Mazar Jordan
53B3 Mazara del Vallo Italy
84B1 Mazar-i-Sharif Afghan
24B2 Mazatlán Mexico
60B2 Mazeikiai USSR

94B3 Mazra Jordan
101C3 Mbabane Swaziland
98B2 Mbaïki CAR
98B3 Mbala Zambia
100B3 Mbalabala Zim
99D2 Mbale Uganda
98B2 Mbalmayo Cam
98B2 Mbam *R* Cam
101C2 Mbamba Bay Tanz
98B2 Mbandaka Zaïre
98B3 Mbanza Congo Angola
98B3 Mbanza-Ngungu Zaïre
99D3 Mbarara Uganda
98C2 Mbéré *R* Cam
98B3 Mbeya Tanz
98B3 Mbinda Congo
97A3 Mbout Maur
98C3 Mbuji-Mayi Zaïre
99D3 Mbulu Tanz
96B2 Mcherrah Region, Alg
101C2 Mchinji Malawi
76D3 Mdrak Viet
96D,L USA
5H4 Meadow Lake Can
14B2 Meadville USA
74A3 Mealy *R* Can
109C1 Meandarra Aust
5G4 Meander River Can
45C2 Meath County, Irish Rep
49C2 Meaux France
16C1 Mechanicville USA
56A2 Mechelen Belg
96B1 Mecheria Alg
56C2 Mecklenburg-Vorpommern *State* Germany
56C2 Mecklenburger Bucht *B* Germany
101C2 Mecúfi Mozam
101C2 Mecubúri Mozam
101D2 Mecufi Mozam
101C2 Mecula Mozam
70A3 Medan Indon
34C3 Medanos Arg
34D2 Medanos Arg
32B2 Medellín Colombia
96D1 Medenine Tunisia
8A2 Medford USA
54C2 Medgidia Rom
34B2 Media Agua Arg
54B1 Medias Rom
20C1 Medical Lake USA
13E2 Medicine Hat Can
35C1 Medina Brazil
80B3 Medina S Arabia
51C1 Medinaceli Spain
50B1 Medina del Campo Spain
50A1 Medina de Rio Seco Spain
85B3 Medinipur India
88E4 Mediterranean S Europe
13F2 Medley Can
61J3 Mednogorsk USSR
86D1 Mêdog China
98B2 Médouneu Gabon
61F3 Medvedista *R* USSR
64E3 Medvezh'yegorsk USSR
106A3 Meekatharra Aust
84D3 Meerut India
99D2 Mega Eth
55B3 Megalópolis Greece
55B3 Mégara Greece
86C1 Meghálaya State, India
86C2 Meghna *R* Bang
94B2 Megiddo *Hist Site* Israel
91B4 Mehran Iran
90B3 Mehriz Iran
35B1 Meia Ponte *R* Brazil
98B2 Meiganga Cam

76B1 Meiktila Burma
47C1 Meiringen Switz
74B2 Meishan China
57C2 Meissen Germany
73D5 Mei Xian China
73D5 Meizhou China
30B3 Mejillones Chile
98B2 Mekambo Gabon
96B1 Meknès Mor
76D3 Mekong *R* Camb
97C3 Mekrou *R* Benin
77C5 Melaka Malay
104F4 Melanesia *Region* Pacific O
78C3 Melawi *R* Indon
107D4 Melbourne Aust
11B4 Melbourne USA
9C4 Melchor Múzguiz Mexico
98B1 Melfi Chad
5H4 Melfort Can
96B1 Melilla N W Africa
29B4 Melimoyu *Mt* Chile
34C2 Melincué Arg
34A2 Melipilla Chile
60E4 Melitopol' USSR
6D2 Melville Bugt *B* Greenland
101H1 Melmoth S Africa
34C2 Melo Arg
29F2 Melo Urug
22B2 Melones Res USA
12D1 Melozitna *R* USA
47C1 Mels Switz
43D3 Melton Mowbray Eng
49C2 Melun France
5H4 Melville Can
27Q2 Melville,C Dominica
4F3 Melville Hills *Mts* Can
106C2 Melville I Aust
4G2 Melville I Can
7E4 Melville,L Can
6B3 Melville Pen Can
45B1 Melvin,L Irish Rep
101C2 Memba Mozam
106A1 Memboro Indon
57C3 Memmingen Germany
78B2 Mempawan Indon
11B3 Memphis Tennessee, USA
19B3 Mena USA
43B3 Menai Str Wales
97C3 Ménaka Mali
14A2 Menasha USA
84R4 Menasha *R* Indon
49C3 Mende France
99D2 Mendebo *Mts* Eth
43C4 Mendip Hills *Upland* Eng
20B2 Mendocino,C USA
105J2 Mendocino Seascarp Pacific O
22B2 Mendota California, USA
29C2 Mendoza Arg
29C3 Mendoza State, Arg
55C3 Menemen Turk
46B1 Menen Belg
72D3 Mengcheng China
78B3 Menggala Indon
76B1 Menghai China
73A5 Mengla China
76B1 Menglian China
73A5 Mengzi China
107D4 Menindee Aust
108B2 Meninde L Aust
108A3 Maningie Aust
14A1 Menominee USA
14A2 Menominee Falls USA
100A2 Menongue Angola
51C1 Menorca *I* Spain
12F2 Mentasta Mts USA
78B3 Mentok Indon
14B2 Mentor USA
46B2 Menu France
72A2 Menyuan China
61H2 Menzelinsk USSR

56B2 Meppen Germany	24C3 México Mexico	59B2 Mielec Pol	12D2 Minchumina,L USA
78D2 Merah Indon	23A2 México State, Mexico	54C1 Miercurea-Ciuc Rom	47D2 Mincio R Italy
18B2 Meramec R USA	18B2 Mexico USA	50A1 Mieres Spain	71D1 Mindanao I Phil
52B1 Merano Italy	24C2 Mexico,G of Cent America	16A2 Mifflintown USA	19B3 Minden Louisiana, USA
71F4 Merauke Indon	94B3 Mezada Hist Site Israel	75A2 Mihara Japan	56B2 Minden Germany
8A3 Merced USA	23B2 Mezcala Mexico	72D1 Mijun Shuiku Res China	100B2 Mindona L Aust
22B2 Merced R USA	64F3 Mezen' USSR	65F4 Mikhayiovka USSR	79B3 Mindoro I Phil
29E2 Mercedario Mt Chile	64G3 Mezhdusharskiy I USSR	55C3 Mikhaylovgrad Bulg	79B3 Mindoro Str Phil
29C2 Mercedes Arg	85D4 Mhow India	61F3 Mikhaylovka USSR	45C3 Mine Hd C Irish Rep
29E2 Mercedes Buenos Aires, Arg	23B2 Miahuatlán Mexico	65J4 Mikhaylovskiy USSR	43C4 Minehead Eng
30E4 Mercedes Corrientes, Arg	11B4 Miami Florida, USA	38K6 Mikkeli Fin	30F2 Mineiros Brazil
29E2 Mercedes Urug	11B4 Miami Oklahoma, USA	55C3 Mikonos I Greece	19A3 Mineola USA
110C1 Mercury B NZ	11B4 Miami Beach USA	59B3 Mikulov Czech	23B1 Mineral de Monte Mexico
110C1 Mercury Is NZ	90A2 Miandowāb Iran	99D3 Mikumi Tanz	16A2 Minersville USA
4F2 Mercy B Can	101D2 Miandrivazo Madag	74D3 Mikuni-sammyaku Mts Japan	108B2 Mingary Aust
6D3 Mercy,C Can	90A2 Mīaneh Iran	75B2 Mikura-jima I Japan	72A2 Minhe China
99E2 Meregh Somalia	84C2 Mianwali Pak	32B4 Milagro Ecuador	87A3 Minicoy I India
76B3 Mergui Burma	73A3 Mianyang China	Milàn = Milano	73D4 Min Jiang R Fujian, China
76B3 Mergui Arch Burma	73C3 Mianyang China	51C2 Milana Alg	73A4 Min Jiang R Sichuan, China
25D2 Mérida Mexico	73A3 Mianzhu China	101C2 Milange Mozam	22C2 Minkler USA
50A2 Mérida Spain	72E2 Miaodao Qundao Arch China	52A1 Milano Italy	108A2 Minlaton Aust
32C2 Mérida Ven	73B4 Miao Ling Upland China	92A2 Milas Turk	72A2 Minle China
11B3 Meridian USA	61K3 Miass USSR	73A5 Mile China	57C2 Minna Nig
109C3 Merimbula Aust	59C3 Michalovce USSR	93D3 Milh, Tharthar L Iraq	10A2 Minneapolis USA
108B2 Meringur Aust	27D3 Miches Dom Rep	107E3 Miles Aust	5J4 Minnedosa Can
95C3 Merowe Sudan	10B2 Michigan State, USA	8C2 Miles City USA	10A2 Minnesota State, USA
106A4 Merredin Aust	14A2 Michigan City USA	16C2 Milford Connecticut, USA	50A1 Miño R Spain
42B2 Merrick Mt Scot	10B2 Michigan,L USA	15C3 Milford Delaware, USA	8C2 Minot USA
14A2 Merrillville USA	7B5 Michipicoten I Can	15D2 Milford Massachusetts, USA	72A2 Minqin China
13C2 Merritt Can	23A2 Michoacan State, Mexico	18A1 Milford Nebraska, USA	72A3 Min Shan Upland China
17B2 Merritt Island USA	65F4 Michunnsk USSR	16B2 Milford Pennsylvania, USA	60C3 Minsk USSR
109D2 Merriwa Aust	54C2 Michurin Bulg	43B4 Milford Haven Wales	58C2 Minsk Mazowiecki Pol
99E1 Mersa Fatma Eth	61F3 Michurinsk USSR	43B4 Milford Haven Sd Wales	12E2 Minto USA
51B2 Mers el Kébir Alg	104F3 Micronesia Region Pacific O	18A2 Milford L USA	4G2 Minto Inlet B Can
42C3 Mersey R Eng	78B2 Midai I Indon	111A2 Milford Sd NZ	7C4 Minto,L Can
42C3 Merseyside County, Eng	102F4 Mid Atlantic Ridge Atlantic O	13E2 Milk River Can	63B2 Minusinsk USSR
92B2 Mersin Turk	46B1 Middelburg Neth	49C3 Millau France	72A3 Min Xian China
77C5 Mersing Malay	20D2 Middle Alkali L USA	16C2 Millbrook USA	7E5 Miquelon Can
85C3 Merta India	16D2 Middleboro USA	17B1 Milledgeville USA	22D3 Mirage L USA
43C4 Merthyr Tydfil Wales	100B4 Middleburg Cape Province, S Africa	12F2 Miller,Mt USA	87A1 Miraj India
50A2 Mertola Port	16A2 Middleburg Pennsylvania, USA	61F4 Millerovo USSR	29E3 Miramar Arg
99D3 Meru Mt Tanz	101G1 Middleburg Transvaal, S Africa	16A2 Millersburg USA	84B2 Miram Shah Pak
60E5 Merzifon Turk	16B1 Middleburgh USA	108A1 Millers Creek Aust	50B1 Miranda de Ebro Spain
46D2 Merzig Germany	15D2 Middlebury USA	16C2 Millers Falls USA	47D2 Mirandola Italy
9B3 Mesa USA	.11B3 Middlesboro USA	16C2 Millerton USA	84B2 Mir Bachchen Küt Afghan
46E1 Meschede Germany	42D2 Middlesbrough Eng	22C2 Millerton L USA	78D1 Miri Malay
93D1 Mescit Dağ Mt Turk	16C2 Middletown Connecticut, USA	108B3 Millicent Aust	23A2 Mirik,C Maur
12C3 Meshik USA	16B3 Middletown Delaware, USA	109D1 Millmerran Aust	63A1 Mirnoye USSR
99C2 Meshra Er Req Sudan	15D2 Middletown New York, USA	45B2 Milltown Malbay Irish Rep	63D1 Mirnyy USSR
47C1 Mesocco Switz	14B3 Middletown Ohio, USA	22A2 Mill Valley USA	112C9 Mirnyy Base Ant
55B3 Mesolóngion Greece	16A2 Middletown Pennsylvania, USA	15D3 Millville USA	84C2 Mirpur Pak
19A3 Mesquite Texas, USA	96B1 Midelt Mor	6H3 Milne Land I Greenland	85B3 Mirpur Khas Pak
101C2 Messalo R Mozam	43C4 Mid Glamorgan County, Wales	21C4 Milolii Hawaiian Is	74B3 Mirtoan S Greece
53C3 Messina Italy	104B4 Mid Indian Basin Indian O	55B3 Milos I Greece	74B3 Miryang S Korea
100B3 Messina S Africa	104B4 Mid Indian Ridge Indian O	107D3 Milparinka Aust	86A1 Mirzapur India
55B3 Messini Greece	7C5 Midland Can	16A2 Milroy USA	23B2 Misantla Mexico
55B3 Messiniakós Kólpos G Greece	14B2 Midland Michigan, USA	111A3 Milton NZ	84C1 Misgar Pak
54B2 Mesta R Bulg	9C3 Midland Texas, USA	16B2 Milton Pennsylvania, USA	14A2 Mishawaka USA
52B1 Mestre Italy	101D3 Midongy Atsimo Madag	10B2 Milwaukee USA	12B1 Misheguk Mt USA
32A1 Meta R Colombia	105G2 Mid Pacific Mts Pacific O	51C2 Mina R Alg	75A2 Mi-shima I Japan
60D2 Meta R USSR	20C2 Midvale USA	93E4 Mînā' al Ahmadī Kuwait	107E2 Misima I Solomon Is
32D2 Meta R Ven	105H2 Midway Is Pacific O	91C4 Mināb Iran	30F4 Misiones State, Arg
6C3 Meta Incognito Pen Can	18A2 Midwest City USA	74C4 Minamata Japan	59C3 Miskolc Hung
19B4 Metairie USA	93D2 Midyat Turk	78A2 Minas Indon	94C2 Mismiyah Syria
20C1 Metaline Falls USA	54B2 Midžor Mt Yugos	29E2 Minas Urug	71E4 Misoöl I Indon
30D4 Metán Arg		31B5 Minas Gerais State, Brazil	95A1 Misrātah Libya
101C2 Metangula Mozam		35C1 Minas Novas Brazil	7B5 Missinaibi R Can
53C2 Metaponto Italy		25C3 Minatitlan Mexico	20B1 Mission City Can
44C3 Methil Scot		76A1 Minbu Burma	15C2 Mississauga Can
16D1 Methuen USA		76A1 Minbya Burma	11A3 Mississippi State, USA
111B2 Methven NZ		34A2 Mincha Chile	11A3 Mississippi R USA
12H3 Metlakatla USA		44A3 Minch,Little Sd Scot	19C3 Mississippi Delta USA
18C2 Metropolis USA		44A2 Minch,North Sd Scot	8B2 Missoula USA
88B2 Mettür India		40B2 Minch,The Sd Scot	96B1 Missour Mor
49D2 Metz France			11A3 Missouri State, USA
70A3 Meulaboh Indon			10A2 Missouri R USA
46A2 Meulan France			10C1 Mistassini,L Can
46C2 Meuse Department, France			85B3 Misti Mt Peru
49D2 Meuse R France			109C1 Mitchell Aust
13A3 Mexia USA			8D2 Mitchell USA
24A1 Mexicali Mexico			107D2 Mitchell R Aust
24B2 Mexico Federal Republic, Cent America			

11B3 Mitchell,Mt USA
45B2 Mitchelstown
  Irish Rep
84C3 Mithankot Pak
55C3 Mitilini Greece
23B2 Mitla Mexico
32C3 Mitu Colombia
99C3 Mitumbar Mts Zaïre
98C3 Mitwaba Zaïre
98B2 Mitzic Gabon
75B1 Miura Japan
72C3 Mi Xian China
69F3 Miyake J Japan
75B2 Miyake-jima I Japan
69E4 Miyako I Japan
74C4 Miyakonojō Japan
74C4 Miyazaki Japan
75B1 Miyazu Japan
74C4 Miyoshi Japan
72D1 Miyun China
99D2 Mizan Teferi Eth
95A1 Mizdah Libya
45B3 Mizen Hd C Irish Rep
54C1 Mizil Rom
86C2 Mizo Hills India
86C2 Mizoram Union
  Territory, India
94B3 Mizpe Ramon Israel
112B11 Mizuho Base Ant
74E3 Mizusawa Japan
39H7 Mjölby Sweden
100B2 Mkushi Zambia
101H1 Mkuzi S Africa
57C2 Mladá Boleslav Czech
58C2 Mława Pol
52C2 Mljet I Yugos
100B3 Mmabatho S Africa
84D2 Mnadi India
97A4 Moa R Sierra Leone
94B3 Moab Region, Jordan
9C3 Moab USA
98B3 Moanda Congo
98B3 Moanda Gabon
99C3 Moba Zaïre
75C1 Mobara Japan
98C2 Mobaye CAR
98C2 Mobayi Zaïre
10A3 Moberly USA
11B3 Mobile USA
11B3 Mobile B USA
8C2 Mobridge USA
101D2 Moçambique Mozam
76C1 Moc Chau Viet
100B3 Mochudi Botswana
101D2 Mocimboa da Praia
  Mozam
32B3 Mocoa Colombia
35B2 Mococa Brazil
34D2 Mocoreta R Arg
23B1 Moctezuma R Mexico
101C2 Mocuba Mozam
47B2 Modane France
101G1 Modder R S Africa
52B2 Modena Italy
46D2 Moder R France
8A3 Modesto USA
22B2 Modesto Res USA
53B3 Modica Italy
59B3 Mödling Austria
107D4 Moe Aust
47C1 Moesa R Switz
42C2 Moffat Scot
84D2 Moga India
35B2 Mogi das Cruzes
  Brazil
60C3 Mogilev USSR
60C4 Mogilev Podolskiy
  USSR
35B2 Mogi-Mirim Brazil
101D2 Mogincual Mozam
47E2 Mogliano Italy
34B2 Mogna Arg
68D1 Mogocha USSR
65K4 Mogochin USSR
50A2 Moguer Spain
110C1 Mohaka R NZ
86C2 Mohanganj Bang
15D2 Mohawk R USA

99D3 Mohoro Tanz
65J5 Mointy USSR
38G5 Mo i Rana Nor
48C3 Moissac France
21B2 Mojave USA
22D3 Mojave R USA
9B3 Mojave Desert USA
78C4 Mojokerto Indon
86B1 Mokama India
110B1 Mokau R NZ
22B1 Mokelumne Aqueduct
  USA
22B1 Mokelumne Hill USA
22B1 Mokelumne North
  Fork R USA
101G1 Mokhotlong Lesotho
96D1 Moknine Tunisia
86C1 Mokokchūng India
98B1 Mokolo Cam
74B4 Mokp'o S Korea
61F3 Moksha R USSR
23B1 Molango Mexico
55B3 Moláoi Greece
60C4 Moldavskaya SSR
  Republic, USSR
38F6 Molde Nor
54B1 Moldoveanu Mt Rom
100B3 Molepolole Botswana
53C2 Molfetta Italy
34A3 Molina Chile
30B2 Mollendo Peru
60C3 Molodechno USSR
112C11 Molodezhnaya Base
  Ant
21C4 Molokai I Hawaiian Is
61G2 Moloma R USSR
109C2 Molong Aust
100B3 Molopo R Botswana
98B2 Moloundou Cam
8D1 Moluccas I USA
71D4 Molucca S Indon
71D4 Moluccas Is Indon
101C2 Moma Mozam
31C3 Mombaca Brazil
99D3 Mombasa Kenya
98C2 Mompono Zaïre
58C2 Mon I Den
44A3 Monach Is Scot
49D3 Monaco
  Principality, Europe
44B3 Monadhliath Mts
  Scot
45C1 Monaghan County,
  Irish Rep
45C1 Monaghan Irish Rep
27D3 Mona Pass
  Caribbean S
13B2 Monarch Mt Can
5G4 Monashee Mts Can
41B3 Monasterevan
  Irish Rep
47B2 Moncalieri Italy
31B2 Monção Brazil
38L5 Monchegorsk USSR
56B2 Mönchen-gladbach
  Germany
24B2 Monclova Mexico
7D5 Moncton Can
9C4 Monctova Mexico
50A1 Mondego R Port
52A2 Mondovi Italy
27H1 Moneague Jamaica
14C2 Monessen USA
18B2 Monett USA
52B1 Monfalcone Italy
50A1 Monforte de Lemos
  Spain
98C2 Monga Zaïre
98C2 Mongala R Zaïre
99D2 Mongalla Sudan
76D1 Mong Cai Viet
98B1 Mongo Chad
68B2 Mongolia Republic,
  Asia
100B3 Mongu Zambia
63D3 Mönhhaan Mongolia
21B2 Monitor Range Mts
  USA

98C3 Monkoto Zaïre
43C4 Monmouth Eng
18B1 Monmouth USA
13C2 Monmouth,Mt Can
97C4 Mono R Togo
21B2 Mono L USA
53C2 Monopoli Italy
51B1 Monreal del Campo
  Spain
19B3 Monroe Louisiana,
  USA
14B2 Monroe Michigan,
  USA
18B1 Monroe Washington,
  USA
18B2 Monroe City USA
97A4 Monrovia Lib
20D3 Monrovia USA
56A2 Mons Belg
52C2 Monselice Italy
16C1 Monson USA
58B1 Mönsterås Sweden
101D2 Montagne d'Ambre
  Mt Madag
96C1 Montagnes des Ouled
  Naïl Mts Alg
12E3 Montague I USA
49C3 Mont Aigoual Mt
  France
48B2 Montaigu France
53C3 Montalto Mt Italy
88B2 Montana State, USA
52A1 Mont Blanc Mt
  France/Italy
49C2 Montceau les Mines
  France
51C1 Montceny Mt Spain
49D3 Mont Cinto Mt Corse
46C2 Montcornet France
48B3 Mont-de-Marsan
  France
52C3 Montdidier France
30D2 Monteagudo Bol
33G4 Monte Alegre Brazil
52B2 Monte Amiata Mt
  Italy
47D2 Monte Baldo Mt Italy
15C1 Montebello Can
106A3 Monte Bello Is Aust
47E2 Montebelluna Italy
49D3 Monte Carlo Monaco
35B1 Monte Carmelo Brazil
34D2 Monte Caseros Arg
52B2 Monte Cimone Mt
  Italy
52A2 Monte Cinto Mt
  Corse
34B2 Monte Coman Arg
52B2 Monte Corno Mt Italy
27C3 Montecristi Dom Rep
52B2 Montecristo I Italy
23A1 Monte Escobedo
  Mexico
53C2 Monte Gargano Mt
  Italy
26B3 Montego Bay Jamaica
47D2 Monte Grappa Mt
  Italy
52B2 Monte Lesima Mt
  Italy
49C3 Montélimar France
53B2 Monte Miletto Mt
  Italy
50A2 Montemo-o-Novo Port
24C2 Montemorelos Mexico
26B5 Montená Colombia
54A2 Montenegro Region,
  Yugos
35D1 Monte Pascoal Mt
  Brazil
34A2 Monte Patria Chile

53C3 Monte Pollino Mt Italy
101C2 Montepuez Mozam
8A3 Monterey California,
  USA
15C3 Monterey Virginia,
  USA
8A3 Monterey B USA
32B2 Montería Colombia
30D2 Montero Bol
47B2 Monte Rosa Mt Italy/
  Switz
24B2 Monterrey Mexico
31C5 Montes Claros Brazil
50B2 Montes de Toledo Mts
  Spain
29E2 Montevideo Urug
52A2 Monte Viso Mt Italy
27P2 Mont Gimie Mt St
  Lucia
11B3 Montgomery
  Alabama, USA
96C2 Mont Gréboun Niger
46C2 Montherme France
47B1 Monthey Switz
19B3 Monticello Arkansas,
  USA
16B2 Monticello New York,
  USA
9C3 Monticello Utah, USA
53A2 Monti del
  Gennargentu Mt
  Sardegna
47D2 Monti Lessini Mts
  Italy
53B3 Monti Nebrodi Mts
  Italy
7C5 Mont-Laurier Can
48C2 Montluçon France
7C5 Montmagny Can
46C2 Montmedy France
49C3 Mont Mézenc Mt
  France
46B2 Montmirail France
50B2 Montoro Spain
49D3 Mont Pelat Mt France
14B2 Montpelier Ohio, USA
10C2 Montpelier Vermont,
  USA
49C3 Montpellier France
7C5 Montréal Can
48C1 Montreuil France
52A1 Montreux Switz
47B1 Mont Risoux Mt
  France
8C3 Montrose Colorado,
  USA
40C2 Montrose Scot
48B2 Mont-St-Michel
  France
96B1 Monts des Ksour Mts
  Alg
51C3 Monts des Ouled Neil
  Mts Alg
51C2 Monts du Hodna Mts
  Alg
27E3 Montserrat I
  Caribbean S
12B1 Monument Mt USA
9B3 Monument V USA
98C2 Monveda Zaïre
76B1 Monywa Burma
52A1 Monza Italy
100B2 Monze Zambia
101H1 Mooi R S Africa
101G1 Mooi River S Africa
108B1 Moomba Aust
109D2 Moonbi Range Mts
  Aust
108B1 Moonda L Aust
109D1 Moonie Aust
109C1 Moonie R Aust
108A2 Moonta Aust
106A4 Moora Aust
106A3 Moore,L Aust
42C2 Moorfoot Hills Scot
8D2 Moorhead USA
22C3 Moorpark USA
7B4 Moose R Can

5H4 Moose Jaw Can
5H4 Moosomin Can
7B4 Moosonee Can
16D2 Moosup USA
101C2 Mopeia Mozam
97B3 Mopti Mali
30B2 Moquegua Peru
39G6 Mora Sweden
31D3 Morada Brazil
84D3 Morādābād India
35B1 Morada Nova de Minas *L* Brazil
101D2 Morafenobe Madag
101D2 Moramanga Madag
27J2 Morant Bay Jamaica
27J2 Morant Pt Jamaica
87B3 Moratuwa Sri Lanka
59B3 Morava *R* Austria/Czech
54B2 Morava *R* Yugos
90C2 Moraveh Tappeh Iran
44D2 Moray Firth *Estuary* Scot
47C1 Morbegno Italy
85C4 Morbi India
93D2 Mor Dağ *Mt* Turk
5J5 Morden Can
61F3 Mordovskaya ASSR Republic, USSR
42C2 Morecambe Eng
42C2 Morecambe B Eng
107D3 Moree Aust
14B3 Morehead USA
47C1 Môrel Switz
24B3 Morelia Mexico
23B2 Morelos State, Mexico
85D3 Morena India
5E4 Moresby I Can
109D1 Moreton I Aust
46B2 Moreuil France
47B1 Morez France
19B4 Morgan City USA
22B2 Morgan Hill USA
14C3 Morgantown USA
101G1 Morgenzon S Africa
47B1 Morges Switz
46D2 Morhange France
74E2 Mori Japan
27K1 Moriatio Tobago
13B2 Morice L Can
13E2 Morinville Can
74E3 Morioka Japan
109D2 Morisset Aust
63D1 Morokoa *R* USSR
48B2 Morlaix France
27Q2 Morne Diablotin *Mt* Dominica
106C2 Mornington I Aust
85B3 Moro Pak
96B2 Morocco Kingdom, Africa
79B4 Moro G Phil
99D3 Morogoro Tanz
23A1 Moroleon Mexico
101D3 Morombe Madag
26B2 Morón Cuba
101D3 Morondava Madag
50A2 Moron de la Frontera Spain
101D2 Moroni Comoros
71D3 Morotai I Indon
99D2 Moroto Uganda
61F4 Morozovsk USSR
42D2 Morpeth Eng
19B2 Morrilton USA
35B1 Morrinhos Brazil
110C1 Morrinsville NZ
16B2 Morristown New Jersey, USA
15C2 Morristown New York, USA
16B2 Morrisville Pennsylvania, USA
21A2 Morro Bay USA
23A2 Morro de Papanoa Mexico
23A2 Morro de Petatlán Mexico

101C2 Morrumbala Mozam
101C3 Morrumbene Mozam
61F3 Morshansk USSR
47C2 Mortara Italy
34C2 Morteros Arg
33G6 Mortes *R* Mato Grosso, Brazil
35C2 Mortes *R* Minas Gerais, Brazil
108B3 Mortlake Aust
27L1 Moruga Trinidad
109D3 Moruya Aust
45C1 Morven Eng
44B3 Morvern *Pen* Scot
109C3 Morwell Aust
76B3 Moscos Is Burma
Moscow = Moskva
20C1 Moscow Idaho, USA
56B2 Mosel *R* Germany
46D2 Moselle Department, France
46D2 Moselle *R* France
20C1 Moses Lake USA
111B3 Mosgiel NZ
99D3 Moshi Tanz
38G5 Mosjøen Nor
63G2 Moskal'vo USSR
64E4 Moskva USSR
35C1 Mosquito *R* Brazil
39G7 Moss Nor
98B3 Mossaka Congo
100B4 Mossel Bay S Africa
98B3 Mossendjo Congo
108B2 Mossgiel Aust
31D3 Mossoró Brazil
57C2 Most Czech
96C1 Mostaganem Alg
54A2 Mostar Yugos
58C2 Mosty USSR
93D2 Mosul Iraq
39H7 Motala Sweden
42C2 Motherwell Scot
86A1 Motihāri India
51B2 Motilla del Palancar Spain
50B2 Motril Spain
111B2 Motueka NZ
111B2 Motueka *R* NZ
47B1 Moudon Switz
98B3 Mouila Gabon
108B2 Moulamein Aust
4G2 Mould Bay Can
47C2 Moulins France
76B2 Moulmein Burma
96B1 Moulouya *R* Mor
17B1 Moultrie USA
17C1 Moultrie,L USA
18C2 Mound City Illinois, USA
18A1 Mound City Missouri, USA
98B2 Moundou Chad
14B3 Moundsville USA
12J1 Mountain *R* Can
17A1 Mountain Brook USA
18B2 Mountain Grove USA
18B2 Mountain Home Arkansas, USA
22A2 Mountain View USA
12B2 Mountain Village USA
16A3 Mount Airy Maryland, USA
16A2 Mount Carmel USA
108A1 Mount Dutton Aust
108A2 Mount Eba Aust
108B3 Mount Gambier Aust
16B3 Mount Holly USA
16A2 Mount Holly Springs USA
108A2 Mount Hope Aust
106C3 Mount Isa Aust
108A2 Mount Lofty Range *Mts* Aust
12D2 Mount McKinley Nat Pk USA
106A3 Mount Magnet Aust
108B2 Mount Manara Aust
107E3 Mount Morgan Aust

19B3 Mount Pleasant Texas, USA
20B1 Mount Rainier Nat Pk USA
43B4 Mounts B Eng
20D1 Mount Shasta USA
11B3 Mount Vernon Illinois, USA
19A3 Mount Vernon Kentucky, USA
20B1 Mount Vernon Washington, USA
45C1 Mourne Mts N Ire
98B1 Moussoro Chad
86B2 Mouths of the Ganga India/Bang
85B4 Mouths of the Indus Pak
77D4 Mouths of the Mekong Viet
97C4 Mouths of the Niger Nig
47B1 Moutier Switz
47B2 Moûtiers France
96C2 Mouydir *Mts* Alg
98B3 Mouyondzi Congo
46C2 Mouzon France
59B3 M'óvár Hung
23A1 Moyahua Mexico
99D2 Moyale Kenya
97A4 Moyamba Sierra Leone
96B1 Moyen Atlas *Mts* Mor
100B4 Moyeni Lesotho
99D2 Moyo Uganda
32B5 Moyobamba Peru
84D1 Moyu China
101C3 Mozambique Republic, Africa
101C3 Mozambique Chan Mozam/Madag
61H2 Mozhga USSR
60C3 Mozyr USSR
99D3 Mpanda Tanz
101C2 Mpika Zambia
100B2 Mposhi Zambia
99D3 Mpulungu Zambia
99D3 Mpwapwa Tanz
96C1 M'Sila Alg
60E3 Mtsensk USSR
101H1 Mtubatuba S Africa
101D2 Mtwara Tanz
76C2 Muang Chainat Thai
76C2 Muang Chiang Rai Thai
76C2 Muang Kalasin Thai
76C2 Muang Khon Kaen Thai
76B2 Muang Lampang Thai
76B2 Muang Lamphun Thai
76C2 Muang Loei Thai
76C2 Muang Lom Sak Thai
76C2 Muang Nakhon Phanom Thai
76B2 Muang Nakhon Sawan Thai
76C2 Muang Nan Thai
76C2 Muang Phayao Thai
76C2 Muang Phetchabun Thai
76C2 Muang Phichit Thai
76C2 Muang Phitsanulok Thai
76C2 Muang Phrae Thai
76C2 Muang Roi Et Thai
76C2 Muang Sakon Nakhon Thai
76C2 Muang Samut Prakan Thai
76C2 Muang Uthai Thani Thai
76C2 Muang Yasothon Thai
77C5 Muar Malay
78C2 Muara Brunei
70B4 Muara Indon
78A3 Muaralakitan Indon
78A3 Muaratebo Indon

78C3 Muaratewah Indon
78A3 Muaremim Indon
76A2 Muaungmaya Burma
99D2 Mubende Uganda
100C2 Muchinga *Mts* Zambia
44A3 Muck I Scot
109C1 Muckadilla Aust
35D1 Mucuri Brazil
35C1 Mucuri *R* Brazil
100B2 Mucusso Angola
69E2 Mudanjiang China
109C2 Mudgee Aust
76E2 Mudon Burma
101C2 Mueda Mozam
107F3 Mueo Nouvelle Calédonie
100B2 Mufulira Zambia
73C4 Mufu Shan *Hills* China
Mugadishu=Muqdisho
61J4 Mugadzhary *Mts* USSR
93C4 Mughayra S Arabia
92A2 Muğla Turk
65G5 Mugodzhary *Mts* USSR
86A1 Mugu Nepal
72A3 Muguaping China
93D3 Muhaywir Iraq
57C3 Mühldorf Germany
57C2 Mühlhausen Germany
38K6 Muhos Fin
77C4 Mui Bai Bung *C* Camb
45C2 Muine Bheag Irish Rep
100B2 Mujimbeji Zambia
59C3 Mukachevo USSR
78C2 Mukah Malay
69G4 Muko-jima I Japan
86A1 Muktinath Nepal
84B2 Mukur Afghan
18B2 Mulberry USA
12C2 Mulchatna *R* USA
34A3 Mulchén Chile
56C2 Mulde *R* Germany
71F5 Mulgrave I Aust
50B2 Mulhacén *Mt* Spain
46D1 Mülheim Germany
46D2 Mulhouse France
73A4 Muli China
44B3 Mull I Scot
87C3 Mullaitivu Sri Lanka
109C2 Mullaley Aust
106A3 Mullewa Aust
16B3 Mullica *R* USA
45C2 Mullingar Irish Rep
42B2 Mull of Kintyre *Pt* Scot
44B3 Mull of Oa *C* Scot
109D1 Mullumbimby Aust
100B2 Mulobezi Zambia
84C2 Multan Pak
100B2 Mumbwa Zambia
61G4 Mumra USSR
71D4 Muna I Indon
57C3 München Germany
14A2 Muncie USA
15C2 Muncy USA
56B2 Münden Germany
109D1 Mundubbera Aust
109C1 Mungallala Aust
109C1 Mungallala *R* Aust
99C2 Mungbere Zaire
86A2 Mungeli India
86B1 Munger India
109C1 Mungindi Aust
Munich = München
14A1 Munising USA
29B6 Muñoz Gomero,Pen Chile
45B2 Münster Region, Irish Rep
47C1 Münster Switz
56B2 Münster Germany
54B1 Muntii Apuseni *Mts* Rom
54B1 Muntii Călimanilor *Mts* Rom

54B1 Muntii Carpaţii
Meridionali *Mts*
Rom
54B1 Muntii Rodnei *Mts*
Rom
54B1 Muntii Zarandului *Mts*
Rom
93C2 Munzur Silsilesi *Mts*
Turk
64D3 Muomio Fin
76C1 Muong Khoua Laos
76D3 Muong Man Viet
76D2 Muong Nong Laos
76C1 Muong Ou Neua Laos
76C1 Muong Sai Laos
76C2 Muong Sen Viet
76C1 Muong Sing Laos
76C1 Muong Son Laos
38J5 Muonio Fin
38J5 Muonio *R*
Sweden/Fin
99E2 Muqdisho Somalia
52B1 Mur *R* Austria
74D3 Murakami Japan
29B5 Murallón *Mt* Arg/
Chile
61G2 Murashi USSR
93D2 Murat *R* Turk
53A3 Muravera Sardegna
75C1 Murayama Japan
90B3 Murcheh Khvort Iran
111B2 Murchison NZ
106A3 Murchison *R* Aust
51B2 Murcia Region, Spain
51B2 Murcia Spain
54B1 Mures *R* Rom
46E2 Murg *R* Germany
65H6 Murgab *R* USSR
84B2 Murgha Kibzai Pak
109D1 Murgon Aust
86B2 Muri India
35C2 Muriaé Brazil
98C3 Muriege Angola
64E3 Murmansk USSR
61F2 Murom USSR
74E2 Muroran Japan
50A1 Muros Spain
74C4 Muroto Japan
75A2 Muroto-zaki *C* Japan
20C2 Murphy Idaho, USA
22B1 Murphys USA
18C2 Murray Kentucky,
USA
108B2 Murray *R* Aust
13C2 Murray *R* Can
108A3 Murray Bridge Aust
71F4 Murray,L PNG
17B1 Murray,L USA
105J2 Murray Seacarp
Pacific O
108B2 Murrumbidgee *R*
Aust
109C2 Murrumburrah Aust
109D2 Murrurundi Aust
47B1 Murten Switz
108B3 Murtoa Aust
110C1 Murupara NZ
86A2 Murwâra India
109D1 Murwillimbah Aust
93D2 Muş Turk
54B2 Musala *Mt* Bulg
74B2 Musan N Korea
91C4 Musandam *Pen*
Oman
Muscat = Masqat
91C5 Muscat Region, Oman
106C3 Musgrave Range *Mts*
Aust
98B3 Mushie Zaïre
14A2 Muskegon USA
14A2 Muskegon *R* USA
14A2 Muskogee USA
15C2 Muskoka,L Can
54C3 Musmar Sudan
99D3 Musoma Tanz
8C2 Musselshell *R* USA
100A3 Mussende Angola
48C2 Mussidan France

55C2 Mustafa-Kemalpasa
Turk
86A1 Mustang Nepal
109D2 Muswellibrook Aust
95B2 Mut Egypt
101C2 Mutarara Mozam
101C2 Mutare Zim
101C2 Mutoko Zim
101D2 Mutsamudu Comoros
100B2 Mutshatsha Zaïre
74E2 Mutsu Japan
74E2 Mutsu-wan *B* Japan
45B2 Mutton *I* Irish Rep
72B2 Mu Us Shamo *Desert*
China
98B3 Muxima Angola
63D2 Muya USSR
38L6 Muyezerskiy USSR
99D3 Muyinga Burundi
98C3 Muyumba Zaïre
82A1 Muyun Kum *Desert*
USSR
84C2 Muzaffarâbad Pak
84C2 Muzaffargarh Pak
84D3 Muzaffarnagar India
86B1 Muzaffarpur India
64H3 Muzhi USSR
82C2 Muzaq *Mt* China
82B2 Muztagata *Mt* China
100C2 Mvuma Zim
99D3 Mwanza Tanz
98C3 Mwanza Zaïre
98C3 Mweka Zaïre
98C3 Mwene Ditu Zaïre
100C3 Mwenezi Zim
99C3 Mwenga Zaïre
99C3 Mweru *L* Zambia
100B2 Mwinilunga Zambia
83D4 Myanaung Burma
59B3 M'yarővár Hung
86D2 Myingyan Burma
76B1 Myingyao Burma
76B3 Myinmoletkat *Mt*
Burma
82D3 Myitkyina Burma
76B3 Myitta Burma
86C2 Mymensingh Bang
69F3 Myojin *I* Japan
39F6 Myrdal Nor
38B2 Myrdalsjökur *Mts*
Iceland
17C1 Myrtle Beach USA
20B2 Myrtle Creek USA
39G7 Mysen Nor
56C2 Nysiloborz Pol
64F3 Mys Kanin Nos *C*
USSR
59B3 Myślenice Pol
69H1 Mys Lopatka *C* USSR
87B2 Mysore India
60D5 Mys Sarych *C* USSR
16D2 Mystic USA
61H5 Mys Tyub-Karagan *Pt*
USSR
63G2 Mys Yelizavety *C*
USSR
64H2 Mys Zhelaniya *C*
USSR
77D3 My Tho Viet
20B2 Mytle Point USA
101C2 Mzimba Malawi
101C2 Mzuzú Malawi

N

21C4 Naalehu Hawaiian Is
39J6 Naantali Fin
45C2 Naas Irish Rep
75B2 Nabari Japan
61H2 Naberezhnyye Chelny
USSR
12F2 Nabesna *R* USA
96D1 Nabeul Tunisia
94B2 Nablus Israel
101D2 Nacala Mozam
20B1 Naches USA
101C2 Nachingwea Tanz

19B3 Nacogdoches USA
76A3 Nacondam *I* Indian O
24B1 Nacozari Mexico
85C4 Nadiãd India
50B2 Nador Mor
90B3 Nadushan Iran
59C3 Nadvornaya USSR
56C1 Naestved Den
95B2 Nafoora Libya
75A2 Nagahama Japan
82D3 Naga Hills Burma
75B1 Nagai Japan
86C1 Nãgãland State, India
74D3 Nagano Japan
74D3 Nagaoka Japan
87B2 Nãgappattinam India
85C4 Nagar Parkar Pak
74B4 Nagasaki Japan
75B2 Nagashima Japan
75A2 Nagato Japan
85C3 Nagaur India
87B3 Nãgercoil India
85B3 Nagha Kalat Pak
84D3 Nagina India
74D3 Nagoya Japan
85D4 Nãgpur India
82D2 Nagqu China
59B3 Nagykanizsa Hung
59B3 Nagykörös Hung
69E4 Naha Japan
8A2 Nahaimo USA
84D2 Nãhan India
4F3 Nahanni Butte Can
94B2 Nahariya Israel
90A3 Nahãvand Iran
46D2 Nahe *R* Germany
72E1 Nahpu China
72E1 Naimen Qi China
7D4 Nain Can
90B3 Na'in Iran
84D3 Naini Tal India
44C3 Nairn Scot
99D3 Nairobi Kenya
90B3 Najafabad Iran
74C2 Najin N Korea
75A2 Nakama Japan
74D3 Nakaminato Japan
75A2 Nakamura Japan
75B1 Nakano Japan
75A1 Nakano-shima *I*
Japan
74C4 Nakatsu Japan
75B1 Nakatsu-gawa Japan
95C3 Nakfa Eth
92C2 Nakhichevan USSR
92B4 Nakhl Egypt
74C2 Nakhodka USSR
76C3 Nakhon Pathom Thai
76C3 Nakhon Ratchasima
Thai
77C4 Nakhon Si Thammarat
Thai
12H3 Nakina Can
7B4 Nakina Ontario, Can
12C3 Naknek USA
12C3 Naknek L USA
4C4 Nakrek USA
39G8 Nakskov Den
99D3 Nakuru Kenya
13D2 Nakusp Can
61F5 Nal'chik USSR
87B1 Nalgonda India
87B1 Nallamala Range *Mts*
India
95A1 Nãlūt Libya
101H1 Namaacha Mozam
65G6 Namak *L* Iran
90C3 Namakzar-e Shadad
Salt Flat Iran
65J5 Namangan USSR
101C2 Namapa Mozam
100A4 Namaqualand Region,
S Africa
109D1 Nambour Aust
109D2 Nambucca Heads Aust
77D4 Nam Can Viet
82D2 Nam Co *L* China
76D1 Nam Dinh Viet

101C2 Nametil Mozam
74H4 Namhae-do *I* S Korea
100A2 Namib Desert
Namibia
100A2 Namibe Angola
100A3 Namibia Dependency,
Africa
82D3 Namjagbarwa Feng
Mt China
71D4 Namlea Indon
109C2 Namoi *R* Aust
13D1 Nampa Can
20C2 Nampa USA
97B3 Nampala Mali
76C2 Nam Phong Thai
74B3 Namp'o N Korea
101C2 Nampula Mozam
38G6 Namsos Nor
76B1 Namton Burma
86D2 Namtu Burma
13B2 Namu Can
101C2 Namuno Mozam
46C1 Namur Belg
100A2 Namutoni Namibia
74B3 Namwŏn S Korea
13C3 Nanaimo Can
74B2 Nanam N Korea
109D1 Nanango Aust
74D3 Nanao Japan
75B1 Nanatsu-jima *I* Japan
73B3 Nanbu China
73D4 Nanchang China
73B3 Nanchong China
72D3 Nancy France
87B1 Nandi India
109D2 Nandewar Range *Mts*
Aust
85C4 Nandurbar India
87B1 Nandyãl India
98B2 Nanga Eboko Cam
84C1 Nanga Parbat *Mt* Pak
78C3 Nangapinoh Indon
78C3 Nangatayap Indon
74B2 Nangnim Sanmaek
Mts N Korea
86C1 Nang Xian China
67F3 Nangzhou China
87B2 Nanjangüd India
72D3 Nanjing China
Nanking = Nanjing
75A2 Nankoku Japan
73C4 Nan Ling Region,
China
76D1 Nanliu China
73B5 Nanning China
6F3 Nanortalik Greenland
73A5 Nanpan Jiang *R*
China
86A1 Nänpāra India
73D4 Nanping China
99D3 Nansio Tanz
48B2 Nantes France
13E2 Nanton Can
72E3 Nantong China
10C2 Nantucket *I* USA
35C1 Nanuque Brazil
72C3 Nanyang China
72D2 Nanyang Hu *L* China
99D2 Nanyuki Kenya
74D3 Naoetsu Japan
85B4 Naokot Pak
22A1 Napa USA
12B2 Napaiskak USA
15C2 Napanee Can
65K4 Napas USSR
6E3 Napassoq Greenland
76D2 Nape Laos
110C1 Napier NZ
Naples = Napoli
17B2 Naples Florida, USA
19B3 Naples Texas, USA
73B5 Napo China
32C4 Napo *R* Peru/Ecuador
53B2 Napoli Italy
90A2 Naqadeh Iran
92C3 Naqb Ishtar Jordan
75B2 Nara Japan

97B3 Nara Mali
107H4 Naracoorte Aust
23B1 Naranjos Mexico
87C1 Narasaräopet India
77C4 Narathiwat Thai
86C2 Narayanganj Bang
87B1 Näräyenpet India
49C3 Narbonne France
84D2 Narendranagar India
6C2 Nares Str Can
58C2 Narew R Pol
75C1 Narita Japan
85C4 Narmada R India
84D3 Narmal India
64H3 Narodnaya Mt USSR
60E2 Naro Fominsk USSR
99D3 Narok Kenya
84C2 Narowal Pak
107D4 Narrabri Aust
109C1 Narran R L Aust
109C1 Narran R Aust
109C2 Narranderra Aust
106A4 Narrogin Aust
109C2 Narromine Aust
85D4 Narsimhapur India
87C1 Narsipatnam India
6F3 Narssalik Greenland
6F3 Narssaq Greenland
6F3 Narssarssuaq Greenland
75C1 Narugo Japan
75A2 Naruto Japan
60C2 Narva USSR
38H5 Narvik Nor
84D3 Narwäna India
64G3 Nar'yan Mar USSR
108R1 Narylico Aust
65J5 Naryn USSR
97C4 Nasarawa Nig
103D5 Nasca Ridge Pacific O
16D1 Nashua USA
19B3 Nashville Arkansas, USA
11B3 Nashville Tennessee, USA
54A1 Našice Yugos
85D4 Nāsik India
99D2 Nasir Sudan
13B1 Nass R Can
26B1 Nassau The Bahamas
16C1 Nassau USA
95C2 Nasser,L Egypt
39G7 Nässjö Sweden
7C4 Nastapoka Is Can
100B3 Nata Botswana
31D3 Natal Brazil
70A3 Natal Indon
101H1 Natal Province, S Africa
90B3 Natanz Iran
7D4 Natashquan Can
7D4 Natashquan R Can
19B3 Natchez USA
19B3 Natchitoches USA
108C3 Nathalia Aust
6H2 Nathorsts Land Region Greenland
13C1 Nation R Can
21B3 National City USA
75C1 Natori Japan
58D2 Natovl'a USSR
99D3 Natron L Tanz
106A4 Naturaliste,C Aust
47D1 Nauders Austria
56C2 Nauen Germany
16C2 Naugatuck USA
57C2 Naumburg Germany
94B3 Naur Jordan
105G4 Nauru I Pacific O
63C2 Naushki USSR
23B1 Nautla Mexico
9C3 Navajo Res USA
50A2 Navalmoral de la Mata Spain
29C7 Navarino I Chile
51B1 Navarra Province, Spain
34D3 Navarro Arg

19A3 Navasota USA
19A3 Navasota R USA
50A1 Navia R Spain
34A2 Navidad Chile
85C4 Navlakhi India
60D3 Navlya USSR
24B2 Navojoa Mexico
55B3 Návpaktos Greece
55B3 Návplion Greece
85C4 Navsäri India
94C2 Nawá Syria
86B2 Nawäda India
84D2 Nawah Afghan
85B3 Nawrabshah Pak
73B4 Naxi China
55C3 Náxos I Greece
23A1 Nayar Mexico
90C3 Nay Band Iran
91B4 Näy Band Iran
74E2 Nayoro Japan
54D1 Nazareth Israel
48B2 Nazay France
32C6 Nazca Peru
92A2 Nazilli Turk
63B2 Nazimovo USSR
13C2 Nazko R Can
65J5 Nazwa Oman
94B3 Nazyvayevsk USSR
98B3 Ndalatando Angola
98C2 Ndélé CAR
98B3 Ndendé Gabon
98B1 Ndjamena Chad
98B3 Ndjolé Gabon
100B2 Ndola Zambia
109C1 Neabul Aust
108A1 Neales R Aust
55B3 Neápolis Greece
43C4 Neath Wales
109C1 Nebine R Aust
65K6 Nebit Dag USSR
8C2 Nebraska State, USA
18A1 Nebraska City USA
13C2 Nechako R Can
19A3 Neches R USA
34D3 Necochea Arg
86C1 Nêdong China
9B3 Needles USA
14A2 Neepawa Can
46C1 Neerpelt Belg
63C2 Neftelensk USSR
99D2 Negelli Eth
94B3 Negev Desert Israel
60B4 Negola Mt Rom
87B3 Negombo Sri Lanka
76A2 Negrais,C Burma
32A4 Negritos Peru
33E4 Negro R Amazonas, Brazil
29C4 Negro R Arg
34D2 Negro R Urug
79B4 Negros I Phil
54C2 Negru Voda Rom
90D3 Nehbandan Iran
73B4 Neijiang China
72B1 Nei Monggol Autonomous Region, China
32B3 Neiva Colombia
99D2 Nejo Eth
60D2 Nelidovo USSR
87B2 Nel'ma USSR
13D3 Nelson Can
111B2 Nelson NZ
7A4 Nelson R Can
108B3 Nelson,C Aust
12B2 Nelson I USA
97B3 Néma Maur
72A1 Nemagt Uul Mt Mongolia
58C1 Neman R USSR
54E1 Nemira Mt Rom
74F2 Nemuro Japan
63E3 Nen R China
41B3 Nenagh Irish Rep
12E2 Nenana USA
12E2 Nenana R USA

43D3 Nene R Eng
69E2 Nenjiang China
18A2 Neodesha USA
18B2 Neosho USA
63C2 Nepa USSR
82C3 Nepal Kingdom, Asia
86A1 Neparganj Nepal
45B1 Nephin Mt Irish Rep
94B3 Neqarot R Israel
34A3 Nequén State, Arg
68D1 Nerchinsk USSR
52C2 Neretva R Yugos
71F2 Nero Deep Pacific O
38C1 Neskaupstaður Iceland
46B2 Nesle France
7E5 Nesleyville Can
55B2 Néstos R Greece
94B2 Netanya Israel
16B2 Netcong USA
56B2 Netherlands Kingdom, Europe
3M7 Netherlands Antilles Is Caribbean S
86C2 Netrakona Bang
6C3 Nettilling L Can
56C2 Neubrandenburg Germany
47B1 Neuchâtel Switz
46C2 Neufchâteau Belg
48C2 Neufchâtel France
46A2 Neufchâtel-en-Bray France
56B2 Neumünster Germany
52C1 Neunkirchen Austria
57B2 Neunkirchen Germany
34B3 Neuquén Arg
29B4 Neuquén State, Arg
34B3 Neuquén R Arg
56B2 Neuruppin Germany
46D1 Neuss Germany
46E2 Neustadt Germany
57B3 Neustadt Germany
56C2 Neustrelitz Germany
46D1 Neuwied Germany
8B3 Nevada State, USA
18B2 Nevada USA
34A3 Nevada de Chillán Mts Arg/Chile
23A2 Nevada de Collima Mexico
23B2 Nevada de Toluca Mt Mexico
94B3 Nevatim Israel
60C2 Nevel' USSR
49C2 Nevers France
109C2 Nevertire Aust
27E3 Nevis I Caribbean S
58D2 Nevis R USSR
92B2 Nevşehir Turk
61K2 Nev'yansk USSR
101C2 Newala Tanz
14A3 New Albany Indiana, USA
19C3 New Albany Mississippi, USA
33F2 New Amsterdam Guyana
109C1 New Angledool Aust
15C3 Newark Delaware, USA
10C2 Newark New Jersey, USA
14B2 Newark Ohio, USA
43D3 Newark-upon-Trent Eng
15D2 New Bedford USA
13B2 New Bella Bella Can
20B1 Newberg USA
11C3 New Bern USA
26B2 New Bight The Bahamas
14B3 New Boston USA
9D4 New Braunfels USA
16C2 New Britain USA
7D5 New Brunswick Province, Can

16B2 New Brunswick USA
9D3 Newburgh USA
43D4 Newbury Eng
16D1 Newburyport USA
16C2 New Canaan USA
109D2 Newcastle Aust
14A3 New Castle Indiana, USA
42B2 Newcastle N Ire
14B2 New Castle Pennsylvania, USA
101G1 Newcastle S Africa
8C2 Newcastle Wyoming, USA
42D2 Newcastle upon Tyne Eng
106C2 Newcastle Waters Aust
45B2 Newcastle West Irish Rep
84D3 New Delhi India
109D2 New England Range Mts Aust
12B3 Newenham,C USA
43D4 New Forest,The Eng
7D4 Newfoundland Can
7E5 Newfoundland I Can
102F2 Newfoundland Basin Atlantic O
18B2 New Franklin USA
42B2 New Galloway Scot
107E1 New Georgia I Solomon Is
7D5 New Glasgow Can
71F4 New Guinea SE Asia
12D3 Newhalen USA
22C3 Newhall USA
10C2 New Hampshire State, USA
101H1 New Hanover S Africa
43E4 Newhaven Eng
15D2 New Haven USA
13B1 New Hazelton Can
19B3 New Iberia USA
10C2 New Jersey State, USA
7C5 New Liskeard Can
16C2 New London USA
106A3 Newman Aust
22B2 Newman USA
43E3 Newmarket Eng
45B2 Newmarket Irish Rep
15C3 New Market USA
9C3 New Mexico State, USA
16C2 New Milford Connecticut, USA
17B1 Newnan USA
109C4 New Norfolk Aust
11A3 New Orleans USA
16B2 New Paltz USA
14B2 New Philadelphia USA
110B1 New Plymouth NZ
18B2 Newport Arkansas, USA
43D4 Newport Eng
14B3 Newport Kentucky, USA
20B2 Newport Oregon, USA
16A2 Newport Pennsylvania, USA
15D2 Newport Rhode Island, USA
15D2 Newport Vermont, USA
43C4 Newport Wales
20C1 Newport Washington, USA
22D4 Newport Beach USA
11C3 Newport News USA
26B1 New Providence I Caribbean S
43B4 Newquay Eng
6C3 New Quebec Crater Can

45C2 New Ross Irish Rep
45C1 Newry N Ire
New Siberian Is =
Novosibirskye
Ostrova
17B2 New Smyrna Beach
USA
107D4 New South Wales
State, Aust
12C3 New Stuyahok USA
18A2 Newton Kansas, USA
16D1 Newton
Massachusetts, USA
19C3 Newton Mississippi,
USA
16B2 Newton New York,
USA
43C4 Newton Abbot Eng
45C1 Newton Stewart N Ire
42B2 Newton Stewart Scot
43C3 Newtown USA
42B2 Newtownards N Ire
16A2 Newville USA
5F5 New Westminster
Can
10C2 New York State, USA
10C2 New York City USA
110 New Zealand
Dominion, SW
Pacific O
105G6 New Zealand Plat
Pacific O
61F2 Neya USSR
91B4 Neyriz Iran
90C2 Neyshabur Iran
98B3 Nezeto Angola
60D3 Nezhin USSR
98B3 Ngabé Congo
100B3 Ngami L Botswana
110C1 Ngaruawahia NZ
110C1 Ngaruroro R NZ
110C1 Ngarunhoe,Mt NZ
98B3 Ngo Congo
76D2 Ngoc Linh Mt Viet
98B2 Ngoko R Cam
68B3 Ngoring Hu L China
99D3 Ngorongoro Crater
Tanz
98B3 N'Gounié R Gabon
98B1 Nguigmi Niger
71E3 Ngulu I Pacific O
97D3 Nguru Nig
76D3 Nha Trang Viet
108B3 Nhill Aust
101H1 Nhlangano Swaziland
76D2 Nhommarath Laos
106C2 Nhulunbuy Aust
97B3 Niafounké Mali
14A1 Niagara USA
15C2 Niagara Falls Can
15C2 Niagara Falls USA
70C3 Niah Malay
97B4 Niakaramandougou
Ivory Coast
97C3 Niamey Niger
99C2 Niangara Zaire
98C2 Nia Nia Zaire
70A3 Nias I Indon
25D3 Nicaragua Republic,
Cent America
53C3 Nicastro Italy
49D3 Nice France
26B1 Nicholl's Town
The Bahamas
83D5 Nicobar Is Indian O
92B2 Nicosia Cyprus
25D3 Nicoya,Pen de
Costa Rica
58C2 Nidzica Pol
46D2 Niederbronn France
56B2 Niedersachsen State,
Germany
99C3 Niemba Zaire
56B2 Nienburg Germany
46D1 Niers R Germany
97B4 Niete,Mt Lib
33F2 Nieuw Amsterdam
Surinam

33F2 Nieuw Nickerie
Surinam
46B1 Nieuwpoort Belg
92B2 Niğde Turk
97C3 Niger Republic, Africa
97A4 Niger R Nig
97C4 Nigeria Federal
Republic, Africa
55B2 Nigrita Greece
75C1 Nihommatsu Japan
74D3 Niigata Japan
74C4 Nihama Japan
75B2 Nii-jima I Japan
74C3 Niimi Japan
74D3 Niitsu Japan
94B3 Nijil Jordan
56B2 Nijmegen Neth
64E3 Nikel' USSR
97C3 Nikki Benin
74D3 Nikko Japan
60D4 Nikolayev USSR
61G4 Nikolayevsk USSR
63G2 Nikolayevsk-na-Amure
USSR
61G2 Nikol'sk RSFSR, USSR
61G3 Nikol'sk USSR
60D4 Nikopol USSR
92C1 Niksar Turk
91D4 Nikshahr Iran
54A2 Nikšić Yugos
71D4 Nila I Indon
80B3 Nile R N E Africa
14A2 Niles USA
87B2 Nilgiri Hills India
85C4 Nimach India
49C3 Nimes France
109C3 Nimmitabel Aust
99D2 Nimule Sudan
83B5 Nine Degree Chan
Indian O
104C4 Ninety-East Ridge
Indian O
109C3 Ninety Mile Beach
Aust
73D4 Ningde China
73D4 Ningdu China
68B3 Ningjing Shan Mts
China
76D1 Ningming China
73A4 Ningnan China
72B2 Ningxia Province,
China
72B2 Ning Xian China
73B5 Ninh Binh Vietnam
107D1 Ninigo Is PNG
12D2 Ninilchik USA
8D2 Niobrara R USA
98B3 Nioki Zaire
97B3 Nioro du Sahel Mali
48B2 Niort France
5H4 Nipawin Can
7B5 Nipigon Can
7B5 Nipigon,L Can
7B5 Nipissing R Can
14B1 Nipissing,L Can
87B1 Nirmal India
86B1 Nirmāli India
54B2 Niš Yugos
81C4 Niṣāb Yemen
69F4 Nishino-shima I
Japan
75A1 Nishino-shima I
Japan
75A2 Nishiwaki Japan
12C2 Nisling R Can
12H2 Nisutlin R Can
7C4 Nitchequon Can
31C6 Niterói Brazil
42C2 Nith R Scot
59B3 Nitra Czech
14B3 Nitro USA
78C2 Niut Mt Malay
46C1 Nivelles Belg
49C2 Nivernais Region,
France
38L5 Nivskiy USSR
87B1 Nizāmābād India
94B3 Nizana Hist Site Israel

61J2 Nizhniye Sergi USSR
61F3 Nizhniy Lomov USSR
65G4 Nizhniy Tagil USSR
63B1 Nizhnyaya Tunguska
R USSR
93C2 Nizip Turk
60D4 Nizmennost USSR
92A2 Njombe Tanz
98B2 Nkambé Cam
101C2 Nkhata Bay Malawi
98B2 Nkongsamba Cam
97C3 N'Konni Niger
86C2 Noakhali Bang
47D1 Noce R Italy
23A1 Nochistlán Mexico
23B2 Nochistlán Mexico
19A3 Nocona USA
24A1 Nogales Sonora,
Mexico
9B3 Nogales USA
23D2 Nogales Veracruz,
Mexico
47D2 Nogara Italy
75A2 Nogata Japan
60E2 Noginsk USSR
34D2 Nogoyá Arg
34D2 Nogoyá R Arg
84C3 Nohar India
75B2 Nojima-zaki C Japan
10A5 Nok Kundi Pak
61G2 Nolinsk USSR
16D2 Nomans Land I USA
12A2 Nome USA
46D2 Nomeny France
72B1 Nomgon Mongolia
5H3 Nonacho L Can
76D2 Nong Khai Thai
101H1 Nongoma S Africa
12B1 Noorvik USA
13B3 Nootka Sd Can
98B3 Noqui Angola
7C5 Noranda Can
46B1 Nord Department,
France
64D2 Nordaustlandet I
Barents S
32C3 Nordegg Can
38F6 Nordfjord Inlet Nor
39F8 Nordfriesische Is
Germany
56C2 Nordhausen Germany
56B2 Nordrhein Westfalen
State, Germany
38J4 Nordkapp C Nor
6E3 Nordre Greenland
38H5 Nord Stronfjället Mt
Sweden
1B9 Nordvik USSR
45C2 Nore R Irish Rep
43E3 Norfolk County, Eng
8D2 Norfolk Nebraska,
USA
11C3 Norfolk Virginia, USA
107F3 Norfolk I Aust
18B2 Norfolk L USA
105G5 Norfolk Ridge
Pacific O
1C10 Noril'sk USSR
18C1 Normal USA
19A2 Norman USA
48B2 Normandie Region,
France
107D2 Normanton Aust
12J1 Norman Wells Can
4B3 Norne USA
15C2 Norristown USA
39H7 Norrköping Sweden
39H6 Norrsundet Sweden
39H7 Norrtälje Sweden
108B3 Norseman Aust
63F2 Norsk USSR
102J2 North S N W Europe
42D2 Northallerton Eng
106A4 Northam Aust

102E3 North American Basin
Atlantic O
106A3 Northampton Aust
43D3 Northampton County,
Eng
43D3 Northampton Eng
15D2 Northampton USA
4G3 North Arm B Can
17B1 North Augusta USA
6D4 North Aulatsivik I Can
13F2 North Battleford Can
7C5 North Bay Can
20B2 North Bend USA
44C3 North Berwick Scot
7D5 North,C Can
7G4 North C NZ
11B3 North Carolina State,
USA
20B1 North Cascade Nat Pk
USA
14B1 North Chan Can
42B2 North Chan Ire/Scot
8C2 North Dakota State,
USA
43E4 North Downs USA
14C2 North East USA
102H2 North East Atlantic
Basin Atlantic O
4B3 Northeast C USA
40B3 Northern Ireland UK
27L1 Northern Range Mts
Trinidad
106C2 Northern Territory
Aust
44C3 North Esk R Scot
16C1 Northfield
Massachusetts, USA
12D2 North Fork B USA
110B1 North I NZ
74B3 North Korea Republic,
S E Asia
North Land =
Severnaya Zemiya
19B3 North Little Rock USA
1B4 North Magnetic Pole
Can
17B2 North Miami USA
17B2 North Miami Beach
USA
8C2 North Platte USA
8C2 North Platte R USA
27B3 North Pt Barbados
14B1 North Pt USA
40B2 North Rona I Scot
44C2 North Ronaldsay I
Scot
13F2 North Saskatchewan
R Can
40D2 North Sea
N W Europe
4D3 North Slope Region
Aust
109D1 North Stradbroke I
Aust
110B1 North Taranaki Bight
B NZ
9C3 North Truchas Peak
Mt USA
44A3 North Uist I Scot
42C2 Northumberland
County, Eng
107E3 Northumberland Is
Aust
7D5 Northumberland Str
Can
20B1 North Vancouver Can
43E3 North Walsham Eng
12F2 Northway USA
106A3 North West C Aust
84C2 North West Frontier
Province, Pak
7D4 North West River Can
4F3 North West Territories
Can
42D2 North York Moors Nat
Pk Eng
12B2 Norton B USA
12B2 Norton Sd USA

112B1	Norvegia,C Ant
16C2	Norwalk Connecticut, USA
14B2	Norwalk Ohio, USA
39F6	Norway Kingdom, Europe
5J4	Norway House Can
6A2	Norwegian B Can
102H1	Norwegian Basin Norwegian S
64A3	Norwegian S N W Europe
16C2	Norwich Connecticut, USA
43E3	Norwich Eng
16D1	Norwood Massachusetts, USA
14B3	Norwood Ohio, USA
54C2	Nos Emine C Bulg
74D2	Noshiro Japan
54C2	Nos Kaliakra C Bulg
44E1	Noss I Scot
91D4	Nosratābād Iran
101D2	Nosy Barren I Madag
101D2	Nosy Bé I Madag
101E2	Nosy Boraha I Madag
101D3	Nosy Varika Madag
58B2	Noteć R Pol
5G4	Notikeuin Can
53C3	Noto Italy
39F7	Notodden Nor
75B1	Noto-hantō Pen Japan
7E5	Notre Dams B Can
43D3	Nottingham County, Eng
43D3	Nottingham Eng
6C3	Nottingham I Can
6C3	Nottingham Island Can
96A2	Nouadhibou Maur
97A3	Nouakchott Maur
107F3	Nouméa Nouvelle Calédonie
97B3	Nouna Burkina
107F3	Nouvelle Calédonie I S W Pacific O
98B3	Nova Chaves Angola
100B2	Nova Chaves Angola
35A2	Nova Esperança Brazil
35C2	Nova Friburgo Brazil
100A2	Nova Gaia Angola
35C1	Nova Granada Brazil
35B2	Nova Horizonte Brazil
35C1	Nova Lima = Huambo
35C1	Nova Lisboa =
35A2	Nova Londrina Brazil
101C3	Nova Mambone Mozam
47C2	Novara Italy
7D5	Nova Scotia Province, Can
22A1	Novato USA
35C1	Nova Venécia Brazil
60D4	Novaya Kakhovka USSR
64G2	Novaya Zemlya I Barents S
54C2	Nova Zagora Bulg
31C2	Nove Russas Brazil
54A1	Nové Zámky Czech
60D2	Novgorod USSR
47C2	Novi Ligure Italy
54C2	Novi Pazar Bulg
54A1	Novi Pazar Yugos
54A1	Novi Sad Yugos
61J3	Novoalekseyevka USSR
61F3	Novoanninskiy USSR
61E4	Novocherkassk USSR
60C3	Novograd Volynskiy USSR
58D2	Novogrudok USSR
30F4	Novo Hamburgo Brazil
65H5	Novokazalinsk USSR
65K4	Novokuznetsk USSR
112B12	Novolazarevskaya Base Ant
52C1	Novo Mesto Yugos
60E3	Novomoskovsk USSR
60E5	Novorossiysk USSR
65K4	Novosibirsk USSR
1B8	Novosibirskiye Ostrova I USSR
61J3	Novotroitsk USSR
61G3	Novo Uzensk USSR
59C2	Novovolynsk USSR
61G2	Novo Vyatsk USSR
60D3	Novozybkov USSR
64J3	Novvy Port USSR
58C2	Novy Dwór Mazowiecki Pol
61K2	Novyy Lyalya USSR
64J3	Novyy Port USSR
61H5	Novyy Uzem USSR
58B2	Nowa Sól Pol
86C1	Nowgong India
12D2	Nowitna R USA
109D2	Nowra Aust
90B2	Now Shahr Iran
84C2	Nowshera Pak
59C3	Nowy Sącz Pol
43E4	Noyes I USA
46B2	Noyon France
97B4	Nsawam Ghana
99D1	Nuba Mts Sudan
81B3	Nubian Desert Sudan
34A3	Nuble R Chile
9D4	Nueces R USA
52A3	Nueltin L Can
26A2	Nueva Gerona Cuba
34A3	Nueva Imperial Chile
9C4	Nueva Laredo Mexico
34D2	Nueva Palmira Urug
24B2	Nueva Rosita Mexico
26B2	Nuevitas Cuba
24B1	Nuevo Casas Grandes Mexico
24C2	Nuevo Laredo Mexico
99E2	Nugaal Region, Somalia
6E2	Nûgâtsiaq Greenland
6E2	Nugssuaq Pen Greenland
6E2	Nûgussaq I Greenland
108A2	Nukey Bluff Mt Aust
93D3	Nukhayb Iraq
65G5	Nukus USSR
5C2	Nulato USA
106B4	Nullarbor Plain Aust
97D4	Numan Nig
75B1	Numata Japan
98C2	Numatinna R Sudan
74D3	Numazu Japan
71E4	Numfoor I Indon
108C3	Numurkah Aust
12B2	Nunapitchuk USA
84D2	Nunkun Mt India
53A2	Nuoro Sardegna
91B3	Nūrābād Iran
47C2	Nure R Italy
108A2	Nuriootpa Aust
84C1	Nūristan Upland Afghan
61H3	Nurlat USSR
38K6	Nurmes Fin
57C3	Nürnberg Germany
108C2	Nurri,Mt Aust
92D2	Nusaybin Turk
86A3	Nushagak R USA
12C3	Nushagak B USA
12C3	Nushagak Pen USA
84B3	Nushki Pak
7D4	Nutak Can
12F2	Nutzotin Mts USA
86A1	Nuwakot Nepal
87C3	Nuwara-Eliya Sri Lanka
16C2	Nyack USA
99D2	Nyahururu Kenya
108B3	Nyah West Aust
4C3	Nyac USA
68B3	Nyainqentanglha Shan Mts China
99D3	Nyakabindi Tanz
98C1	Nyala Sudan
86B1	Nyalam China
98C2	Nyamlell Sudan
100C3	Nyanda Zim
64F3	Nyandoma USSR
98B3	Nyanga R Gabon
101C2	Nyasa L Malawi/ Mozam
76B2	Nyaunglebin Burma
61J2	Nyazepetrovsk USSR
39G7	Nyborg Den
39H7	Nybro Sweden
64J3	Nyda USSR
6D1	Nyeboes Land Region Can
99D3	Nyeri Kenya
101C2	Nyimba Zambia
82D3	Nyingchi China
59C3	Nyiregyháza Hung
99D2	Nyiru,Mt Kenya
38J6	Nykarleby Fin
39F7	Nykøbing Den
39G8	Nykøbing Den
39H7	Nyköping Sweden
101C2	Nylstroom S Africa
109C2	Nymagee Aust
39H7	Nynäshamn Sweden
109C2	Nyngan Aust
47B1	Nyon Switz
98B2	Nyong R Cam
49C2	Nyons France
59B2	Nysa Pol
20C2	Nyssa USA
99D3	Nyurba USSR
99D3	Nzega Tanz
97B4	Nzérékore Guinea

O

6F3	Oaggsimiut Greenland
8C2	Oahe Res USA
4C3	Oahu I Hawaiian Is
108B2	Oakbank Aust
22B2	Oakdale USA
109D1	Oakey Aust
21A2	Oakland California, USA
20B2	Oakland Oregon, USA
14A3	Oakland City USA
22B2	Oakley California, USA
20B2	Oakridge USA
14C2	Oakville Can
111B3	Oamaru NZ
112B7	Oates Land Region, Ant
109C4	Oatlands Aust
23B2	Oaxaca Mexico
23B2	Oaxaca State, Mexico
65J3	Ob' R USSR
74D3	Obama Japan
44B3	Oban Scot
75C1	Obanazawa Japan
47D1	Oberammergau Germany
46D1	Oberhausen Germany
47D1	Oberstdorf Germany
71D4	Obi I Indon
33F4	Obidos Brazil
74E2	Obihiro Japan
98C2	Obo CAR
99E1	Obock Djibouti
58B2	Oborniki Pol
60E3	Oboyan USSR
20B2	O'Brien USA
61H3	Obshchiy Syrt Mts USSR
64J3	Obskaya Guba B USSR
97B4	Obuasi Ghana
17B2	Ocala USA
32C2	Ocana Colombia
50B2	Ocaña Spain
12G3	Ocean C USA
15C3	Ocean City Maryland, USA
16B3	Ocean City New Jersey, USA
5F4	Ocean Falls Can
22D4	Oceanside USA
19C3	Ocean Springs USA
61H2	Ocher USSR
44C3	Ochil Hills Scot
17B1	Ochlockonee R USA
27H1	Ocho Rios Jamaica
17B1	Ocmulgee R USA
17B1	Oconee R USA
14A2	Oconto USA
23A1	Ocotlán Jalisco, Mexico
23B2	Ocotlán Oaxaca, Mexico
97B4	Oda Ghana
75A1	Oda Japan
	Ódáðáhraun Region, Iceland
74E2	Odate Japan
74D3	Odawara Japan
39F6	Odda Nor
50A2	Odemira Port
54C2	Ödemiş Turk
101G1	Odendaalsrus S Africa
39G7	Odense Den
56C2	Oder R Pol/Germany
9C3	Odessa Texas, USA
60D4	Odessa USSR
20C1	Odessa Washington, USA
97B4	Odienné Ivory Coast
59B2	Odra R Pol
33E4	Oeiras Brazil
106B1	Oekusi Indon
53C2	Ofanto R Italy
94B3	Ofaqim Israel
45C2	Offaly County, Irish Rep
49D1	Offenbach Germany
49D2	Offenburg Germany
74D3	Oga Japan
99E2	Ogaden Region, Eth
74D3	Ogaki Japan
82C2	Ogallala USA
69G4	Ogasawara Gunto Is Japan
97C4	Ogbomosho Nig
8B2	Ogden Utah, USA
15C2	Ogdensburg USA
17B1	Ogeechee R USA
12G1	Ogilvie Can
4E3	Ogilvie Mts Can
17B1	Oglethorpe,Mt USA
47D2	Oglio R Italy
47B1	Ognon R France
97C4	Ogoja Nig
98A3	Ogooué R Gabon
58C1	Ogre USSR
96B2	Oguilet Khenachich Well Mali
52C1	Ogulin Yugos
113A3	Ohai NZ
110C1	Ohakune NZ
96C2	Ohanet Alg
111A2	Ohau,L NZ
10B2	Ohio State, USA
14A3	Ohio R USA
100A2	Ohopoho Namibia
57C2	Ohre R Czech
55B2	Ohrid Yugos
55B2	Ohridsko Jezero L Yugos/Alb
110B1	Ohura NZ
33G3	Oiapoque French Guiana
68B2	Oijiaojing China
12C2	Oil City USA
21B2	Oildale USA

46B2 Oise Department, France
49C2 Oise R France
74C4 Oita Japan
22C3 Ojai USA
24B2 Ojinaga Mexico
23B2 Ojitlán Mexico
75B1 Ojiya Japan
30C4 Ojos del Salado Mt Arg
23A1 Ojueloz Mexico
60E3 Oka R USSR
100A3 Okahandja Namibia
20C1 Okanagan Falls Can
13D2 Okanagan L Can
20C1 Okanogan USA
20C1 Okanogan R USA
20B1 Okanogan Range Mts Can/USA
84C2 Okara Pak
100A2 Okavango R Angola/Namibia
100B2 Okavango Delta Marsh Botswana
74D3 Okaya Japan
74C4 Okayama Japan
75B2 Okazaki Japan
17B2 Okeechobee USA
17B2 Okeechobee,L USA
17B1 Okefenokee Swamp USA
97C4 Okene Nig
18A4 Okha India
69G1 Okha USSR
86B1 Okhaldunga Nepal
62J3 Okhotsk,S of USSR
69E4 Okinawa I Japan
69E4 Okinawa gunto Arch Japan
74C3 Oki-shoto Is Japan
9D3 Oklahoma State, USA
18A2 Oklahoma City USA
18A2 Okmulgee USA
98B3 Okondja Gabon
98B3 Okoyo Congo
97C4 Okpara R Nig
61J4 Oktyabr'sk USSR
61H3 Oktyabr'skiy Bashkirskaya, USSR
74D2 Okushiri-tō I Japan
38A2 Olafsvik Iceland
39H7 Öland I Sweden
108B2 Olary Aust
18B2 Olathe USA
29D3 Olavarría Arg
53A2 Olbia Sardegna
12G1 Old Crow Can
56B2 Oldenburg Niedersachsen, Germany
56C2 Oldenburg Schleswig-Holstein, Germany
15C2 Old Forge USA
42C3 Oldham Eng
12D3 Old Harbor USA
41B3 Old Head of Kinsale C Scot
16C2 Old Lyme USA
13E2 Olds Can
15C2 Olean USA
63E2 Olekma R USSR
63D1 Olekminsk USSR
38L5 Olenegorsk USSR
58D2 Olevsk USSR
69F2 Ol'ga USSR
100A3 Olifants R Namibia
55B2 Ólimbos Mt Greece
35B2 Olímpia Brazil
23B2 Olinala Mexico
31E3 Olinda Brazil
34C2 Oliva Arg
29C2 Olivares Mt Arg
35C2 Oliveira Brazil
13D3 Oliver Can
30C3 Ollagüe Chile
30C3 Ollagüe Mt Bol
18C2 Olney USA
68E1 Olochi USSR

39G7 Olofstrom Sweden
98B3 Olombo Congo
59B3 Olomouc Czech
60D1 Olonets USSR
79B3 Olongapo Phil
48B3 Oloron Ste Marie France
68D1 Olovyannaya USSR
46D1 Olpe Germany
58C2 Olsztyn Pol
47B1 Olten Switz
54B2 Oltul R Rom
20B1 Olympia USA
20B1 Olympic Nat Pk USA
20B1 Olympus = Olimbos
20B1 Olympus,Mt USA
65J4 Om' R USSR
75B1 Omachi Japan
75B2 Omae-zaki C Japan
45C1 Omagh N Ire
18A1 Omaha USA
20C1 Omak USA
91C5 Oman Sultanate, Arabian Pen
91C4 Oman,G of UAE
98A3 Omboue Gabon
99D1 Omdurman Sudan
23B2 Ometepec Mexico
13B1 Omineca R Can
13B1 Omineca Mts Can
75B1 Omiya Japan
12H3 Ommaney,C USA
4J4 Ommanney B Can
99D2 Omo R Eth
65J4 Omsk USSR
74B4 Omura Japan
74C4 Omuta Japan
61H2 Omutninsk USSR
78D3 Onang Indon
14B1 Onaping L Can
100A2 Oncócua Angola
100A2 Ondangua Namibia
59C3 Ondava R Czech
68D2 Öndörhaan Molgolia
83B5 One and Half Degree Chan Indian O
64E3 Onega USSR
64E3 Onega R USSR
15C2 Oneida L USA
8D2 O'Neill USA
69H2 Onekotan I USSR
98C3 Onema Zaïre
15D2 Oneonta USA
64E3 Onezhskoye Ozero L USSR
100A2 Ongiva Angola
74B3 Ongjin N Korea
72D1 Ongniud Qi China
87A1 Ongole India
15C2 Onieda L USA
101D3 Onilahy R Madag
97C4 Onitsha Nig
68C2 Onjüül Mongolia
75B1 Ono Japan
75B2 Onohara-jima I Japan
74C4 Onomichi Japan
106A3 Onslow Aust
17C1 Onslow B USA
75B1 Ontake-san Mt Japan
22D3 Ontario California, USA
20C2 Ontario Oregon, USA
7A4 Ontario Province, Can
15C2 Ontario,L Can/USA
51B2 Onteniente Spain
106C3 Oodnadatta Aust
106C4 Ooldea Aust
18A2 Oologah L USA
46B1 Oostende Belg
46B1 Oosterschelde Estuary Neth
87B2 Ootacamund India
13B2 Ootsa L Can
69H1 Opala USSR
98C3 Opala Zaïre
87C3 Opanake Sri Lanka
61G2 Oparino USSR
59B3 Opava Czech

17A1 Opelika USA
19B3 Opelousas USA
12C2 Ophir USA
58D1 Opochka USSR
59B2 Opole Pol
Oporto = Porto
110C1 Opotiki NZ
17A1 Opp USA
38F6 Oppdal Nor
110B1 Opunake NZ
50B1 Oradea Rom
38B2 Oraefajökull Mts Iceland
30D3 Orai India
96B1 Oran Alg
30D3 Orán Arg
109C2 Orange Aust
22D4 Orange California, USA
49C3 Orange France
19B3 Orange Texas, USA
100A3 Orange R S Africa
17B1 Orangeburg USA
101G1 Orange Free State Province, S Africa
17B1 Orange Park USA
14B2 Orangeville Can
23B2 Oranienburg Germany
79C3 Oras Phil
54B1 Orǎstie Rom
54B1 Oravita Rom
52B2 Orbetello Italy
109C3 Orbost Aust
46B1 Orchies France
47B2 Orco R Italy
106B2 Ord R Aust
106B2 Ord,Mt Aust
93C1 Ordu Turk
39H7 Örebro Sweden
8A2 Oregon State, USA
14B2 Oregon USA
20B1 Oregon City USA
39H6 Oregrund Sweden
60E2 Orekhovo Zuyevo USSR
60E3 Orel USSR
61H3 Orenburg USSR
34D3 Orense Arg
50A1 Orense Spain
56C1 Øresund Str Den/Sweden
111A3 Oreti R NZ
55C3 Orhaneli R Turk
68C2 Orhon Gol R Mongolia
23B2 Oriental Mexico
108B1 Orientos Aust
51B2 Orihuela Spain
15C2 Orillia Can
33E2 Orinoco R Ven
86A2 Orissa State, India
53A3 Oristano Sardegna
38K6 Orivesi L Fin
33F4 Oriximina Brazil
23B2 Orizaba Mexico
35B1 Orizona Brazil
44C2 Orkney I Scot
35B2 Orlândia Brazil
17B2 Orlando USA
22D3 Orléanais Region France
48C2 Orléans France
63B2 Orlik USSR
82A3 Ormara Pak
79B3 Ormoc Phil
17B2 Ormond Beach USA
46C2 Ornain R France
47B1 Ornans France
48B2 Orne R France
38H6 Örnsköldsvik Sweden
32C3 Orocué Colombia
94B3 Oron Israel
Orontes = 'Āşī
79B4 Oroquieta Phil
59C3 Oroszlá Hung
21A2 Oroville California, USA

20C1 Oroville Washington, USA
47B1 Orsières Switz
65G4 Orsk USSR
38F6 Orsta Nor
48B3 Orthez France
50A1 Ortigueira Spain
47D1 Ortles Mts Italy
27L1 Ortoire R Trinidad
93E2 Orümiyeh Iran
30C2 Oruro Bol
61J2 Osa USSR
18B2 Osage R USA
75B1 Osaka Japan
25D4 Osa,Pen de Costa Rica
18C2 Osceola Arkansas, USA
18B1 Osceola Iowa, USA
20C2 Osgood Mts USA
15C2 Oshawa Can
75B2 Ō-shima I Japan
10B2 Oshkosh USA
97C4 Oshogbo Nig
7B5 Oshosh USA
98B3 Oshwe Zaïre
54A1 Osijek Yugos
65K5 Osinniki USSR
58D2 Osipovichi USSR
18B1 Oskaloosa USA
60A2 Oskarshamn Sweden
39G7 Oslo Nor
92C2 Osmaniye Turk
56B2 Osnabrück Germany
30F4 Osório Brazil
29B4 Osorno Chile
50B1 Osorno Spain
20C1 Osoyoos Can
13C1 Ospika R Can
107D5 Ossa,Mt Aust
16C2 Ossining USA
60D2 Ostashkov USSR
Ostend = Oostende
38G6 Østerdalen V Nor
38G6 Östersund Sweden
56B2 Ostfriesische Inseln Is Germany
39H6 Östhammar Sweden
52B2 Ostia Italy
47D2 Ostiglia Italy
59B3 Ostrava Czech
58B2 Ostróda Pol
60C2 Ostrov USSR
64J2 Ostrov Belyy I USSR
64H1 Ostrov Greem Bell I USSR
64F3 Ostrov Kolguyev I USSR
74F2 Ostrov Kunashir I USSR
64F2 Ostrov Mechdusharskiy I Barents S
90B2 Ostrov Ogurchinskiy I USSR
64G1 Ostrov Rudol'fa I Barents S
64G2 Ostrov Vaygach I USSR
1B7 Ostrov Vrangelya I USSR
58B2 Ostrów Pol
59C2 Ostrowiec Pol
58C2 Ostrów Mazowiecka Pol
50A2 Osuna Spain
15C2 Oswego USA
15C2 Oswego R USA
43C3 Oswestry Eng
59B2 Oświęcim Pol
75B1 Ota Japan
111B3 Otago Pen NZ
110C2 Otaki NZ
74E2 Otaru Japan
32B3 Otavalo Ecuador
100A2 Otavi Namibia
75C1 Otawara Japan
20C1 Othello USA

55B3 Óthris *Mt* Greece
16C1 Otis Massachusetts, USA
10C1 Otish Mts Can
16B2 Otisville USA
100A3 Otjiwarongo Namibia
72B2 Otog Qi China
110C1 Otorohanga NZ
55A2 Otranto Italy
55A2 Otranto,Str of *Chan* Italy/Alb
14A2 Otsego USA
75B1 Otta Nor
39F6 Otta Nor
39F7 Otta *R* Nor
15C1 Ottawa Can
18A2 Ottawa Kansas, USA
15C1 Ottawa *R* Can
7B4 Ottawa Is Can
7B4 Otter Rapids Can
6B1 Otto Fjord Can
101G1 Ottosdal S Africa
18B1 Ottumwa USA
46B2 Ottweiler Germany
97C4 Oturkpo Nig
32B5 Otusco Peru
108B3 Otway,C Aust
58C2 Otwock Pol
47D1 Ötz Austria
47C1 Ötzal Mts Austria
76C1 Ou *R* Laos
19B3 Ouachita *R* USA
19B3 Ouachita,L USA
19B3 Ouachita Mts USA
96A2 Ouadane Maur
98C2 Ouadda CAR
98C1 Ouaddaï *Desert Region* Chad
97B3 Ouagadougou Burkina
97B3 Ouahigouya Burkina
98C2 Ouaka CAR
97C3 Oualam Niger
98C2 Ouallen Alg
98C2 Ouanda Djallé CAR
96A2 Ouarane Region, Maur
97C4 Ouargla Alg
98C2 Ouarra *R* CAR
96B1 Ouarzazate Mor
51C2 Ouassel *R* Alg
98B2 Oubangui *R* Congo
46B1 Oudenaarde Belg
100B4 Oudtshoorn S Africa
51B2 Oued Tlélat Alg
96B1 Oued Zem Mor
98B2 Ouesso Congo
96B1 Ouezzane Mor
98B2 Ouham *R* Chad
97C4 Ouidah Benin
96B1 Oujda Mor
38J6 Oulainen Fin
38K5 Oulu Fin
38K6 Oulu *R* Fin
38K6 Oulujärvi *L* Fin
95B3 Oum Chalouba Chad
98B1 Oum Hadjer Chad
95B3 Oum Haouach *Watercourse* Chad
38K5 Ounas *R* Fin
95B3 Ounianga Kébir Chad
46D1 Our *R* Germany
47F3 Ourcq *R* France
31C3 Ouricuri Brazil
35B2 Ourinhos Brazil
35C2 Ouro Prêto Brazil
46C1 Ourthe *R* Belg
42D2 Ouse *R* Eng
43E3 Ouse *R* Eng
40B2 Outer Hebrides *Is* Scot
22C4 Outer Santa Barbara *Chan* USA
100A3 Outjo Namibia
38K6 Outokumpu Fin
108B3 Ouyen Aust
47C2 Ovada Italy
34A2 Ovalle Chile
100A2 Ovamboland Region, Namibia

61H5 Ova Tyuleni *Is* USSR
38J5 Övertorneä Sweden
50A1 Oviedo Spain
60C3 Ovruch USSR
63E2 Ovsyanka USSR
111A3 Owaka NZ
75B2 Owase Japan
11B3 Owensboro USA
21B2 Owens L USA
14B2 Owen Sound Can
107D1 Owen Stanley Range *Mts* PNG
97C4 Owerri Nig
97C4 Owo Nig
14B2 Owosso USA
20C2 Owyhee *R* USA
20C2 Owyhee Mts USA
32B6 Oxapampa Peru
39H7 Oxelösund Sweden
43D4 Oxford County, Eng
43D4 Oxford Eng
16D1 Oxford Massachusetts, USA
19C3 Oxford Mississippi, USA
45B1 Ox Mts Irish Rep
22C3 Oxnard USA
74D3 Oyama Japan
13E2 Oyen Can
98B2 Oyem Gabon
44B3 Oykel *R* Scot
39F6 Øyre Nor
109C4 Oyster B Aust
79A3 Oyamiz Phil
17A1 Ozark USA
18B2 Ozark Plat USA
18B2 Ozarks,L of the USA
59C3 Ozd Hung
65K5 Ozero Alakol *L* USSR
65J5 Ozero Balkhash *L* USSR
63C2 Ozero Baykal *L* USSR
65J4 Ozero Chany *L* USSR
60C2 Ozero Chudskoye *L* USSR
60D2 Ozero Il'men *L* USSR
38L5 Ozero Imandra *L* USSR
82B1 Ozero Issyk Kul' *L* USSR
69F2 Ozero Khanka *L* China/USSR
38L5 Ozero Kovdozero *L* USSR
38L5 Ozero Kuyto *L* USSR
38L5 Ozero Pyaozero *L* USSR
65H4 Ozero Tengiz *L* USSR
38L5 Ozero Topozero *L* USSR
65K5 Ozero Zaysan USSR
23B1 Ozuluama Mexico

P

100A4 Paarl S Africa
44A3 Pabbay *I* Scot
58B2 Pabianice Pol
86B2 Pabna Bang *I*
58D2 Pabrade USSR
32B5 Pacasmayo Peru
23B1 Pachuca Mexico
105K6 Pacific-Antarctic Ridge Pacific O
22B2 Pacific Grove USA
78C4 Pacitan Indon
35C1 Pacuí *R* Brazil
70B4 Padang Indon
56B2 Paderborn Germany
5J3 Padlei Can
86C2 Padma *R* Bang
47D2 Padova Italy
9D4 Padre I USA
43B4 Padstow Eng
108B3 Padthaway Aust
Padua = Padova
14A3 Paducah Kentucky, USA

11B3 Paducah USA
38L5 Padunskoye More *L* USSR
74A3 Paengnyöng-do *I* S Korea
110C1 Paeroa NZ
100C3 Pafuri Mozam
52B2 Pag *I* Yugos
79B4 Pagadian Phil
70B4 Pagai Selatan *I* Indon
70B4 Pagai Utara *I* Indon
71F2 Pagan *I* Pacific O
78D3 Pagatan Indon
55C3 Pagondhas Greece
110C2 Pahiatua NZ
21C4 Pahoa Hawaiian Is
17B2 Pahokee USA
39K6 Päijänne *L* Fin
21C4 Pailola Chan Hawaiian Is
14B2 Painesville USA
9B3 Painted Desert USA
42B2 Paisley Scot
32A5 Paita Peru
38J5 Pajala Sweden
80E3 Pakistan Republic, Asia
76C2 Pak Lay Laos
86D2 Pakokku Burma
13E2 Pakowki L Can
52C1 Pakrac Yugos
54A1 Paks Hung
76C2 Pak Sane Laos
76C2 Pakse Laos
99D2 Pakwach Uganda
98B2 Pala Chad
52C2 Palagruža *I* Yugos
46B2 Palaiseau France
78C3 Palangkaraya Indon
87B2 Palani India
85C4 Pālanpur India
100B3 Palapye Botswana
17B2 Palatka USA
71E3 Palau Is Pacific O
76B3 Palaw Burma
79A4 Palawan *I* Phil
79A4 Palawan Pass Phil
87B3 Palayankottai India
39J7 Paldiski USSR
78A3 Palembang Indon
50B1 Palencia Spain
94A1 Paleokhorio Cyprus
53B3 Palermo Italy
94B3 Palestine Region, Israel
19A3 Palestine USA
86C2 Paletwa Burma
87B2 Pālghāt India
85C3 Pali India
85C4 Pālitāna India
87B3 Palk Str India/Sri Lanka
61G3 Pallasovka USSR
38J5 Pallastunturi *Mt* Fin
11B2 Palliser B NZ
11C2 Palliser,C NZ
101D2 Palma Mozam
51C2 Palma de Mallorca Spain
31D3 Palmares Brazil
26A5 Palmar Sur Costa Rica
97B4 Palmas,C Lib
26B2 Palma Soriano Cuba
17B2 Palm Bay USA
17B2 Palm Beach USA
22C3 Palmdale USA
31D3 Palmeira dos Indos Brazil
12E2 Palmer USA
112C3 Palmer *Base* Ant
112C3 Palmer Arch Ant
112B3 Palmer Land *Region* Ant
111B3 Palmerston NZ
110C2 Palmerston North NZ
16B2 Palmerton USA
17B2 Palmetto USA
53C3 Palmi Italy

32B3 Palmira Colombia
107D2 Palm Is Aust
21B3 Palm Springs USA
18B2 Palmyra Missouri, USA
16A2 Palmyra Pennsylvania, USA
86B2 Palmyras Pt India
22A2 Palo Alto USA
99D1 Paloich Sudan
21B3 Palomar Mt USA
70D4 Palopo Indon
70C4 Palu Indon
93C2 Palu Turk
84D3 Palwal India
96A3 Pama Burkina
70C4 Pamekasan Indon
78B4 Pameungpeuk Indon
48C3 Pamiers France
82B2 Pamir *Mts* China
65J6 Pamir *R* USSR
11C3 Pamlico Sd USA
9C3 Pampa USA
8B2 Pampa de la Salinas *Salt pan* Arg
34B3 Pampa de la Varita *Plain* Arg
32C2 Pamplona Colombia
50B1 Pamplona Spain
18C2 Pana USA
54B2 Panagyurishte Bulg
87A1 Panaji India
32B2 Panama Panama
32A2 Panama Republic, Cent America
26B5 Panama Canal Panama
71A1 Panama City USA
21B2 Panamint Range *Mts* USA
21B2 Panamint V USA
47D2 Panaro *R* Italy
79B3 Panay *I* Phil
54B2 Pancevo Yugos
79B3 Pandan Phil
87B1 Pandharpur India
108A1 Pande Pandie Aust
58C1 Panevežys USSR
65K5 Panfilov USSR
76B1 Pang *R* Burma
99D3 Pangani Tanz
99D3 Pangani *R* Tanz
98C3 Pangi Zaire
78B3 Pangkalpinang Indon
6D3 Pangnirtung Can
76B1 Pangtara Burma
79B4 Pangutaran Group *Is* Phil
84D3 Panipat India
84B2 Panjao Afghan
78D4 P'anmunjŏm N Korea
86A2 Panna India
35A2 Panorama Brazil
53B3 Pantelleria *I* Medit S
23B1 Pantepec Mexico
23B1 Panuco Mexico
23B1 Pánuco *R* Mexico
73A4 Pan Xian China
53C3 Paola Italy
18B2 Paola USA
14A3 Paoli USA
59B3 Pápa Hung
110B1 Papakura NZ
23B2 Papaloapan *R* Mexico
23B1 Papantla Mexico
44E1 Papa Stour *I* Scot
110B1 Papatoetoe NZ
44C2 Papa Westray *I* Scot
107D1 Papua,G of PNG
107D1 Papua New Guinea Republic, S E Asia
34A2 Papudo Chile
76B2 Papun Burma
33G4 Para State, Brazil
31B2 Pará *R* Brazil
106A3 Paraburdoo Aust

32B6 Paracas,Pen de Peru
35B1 Paracatu Brazil
35B1 Paracatu R Brazil
108A2 Parachilna Aust
84C2 Parachinar Pak
54B2 Parachute USA
35C1 Para de Minas Brazil
21A2 Paradise California, USA
18B2 Paragould USA
33E6 Paragua R Bol
33E2 Paragua R Ven
30E2 Paraguai R Brazil
30E4 Paraguari Par
30E3 Paraguay Republic, S America
30E3 Paraguay R Par
31D3 Paraiba State, Brazil
35B2 Paraiba Brazil
35C2 Paraiba do Sul R Brazil
97C4 Parakou Benin
108A2 Parakylia Aust
87B3 Paramakkudi India
33F2 Paramaribo Surinam
69H1 Paramushir I USSR
30F3 Paraná State, Brazil
34C2 Paraná Urug
29E2 Paraná R Urug
31B4 Paraná R Brazil
35A2 Paraná R Brazil
30G4 Paranaguá Brazil
35A1 Paranaiba Brazil
35A1 Paranaiba R Brazil
35A2 Paranapanema R Brazil
35A2 Paranavai Brazil
79B4 Parang Phil
35C1 Paraope R Brazil
110B2 Paraparaumu NZ
87B1 Parbhani India
94B2 Pardes Hanna Israel
34D3 Pardo R
35D1 Pardo R Bahia, Brazil
35A2 Pardo R Mato Grosso do Sul, Brazil
35B1 Pardo R Minas Gerais, Brazil
35B2 Pardo R Sao Paulo, Brazil
59B2 Pardubice Czech
69F4 Parece Vela Reef Pacific O
10C2 Parent Can
70C4 Parepare Indon
34C3 Parera Arg
70B4 Pariaman Indon
33E1 Paria,Pen de Ven
48C2 Paris France
14B3 Paris Kentucky, USA
19A3 Paris Texas, USA
14B3 Parkersburg USA
109C2 Parkes Aust
16B3 Parksburg USA
14A2 Park Forest USA
20B1 Parksville Can
87B1 Parli India
47D2 Parma Italy
14B2 Parma USA
31C2 Parnaiba Brazil
31C2 Parnaiba R Brazil
55B3 Párnon Óros Mts Greece
60B2 Pärnu USSR
86B1 Paro Bhutan
108B1 Paroo R Aust
108B2 Paroo Channel R Aust
55C3 Páros I Greece
47B2 Parpaillon Mts France
34A3 Parral Chile
109D2 Parramatta Aust
9C4 Parras Mexico
6B3 Parry B Can
4G2 Parry Is Can
7C5 Parry Sd Can
14B1 Parry Sound Can
57C3 Parsberg Germany
5F4 Parsnip R Can

18A2 Parsons Kansas, USA
14C3 Parsons West Virginia, USA
48B2 Parthenay France
53B3 Partinico Italy
74C2 Partizansk USSR
33G4 Paru R Brazil
101G1 Parys S Africa
19A4 Pasadena Texas, USA
22C3 Pasadena California, USA
78D3 Pasangkayu Indon
76B2 Pasawing Burma
19C3 Pascagoula USA
54C1 Pașcani Rom
20C1 Pasco USA
46B1 Pas-de-Calais Department, France
39G8 Pasewalk Germany
91C4 Pashu'iyeh Iran
106B4 Pasley,C Aust
29E2 Paso de los Toros Urug
29B4 Paso Limay Arg
21A2 Paso Robles USA
45B3 Passage West Irish Rep
16B2 Passaic USA
57C3 Passau Germany
30E4 Passo de los Libres Arg
47D1 Passo di Stelvio Mt Italy
30F4 Passo Fundo Brazil
35B2 Passos Brazil
47B2 Passy France
32B4 Pastaza R Peru
34C3 Pasteur Arg
5H4 Pas,The Can
32B3 Pasto Colombia
12B2 Pastol B USA
47D2 Pasubio Mt Italy
78C4 Pasuruan Indon
58C1 Pasvalys USSR
85C4 Patan India
86B1 Patan Nepal
108B3 Patchewollock Aust
110B1 Patea NZ
111B2 Patea R NZ
53B3 Paterno Italy
16B2 Paterson USA
111A3 Paterson Inlet B NZ
84D2 Pathankot India
84D2 Patiala India
32B6 Pativilca Peru
55C3 Pátmos I Greece
86B1 Patna India
93D2 Patnos Turk
31D3 Patos Brazil
35B1 Patos de Minas Brazil
34B2 Patquia Arg
55B3 Pátrai Greece
35B1 Patrocinio Brazil
99E3 Patta I Kenya
78D4 Pattallasang Indon
77C4 Pattani Thai
22B2 Patterson California, USA
19B4 Patterson Louisiana, USA
13C1 Patterson,Mt Can
12C2 Patterson Mt USA
13B1 Pattullo,Mt Can
31D3 Patu Brazil
86C2 Patuakhali Bang
25D3 Patuca R Honduras
23A2 Patzcuaro Mexico
48B3 Pau France
4F3 Paukatuk Can
31C3 Paulistana Brazil
101H1 Paulpietersburg S Africa
19A3 Pauls Valley USA
76B2 Paungde Burma
84D2 Pauri India
38H5 Pauskie Nor
35C1 Pavão Brazil
47C2 Pavia Italy

65J4 Pavlodar USSR
63E2 Pavlovich USSR
61J2 Pavlovka USSR
61F2 Pavlovo USSR
61F3 Pavlovsk USSR
78C3 Pawan R Indon
18A2 Pawhuska USA
16D2 Pawtucket USA
47B1 Payerne Switz
20C2 Payette USA
64H3 Pay-Khoy,Khrebet Mts USSR
7C4 Payne,L Can
34D2 Paysandu Urug
46A2 Pays-de-Bray Region, France
54B2 Pazardzhik Bulg
13D1 Peace R Can
17B2 Peace R USA
13D1 Peace River Can
43D3 Peak District Nat Pk Eng
108A1 Peake R Aust
109C2 Peak Hill Aust
71E4 Peak Mandala Mt Indon
42D3 Peak,The Mt Eng
19B3 Pearl R USA
21C4 Pearl City Hawaiian Is
21C4 Pearl Harbor Hawaiian Is
4H2 Peary Chan Can
101C2 Pebane Mozam
54B2 Peć Yugos
35C1 Peçanha Brazil
19B4 Pecan Island USA
38L5 Pechenga USSR
64F3 Pechora R USSR
53C3 Pecoraro Mt Italy
9C3 Pecos USA
9C3 Pecos R USA
59B3 Pécs Hung
108A1 Pedirka Aust
35C1 Pedro Azul Brazil
35B2 Pedregulho Brazil
26B3 Pedro Cays Is Caribbean S
30C3 Pedro de Valdivia Chile
30E3 Pedro Juan Caballero Par
34C3 Pedro Luro Arg
23B1 Pedro Mentova Mexico
87C3 Pedro,Pt Sri Lanka
108B2 Peebinga Aust
42C2 Peebles Scot
17C1 Pee Dee R USA
16C2 Peekskill USA
42B2 Peel Eng
12H1 Peel R Can
4J2 Peel Sd Can
108A1 Peera Peera Poolanna L Aust
13E1 Peerless L Can
71E4 Peg Arfak Mt Indon
111B2 Pegasus B NZ
83D4 Pegu Burma
78A3 Pegunungan Barisan Mts Indon
78C2 Pegunungan Iran Mts Malay/Indon
71E4 Pegunungan Maoke Mts Indon
78D3 Pegunungan Meratus Mts Indon
78D3 Pegunungan Muller Mts Indon
78C3 Pegunungan Schwaner Mts Indon
78A3 Pegunungan Tigapuluh Mts Indon
76B2 Pegu Yoma Mts Burma

34C3 Pehuajó Arg
35A2 Peixe R Sao Paulo, Brazil
72D3 Pei Xian China
78B4 Pekalongan Indon
77C5 Pekan Malay
78B4 Pekanbaru Indon
18C1 Pekin USA
Peking = Beijing
77C5 Pelabohan Kelang Malay
78D4 Pelau Pelau Kangean Is Indon
78C4 Pelau Pelau Karimunjawa Arch Indon
78D4 Pelau Pelau Postilyon Is Indon
54B1 Peleaga Mt Rom
63D2 Peleduy USSR
14B2 Pelee I Can
71D4 Peleng I Indon
12G3 Pelican USA
69F1 Peliny Osipenko USSR
34C3 Pellegrini Arg
38J5 Pello Fin
12H2 Pelly R Can
6A3 Pelly Bay Can
12G2 Pelly Crossing Can
12H2 Pelly Mts Can
30F5 Pelotas Brazil
30F4 Pelotas R Brazil
47B2 Pelvoux Region, France
78B4 Pemalang Indon
78B4 Pematang Indon
101D2 Pemba Mozam
99D3 Pemba I Tanz
20C1 Pemberton Can
13D2 Pembina R Can
15C1 Pembroke Can
17B1 Pembroke USA
43B4 Pembroke Wales
34A3 Pemuco Chile
78D2 Penambo Range Mts Malay
35A2 Penápolis Brazil
50A2 Peñarroya Spain
51B1 Peñarroya Mt Spain
50A1 Peña Trevina Mt Spain
98B2 Pende R Chad
12J3 Pendleton,Mt Can
20C1 Pendleton USA
20C1 Pend Oreille R USA
31D4 Pendozinho Brazil
85D5 Penganga R India
73D5 P'eng-hu Lieh-tao Is Taiwan
72E2 Penglai China
73B4 Pengshui China
71E4 Pengunungan Maoke Mts Indon
26C4 Peninsula de la Guajiri Pen Colombia
27E4 Peninsula de Paria Pen Ven
77C5 Peninsular Malaysia Malay
23A1 Penjamo Mexico
87B2 Penner R India
42C2 Pennine Chain Mts Eng
16B3 Penns Grove USA
10C2 Pennsylvania State, USA
6D3 Penny Highlands Can
108B3 Penola Aust
106C4 Penong Aust
42C2 Penrith Eng
11B3 Pensacola USA
112A Pensacola Mts Ant
78D1 Pensiangan Malay
13D3 Penticton Can
44C2 Pentland Firth Chan Scot
42C2 Pentland Hills Scot

61G3 Penza USSR
43B2 Penzance Eng
10B2 Peoria USA
78A3 Perabumulih Indon
77C5 Perak R Malay
78A2 Perawang Indon
32B3 Pereira Colombia
35A2 Pereira Barreto Brazil
61F4 Perelazovskiy USSR
12D3 Perenosa B USA
34C2 Pergamino Arg
7C4 Peribonca R Can
48C2 Périgueux France
25E4 Perlas Arch de Is Panama
61J2 Perm' USSR
Pernambuco = Recife
Pernambuco State, Brazil
108A2 Pernatty Lg Aust
54B2 Pernik Bulg
46B2 Péronne France
23B2 Perote Mexico
49C3 Perpignan France
22D4 Perris USA
17B1 Perry Florida, USA
17B1 Perry Georgia, USA
18A2 Perry Oklahoma, USA
4H3 Perry River Can
14B2 Perrysburg USA
12C3 Perryville Alaska, USA
12C3 Perryville Missouri, USA
106A4 Perth Aust
15C2 Perth Can
44C3 Perth Scot
14B1 Perth Amboy USA
32C6 Peru Republic, S America
18C1 Peru USA
103E1 Peru-Chile Trench Pacific O
52B2 Perugia Italy
52C2 Perušic Yugos
93D2 Pervari Turk
61F3 Pervomaysk RSFSR, USSR
60D4 Pervomaysk Ukraine SSR, USSR
61J2 Pervoural'sk USSR
52B2 Pesaro Italy
22A2 Pescadero USA
Pescadores = P'eng-hu Lieh-tao
52B2 Pescara Italy
47D2 Peschiera Italy
84C2 Peshawar Pak
54B2 Peshkopi Alb
14A1 Peshtigo USA
60E2 Pestovo USSR
94B2 Petah Tiqwa Israel
21A2 Petaluma USA
46C2 Pétange Lux
23A2 Petatlán Mexico
101C2 Petauke Zambia
108A2 Peterborough Aust
15C2 Peterborough Can
43D3 Peterborough Eng
44D3 Peterhead Scot
6D1 Petermann Gletscher Gl Greenland
106B3 Petermann Range Mts Aust
29B3 Peteroa Mt Arg/Chile
13F1 Peter Pond L Can
12H3 Petersburg Alaska, USA
85C4 Petlad India
23B2 Petlalcingo Mexico
25D2 Peto Mexico
63D2 Petomskoye Nagor'ye Upland USSR
34A2 Petorca Chile
14B1 Petoskey USA
31C3 Petrolina Brazil
65H4 Petropavlovsk USSR
35C2 Petrópolis Brazil
64E3 Petrovadovsk USSR

61G3 Petrovsk USSR
68C1 Petrovsk Zabaykal'skiy USSR
64E3 Petrozavodsk USSR
101G1 Petrus S Africa
101G1 Petrus S Africa
1B7 Pevek USSR
46D2 Pfälzer Wald Region, Germany
57B3 Pforzheim Germany
84D2 Phagwara India
85C3 Phalodi India
46D2 Phalsbourg France
87A1 Phaltan India
77B4 Phangnga Thai
76C3 Phanom Dang Mts Camb
76D3 Phan Rang Viet
76D3 Phan Thiet Viet
17A1 Phenix City USA
76B3 Phet Buri Thai
76D3 Phiafay Laos
19C3 Philadelphia Mississippi, USA
16B2 Philadelphia Pennsylvania, USA
Philippeville = Skikda
46C1 Philippeville Belg
71D2 Philippine S Pacific O
71D2 Philippines Republic, S E Asia
104E3 Philippine Trench Pacific O
15C2 Philipsburg Pennsylvania, USA
12E1 Philip Smith Mts USA
79B2 Phillipe S Phil
6B1 Phillips USA
6B2 Phillipsburg New Jersey, USA
6B2 Philpots Pen Can
76C3 Phnom Penh Camb
9B3 Phoenix Arizona, USA
15C2 Phoenixville USA
76C1 Phong Saly Laos
76C2 Phu Bia Mt Laos
76D3 Phu Cuong Viet
77B4 Phuket Thai
86A2 Phulbãni India
76C2 Phu Miang Mt Thai
76D2 Phu Set Mt Laos
76D1 Phu Tho Viet
77D4 Phu Vinh Viet
47C2 Piacenza Italy
109C2 Pian R Aust
52B2 Pianosa I Italy
52B2 Pianosa I Italy
58C2 Piaseczno Pol
54C1 Piatra-Neamt Rom
31C3 Piauí State, Brazil
47E2 Piave R Italy
99D2 Pibor R Sudan
99D2 Pibor Post Sudan
46B1 Picardie Region, France
19C3 Picayune USA
47B2 Pic de Rochebrune Mt France
34A2 Pichilemu Chile
34C3 Pichi Mahuida Arg
42C2 Pickering Eng
7A4 Pickle Lake Can
96A1 Pico I Acores
47C1 Pico Bernina Mt Switz
51C1 Pico de Anito Mt Spain
24B3 Pico del Infiernillo Mt Mexico
27C3 Pico Duarte Mt Dom Rep
25B3 Pico Brazil
50B1 Picos de Europa Mt Spain
109D2 Picton Aust
111B2 Picton NZ
95A2 Pic Toussidé Mt Chad
35B2 Piedade Brazil
22C2 Piedra Chile

24B2 Piedras Negras Mexico
38K6 Pieksämäki Fin
38K6 Pielinen L Fin
47B2 Piemonte Region, Italy
8C2 Pierre USA
59B3 Pieštany Czech
101H1 Pietermaritzburg S Africa
100B3 Pietersburg S Africa
101H1 Piet Retief S Africa
60B4 Pietrosu Mt Rom
47E1 Pieve di Cadore Italy
13E2 Pigeon L Can
18B2 Piggott USA
34C3 Pigüé Arg
77A4 Pikanglkum L Can
8C3 Pikes Peak USA
100A4 Piketberg S Africa
6F3 Pikintaleq Greenland
82B2 Pik Kommunizma Mt USSR
98B2 Pikounda Congo
82C1 Pik Pobedy Mt China/ USSR
34D3 Pila Arg
58B2 Pila Pol
30E4 Pilar Par
30D3 Pilcomayo R Arg/Par
84D3 Pilibhit India
59B2 Pilica R Pol
109C4 Pillar,C Aust
55B3 Pilos Greece
12C3 Pilot Point USA
12B2 Pilot Station USA
19C3 Pilottown USA
33F4 Pimenta Brazil
77C4 Pinang I Malay
26A2 Pinar del Rio Cuba
34B2 Pinas Arg
46C1 Pinche Belg
13E2 Pincher Creek Can
31B2 Pindaré R Brazil
55B3 Pindhos Mts Greece
19B3 Pine Bluff USA
106C2 Pine Creek Aust
22C1 Pinecrest USA
22C2 Pinedale California, USA
22C2 Pine Flat Res USA
64F3 Pinega R USSR
16A2 Pine Grove USA
17B2 Pine Hills USA
17B2 Pine I USA
19B3 Pineland USA
17B2 Pinellas Park USA
5G3 Pine Point Can
22C2 Pinerolo Italy
31B2 Pinheiro Brazil
70A3 Pini I Indon
55B3 Piniós R Greece
106A4 Pinjarra Aust
13C1 Pink Mountain Can
108B3 Pinnaroo Aust
Pinos,I de, I = Isla de la Juventud
21A2 Pinos,Pt USA
23B2 Pinotepa Nacional Mexico
70C4 Pinrang Indon
60C3 Pinsk USSR
32J7 Pinta I Ecuador
61G1 Pinyug USSR
8B3 Pioche USA
52B2 Piombino Italy

6H3 Piórsá Iceland
59B2 Piotrków Trybunalski Pol
44E2 Piper Oilfield N Sea
21B2 Piper Peak Mt USA
70C4 Pipmuacan Res Can
14B2 Piqua USA
35B1 Piracanjuba Brazil
35B2 Piracicaba Brazil
35B2 Piraçununga Brazil
55B3 Piraiévs Greece
35B2 Pirajuí Brazil
35A1 Piranhas Brazil
35C1 Pirapora Brazil
35B1 Pirenópolis Brazil
35B1 Pires do Rio Brazil
55B3 Pírgos Greece
Pirineos = Pyrénées
31C2 Piripiri Brazil
46D2 Pirmasens Germany
54B2 Pirot Yugos
84C2 Pir Panjál Range Mts India
71D4 Piru Indon
22C3 Piru Creek R USA
42C2 Pisa Italy
32B6 Pisco Peru
57C3 Písek Czech
84B2 Pishin Pak
30C4 Pissis Mt Arg
49E3 Pistoia Italy
50B1 Pisuerga R Spain
28B2 Pit R USA
32B3 Pitalito Colombia
105K5 Pitcairn I Pacific O
38H5 Pite R Sweden
38J5 Piteå Sweden
54B2 Piteşti Rom
63B2 Pit Gorodok USSR
38L6 Pitkyaranta USSR
44C3 Pitlochry Scot
34A3 Pitrutquén Chile
13B2 Pitt I Can
22B1 Pittsburg California, USA
18B2 Pittsburg Kansas, USA
14C2 Pittsburgh USA
18B2 Pittsfield Illinois, USA
16C1 Pittsfield Massachusetts, USA
109D1 Pittsworth Aust
86A1 Piuthan Nepal
47D1 Pizzo Redorta Mt Italy
38B2 Pjórsá Iceland
32A5 Piura Peru
7E5 Placentia B Can
22B1 Placerville USA
46B1 Plaine des Flandres Plain Belg/France
96C2 Plaine du Tidikelt Desert Region, Alg
9C3 Plainview Texas, USA
22B2 Planada USA
31D3 Planalto de Mato Grosso Plat Brazil
31D3 Planalto do Borborema Plat Brazil
32A1 Planalto do Mato Grosso Mts Brazil
19A3 Plano USA
17B2 Plantation USA
17B2 Plant City USA
50A1 Plasencia Spain
61K3 Plast USSR
69F2 Plastun USSR
96C2 Plateau du Tademait Alg
46D2 Plateau Lorrain Plat France
48C2 Plateaux de Limousin Plat France
51C2 Plateaux du Sersou Plat Alg
26C5 Plato Colombia
65G5 Plato Ustyurt Plat

8C2 Platte *R* USA
15D2 Plattsburgh USA
18A1 Plattsmouth USA
57C2 Plauen Germany
60E3 Plavsk USSR
23A2 Playa Azul Mexico
32A4 Playas Ecuador
23B2 Playa Vicente Mexico
50A1 Plaza de Moro
Almanzor *Mt* Spain
22B2 Pleasanton California,
USA
16B3 Pleasantville USA
14A3 Pleasure Ridge Park
USA
76D3 Pleiku Viet
110C1 Plenty,B *R* NZ
58B2 Pleszew Pol
7C4 Pletipi,L Can
54B2 Pleven Bulg
54A2 Pljevlja Yugos
52C2 Ploče Yugos
58B2 Płock Pol
48B2 Ploërmel France
54C2 Ploieşti Rom
60B3 Płońsk Pol
54B2 Plovdiv Bulg
20C1 Plummer USA
12C2 Plummer,Mt USA
100B3 Plumtree Zim
22B1 Plymouth California,
USA
43B4 Plymouth Eng
14A2 Plymouth Indiana,
USA
16D2 Plymouth
Massachusetts, USA
15C2 Plymouth
Pennsylvania, USA
43B4 Plymouth Sd Eng
43C3 Plynlimon *Mt* Wales
57C3 Plzeň Czech
58B2 Pniewy Pol
38K6 Pnyäselkä *L* Fin
97B3 Pô Burkina
47E2 Po *R* Italy
97C4 Pobé Benin
69G2 Pobedino USSR
8B2 Pocatello USA
15C3 Pocomoke City USA
35B2 Pocos de Caldas Brazil
47D2 Po di Volano *R* Italy
63B1 Podkamennaya *R*
USSR
60E2 Podolsk USSR
59D3 Podol'skaya
Vozvyshennost'
Upland USSR
60D1 Podporozh'ye USSR
61F1 Podyuga USSR
100A3 Pofadder S Africa
74B3 P'ohang S Korea
112C9 Poinsett,C Ant
108C2 Point Aust
27E3 Pointe-à-Pitre
Guadeloupe
48B2 Pointe de Barfleur *Pt*
France
98B3 Pointe Noire Congo
98A2 Pointe Pongara *Pt*
Gabon
108B3 Point Fairy Aust
27L1 Point Fortin Trinidad
4B3 Point Hope USA
4G3 Point L Can
12B1 Point Lay USA
16B2 Point Pleasant
New Jersey, USA
14B3 Point Pleasant
W Virginia, USA
47B2 Point St Bernard *Mt*
France
48C2 Poitiers France
48B2 Poitou Region, France
46A2 Poix France
85C3 Pokaran India
109C1 Pokataroo Aust
63E1 Pokrovsk USSR

58B2 Poland
Republic, Europe
92B2 Polatlı Turk
78D3 Polewali Indon
47A1 Poligny France
55B2 Políyiros Greece
39J6 Pori Fin
79B3 Polollo Is Phil
52D1 Polonnye USSR
58D1 Polotsk USSR
60D4 Poltava USSR
52C1 Pölten Austria
64F3 Poluostrov Kanin *Pen*
USSR
61H5 Poluostrov
Mangyshlak *Pen*
USSR
38L5 Poluostrov Rybachiy
Pen USSR
64H2 Poluostrov Yamal *Pen*
USSR
38L5 Polyarnyy Murmansk,
USSR
1B8 Polyarnyy Yakutskaya,
USSR
105H3 Polynesia *Region*
Pacific O
32B5 Pomabamba Peru
35C2 Pomba *R* Brazil
22D3 Pomona USA
18A2 Pomona Res USA
17B2 Pompano Beach USA
16B2 Pompton Lakes USA
18A2 Ponca City USA
27D3 Ponce Puerto Rico
17B2 Ponce de Leon B USA
87B2 Pondicherry India
6C2 Pond Inlet Can
50A1 Ponferrada Spain
98C2 Pongo *R* Sudan
101H1 Pongola *R* S Africa
87B2 Ponnani India
86C2 Ponnyadoung Range
Mts Burma
13E2 Ponoka Can
64F3 Ponoy USSR
48B2 Pons France
35D1 Ponta da Baleia *Pt*
Brazil
96A1 Ponta Delgada Açores
98B3 Ponta do Padrão *Pt*
Angola
35C2 Ponta dos Búzios *Pt*
Brazil
30F4 Ponta Grossa Brazil
35B2 Pontal Brazil
46D2 Pont-à-Mousson
France
30E3 Ponta Pora Brazil
49D2 Pontarlier France
19B3 Pontchartrain,L USA
52B2 Pontedera Italy
52A2 Ponte Leccia Corse
50A1 Pontevedra Spain
18C1 Pontiac Illinois, USA
14B2 Pontiac Michigan,
USA
78B3 Pontianak Indon
48B2 Pontivy France
48B2 Pontoise France
19C3 Pontotoc USA
43C4 Pontypool Wales
43C4 Pontypridd Wales
43B4 Poole Eng
Poona = Pune
108B2 Pooncarie Aust
108B2 Poopelloe,L *L* USA
12C2 Poorman USA
32B3 Popayán Colombia
46B1 Poperinge Belg
19C3 Poplar Bluff USA
18B2 Poplar Bluff USA
19C3 Poplarville USA
107D1 Popndetta PNG
23B2 Popocatepetl *Mt*
Mexico
98B3 Popokabaka Zaïre
71F4 Popondetta PNG

54C2 Popovo Bulg
85B4 Porbandar India
13A2 Porcher I Can
12F1 Porcupine *R* Can/USA
52B1 Poreč Yugos
35A2 Porecatu Brazil
39J6 Pori Fin
111B2 Porirua NZ
38H5 Porjus Sweden
69G2 Poronaysk USSR
47B1 Porrentruy Switz
38K4 Porsangen *Inlet* Nor
39F7 Porsgrunn Nor
45C1 Portadown N Ire
8D2 Portage la Prairie Can
13C3 Port Alberni Can
50A2 Portalegre Port
9C3 Portales USA
7C5 Port Alfred Can
100B4 Port Alfred S Africa
13B2 Port Alice Can
19B3 Port Allen USA
20B1 Port Angeles USA
26B3 Port Antonio Jamaica
45C2 Portarlington
Irish Rep
107D4 Port Arthur USA
108A2 Port-au-Prince Haiti
26C3 Port-au-Prince Haiti
14B2 Port Austin USA
100B3 Port Campbell Aust
86B2 Port Canning India
7D5 Port Cartier Can
111B3 Port Chalmers NZ
17B2 Port Charlotte USA
16C2 Port Chester USA
15C2 Port Colborne Can
15C2 Port Credit Can
109C4 Port Davey Aust
26C3 Port-de-Paix Haiti
77C5 Port Dickson Malay
100C4 Port Edward S Africa
35C1 Porteirinha Brazil
108A4 Port Elizabeth S Africa
27N2 Porter Pt St Vincent
21B2 Porterville USA
107D4 Port Fairy Aust
98A3 Port Gentil Gabon
19B3 Port Gibson USA
12D3 Port Graham USA
20B1 Port Hammond USA
89E7 Port Harcourt Nig
13B2 Port Hardy Can
7D5 Port Hawkesbury Can
106A3 Port Hedland Aust
Port Heiden = Meshik
43B3 Porthmadog Wales
7E4 Port Hope Simpson
Can
22C3 Port Hueneme USA
14B2 Port Huron USA
50A2 Portimão Port
109D2 Port Jackson *B* Aust
16C2 Port Jefferson USA
16B2 Port Jervis USA
109D2 Port Kembla Aust
14B2 Portland Indiana, USA
10C2 Portland Maine, USA
109C2 Portland New South
Wales, Aust
20B1 Portland Oregon, USA
108B3 Portland Victoria, Aust
27H2 Portland Bight *B*
Jamaica
43C4 Portland Bill *Pt* Eng
109C4 Portland,C Aust
13A1 Portland Canal Can/
USA
110C1 Portland I NZ
27H2 Portland Pt Jamaica
45C2 Port Laoise Irish Rep
108A2 Port Lincoln Aust
97A4 Port Loko Sierra
Leone
101E3 Port Louis Mauritius
108B3 Port MacDonnell Aust
13B2 Port McNeill Can

109D2 Port Macquarie Aust
12B3 Port Moller USA
107D1 Port Moresby PNG
100A3 Port Nolloth S Africa
16B3 Port Norris USA
89E7 Port Novo Benin
50A1 Porto Port
30F5 Pôrto Alegre Brazil
33F6 Pôrto Artur Brazil
35A2 Pôrto 15 de Novembro
Brazil
30F3 Pôrto E Cunha Brazil
52B2 Portoferraio Italy
27E4 Port of Spain Trinidad
47D2 Portomaggiore Italy
97C4 Porto Novo Benin
21B2 Port Orchard USA
20B2 Port Orford USA
96A1 Pôrto Santo *I* Medeira
31D5 Pôrto Seguro Brazil
53A2 Porto Torres
Sardegna
53A2 Porto Vecchio Corse
33E5 Pôrto Velho Brazil
111A3 Port Pegasus *B* NZ
108B3 Port Phillip *B* Aust
108A2 Port Pirie Aust
44A3 Portree Scot
20B1 Port Renfrew Can
27J2 Port Royal Jamaica
17B1 Port Royal Sd USA
45C1 Portrush N Ire
92B3 Port Said Egypt
17A2 Port St Joe USA
100B4 Port St Johns S Africa
7E4 Port Saunders Can
100C4 Port Shepstone
S Africa
13A2 Port Simpson Can
27O2 Portsmouth Dominica
43D4 Portsmouth Eng
14B3 Portsmouth Ohio,
USA
11C3 Portsmouth Virginia,
USA
109D2 Port Stephens *B* Aust
95C3 Port Sudan Sudan
19C3 Port Sulphur USA
38K5 Porttipahdan Tekojärvi
Res Fin
50A2 Portugal
Republic, Europe
14A2 Port Washington USA
77C5 Port Weld Malay
32D6 Porvenir Bol
39K6 Porvoo Fin
30E4 Posadas Arg
50A2 Posadas Spain
47D1 Poschiavo Switz
6B2 Posheim Pen Can
90C3 Posht-e Badam Iran
71D4 Poso Indon
58D1 Posvy USSR
14B2 Post Clinton USA
7C4 Poste-de-la-Baleine
Can
100B3 Postmasburg S Africa
52B1 Postojna Yugos
74C2 Pos'yet USSR
101G1 Potchefstroom
S Africa
19B2 Poteau USA
53C2 Potenza Italy
100B3 Potgietersrus S Africa
97D3 Potiskum Nig
20C1 Potlatch USA
15C3 Potomac *R* USA
30C2 Potosi Bol
30C4 Potrerillos Chile
56C2 Potsdam Germany
16B2 Pottstown USA
16A2 Pottsville USA
16C2 Poughkeepsie USA
35B2 Pouso Alegre Brazil
71P9 Poverty B NZ
61F3 Povorino USSR
7C4 Povungnituk Can
8C2 Powder *R* USA

106C2 Powell Creek Aust
9B3 Powell,L USA
13C3 Powell River Can
82C Power R USA
43C3 Powys County, Wales
73D4 Poyang Hu L China
92B2 Pozantı Turk
23B1 Poza Rica Mexico
58B2 Poznań Pol
30E3 Pozo Colorado Par
53B2 Pozzuoli Italy
97B4 Pra R Ghana
76C3 Prachin Buri Thai
76C3 Prachuap Khiri Khan Thai
59B2 Praděd Mt Czech
49C3 Pradelles France
35D1 Prado Brazil
Prague = Praha
57C2 Praha Czech
97A4 Praia Cape Verde
33E5 Prainha Brazil
18B2 Prairie Village USA
76C3 Prakhon Chai Thai
35B1 Prata Brazil
35B1 Prata R Brazil
Prates = Dongsha Qundao
49E3 Prato Italy
16B1 Prattsville USA
17A1 Prattville USA
48B1 Prawle Pt Eng
47D1 Praya Indon
47D1 Predazzo Italy
63B2 Predivinsk USSR
58C2 Pregolyu R USSR
76D3 Prek Kak Camb
56C2 Prenzlau Germany
76A3 Preparis I Burma
76A2 Preparis North Chan Burma
59B3 Přerov Czech
23A2 Presa del Infiernillo Mexico
9B3 Prescott Arizona, USA
19B3 Prescott Arkansas, USA
15C2 Prescott Can
30D4 Presidencia Roque Sáenz Peña Arg
35A2 Presidente Epitácio Brazil
112C2 Presidente Frei Base Ant
23B2 Presidente Miguél Aleman L Mexico
35A2 Presidente Prudente Brazil
30F3 Presidenté Vargas Brazil
35A2 Presidente Venceslau Brazil
59C3 Prešov Czech
55B2 Prespansko Jezero L Yugos
10D2 Presque Isle USA
42C3 Preston Eng
8B2 Preston Idaho, USA
18B2 Preston Missouri, USA
42B2 Prestwick Scot
31B6 Prêto Brazil
35B1 Prêto R Brazil
101G1 Pretoria S Africa
55B3 Préveza Greece
76D3 Prey Veng Camb
8B3 Price USA
13B2 Price I Can
60D4 Prichernomorskaya Nizmennost' Lowland USSR
27M2 Prickly Pt Grenada
58C1 Priekule USSR
100B3 Prieska S Africa
20C1 Priest L USA
20C1 Priest River USA

61G4 Prikaspiyskaya Nizmennost' Region USSR
55B2 Prilep Yugos
60D3 Priluki USSR
34C2 Primero R Arg
39K6 Primorsk USSR
60E4 Primorsko-Akhtarsk USSR
13F2 Primrose L Can
5H4 Prince Albert Can
4F2 Prince Albert,C Can
55C3 Psará I Greece
60C2 Pskov USSR
58D2 Ptich R USSR
55B2 Ptolemaïs Greece
32C5 Pucallpa Peru
73D4 Pucheng China
34A3 Pucón Chile
39K5 Pudasjärvi Fin
87B2 Pudukkottai India
23B2 Puebla Mexico
23B2 Puebla State, Mexico
50A1 Puebla de Sanabria Spain
50A1 Puebla de Trives Spain
9C2 Pueblo USA
34B3 Puelches Arg
34B3 Puelén Arg
23A2 Puente Ixbapa Mexico
32A5 Puente del Inca Arg
32A5 Puerta Aguja Peru
30B2 Puerta Coles Peru
34B2 Puerta de los Llanos Arg
31D3 Puerta do Calcanhar Pt Brazil
32C1 Puerta Gallinas Colombia
23B2 Puerta Maldonado Pt Mexico
32A2 Puerta Mariato Panama
29C5 Puerta Médanosa Pt Arg
23A2 Puerta Mongrove Mexico
25E4 Puerta San Blas Pt Panama
23A2 Puerta San Telmo Mexico
29B5 Puerto Aisén Chile
25D4 Puerto Armuelles Panama
33F6 Puerto Artur Brazil
32B3 Puerto Asis Colombia
32D2 Puerto Ayacucho Ven
25D3 Puerto Barrios Guatemala
32C2 Puerto Berrio Colombia
32D1 Puerto Cabello Ven
25D3 Puerto Cabezas Nic
32D2 Puerto Carreño Colombia
25D4 Puerto Cortes Costa Rica
25D3 Puerto Cortés Honduras
96A2 Puerto del Rosario Canary Is
30F3 Puerto E Cunha Brazil
32C1 Puerto Fijo Ven
31B3 Puerto Franco Brazil
32D6 Puerto Heath Bol
25D2 Puerto Juarez Mexico
33E1 Puerto la Cruz Ven
50B2 Puertollano Spain
27C4 Puerto Lopez Colombia
29D4 Puerto Madryn Arg
32D6 Puerto Maldonado Peru
23B2 Puerto Marquéz Mexico
29B4 Puerto Montt Chile
30E3 Puerto Murtinho Brazil

49C2 Provins France
8B2 Provo USA
13E2 Provost Can
4D2 Prudhoe Bay USA
6D2 Prudhon Land Greenland
81C2 Pruszkow Pol
60C4 Prutul R USSR
58C2 Pruzhany USSR
18A2 Pryor USA
57A1 Przemysl'1 Pol
55C3 Psará I Greece
52B2 Pula Yugos
15C2 Pulaski New York, USA
71E4 Pulau Kolepom I Indon
70A4 Pulau Pulau Batu Is Indon
58C2 Pulawy Pol
87C2 Pulicat,L India
84B1 Pul-i-Khumri Afghan
87B3 Puliyangudi India
20C1 Pullman USA
71E3 Pulo Anna Merir I Pacific O
79B2 Pulog,Mt Phil
38L5 Pulozero USSR
58C2 Pultusk Pol
30C4 Puna de Atacama Arg
86B1 Punakha Bhutan
84C2 Punch Pak
87A1 Pune India
23A2 Punéper Mexico
98C3 Punia Zaïre
34A2 Punitaqui Chile
79C4 Punjab Province, Pak
84D2 Punjab State, India
30B2 Puno Peru
24A2 Punta Abreojos Pt Mexico
53C3 Punta Alice Pt Italy
32A2 Punta Alta Arg
29B6 Punta Arenas Chile
34A2 Punta Baja Pt Mexico
34A2 Punta Curaumilla Pt Chile
100A2 Punta da Marca Pt Angola
101C3 Punta de Barra Falsa Pt Mozam
29F2 Punta del Este Urug
23A2 Punta Eugenia Pt Mexico
25D3 Punta Gorda Belize
17B2 Punta Gorda USA
34A3 Punta Lavapié Pt Chile
34A2 Punta Lengua de Vaca Pt Chile
53B2 Punta Licosa Pt Italy
34A1 Punta Poroto Pt Chile
9B4 Punta San Antonia Pt Mexico
34A2 Punta Topocalma Chile
73C4 Puqi China
64J3 Pur R USSR
19A2 Purcell USA
12C1 Purcell Mt USA
13D2 Purcell Mts Can
34A3 Purén Chile

29B6 Puerto Natales Chile
24A1 Puerto Peñasco Mexico
29D4 Puerto Pirámides Arg
27C3 Puerto Plata Dom Rep
79A4 Puerto Princesa Phil
32B3 Puerto Rico Colombia
27D3 Puerto Rico I Caribbean S
27D3 Puerto Rico Trench Caribbean S
23A2 Puerto San Juan de Lima Mexico
33G4 Puerto Santanga Brazil
30E2 Puerto Suárez Bol
24B2 Puerto Vallarta Mexico
29B4 Puerto Varas Chile
30D2 Puerto Villarroel Bol
61G3 Pugachev USSR
84C3 Pugal India
51C1 Puigcerdá Spain
111B2 Pukaki,L L NZ
74B2 Pukch'ŏng N Korea
110B1 Pukekobe NZ
111B2 Puketeraki Range Mts NZ

86B2 Puri India
87B1 Pūrna India
86B1 Pūrnia India
76C3 Pursat Camb
23A1 Puruandiro Mexico
33E4 Purus R Brazil
19C3 Purvis USA
78B4 Purwokerto Indon
78C4 Purworejo Indon
85D5 Pusad India
74B3 Pusan S Korea
60D2 Pushkin USSR
58D1 Pustochka USSR
82D3 Puta Burma
34A2 Putaendo Chile
110C1 Putaruru NZ
73D4 Putian China
16D2 Putnam USA
87B3 Puttalam Sri Lanka
56C2 Puttgarden Germany
32B4 Putumayo R Ecuador
78C2 Putussibau Indon
38K6 Puulavesi L Fin
20B1 Puyallup USA
49C2 Puy de Sancy Mt
  France
111A3 Puysegur Pt NZ
99C3 Pweto Zaire
43B3 Pwllheli Wales
76B2 Pyapon Burma
61F5 Pyatigorsk USSR
74B3 P'yŏngyang N Korea
108B3 Pyramid Hill Aust
75D4 Pyramid L USA
111A2 Pyramid,Mt NZ
48B3 Pyrénées Mts France
58D1 Pytalovo USSR
76B2 Pyu Burma

Q

94B2 Qabatiya Israel
94C3 Qā'el Hafira Mud Flats
  Jordan
94C3 Qā'el Jinz Mud Flats
  Jordan
68B3 Qaidam Pendi Salt
  Flat China
94C2 Qa Khanna Salt Marsh
  Jordan
99D1 Qala'en Nahl Sudan
84B2 Qalat Afghan
94C1 Qal'at al Hisn Syria
81C3 Qal'at Bishah
  S Arabia
93E3 Qal'at Sālih Iraq
68B3 Qamdo China
99E2 Qardho Somalia
90A3 Qareh Iran
91A4 Qaryat al Ulyā
  S Arabia
94C3 Qasr el Kharana
  Jordan
91D4 Qasr-e-Qand Iran
95B2 Qasr Farafra Egypt
94C2 Qatana Syria
91B4 Qatar Emirate,
  Arabian Pen
94C3 Qatrāna Jordan
95B2 Qattāra Depression
  Egypt
90C3 Qāyen Iran
90A2 Qazvin Iran
95C2 Qena Egypt
90A2 Qeydār Iran
91B4 Qeys I Iran
94B3 Qeziot Israel
73B5 Qian Jiang R China
72E1 Qian Shan Upland
  China
72E3 Qidong China
73B4 Qijiang China
84B2 Qila Saifullah Pak
72A2 Qilian China
68B3 Qilian Shan China
72B3 Qin'an China

72E2 Qingdao China
72A2 Qinghai Province,
  China
68B3 Qinghai Hu L China
72D3 Qingjiang Jiangsu,
  China
73D4 Qingjiang Jiangxi,
  China
72B3 Qing Jiang R China
72C2 Qingshuihe China
72B2 Qingshui He R China
72B2 Qingtonxia China
72D2 Qingyang China
74B2 Qingyuan Liaoning,
  China
73D4 Qingyuan Zhejiang,
  China
82C2 Qing Zang Upland
  China
72D2 Qinhuangdao China
72B3 Qin Ling Mts China
73B5 Qinzhou China
76E2 Qionghai China
73A3 Qiongdai Shan Upland
  China
76D1 Qiongzhou Haixia Str
  China
69E2 Qiqihar China
94B3 Qiryat Ata Israel
94B3 Qiryat Gat Israel
94B2 Qiryat Shemona Israel
94B2 Qiryat Yam Israel
94B2 Qishon R Israel
63A3 Qitai China
73C4 Qiyang China
72B1 Qog Qi China
90B2 Qolleh-ye Damavand
  Mt Iran
90B3 Qom Iran
90B3 Qomisheh Iran
  Qomolangma Feng =
  Everest,Mt
94C1 Qornet es Saouda Mt
  Leb
6E3 Qôrnoq Greenland
91C4 Qotbābad Iran
16C1 Quabbin Res USA
16B2 Quakertown USA
77C3 Quam Phu Quoc I Viet
76D2 Quang Ngai Viet
76D2 Quang Tri Viet
77D4 Quan Long Viet
73D5 Quanzhou Fujian,
  China
73C4 Quanzhou Guangxi,
  China
5H4 Qu' Appelle R Can
91C5 Quaraiyyāt Oman
13B2 Quatsino Sd Can
90C2 Quchan Iran
109C3 Queanbeyan Aust
15D1 Québec Can
7C4 Quebec Province, Can
35B1 Quebra-Anzol R Brazil
34D2 Quebracho Urug
30F4 Quedas do Iguaçu
  Brazil/Arg
16A3 Queen Anne USA
13B2 Queen Bess,Mt Can
5E4 Queen Charlotte Is
  Can
13B2 Queen Charlotte Sd
  Can
13B2 Queen Charlotte Str
  Can
4H1 Queen Elizabeth Is
  Can
112B9 Queen Mary Land
  Region, Ant
4H3 Queen Maud G Can
112A Queen Maud Mts Ant
16C2 Queens Borough, New
  York, USA
108B3 Queenscliff Aust
107D3 Queensland State,
  Aust
109C4 Queenstown Aust

111A3 Queenstown NZ
100B4 Queenstown S Africa
16A3 Queenstown USA
98B3 Quela Angola
101C2 Quelimane Mozam
34C3 Quemuquemi Arg
13C2 Quensel L Can
34D3 Quequén Arg
34D3 Quequén R Arg
23A1 Querétaro Mexico
23A1 Querétaro State,
  Mexico
13C2 Quesnel Can
84B2 Quetta Pak
25C3 Quezaltenango
  Guatemala
79B3 Quezon City Phil
100A2 Quibala Angola
98B3 Quibaxe Angola
32B2 Quibdó Colombia
48B2 Quiberon France
98B3 Quicama Nat Pk
  Angola
73A4 Quijing China
34A2 Quilima Chile
34C2 Quilino Arg
32C6 Quillabamba Peru
30C2 Quillacollo Bol
48C3 Quillan France
5H4 Quill L Can
5H4 Quill Lakes Can
34A2 Quillota Chile
87B3 Quilon India
108B1 Quilpie Aust
34A2 Quilpué Chile
98B3 Quimbele Angola
48B2 Quimper France
48B2 Quimperlé France
21A2 Quincy California,
  USA
10A3 Quincy Illinois, USA
16D1 Quincy
  Massachusetts, USA
34A2 Quines Arg
12B3 Quinhagak USA
01 Qui Nhon Viet
50B2 Quintanar de la Orden
  Spain
34A2 Quintero Chile
34C2 Quinto R Arg
34A3 Quirihue Chile
100A2 Quirima Angola
109D2 Quirindi Aust
101D2 Quissanga Mozam
101C3 Quissico Mozam
32B4 Quito Ecuador
31D2 Quixadá Brazil
108A2 Quorn Aust
95C2 Quseir Egypt
6E3 Qutdligssat Greenland
  Quthing = Moyeni
73B3 Qu Xian Sichuan,
  China
73D4 Qu Xian Zhejiang,
  China
76D2 Quynh Luu Viet
72C2 Quzhou Viet
86C1 Qüzü China

R

38J6 Raahe Fin
44A3 Raasay I Scot
44A3 Raasay,Sound of Chan
  Scot
52B2 Rab I Yugos
78D4 Raba Indon
59B3 Rába R Hung
96B1 Rabat Mor
94B3 Rabba Israel
80B3 Rabigh S Arabia
47B2 Racconigi Italy
7E5 Race,C Can
75B3 Rachaya Leb
57C3 Rachel Mt Germany
76D3 Rach Gia Viet
14A2 Racine USA

59D3 Rădăuti Rom
85C4 Radhanpur India
27L1 Radix,Pt Trinidad
58C2 Radom Pol
59B2 Radomsko Pol
58C1 Radviliškis Latvia
4G3 Rae Can
86A1 Rãe Bareli India
6B3 Rae Isthmus Can
4G3 Rae L Can
110C1 Raetihi NZ
34C2 Rafaela Arg
94B3 Rafah Egypt
98C2 Rafai CAR
93D3 Rafhã Al Jumaymah
  S Arabia
91C3 Rafsanjän Iran
98C2 Raga Sudan
27R3 Ragged Pt Barbados
95A2 Raguba Libya
53B3 Ragusa Italy
99D1 Rahad R Sudan
84C3 Rahimyar Khan Pak
90B3 Rãhjerd Iran
34D2 Raíces Arg
87B1 Rãichur India
86A2 Rãigarh India
85D5 Raigarh India
108B3 Rainbow Aust
17A1 Rainbow City USA
20B1 Rainier USA
20B1 Rainier,Mt USA
12D2 Rainy P USA
10A2 Rainy River Can
86A2 Raipur India
87C1 Rãjahmundry India
78C2 Rajang R Malay
84C3 Rajanpur Pak
87B3 Rãjapalaiyam India
85C3 Rãjasthan State, India
84D3 Rãjgarh India
85D4 Rãjgarh State, India
85C4 Rãjkot India
86B2 Rãjmahãl Hills India
86A2 Rãj Nandgaon India
85C4 Rãjpipla India
86B2 Rãjshahi Bang
85D4 Rajur India
111B2 Rakaia R NZ
78B4 Rakata I Indon
82C3 Raka Zangbo R China
59C3 Rakhov USSR
100B3 Rakops Botswana
58D2 Rakov USSR
11C3 Raleigh USA
7A5 Ralny L Can
94B2 Rama Israel
94B3 Ramallah Israel
87B3 Rãmanãthapuram
  India
69G2 Ramapo Deep
  Pacific O
94B2 Ramat Gan Israel
46A2 Rambouillet France
86B2 Rãmgarh Bihar, India
85C3 Rãmgarh Rajasthan,
  India
90A3 Rãmhormoz Iran
94B3 Ramla Israel
91C5 Ramlat Al Wahibah
  Region, Oman
21B3 Ramona USA
84D3 Rãmpur India
85D4 Rãmpura India
90B2 Rãmsar Iran
42B2 Ramsey Eng
16B2 Ramsey USA
43B4 Ramsey I Wales
43E4 Ramsgate Eng
94C2 Ramtha Jordan
71F4 Ramu R PNG
34A2 Rancagua Chile
86B2 Rãnchi India
86A2 Rãnchi Plat India
39G7 Randers Den
101G1 Randfontein S Africa
15D2 Randolph Vermont,
  USA

111B3 Ranfurly NZ
86C2 Rangamati Bang
111B2 Rangiora NZ
110C1 Rangitaiki R NZ
111B2 Rangitata R NZ
110C1 Rangitikei R NZ
76B2 Rangoon Burma
86B1 Rangpur India
87B2 Rānibennur India
86B2 Rāniganj India
109C2 Rankins Springs Aust
6A3 Ranklin Inlet Can
85B4 Rann of Kachchh
    Flood Area India
77B4 Ranong Thai
70A3 Rantauparapat Indon
18C1 Rantoul USA
49D3 Rapallo Italy
34A2 Rapel R Chile
6D3 Raper,C Can
8C2 Rapid City USA
14A1 Rapid River USA
15C3 Rappahannock R USA
47C1 Rapperswil Switz
16B2 Raritan B US
95C2 Ras Abu Shagara C
    Sudan
93D2 Ra's al 'Ayn Syria
91C5 Ra's al Hadd C Oman
91C4 Ras al Kaimah UAE
91C5 Ras-al-Kuh C Iran
81D4 Ra's al Madrakah C
    Oman
91A4 Ra's az Zawr C
    S Arabia
95C2 Rãs Bânâs C Egypt
94A3 Ras Burūn C Egypt
99D1 Ras Dashan Mt Eth
90A3 Ra's e-Barkan Pt Iran
92A3 Rãs el Kenâyis Pt
    Egypt
81D4 Ra's Fartak C Yemen
95C2 Rãs Ghârib Egypt
99D1 Rashad Sudan
94B3 Rashādīya Jordan
92B3 Rashid Egypt
90A2 Rasht Iran
91C5 Ra's Jibish C Oman
99E1 Ras Khanzira C
    Somalia
84B3 Ras Koh Mt Pak
95C2 Rãs Muhammad C
    Egypt
96A2 Ras Nouadhibou C
    Maur
69H2 Rasshua I USSR
61F3 Rasskazovo USSR
91A4 Ra's Tanãqib C
    S Arabia
91B4 Ra's Tannūrah
83B3 Rastatt Germany
    Ras Uarc = Cabo Tres
    Forcas
99F1 Ras Xaafuun C
    Somalia
84C3 Ratangarh India
76B3 Rat Buri Thai
85D3 Rath India
56C2 Rathenow Germany
45B2 Rathkeale Irish Rep
45C1 Rathlin I N Ire
45B2 Rath Luirc Irish Rep
80B3 Ratlām India
87A1 Ratnāgiri India
87C3 Ratnapura Sri Lanka
58C2 Ratno USSR
47D1 Rattenberg Austria
39H6 Rättvik Sweden
12H3 Ratz,Mt Can
37H9 Rauch Arg
110C1 Raukumara Range NZ
35C2 Raul Soares Brazil
39J6 Rauma Fin
86A2 Raurkela India
90A3 Ravānsar Iran

90C3 Rãvar Iran
59C2 Rava Russkaya USSR
16C1 Ravena USA
52B2 Ravenna Italy
57B3 Ravensburg Germany
107D2 Ravenshoe Aust
84C2 Ravi R Pak
84C2 Rawalpindi Pak
58B2 Rawicz Pol
106B4 Rawlinna Aust
8C2 Rawlins USA
93D2 Rawndiz Iraq
29C4 Rawson Arg
78C3 Raya Mt Indon
87B2 Rãyadurg India
94C2 Rayak Leb
7E5 Ray,C Can
91C4 Rãyen Iran
22C2 Raymond California,
    USA
20B1 Raymond
    Washington, USA
109D2 Raymond Terrace
    Aust
12D1 Ray Mts USA
23B1 Rayon Mexico
90A2 Razan Iran
54C2 Razgrad Bulg
54C2 Razim L Rom
43D4 Reading Eng
16C2 Reading USA
4G3 Read Island Can
16C1 Readsboro USA
34B2 Real de Padre Arg
34C3 Realicó Arg
95B2 Rebiana Well Libya
95B2 Rebiana Sand Sea
    Libya
38L6 Reboly USSR
106B4 Recherche,Arch of the
    Is Aust
31E3 Recife Brazil
107F2 Récifs D'Entrecasteaux
    Nouvelle Calédonie
46D1 Recklinghausen
    Germany
30E4 Reconquista Arg
19B3 Red R USA
77C4 Redang I Malay
16B2 Red Bank New Jersey,
    USA
21A1 Red Bluff USA
42D2 Redcar Eng
13E2 Redcliff Can
109D1 Redcliffe Aust
108B2 Red Cliffs Aust
13E2 Red Deer Can
13E2 Red Deer R Can
20B2 Redding USA
10A2 Red L USA
7A4 Red Lake Can
22D3 Redlands USA
16A3 Red Lion USA
20B2 Redmond USA
18A1 Red Oak USA
48B2 Redon France
22C4 Redondo Beach USA
12D2 Redoubt V USA
61K3 Redva USSR
73B5 Red River Delta
    Vietnam
80B3 Red Sea Africa/
    Arabian Pen
13E2 Redwater Can
22A2 Redwood City USA
14A2 Reed City USA
22C2 Reedley USA
20B2 Reedsport USA
111B2 Reefton NZ
93C2 Refahiye Turk
35D1 Regência Brazil
57C3 Regensburg Germany
96C2 Reggane Alg
53C3 Reggio di Calabria
    Italy
47D2 Reggio Nell'Emilia
    Italy
54B1 Reghin Rom
5H4 Regina Can

100A3 Rehoboth Namibia
15C3 Rehoboth Beach USA
94B3 Rehovot Israel
32D1 Reicito Ven
43C4 Reigate Eng
48C2 Reims France
5H4 Reindeer R Can
50B1 Reinosa Spain
16A3 Reisterstown USA
101G1 Reitz S Africa
4H3 Reliance Can
108A2 Remarkable,Mt Aust
78C4 Rembang Indon
91C4 Remeshk Iran
46D1 Remscheid Germany
18C2 Rend,L USA
56B2 Rendsburg Germany
15C2 Renfrew Can
78A3 Rengat Indon
34A2 Rengo Chile
59D3 Reni USSR
99D1 Renk Sudan
6H2 Renland Pen
    Greenland
108B2 Renmark Aust
107F2 Rennell I Solomon Is
48B2 Rennes France
21B2 Reno USA
47D2 Reno R Italy
15C2 Renovo USA
16C1 Rensselaer USA
70D4 Reo Indon
35B2 Represa de Furnas
    Dam Brazil
35B1 Represa Três Marias
    Dam Brazil
20C1 Republic USA
41B3 Republic of Ireland
    NW Europe
6B3 Repulse Bay Can
15C1 Réservoir Baskatong
    Res Can
7C5 Réservoire Cabonga
    Res Can
7C5 Réservoire Gouin Res
    Can
10D1 Réservoire
    Manicouagan Res
    Can
90B2 Reshteh-ye Alborz
    Mts Iran
72A2 Reshui China
30E4 Resistencia Arg
54B1 Resita Rom
111A3 Resolution I NZ
6D3 Resolution Island Can
101H1 Ressano Garcia
    Mozam
34B2 Retamito Arg
46C2 Rethel France
54C3 Réthimnon Greece
89K10 Reunion I Indian O
51C1 Reus Spain
47C1 Reuss R Switz
47D1 Reutte Austria
61K3 Revda USSR
13D2 Revelstoke Can
24A3 Revillagigedo Is
    Mexico
12H3 Revillagigedo I USA
46C2 Revin France
94B3 Revivim Israel
86A2 Rewa India
84B3 Rewari India
8B2 Rexburg USA
38A2 Reykjavik Iceland
24C2 Reynosa Mexico
48B2 Rezé France
48B2 Reze France
58D1 Rezekne USSR
61K2 Rezh USSR
47C1 Rhätikon Mts Austria/
    Switz
94B1 Rhazir Republic, Leb
56B2 Rhein R W Europe
56B2 Rheine Germany
47B1 Rheinfielden Switz

49D2 Rheinland Pfalz
    Region, Germany
47C1 Rheinwaldhorn Mt
    Switz
    Rhine = Rhein
16C2 Rhinebeck USA
10B2 Rhinelander USA
49C2 Rho Italy
15D2 Rhode Island State,
    USA
16D2 Rhode Island Sd USA
    Rhodes = Ródhos
49C3 Rhône R France
43C3 Rhyl Wales
31D4 Riachão do Jacuipe
    Brazil
50A1 Ria de Arosa B Spain
50A1 Ria de Betanzos B
    Spain
50A1 Ria de Corcubion B
    Spain
50A1 Ria de Lage B Spain
50A1 Ria de Sta Marta B
    Spain
50A1 Ria de Vigo B Spain
84C2 Riasi Pak
50A1 Ribadeo Spain
35A2 Ribas do Rio Pardo
    Brazil
101C2 Ribauè Mozam
42C3 Ribble R Eng
35B2 Ribeira Brazil
35B2 Ribeirão Prêto Brazil
32D6 Riberalta Bol
15C2 Rice L Can
10A2 Rice Lake USA
101H1 Richard's Bay S Africa
19A3 Richardson USA
12C1 Richardson Mts Can
8B3 Richfield USA
20C1 Richland USA
22A2 Richmond California,
    USA
11H1 Richmond Natal,
    S Africa
109D2 Richmond New South
    Wales, Aust
111B2 Richmond NZ
107D3 Richmond
    Queensland, Aust
10C3 Richmond Virginia,
    USA
111B2 Richmond Range Mts
    NZ
15C2 Rideau,L Can
17B1 Ridgeland USA
15C2 Ridgway USA
27D4 Riecito Ven
47C1 Rienza R Italy
57C2 Riesa Germany
29B6 Riesco I Chile
101F1 Riet R S Africa
52B2 Rieti Italy
50B2 Rif Mts Mor
58C1 Riga USSR
58C1 Riga,G of USSR
91C4 Rigan Iran
20C1 Riggins USA
7E4 Rigolet Can
39J6 Riihimaki Fin
52B1 Rijeka Yugos
13E2 Rimbey Can
39H7 Rimbo Sweden
52B2 Rimini Italy
54C1 Rimnicu Sărat Rom
54B1 Rimnicu Vilcea Rom
10D2 Rimouski Can
23A1 Rincón de Romos
    Mexico
39F7 Ringkøbing Den
98A2 Rio Benito Eq Guinea
32D5 Rio Branco Brazil
24B1 Rio Bravo del Norte R
    Mexico/USA
32C1 Riochacha Colombia
35B2 Rio Claro Brazil
27L1 Rio Claro Trinidad
34C3 Rio Colorado Arg

34C2 Rio Cuarto Arg
31D4 Rio de Jacuipe Brazil
35C2 Rio de Janeiro Brazil
35C2 Rio de Janeiro State, Brazil
29E3 Rio de la Plata Est Arg/Urug
29C6 Rio Gallegos Arg
29C6 Rio Grande Arg
30F5 Rio Grande Brazil
26A4 Rio Grande Nic
25D3 Rio Grande R Nic
24B2 Rio Grande R Mexico/USA
23A1 Rio Grande de Santiago Mexico
31D3 Rio Grande do Norte State, Brazil
30F4 Rio Grande do Sul State, Brazil
103G6 Rio Grande Rise Atlantic O
26C4 Riohacha Colombia
49C2 Riom France
32B4 Riombamba Ecuador
30C2 Rio Mulatos Bol
29C3 Rio Negro State, Arg
30F4 Rio Pardo Brazil
34C2 Rio Tercero Arg
33E6 Rio Theodore Roosevelt R Brazil
29B6 Rio Turbio Arg
35A1 Rio Verde Brazil
23A1 Rio Verde Mexico
14B3 Ripley Ohio, USA
14B3 Ripley West Virginia, USA
42D2 Ripon Eng
22B2 Ripon USA
94B3 Rishon le Zion Israel
16A3 Rising Sun USA
39F7 Riser Nor
6E2 Ritenbenk Greenland
22C2 Ritter,Mt USA
20C1 Ritzville USA
34B2 Rivadavia Arg
34A1 Rivadavia Chile
34C3 Rivadavia Gonzalez Moreno Arg
47D2 Riva de Garda Italy
34C3 Rivera Arg
29E2 Rivera Urug
22B2 Riverbank USA
97B4 River Cess Lib
16C2 Riverhead USA
108B3 Riverina Aust
111A3 Riverdale NZ
22D4 Riverside USA
13B2 Rivers Inlet Can
111A3 Riverton NZ
8C2 Riverton USA
17B2 Riviera Beach USA
7C4 Rivière aux Feuilles R Can
7D4 Rivière de la Baleine R Can
7D4 Rivière du Petit Mécatina R Can
46C2 Rivigny-sur-Ornain France
93D1 Rize Turk
72D2 Rizhao China
Rizhskiy Zaliv = Riga,G of
39F7 Rjukan Nor
6B2 Roanes Pen Can
49C2 Roanne France
17A1 Roanoke Alabama, USA
11C3 Roanoke Virginia, USA
11C3 Roanoke R USA
45B3 Roaringwater B Irish Rep
38J6 Robertson Sweden
19B2 Robert S Kerr Res USA
97A4 Robertsport Lib

7C5 Roberval Can
30H6 Robinson Crusoe I Chile
108B2 Robinvale Aust
13D2 Robson,Mt Can
24A3 Roca Partida I Mexico
103G5 Rocas I Atlantic O
31E2 Rocas I Brazil
29F2 Rocha Urug
42C3 Rochdale Eng
31E2 Rochefort France
5G3 Rocher River Can
108B3 Rochester Aust
7C5 Rochester Can
43E4 Rochester Eng
10A2 Rochester Minnesota, USA
15D2 Rochester New Hampshire, USA
10C2 Rochester New York, USA
10B2 Rockford USA
11B3 Rock Hill USA
10A2 Rock Island USA
108B3 Rocklands Res Aust
17B2 Rockledge USA
8C2 Rock Springs Wyoming, USA
110B2 Rocks Pt NZ
109C3 Rock,The Aust
16C2 Rockville Connecticut, USA
14A3 Rockville Indiana, USA
16A3 Rockville Maryland, USA
14B1 Rocky Island L Can
13E2 Rocky Mountain House Can
8B1 Rocky Mts Can/USA
12B2 Rocky Pt USA
56C2 Rødbyhavn Den
56C2 Rodeo Arg
49C3 Rodez France
55C3 Ródhos Greece
55C3 Ródhos I Greece
52C2 Rodi Garganico Italy
54B3 Rodopi Mts Bulg
106A3 Roebourne Aust
46C1 Roermond Neth
46B1 Roeselare Belg
6B3 Roes Welcome Sd Can
18B2 Rogers USA
14B1 Rogers City USA
20B2 Rogue R USA
85B3 Rohn Pak
84D3 Rohtak India
58C1 Roja USSR
35A2 Rolândia Brazil
18B2 Rolla USA
109C1 Roma Aust
47C2 Romagnano Italy
17C1 Romain,C USA
54C1 Roman Rom
103H5 Romanche Gap Atlantic O
71D4 Romang I Indon
60B4 Romania Republic, E Europe
17B2 Romano,C USA
49D2 Romans sur Isère France
79B3 Romblon Phil
Rome = Roma
17A1 Rome Georgia, USA
15C2 Rome New York, USA
49C2 Romilly-sur-Seine France
15C3 Romney USA
60D3 Romny USSR
56B1 Rømø I Den
47B1 Romont Switz
48C2 Romoratin France
50A2 Ronda Spain
33E6 Rondónia Brazil
24F6 Rondônia State, Brazil

30F2 Rondonópolis Brazil
73B4 Rong'an China
73B4 Rongchang China
72E2 Rongcheng China
73B4 Rongjiang China
73B4 Rong Jiang R China
76A1 Rongklang Range Mts Burma
39G7 Rønne Den
39H7 Ronneby Sweden
112B2 Ronne Ice Shelf Ant
46B1 Ronse Belg
48A2 Ronthieu Region, France
9C3 Roof Butte Mt USA
84D3 Roorkee India
16C1 Roosendaal Neth
112B6 Roosevelt I Ant
106C2 Roper R Aust
33E3 Roraima State, Brazil
33E2 Roraima Mt Ven
38G6 Røros Nor
47C1 Rorschach Switz
38G6 Rørvik Nor
27Q2 Roseau Dominica
22C3 Rosamond L USA
34C2 Rosario Arg
31C2 Rosário Brazil
34D2 Rosario del Tala Arg
48B2 Roscoff France
45B2 Roscommon County, Irish Rep
41B3 Roscommon Irish Rep
45C2 Roscrea Irish Rep
27E3 Roseau Dominica
109C4 Rosebery Aust
20B2 Roseburg USA
19A4 Rosenberg USA
57C3 Rosenheim Germany
13F2 Rosetown Can
54B2 Roșiori de Vede Rom
39G7 Røskilde Den
61E2 Roslyatino USSR
111B2 Ross NZ
12H2 Ross R Can
40B3 Rossan Pt Irish Rep
53C3 Rossano Italy
19C3 Ross Barnet Res USA
15C1 Rosseau L L Can
107E2 Rossel I Solomon Is
112A Ross Ice Shelf Ant
60D2 Rossiyskaya S.F.S.R. Republic, USSR
20B1 Ross L USA
13D3 Rossland Can
45C2 Rosslare Irish Rep
111C2 Ross,Mt NZ
97A3 Rosso Maur
43C4 Ross-on-Wye Eng
60E4 Rossosh USSR
4E3 Ross River Can
112B6 Ross S Ant
56C2 Rostock Germany
Rostov = Rostov-na-Donu
61E4 Rostov-na-Donu USSR
17B1 Roswell Georgia, USA
9C3 Roswell New Mexico, USA
71F2 Rota Pacific O
56B2 Rotenburg Niedersachsen, Germany
46E1 Rothaar-Geb Region Germany
112C3 Rothera Base Ant
42D3 Rotherham Eng
42B2 Rothesay Scot
71D5 Roti I Indon
109C2 Roto Aust
110C1 Rotoroa,L NZ
110C1 Rotorua NZ
110C1 Rotorua,L NZ
56A2 Rotterdam Neth

46B1 Roubaix France
48C2 Rouen France
42E3 Rough Oilfield N Sea
Roulers = Roeselare
101E3 Round I Mauritius
109D2 Round Mt Aust
8C2 Roundup USA
44C2 Rousay I Scot
43C3 Roussillon Region, France
28K5 Rovaniemi Fin
47D2 Rovereto Italy
47D2 Rovigo Italy
52B1 Rovinj Yugos
59D2 Rovno USSR
90A2 Row'an Iran
109C1 Rowena Aust
6C3 Rowley I Can
106A2 Rowley Shoals Aust
79A3 Roxas Palawan, Phil
79B3 Roxas Panay, Phil
111A3 Roxburgh NZ
45C2 Royal Canal Irish Rep
43D3 Royal Leamington Spa Eng
14B2 Royal Oak USA
43E4 Royal Tunbridge Wells Eng
48B2 Royan France
46B2 Roye France
43D3 Royston Eng
59C3 Rožňava Czech
46B2 Rozoy France
61F3 Rtishchevo USSR
99D3 Ruaha Nat Pk Tanz
110C1 Ruahine Range Mts NZ
110C1 Ruapehu,Mt NZ
65D3 Rub al Khālī Desert S Arabia
44A3 Ruaha Hunish Scot
35A2 Rubineia Brazil
65K4 Rubtsoysk USSR
12C2 Ruby USA
91C4 Rudan Iran
90A2 Rūdbar Iran
69F2 Rudnaya Pristan' USSR
54B2 Rudoka Planina Mt Yugos
72E3 Rudong China
14B1 Rudyard USA
46A1 Rue France
47C2 Ruffec France
99D3 Rufiji R Tanz
34C2 Rufino Arg
97A3 Rufisque Sen
100B2 Rufunsa Zambia
43D3 Rugby Eng
39G8 Rügen I Germany
56B3 Ruhr R Germany
73D4 Rujin China
54B2 Rujen Mt Bulg/Yugos
99D3 Rukwa L Tanz
44A3 Rum I Scot
54A1 Ruma Yugos
91A4 Rumāh S Arabia
98C2 Rumbek Sudan
26C2 Rum Cay I Caribbean S
47C2 Rumilly France
106C2 Rum Jungle Aust
101C2 Rumphi Malawi
111C2 Runanga NZ
110C1 Runaway,C NZ
100A2 Rundu Namibia
99D3 Rungwa Tanz
99D3 Rungwa R Tanz
99D3 Rungwe Mt Tanz
82C2 Ruoqiang China
82C2 Ruo Shui R China
54C1 Rupea Rom
7C4 Rupert R Can
46D1 Rur R Germany
32D6 Rurrenabaque Bol
101C2 Rusape Zim
54C2 Ruse Bulg

18B1 **Rushville** Illinois, USA
108B3 **Rushworth** Aust
19A3 **Rusk** USA
17B2 **Ruskin** USA
110B1 **Russell** NZ
18B2 **Russellville** Arkansas, USA
18C2 **Russellville** Kentucky, USA
21A2 **Russian** R USA
60B3 **Russian Socialist Federated Soviet Rep** USSR
93E1 **Rustavi** USSR
101G1 **Rustenburg** S Africa
19B3 **Ruston** USA
99C3 **Rutana** Burundi
46E1 **Rüthen** Germany
23B2 **Rutla** Mexico
15D2 **Rutland** USA
84D2 **Rutog** China
Ruvu = Pangani
101D2 **Ruvuma** R Tanz/Mozam
99D2 **Ruwenzori Range** Mts Uganda/Zaire
101C2 **Ruya** R Zim
59B3 **Ružomberok** Czech
99C3 **Rwanda** Republic, Africa
60E3 **Ryazan'** USSR
61F3 **Ryazhsk** USSR
60E2 **Rybinsk** USSR
60E2 **Rybinskoye Vodokhranilishche** Res USSR
13D1 **Rycroft** Can
43E4 **Rye** Eng
20C2 **Rye Patch Res** USA
60D3 **Ryl'sk** USSR
61G4 **Ryn Peskt** Desert USSR
74D3 **Ryōtsu** Japan
59D3 **Ryskany** USSR
69E4 **Ryūkyū Retto** Arch Japan
59C2 **Rzeszów** Pol
60D2 **Rzhev** USSR

S

91B3 **Sa'ādatābād** Iran
56C2 **Saale** R Germany
47B1 **Saanen** Switz
46D2 **Saar** R Germany
46D2 **Saarbrücken** Germany
46D2 **Saarburg** Germany
39J7 **Saaremaa** I USSR
46D2 **Saarland** State, Germany
46D2 **Saarlouis** Germany
34C3 **Saavedra** Arg
54A2 **Šabac** Yugos
51C1 **Sabadell** Spain
75B1 **Sabae** Japan
78D1 **Sabah** State, Malay
26C4 **Sabanalarga** Colombia
70A3 **Sabang** Indon
87C1 **Sabari** R India
94B2 **Sabastiya** Israel
30C2 **Sabaya** Bol
93C3 **Sab'Bi'ār** Syria
94C2 **Sabhā** Jordan
95A2 **Sabhā** Libya
101C3 **Sabi** R Zim
24B2 **Sabinas** Mexico
24B2 **Sabinas Hidalgo** Mexico
19A3 **Sabine** R USA
19B4 **Sabine** L USA
91B5 **Sabkhat Maṭṭi** Salt Marsh UAE
94A3 **Sabkhet El Bardawil** Lg Egypt
79B3 **Sablayan** Phil

7D5 **Sable,C** Can
17B2 **Sable,I** Can
7D5 **Sable I** Can
90C2 **Sabzevār** Iran
20C1 **Sacajawea Peak** USA
10A1 **Sachigo** R Can
57C2 **Sachsen** State, Germany
56C2 **Sachsen-Anhalt** State, Germany
4F2 **Sachs Harbour** Can
47B1 **Säckingen** Germany
22B1 **Sacramento** USA
22A1 **Sacramento** R USA
21A1 **Sacramento** V USA
9C3 **Sacramento Mts** USA
81C4 **Sa'dah** Yemen
54B2 **Sadanski** Bulg
82D3 **Sadiya** India
50A2 **Sado** R Port
74D3 **Sado-shima** I Japan
85C3 **Sādri** India
Safad = Zefat
84A2 **Safed Koh** Mts Afghan
39G7 **Saffle** Sweden
92C3 **Safi** Jordan
96B1 **Safi** Mor
90D3 **Safīdabeh** Iran
94C1 **Sāfītā** Syria
93E3 **Safwān** Iraq
75A2 **Saga** Japan
76B1 **Sagaing** Burma
75B2 **Sagami-nada** B Japan
85D4 **Sagar** India
16C2 **Sag Harbor** USA
14B2 **Saginaw** USA
14B2 **Saginaw B** USA
26B2 **Sagua de Tánamo** Cuba
26B2 **Sagua la Grande** Cuba
7C5 **Saguenay** R Can
51B2 **Sagunto** Spain
94C3 **Sahāb** Jordan
50A1 **Sahagún** Spain
96C2 **Sahara** Desert N Africa
84D3 **Saharanpur** India
84C2 **Sahiwal** Pak
93D3 **Şahrā al Hijārah** Desert Region Iraq
23A1 **Sahuayo** Mexico
107D1 **Saibai** I Aust
96C1 **Saïda** Alg
94B2 **Sāïda** Leb
91C4 **Sa'idabad** Iran
51B2 **Saidia** Mor
86B1 **Saidpur** India
84C2 **Saidu** Pak
75A1 **Saigō** Japan
76D3 **Saigon** Viet
85A1 **Saiha** India
88C2 **Saihan Tal** China
75A2 **Saijo** Japan
74C4 **Saiki** Japan
42C2 **St Abb's Head** Pt Scot
43D4 **St Albans** Eng
15D2 **St Albans** Vermont, USA
14B3 **St Albans** West Virginia, USA
43C4 **St Albans Head** C Eng
13E2 **St Albert** Can
46B1 **St Amand-les-Eaux** France
48C2 **St Amand-Mont Pond** France
101D2 **St André** C Madag
17A2 **St Andrew B** USA
44C3 **St Andrews** Scot
27H1 **St Ann's Bay** Jamaica
7E4 **St Anthony** Can
108B3 **St Arnaud** Aust
17B2 **St Augustine** USA
43B4 **St Austell** Eng
46D2 **St-Avold** France
42C2 **St Bees Head** Pt Eng

47B2 **St-Bonnet** France
43B4 **St Brides B** Wales
48B2 **St-Brieuc** France
15C2 **St Catharines** Can
27M2 **St Catherine,Mt** Grenada
17B1 **St Catherines I** USA
43D4 **St Catherines Pt** Eng
49C2 **St Chamond** France
18B2 **St Charles** Missouri, USA
14B2 **St Clair** USA
14B2 **St Clair,L** Can/USA
14B2 **St Clair Shores** USA
49D2 **St Claud** France
10A2 **St Cloud** USA
47B1 **Ste Croix** Switz
27E3 **St Croix** I Caribbean S
43B4 **St Davids Head** Pt Wales
46B2 **St Denis** France
101E3 **St Denis** Réunion
46C2 **St Dizier** France
12F2 **St Elias,Mt** USA
12G2 **St Elias Mts** Can
48B2 **Saintes** France
49C2 **St Étienne** France
18B2 **St Francis** R USA
100B4 **St Francis,C** S Africa
47C1 **St Gallen** Switz
48C3 **St-Gaudens** France
109C1 **St George** Aust
17B2 **St George** South Carolina, USA
9B3 **St George** Utah, USA
17B2 **St George I** Florida, USA
20B2 **St George,Pt** USA
15D1 **St-Georges** Can
27E4 **St George's** Grenada
45C3 **St George's Chan** Irish Rep/Wales
46A2 **St Germain-en-Laye** France
47B2 **St-Gervais** France
47C1 **St Gotthard P** Switz
43B4 **St Govans Head** Pt Wales
22A1 **St Helena** USA
103H5 **St Helena** I Atlantic O
100A4 **St Helena B** S Africa
17B1 **St Helena Sd** USA
109C4 **St Helens** Aust
42C3 **St Helens** Eng
20B1 **St Helens** USA
20B1 **St Helens,Mt** USA
48B2 **St Helier** Jersey
47B1 **St Hippolyte** France
46C1 **St-Hubert** Belg
7C5 **St-Hyacinthe** Can
14B1 **St Ignace** USA
43B4 **St Ives** Eng
18B2 **St James** Missouri, USA
5E4 **St James,C** Can
15D1 **St Jean** Can
48B2 **St Jean-d'Angely** France
47B2 **St-Jean-de-Maurienne** France
10C2 **St Jean,L** Can
15D1 **St-Jérôme** Can
20C1 **St Joe** R USA
7D5 **Saint John** Can
7E5 **St John's** Can
14B2 **St Johns** Michigan, USA
17B2 **St Johns** R USA
15D2 **St Johnsbury** USA
15D1 **St-Joseph** Can
19B3 **St Joseph** Louisiana, USA
14A2 **St Joseph** Michigan, USA
18B2 **St Joseph** Missouri, USA
27L1 **St Joseph** Trinidad

14B2 **St Joseph** R USA
14B1 **St Joseph,L** Can
7A4 **St Joseph,L** Can
47B1 **St Julien** France
48C2 **St-Junien** France
46B2 **St-Just-en-Chaussée** France
44A2 **St Kilda** I Scot
27E3 **St Kitts** I Caribbean S
47E1 **St-Laurent** France
7D5 **St Lawrence** R Can
7D5 **Saint Lawrence,G of** Can
4A3 **St Lawrence I** USA
7E4 **St Lawrence Seaway** Can/USA
48B2 **St Lô** France
97A3 **St Louis** Sen
11A3 **St Louis** USA
27E4 **St Lucia** I Caribbean S
101H1 **St Lucia,S** S Africa
44E1 **St Magnus B** Scot
48B2 **St Malo** France
101D3 **Ste Marie** C Madag
20C1 **St Maries** USA
27E3 **St Martin** I Caribbean S
108A2 **St Mary Peak** Mt Aust
109C4 **St Marys** Aust
15C2 **St Marys** USA
17B1 **St Marys** R USA
46C2 **Ste-Menehould** France
12B2 **St Michael** USA
16A3 **St Michaels** USA
47B2 **St-Michel** France
46C2 **St-Mihiel** France
47C1 **St Moritz** Switz
48B2 **St-Nazaire** France
57C1 **St-Niklaas** Belg
46B1 **St-Omer** France
13E2 **St Paul** Can
10A2 **St Paul** Minnesota, USA
97A4 **St Paul** R Lib
17B2 **St Petersburg** USA
15D1 **St Pierre,L** Can
46B1 **St-Pol-Sur-Ternoise** France
59B3 **St Pölten** Austria
15D1 **St Quentin** France
49D3 **St Raphaël** France
101D2 **St Sébastien** C Madag
17B1 **St Simons I** USA
17B1 **St Stephen** USA
14B2 **St Thomas** Can
49D3 **St-Tropez** France
46C1 **St Truiden** Belg
46A1 **St-Valery-sur-Somme** France
101D3 **St Vincent** C Madag
27E4 **St Vincent** I Caribbean S
108A2 **St Vincent,G** Aust
46D1 **St-Vith** Germany
46D2 **St Wendel** Germany
71F2 **Saipan** I Pacific O
84B2 **Saiydabad** Afghan
30C2 **Sajama** Mt Bol
74D4 **Sakai** Japan
75A2 **Sakaidi** Japan
75A1 **Sakaiminato** Japan
93D4 **Sakākah** S Arabia
10C1 **Sakami,L** Can
100B2 **Sakania** Zaïre
101D3 **Sakaraha** Madag
60D5 **Sakarya** R Turk
58C1 **Sakasleja** USSR
74D3 **Sakata** Japan
97C4 **Saketél** Benin
69J2 **Sakhalin** I USSR
69E4 **Sakishima gunto** Is Japan
97A4 **Sal** I Cape Verde
61F4 **Sal** R USSR

39H7 **Sala** Sweden
34D3 **Saladillo** R Arg
34C2 **Saladillo** R Arg
34D3 **Salado** R
    Buenos Aires, Arg
34B3 **Salado** R Mendoza/
    San Luis, Arg
30D4 **Salado** R Sante Fe,
    Arg
97B4 **Salaga** Ghana
76C3 **Sala Hintoun** Camb
98B1 **Salal** Chad
81D4 **Salālah** Oman
34A2 **Salamanca** Chile
23A1 **Salamanca** Mexico
50A1 **Salamanca** Spain
15C2 **Salamanca** USA
98B2 **Salamat** R Chad
71F4 **Salamaua** PNG
15C2 **Salamonica** USA
78D1 **Salang** Indon
38H5 **Salangen** Nor
30C3 **Salar de Arizaro** Arg
30C3 **Salar de Atacama**
    Salt Pan Chile
30C2 **Salar de Coipasa**
    Salt Pan Bol
30C3 **Salar de Uyuni**
    Salt Pan Bol
47C2 **Salasomaggiore** Italy
61J3 **Salavat** USSR
70D4 **Salayar** Indon
105L5 **Sala y Gomez** I
    Pacific O
34C3 **Salazar** Arg
48C2 **Salbris** France
12E2 **Salcha** R USA
100A4 **Saldanha** S Africa
94C2 **Saldhad** Syria
34C3 **Saldungaray** Arg
58C1 **Saldus** USSR
109C3 **Sale** Aust
18C2 **Salem** Illinois, USA
87B2 **Salem** India
16D1 **Salem** Massachusetts,
    USA
16B3 **Salem** New Jersey,
    USA
20B2 **Salem** Oregon, USA
78C4 **Salembu Besar** I
    Indon
39G6 **Salen** Sweden
53B2 **Salerno** Italy
42C3 **Salford** Eng
54A1 **Salgót** Hung
59B3 **Salgótarjan** Hung
31D3 **Salgueiro** Brazil
55C5 **Salihli** Turk
101C2 **Salima** Malawi
39K6 **Salina** I, USA
14A1 **Salina** Kansas, USA
53B3 **Salina** I Italy
23B2 **Salina Cruz** Mexico
30C3 **Salina de Arizato** Arg
34B3 **Salina Grande**
    Salt Pan Arg
34B2 **Salina La Antigua**
    Salt Pan Arg
35C1 **Salinas** Brazil
22B2 **Salinas** USA
22B2 **Salinas** R USA
34B3 **Salinas de Llancaneb**
    Salt Pan Arg
34B2 **Salinas Grandes**
    Salt Pan Arg
19B3 **Saline** R Arkansas,
    USA
27M2 **Salines,Pt** Grenada
31B2 **Salinópolis** Brazil
47A1 **Salins** France
    Salisbury = Harare
43D4 **Salisbury** Eng
15C3 **Salisbury** Maryland,
    USA
6C3 **Salisbury** I Can
43D4 **Salisbury Plain** Eng
38K5 **Salla** Fin
47B2 **Sallanches** France

18B2 **Sallisaw** USA
6C3 **Salluit** Can
86A1 **Sallyana** Nepal
93D2 **Salmas** Iran
38L6 **Salmi** USSR
20C1 **Salmo** Can
8B2 **Salmon** USA
13D2 **Salmon Arm** Can
8B2 **Salmon River Mts**
    USA
39J6 **Salo** Fin
47D2 **Salò** Italy
49D3 **Salon-de-Provence**
    France
    Salonica =
    Thessaloniki
54B1 **Salonta** Rom
38K6 **Salpausselka** Region,
    Fin
34B2 **Salsacate** Arg
61F4 **Sal'sk** USSR
94B2 **Salt** Jordan
30C3 **Salta** Arg
30C3 **Salta** State, Arg
24B2 **Saltillo** Mexico
8B2 **Salt Lake City** USA
30C2 **Salto** Arg
34D2 **Salto** Uru
32C3 **Salto Angostura**
    Waterfall Colombia
35D1 **Salto da Divisa** Brazil
33E2 **Salto del Angel**
    Waterfall Ven
30E3 **Salto del Guaira**
    Waterfall Brazil
32C4 **Salto Grande**
    Waterfall Colombia
84C2 **Salt Range** Mts Pak
27H2 **Salt River** Jamaica
17B1 **Saluda** USA
17B2 **Saluzzo** Italy
31D4 **Salvador** Brazil
19B4 **Salvador,L** USA
23A1 **Salvatierra** Mexico
91B5 **Salwah** Qatar
76B1 **Salween** R Burma
93E2 **Sal'yany** USSR
57C3 **Salzburg** Austria
56C2 **Salzgitter** Germany
56C2 **Salzwedel** Germany
68B1 **Samagaltay** USSR
79B4 **Samales Group** Is Phil
27D3 **Samaná** Dom Rep
92C2 **Samandaği** Turk
84B1 **Samangan** Afghan
79C3 **Samar** I Phil
107E2 **Samarai** PNG
78D3 **Samarinda** USSR
80E2 **Samarkand** USSR
93D3 **Sāmarrā'** Iraq
79B3 **Samar** S Phil
86A2 **Sambalpur** India
78B2 **Sambas** Indon
101E2 **Sambava** Madag
84D3 **Sambhal** India
78D3 **Samboja** Indon
59C3 **Sambor** USSR
46B1 **Sambre** R France
74B3 **Samch'ŏk** S Korea
99D3 **Same** Tanz
47C1 **Samedan** Switz
46A1 **Samer** France
100B2 **Samfya** Zambia
76B1 **Samka** Burma
76C1 **Sam Neua** Laos
55C3 **Sámos** I Greece
55C2 **Samothráki** I Greece
34C2 **Sampacho** Arg
78D3 **Sampaga** Indon
78C3 **Sampit** Indon
78C3 **Sampit** R Indon
19B3 **Sam Rayburn Res**
    USA
76C3 **Samrong** Camb
56C1 **Samsø** I Den
92C1 **Samsun** Turk
97B3 **San** Mali
76D3 **San** R Camb

59C2 **San** R Pol
81C4 **San'a'** Yemen
98B2 **Sanaga** R Cam
29C2 **San Agustin** Arg
79C4 **San Agustin,C** Phil
90A2 **Sanandaj** Iran
22B1 **San Andreas** USA
25C3 **San Andrés Tuxtla**
    Mexico
9C3 **San Angelo** USA
53A3 **San Antioco** Sardegna
53A3 **San Antioco** I Medit S
34A2 **San Antonio** Chile
9C3 **San Antonio** New
    Mexico, USA
79B2 **San Antonio** Phil
9D4 **San Antonio** R Texas,
    USA
51C2 **San Antonio Abad**
    Spain
25D2 **San Antonio,C** Cuba
26A2 **San Antonio de los**
    Banos Cuba
22D3 **San Antonio,Mt** USA
29C4 **San Antonio Oeste**
    Arg
34D3 **San Agustin** Arg
34B2 **San Agustin de Valle**
    Féril Arg
85A3 **Sanawad** India
23A1 **San Bartolo** Mexico
24A3 **San Benedicto** I
    Mexico
22B2 **San Benito** R USA
22B2 **San Benito Mt** USA
22D3 **San Bernardino** USA
34A2 **San Bernardo** Chile
17A2 **San Blas,C** USA
34A3 **San Carlos** Chile
32A1 **San Carlos** Nic
79B2 **San Carlos** Phil
29B4 **San Carlos de**
    Bariloche Arg
69E4 **San-chung** Taiwan
61G2 **Sanchursk** USSR
34A3 **San Clemente** Chile
22D4 **San Clemente** USA
21B3 **San Clemente** I USA
34C2 **San Cristóbal** Arg
25C3 **San Cristóbal** Mexico
32C2 **San Cristóbal** Ven
32J7 **San Cristóbal** I
    Ecuador
107F2 **San Cristóbal** I
    Solomon Is
25E2 **Sancti Spíritus** Cuba
78C3 **Sandai** Indon
70C3 **Sandakan** Malay
44C2 **Sanday** I Scot
9C3 **Sanderson** USA
13F1 **Sandfly L** Can
21B3 **San Diego** USA
92B2 **Sandikli** Turk
86A1 **Sandila** India
39F7 **Sandnes** Nor
38G5 **Sandnessjøen** Nor
98C3 **Sandoa** Zaire
59C2 **Sandomierz** Pol
38D3 **Sandoy** Føroyar
20C1 **Sandpoint** USA
49D2 **Sandrio** Italy
18A2 **Sand Springs** USA
106A3 **Sandstone** Aust
73C4 **Sandu** China
14B2 **Sandusky** USA
39H6 **Sandviken** Sweden
7A4 **Sandy L** Can
34C2 **San Elcano** Arg
9B3 **San Felipe** Baja Cal,
    Mexico
34A2 **San Felipe** Chile
23A1 **San Felipe**
    Guanajuato, Mexico
27D4 **San Felipe** Ven
51C1 **San Feliu de Guixols**
    Spain
28A5 **San Felix** I Pacific O
34A2 **San Fernando** Chile

79B2 **San Fernando** Phil
79B2 **San Fernando** Phil
50A2 **San Fernando** Spain
27E4 **San Fernando**
    Trinidad
22C3 **San Fernando** USA
32D2 **San Fernando** Ven
17B2 **Sanford** Florida, USA
12F2 **Sanford,Mt** USA
34C2 **San Francisco** Arg
27C3 **San Francisco** Dom
    Rep
22A2 **San Francisco** USA
22A2 **San Francisco B** USA
24B2 **San Francisco del Oro**
    Mexico
23A1 **San Francisco del**
    Rincon Mexico
22D3 **San Gabriel Mts** USA
85C5 **Sangamner** India
18C2 **Sangamon** R USA
71F2 **Sangan** I Pacific O
87B1 **Sangāreddi** India
78D4 **Sangeang** I Indon
22C2 **Sanger** USA
72C2 **Sanggan He** R China
78C2 **Sanggau** Indon
98B2 **Sangha** R Congo
85B3 **Sanghar** Pak
78B2 **Sangkhla Buri** Thai
78D2 **Sangkulirang** Indon
87A1 **Sāngli** India
98B2 **Sangmélima** Cam
9B3 **San Gorgonio Mt** USA
9C3 **Sangre de Cristo** Mts
    USA
34C2 **San Gregorio** Chile
22A2 **San Gregorio** USA
84D2 **Sangrūr** India
30E4 **San Ignacio** Arg
79B3 **San Isidro** Phil
32B2 **San Jacinto** Colombia
21B3 **San Jacinto Peak** Mt
    USA
34A3 **San Javier** Chile
34D2 **San Javier** Sante Fe,
    Arg
74D3 **Sanjo** I Japan
31C6 **São João del Rei**
    Brazil
22B2 **San Joaquin** R USA
22B2 **San Joaquin Valley**
    USA
32A1 **San José** Costa Rica
25C3 **San José** Guatemala
79B2 **San José** Luzon, Phil
79B3 **San José** Mindoro,
    Phil
22B2 **San José** USA
9B4 **San Jose** I Mexico
30D2 **San José de Chiquitos**
    Bol
34D2 **San José de Feliciano**
    Arg
34B2 **San José de Jachal**
    Arg
34C2 **San José de la**
    Dormida Arg
31B6 **San José do Rio Prêto**
    Brazil
24B2 **San José del Cabo**
    Mexico
34B2 **San Juan** Arg
27D3 **San Juan** Puerto Rico
34B2 **San Juan** State, Arg
27L1 **San Juan** Trinidad
32D2 **San Juan** Ven
26B2 **San Juan** Mt Cuba
8C3 **San Juan** Mts USA
34B2 **San Juan** R Arg
23B2 **San Juan** R Mexico
25D3 **San Juan** R Nic/
    Costa Rica
23B2 **San Juan Bautista**
    Mexico
30E4 **San Juan Bautista** Par
34A2 **San Juan Bautista**
    USA

25D3 San Juan del Norte Nic
27D4 San Juan de los Cayos Ven
23A1 San Juan de loz Lagoz Mexico
23A1 San Juan del Rio Mexico
25D3 San Juan del Sur Nic
20B1 San Juan Is USA
23B2 San Juan Tepozcolula Mexico
29C5 San Julián Arg
34C2 San Justo Arg
98C3 Sankuru R Zaire
22A2 San Leandro USA
32B3 San Lorenzo Ecuador
34C2 San Lorenzo Arg
22B2 San Lucas Arg
34B2 San Luis Arg
34B2 San Luis State, Arg
23A1 San Luis de la Paz Mexico
21A2 San Luis Obispo USA
23A1 San Luis Potosi Mexico
22B2 San Luis Res USA
53A3 Sanluri Sardegna
33D2 San Maigualida Mts Ven
34D3 San Manuel Arg
34A2 San Marcos Chile
23B2 San Marcos Mexico
52B2 San Marino Republic, Europe
34B2 San Martin Mendoza, Arg
112C3 San Martin Base Ant
47D1 San Martino di Castroza Italy
23B2 San Martin Tuxmelucan Mexico
22A2 San Mateo USA
30E2 San Matias Bol
72C3 Sanmenxia China
25D3 San Miguel El Salvador
22B3 San Miguel I USA
23A1 San Miguel del Allende Mexico
34D3 San Miguel del Monte Arg
30C4 San Miguel de Tucumán Arg
73D4 Sanming China
9B3 San Nicolas I USA
34C2 San Nicolás de los Arroyos Arg
101G1 Sannieshof S Africa
97B4 Sanniquellie Lib
59C3 Sanok Pol
26B5 San Onofre Colombia
22D4 San Onofre USA
79B3 San Pablo Phil
22A1 San Pablo B USA
34D2 San Pedro Buenos Aíres, Arg
97B4 San Pedro Ivory Coast
30D3 San Pedro Jujuy, Arg
30E3 San Pedro Par
22C4 San Pedro Chan USA
9C4 San Pedro de los Colonias Mexico
25D3 San Pedro Sula Honduras
53A3 San Pietro I Medit S
24A1 San Quintin Mexico
34B2 San Rafael Arg
22A2 San Rafael USA
22C3 San Rafael Mts USA
49D3 San Remo Italy
34D2 San Salvador Arg
25D3 San Salvador I Caribbean S
32J7 San Salvador I Ecuador
30C3 San Salvador de Jujuy Arg
51B1 San Sebastian Spain
53C2 San Severo Italy
30C2 Santa Ana Bol
25C3 Santa Ana Guatemala
22D4 Santa Ana USA
22C3 Santa Ana Mts USA
34A3 Santa Bárbara Chile
24B2 Santa Barbara Mexico
22C3 Santa Barbara I USA
22C4 Santa Barbara USA
22C3 Santa Barbara Chan USA
22C3 Santa Barbara Res USA
22C4 Santa Catalina I USA
22C4 Santa Catalina,G of USA
30F4 Santa Catarina State, Brazil
26B2 Santa Clara Cuba
22B2 Santa Clara USA
22C3 Santa Clara R USA
29C6 Santa Cruz Arg
30D2 Santa Cruz Bol
34A2 Santa Cruz Chile
79B3 Santa Cruz Phil
29B5 Santa Cruz State, Arg
22A2 Santa Cruz USA
22C4 Santa Cruz I USA
35D1 Santa Cruz Cabrália Brazil
22C3 Santa Cruz Chan USA
96A2 Santa Cruz de la Palma Canary Is
26B2 Santa Cruz del Sur Cuba
96A2 Santa Cruz de Tenerife Canary Is
100B2 Santa Cruz do Cuando Angola
35B2 Santa Cruz do Rio Pardo Brazil
22A2 Santa Cruz Mts USA
34D2 Santa Elena Arg
33E3 Santa Elena Ven
34C2 Santa Fe Arg
34C2 Santa Fe State, Arg
9C3 Santa Fe USA
35A1 Santa Helena de Goiás Brazil
73B3 Santai China
29B6 Santa Inés I Chile
34B3 Santa Isabel La Pampa, Arg
34C2 Santa Isabel Sante Fe, Arg
107E1 Santa Isabel I Solomon Is
21A2 Santa Lucia Ra USA
21A2 Santa Lucia Range Mts USA
97A4 Santa Luzia I Cape Verde
9B4 Santa Margarita I Mexico
22D4 Santa Margarita R USA
30F4 Santa Maria Brazil
26C4 Santa Maria Colombia
21A3 Santa Maria USA
96A1 Santa Maria I Açores
23B1 Santa Maria R Queretaro, Mexico
23A1 Santa Maria del Rio Mexico
32C1 Santa Marta Colombia
22C3 Santa Monica USA
22C4 Santa Monica B USA
29E2 Santana do Livramento Brazil
32B3 Santander Colombia
50B1 Santander Spain
51C2 Santañy Spain
22C3 Santa Paula USA
31C2 Santa Quitéria Brazil
33G4 Santarem Brazil
50A2 Santarém Port
22A1 Santa Rosa California, USA
25D3 Santa Rosa Honduras
34C3 Santa Rosa La Pampa, Arg
34B2 Santa Rosa Mendoza, Arg
34B2 Santa Rosa San Luis, Arg
22B3 Santa Rosa I USA
24A2 Santa Rosalía Mexico
20C2 Santa Rosa Range Mts USA
31D3 Santa Talhada Brazil
35C1 Santa Teresa Brazil
53A2 Santa Teresa di Gallura Sardegna
22B3 Santa Ynez I USA
22B3 Santa Ynez Mts USA
17C1 Santee R USA
47C2 Santhia Italy
34A2 Santiago Chile
27C3 Santiago Dom Rep
32A2 Santiago Panama
79B2 Santiago Phil
32B4 Santiago R Peru
50A1 Santiago de Compostela Spain
26B2 Santiago de Cuba Cuba
30D4 Santiago del Estero Arg
34C2 Santiago del Estero State, Arg
22D4 Santiago Peak Mt USA
31C5 Santo State, Brazil
35C2 Santo Anastácio Brazil
30F4 Santo Angelo Brazil
97A4 Santo Antão I Cape Verde
35A2 Santo Antonio da Platina Brazil
27D3 Santo Domingo Dom Rep
35B2 Santos Brazil
35C2 Santos Dumont Brazil
30E4 Santo Tomé Brazil
29B5 San Valentin Mt Chile
34A2 San Vicente Chile
98B3 Sanza Pomba Angola
35B2 São Borja Brazil
35B2 São Carlos Brazil
33G5 São Félix Mato Grosso, Brazil
35C2 São Fidélis Brazil
35C1 São Francisco Brazil
31D3 São Francisco R Brazil
30G4 São Francisco do Sul Brazil
35B1 São Gotardo Brazil
99D3 São Hill Tanz
35C2 São João da Barra Brazil
35B2 São João da Boa Vista Brazil
35C1 São João da Ponte Brazil
35C2 São João del Rei Brazil
35B2 São Joaquim da Barra Brazil
96A1 São Jorge I Açores
35B2 São José do Rio Prêto Brazil
35B2 São José dos Campos Brazil
31C2 São Luis Brazil
35B1 São Marcos R Brazil
35B1 São Maria do Suaçui Brazil
35D1 São Mateus Brazil
35C1 São Mateus R Brazil
96A1 São Miguel I Açores
49C2 Saône R France
97A4 São Nicolau I Cape Verde
35B2 São Paulo Brazil
35A2 São Paulo State, Brazil
31C3 São Raimundo Nonato Brazil
35B1 São Romão Brazil
35B2 São Sebastião do Paraiso Brazil
35A1 São Simão Goias, Brazil
35B2 São Simão Sao Paulo, Brazil
97A4 São Tiago I Cape Verde
97C4 São Tomé I W Africa
97C4 São Tomé and Principe Republic, W Africa
96B2 Saoura Watercourse Alg
35B2 São Vicente Brazil
97A4 São Vincente I Cape Verde
55C2 Sápai Greece
78D4 Sape Indon
97C4 Sapele Nig
74E2 Sapporo Japan
53C2 Sapri Italy
18A2 Sapulpa USA
90A2 Saqqez Iran
10C2 Saquenay R Can
90A2 Sarāb Iran
54C1 Sarata USSR
54A2 Sarajevo Yugos
90D2 Sarakhs Iran
61J3 Saraktash USSR
63A2 Sarala USSR
15D2 Saranac L USA
15D2 Saranac Lake USA
55B3 Sarandë Alb
55B2 Saransk Indon
63H2 Saransk USSR
61H2 Sarapul USSR
17B2 Sarasota USA
15D2 Saratoga Springs USA
78C2 Saratok Malay
61G3 Saratov USSR
61G3 Saratovskoye Vodokhranilishche Res USSR
67F4 Sarawak State, Malay
92A2 Saraykoy Turk
90C3 Sarbisheh Iran
47D1 Sarca R Italy
84C2 Sargodha Pak
98B2 Sarh Chad
90B2 Sāri Iran
94B2 Sarida R Isreal
93D1 Sarikamiş Turk
107D3 Sarina Aust
47B1 Sarine R Switz
84B1 Sar-i-Pul Afghan
95A2 Sarir Tibesti Desert Libya
74B3 Sariwŏn N Korea
48B2 Sark I UK
92C2 Sarkişla Turk
71E4 Sarmi Indon
29C5 Sarmiento Arg
38G6 Sårna Sweden
47C1 Sarnen Switz
14B2 Sarnia Can
58D2 Sarny USSR
6E2 Saroaq Greenland
84B2 Sarobi Afghan
78A3 Sarolangun Indon
55B3 Saronikós Kólpos G Greece
47C2 Saronno Italy
55C2 Saros Körfezi B Turk
39G7 Sarpsborg Nor

46D2 **Sarralbe** France
46D2 **Sarrebourg** France
46D2 **Sarreguemines** France
46D2 **Sarre-Union** France
51B1 **Sarrion** Spain
85B3 **Sartanahu** Pak
53A2 **Sartène** Corse
48B2 **Sarthe** R France
61H4 **Sarykamys** USSR
65H5 **Sarysu** R USSR
86A2 **Sasarām** India
74B4 **Sasebo** Japan
5H4 **Saskatchewan**
　　Province, Can
5H4 **Saskatchewan** R Can
13F2 **Saskatoon** Can
101G1 **Sasolburg** S Africa
61F3 **Sasovo** USSR
97B4 **Sassandra** Ivory Coast
97B4 **Sassandra** R Ivory
　　Coast
53A2 **Sassari** Sardegna
56C2 **Sassnitz** Germany
47D2 **Sassuolo** Italy
34C2 **Sastre** Arg
87A1 **Sātāra** India
4G2 **Satellite B** Can
78D4 **Satengar** Is Indon
39H6 **Säter** Sweden
17B1 **Satilla** R USA
61J2 **Satka** USSR
84D2 **Satluj** R India
86A2 **Satna** India
85C4 **Satpura Range** Mts
　　India
54B1 **Satu Mare** Rom
34D2 **Sauce** Arg
39F7 **Sauda** Nor
80C3 **Saudi Arabia**
　　Kingdom,
　　Arabian Pen
46D2 **Sauer** R Germany/Lux
46D1 **Sauerland** Region,
　　Germany
38B1 **Sauðárkrókur** Iceland
14A2 **Saugatuck** USA
16C1 **Saugerties** USA
13B2 **Saugstad,Mt** Can
7B5 **Sault Sainte Marie**
　　Can
14B1 **Sault Ste Marie** Can
14B1 **Sault Ste Marie** USA
71E4 **Saumlaki** Indon
48B2 **Saumur** France
98C3 **Saurimo** Angola
27M2 **Sauteurs** Grenada
54A2 **Sava** R Yugos
97C4 **Savalou** Benin
17B1 **Savannah** Georgia,
　　USA
17B1 **Savannah** R USA
76C2 **Savannakhet** Laos
26B3 **Savanna la Mar**
　　Jamaica
7A4 **Savant Lake** Can
76D2 **Savarane** Laos
47B2 **Savigliano** Italy
48B2 **Savigny** France
49D2 **Savoie** Region France
49D3 **Savona** Italy
38K6 **Savonlinna** Fin
4A3 **Savoonga** USA
38K5 **Savukoski** Fin
71D4 **Savu S** Indon
76A1 **Saw** Burma
85D3 **Sawai Mādhopur**
　　India
78A2 **Sawang** Indon
76B2 **Sawankhalok** Thai
75C1 **Sawara** Japan
95A2 **Sawknah** Libya
12E1 **Sawtooth Mt** USA
106B2 **Sawu** I Indon
97C3 **Say** Niger

84B1 **Sayghan** Afghan
72B1 **Sayhandulaan**
　　Mongolia
91B5 **Sayhut** Yemen
61G4 **Saykhin** USSR
68D2 **Saynshand** Mongolia
61H5 **Say-Utes** USSR
16C2 **Sayville** USA
13B2 **Sayward** Can
57C3 **Sázava** R Czech
51C2 **Sbisseb** R Alg
42C2 **Scafell Pike** Mt Eng
44E1 **Scalloway** Scot
44C2 **Scapa Flow** Sd Scot
15C2 **Scarborough** Can
42D2 **Scarborough** Eng
27E4 **Scarborough** Tobago
44A2 **Scarp** I Scot
45B2 **Scarriff** Irish Rep
52A1 **Schaffhausen** Switz
57C3 **Scharding** Austria
56B2 **Scharteberg** Mt
　　Germany
7D4 **Schefferville** Can
46B1 **Schelde** R Belg
10C2 **Schenectady** USA
47D2 **Schio** Italy
56C1 **Schleiden** Germany
56B2 **Schleswig** Germany
56B2 **Schleswig Holstein**
　　State, Germany
16B1 **Schoharie** USA
71F4 **Schouten** Is PNG
56B2 **Schreiber** Can
21B2 **Schurz** USA
16A2 **Schuykill Haven** USA
16B2 **Schuylkill** R USA
57B3 **Schwabische Alb**
　　Upland Germany
57B3 **Schwarzwald** Upland
　　Germany
12C1 **Schwatka Mts** USA
47D1 **Schwaz** Austria
57C2 **Schweinfurt** Germany
101G1 **Schweizer Reneke**
　　S Africa
56C2 **Schwerin** Germany
47C1 **Schwyz** Switz
53B3 **Sciacca** Italy
14B3 **Scioto** R USA
109D2 **Scone** Aust
6H2 **Scoresby Sd**
　　Greenland
103F7 **Scotia Ridge**
　　Atlantic O
103F7 **Scotia S** Atlantic O
44B3 **Scotland** Country, UK
112B7 **Scott** Base Ant
13B2 **Scott,C** Can
9C2 **Scott City** USA
112C6 **Scott I** Ant
6C2 **Scott Inlet** B Can
20B2 **Scott,Mt** USA
106B2 **Scott Reef** Timor S
8C2 **Scottsbluff** USA
17A1 **Scottsboro** USA
109C4 **Scottsdale** Aust
10C2 **Scranton** USA
47D1 **Scuol** Switz
5J4 **Seal** R Can
108B3 **Sea Lake** Aust
18B2 **Searcy** USA
22B2 **Seaside** California,
　　USA
20B1 **Seaside** Oregon, USA
16B3 **Seaside Park** USA
20B1 **Seattle** USA
22A1 **Sebastopol** USA
58D1 **Sebez** USSR
17B2 **Sebring** USA
111A3 **Secretary I** NZ
18B2 **Sedalia** USA
46C2 **Sedan** France
111B2 **Seddonville** NZ
94B3 **Sede Boqer** Israel
94B3 **Sederot** Israel
97A3 **Sédhiou** Sen

94B3 **Sedom** Israel
100A3 **Seeheim** Namibia
111B2 **Sefton,Mt** NZ
77C5 **Segamat** Malay
51B2 **Segorbe** Spain
97B3 **Ségou** Mali
　　Segovia = Coco
50B1 **Segovia** Spain
51C1 **Segre** R Spain
97B4 **Séguéla** Ivory Coast
96A2 **Seguia el Hamra**
　　Watercourse Mor
34C2 **Segundo** R Arg
50B2 **Seguntur** Indon
50B2 **Segura** R Spain
85B3 **Sehwan** Pak
51B2 **Seille** R France
38J6 **Seinäjoki** Fin
48C2 **Seine** R France
48C2 **Seine-et-Marne**
　　Department, France
99D3 **Sekenke** Tanz
20B1 **Selah** USA
21E4 **Selaru** I Indon
8D4 **Selat Alas** Str Indon
78B3 **Selat Bangka** Str
　　Indon
78A3 **Selat Berhala** B Indon
71E4 **Selat Dampier** Str
　　Indon
78B3 **Selat Gaspar** Str
　　Indon
78D4 **Selat Lombok** Str
　　Indon
78D4 **Selat Sape** Str Indon
78B4 **Selat Sunda** Str Indon
71D4 **Selat Wetar** Chan
　　Indon
12B1 **Selawik** USA
12C1 **Selawik** R USA
12B1 **Selawik L** USA
42D3 **Selby** Eng
55C3 **Selçuk** Turk
12D3 **Seldovia** USA
100B3 **Selebi Pikwe**
　　Botswana
6H3 **Selfoss** Iceland
95B2 **Selima Oasis** Sudan
5J4 **Selkirk** Can
42C2 **Selkirk** Scot
13D2 **Selkirk Mts** Can
22C2 **Selma** California, USA
50B2 **Selouane** Mor
12H2 **Selous,Mt** Can
71B3 **Selta Karimata** Str
　　Indon
32C5 **Selvas** Region, Brazil
107D3 **Selwyn** Aust
4E3 **Selwyn Mts** Can
78C4 **Semarang** Indon
61E2 **Semenov** USSR
12C3 **Semidi Is** USA
60E3 **Semiluki** USSR
19A2 **Seminole** Oklahoma,
　　USA
17B1 **Seminole,L** USA
65K4 **Semipalatinsk** USSR
79B3 **Semirara Is** Phil
90B3 **Semirom** Iran
78C2 **Semnan** Iran
90B2 **Semnān** Iran
46C2 **Semois** R Belg
23B2 **Sempoala** Hist Site,
　　Mexico
32D5 **Sena Madureira** Brazil
100B2 **Senanga** Zambia
19C3 **Senatobia** USA
74E3 **Sendai** Honshū, Japan
74C4 **Sendai** Kyūshū, Japan
85D4 **Sendwha** India
15C2 **Seneca Falls** USA
97A3 **Senegal** Republic,
　　Africa
97A3 **Sénégal** R Maur Sen
101G1 **Senekal** S Africa
31D4 **Senhor do Bonfim**
　　Brazil
52B2 **Senigallia** Italy

52C2 **Senj** Yugos
69E4 **Senkaku Gunto** Is
　　Japan
46B2 **Senlis** France
99D1 **Sennar** Sudan
7C5 **Senneterre** Can
49C2 **Sens** France
54A1 **Senta** Yugos
98C3 **Sentery** Zaïre
13C2 **Sentinel Peak** Mt Can
85D4 **Seoni** India
　　Seoul = Soul
110B2 **Separation Pt** NZ
76D2 **Sepone** Laos
7D4 **Sept-Iles** Can
95A2 **Séquédine** Niger
21B2 **Sequoia** Nat Pk, USA
71D4 **Seram** I Indon
78B4 **Serang** Indon
78B2 **Serasan** I Indon
54A2 **Serbia** Region, Yugos
61F3 **Serdobsk** USSR
77C5 **Seremban** Malay
99D3 **Serengeti Nat Pk**
　　Tanz
100C2 **Serenje** Zambia
59D3 **Seret** R USSR
61G2 **Sergach** USSR
65H3 **Sergino** USSR
31D4 **Sergipe** State, Brazil
78C2 **Seria** Brunei
78C2 **Serian** Malay
55B3 **Sérifos** I Greece
47C2 **Serio** R Italy
95B2 **Serir Calanscio** Desert
　　Libya
46C2 **Sermaize-les-Bains**
　　France
71D4 **Sermata** I Indon
61H3 **Sernovodsk** USSR
65H4 **Serov** USSR
100B3 **Serowe** Botswana
50A2 **Serpa** Port
60E3 **Serpukhov** USSR
35B2 **Serra da Canastra** Mts
　　Brazil
50A1 **Serra da Estrela** Mts
　　Port
35B2 **Serra da Mantiqueira**
　　Mts Brazil
35A1 **Serra da Mombuca**
　　Brazil
35C1 **Serra do Cabral** Mt
　　Brazil
33F5 **Serra do Cachimbo**
　　Mts Brazil
35A1 **Serra do Caiapó** Mts
　　Brazil
35A2 **Serra do Cantu** Mts
　　Brazil
35C2 **Serra do Caparaó** Mts
　　Brazil
31C5 **Serra do Chifre** Brazil
35C1 **Serra do Espinhaço**
　　Mts Brazil
35B2 **Serra do Mar** Mts
　　Brazil
35A2 **Serra do Mirante** Mts
　　Brazil
33G3 **Serra do Navio** Brazil
35B2 **Serra do**
　　Paranapiacaba Mts
　　Brazil
33F6 **Serra dos Caiabis** Mts
　　Brazil
35A2 **Serra dos Dourados**
　　Mts Brazil
33E6 **Serra dos Parecis** Mts
　　Brazil
35B1 **Serra dos Pilões** Mts
　　Brazil
35A1 **Serra Dourada** Mts
　　Brazil
33F6 **Serra Formosa** Mts
　　Brazil
55B2 **Sérrai** Greece
25D3 **Serrana Bank** Is
　　Caribbean S

51B1 Serrana de Cuenca *Mts* Spain
35A1 Serranópolis Brazil
33E3 Serra Pacaraima *Mts* Brazil/Ven
33E3 Serra Parima *Mts* Brazil
33G3 Serra Tumucumaque Brazil
46B2 Serre R France
34B2 Serrezuela Arg
6G3 Serrmilik Greenland
35C1 Serro Brazil
35A2 Sertanópolis Brazil
72A3 Sértar China
78C3 Seruyan R Indon
100A2 Sesfontein Namibia
100B2 Sesheke Zambia
47B2 Sestriere Italy
74D2 Setana Japan
49C3 Sète France
75B1 Seto Japan
75A2 Seto Naikai S Japan
96B1 Settat Mor
42C2 Settle Eng
5G4 Settler Can
50A2 Sétubal Port
93E1 Sevan,Oz L USSR
60D5 Sevastopol' USSR
7B4 Severn R Can
43C3 Severn R Eng
1B9 Severnaya Zemlya I USSR
63C2 Severo-Baykalskoye Nagorye *Mts* USSR
60E4 Severo Donets USSR
60E3 Severodvinsk USSR
64H3 Severo Sos'va R USSR
8B3 Sevier R USA
8B3 Sevier L USA
50A2 Sevilla Spain
Seville = Sevilla
54C2 Sevlievo Bulg
97A4 Sewa R Sierra Leone
12E2 Seward Alaska, USA
18A1 Seward Nebraska, USA
12A1 Seward Pen USA
13D1 Sexsmith Can
89K8 Seychelles *Is* Indian O
38C1 Seyðisfjördur Iceland
92C2 Seyhan Turk
60E3 Seym R USSR
108C3 Seymour Aust
54C2 Seymour Connecticut, USA
14A3 Seymour Indiana, USA
46B2 Sézanne France
96D1 Sfax Tunisia
54C1 Sfíntu Gheorghe Rom
56A2 's-Gravenhage Neth
72B3 Shaanxi China
98C3 Shabunda Zaïre
82B2 Shache China
112C9 Shackleton Ice Shelf Ant
85B3 Shadadkot Pak
91B3 Shādhām R Iran
43C4 Shaftesbury Eng
29G8 Shag Rocks *Is* South Georgia
90A3 Shāhābād Iran
94C2 Shahdol India
91C3 Shahdāp Iran
86A2 Shahdol India
90A2 Shāhīn Dezh Iran
90C3 Shāh Kūh Iran
91C3 Shahr-e Bābak Iran
Shahresa = Qomisheh
90B3 Shahr Kord Iran
87B1 Shājābād India
84D3 Shājahānpur India

85D4 Shājāpur India
61F4 Shakhty USSR
72E1 Shakhun'ya USSR
97C4 Shaki Nig
12B2 Shaktoolik USA
61J2 Shamary USSR
99D2 Shambe Sudan
16A2 Shandon USA
16B1 Shandaken USA
72D2 Shandong Province, China
73C5 Shangchuan Dao I China
72C1 Shangdu China
73E3 Shanghai China
73C5 Shangnan China
100B2 Shangombo Zambia
73D4 Shangra China
73B5 Shangsi China
72C3 Shang Xian China
41B3 Shannon R Irish Rep
72D3 Shanrāju China
74B2 Shansonggang China
63F2 Shantarskiye Ostrova I USSR
73D5 Shantou China
72C2 Shanxi Province, China
72D3 Shan Xian China
73C5 Shaoguan China
73E4 Shaoxing China
73C4 Shaoyang China
44C2 Shapinsay I Scot
94C2 Shaqqā Syria
90C2 Sharīfābād Iran
91CA Sharjah UAE
90C2 Sharlauk USSR
94B2 Sharon,Plain of Israel
61G2 Sharya USSR
99D2 Shashamanna Eth
73C3 Shashi China
20B2 Shasta L USA
20B2 Shasta,Mt USA
93E3 Shaṭṭ al Gharrat R Iraq
94B3 Shaubak Jordan
13F3 Shaunavon Can
22C2 Shaver L USA
16B2 Shawangunk Mt USA
15D1 Shawinigan Can
19A2 Shawnee Oklahoma, USA
94C1 Shinshār Syria
99D3 Shinyanga Tanz
74E3 Shiogama Japan
75B2 Shiono-misaki C Japan
73A5 Shiping China
16A2 Shippensburg USA
72B3 Shiquan China
75C1 Shirakawa Japan
74E3 Shirane-san Mt Japan
75B1 Shirani-san Mt Japan
91B4 Shīrāz Iran
90B3 Shīr Kūh Iran
75B1 Shirotori Japan
90C2 Shirvān Iran
12A1 Shishmaref USA
12A1 Shishmaref Inlet USA
4B3 Shisanjan China
73C3 Shitanjing China
14A3 Shively USA
85D3 Shivpuri India
94B3 Shivta Hist Site Israel
101C2 Shiwa Ngandu Zambia
72C3 Shiyan China
72B2 Shizuishan China
74D4 Shizuoka Japan
54A2 Shkodër Alb
109D2 Shoalhaven R Aust
75A2 Shobara Japan
87B2 Shoranur India
87B1 Shorāpur India
21B2 Shoshone Mts USA
60D3 Shoshta USSR
19B3 Shreveport USA
43C3 Shrewsbury Eng

95C2 Shendi Sudan
72C2 Shenmu China
72E1 Shenyang China
73C5 Shenzhen China
85D3 Sheopur India
59D2 Shepetovka USSR
108C3 Shepparton Aust
6B2 Sherard,C Can
43C4 Sherborne Eng
97A4 Sherbro I Sierra Leone
15D1 Sherbrooke Can
85C3 Shergarh India
19B3 Sheridan Arkansas, USA
8C2 Sheridan Wyoming, USA
19A3 Sherman USA
56B2 s-Hertogenbosch Neth
12H3 Sheslay Can
40C1 Shetland Is Scot
61H5 Shevchenko USSR
91B4 Sheyk Sho'eyb I Iran
69H2 Shiashkotan I USSR
84B1 Shibarghan Afghan
74D3 Shibata Japan
99E2 Shibeli R Eth
95C1 Shibin el Kom Egypt
75B1 Shibukawa Japan
72C2 Shijiazhuang China
84B3 Shikarpur Pak
67G3 Shikoku I Japan
75A2 Shikoku-sanchi Mts Japan
86B1 Shiliguri India
68D1 Shilka USSR
68D1 Shilka R USSR
16B2 Shillington USA
86C1 Shillong India
61F3 Shilovo USSR
75A2 Shimabara Japan
75A2 Shimada Japan
69E1 Shimanovsk USSR
75B2 Shimizu Japan
75B2 Shimoda Japan
87B2 Shimoga India
74C4 Shimonoseki Japan
75B1 Shinano R Japan
91C5 Shinas' Oman
74D4 Shingū Japan
75C1 Shinjō Japan
74D3 Shinminato Japan

43C3 Shropshire County, Eng
72E1 Shuanglia China
69F2 Shuangyashan China
61J4 Shubar kuduk USSR
72D2 Shu He R China
73A4 Shuicheng China
84C3 Shujaabad Pak
85D4 Shujalpur India
88B2 Shule He China
54C2 Shumen Bulg
61G2 Shumerlya USSR
73D4 Shuncheng China
12C1 Shungnak USA
72C2 Shuo Xian China
91C4 Shūr Gaz Iran
100B2 Shurugwi Zim
13D2 Shuswap L Can
61F2 Shuya USSR
12D3 Shuyak I USA
82D3 Shwebo Burma
82B2 Shwegyin Burma
84A2 Siah Koh Mts Afghan
84C2 Sialkot Pak
Sian = Xi'an
79C4 Siarao I Phil
79B4 Siaton Phil
58C1 Šiauliai USSR
65G4 Sibay USSR
101H1 Sibayi L S Africa
52C2 Šibenik Yugos
70A4 Siberut I Indon
84B3 Sibi Pak
98C3 Sibiti Congo
98E3 Sibiti R Tanz
54B1 Sibiu Rom
70A3 Sibolga Indon
86C1 Sibsāgār India
70B2 Sibu Malay
79B4 Sibuguey B Phil
98B2 Sibut CAR
79B3 Sibuyan I Phil
79B3 Sibuyan S Phil
73A3 Sichuan Province, China
53B3 Sicilia I Medit S
53B3 Sicilian Chan Italy/ Tunisia
Sicily = Sicilia
32C6 Sicuani Peru
85C4 Siddhapur India
87B1 Siddipet India
86A2 Sidhi India
95B1 Sidi Barrani Egypt
96B1 Sidi Bel Abbès Alg
44C5 Sidlaw Hills Scot
112B5 Sidley,Mt Ant
20B1 Sidney Can
5C2 Sidney Nebraska, USA
15C2 Sidney New York, USA
15C2 Sidney Ohio, USA
17B1 Sidney Lanier,L USA
Sidon = Säida
58C2 Siedlce Pol
46D1 Sieg R Germany
46D1 Siegburg Germany
46D1 Siegen Germany
76C3 Siem Reap Camb
52B2 Siena Italy
58B2 Sierpc Pol
23B2 Sierra Andrés Tuxtla Mexico
34B3 Sierra Auca Mahuida Mts Arg
51B3 Sierra Blanca USA
51B1 Sierra de Albarracin Mts Spain
50B2 Sierra de Alcaraz Mts Spain
34B2 Sierra de Cordoba Mts Arg
50A1 Sierra de Gredos Mts Spain
50A2 Sierra de Guadalupe Mts Spain

50B1 Sierra de Guadarrama Mts Spain
51B1 Sierra de Guara Mts Spain
51B1 Sierra de Gudar Mts Spain
23B2 Sierra de Juárez Mexico
34C3 Sierra de la Ventana Mts Arg
51C1 Sierra del Codi Mts Spain
34B2 Sierra del Morro Mt Arg
34B3 Sierra del Nevado Mts Arg
24B2 Sierra de los Alamitos Mts Mexico
50B2 Sierra de los Filabres Spain
23A1 Sierra de los Huicholes Mexico
23B2 Sierra de Miahuatlán Mexico
23A1 Sierra de Morones Mts Mexico
50A2 Sierra de Ronda Mts Spain
34B2 Sierra de San Luis Arg
50B2 Sierra de Segura Spain
50B1 Sierra de Urbion Mts Spain
34B2 Sierra de Uspallata Mts Arg
34B2 Sierra de Valle Fértil Mts Arg
23B2 Sierra de Zongolica Mexico
34C2 Sierra Grande Arg
97A4 Sierra Leone Republic, Africa
97A4 Sierra Leone,C Sierra Leone
79B2 Sierra Madre Mts Phil
23A2 Sierra Madre del Sur Mts Mexico
24B2 Sierra Madre Occidental Mts Mexico
24C2 Sierra Madre Oriental Mts Mexico
34B2 Sierra Malanzan Mts Arg
9C4 Sierra Mojada Mexico
50A2 Sierra Morena Mts Spain
50B2 Sierra Nevada Spain
21A2 Sierra Nevada Mts USA
32C1 Sierra Nevada de Santa Marta Colombia
34B2 Sierra Pié de Palo Mts Arg
47B1 Sierre Switz
55B3 Sifnos I Greece
59C3 Sighet Rom
54B1 Sighișoara Rom
38B1 Siglufjörður Iceland
50B1 Sigüenza Spain
97B3 Siguiri Guinea
85E4 Sihora India
93D2 Siirt Turk
68B3 Sikai Hu L China
85D3 Sikar India
84B2 Sikaram Mt Afghan
97B3 Sikasso Mali
18C2 Sikeston USA
55C3 Sikinos I Greece
55B3 Sikionia Greece
86B1 Sikkim State, India
50A1 Sil R Spain
47D1 Silandro Italy
23A1 Silao Mexico

79B3 Silay Phil
86C2 Silchar India
96C2 Silet Alg
86A1 Silgarhi Nepal
92B2 Silifke Turk
82C2 Siling Co L China
54C2 Silistra Bulg
39F7 Silkeborg Den
47E1 Sillian Austria
111B2 Siloam Springs USA
11B3 Silsbee USA
95A3 Siltou Well Chad
58C1 Šilute USSR
93D2 Silvan Turk
35B1 Silvania Brazil
85C4 Silvassa India
21B2 Silver City Nevada, USA
9C3 Silver City New Mexico, USA
20B2 Silver Lake USA
16A3 Silver Spring USA
13B2 Silverthrone Mt Can
108B2 Silverton Aust
47C1 Silvretta Mts Austria/Switz
78C2 Simanggang Malay
76C1 Simao China
90A3 Simareh R Iran
55C3 Simav Turk
55C3 Simav R Turk
15C2 Simcoe,L Can
70A3 Simeulue I Indon
60D5 Simferopol' USSR
55C3 Simi I Greece
84D2 Simla India
46D1 Simmern Germany
13B2 Simoon Sound Can
49D2 Simplon Mt Switz
47C1 Simplon P Switz
47C2 Simplon,C USA
106C3 Simpson Desert Aust
6B3 Simpson Pen Can
39G7 Simrishamn Sweden
69H2 Simushir I USSR
99E2 Sinadogo Somalia
92B4 Sinai Pen Egypt
32B2 Sincelejo Colombia
17B1 Sinclair,L USA
85D3 Sind R India
85B3 Sindh Region, Pak
55C3 Sindirği Turk
86B2 Sindri India
50A2 Sines Port
99D1 Singa Sudan
77C5 Singapore Republic, S E Asia
77C5 Singapore,Str of S E Asia
78D4 Singaraja Indon
99D3 Singida Tanz
78B2 Singkawang Indon
109D2 Singleton Aust
78A3 Singtep I Indon
76B1 Singu Burma
53A2 Siniscola Sardegna
93D2 Sinjär Iraq
84B2 Sinkai Hills Mts Afghan
95C3 Sinkat Sudan
82C1 Sinkiang Autonomous Region, China
33G2 Sinnamary French Guiana
92C1 Sinop Turk
54B1 Sintana Rom
78C2 Sintang Indon
50A2 Sintra Port
32B2 Sinú R Colombia
74A2 Sinüiju N Korea
53B4 Siofok Hung
47B1 Sion Switz
8D2 Sioux City USA
8D2 Sioux Falls USA
10A2 Sioux Lookout Can
79B4 Sipalay Phil
27L1 Siparia Trinidad
69E2 Siping China

112B3 Siple Base Ant
112B5 Siple I Ant
79B3 Sipocot Phil
70A4 Sipora Indon
79B4 Siquijor I Phil
87B2 Sira India
53C3 Siracusa Italy
86B2 Sirajgonj Bang
13C2 Sir Alexander,Mt Can
91B5 Sir Bani Yas I UAE
106C2 Sir Edward Pellew Group Is Aust
54C1 Siret R Rom
12J2 Sir James McBrien,Mt Can
87B2 Sir Kälahasti India
13D2 Sir Laurier,Mt Can
93D2 Širnak Turk
85C4 Sirohi India
87B1 Sironcha India
85D4 Sironj India
55B3 Siros I Greece
91B4 Sirri I Iran
84D3 Sirsa India
13D2 Sir Sandford,Mt Can
87A2 Sirsi India
95A1 Sirt Libya
95A1 Sirte Desert Libya
95A1 Sirte,G of Libya
52C1 Sisak Yugos
76C2 Sisaket Thai
76C3 Sisophon Camb
46B2 Sissonne France
90D3 Sistan Region, Iran/Afghan
49D3 Sisteron France
63B2 Sistig Khem USSR
86A1 Sitäpur India
55C3 Sitia Greece
4E4 Sitka USA
12D3 Sitkalidak I USA
12D3 Sitkinak I USA
76B2 Sittang R Burma
46C1 Sittard Neth
86A1 Sittwe Burma
78C4 Situbondo Indon
92C2 Sivas Turk
93C2 Siverek Turk
92B2 Sivrihisar Turk
95B2 Siwa Egypt
84D2 Siwalik Range Mts India
86A1 Siwalik Range Mts Nepal
72D3 Siyang China
15C2 Sjaelland I Den
39G7 Skagen Den
39F7 Skagerrak Str Nor/Den
20B1 Skagit R USA
20B1 Skagit Mt Can
4E4 Skagway USA
39G7 Skara Sweden
59C2 Skarzysko-Kamienna Pol
5F4 Skeena R Can
13B1 Skeena Mts Can
4D3 Skeenjek R USA
42E3 Skegness Eng
38H5 Skellefte R Sweden
38J6 Skellefteå Sweden
55B3 Skiathos I Greece
45B3 Skibbereen Irish Rep
5E4 Skidegate Can
58C2 Skierniewice Pol
39F7 Skien Nor
96C1 Skikda Alg
74C4 Skikoku I Japan
42D3 Skipton Eng
55B3 Skiros I Greece
39F7 Skive Den
56B1 Skjern Den
6H3 Skjoldungen Greenland
14A2 Skokie USA
55B3 Skópelos I Greece
54B2 Skopje Yugos
39G7 Skövde Sweden

63E2 Skovorodino USSR
4C3 Skwentna USA
58B2 Skwierzyna Pol
40B2 Skye I Scot
39G7 Slagelse Den
45C2 Slaney R Irish Rep
54B2 Slatina Rom
54B2 Slatina Rom
5G3 Slave R Can
13E1 Slave Lake Can
65J4 Slavgorod Rossiyskaya, USSR
59D2 Slavuta USSR
60E4 Slavyansk USSR
44B3 Sleat,Sound of Chan Scot
12C2 Sleetmute USA
19C3 Slidell USA
16B2 Slide Mt USA
45C2 Slieve Bloom Mts Irish Rep
45B1 Sligo County, Irish Rep
41B3 Sligo Irish Rep
41B3 Sligo B Irish Rep
54C2 Sliven Bulg
54C2 Slobozia Rom
13D3 Slocan Can
58D2 Slonim USSR
43D4 Slough Eng
22B2 Slough R USA
59B3 Slovensko Region, Czech
56C2 Słubice Pol
59D2 Sluch' R USSR
68C1 Sludyanka USSR
58B2 Słupsk Pol
58B2 Słutsk USSR
58D2 Slutsk R USSR
41A3 Slyne Head Pt Irish Rep
63C2 Slyudyanka USSR
7D4 Smallwood Res Can
54B2 Smederevo Yugos
54B2 Smederevska Palanka Yugos
60D4 Smela USSR
99F2 Smerth USA
13E1 Smith Can
4F3 Smith Arm B Can
13B2 Smithers Can
7C3 Smith I Can
13B2 Smith Sd Can
15C2 Smiths Falls Can
15C2 Smithton Aust
13D1 Smoky R Can
109D2 Smoky C Aust
13E2 Smoky Lake Can
38F6 Smøla I Nor
60D3 Smolensk USSR
55B2 Smólikas Mt Greece
54B2 Smolyan Bulg
58D2 Smorgon' USSR
16B3 Smyrna Delaware, USA
17B1 Smyrna Georgia, USA
42B2 Snaefell Mt Eng
38B2 Snafell Mt Iceland
8B2 Snake R USA
8B2 Snake River Canyon USA
56B2 Sneek Neth
45B3 Sneem Irish Rep
22B2 Snelling USA
59B2 Sněžka Mt Pol/Czech
38F6 Snøhetta Mt Nor
20B1 Snohomish USA
20B1 Snoqualmie P USA
76D3 Snoul Camb
43B3 Snowdon Mt Wales
43B3 Snowdonia Nat Pk Wales
4G3 Snowdrift Can
5H4 Snow Lake Can
108A2 Snowtown Aust
109C3 Snowy Mts Aust
9C3 Snyder USA
74B4 Soan-kundo I S Korea

Sobat

99D2 **Sobat** *R* Sudan
31C2 **Sobral** Brazil
58C2 **Sobchazew** Pol
61E5 **Sochi** USSR
9C3 **Socorro** USA
24A3 **Socorro** *I* Mexico
34A2 **Socos** Chile
81D4 **Socotra** *I* Yemen
38K5 **Sodankyla** Fin
99D2 **Soddo** Eth
39H6 **Soderhamn** Sweden
39H7 **Södertälje** Sweden
99C1 **Sodiri** Sudan
46E1 **Soest** Germany
101C2 **Sofala** Mozam
   Sofia = Sofiya
54B2 **Sofiya** Bulg
69G4 **Sofu Gan** *I* Japan
32C2 **Sogamoso** Colombia
39F6 **Sognefjorden** *Inlet* Nor
82D2 **Sog Xian** China
95C2 **Sohâg** Egypt
84D3 **Sohipat** India
46B2 **Soignies** Belg
46B2 **Soissons** France
85C3 **Sojat** India
74A3 **Sõjosõn-man** *B* N Korea
92A2 **Söke** Turk
97C4 **Sokode** Togo
61E2 **Sokol** USSR
58C2 **Sokołka** Pol
97B3 **Sokolo** Mali
6H3 **Søkongens Øy** *I* Greenland
99D1 **Sokota** Eth
97C3 **Sokoto** Nig
97C3 **Sokoto** *R* Nig
111A3 **Solander** *I* NZ
79B2 **Solana** Phil
87B1 **Solapur** India
47D1 **Solbad Hall** Austria
47D1 **Sölden** Austria
12D2 **Soldotna** USA
26C4 **Soledad** Colombia
43D4 **Solent** *Sd* Eng
46B1 **Solesmes** France
58D2 **Soligorsk** USSR
61J2 **Solikamsk** USSR
32C4 **Solimões** *R* Peru
46D1 **Solingen** Germany
65G4 **Sol'Itesk** USSR
38H6 **Solleftea** Sweden
61H3 **Sol'Iletsk** USSR
71B3 **Solok** Indon
105G4 **Solomon Is** Pacific O
47B1 **Solothurn** Switz
39F8 **Soltau** Germany
22B3 **Solvang** USA
42C2 **Solway Firth** *Estuary* Eng/Scot
100B2 **Solwezi** Zambia
75C1 **Sōma** Japan
55C3 **Soma** Turk
81C5 **Somalia** Republic, E Africa
54A1 **Sombor** Yugos
107D2 **Somerset** Aust
43C4 **Somerset** County, Eng
16D2 **Somerset** Massachusetts, USA
15C2 **Somerset** Pennsylvania, USA
100B4 **Somerset East** S Africa
6A2 **Somerset I** Can
16B3 **Somers Point** USA
16B2 **Somerville** USA
19A3 **Somerville Res** USA
54B1 **Somes** *R* Rom
46B2 **Somme** Department, France
46B2 **Somme** *R* France
46C2 **Sommesous** France
86A2 **Son** *R* India
74A3 **Sônch'ôn** N Korea
39F8 **Sønderborg** Den

6E3 **Søndre Strømfjord** Greenland
47C1 **Sondrio** Italy
76D3 **Song Ba** *R* Viet
76D3 **Song Cau** Viet
101C2 **Songea** Tanz
73E3 **Songjiang** China
77C4 **Songkhla** Thai
74B3 **Songnim** N Korea
77C5 **Song Pahang** *R* Malay
72A3 **Songpan** China
72C1 **Sonid Youqi** China
76C1 **Son La** Viet
85B3 **Sonmiani** Pak
85B3 **Sonmiani Bay** Pak
22A1 **Sonoma** USA
22B2 **Sonora** California, USA
22B2 **Sonora** *R* Mexico
24A2 **Sonora** *R* Mexico
9B3 **Sonoran Desert** USA
22C1 **Sonora P** USA
25D3 **Sonsonate** El Salvador
71E3 **Sonsorol** *I* Pacific O
10B2 **Soo Canals** Can/USA
13C3 **Sooke** Can
58B2 **Sopot** Pol
52D2 **Sopron** Hung
32B2 **Soquel** USA
53B2 **Sora** Italy
94B3 **Sored** *R* Israel
15D1 **Sorel** Can
109C4 **Sorel** Aust
92C2 **Sorgun** Turk
50B1 **Soria** Spain
38J6 **Sørkjosen** Nor
64C2 **Sørksop** *I* Barents S
61H4 **Sor Mertvyy Kultuk** *Plain* USSR
35B2 **Sorocaba** Brazil
61H3 **Sorochinsk** USSR
71F3 **Soroi** *I* Pacific O
60C4 **Soroki** USSR
71E4 **Sorong** Indon
71E4 **Sorong** Province, Indon
99D2 **Soroti** Uganda
38J4 **Sørøya** *I* Nor
53B2 **Sorrento** Italy
38K5 **Sorsatunturi** *Mt* Fin
38H5 **Sorsele** Sweden
79B3 **Sorsogon** Phil
38L6 **Sortavala** USSR
74B3 **Sösan** S Korea
59B3 **Sosnowiec** Pol
65H4 **Sos'va** USSR
64H4 **Sos'va** *R* USSR
98B2 **Souanké** Congo
97B4 **Soubré** Ivory Coast
16B2 **Souderton** USA
77C2 **Soufrière** St Lucia
27N2 **Soufrière** *V* St Vincent
48C3 **Souillac** France
96C1 **Souk Ahras** Alg
74B3 **Soul** S Korea
51C2 **Soummam** *R* Alg
   Sour = Tyr
101G1 **Sources,Mt aux** Lesotho
31D3 **Sousa** Brazil
96D1 **Sousse** Tunisia
100B4 **South Africa** Republic, Africa
14B2 **Southampton** Can
43D4 **Southampton** Eng
16C2 **Southampton** Eng
6B3 **Southampton I** Can
28F6 **South Atlantic O**
7D4 **South Aulatsivik I** Can
106C3 **South Australia** State, Aust
14E5 **South Australian Basin** Indian O
19C3 **Southaven** USA
17B2 **South Bay** USA
14B1 **South Baymouth** Can

14A2 **South Bend** Indiana, USA
20B1 **South Bend** Washington, USA
16D1 **Southbridge** USA
   South Cape = Ka Lae
11B3 **South Carolina** State, USA
70C2 **South China S** S E Asia
8C2 **South Dakota** State, USA
16C1 **South Deerfield** USA
43D4 **South Downs** Eng
109C4 **South East C** Aust
111A2 **Southern Alps** *Mts* NZ
5H4 **Southend** Can
43E4 **Southend-on-Sea** Eng
111A2 **Southern Alps** *Mts* NZ
106A4 **Southern Cross** Aust
5J4 **Southern Indian L** Can
27H2 **Southfield** Jamaica
105G5 **South Fiji Basin** Pacific O
12D2 **South Fork** *R* Alaska, USA
22B1 **South Fork** *R* California, USA
28F8 **South Georgia** *I* S Atlantic O
43C4 **South Glamorgan** County, Wales
14A2 **South Haven** USA
5J3 **South Henik L** Can
104F3 **South Honshu Ridge** Pacific O
111A2 **South I** NZ
16C2 **Southington** USA
74B3 **South Korea** Republic, S E Asia
21A2 **South Lake Tahoe** USA
112C8 **South Magnetic Pole** Ant
17B2 **South Miami** USA
16A3 **South Mt** USA
4F3 **South Nahanni** *R* Can
27J1 **South Negril Pt** Jamaica
103F8 **South Orkney** *Is* Atlantic O
8C2 **South Platte** *R* USA
80E **South Pole** Ant
42C3 **Southport** Eng
27R3 **South Pt** Barbados
16B2 **South River** USA
44C2 **South Ronaldsay** *I* Scot
103G7 **South Sandwich Trench** Atlantic O
22A2 **South San Francisco** USA
5H4 **South Saskatchewan** *R* Can
42D2 **South Shields** Eng
110B1 **South Taranaki Bight** NZ
44A3 **South Uist** *I* Scot
   South West Africa = Namibia
107D5 **South West C** Aust
105J5 **South West Pacific Basin** Pacific O
103D5 **South West Peru Ridge** Pacific O
43D3 **South Yorkshire** County, Eng
58C1 **Sovetsk** RSFSR, USSR
61G2 **Sovetsk** RSFSR, USSR
98B3 **Soyo Congo** Angola
60D3 **Sozh** *R* USSR
46C1 **Spa** Belg
50A1 **Spain** Kingdom
   Spalato = Split
43D3 **Spalding** Eng
14B1 **Spanish** *R* Can

26B3 **Spanish Town** Jamaica
21B2 **Sparks** USA
11B3 **Spartanburg** USA
55B3 **Sparti** Greece
69F2 **Spassk Dal'niy** USSR
27R3 **Speightstown** Barbados
12E2 **Spenard** USA
14A3 **Spencer** Indiana, USA
8D2 **Spencer** Iowa, USA
6A3 **Spencer Bay** Can
108A3 **Spencer,C** Aust
108A2 **Spencer G** Aust
6C3 **Spencer I** Can
111B2 **Spencer Mts** NZ
45C1 **Sperrin Mts** N Ire
44C3 **Spey** *R* Scot
57B3 **Speyer** Germany
27K1 **Speyside** Tobago
47B1 **Spiez** Switz
12F1 **Spike Mt** USA
20C1 **Spirit Lake** USA
5G4 **Spirit River** Can
   Spitsbergen = Svalbard
57C3 **Spittal** Austria
38F6 **Spjelkavik** Nor
52C2 **Split** Yugos
47C1 **Splügen** Switz
20C1 **Spokane** USA
55C3 **Sporádhes** *Is* Greece
20C2 **Spray** USA
56C2 **Spree** *R* Germany
100A3 **Springbok** S Africa
18B2 **Springdale** USA
10B3 **Springfield** Illinois, USA
10C2 **Springfield** Massachusetts, USA
18B2 **Springfield** Missouri, USA
14B3 **Springfield** Ohio, USA
20B2 **Springfield** Oregon, USA
15D2 **Springfield** Vermont, USA
100B4 **Springfontein** S Africa
101G1 **Springs** S Africa
41D3 **Spurn Head** *Pt* Eng
13C3 **Squamish** Can
60E2 **Sredne-Russkaya Vozvyshennost** *Upland* USSR
63B1 **Sredne Sibirskoye Ploskogorye** *Tableland* USSR
61J2 **Sredniy Ural** *Mts* USSR
76D3 **Srepok** *R* Camb
68D1 **Sretensk** USSR
76C3 **Sre Umbell** Camb
83C5 **Sri Lanka** Republic, S Asia
84C2 **Srinagar** Pak
87A1 **Srivardhan** India
58B2 **Sroda** Pol
30H6 **Sta Clara** *I* Chile
32J7 **Sta Cruz** *I* Ecuador
56B2 **Stade** Germany
44A3 **Staffa** *I* Scot
43C3 **Stafford** County, Eng
43C3 **Stafford** Eng
16C2 **Stafford Springs** USA
   Stalingrad = Volgograd
6A1 **Stallworthy,C** Can
59C2 **Stalowa Wola** Pol
32J7 **Sta Maria** *I* Ecuador
16C2 **Stamford** Connecticut, USA
16B1 **Stamford** New York, USA
100A3 **Stampriet** Namibia
101G1 **Standerton** S Africa
14B2 **Standish** USA
101H1 **Stanger** S Africa
22B2 **Stanislaus** *R* USA

54B2 Stanke Dimitrov Bulg
109C4 Stanley Aust
29E6 Stanley Falkland Is
87B2 Stanley Res India
Stanleyville = Kisangani
25D3 Stann Creek Belize
63E2 Stanovoy Khrebet Mts USSR
47C1 Stans Switz
109D1 Stanthorpe Aust
59C2 Starachowice Pol
54B2 Stara Planiná Mts Bulg
60D2 Staraya Russa USSR
54C2 Stara Zagora Bulg
58B2 Stargard Pol
19C3 Starkville USA
57C3 Starnberg Germany
58B2 Starogard Gdanski Pol
59D3 Starokonstantinov USSR
43C4 Start Pt Eng
60E3 Staryy Oskol USSR
15C2 State College USA
16B2 Staten I USA
17B1 Statesboro USA
15C3 Staunton USA
39H7 Stavanger Nor
46C1 Stavelot Belg
61F4 Stavropol' USSR
108B3 Stawell Aust
58B2 Stawno Pol
20B2 Stayton USA
12B2 Stebbins USA
12F2 Steele,Mt Can
16A2 Steelton USA
20C2 Steens Mt USA
6E2 Steenstrups Gletscher Gl Greenland
4H2 Stefansson I Can
101H1 Stegi Swaziland
47D1 Steinach Austria
8D2 Steinbach Can
38G6 Steinkjer Nor
13C2 Stein Mt USA
23B2 Stemaco Mexico
46C2 Stenay France
56C2 Stendal Germany
110B2 Stephens,C NZ
108B2 Stephens Creek Aust
14A1 Stephenson USA
12H3 Stephens Pass USA
7E5 Stephenville Can
100B4 Sterkstroom S Africa
8C2 Sterling Colorado, USA
14B2 Sterling Heights USA
61J3 Sterlitamak USSR
13E2 Stettler Can
14D2 Steubenville USA
4D3 Stevens Village USA
13B1 Stewart Can
21B2 Stewart R Can
12G2 Stewart R Can
12G2 Stewart Crossing Can
111A3 Stewart I NZ
107F1 Stewart Is Solomon Is
4E3 Stewart River Can
16A3 Stewartstown USA
101G1 Steyn S Africa
57C3 Steyr Austria
12G3 Stika USA
12H3 Stikine R Can
12H3 Stikine Ranges Mts Can
18A2 Stillwater Oklahoma, USA
21B2 Stillwater Range Mts USA
108A2 Stirling Aust
44C3 Stirling Scot
16C1 Stockbridge USA
59B3 Stockerau Austria
39H7 Stockholm Sweden
42C3 Stockport Eng
22B2 Stockton California, USA

42D2 Stockton Eng
18B2 Stockton L USA
43C3 Stoke-on-Trent Eng
38A2 Stokkseyri Iceland
38G5 Stokmarknes Nor
39K8 Stolbtsy USSR
58D2 Stolin USSR
16B3 Stone Harbor USA
44C3 Stonehaven Scot
19A3 Stonewall USA
12D2 Stony R USA
38H5 Storavan L Sweden
38G6 Støren Nor
109C4 Storm B Aust
42A2 Stornoway Scot
59D3 Storozhinets USSR
16C2 Storrs USA
38G6 Storsjon L Sweden
38H5 Storuman Sweden
16D1 Stoughton USA
43E3 Stowmarket Eng
45C1 Strabane N Ire
109C4 Strahan Aust
56C2 Stralsund Germany
38F6 Stranda Nor
39H7 Strängnäs Sweden
42B2 Stranraer Scot
49D2 Strasbourg France
15C3 Strasburg USA
14B2 Stratford Can
16C2 Stratford Connecticut, USA
110B1 Stratford NZ
43D3 Stratford-on-Avon Eng
108A3 Strathalbyn Aust
42B2 Strathclyde Region, Scot
13E2 Strathmore Can
18C1 Streator USA
47C2 Stresa Italy
53C3 Stretto de Messina Str Italy/Sicily
38D3 Streymoy Føroyar
53C3 Stroboli I Italy
6E3 Strømfjord Greenland
44C2 Stromness Scot
41B3 Stronsay I Scot
38H6 Stromsund Sweden
38G6 Ströms Vattudal L Sweden
44C2 Stronsay I Scot
43C4 Stroud Eng
16B2 Stroudsburg USA
54B2 Struma R Bulg
43B3 Strumble Head Pt Wales
54B2 Strumica Yugos
59C3 Stryy USSR
59C3 Stryy R USSR
108B1 Strzelecki Creek R Aust
17B2 Stuart Florida, USA
13C2 Stuart R Can
13C2 Stuart I USA
13C2 Stuart L Can
47D1 Stubaier Alpen Mts Austria
60C3 Stuch R USSR
76D3 Stung Sen Camb
76D3 Stung Treng Camb
52A2 Stura R Italy
112C2 Sturge I Ant
14A2 Sturgeon Bay USA
14C1 Sturgeon Falls Can
14B2 Sturgis Kentucky, USA
14A2 Sturgis Michigan, USA
106B2 Sturt Creek R Aust
108B1 Sturt Desert Aust
100B4 Stutterheim S Africa
19B3 Stuttgart USA
57B3 Stuttgart Germany
38A1 Stykkishólmur Iceland
59D2 Styr R USSR
35C1 Suaçuí Grande R Brazil

81B4 Suakin Sudan
73E5 Su-ao Taiwan
34C2 Suardi Arg
78B2 Subi I Indon
54A1 Subotica Yugos
60C4 Suceava Rom
45B2 Suck R Irish Rep
30C2 Sucre Bol
35A1 Sucuriú R Brazil
98C1 Sudan Republic, Africa
14B1 Sudbury Can
43E3 Sudbury Eng
99C2 Sudd Swamp Sudan
98C2 Sue R Sudan
4H2 Suerdrup Is Can
92B4 Suez Egypt
92B3 Suez Canal Egypt
92B3 Suez,G of Egypt
16B2 Suffern USA
43E3 Suffolk County, Eng
109J2 Sugarloaf Pt Aust
91C5 Suhar Oman
68C1 Sühbaatar Mongolia
84B3 Sui Pak
72C2 Suide China
69E2 Suihua China
73B3 Suining China
46C2 Suippes France
41B3 Suir R Irish Rep
73C3 Sui Xian China
72E1 Suizhong China
85C3 Sujāngarh India
78B4 Sukabumi Indon
78D4 Sukadana Borneo, Indon
78B4 Sukadana Sumatra, Indon
74E3 Sukagawa Japan
78C3 Sukaraya Indon
60E3 Sukhinichi Shchekino USSR
61F2 Sukhona R USSR
61F5 Sukhumi USSR
6E3 Sukkertoppen Greenland
6E3 Sukkertoppen L Greenland
38L6 Sukkozero USSR
85B3 Sukkur Pak
87C1 Sukma India
100A3 Sukses Namibia
75A2 Sukumo Japan
13C1 Sukunka R Can
84B3 Sulaiman Range Mts Pak
70C4 Sulawesi I Indon
93E3 Sulaymaniyah Iraq
54C1 Sulina Rom
38H5 Sulitjelma Nor
32A4 Sullana Peru
18B2 Sullivan USA
13B2 Sullivan Bay Can
13E2 Sullivan L Can
52B2 Sulmona Italy
19B3 Sulphur Louisiana, USA
19A3 Sulphur Oklahoma, USA
19A3 Sulphur Springs USA
86A1 Sultänpur India
79B4 Sulu Arch Phil
70C3 Sulu S Philip
30D4 Sumampa Arg
70B4 Sumatera I Indon
70C4 Sumba I Indon
78D4 Sumbawa I Indon
78D4 Sumbawa Besar Indon
99D3 Sumbawanga ...
100A2 Sumbe An...
44E2 Sumburgh ... Scot
78C4 Sumen...
69G3 Sumis...
13D3 Sumr...

5F4 Summit Lake Can
21B2 Summit Mt USA
111B2 Sumner,L NZ
75A2 Sumoto Japan
17B1 Sumter USA
60D3 Sumy USSR
16A2 Sunbury USA
34C2 Sunchales Arg
74B3 Sunch'ŏn N Korea
74B4 Sunch'ŏn S Korea
86A2 Sundargarh India
86B2 Sunderbans Swamp India
42D2 Sunderland Eng
13E2 Sundre Can
15C1 Sundridge Can
38H6 Sundsvall Sweden
38D3 Suduroy Føroyar
78D3 Sungaianyar Indon
78A3 Sungaisalak Indon
20C1 Sunnyside USA
21A2 Sunnyvale USA
63D1 Suntar USSR
97B4 Sunyani Ghana
75A2 Suŏ-nada B Japan
38K6 Suonejoki Fin
86B1 Supaul India
18A1 Superior Nebraska, USA
10A2 Superior Wisconsin, USA
10B2 Superior,L Can/USA
76C3 Suphan Buri Thai
93D2 Süphan Daği Turk
11E4 Supiori I Indon
93E3 Suq ash Suyukh Iraq
72D3 Suqian China
Suqutra = Socotra
91C5 Sur Oman
78C4 Surabaya Indon
75B2 Suraga-wan B Japan
78C4 Surakarta Indon
61G3 Surar R USSR
109C1 Surat Aust
85C4 Sürat India
84C3 Süratgarh India
77B4 Surat Thani Thai
85C4 Surendranagar India
16B3 Surf City USA
64J3 Surgut USSR
87B1 Süriäpet India
49D2 Sürich Switz
79C4 Surigao Phil
76C3 Surin Thai
33F3 Surinam Republic, S America
43D4 Surrey County, Eng
47C1 Sursee Switz
38A2 Surtsey I Iceland
78A3 Surulangan Indon
52A2 Susa Italy
75A2 Susa Japan
75A2 Susaki Japan
21A1 Susanville USA
47D1 Süsch Switz
12E2 Susitna R USA
16A3 Susquehanna R USA
16B2 Sussex USA
43D4 Sussex West Eng
13B1 Sutcut Peak Mt Can
100B4 Sutherland S Africa
84C2 Sutlej R Pak
21A2 Sutter USA
14B3 Sut...
12C3 ... Japan
74... S
... Is Barents S
...yava USSR

38G5	Svartisen *Mt* Nor
76D3	Svay Rieng Camb
38G6	Sveg Sweden
39G7	Svendborg Den
65H4	Sverdlovsk USSR
6A1	Sverdrup Chan Can
69F2	Svetlaya USSR
58C2	Svetlogorsk USSR
39K6	Svetogorsk USSR
54B2	Svetozarevo Yugos
54C2	Svilengrad Bulg
58D2	Svir' USSR
79B3	Svitavy Czech
69E1	Svobodnyy USSR
38G5	Svolvaer Nor
107E3	Swain Reefs Aust
17B1	Swainsboro USA
100A3	Swakopmund Namibia
42D2	Swale *R* Eng
70C3	Swallow Reef *I* S E Asia
87B2	Swamihalli India
25D3	Swan *I* Honduras
43C4	Swanage Eng
108B3	Swan Hill Aust
13D2	Swan Hills Can
13D2	Swan Hills *Mts* Can
26A3	Swan *I* Caribbean S
5H4	Swan River Can
43C4	Swansea Wales
43C4	Swansea B Wales
101G1	Swartruggens S Africa
	Swatow = Shantou
101H1	Swaziland Kingdom, S Africa
39G7	Sweden Kingdom, N Europe
20B2	Sweet Home USA
9C3	Sweetwater USA
100B4	Swellendam S Africa
59B2	Swidnica Pol
58B2	Swidwin Pol
58B2	Swiebodzin Pol
58B2	Swiecie Pol
5H4	Swift Current Can
43D4	Swindon Eng
45B2	Swinford Irish Rep
58C2	Swinoujscie Pol
52B1	Switzerland Federal Republic, Europe
45C2	Swords Irish Rep
109D2	Sydney Aust
7D5	Sydney Can
64G3	Syktyvkar USSR
17A1	Sylacauga USA
38G6	Sylarna *Mt* Sweden
86C2	Sylhet Bang
56B1	Sylt *I* Germany
14B2	Sylvania USA
112C11	Syowa *Base* Ant
	Syracuse = Siracusa
15C2	Syracuse USA
65H5	Syrdal'ya *R* USSR
93C2	Syria Republic, S W Asia
61J2	Sysert' USSR
61G3	Syzran' USSR
58B2	Szczecin Pol
58B2	Szczecinek Pol
58C2	Szczytno Pol
59C3	Szeged Hung
59B3	Székesfehérvár Hung
59B3	Szekszard Hung
59B3	Szolnok Hung
59B3	Szombathely Hung
58B2	Szprotawa Pol

79B3	Tablas *I* Phil
100A4	Table Mt S Africa
12F1	Table Mt USA
18B2	Table Rock Res USA
78B3	Taboali Indon
57C3	Tábor Czech
99D3	Tabora Tanz
97B4	Tabou Ivory Coast
90C2	Tabriz Iran
92C4	Tabuk S Arabia
23A2	Tacámbaro Mexico
82C1	Tacheng China
79C3	Tacloban Phil
30B2	Tacna Peru
8A2	Tacoma USA
99E1	Tadjoura Djibouti
87B2	Tadpatri India
65H6	Tadzhen USSR
82A2	Tadzhikskaya SSR Republic, USSR
74B3	Taebaek Sanmaek *Mts* S Korea
74B3	Taeback S Korea
74B4	Taehŭksan *I* S Korea
74B3	Taejŏn S Korea
51B1	Tafalla Spain
96C2	Tafassaet *Watercourse* Alg
43C4	Taff *R* Wales
94B3	Tafila Jordan
97A3	Tagant Region, Maur
79B4	Tagbilaran Phil
96B2	Taguenout Hagguerete *Well* Maur
107E2	Tagula *I* Solomon Is
79C4	Tagum Phil
	Tagus = Tejo
96C2	Tahat *Mt* Alg
105J4	Tahiti *I* Pacific O
18A2	Tahlequah USA
21A2	Tahoe City USA
21A2	Tahoe,L USA
97C3	Tahoua Niger
71D3	Tahuna Indon
72D2	Tai'an China
72B3	Taibai Shan *Mt* China
72D1	Taibus Qi China
73E5	T'ai-chung Taiwan
111B3	Taieri *R* NZ
72C2	Taihang Shan China
110C1	Taihape NZ
72E3	Tai Hu *L* China
108A3	Tailem Bend Aust
44B3	Tain Scot
73E5	T'ai-nan Taiwan
35C1	Taiobeiras Brazil
73E5	T'ai pei Taiwan
77C5	Taiping Malay
75C1	Taira Japan
78A3	Tais Indon
75A1	Taisha Japan
29B5	Taitao,Pen de Chile
73E5	T'ai-tung Taiwan
38K5	Taivelkoski Fin
69E4	Taiwan Republic, China
	Taiwan Haixia = Formosa Str
72C2	Taiyuan China
72D3	Taizhou China
81C4	Ta'izz Yemen
50B1	Tajo *R* Spain
76B2	Tak Thai
74D3	Takada Japan
75A2	Takahashi Japan
110B2	Takaka NZ
74C4	Takamatsu Japan
74D3	Takaoka Japan
110B1	Takapuna NZ
74D3	Takasaki Japan
75B1	Takayama Japan
74D3	Takefu Japan
76C3	Takeo Camb
75A2	Takeo Japan
	Take-shima = Tok-do
90A2	Takestan Iran
75A2	Taketa Japan
	Takingeun Indon

4G3	Takjvak L Can
99D1	Takkaze *R* Eth
13B1	Takla L Can
13B1	Takla Landing Can
12B2	Takslesluk L USA
12H2	Taku Arm *R* Can
23A1	Tala Mexico
59B3	Talabanya Hung
34A2	Talagang Pak
34A2	Talagante Chile
54C1	Talaimannar Sri Lanka
97C3	Talak *Desert Region*, Niger
78A3	Talangbetutu Indon
32A4	Talara Peru
50B2	Talavera de la Reina Spain
34A3	Talca Chile
34A3	Talcahuano Chile
86B2	Tālcher India
82B1	Taldy Kurgan USSR
91D4	Taliabu Indon
84B1	Taligan Afghan
91D4	Tali Post Sudan
78D4	Taliwang Indon
12D2	Talkeetna USA
12E2	Talkeetna Mts USA
17A1	Talladega USA
17A1	Tallahassee USA
94C1	Tall Bisah Syria
60B2	Tallinn USSR
92C3	Tall Kalakh Syria
19B3	Tallulah USA
60D4	Tal'noye USSR
78D1	Talpaki USSR
30B4	Taltal Chile
109C1	Talwood Aust
78D1	Tamabo Range *Mts* Malay
97B4	Tamale Ghana
96C2	Tamanrasset Alg
96C2	Tamanrasset *Watercourse* Alg
16B2	Tamaqua USA
	Tamatave = Toamasina
23A2	Tamazula Jalisco, Mexico
23B2	Tamazulapan Mexico
23B1	Tamazunchale Mexico
97A3	Tambacounda Sen
61F3	Tambov USSR
50A1	Tambre *R* Spain
98C2	Tambura Sudan
97C3	Tamchaket Maur
50A1	Tamega *R* Port
23B1	Tamiahua Mexico
87B2	Tamil Nādu State, India
54B1	Tamiş *R* Rom
76B2	Tam Ky Viet
17B2	Tampa USA
17B2	Tampa B USA
39J6	Tampere Fin
23B1	Tampico Mexico
68D2	Tamsagbulag Mongolia
86C2	Tamu Burma
23B1	Tamuis Mexico
109D2	Tamworth Aust
43D3	Tamworth Eng
38K4	Tana Nor
99D1	Tana *L* Eth
99E3	Tana *R* Kenya
38K5	Tana *R* Nor/Fin
75B2	Tanabe Japan
38K4	Tanafjord *Inlet* Nor
78D3	Tanahgrogot Indon
71E4	Tanahmerah Indon
12D1	Tanana USA
12E2	Tanana *R* USA
	Tananarive = Antananarivo
47C2	Tanaro *R* Italy
74B2	Tanch'ŏn N Korea
99E1	Tandaho Eth
34D3	Tandil Arg

78B2	Tandjong Datu *Pt* Indon
71E4	Tandjung d'Urville *C* Indon
78D3	Tandjung Layar *C* Indon
78B3	Tandjung Lumut *C* Indon
78D2	Tandjung Mangkalihet *C* Indon
78C3	Tandjung Sambar *C* Indon
78C2	Tandjung Sirik *C* Malay
71E4	Tandjung Vals *C* Indon
85B3	Tando Adam Pak
85B3	Tando Muhammad Khan Pak
108B2	Tandou L Aust
87B1	Tāndūr India
110C1	Taneatua NZ
76B2	Tanen Range *Mts* Burma/Thai
96B2	Tanezrouft *Desert Region* Alg
91C4	Tang Iran
99D3	Tanga Tanz
60E4	Tanganrog USSR
99C3	Tanganyika,L Tanz/Zaire
86B1	Tanger Mor
82C2	Tanggula Shan *Mts* China
	Tangier = Tanger
78A2	Tangjungpinang Indon
82C2	Tangra Yumco *L* China
72D2	Tangshan China
79B4	Tangub Phil
63C2	Tanguy USSR
78C4	Tanjay Phil
78C4	Tanjong Bugel *C* Indon
78A4	Tanjong Cangkuang *C* Indon
78C3	Tanjong Puting *C* Indon
78C3	Tanjong Selatan *C* Indon
78D3	Tanjung Indon
70A3	Tanjungbalai Indon
78A3	Tanjung Jabung *C* Indon
78B3	Tanjungpandan Indon
78A4	Tanjung Priok Indon
78D2	Tanjungredeb Indon
78D2	Tanjungselor Indon
84C2	Tank Pak
68B1	Tannu Ola *Mts* USSR
67A1	Tano *R* Ghana
97C3	Tanout Niger
23B1	Tanquián Mexico
73E4	Tan-shui Taiwan
86A1	Tansing Nepal
95C1	Tanta Egypt
96A2	Tan-Tan Mor
99D3	Tanzania Republic, Africa
72A3	Tao He *R* China
101D3	Taolañaro Madag
72B2	Taole China
86B1	Taourirt Mor
60C2	Tapa USSR
25C3	Tapachula Mexico
33F4	Tapajós *R* Brazil
34C3	Tapalquén Arg
78B3	Tapan Indon
111A3	Tapanui NZ
33D5	Tapaua *R* Brazil
85D4	Tapi *R* India
86B1	Taplejung Nepal
111B2	Tapuaenuku *Mt* NZ
35B2	Tapuaritinga Brazil
78B4	Tapul Group *Is* Phil
33E4	Tapurucuara Brazil

109D1 Tara Aust
65J4 Tara USSR
65J4 Tara R USSR
54A2 Tara R Yugos
97D4 Taraba R Nig
30D2 Tarabuco Bol
Tarābulus = Tripoli
50B1 Taracón Spain
110C1 Taradale NZ
78D2 Tarakan Indon
44A3 Taransay I Scot
53C2 Taranto Italy
32B5 Tarapoto Peru
47C2 Tarare France
110C2 Tararua Range Mts NZ
96C2 Tarat Alg
110C1 Tarawera NZ
51B1 Tarazona Spain
44C3 Tarbat Ness Pen Scot
84C2 Tarbela Res Pak
42B2 Tarbert Strathclyde, Scot
44A3 Tarbert Western Isles, Scot
48C3 Tarbes France
106C4 Tarcoola Aust
109C2 Tarcoon Aust
109D2 Taree Aust
96A2 Tarfaya Mor
95A1 Tarhūnah Libya
91B5 Tarif UAE
30D3 Tarija Bol
87B2 Tarikere India
81C4 Tarim Yemen
99D3 Tarime Tanz
82C1 Tarim He R China
82C2 Tarim Pendi Basin China
84B2 Tarin Kut Afghan
18A1 Tarkio USA
79B2 Tarlac Phil
32B6 Tarma Peru
49C3 Tarn R France
59C2 Tarnobrzeg Pol
59C3 Tarnów Pol
107D3 Taroom Aust
51C1 Tarragona Spain
109C4 Tarraleah Aust
51C1 Tarrasa Spain
16C2 Tarrytown USA
92B2 Tarsus Turk
44D2 Tartan Oilfield N Sea
47D2 Tartaro R Italy
60C2 Tartu USSR
92C3 Tartūs Syria
35C1 Tarumirim Brazil
70A3 Tarutung Indon
52B1 Tarvisio Italy
80D1 Tashauz USSR
86C1 Tashigang Bhutan
82A1 Tashkent USSR
65K4 Tashtagol USSR
63A2 Tashtyp USSR
78B4 Tasikmalaya Indon
94B2 Tasil Syria
6E2 Tasiussaq Greenland
95A3 Tasker Well Niger
110B2 Tasman B NZ
107D5 Tasmania I Aust
111B2 Tasman Mts NZ
109C4 Tasman Pen Aust
107E4 Tasman S NZ/Aust
92C1 Taşova Turk
92C2 Tassili du Hoggar Desert Region, Alg
96C2 Tassili N'jjer Desert Region, Alg
96B2 Tata Mor
96D1 Tataouine Tunisia
65J4 Tatarsk USSR
61G2 Tatarskaya ASSR Republic, USSR
69G2 Tatarskiy Proliv Str USSR
75B1 Tateyama Japan
5G3 Tathlina L Can
12E2 Tatitlek USA

13C2 Tatla Lake Can
59B3 Tatry Mts Pol/Czech
75A2 Tatsuno Japan
85B4 Tatta Pak
35B2 Tatui Brazil
93D2 Tatvan Turk
31C3 Tauá Brazil
35B2 Taubate Brazil
110C1 Taumarunui NZ
101F1 Taung S Africa
76B2 Taungdwingyi Burma
76B1 Taung-gyi Burma
76B2 Taungup Burma
84C2 Tauns Pak
43C4 Taunton Eng
16D2 Taunton USA
46E1 Taunus Region, Germany
110C1 Taupo NZ
110C1 Taupo,L NZ
58C1 Taurage USSR
110C1 Tauranga NZ
110C1 Tauranga Harbour B NZ
110B1 Tauroa Pt NZ
7A3 Tavani Can
7A3 Tavani Can
65H4 Tavda R USSR
43B4 Tavistock Eng
76B3 Tavoy Burma
76B3 Tavoy Pt Burma
92A2 Tavsanli Turk
111B2 Tawa NZ
19A3 Tawakoni,L USA
14B2 Tawas City USA
70C3 Tawau Malay
98C1 Taweisha Sudan
79B4 Tawitawi I Phil
79B4 Tawitawi Group Is Phil
23B2 Taxco Mexico
23B2 Taxcoco Mexico
44C3 Tay R Scot
78C3 Tayan Indon
12B1 Taylor Alaska, USA
13C1 Taylor Can
14B2 Taylor Michigan, USA
19A3 Taylor Texas, USA
18C2 Taylorville USA
80B3 Taymā' S Arabia
63B1 Taymyr R USSR
76D3 Tay Ninh Viet
23B2 Tayshet USSR
68B2 Tayshir Mongolia
44C3 Tayside Region, Scot
79D3 Taytay Phil
91A3 Tayyebāt Iran
96B1 Taza Mor
95B2 Tazerbo Region, Libya
12E2 Tazline L USA
64J3 Tazovskiy USSR
65F5 Tbilisi USSR
98B3 Tchibanga Gabon
95A2 Tchigai,Plat du Niger
97C3 Tchin Tabaradene Niger
98B2 Tcholliré Cam
58B2 Tczew Pol
111A3 Te Anau NZ
111A3 Te Anau,L NZ
110C1 Te Aroha NZ
110C1 Te Awamutu NZ
96C1 Tébessa Alg
23A2 Tebonan Mexico
23A2 Tecaitlán Mexico
21B3 Tecate Mexico
61K2 Techa R USSR
23A1 Tecolotlán Mexico
23A2 Tecpan Mexico
54C1 Tecuci Rom
18A1 Tecumseh USA
80E2 Tedzhen USSR
65H6 Tedzhen R USSR
42D2 Tees R Eng
33E4 Tefé Brazil
78B4 Tegal Indon
78B4 Tegineneng Indon
25D3 Tegucigalpa Honduras

21B3 Tehachapi Mts USA
21B2 Tehachapi P USA
4J3 Tehek L Can
90B2 Tehrān Iran
23B2 Tehuacán Mexico
23B2 Tehuantepec Mexico
23B2 Tehuitzingo Mexico
43B3 Teifi R Wales
50A2 Tejo R Port
23A2 Tejupilco Mexico
111B2 Tekapo,L NZ
82B1 Tekeli USSR
92A1 Tekirdağ Turk
55C2 Tekir Dağlari Mts Turk
86C2 Teknaf Bang
110C1 Te Kuiti NZ
25D3 Tela Honduras
94B2 Tel Aviv Yafo Israel
34B3 Telén Arg
21B2 Telescope Peak Mt USA
33F5 Teles Pires R Brazil
47D1 Telfs Austria
63A2 Tell USSR
94B3 Tell el Meise Mt Jordan
12A1 Teller USA
87B2 Tellicherry India
77C5 Telok Anson Malay
78D2 Telok Darvel Malay
71E4 Telok Flamingo B Indon
78C3 Telok Kumai B Indon
78B4 Telok Pelabuanratu B Indon
78D4 Telok Saleh B Indon
78A3 Telok Sampit B Indon
78B3 Telok Sukadona B Indon
23B2 Teloloapán Mexico
64G3 Tel'pos-iz Mt USSR
58C1 Telšiai USSR
78C3 Telukbatang Indon
71E4 Teluk Berau B Indon
78B4 Telukbetung Indon
70D4 Teluk Bone B Indon
71E4 Teluk Cendrawasih B Indon
78D3 Teluk Mandar B Indon
71D4 Teluk Tolo B Indon
70D4 Teluk Tomini B Indon
71D3 Teluk Weda B Indon
14B1 Temagami,L Can
23B2 Temascal Mexico
78A3 Tembesi R Indon
78A3 Tembilahan Indon
27E5 Temblador Ven
76C1 Temerloh Malay
65G5 Temir USSR
65J4 Temirtau USSR
15C1 Temiscaming Can
109C2 Temora Aust
9B3 Tempe USA
19A3 Temple USA
45C2 Templemore Irish Rep
23B1 Tempoal Mexico
34A3 Temuco Chile
111B2 Temuka NZ
32B4 Tena Ecuador
87C1 Tenali India
23B2 Tenancingo Mexico
76B3 Tenasserim Burma
43B4 Tenby Wales
83D5 Ten Degree Chan Indian O
98B1 Ténéré Desert Region Niger
96A2 Tenerife I Canary Is
96C1 Ténès Alg
78C3 Tengah Indon
76B1 Teng R Burma
78D3 Tenggarong Indon
72A2 Tengger Shamo Desert China
87B3 Tenkāsi India
100B2 Tenke Zaïre
97B3 Tenkodogo Burkina
106C2 Tennant Creek Aust

11B3 Tennessee State, USA
18C2 Tennessee R USA
34A2 Teno Chile
78D1 Tenom Malay
25C3 Tenosique Mexico
109D1 Tenterfield Aust
72B1 Ten Thousand Is USA
23A1 Teocaltiche Mexico
35C1 Teófilo Otóni Brazil
23B2 Teotihiucan Hist Site, Mexico
23B2 Teotitlan Mexico
23A1 Tepatitlan Mexico
24B2 Tepehuanes Mexico
23B2 Tepeji Mexico
23A1 Tepic Mexico
57C2 Teplice Czech
110C1 Te Puke NZ
23A1 Tequila Mexico
23B2 Tequistepec Mexico
51C1 Ter R Spain
97C3 Téra Niger
75B1 Teradomari Japan
52B2 Teramo Italy
96A1 Terceira I Açores
35E6 Tereboviya USSR
31C3 Teresina Brazil
35C2 Teresópolis Brazil
92C1 Termse USSR
80E2 Termez USSR
52B2 Termoli Italy
71D3 Ternate Indon
52B2 Terni Italy
59D3 Ternopol USSR
13B2 Terrace Can
53B2 Terracina Italy
53B2 Terralba Italy
100B3 Terra Firma S Africa
112C8 Terre Adélie Region, Ant
19B4 Terre Bonne B USA
14A3 Terre Haute USA
19A3 Terrell USA
56B2 Terschelling I Neth
51B1 Teruel Spain
4C2 Teshekpuk L USA
4C2 Teshekpuk L USA
74E2 Teshio R Japan
68B2 Tesiyn Gol Mts Mongolia
12H2 Teslin Can
12H3 Teslin R Can
12H2 Teslin L Can
63B3 Teslyn Gol R Mongolia
96C2 Tessalit Mali
97C3 Tessaoua Niger
101C2 Tete Mozam
23A2 Tetela Mexico
96B1 Tetouan Mor
61G2 Tetyushi USSR
30D3 Teuco R Arg
23A1 Teúl de Gonzalez Ortega Mexico
71D4 Teun I Indon
52B2 Tevere R Italy
42C2 Teviot R Scot
65J4 Tevriz USSR
113A3 Te Waewae B NZ
78C3 Tewah Indon
109D1 Tewantin Aust
72A3 Têwo China
19B3 Texarkana USA
19B3 Texarkana,L USA
19D1 Texas Aust
9C3 Texas State, USA
19B4 Texas City USA
56A2 Texel I Neth
19A3 Texoma,L USA
101G1 Teyateyaneng Lesotho
23B2 Teziutlán Mexico
86C1 Tezpur India
76C1 Tha Laos
101G1 Thabana Ntlenyana Mt Lesotho
101G1 Thaba Putsoa Mt Lesotho
76B3 Thagyettaw Burma

76D1 Thai Binh Viet
76C2 Thailand Kingdom,
 S E Asia
76C3 Thailand,G of Thai
76D1 Thai Nguyen Viet
76C2 Thakhek Laos
84C2 Thal Pak
77C4 Thale Luang L Thai
109C1 Thallon Aust
110C1 Thames NZ
43E4 Thames R Eng
76D2 Thanh Hoah Viet
87B2 Thanjavur India
85C3 Thar Desert India
108B1 Thargomindah Aust
55B2 Thásos I Greece
76B2 Thaton Burma
76B2 Thayetmyo Burma
5F5 The Dalles USA
91B4 The Gulf S W Asia
4H3 Thelon R Can
107E3 Theodore Aust
9B3 Theodore Roosevelt L
 USA
55B2 Thermaikós Kólpos G
 Greece
8C2 Thermopolis USA
4F2 Thesiger B Can
14B1 Thessalon Can
55B2 Thessaloníki Greece
43E3 Thetford Eng
15D1 Thetford Mines Can
101G1 Theunissen S Africa
19B4 Thibodaux USA
5J4 Thicket Portage Can
8D2 Thief River Falls USA
20B2 Thielsen,Mt USA
49C2 Thiers France
97A3 Thiès Sen
99D3 Thika Kenya
86B1 Thimphu Bhutan
49D2 Thionville France
55C3 Thíra I Greece
42D2 Thirsk Eng
39F7 Thisted Den
55B3 Thívai Greece
48C2 Thiviers France
21F1 Thomaston Georgia,
 USA
17B1 Thomasville Georgia,
 USA
6A2 Thom Bay Can
5J4 Thompson R Can
18B1 Thompson R USA
4G3 Thompson Landing
 Can
13C2 Thompson R Can
17B1 Thompsonville USA
17B1 Thomson USA
107D3 Thomson R Aust
76C3 Thon Buri Thai
76B2 Thongwa Burma
47B1 Thonon-les-Bains
 France
42C2 Thornhill Scot
48B2 Thouars France
15C2 Thousand Is Can/USA
13E2 Three Hills Can
7G4 Three Kings Is NZ
76B2 Three Pagodas P Thai
14A2 Three Rivers
 Michigan, USA
20B2 Three Sisters Mt USA
6D2 Thule Greenland
47B1 Thun Switz
47B1 Thunder Bay Can
47B1 Thuner See L Switz
77B4 Thung Song Thai
47C1 Thur R Switz
57C2 Thüringen State,
 Germany
57C2 Thüringen Wald
 Upland Germany
45C2 Thurles Irish Rep
71F5 Thursday I Aust
44C2 Thurso Scot

112B4 Thurston I Ant
47C1 Thusis Switz
108B1 Thylungra Aust
73B5 Tianjing China
73B5 Tian'e China
72D2 Tianjin China
73B5 Tianlin China
82C1 Tian Shan Mts C Asia
72B3 Tianshui China
72A2 Tianzhu China
96C1 Tiaret Alg
35A2 Tibagi R Brazil
94B2 Tiberias Israel
94B2 Tiberias,L Israel
 Tiber,R = Tevere,R
95A2 Tibesti Massif
 Region Chad
82C2 Tibet Autonomous
 Region, China
108B1 Tibooburra Aust
86A1 Tibrikot Nepal
24A2 Tiburón I Mexico
97B3 Tichitt Maur
96A2 Tichla Mor
47C2 Ticino R Italy/Switz
15D2 Ticonderoga USA
25D2 Ticul Mexico
97A3 Tidjikja Maur
47C1 Tiefencastel Switz
74A2 Tieling China
46B1 Tielt Belg
46C1 Tienen Belg
65J5 Tien Shan Mts China/
 USSR
72D2 Tientsin China
39H6 Tierp Sweden
23B2 Tierra Blanca Mexico
23B2 Tierra Colorada
 Mexico
29C6 Tierra del Fuego
 Territory, Arg
28C8 Tierra del Fuego I
 Arg/Chile
35B2 Tietê Brazil
35A2 Tietê R Brazil
14B2 Tiffin USA
17B1 Tifton USA
32E3 Tigre R Peru
33E2 Tigre R Ven
93E3 Tigris R Iraq
23B1 Tihuatlán Mexico
21B3 Tijuana Mexico
85D4 Tikamgarh India
60D2 Tikhin USSR
61F4 Tikhoretsk USSR
93D3 Tikrit Iraq
1B8 Tiksi USSR
46C1 Tilburg Neth
43E4 Tilbury Eng
30C3 Tilcara Arg
108B1 Tilcha Aust
76A1 Tilin Burma
97C3 Tillabéri Niger
20B1 Tillamook USA
73B1 Tilsa Niger
55C3 Tílos I Greece
108B2 Tilpa Aust
32B3 Tiluá Colombia
64G3 Timanskiy Kryazh Mts
 USSR
111B2 Timaru NZ
60E4 Timashevsk USSR
55B3 Timbákion Greece
19B4 Timbalier B USA
97B3 Timbédra Maur
 Timbuktu =
 Tombouctou
97B3 Timétrine Monts Mts
 Mali
97C3 Timia Niger
96C2 Timimoun Alg
54B1 Timişoara Rom
10B2 Timmins Can
106B1 Timor I Indon
106B2 Timor S Aust/Indon
34C3 Timote Arg
27D5 Tinaco Ven

87B2 Tindivanam India
96B2 Tindouf Alg
96B2 Tinfouchy Alg
96C2 Tin Fouye Alg
6F3 Tingmiarmiut
 Greenland
32B5 Tingo Maria Peru
97B3 Tingrela Ivory Coast
86B1 Tingri China
71F2 Tinian Pacific O
30C4 Tinogasta Arg
55C3 Tínos I Greece
43B4 Tintagel Head Pt Eng
96C2 Tin Tarabine
 Watercourse Alg
108B3 Tintinara Aust
96C2 Tin Zaouaten Alg
22C2 Tioga P USA
77C5 Tioman I Malay
47D1 Tione Italy
45C2 Tipperary County,
 Irish Rep
41B3 Tipperary Irish Rep
18B2 Tipton Missouri, USA
87B2 Tiptur India
23A2 Tiquicheo Mexico
55A2 Tiranë Alb
47D1 Tirano Italy
60C4 Tiraspol USSR
87B2 Tirchchiräppalli India
55C3 Tire Turk
93C1 Tirebolu Turk
44A3 Tiree I Scot
54C2 Tîrgoviste Rom
54B1 Tîrgu Jiu Rom
54B1 Tîrgu Mureş Rom
84C1 Tirich Mir Mt Pak
96A2 Tiris Region, Mor
61J3 Tirlyanskiy USSR
54B1 Tîrnăveni Rom
55B3 Tírnavos Greece
85D4 Tirodi India
47D1 Tirol Province, Austria
53A2 Tirso R Sardegna
87B3 Tiruchendür India
87B3 Tirunelveli India
87B2 Tirupati India
87B2 Tiruppattur India
87B2 Tiruppur India
87B2 Tiruvannamalai India
19A3 Tishomingo USA
94C2 Tisiyah Syria
59C3 Tisza R Hung
86A2 Titāgarh India
54B2 Titograd Yugos
54B2 Titova Mitrovica
 Yugos
54A2 Titovo Užice Yugos
52C1 Titovo Velenje Yugos
54B2 Titov Veles Yugos
99B3 Titule Zaire
17B2 Titusville USA
43C4 Tiverton Eng
52B2 Tívoli Italy
23B2 Tixtla Mexico
99E2 Tiyeglow Somalia
23B2 Tizayuca Mexico
25D2 Tizimin Mexico
96C1 Tizi Ouzou Alg
96B2 Tiznit Mor
23A1 Tizpan el Alto Mexico
23B2 Tlacolula Mexico
23B2 Tlacotalpan Mexico
23B2 Tlalchapa Mexico
23B2 Tlalnepantla Mexico
23B2 Tlalpan Mexico
23A1 Tlaltenango Mexico
23B2 Tlancualpican Mexico
23B2 Tlapa Mexico
23B2 Tlapacoyan Mexico
23B2 Tlaquepaque Mexico
23B2 Tlaxcala Mexico
23B2 Tlaxcala State, Mexico
23B2 Tlaxiaco Mexico
96B1 Tlemcen Alg
101D2 Toamasina Madag
34C3 Toay Arg
75B2 Toba Japan

84B2 Toba and Kakar
 Ranges Mts Pak
27E4 Tobago I Caribbean S
13C2 Toba Inlet Sd Can
65H4 Tobal R USSR
71D3 Tobelo Indon
14B1 Tobermory Can
44A3 Tobermory Scot
71E3 Tobi I Pacific O
21B1 Tobin,Mt USA
65H4 Tobol R USSR
70D4 Toboli Indon
65H4 Tobol'sk USSR
 Tobruk = Tubruq
31B2 Tocantins R Brazil
17B1 Toccoa USA
47C1 Toce R Italy
30B3 Tocopilla Chile
30C3 Tocorpuri Mt Chile
32D1 Tocuyo R Ven
85D3 Toda India
47C1 Tödi Mt Switz
75A1 Todong S Korea
9B4 Todos Santos Mexico
13E2 Tofield Can
13B3 Tofino Can
12B3 Togiak B USA
97C4 Togo Republic, Africa
72C1 Togtoh China
12F2 Tok USA
74E2 Tokachi R Japan
75B1 Tokamachi Japan
95C3 Tokar Sudan
69E4 Tokara Retto Arch
 Japan
92C1 Tokat Turk
74B3 Tŏkchŏk-kundo Arch
 S Korea
75A1 Tok-do I S Korea
82B1 Tokmak USSR
110C1 Tokomaru Bay NZ
12H3 Toku R Can/USA
78C3 Tokung Indon
69E4 Tokuno I Japan
74C4 Tokushima Japan
75A2 Tokuyama Japan
74D3 Tökyö Japan
110C1 Tolaga Bay NZ
30F3 Toledo Brazil
50B2 Toledo Spain
14B2 Toledo USA
19B3 Toledo Bend Res USA
101D3 Toliara Madag
23B1 Toliman Mexico
32B3 Tolima Mt Colombia
51B1 Tolosa Spain
29B3 Toltén Chile
23B2 Toluca Mexico
99E2 Tol'yatti USSR
74E2 Tomakomai Japan
78D1 Tomani Malay
58C2 Tomaszów
 Mazowiecka Pol
11B3 Tombigbee R USA
98B3 Tomboco Angola
35C2 Tombos Brazil
97B3 Tombouctou Mali
100A2 Tombua Angola
34A3 Tomé Chile
50B2 Tomelloso Spain
50A2 Tomer Port
106B3 Tomkinson Range Mts
 Aust
63E2 Tommot USSR
55B2 Tomorrit Mt Alb
65K4 Tomsk USSR
16B3 Toms River USA
25C3 Tonalá Mexico
15C2 Tonawanda USA
105H4 Tonga I Pacific O
101H1 Tongaat S Africa
73D3 Tongcheng China
72B2 Tongchuan China
72A2 Tongde China
46C1 Tongeren Belg
66E2 Tonggu Jiao I China

73A5 Tonghai China
74B2 Tonghua China
74B3 Tongjosŏn-man N Korea
76D1 Tongkin,G of China/Viet
72E1 Tonglia China
73D3 Tongling China
108B2 Tongo Aust
34A2 Tongoy Chile
73B4 Tongren Guizhou, China
72A2 Tongren Qinghai, China
86C1 Tongsa Bhutan
76B1 Tongta Burma
68B3 Tongtian He R China
44B2 Tongue Scot
72D2 Tong Xian China
72B2 Tongxin China
73B4 Tongzi China
63B3 Tonhil Mongolia
9C4 Tonich Mexico
99C2 Tonj Sudan
85D3 Tonk India
18A2 Tonkawa USA
76C3 Tonle Sap L Camb
21B2 Tonopah USA
12E2 Tonsina USA
8B2 Tooele USA
109D1 Toogoolawah Aust
108B1 Toompine Aust
109D1 Toowoomba Aust
22C1 Topaz L USA
18A2 Topeka USA
9C4 Topolobampo Mexico
20B1 Toppenish USA
55C3 Torbali Turk
90C2 Torbat-e-Heydarīyeh Iran
90D2 Torbat-e Jām Iran
43C4 Torbay Eng
12D2 Torbert,Mt USA
50A1 Tordesillas Spain
56C2 Torgau Germany
46B1 Torhout Belg
99D2 Tori I
69G3 Tori I Japan
47B2 Torino Italy
99D2 Torit Sudan
35A1 Torixoreu Brazil
50A1 Tormes R Spain
13E2 Tornado Mt Can
38J5 Torne L Sweden
38H5 Torneträsk Sweden
7D4 Torngat Mts Can
38J5 Tornio Fin
34C3 Tornquist Arg
15C2 Toronto Can
60D2 Toropets USSR
99D2 Tororo Uganda
92B2 Toros Dağlari Mts Turk
22C4 Torrance USA
50A2 Torrão Port
51C1 Torreblanca Spain
53B2 Torre del Greco Italy
50B1 Torrelavega Spain
50B2 Torremolinos Spain
108A2 Torrens,L Aust
24B2 Torreón Mexico
47B2 Torre Pellice Italy
107D2 Torres Str Aust
50A2 Torres Vedras Port
16C2 Torrington Connecticut, USA
8C2 Torrington Wyoming, USA
9C4 Torrón Mexico
38D3 Torshavn Faroyar
47C2 Tortona Italy
51C1 Tortosa Spain
90C2 Torūd Iran
58B2 Toruń Pol
40B2 Tory I Irish Rep
60D2 Torzhok USSR
75A2 Tosa Japan
74C4 Tosa-shimizu Japan

74C4 Tosa-wan B Japan
75B2 To-shima I Japan
39L7 Tosno USSR
60D2 Tosno USSR
75A2 Tosu Japan
92B1 Tosya Turk
61F1 Tot'ma USSR
43C4 Totnes Eng
33F2 Totness Surinam
23B2 Totolapan Mexico
51B2 Totana Spain
109C2 Tottenham Aust
74C3 Tottori Japan
97B4 Touba Ivory Coast
97A3 Touba Sen
96B1 Toubkal Mt Mor
97B3 Tougan Burkina
96C1 Touggourt Alg
97A3 Tougue Guinea
46C2 Toul France
49D3 Toulon France
48C3 Toulouse France
97B4 Toumodi Ivory Coast
76B2 Toungoo Burma
46B1 Tourcoing France
96A2 Tourine Maur
46B1 Tournai Belg
48C2 Tours France
74E2 Towada Japan
74E2 Towada-ko L Japan
15C2 Towanda USA
107D2 Townsville Aust
16A3 Towson USA
43C4 Towy R Wales
74D3 Toyama Japan
75B1 Toyama-wan B Japan
75B2 Toyohashi Japan
75B2 Toyonaka Japan
75A1 Toyooka Japan
74D3 Toyota Japan
96C1 Tozeur Tunisia
46D2 Traben-Trarbach Germany
93C1 Trabzon Turk
22B2 Tracy California, USA
34A3 Traiguén Chile
13D3 Trail Can
41B3 Tralee Irish Rep
45B2 Tralee B Irish Rep
45C2 Tramore Irish Rep
39G7 Tranås Sweden
57B4 Trang Thai
71E4 Trangan I Indon
109C2 Trangie Aust
12E2 Transalaskan Pipeline USA
100B3 Transvaal Province, S Africa
Transylvanian Alps = Muntii Carpaţii Meridionali
53B2 Trapani Italy
109C3 Traralgon Aust
97A3 Trarza Region, Maur
75A2 Trat Thai
108B2 Traveller's L Aust
56C2 Travemünde Germany
14A2 Traverse City USA
12C1 Traverse Peak Mt USA
111B2 Travers,Mt NZ
47C2 Trebbia R Italy
59B3 Třebíč Czech
54A2 Trebinje Yugos
57C3 Trebon Czech
29F2 Treinta y Tres Urug
29C4 Trelew Arg
39G7 Trelleborg Sweden
43B3 Tremadog B Wales
15D1 Tremblant,Mt Can
13C2 Trembleur L Can
16A2 Tremont USA
59B3 Trenčín Czech
34C3 Trenque Lauquén Arg
43D3 Trent R Eng
47D1 Trentino Region, Italy
47D1 Trento Italy
15C2 Trenton Can

18B1 Trenton Missouri, USA
16B2 Trenton New Jersey, USA
7E5 Trepassey Can
34C3 Tres Arroyos Arg
33C2 Três Corações Brazil
30F3 Três Lagoas Brazil
34C3 Tres Lomas Arg
22B2 Tres Pinos USA
35C2 Três Rios Brazil
47C2 Treviglio Italy
47E2 Treviso Italy
47B2 Trezzo Italy
87B2 Trichūr India
108C2 Trida Aust
46D2 Trier Germany
52B1 Trieste Italy
45C2 Trim Irish Rep
87C3 Trincomalee Sri Lanka
33E6 Trinidad Bol
29E2 Trinidad Urug
9C3 Trinidad USA
34C3 Trinidad I Arg
27E4 Trinidad I Caribbean S
103G6 Trinidade I Atlantic O
27E4 Trinidad & Tobago Republic, Caribbean S
19A3 Trinity USA
9D3 Trinity R USA
7E5 Trinity B Can
12D3 Trinity Is USA
17A1 Trion USA
94B1 Tripoli Leb
95A1 Tripoli Libya
55B3 Trípolis Greece
86C2 Tripura State, India
103H6 Tristan da Cunha Is Atlantic O
87B3 Trivandrum India
59B3 Trnava Czech
107E1 Trobriand Is PNG
15D1 Trois-Rivières Can
65H4 Troitsk USSR
39G7 Trollhättan Sweden
38F6 Trollheimen Mt Nor
89K9 Tromelin I Indian O
38H5 Tromsø Nor
38H6 Trondheim Nor
38G6 Trondheimfjord Inlet Nor
42B2 Troon Scot
102J3 Tropic of Cancer
103J6 Tropic of Capricorn
96B2 Troudenni Mali
7A4 Trout L Ontario, Can
17A1 Troy Alabama, USA
16C1 Troy New York, USA
14B2 Troy Ohio, USA
54B2 Troyan Bulg
49C2 Troyes France
91B5 Trucial Coast Region, UAE
21A2 Truckee R USA
25D3 Trujillo Honduras
32B5 Trujillo Peru
50B2 Trujillo Spain
32C2 Trujillo Ven
109C2 Trundle Aust
7D5 Truro Can
43B4 Truro Eng
71E3 Trust Territories of the Pacific Is Pacific O
68B2 Tsagaan Nuur L Mongolia
68B1 Tsagan-Tologoy USSR
101D2 Tsaratanana Madag
100B3 Tsau Botswana
99D3 Tsavo Kenya
99D3 Tsavo Nat Pk Kenya
65J4 Tselinograd USSR
100A3 Tses Namibia
68C2 Tsetserleg Mongolia
68C2 Tsetserleg Mongolia
97C4 Tsévié Togo
100B3 Tshabong Botswana

100B3 Tshane Botswana
98B3 Tshela Zaïre
98C3 Tshibala Zaïre
98C3 Tshikapa Zaïre
98C3 Tshuapa R Zaïre
101D3 Tsihombe Madag
61F4 Tsimlyanskoye Vodokhranilishche Res USSR
Tsinan = Jinan
Tsingtao = Qingdao
101D2 Tsiroanomandidy Madag
13B2 Tsitsutl Peak Mt Can
58D2 Tsna R USSR
72B1 Tsogt Ovoo Mongolia
75B2 Tsu Japan
75B1 Tsubata Japan
74E3 Tsuchira Japan
74E2 Tsugaru-kaikyō Str Japan
100A2 Tsumeb Namibia
100A3 Tsumis Namibia
75B1 Tsurugi Japan
74D3 Tsuruga Japan
74D3 Tsuruoka Japan
75B1 Tsushima Japan
74B4 Tsushima I Japan
74C4 Tsuyama Japan
50A1 Tua R Port
13A2 Tuam Irish Rep
60E5 Tuapse USSR
111A3 Tuatapere NZ
30G4 Tubarão Brazil
94B2 Tubas Israel
79A4 Tubbataha Reefs Is Phil
57B3 Tübingen Germany
95B1 Tubruq Libya
16B3 Tuckerton USA
9B3 Tucson USA
30C4 Tucuman State, Arg
34B2 Tucunuco Arg
33E2 Tucupita Ven
51B1 Tudela Spain
93C3 Tudmur Syria
101H1 Tugela R S Africa
109D2 Tuggerah L Aust
12D3 Tugidak I
79B2 Tuguegarao Phil
63F2 Tugur USSR
72D2 Tuhai He R China
4E3 Tuktoyaktuk USA
58C1 Tukums USSR
99D3 Tukuyu Tanz
84B1 Tukzar Afghan
60E3 Tula USSR
23B1 Tulancingo Mexico
78A3 Tulangbawang R Indon
32B3 Tulcán Colombia
60C5 Tulcea Rom
100B3 Tuli Zim
94B2 Tulkarm Israel
48C2 Tulle France
19B3 Tullos USA
45C2 Tullow Irish Rep
18A2 Tulsa USA
93C3 Tulūl ash Shāmīyah Desert Region Syria/S Arabia
63C2 Tulun USSR
78C4 Tulungagung Indon
32B3 Tumaco Colombia
109C3 Tumbarumba Aust
32A4 Tumbes Ecuador
108A2 Tumby Bay Aust
74B2 Tumen China
87B2 Tumkur India
77C4 Tumpat Malay
85D4 Tumsar India
97B3 Tumu Ghana
109C3 Tumut Aust
27L1 Tunapuna Trinidad
93C2 Tunceli Turk
99D3 Tunduma Zambia
101C2 Tunduru Tanz

54C2 Tundzha R Bulg
87B1 Tungabhadra R India
68D4 Tung-Chiang Taiwan
38B2 Tungnafellsjökull Mts Iceland
12J2 Tungsten Can
63B1 Tunguska R USSR
87C1 Tuni India
96D1 Tunis Tunisia
88E4 Tunisia Republic, N Africa
32C2 Tunja Colombia
12B2 Tuntutuliak USA
12B2 Tunuak USA
34B2 Tunuyán Arg
34B2 Tunuyán R Arg
73D4 Tunxi China
22C2 Tuolumne Meadows USA
35A2 Tupã Brazil
35B1 Tupaciguara Brazil
19C3 Tupelo USA
30C3 Tupiza Bol
15D2 Tupper Lake USA
34B2 Tupungato Arg
29C2 Tupungato Mt Arg
86C1 Tura India
63C1 Tura USSR
61K2 Tura R USSR
90C2 Turán Iran
63B2 Turan USSR
93C3 Turayf S Arabia
80E3 Turbat Pak
32B2 Turbo Colombia
54B1 Turda Rom
63A3 Turfan Depression China
65H4 Turgay USSR
63B3 Turgen Uul Mt Mongolia
54C2 Turgovishte Bulg
92A2 Turgutlu Turk
92C1 Turhal Turk
39K7 Turi USSR
51B2 Turia R Spain
 Turin = Torino
61K2 Turinsk USSR
69F2 Turiy Rog USSR
99D2 Turkana,L Kenya/Eth
80E1 Turkestan Region, C Asia
82A1 Turkestan USSR
92C2 Turkey Republic, W Asia
80D1 Turkmenskaya SSR Republic, USSR
90B2 Turkmenskiy Zaliv B USSR
27C2 Turks Is Caribbean S
39J6 Turku Fin
99D2 Turkwel R Kenya
22B2 Turlock USA
22B2 Turlock L USA
110C2 Turnagain,C NZ
24D3 Turneffe I Belize
16C1 Turners Falls USA
46C1 Turnhout Belg
13F1 Turnor L Can
54B2 Turnu Măgurele Rom
63A3 Turpan China
26B2 Turquino Mt Cuba
80E1 Turtkul' USSR
18A2 Turtle Creek Res USA
13F2 Turtle L Can
63A1 Turukhansk USSR
68C1 Turuntayevo USSR
35A1 Turvo R Goias, Brazil
35B2 Turvo R São Paulo, Brazil
58C2 Tur'ya R USSR
19C3 Tuscaloosa USA
19C3 Tuscola USA
90C3 Tusharik Iran
87B3 Tuticorin India
54C2 Tutrakan Bulg
57B3 Tuttlingen Germany
68C2 Tuul Gol R Mongolia
105G4 Tuvalu Is Pacific O

63B2 Tuvinskaya Republic, USSR
23A2 Tuxpan Jalisco, Mexico
24B2 Tuxpan Nayarit, Mexico
23B1 Tuxpan Veracruz, Mexico
23B2 Tuxtepec Mexico
25C3 Tuxtla Gutiérrez Mexico
50A1 Túy Spain
76D3 Tuy Hoa Viet
92B2 Tuz Gölü Salt L Turk
93D3 Tuz Khurmātū Iraq
54A2 Tuzla Yugos
42C2 Tweed R Eng/Scot
109D1 Tweed Heads Aust
42C2 Tweedsmuir Hills Scot
7E5 Twillingate Can
8B2 Twin Falls USA
111B2 Twins,The Mt NZ
14A2 Two Rivers USA
63E2 Tygda USSR
19A3 Tyler USA
65K3 Tym R USSR
69G1 Tymovskoye USSR
42D2 Tyne R Eng
42D2 Tyne and Wear County, Eng
42D2 Tynemouth Eng
38G6 Tynset Nor
12D3 Tyonek USA
94B2 Tyr Leb
 Tyre = Tyr
45C1 Tyrone County, N Ire
108B3 Tyrrell,L Aust
53B2 Tyrrhenian S Italy
65K3 Tyumen' USSR
43B3 Tywyn Wales
55B3 Tzoumérka Mt Greece

U
99E2 Uarsciek Somalia
35C2 Ubá Brazil
35C1 Ubaí Brazil
98B2 Ubangi R CAR
47B2 Ubaye R France
75A2 Ube Japan
50B2 Ubeda Spain
6E2 Ubekendt Ejland I Greenland
35B1 Uberaba Brazil
35B1 Uberlândia Brazil
76C2 Ubon Ratchathani Thai
58D2 Ubort R USSR
98C3 Ubundi Zaire
32C5 Ucayali R Peru
84C3 Uch Pak
74E2 Uchiura-wan B Japan
63F2 Uchur R USSR
85C4 Udaipur India
86B1 Udaipur Garhi Nepal
34D3 Udaquoila Arg
39G7 Uddevalla Sweden
38H5 Uddjaur L Sweden
87B1 Udgir India
84D2 Udhampur India
61H2 Udmurtskaya ASSR Republic, USSR
76C2 Udon Thani Thai
63F2 Udskaya Guba B USSR
87A2 Udupi India
75B1 Ueda Japan
99C2 Uele R Zaire
99D2 Uelen USSR
56C2 Uelzen Germany
98C2 Uere R Zaire
61J3 Ufa USSR
61J2 Ufa R USSR
100A3 Ugab R Namibia
99D3 Ugalla R Tanz
12D3 Ugak B USA
99D2 Uganda Republic, Africa
12C3 Ugashik B USA
12C3 Ugashik L USA

47B2 Ugine France
69G2 Uglegorsk USSR
60E2 Uglich USSR
60E3 Ugra R USSR
44A3 Uig Scot
98B3 Uige Angola
61H4 Uil USSR
8B2 Uinta Mts USA
100B4 Uitenhage S Africa
59C3 Ujfehértó Hung
75B2 Uji Japan
19A3 Ujiji Tanz
30C3 Ujina Chile
85D4 Ujjain India
70C4 Ujung Pandang Indon
99D3 Ukerewe I Tanz
86C1 Ukhrul India
21A2 Ukiah California, USA
21B3 Ukiah Oregon, USA
58C1 Ukmerge USSR
60C4 Ukrainskaya Republic, USSR
68C2 Ulaanbaatar Mongolia
68B2 Ulaangom Mongolia
72C1 Ulan Uul Mongolia
82C1 Ulangar Hu L China
68C1 Ulan Ude USSR
68B3 Ulan Ul China
34B2 Ulapes Arg
74B3 Ulchin S Korea
54A2 Ulcinj Yugos
68B2 Uliastay Mongolia
58D1 Ulla R USSR
109D3 Ulladulla Aust
44B3 Ullapool Scot
38H5 Ullsfjorden Inlet Nor
42C2 Ullswater L Eng
74C2 Ullung-do I S Korea
57C3 Ulm Germany
108A1 Ulooowaranie,L Aust
74B3 Ulsan S Korea
45C1 Ulster Region, N Ire
65K5 Ulungur He R China
65K5 Ulungur Hu L China
44A3 Ulva I Scot
42C2 Ulverston Eng
109C4 Ulverstone Aust
63G2 Ulya R USSR
61G3 Ul'yanovsk USSR
60D4 Uman USSR
6E2 Umanak Greenland
86A2 Umaria India
85B3 Umarkot Pak
108A1 Umaroona,L Aust
20C1 Umatilla USA
38L5 Umba USSR
99D3 Umba R Tanz
38H6 Ume R Sweden
38J6 Umea Sweden
101H1 Umfolozi R S Africa
4C3 Umiat USA
91C4 Umm al Qaiwain UAE
91C5 Umm al Samim Salt Marsh Oman
99C1 Umm Bell Sudan
99D1 Umm Hagar Eth
98C1 Umm Keddada Sudan
99D1 Umm Ruwaba Sudan
91B5 Umm Sa'id Qatar
100B2 Umnaiti R Zim
20B2 Umpqua R USA
85D4 Umred India
100B3 Umtata S Africa
35A2 Umuarama Brazil
52C1 Una R Yugos
35B1 Unai Brazil
12B2 Unalakleet USA
80C3 Unayzah S Arabia
16C2 Uncasville USA
101G1 Underberg S Africa
60D3 Unecha USSR
94B3 Uneisa Jordan
7D4 Ungava B Can
30F4 União de Vitória Brazil
34B3 Unión Arg
34B2 Union Missouri, USA
17B1 Union S Carolina, USA

14C2 Union City Pennsylvania, USA
62C3 Union of Soviet Socialist Reps Asia
17A1 Union Springs USA
15C3 Uniontown USA
91B5 United Arab Emirates Arabian Pen
36C3 United Kingdom Kingdom, W Europe
2H4 United States of America
6B1 United States Range Mts Can
13F2 Unity Can
20C2 Unity USA
46D1 Unna Germany
86A1 Unnao India
44E1 Unst I Scot
13A1 Unuk R USA
92C1 Ünye Turk
61F2 Unzha R USSR
33E2 Upata Ven
93C4 Upemba Nat Pk Zaïre
6E2 Upernavik Greenland
22D3 Upland USA
100B3 Uplington S Africa
14B2 Upper Arlington USA
13D2 Upper Arrow L Can
111C2 Upper Hutt NZ
20B2 Upper Klamath L USA
20B2 Upper L USA
45C1 Upper Lough Erne L N Ire
27L1 Upper Manzanilla Trinidad
7C4 Upper Seal,L Can
39H7 Uppsala Sweden
72B1 Urad Qianqi China
91A4 Urairah S Arabia
61H3 Ural R USSR
109D2 Uralla Aust
61H3 Ural'sk USSR
65G4 Uralskiy Khrebet Mts USSR
5H4 Uranium City Can
75B1 Urawa Japan
14B2 Urbana Illinois, USA
14B2 Urbana Ohio, USA
52B2 Urbino Italy
42C2 Ure R Eng
61G2 Uren' USSR
93C2 Urfa Turk
80E1 Urgench USSR
80E2 Urgun Afghan
55C3 Urla Turk
54B2 Uroševac Yugos
33A2 Uruaçu Brazil
23A2 Uruapan Mexico
35B1 Urucuia R Brazil
30E4 Uruguaiana Brazil
29E2 Uruguay Republic, S America
29E2 Uruguay R Urug
82C1 Ürümqi China
69H2 Urup I USSR
84B2 Uruzgan Afghan
61F3 Uryupinsk USSR
61H2 Urzhum USSR
54C1 Urziceni Rom
82C1 Usa China
75A2 Usa Japan
64G3 Usa R USSR
92A2 Uşak Turk
100A3 Usakos Namibia
99D3 Ushashi Tanz
65J5 Ush Tobe USSR
29C6 Ushuaia Arg
63E2 Ushumun USSR
43C4 Usk R Wales
92A1 Üsküdar Turk
63C2 Usolye Sibirskoye USSR
34B2 Uspallata Arg
69F2 Ussuriysk USSR
47C1 Uster Switz
53B3 Ustica I Italy
57C2 Ústi nad Labem Czech

65J4 Ust'Ishim USSR
58B2 Ustka Pol
65K5 Ust'-Kamenogorsk
  USSR
63B2 Ust Karabula USSR
61J2 Ust'Katav USSR
63C2 Ust'-Kut USSR
61E4 Ust Labinsk USSR
63F1 Ust'Maya USSR
1C8 Ust'Nera USSR
63E2 Ust'Nyukzha USSR
63C2 Ust'Ordynskiy USSR
64G3 Ust'Tsil'ma USSR
63F2 Ust'Umal'ta USSR
75A2 Usuki Japan
25C3 Usumacinta R
  Guatemala/Mexico
101H1 Usutu R Swaziland
8B3 Utah State, USA
8B2 Utah L USA
58D1 Utena USSR
85B3 Uthal Pak
10C2 Utica USA
51B2 Utiel Spain
13D1 Utikuma L Can
56B2 Utrecht Neth
101H1 Utrecht S Africa
50A2 Utrera Spain
38K5 Utsjoki Fin
74D3 Utsunomiya Japan
76C2 Uttaradit Thai
86A1 Uttar Pradesh State,
  India
65H4 Uvel USSR
107F3 Uvéa I / Nouvelle
  Calédonie
99D3 Uvinza Tanz
99C3 Uvira Zaïre
6E2 Uvkusigssat
  Greenland
39J6 Uusikaupunki Fin
68B1 Uvs Nuur L China
74C4 Uwajima Japan
72B2 Uxin Qi China
63B2 Uyar USSR
30C3 Uyuni Bol
80E1 Uzbekskaya S.S.R.
  Republic, USSR
48C2 Uzerche France
59C3 Uzhgorod USSR
60E3 Uzlovaya USSR
92A1 Uzunköprü Turk

V

101F1 Vaal R S Africa
101G1 Vaal Dam Res
  S Africa
100B3 Vaalwater S Africa
38J6 Vaasa Fin
59B3 Vác Hung
30F4 Vacaria Brazil
35C1 Vacaria R Minas
  Gerais, Brazil
21A2 Vacaville USA
85C4 Vadodara India
38K4 Vadsø Nor
47C1 Vaduz Leichtenstein
38D3 Vågar Føroyar
29E3 Va Gesell Arg
59B3 Váh R Czech
87B2 Vaigai R India
65K3 Vakh R USSR
60B4 Vălcea Rom
29C4 Valcheta Arg
47D2 Valdagno Italy
60D2 Valday USSR
60D2 Valdayskaya
  Vozvyshennost'
  Upland USSR
32D2 Val de la Pascua Ven
50B2 Valdepeñas Spain
12E2 Valdez USA
29B3 Valdivia Chile
46B2 Val d'Oise Department
  France
17B1 Valdosta USA

20C2 Vale USA
13D2 Valemount Can
31D4 Valença Bahia, Brazil
35C2 Valença Rio de
  Janeiro, Brazil
49C3 Valence France
51B2 Valencia Region, Spain
51B2 Valencia Spain
32D1 Valencia Ven
45A3 Valencia I / Irish Rep
50A2 Valencia de Alcantara
  Spain
46B1 Valenciennes France
47C2 Valenza Italy
32C2 Valera Ven
39K7 Valga USSR
64E4 Valikiyo USSR
54A2 Valjevo Yugos
39J6 Valkeakoski Fin
25D2 Valladolid Mexico
50B1 Valladolid Spain
47B2 Valle d'Aosta Region,
  Italy
27D5 Valle de la Pascua Ven
23A1 Valle de Santiago
  Mexico
47B2 Valle d'Isère France
32C1 Valledupar Colombia
97C3 Vallée de l'Azaouak V
  Niger
97C3 Vallée Tilemsi V Mali
30D2 Valle Grande Bol
22A1 Vallejo USA
30B4 Vallenar Chile
53B3 Valletta Malta
8D2 Valley City USA
20B2 Valley Falls USA
15D1 Valleyfield Can
13D1 Valleyview Can
47E2 Valli di Comacchio Lg
  Italy
51C1 Valls Spain
58D1 Valmiera USSR
35A2 Valparaiso Brazil
34A2 Valparaiso Chile
23A1 Valparaiso Mexico
17A1 Valparaiso USA
101G1 Vals R S Africa
85C4 Valsad India
60E3 Valuyki USSR
50A2 Valverde del Camino
  Spain
38J6 Vammala Fin
93D2 Van Turk
63C1 Vanavara USSR
18B2 Van Buren Arkansas,
  USA
13C3 Vancouver Can
20B1 Vancouver USA
5G5 Vancouver I Can
12G2 Vancouver,Mt Can
18C2 Vandalia Illinois, USA
14B3 Vandalia Ohio, USA
13C2 Vanderhoof Can
106C2 Van Diemen G Aust
39G7 Vänern L Sweden
39G7 Vänersborg Sweden
101D3 Vangaindrano Madag
93D2 Van Gölü Salt L Turk
76C2 Vang Vieng Laos
9C3 Van Horn USA
15C1 Vanier Can
1C6 Vankarem USSR
38H6 Vännäs Sweden
48B2 Vannes France
47B2 Vanoise Mts France
100A4 Vanrhynsdorp S Africa
6B3 Vansittart I Can
105G4 Vanuatu Is Pacific O
14B2 Van Wert USA
90B2 Varamin Iran
86A1 Vārānasi India
38K4 Varangerfjord Inlet
  Nor
38K4 Varangerhalvøya Pen
  Nor
52C1 Varazdin Yugos

39G7 Varberg Sweden
39F7 Varde Den
38L4 Vardø Nor
58C2 Varéna USSR
47C2 Varenna Italy
47C2 Varese Italy
35B2 Varginha Brazil
38K6 Varkaus Fin
54B2 Varna Bulg
39G7 Värnamo Sweden
17B1 Varnville USA
35C1 Várzea da Palma
  Brazil
50B1 Vascongadas Region,
  Spain
60D3 Vasil'kov USSR
14B2 Vassar USA
39H7 Västerås Sweden
39H7 Västervik Sweden
52B2 Vasto Italy
65J4 Vasyugan R USSR
6B2 Vatnajökull Mts
  Iceland
38A1 Vatneyri Iceland
54C1 Vatra Dornei Rom
39G7 Vättern L Sweden
9C3 Vaughn USA
32C3 Vaupés R Colombia
13E2 Vauxhall Can
72C3 Vavuniya Sri Lanka
39G7 Växjö Sweden
64G2 Vaygach, Ostrov /
  USSR
34C2 Vedia Arg
38G5 Vega / Nor
13E2 Vegreville Can
50A2 Vejer de la Frontera
  Spain
39F7 Vejle Den
52C2 Velebit Mts Yugos
51B2 Velhas R Brazil
39K7 Velikaya R USSR
60D2 Velikiye Luki USSR
61G1 Velikiy Ustyug USSR
54B2 Veliko Türnovo Bulg
97A3 Vélingara Sen
87B2 Vellore India
61F1 Vel'sk USSR
87B3 Vembanad L India
34C2 Venado Tuerto Arg
35B2 Vençeslau Braz Brazil
49C2 Vendôme France
12E1 Venetie USA
47D2 Veneto Region, Italy
47E2 Venezia Italy
32D2 Venezuela Republic,
  S America
87A1 Vengurla India
12C3 Veniaminof V USA
  Venice = Venezia
72B2 Venkatagiri India
56B2 Venlo Neth
58C1 Venta R USSR
101G1 Ventersburg S Africa
58C1 Ventspils USSR
32D3 Venturi R Ven
22C3 Ventura USA
60D1 Vepsovskaya
  Vozvyshennost'
  Upland USSR
30D4 Vera Arg
51B2 Vera Spain
23B2 Veracruz Mexico
23B1 Veracruz State,
  Mexico
85C4 Verāval India
47B2 Verbania Italy
47C2 Vercelli Italy
35A1 Verde R Goias, Brazil
23A1 Verde R Jalisco,
  Mexico
35A1 Verde R Mato Grosso
  do Sul, Brazil
23B2 Verde R Oaxaca,
  Mexico
  Verde,C = Cap Vert
35C1 Verde Grande R Brazil

34C3 Verde,Pen Arg
49D3 Verdon R France
46C2 Verdun France
101G1 Vereeniging S Africa
61H2 Vereshchagino USSR
97A3 Verga,C Guinea
34D3 Vergara Arg
50A1 Verin Spain
98C3 Verissimo Sarmento
  Angola
63D2 Verkh Angara R
  USSR
61J3 Verkhneural'sk USSR
63E1 Verkhnevilyuysk
  USSR
1C8 Verkhoyansk USSR
35A1 Vermelho R Brazil
13E2 Vermilion Can
10C2 Vermont State, USA
22B2 Vernalis USA
13D2 Vernon Can
46A2 Vernon France
9D3 Vernon USA
17B2 Vero Beach USA
54C2 Véroia Greece
47D2 Veronalnuova Italy
47D2 Verona Italy
46B2 Versailles France
101H1 Verulam S Africa
46C1 Vervins Belg
46C1 Vervins France
46C2 Vesle R France
49D2 Vesoul France
38G5 Vesterålen Is Nor
38G5 Vestfjorden Inlet Nor
38A2 Vestmannaeyjar
  Iceland
53B2 Vesuvio Mt Italy
59B3 Veszprém Hung
39H7 Vetlanda Sweden
61F2 Vetluga R USSR
46B1 Veurne Belg
47B1 Vevey Switz
46A2 Vexin Region, France
47D2 Veynes France
50A1 Viana do Castelo Port
49E3 Viareggio Italy
39F7 Viborg Den
53C3 Vibo Valentia Italy
112C2 Vice-commodoro
  Marambio Base Ant
52B1 Vicenza Italy
51C1 Vich Spain
32D3 Vichada R Colombia
61F2 Vichuga USSR
49C2 Vichy France
19B3 Vicksburg USA
35C2 Viçosa Brazil
106C4 Victor Harbour Aust
34C2 Victoria Arg
13C3 Victoria Can
34A3 Victoria Chile
73C5 Victoria Hong Kong
78D1 Victoria Malay
108B3 Victoria State, Aust
9D4 Victoria USA
106C2 Victoria R Aust
107D4 Victoria State Aust
26B2 Victoria de las Tunas
  Cuba
100B2 Victoria Falls Zambia/
  Zim
4G2 Victoria I Can
108B2 Victoria,L Aust
99D3 Victoria,L C Africa
112B7 Victoria Land Region,
  Ant
86C2 Victoria,Mt Burma
99D2 Victoria Nile R
  Uganda
111B2 Victoria Range Mts
  NZ
106C2 Victoria River Downs
  Aust
4H3 Victoria Str Can
15D1 Victoriaville Can
100B4 Victoria West S Africa
34B3 Victorica Arg

21B3	**Victorville** USA
34A2	**Vicuña** Chile
34C2	**Vicuña Mackenna** Arg
17B1	**Vidalia** USA
54C2	**Videle** Rom
54B2	**Vidin** Bulg
85D4	**Vidisha** India
58D1	**Vidzy** USSR
29D4	**Viedma** Arg
26A4	**Viejo** Costa Rica
51C1	**Viella** Spain
	Vienna = Wien
18C2	**Vienna** Illinois, USA
14B3	**Vienna** W Virginia, USA
49C2	**Vienne** France
48C2	**Vienne** *R* France
76C2	**Vientiane** Laos
47C1	**Vierwaldstätter See** *L* Switz
48C2	**Vierzon** France
53C2	**Vieste** Italy
70B2	**Vietnam** Republic, S E Asia
76D1	**Vietri** Viet
27P2	**Vieux Fort** St Lucia
79B2	**Vigan** Phil
47C2	**Vigevano** Italy
48B3	**Vignemale** *Mt* France
50A1	**Vigo** Spain
87C1	**Vijayawada** India
55A2	**Vijosë** *R* Alb
38B2	**Vik** Iceland
54B2	**Vikhren** *Mt* Bulg
13E2	**Viking** Can
38G6	**Vikna** *I* Nor
101C2	**Vila da Maganja** Mozam
101C2	**Vila Machado** Mozam
101C3	**Vilanculos** Mozam
50A1	**Vila Real** Port
101C2	**Vila Vasco da Gama** Mozam
35C2	**Vila Velha** Brazil
58D2	**Vileyka** USSR
38H6	**Vilhelmina** Sweden
33E6	**Vilhena** Brazil
60C2	**Viljandi** USSR
101G1	**Viljoenskroon** S Africa
59D3	**Vilkovo** USSR
9C3	**Vila Ahumada** Mexico
34B2	**Villa Atuel** Arg
50A1	**Villalba** Spain
23A2	**Villa Carranza** Mexico
52B1	**Villach** Austria
34B2	**Villa Colon** Arg
34C2	**Villa Constitución** Arg
34C1	**Vila de Maria** Arg
23A1	**Villa de Reyes** Mexico
34B2	**Villa Dolores** Arg
47D2	**Villafranca di Verona** Italy
34C2	**Villa General Mitre** Arg
34B2	**Villa General Roca** Arg
34D2	**Villaguay** Arg
25C3	**Villahermosa** Mexico
23A1	**Villa Hidalgo** Mexico
34C2	**Villa Huidobro** Arg
34C3	**Villa Iris** Arg
30D3	**Villa Montes** Bol
23A1	**Villanueva** Mexico
50A1	**Villa Nova de Gaia** Port
50A2	**Villanueva de la Serena** Spain
51C1	**Villanueva-y-Geltrú** Spain
34B3	**Villa Regina** Arg
51B2	**Villarreal** Spain
29B3	**Villarrica** Chile
30E4	**Villarrica** Par
50D2	**Villarrobledo** Spain
34D2	**Villa San José** Arg
34C2	**Villa Valeria** Arg
32C3	**Villavicencio** Colombia

49C2	**Villefranche** France
7C5	**Ville-Marie** Can
51B2	**Villena** Spain
46B2	**Villeneuve-St-Georges** France
48C3	**Villeneuve-sur-Lot** France
19B3	**Ville Platte** USA
46B2	**Villers-Cotterêts** France
49C2	**Villeurbanne** France
101G1	**Villiers** S Africa
87B2	**Villupuram** India
52C2	**Vilnius** USSR
63D1	**Vilyuy** USSR
63E1	**Vilyuysk** USSR
34A2	**Viña del Mar** Chile
51C1	**Vinaroz** Spain
14A3	**Vincennes** USA
38H5	**Vindel** *R* Sweden
85D4	**Vindhya Range** *Mts* India
16B3	**Vineland** USA
16D2	**Vineyard Haven** USA
76D2	**Vinh** Viet
76D3	**Vinh Cam Ranh** *B* Viet
77D4	**Vinh Loi** Viet
77D3	**Vinh Long** Viet
18A2	**Vinita** USA
54A1	**Vinkovci** Yugos
60C4	**Vinnitsa** USSR
112B3	**Vinson Massif** *Upland* Ant
100A3	**Vioolsdrift** S Africa
47D1	**Vipiteno** Italy
79B3	**Virac** Phil
87B2	**Virddhāchalam** India
100A2	**Virei** Angola
35C1	**Virgem da Lapa** Brazil
11C3	**Virginia** S Africa
10C3	**Virginia** State, USA
10A2	**Virginia** USA
21B2	**Virginia City** USA
27E3	**Virgin Is** Caribbean S
52C1	**Virovitica** Yugos
46C2	**Virton** Belg
87B3	**Virudunagar** India
52C2	**Vis** *I* Yugos
21B2	**Visalia** USA
79B3	**Visayan S** Phil
39H7	**Visby** Sweden
4H2	**Viscount Melville Sd** Can
54A2	**Višegrad** Yugos
50A1	**Viseu** Port
83C4	**Vishākhapatnam** India
47B1	**Visp** Switz
21B3	**Vista** USA
	Vistula = Wisla
57C3	**Vitava** *R* Czech
87A1	**Vite** India
60D2	**Vitebsk** USSR
52B2	**Viterbo** Italy
50A1	**Vitigudino** Spain
63D2	**Vitim** *R* USSR
50B1	**Vitora** Spain
31C6	**Vitória** Brazil
31C4	**Vitória da Conquista** Brazil
48B2	**Vitré** France
46C2	**Vitry-le-Francois** France
38J5	**Vittangi** Sweden
53B3	**Vittoria** Italy
47E2	**Vittorio Veneto** Italy
69H2	**Vityaz Depth** Pacific O
50A1	**Vivero** Spain
63B1	**Vivi** *R* USSR
34D3	**Vivorata** Arg
63C4	**Vizhne-Angarsk** USSR
83C4	**Vizianagaram** India
54B1	**Vladeasa** *Mt* Rom
61F5	**Vladikavkaz** USSR
65F4	**Vladimir** USSR
59C2	**Vladimir Volynskiy** USSR
74C2	**Vladivostok** USSR
56A2	**Vlieland** *I* Neth

46B1	**Vlissingen** Neth
55A2	**Vlorë** Alb
57C3	**Vöcklabruck** Austria
76D3	**Voeune Sai** Camb
47C2	**Voghera** Italy
101D2	**Vohibinany** Madag
101E2	**Vohimarina** Madag
99D3	**Voi** Kenya
97B4	**Voinjama** Lib
49D2	**Voiron** France
26A5	**Volcán Baru** *Mt* Panama
23B2	**Volcán Citlaltepetl** *Mt* Mexico
30C3	**Volcán Lullaillaco** *Mt* Chile
34A3	**Volcáno Copahue** *Mt* Chile
34A3	**Volcáno Domuyo** *Mt* Arg
	Volcano Is = Kazan Retto
29B3	**Volcáno Lanin** *Mt* Arg
30C3	**Volcán Ollagüe** *Mt* Chile
34A3	**Volcán Llaima** *Mt* Chile
34B2	**Volcán Maipo** *Mt* Arg
34A3	**Volcáno Peteroa** *Mt* Chile
34B3	**Volcáno Tromen** *V* Arg
23A2	**Volcán Paracutin** *Mt* Mexico
32B3	**Volcán Puracé** *Mt* Colombia
34A2	**Volcán Tinguiririca** *Mt* Arg/Chile
61J2	**Volchansk** USSR
61G4	**Volga** *R* USSR
61G4	**Volgodonsk** USSR
61F4	**Volgograd** USSR
61G3	**Volgogradskoye Vodokhranilishche** *Res* USSR
60D2	**Volkhov** USSR
60D2	**Volkhov** *R* USSR
58C2	**Volkovysk** USSR
101G1	**Volksrust** S Africa
61F2	**Vologda** USSR
48B2	**Volognes** France
55B3	**Vólos** Greece
61G3	**Vol'sk** USSR
22B2	**Volta** USA
97B3	**Volta Blanche** *R* Burkina
97B4	**Volta,L** Ghana
97B3	**Volta Noire** *R* Burkina
35C2	**Volta Redonda** Brazil
97B3	**Volta Rouge** *R* Burkina
60C3	**Volynskiy** USSR
61F4	**Volzhskiy** USSR
12D2	**Von Frank Mt** USA
6J3	**Vopnafjördur** Iceland
47C1	**Voralberg** Province, Austria
47C1	**Vorder Rhein** *R* Switz
56C1	**Vordingborg** Den
64H3	**Vorkuta** USSR
39G6	**Vorma** *R* Nor
60E3	**Voronezh** USSR
38M5	**Voron'ya** *R* USSR
39K7	**Võru** USSR
49D2	**Vosges** *Mt* France
68B1	**Voshnyy Saytocan** *Mts* USSR
39F6	**Voss** Nor
63B2	**Vostochnyy Sayan** *Mts* USSR
112B9	**Vostok** *Base* Ant
61H2	**Votkinsk** USSR
46C2	**Vouziers** France
60D4	**Voznesensk** USSR
54B2	**Vranje** Yugos
54B2	**Vratsa** Bulg
54A1	**Vrbas** Yugos

52C2	**Vrbas** *R* Yugos
52B1	**Vrbovsko** Yugos
101G1	**Vrede** S Africa
33F2	**Vreed en Hoop** Guyana
54B1	**Vršac** Yugos
52C2	**Vrtoče** Yugos
100B3	**Vryburg** S Africa
101H1	**Vryheid** S Africa
54A1	**Vukovar** Yugos
13E2	**Vulcan** Can
53B3	**Vulcano** *I* Italy
77D3	**Vung Tau** Viet
38J5	**Vuollerim** Sweden
54B1	**Vyartsilya** USSR
61H2	**Vyatka** *R* USSR
69F2	**Vyazemskiy** USSR
60D2	**Vyaz'ma** USSR
61F2	**Vyazniki** USSR
60C1	**Vyborg** USSR
64G3	**Vym'** *R* USSR
43C3	**Vyrnwy** *R* Wales
60D2	**Vyshiy Volochek** USSR
57B3	**Vyškov** Czech
60E1	**Vytegra** USSR

W

97B3	**Wa** Ghana
13E1	**Wabasca** Can
5G4	**Wabasca** *R* Can
13E1	**Wabasca L** Can
14A2	**Wabash** USA
14A3	**Wabash** *R* USA
5J4	**Wabowden** Can
7D4	**Wabush** Can
17B2	**Waccasassa B** USA
16D1	**Wachusett Res** USA
19A3	**Waco** USA
85B3	**Wad** Pak
95A2	**Waddān** Libya
5F4	**Waddington,Mt** Can
93E4	**Wadi al Bātin** *Watercourse* Iraq
93D3	**Wadi al Ghudaf** *Watercourse* Iraq
94C2	**Wadi al Harir** *V* Syria
93D3	**Wadi al Mirah** *Watercourse* Iraq/ S Arabia
93D3	**Wadi al Ubayyid** *Watercourse* Iraq
93D3	**Wadi Ar'ar** *Watercourse* S Arabia
91A5	**Wadi as Hsabā'** *Watercourse* S Arabia
92C3	**Wadi as Sirhān** *V* S Arabia
94C2	**Wadi az Zaydi** *V* Syria
94C3	**Wadi edh Dhab'ī** *V* Jordan
94A3	**Wadi el 'Arish** *V* Egypt
94C3	**Wadi al Ghadaf** *V* Jordan
94B3	**Wadi el Hasa** *V* Jordan
94B3	**Wadi el Janab** *V* Jordan
94B3	**Wadi el Jeib** *V* Israel/ Jordan
95B3	**Wadi el Milk** *Watercourse* Sudan
92A3	**Wadi el Natrun** *Watercourse* Egypt
94B3	**Wadi es Sir** Jordan
94B3	**Wadi Fidan** *V* Jordan
94B3	**Wadi Hareidin** *V* Egypt
93D3	**Wadi Hawrān** *R* Iraq
95B3	**Wadi Howa** *Watercourse* Sudan
98C1	**Wadi Ibra** *Watercourse* Sudan

94C2 Wadi Luhfi
   Watercourse Jordan
94B3 Wadi Mujib *V* Jordan
94B3 Wadi Qîtaiya *V* Egypt
80B3 Wadi Sha'it
   Watercourse Egypt
99D1 Wad Medani Sudan
93E4 Wafra Kuwait
6B3 Wager B Can
6A3 Wager Bay Can
109C3 Wagga Wagga Aust
106A4 Wagin Aust
95A2 Waha Libya
21C4 Wahaiwa Hawaiian Is
18A1 Wahoo USA
8D2 Wahpeton USA
87A1 Wai India
111B2 Waiau R NZ
111A3 Waiau NZ
111B2 Waiau R NZ
71E3 Waigeo I Indon
110C1 Waihi NZ
110C1 Waikaremoana,L NZ
110C1 Waikato R NZ
108A2 Waikerie Aust
111B3 Waikouaiti NZ
21C4 Wailuku Hawaiian Is
111B2 Waimakariri R NZ
111B2 Waimate NZ
21C4 Waimea Hawaiian Is
106B1 Waingapu Indon
13E2 Wainwright Can
4B2 Wainwright USA
111B2 Waipara NZ
110C2 Waipukurau NZ
111C2 Wairarapa,L NZ
111B2 Wairau R NZ
110C1 Wairoa R NZ
110C1 Wairoa R NZ
111B2 Waitaki R NZ
110B1 Waitara NZ
110C1 Waitomo NZ
110B1 Waiuku NZ
75B1 Wajima Japan
99E2 Wajir Kenya
95B2 Wakasa-wan B
   Japan
111A3 Wakatipu,L NZ
74D4 Wakayama Japan
42D3 Wakefield Eng
27H1 Wakefield Jamaica
16D2 Wakefield Rhode
   Island, USA
76B2 Wakema Burma
69G2 Wakkanai Japan
108B3 Wakool R Aust
59B2 Walbrzych Pol
109D2 Walcha Aust
58B2 Walcz Pol
46D1 Waldbröl Germany
16B2 Walden USA
99D1 Waldia Eth
43C3 Wales Country, UK
12A1 Wales USA
6B3 Wales I Can
109C2 Walgett Aust
112B4 Walgreen Coast
   Region, Ant
99C3 Walikale Zaire
21B2 Walker L USA
14B2 Walkerton Can
8B2 Wallace USA
108A2 Wallaroo Aust
109C3 Walla Walla Aust
20C1 Walla Walla USA
16C2 Wallingford USA
105H4 Wallis and Futuna Is
   Pacific O
20C1 Wallowa USA
20C1 Wallowa Mts Mts
   USA
109C1 Wallumbilla Aust
18B2 Walnut Ridge USA
110C1 Walouru NZ
43D3 Walsall Eng
9C3 Walsenburg USA
9C3 Walsenburgh USA
17B1 Walterboro USA

17A1 Walter F George Res
   USA
16D1 Waltham USA
100A3 Walvis Bay S Africa
103J6 Walvis Ridge
   Atlantic O
97C4 Wamba Nig
98B3 Wamba R Zaïre
18A2 Wamego USA
84B2 Wana Pak
108B1 Wanaaring Aust
111A2 Wanaka NZ
111A3 Wanaka,L NZ
14B1 Wanapitei L Can
109C1 Wandoan Aust
108B3 Wanganella Aust
110C1 Wanganui NZ
110C1 Wanganui R NZ
109C3 Wangaratta Aust
99E2 Wanle Weyne Somalia
76E2 Wanning China
87B1 Wanparti India
73B3 Wanxian China
73B3 Wanyuan China
13D2 Wapiti R Can
16C2 Wappapello,L USA
87B1 Warangal India
109C4 Waratah Aust
108C3 Waratah B Aust
108A1 Warburton R Aust
109C1 Ward R Aust
101G1 Warden S Africa
99E2 Warder Eth
85D4 Wardha India
111A3 Ward,Mt NZ
5F4 Ware Can
16C1 Ware USA
16D2 Wareham USA
109D1 Warialda Aust
76C2 Warin Chamrap Thai
100B3 Warmbad S Africa
16B2 Warminster USA
21B2 Warm Springs USA
56C2 Warnemünde
   Germany
20B2 Warner Mts USA
17B1 Warner Robins USA
108B3 Warracknabeal Aust
108A1 Warrandirinna,L Aust
107D3 Warrego R Aust
19B3 Warren Arkansas,
   USA
109C2 Warren Aust
16D2 Warren
   Massachusetts, USA
14B2 Warren Ohio, USA
15C2 Warren Pennsylvania,
   USA
45C1 Warrenpoint N Ire
18B2 Warrensburg USA
101F1 Warrenton S Africa
15C3 Warrenton USA
97C4 Warri Nig
108A1 Warrina Aust
42C3 Warrington Eng
108B3 Warrnambool Aust
   Warsaw = Warszawa
58C2 Warszawa Pol
59B2 Warta R Pol
109D1 Warwick Aust
43D3 Warwick County, Eng
43D3 Warwick Eng
16B2 Warwick New York,
   USA
16D2 Warwick Rhode
   Island, USA
8B3 Wasatch Range Mts
   USA
101H1 Wasbank S Africa
21B2 Wasco USA
4H2 Washburn L Can
85D4 Wāshīm India
10C3 Washington District of
   Columbia, USA
17B1 Washington Georgia,
   USA

14A3 Washington Indiana,
   USA
18B2 Washington Missouri,
   USA
16B2 Washington New
   Jersey, USA
14B2 Washington
   Pennsylvania, USA
8A2 Washington State,
   USA
14B3 Washington Court
   House USA
6D1 Washington Land Can
15D2 Washington,Mt USA
43E3 Wash,The Eng
85A3 Washuk Pak
12E2 Wasilla USA
26A4 Waspán Nic
70D4 Watampone Indon
16C2 Waterbury USA
45C2 Waterford County,
   Irish Rep
41B3 Waterford Irish Rep
45C2 Waterford Harbour
   Irish Rep
46C1 Waterloo Belg
14A2 Waterloo USA
15C2 Watertown New York,
   USA
101H1 Waterval-Boven
   S Africa
10D2 Waterville Maine, USA
15C1 Watervliet USA
5G4 Waterways Can
43D3 Watford Eng
15C2 Watkins Glen USA
8C1 Watrous Can
99C2 Watsa Zaïre
12J2 Watson Lake Can
22B2 Watsonville USA
71F4 Wau PNG
99C2 Wau Sudan
7B5 Waua Can
109D2 Wauchope Aust
17B2 Wauchula USA
14A2 Waukegan USA
10B2 Wausau USA
14A2 Wauwatosa USA
106C2 Wave Hill Aust
43E3 Waveney R Eng
14B3 Waverly Ohio, USA
46C1 Wavre Belg
10B2 Wawa Can
95A2 Wāw Al Kabir Libya
95A2 Wāw an Nāmūs Well
   Libya
22C2 Wawona USA
19A3 Waxahachie USA
17B1 Waycross USA
17B1 Waynesboro Georgia,
   USA
19C3 Waynesboro
   Mississippi, USA
16A3 Waynesboro
   Pennsylvania, USA
15C3 Waynesboro Virginia,
   USA
18B2 Waynesville Missouri,
   USA
84B2 Wazi Khwa Afghan
43E4 Weald,The Upland
   Eng
42C2 Wear R Eng
19A3 Weatherford Texas,
   USA
20B2 Weaverville USA
14B1 Webbwood Can
16D1 Webster USA
18B2 Webster Groves USA
29D6 Weddell I Falkland Is
112C2 Weddell S Ant
13C2 Wedge Mt Can
20B2 Weed USA
101H1 Weenen S Africa
109C2 Wee Waa Aust
72D1 Weichang China
57C3 Weiden Germany
72D2 Weifang China

72E2 Weihai China
72C3 Wei He R Henan,
   China
72C2 Wei He R Shaanxi,
   China
109C1 Weilmoringle Aust
73A4 Weining China
107D2 Weipa Aust
14B2 Weirton USA
20C2 Weiser USA
72D3 Weishan Hu L China
57C2 Weissenfels
   Germany
17A1 Weiss L USA
101G1 Welkom S Africa
15C2 Welland Can
43D3 Welland R Eng
43D3 Welland R Eng
109C2 Wellesley Is Aust
12G2 Wellesley L Can
43D3 Wellingborough Eng
109C2 Wellington Aust
18A2 Wellington Kansas,
   USA
111B2 Wellington NZ
6A2 Wellington Chan Can
13C2 Wells Can
43C4 Wells Eng
110B1 Wellsford NZ
106B3 Wells,L Aust
57C3 Wels Austria
43C3 Welshpool Wales
13D1 Wembley Can
7C4 Wemindji Can
20B1 Wenatchee USA
20C1 Wenatchee R USA
97B4 Wenchi Ghana
72E2 Wenden China
73E4 Wenling China
32J7 Wenman I Ecuador
73A5 Wenshan China
107D4 Wenthaggi Aust
108B2 Wentworth Aust
72A3 Wen Xian China
73E4 Wenzhou China
73C4 Wenzhu China
101G1 Wepener S Africa
12G1 Werneche Mts Can
57C2 Werra R Germany
109D2 Werris Creek Aust
56B2 Wesel Germany
56B2 Weser R Germany
106C2 Wessel Is Aust
14A2 West Allis USA
104C4 West Australian Basin
   Indian O
104C5 West Australian Ridge
   Indian O
19C3 West B USA
86B2 West Bengal State,
   India
43D3 West Bromwich Eng
16B3 West Chester USA
46D1 Westerburg Germany
56B2 Westerland Germany
106A3 Western Australia
   State, Aust
87A1 Western Ghats Mts
   India
44A3 Western Isles Scot
96A2 Western Sahara
   Region, Mor
105H4 Western Samoa Is
   Pacific O
46B1 Westerschelde
   Estuary Neth
46D1 Westerwald Region,
   Germany
49D1 Westfalen Region,
   Germany
29D6 West Falkland I
   Falkland Is
16C1 Westfield
   Massachusetts, USA
15C2 Westfield New York,
   USA
18C2 West Frankfort USA
109C1 Westgate Aust

43C4 West Glamorgan County, Wales
102E3 West Indies Is Caribbean S
13E2 Westlock Can
14B2 West Lorne Can
45C2 Westmeath County, Irish Rep
18B2 West Memphis USA
43D3 West Midlands County, Eng
43D4 Westminster Eng
16A3 Westminster Maryland, USA
17B1 Westminster S Carolina, USA
100B3 West Nicholson Zim
78D1 Weston Malay
14B3 Weston USA
43C4 Weston-super-Mare Eng
17B2 West Palm Beach USA
18B2 West Plains USA
22B1 West Point California, USA
19C3 West Point Mississippi, USA
16C2 West Point New York, USA
12F2 West Point Mt USA
45B2 Westport Irish Rep
111B2 Westport NZ
40C2 Westray J Scot
13C2 West Road R Can
42E3 West Side Oilfield N Sea
11B3 West Virginia State, USA
22C1 West Walker R USA
109C2 West Wyalong Aust
42D3 West Yorkshire County, Eng
71D4 Wetar J Indon
13E2 Wetaskiwin Can
99D3 Wete Tanz
46E1 Wetzlar Germany
Wevok = Cape Lisburne
71F4 Wewak PNG
19A2 Wewoka USA
45C2 Wexford County, Irish Rep
45C2 Wexford Irish Rep
5H5 Weyburn Can
43C4 Weymouth Eng
110C1 Whakatane NZ
110C1 Whakatane R NZ
44E1 Whalsay J Scot
110B1 Whangarei NZ
42D3 Wharfe R Eng
19A4 Wharton USA
111B2 Whataroa NZ
16A3 Wheaton Maryland, USA
8B3 Wheeler Peak Mt Nevada, USA
9C3 Wheeler Peak Mt New Mexico, USA
14B2 Wheeling USA
13C3 Whistler Can
15C2 Whitby Can
42D2 Whitby Eng
18B2 White R Arkansas, USA
12F2 White R Can
14A3 White R Indiana, USA
8C2 White R S Dakota, USA
7E4 White B Can
108B2 White Cliffs Aust
40C2 White Coomb Mt Scot
13D2 Whitecourt Can
14A1 Whitefish Pt USA
7D4 Whitegull L Can
15D2 Whitehall New York, USA

16B2 Whitehall Pennsylvania, USA
42C2 Whitehaven Eng
12G2 Whitehorse Can
110C1 White I NZ
19B4 White L USA
109C4 Whitemark Aust
21B2 White Mountain Peak Mt USA
12E1 White Mts Alaska, USA
15D2 White Mts New Hampshire, USA
99D1 White Nile R Sudan
16C2 White Plains USA
7B5 White River USA
15D2 White River Junction USA
White S = Beloye More
13B2 Whitesail L Can
20B1 White Salmon USA
17C1 Whiteville USA
97B4 White Volta R Ghana
42B2 Whithorn Scot
17B1 Whitmire USA
21B2 Whitney,Mt USA
12E2 Whittier Alaska, USA
22C4 Whittier California, USA
5H3 Wholdia L Can
108A2 Whyalla Aust
14B2 Wiarton Can
18A2 Wichita USA
9D3 Wichita Falls USA
44C2 Wick Scot
45C2 Wicklow County, Irish Rep
45C2 Wicklow Irish Rep
45C2 Wicklow Mts Irish Rep
109C1 Widgeegoara R Aust
46D1 Wied R Germany
59B2 Wielun Pol
59B3 Wien Austria
59B3 Wiener Neustadt Austria
58C2 Wieprz R Pol
46E1 Wiesbaden Germany
42C3 Wigan Eng
19C3 Wiggins USA
42B2 Wigtown Scot
42B2 Wigtown B Scot
47C1 Wil Switz
20C1 Wilbur USA
108B2 Wilcannia Aust
21B2 Wildcat Peak Mt USA
47B1 Wildhorn Mt Switz
13E2 Wild Horse Can
47D1 Wildspitze Mt Austria
17D2 Wildwood Florida, USA
16B3 Wildwood New Jersey, USA
101G1 Wilge R S Africa
56B2 Wilhelmshaven Germany
15C2 Wilkes-Barre USA
112B8 Wilkes Land Ant
13F2 Wilkie Can
20B2 Willamette R USA
108B2 Willandra R Aust
9C3 Willcox USA
27D4 Willemstad Curaçao
108A1 William Creek Aust
108B3 William,Mt Aust
21A2 Williams California, USA
13C2 Williams Lake Can
15C2 Williamsport USA
16C1 Williamstown Massachusetts, USA
14B3 Williamstown W Virginia, USA
16C2 Willimantic USA
16B2 Willingboro USA
13D2 Willingdon,Mt Can

107E2 Willis Group Is Aust
17B2 Williston Florida, USA
100B4 Williston S Africa
13C1 Williston L Can
8D2 Willmar USA
108A3 Willoughby,C Aust
13C2 Willow R Can
20B2 Willow Ranch USA
21A2 Willows USA
18B2 Willow Springs USA
108A2 Wilmington Aust
16B3 Wilmington Delaware, USA
17C1 Wilmington N Carolina, USA
7A5 Wilnona USA
11C3 Wilson R Aust
68B1 Wilson R Aust
22C3 Wilson,Mt California, USA
20B1 Wilson,Mt Oregon, USA
109C4 Wilsons Promontory Pen Aust
43D4 Wiltshire County, Eng
42C2 Wilts Lux
106B3 Wiluna Aust
14A2 Winamac USA
101G1 Winburg S Africa
16C1 Winchendon USA
15C1 Winchester Can
43D4 Winchester Eng
15C3 Winchester New Hampshire, USA
15C3 Winchester Virginia, USA
42C2 Windermere Eng
100A3 Windhoek Namibia
107D3 Windorah Aust
8C2 Wind River Range Mts USA
109D2 Windsor Aust
12C2 Windsor Connecticut, USA
43D4 Windsor Eng
7D5 Windsor Nova Scotia, Can
14B2 Windsor Ontario, Can
15D1 Windsor Quebec, Can
17B1 Windsor Forest USA
16C2 Windsor Locks USA
27E4 Windward Is Caribbean S
26C3 Windward Pass Caribbean S
13E1 Winefred L Can
18A2 Winfield Kansas, USA
109D2 Wingham Aust
34C3 Winifreda Arg
7B4 Winisk R Can
7B4 Winisk L Can
76B2 Winkana Burma
20B1 Winlock USA
97B4 Winneba Ghana
14A2 Winnebago,L USA
20C2 Winnemucca USA
19B3 Winnfield USA
5J4 Winnipeg Can
5J4 Winnipeg,L Can
5J4 Winnipegosis Can
4J4 Winnipegosis,L Can
15D2 Winnipesaukee,L USA
7 Winona Minnesota, USA
19C3 Winona Mississippi, USA
15D2 Winooski USA
9B3 Winslow USA
16C2 Winsted USA
11B3 Winston-Salem USA
46E1 Winterberg Germany
17B2 Winter Garden USA
17B2 Winter Park USA
22B1 Winters USA
47C1 Winterthur Switz
107D3 Winton Aust
111A3 Winton NZ

43E3 Wisbech Eng
10B2 Wisconsin State, USA
7B5 Wisconsin Rapids USA
12D1 Wiseman USA
58B2 Wisła R Pol
56C2 Wismar Germany
33F2 Witagron Surinam
101G1 Witbank S Africa
9D3 Witchita Falls USA
43D3 Witham R Eng
42E3 Withernsea Eng
43D4 Witney Eng
46D1 Witten Germany
56C2 Wittenberg Germany
108A3 Wittenoom Aust
46D1 Wittlich Germany
58B2 Władysławowo Pol
58B2 Włocławek Pol
58B2 Włodawa Pol
109C3 Wodonga Aust
47C1 Wohlen Switz
71E4 Wokam Indon
43D4 Woking Eng
71F3 Woleai I Pacific O
20D2 Wolf Creek USA
8C2 Wolf Point USA
57C3 Wolfsberg Austria
56C2 Wolfsburg Germany
5H4 Wollaston L Can
5H4 Wollaston Lake Can
4G3 Wollaston Pen Can
109D2 Wollongong Aust
101G1 Wolmaranstad S Africa
58B2 Wolow Pol
108B3 Wolseley Aust
43E3 Wolverhampton Eng
16A2 Womelsdorf USA
100D1 Wondai Aust
74B3 Wŏnju S Korea
108B2 Wonominta R Aust
13C1 Wonowon Can
74B3 Wŏnsan N Korea
108C3 Wonthaggi Aust
108A2 Woocalla Aust
16B3 Woodbine USA
15C3 Woodbridge USA
5G4 Wood Buffalo Nat Pk Can
109D1 Woodburn Aust
20B1 Woodburn USA
16B3 Woodbury USA
12F1 Woodchopper USA
21A2 Woodland California, USA
20B1 Woodland Washington, USA
107E1 Woodlark I PNG
106C4 Woodmera Aust
106C3 Woodroffe,Mt Aust
14B2 Woodstock Ontario, Can
14B2 Woodstown USA
110C2 Woodville NZ
19B3 Woodville USA
106A4 Woomera Aust
15D2 Woonsocket USA
14B2 Wooster USA
43C3 Worcester Eng
100A4 Worcester S Africa
16D1 Worcester USA
47C1 Wörgl Austria
42C2 Workington Eng
8C2 Worland USA
46E2 Worms Germany
43B4 Worms Head Pt Wales
43D4 Worthing Eng
8D2 Worthington USA
71D4 Wowoni I Indon
12H3 Wrangell USA
12H3 Wrangell I USA
12F2 Wrangell Mts USA
40B2 Wrath,C Scot
43C3 Wrexham Wales
17B1 Wrightsville USA
22D3 Wrightwood USA

4F3 Wrigley Can
59B2 Wrocław Pol
58B2 Września Pol
69E2 Wuchang China
76E1 Wuchuan China
72C2 Wuda China
76E1 Wuding He *R* China
72A3 Wuda China
73C4 Wugang China
72B2 Wuhai China
73C3 Wuhan China
73D3 Wuhu China
73D5 Wuhu China
84D2 Wujiang China
72B1 Wujia He *R* China
73B4 Wu Jiang *R* China
97C4 Wukari Nig
73B4 Wuling Shan *Mts*
　　　 China
97D4 Wum Cam
73A4 Wumeng Shan
　　　 Upland China
46D1 Wuppertal Germany
72B2 Wuqi China
72D2 Wuqing China
57B3 Würzburg Germany
57C2 Wurzen Germany
72C2 Wutai Shan *Mt* China
71F4 Wuvulu *I* Pacific O
72A2 Wuwei China
73E3 Wuxi China
73E3 Wuxing China
72C2 Wuyang China
73B4 Wuyi Shan *Mts* China
72B1 Wuyuan China
76D2 Wuzhi Shan *Mts*
　　　 China

72B2 Wuzhong China
73C5 Wuzhou China
14B2 Wyandotte USA
109C1 Wyandra Aust
43C4 Wye *R* Eng
43C4 Wylye *R* Eng
43C4 Wymondham Eng
106B2 Wyndham Aust
18F2 Wynne USA
4G2 Wynniatt B Can
109C4 Wynyard Aust
8C2 Wyoming State, USA
14A2 Wyoming USA
109D2 Wyong Aust

X

84D1 Xaidulla China
72D1 Xai Moron He *R*
　　　 China
101C3 Xai Xai Mozam
23B2 Xaltinguis Mexico
100A2 Xangongo Angola
46D1 Xanten Germany
55B2 Xánthi Greece
100B3 Xau,L Botswana
14B3 Xenia USA
68B4 Xiaguan China
72A2 Xiahe China
73D5 Xiamen China
72B3 Xi'an China
73B4 Xianfeng China
73C3 Xiangfan China
73C4 Xiang Jiang *R* China
73C4 Xiangtan Province,
　　　 China
73C4 Xianning China
72B3 Xianyang China
73C4 Xiao Shui *R* China
73D4 Xiapu China
73A4 Xichang China
23B1 Xicotepec Mexico
76C2 Xieng Khouang Laos
73B4 Xifeng China
86B1 Xigazê China
72A1 Xi He *R* China
72B2 Xiji China
73C5 Xi Jiang *R* China
72E1 Xiliao He *R* China
73B5 Xilin China

23B1 Xilitla Mexico
73D4 Xinfeng China
72C1 Xinghe China
73D5 Xingning China
73B4 Xingren China
72C2 Xingtai China
33G4 Xingu *R* Brazil
68B2 Xingxingxia China
73A4 Xingyi China
72A2 Xining China
72E2 Xinjin Liaoning, China
73A3 Xinjin Sichuan, China
72D2 Xinwen China
72C1 Xin Xian China
72C2 Xinxiang China
73C3 Xinyang China
73C5 Xinyi Guangdong,
　　　 China
72D3 Xinyi Jiangsu, China
72D1 Xi Ujimqin Qi China
74A2 Xiuyan China
23B2 Xochimilco Mexico
73D3 Xuancheng China
73B3 Xuanhan China
72D1 Xuanhua China
73A4 Xuanwei China
72C3 Xuchang China
99E2 Xuddur Somalia
72A2 Xunhua China
73C5 Xun Jiang *R* China
69E2 Xunke China
73D5 Xunwu China
73C4 Xupu China
16E1 Xuwen China
73B4 Xuyong China
72D3 Xuzhou China

Y

73A4 Ya'an China
108B3 Yaapeet Aust
98B2 Yabassi Cam
68C1 Yablonovyy Khrebet
　　　 Mts USSR
94C2 Yabrūd Syria
20B2 Yachats USA
30D3 Yacuiba Bol
87B1 Yādgīr India
95A1 Yafran Libya
23A1 Yahualica Mexico
98C2 Yahuma Zaire
75B1 Yaita Japan
75B2 Yaizu Japan
73A4 Yajiang China
20B1 Yakima USA
20B1 Yakima *R* USA
97B3 Yako Burkina
98C2 Yakoma Zaire
74E2 Yakumo Japan
12G3 Yakutat USA
12G3 Yakutat B USA
63E1 Yakutsk USSR
77C4 Yala Thai
23B2 Yalalag Mexico
98C3 Yalinga CAR
109C3 Yalkubul Aust
68B3 Yalong *R* China
73A4 Yalong Jiang *R* China
54C2 Yalova Turk
60D5 Yalta USSR
74B2 Yalu Jiang *R* China
74C4 Yamagata Japan
74C4 Yamaguchi Japan
68D1 Yamarovka USSR
109D1 Yamba New S Wales,
　　　 Aust
108B2 Yamba S Australia,
　　　 Aust
99C2 Yambio Sudan
54C2 Yambol Bulg
71E4 Yamdena *I* Indon
　　　 Yam Kinneret =
　　　 Tiberias,L
108B1 Yamma Yamma,L
　　　 Aust
97B4 Yamoussoukro Ivory
　　　 Coast

85D3 Yamuna *R* India
86C1 Yamzho Yumco *L*
　　　 China
63F1 Yana *R* USSR
108B3 Yanac Aust
75A2 Yanagawa Japan
87C1 Yanam India
72B2 Yan'an China
80B3 Yanbu'al Bahr
　　　 S Arabia
108B2 Yancannia Aust
72E3 Yancheng China
72B2 Yanchi China
108B1 Yandama *R* Aust
98C2 Yangambi Zaïre
72C1 Yang He *R* China
73C5 Yangjiang China
72C2 Yangquan China
73C5 Yangshan China
72E3 Yangtze Gorges
　　　 China
72E3 Yangtze,Mouths of the
　　　 China
72D3 Yangzhou China
73B4 Yanhe China
14B2 Yankton USA
108C3 Yanko *R* Aust
8D2 Yankton USA
68A2 Yanqqi China
72D1 Yan Shan *Hills*
108B1 Yantabulla Aust
72E2 Yantai China
72D2 Yanzhou China
98B2 Yaoundé Cam
71E4 Yapen *I* Indon
71E3 Yap Is Pacific O
24B2 Yaqui *R* Mexico
61G2 Yaransk USSR
32C3 Yarí *R* Colombia
74D3 Variga-dake *Mt* Japan
82B2 Yarkant He *R* China
86C1 Yarlung Zangbo Jiang
　　　 R China
7D5 Yarmouth Can
94B2 Yarmūk *R* Syria/Jordan
61E2 Yaroslavl' USSR
94B2 Yarqon *R* Israel
109C3 Yarram Aust
109D1 Yarraman Aust
109C3 Yarrawonga Aust
60D2 Yartsevo USSR
63B1 Yartsevo USSR
32B2 Yarumal Colombia
97C3 Yashi Nig
97C4 Yashikera Nig
61F4 Yashkul' USSR
84C1 Yasin Pak
59C3 Yasinya USSR
109C2 Yass Aust
109C2 Yass *R* Aust
75A1 Yasugi Japan
18A2 Yates Center USA
98C2 Yatolema Zaïre
74C4 Yatsushiro Japan
94B3 Yatta Israel
32C4 Yavari Peru
85D4 Yavatmāl India
74C4 Yawatahama Japan
76D2 Ya Xian China
90B3 Yazd Iran
90B3 Yazd-e Khvāst Iran
19B3 Yazoo *R* USA
19B3 Yazoo City USA
76B2 Ye Burma
59D3 Yedintsy USSR
108A2 Yeelanna Aust
60E3 Yefremov USSR
61F4 Yegorlyk *R* USSR
99D2 Yei Sudan
63E0 Yelets USSR
44E1 Yell *I* Scot
87C1 Yellandu India
　　　 Yellow = Huang He
8B1 Yellowhead P Can
4G3 Yellowknife Can
5G4 Yellowknife *R* Can
109C2 Yellow Mt *Aust*
69E3 Yellow Sea China/Korea

8C2 Yellowstone *R* USA
8B2 Yellowstone L USA
6B1 Yelverton B Can
97C3 Yelwa Nig
81C4 Yemen Republic,
　　　 Arabian Pen
76C1 Yen Bai Viet
97B4 Yendi Ghana
76B1 Yengan Burma
63B2 Yeniseysk USSR
63B1 Yeniseyskiy Kryazh
　　　 Ridge USSR
64J2 Yeniseyskiy Zal *B*
　　　 USSR
12D2 Yentna *R* USA
43C4 Yeo *R* Eng
109C2 Yeoval Aust
43C4 Yeovil Eng
63C1 Yerbogachen USSR
65F5 Yerevan USSR
21B2 Yerington USA
21B3 Yermo USA
63E2 Yerofey USSR
69E1 Yerofey-Pavlovich
　　　 USSR
94B3 Yeroham Israel
61G3 Yershov USSR
　　　 Yerushalayim =
　　　 Jerusalem
92C1 Yeşil *R* Turk
94B2 Yesud Hama'ala
　　　 Israel
109D1 Yetman Aust
96B2 Yetti Maur
93E1 Yevlakh USSR
60D4 Yevpatoriya USSR
72E2 Ye Xian China
60E4 Yeysk USSR
55B2 Viánnitsá Greece
73A4 Yibin China
73C3 Yichang China
69E2 Yichun China
72B2 Yijun China
73A4 Yildiz Dağları *Upland*
92C2 Yıldızeli Turk
73A5 Yiliang China
72B2 Yinchuan China
72D3 Ying He *R* China
72E1 Yingkou China
73D3 Yingshan Hubei,
　　　 China
72B3 Yingshan Sichuan,
　　　 China
73D4 Yingtan China
82C1 Yining China
72B1 Yin Shan *Upland*
99D2 Yirga Alem Eth
99D2 Yirol Sudan
63D3 Yirshi China
73B5 Yishan China
72D2 Yishui China
55B3 Yíthion Greece
38J6 Yivieska Fin
73C4 Yiyang China
38K5 Yli-Kitka *L* Fin
38J5 Ylilornio Sweden
19A4 Yoakum USA
23B2 Yogope Mexico
78C4 Yogyakarta Indon
98B3 Yokadouma Cam
98B2 Yokadouma Cam
75B2 Yokkaichi Japan
75B2 Yokohama Japan
75B1 Yokosuka Japan
74C3 Yonago Japan
74B3 Yonezawa Japan
73D4 Yong'an China
72A2 Yongchang China
74B3 Yŏngch'on S Korea
73A4 Yongchuan China
72A2 Yongdeng China
73D5 Yongding China
72D2 Yongding He *R*
　　　 China
74B3 Yŏngdŏk S Korea
74B3 Yŏnghŭng N Korea

74B3 Yongju S Korea
72B2 Yongning China
16C2 Yonkers USA
49C2 Yonne R France
42D3 York Eng
18A1 York Nebraska, USA
16A3 York Pennsylvania, USA
107D2 York,C Aust
108A2 Yorke Pen Aust
108A3 Yorketown Aust
74C4 York Factory Can
41C3 Yorkshire Moors Moorland Eng
42D2 Yorkshire Wolds Upland Eng
5H4 Yorkton Can
72B2 Yosemite L USA
22C1 Yosemite Nat Pk USA
75A2 Yoshii R Japan
75A2 Yoshino R Japan
61G2 Yoshkar Ola USSR
74B4 Yŏsu S Korea
41B3 Youghal Irish Rep
45C3 Youghal Harb Irish Rep
73B5 You Jiang R China
109C2 Young Aust
34D2 Young Urug
111A2 Young Range Mts NZ
13E2 Youngstown USA
14B2 Youngstown Ohio, USA
22A1 Yountville USA
73B4 Youyang China
80B2 Yozgat Turk
39G7 Ystad Sweden
43C3 Ystwyth R Wales
44C3 Ythan R Scot
73C4 Yuan Jiang R Hunan, China
73A5 Yuan Jiang R Yunnan, China
73A4 Yuanmu China
72C2 Yuanping China
21A2 Yuba City USA
74E2 Yūbari Japan
25D3 Yucatan Pen Mexico
25D2 Yucatan Chan Mexico/Cuba
72C2 Yuci China
63F2 Yudoma R USSR
73D4 Yuexi China
73A4 Yuexi China
73C4 Yueyang China
54A2 Yugoslavia Federal Republic, Europe
73B5 Yu Jiang R China
12C2 Yukon R Can/USA
4E3 Yukon Territory Can
76E1 Yulin Guangdong, China
73C5 Yulin Guangxi, China
72B2 Yulin Shaanxi, China
9B3 Yuma USA
68B3 Yumen China
72D2 Yunan China
34A3 Yungay Chile
73C5 Yunkai Dashan Hills China
108A2 Yunta Aust
72C3 Yunxi China
72C3 Yun Xian China
73B3 Yunyang China
32B5 Yurimaguas Peru
73C5 Yu Shan Mt Taiwan
38L6 Yushkozero USSR
82D2 Yushu Tibet, China
73A5 Yuxi China
74F2 Yuzhno-Kuril'sk USSR
69G2 Yuzhno-Sakhalinsk USSR
61J3 Yuzh Ural Mts USSR

46A2 Yvelines Department, France
47B1 Yverdon Switz

Z

56A2 Zaandam Neth
63C2 Zabakalskiy USSR
93D2 Zāb al Babir R Iraq
93D2 Zāb as Saghir R Iraq
68D2 Zabaykal'sk USSR
59B3 Zabreh Czech
59B2 Zabrze Pol
23A2 Zacapu Mexico
24B2 Zacatecas USSR
23B2 Zacatepec Morelos, Mexico
23B2 Zacatepec Oaxaca, Mexico
23B2 Zacatlan Mexico
23A1 Zacoalco Mexico
23B1 Zacualtipan Mexico
52C2 Zadar Yugos
76B3 Zadetkyi I Burma
50A2 Zafra Spain
95C1 Zagazig Egypt
96B1 Zagora Mor
60E2 Zagorsk USSR
52C1 Zagreb Yugos
91D4 Zāhedān Iran
94B2 Zahle Leb
51C2 Zahrez Chergui Marshland Alg
61H2 Zainsk USSR
98C3 Zaire Republic, Africa
98B3 Zaire R Zaire/Congo
98C1 Zajecâr Yugos
68C1 Zakamensk USSR
93D2 Zakho Iraq
55B3 Zákinthos I Greece
59B3 Zakopane Pol
59B3 Zalaegerszeg Hung
54B1 Zalău Rom
56C2 Zalew Szczeciński Lg Pol
98C1 Zalingei Sudan
63F2 Zaliv Akademii G B USSR
65G5 Zaliv Kara-Bogaz Gol B USSR
74C2 Zaliv Petra Velikogo B USSR
69G2 Zaliv Turpeniya G USSR
89H9 Zambesi R Mozam
100B2 Zambezi Zambia
100B2 Zambezi R Zambia
100B2 Zambia Republic, Africa
79B4 Zamboanga Phil
79B4 Zamboanga Pen Phil
58C2 Zambrów Pol
32B4 Zamora Ecuador
23A2 Zamora Mexico
50A1 Zamora Spain
59C2 Zamość Pol
72A3 Zamtang China
98B3 Zanaga Congo
50B2 Záncara R Spain
24D2 Zanda China
14B3 Zanesville USA
84D2 Zangla India
90A2 Zanjan Iran
34B2 Zanjitas Arg
34B2 Zanjon R Arg
99D3 Zanzibar Tanz
99D3 Zanzibar I Tanz
96C2 Zaouiaallaz Alg
72D3 Zaozhuang China
93D2 Zap R Turk
39K7 Zapadnaja Dvina R USSR
63B2 Zapadno Dvina R USSR
65H3 Zapadno-Sibirskaya Nizmennost' Lowland USSR

63B2 Zapadnyy Sayan Mts USSR
34A3 Zapala Arg
65H4 Zaporozh'ye USSR
93C2 Zara Turk
23A1 Zaragoza Mexico
50B1 Zaragoza Spain
90B2 Zarand Iran
90C3 Zarand Iran
80E2 Zaranj Afghan
33D2 Zaraza Ven
58D1 Zarasai USSR
34D2 Zárate Arg
90B3 Zard Kuh Mt Iran
12H3 Zaremboi I USA
84B2 Zarghun Shahr Afghan
84B2 Zargun Mt Pak
97C3 Zaria Nig
92C3 Zarqa Jordan
94B2 Zarqa R Jordan
32B4 Zaruma Ecuador
58B2 Zary Pol
96D1 Zarzis Tunisia
84D2 Zāskar R India
84D2 Zāskār R India
94C2 Zatara R Jordan
Zatoka Gdańska = Gdańsk,G of
69E1 Zavitinsk USSR
59B2 Zawiercie Pol
95A2 Zawilah Libya
63C2 Zayarsk USSR
65K5 Zaysan USSR
82C1 Zaysan USSR
82D3 Zayü China
73C3 Zayü China
58B2 Zduńska Wola Pol
46B1 Zeebrugge Belg
94B3 Zeelim Israel
101G1 Zeerust S Africa
94B2 Zefat Israel
97C3 Zegueren Watercourse Mali
99E1 Zeila Somalia
57C2 Zeitz Germany
72A2 Zekog China
61G2 Zelenodol'sk USSR
39K6 Zelenogorsk USSR
47D1 Zell Austria
58B1 Zelten Libya
98C2 Zemio CAR
64F2 Zemlya Aleksandry I Barents S
64F1 Zemlya Georga I Barents S
64H1 Zemlya Vil'cheka I Barents S
73B4 Zenning China
47B1 Zermatt Switz
63E2 Zeya USSR
63E2 Zeya Res USSR
47C1 Zèzere R Port
94B1 Zghorta Leb
58B2 Zgierz Pol
72D1 Zhangjiakou China
73D4 Zhangping China
72D2 Zhangwei He R China
72C1 Zhangwu China
72A2 Zhangye China
73D5 Zhangzhou China
73A4 Zhanyi China
73C5 Zhaoqing China
73A4 Zhaotong China
73D2 Zhaoyang Hu L China
61J4 Zharkamys USSR
61E3 Zhatay USSR
73D4 Zhejiang Province, China

73C3 Zhicheng China
68C1 Zhigalovo USSR
73B4 Zhijin China
58D2 Zhitkovichi USSR
60C3 Zhitomir USSR
60D3 Zhlobin USSR
60C4 Zhmerinka USSR
84B2 Zhob Pak
58D2 Zhodino USSR
72B2 Zhongning China
73C5 Zhongshan China
73B2 Zhongwei China
68B4 Zhougdian China
73E3 Zhoushan Quandao Arch China
72C2 Zhuanghe China
72A3 Zhuggu China
73C2 Zhushan China
73C4 Zhuzhou China
72D2 Zibo China
106C3 Ziel,Mt Aust
58B2 Zielona Gora Pol
76A1 Zigaing Burma
73A4 Zigong China
97A3 Ziguinchor Sen
23A2 Zihuatanejo Mexico
94B2 Zikhron Ya'aqov Israel
59B3 Žilina Czech
47D1 Ziller R Austria
47D1 Zillertaler Alpen Mts Austria
58D1 Zilupe USSR
63C2 Zima USSR
23A2 Zimapan Mexico
23B2 Zimatlan Mexico
100B2 Zimbabwe Republic, Africa
94B3 Zin R Israel
23A2 Zinacatepec Mexico
23A2 Zinapécuaro Mexico
97C3 Zinder Niger
73C4 Zi Shui China
23A2 Zitácuaro Mexico
57C2 Zittau Germany
72D2 Ziya He R China
72A3 Ziyang China
61J2 Zlatoust USSR
59B3 Zlin Czech
65K4 Zmeinogorsk USSR
58B2 Znin Pol
59B3 Znoimo Czech
100B3 Zoekmekaar S Africa
47B1 Zofingen Switz
47A2 Zoige China
59D3 Zolochev USSR
101C2 Zomba Malawi
98B2 Zongo Zaire
92B1 Zonguldak Turk
97B4 Zorzor Lib
96A2 Zouerate Maur
54B1 Zrenjanin Yugos
47C1 Zug Switz
47D1 Zugspitze Mt Germany
50A2 Zújar R Spain
100C2 Zumbo Mozam
23B2 Zumpango Mexico
97C4 Zungeru Nig
73B4 Zunyi China
76D1 Zuo R China
73B5 Zuo Jiang R China
47C1 Zürich Switz
47C1 Zürichsee L Switz
95A1 Zuwārah Libya
61H2 Zuyevka USSR
100B4 Zvishavane Zim'
59B3 Zvolen Czech
94B1 Zwelle Neth
58C2 Zyrardow Pol
65K5 Zyryanovsk USSR
59B3 Żywiec Pol
94A1 Zyyi Cyprus